Media Studies: A Reader

MEDIA STUDIES: A READER

Edited and Introduced by
Paul Marris
and
Sue Thornham

EDINBURGH UNIVERSITY PRESS

Selection and editorial material © 1996 Paul Marris and Sue Thornham
The texts are reprinted by permission of other publishers.

Reprinted 1997

Edinburgh University Press Ltd
22 George Square, Edinburgh

Typeset in Monotype Garamond by Bibliocraft, Dundee,
and printed and bound in Great Britain

A CIP record for this book is available from the British Library

ISBN 0 7486 0778 1

CONTENTS

PART TWO: CASE STUDIES

PREFACE

We should like to take this opportunity to thank staff and students on the BA (Hons) Media Studies and BA (Hons) Communication Studies degrees at the University of Sunderland for their contributions to the planning of this reader. We should also like to thank the School of Arts, Design and Communications for granting us sabbatical leave to complete the book; and colleagues in Media and Cultural Studies for being willing to add further administrative burdens to already heavy loads in order to make that leave possible. Thanks also go to Jackie Jones of Edinburgh University Press for her support and encouragement, to Nicola Carr for the efficiency of her detective work, and to Melanie Gibson for her help in the final stages of preparation. Finally, we should like to thank our families for their support throughout the preparation of this reader.

INTRODUCTION

ABOUT THIS READER

As part of the process by which any book reaches print, the outline proposal for this one was sent to a number of academic readers for comment. Those of one American reader, Jane Feuer, included the following: 'it combines a wide spectrum of what might be labelled cultural studies approaches to the media; it is very British and very lefty/Marxist/feminist' – though she did add, 'I think that's good . . .' The comment seems a useful one on which to begin this introduction, not because of its accuracy as a summary, but because it draws attention to the fact that the study of the mass media has always been a politically, as well as a theoretically, engaged enterprise (though, in the case of some research traditions, not always explicitly so), and that the particular inflection of that study in Britain is a distinctive one. What this book seeks to do, then, is to map a field, its varied, and often conflicting, histories, and its current debates. However, like any other, it is a map sketched from a particular perspective. That perspective is one which draws centrally on certain key political/theoretical assumptions to provide its academic coherence and its structural framework, assumptions which are, as our reader suggests, grounded in cultural studies approaches to the media.

The opening section 'Some Introductions' begins by outlining the different, and often theoretically and methodologically opposed, origins of the field as it is now constituted in Britain. From the arguments between the American mass communication tradition and the Europe-centred Frankfurt School in the 1940s, to the very different analyses of communication technologies by Marshall McLuhan and Raymond Williams in the 1960s, these differences have centred not only on the relative importance of the theoretical and the empirical in media research, but also – and always (even if only implicitly) underpinning these more overt arguments – on the political assumptions within the different traditions about the role and function of the mass media in society. Crudely summarised, the approaches of both the American mass communication tradition and McLuhan's work in the 1960s derive from a position broadly supportive of the directions in which Western society was moving, whereas those of the Frankfurt School and the English culturalist tradition are profoundly critical. Thus, in Tony Bennett's words, 'the sorts of assumptions made about the broader structure of society within different bodies of theory have determined both the sorts of questions that have been posed in relation to the media and the way in which those questions have been pursued'.[1]

The work of Stuart Hall at the Birmingham Centre for Contemporary Cultural Studies in the 1970s (see Chapter 5) constitutes a crucial moment in the development of media studies in Britain, drawing as it does upon paradigms from both the American and the European strands of thought and adding to them an attention to the media text which has its origins partly in a specifically English tradition of literary criticism and partly in 1970's British film theory. But Hall's work does not represent merely a synthesis of hitherto opposed traditions. Rather, through his use of Antonio Gramsci's concept of hegemony,[2] he provides a framework by which the operation of mass media in society can be understood as a series of 'articulated' (in the term's double sense of 'expressed' and 'joined together') moments, each of which is also the site of cultural struggle, or 'negotiation', over meaning. Within such a framework, earlier traditions of research are both drawn upon and critiqued, positioned within a field of study which is now reconstituted around a model which is at once a theoretical and a political analysis.

It is Hall's model – with its three 'moments' of production ('encoding'), text ('meaningful discourse') and reception ('decoding'), each of which may be viewed (and studied) as 'relatively autonomous', but which are also part of a wider process – which provides the central organising principle of this book. This is not to say, however, either that Hall's model has been uncontested or that the division between production, text and reception is unproblematic. Three difficulties should be mentioned here. The first is that many of the writers included in this volume would deny the equivalence of Hall's 'moments', seeing the primary determining element in the production of meaning as being, for example, the processes of production or the processes of reception/consumption. The second difficulty concerns the boundaries between the divisions. In the case of soap opera, for example, where the programme itself is a continuous serial, where its storylines and characters are mediated for us by magazines and the press, and where viewers 'remake' the text in their viewing processes and discussions, the boundary between 'text' and 'reception' becomes uncertain, and much research has focused on this issue. Finally, in more recent work, particularly that which centres on theories of the postmodern, the Gramscian paradigm which underpins Hall's model has been more fundamentally challenged. The two chapters which close the opening section of this book (Chapters 7 and 8) represent two very different forms of this challenge. Jürgen Habermas calls for a return to a focus on the media as the site of the 'public sphere' of information and debate – away, therefore, from an emphasis on the media as site of popular culture, where Hall's model has proved so fruitful and where many of the chapters in this volume would be placed. For Jean Baudrillard, however, the mass media *cannot* operate in this public sphere, since theirs is a structure not of meaning but of simulation. Moreover, this world of simulation and spectacle has now absorbed the realm of the social, so that a separate sphere of resistance no longer exists. In this vision, Hall's model of 'articulated moments' no longer applies, and with its disappearance go the possibilities of negotiation and resistance which are built in at each 'moment' of the operation of the mass media in society.

There are other debates and divisions which are represented in this volume. One concerns the position of feminist theory and research within media studies. None of the approaches outlined so far employs gender as a central organising principle. Indeed, most are, at least in their original form, notably gender-blind, operating a model within which the crucial issues for feminist analysis – such as the gendered nature of access to public power and discourses or the centrality of women's bodies as a site of struggle over control and meaning – cannot be inserted without a radical questioning of the model itself. Yet, as Annette Kuhn argues (Chapter 6), issues of power and representation within the operation of mass media have been a central concern of feminist cultural analyses, and feminist theories have challenged, used and transformed approaches and models produced elsewhere. Moreover, feminists have been active within media research and theory, shifting the focus of Hall's model, for example, away from its original class-based analysis and towards a model of social power and dominance which can account for a range of differences in the structuring of social and discursive power, and a range of negotiations at the level of production, text and audience. The result is an uneven picture, in which feminist analyses are positioned as central in some areas of media research and theory – notably those which focus upon the text–reader relationship within forms of popular culture – and as notably 'off-centre' within others.[3] The reader may trace the contours of this debate through the different sections of this book.

One further debate should be highlighted here, and this concerns the directions which research has taken *within* the broad framework provided by Hall's model. Its elaboration into a paradigm in which the 'relative autonomy' of its different moments could facilitate the separate study of the text as a complex discursive structure, and of the processes of reception as ones in which resistant, or oppositional, meanings and pleasures could be produced, can be seen as leading to the disappearance from sight of the framework as a whole. In particular, an increasing focus on theories of pleasure in studies both of the text and of processes of reception poses problems for a model which was founded on an analysis of the operations of *power*. The result, it has been argued, is that a model which began from a perspective critical of the structure and operations of contemporary Western society has ended in an often uncritical celebration of that society's mass media output.[4] This debate, too, is one which can be traced within this book both implicitly – in the difference between arguments to be found within the different sections (notably between those outlined in the section on 'Production' and those to be found in the later parts of the sections on 'Text' and 'Reception' – and explicitly – within individual sections.

Nevertheless, if one function of a reader of this nature is to draw attention to debates and differences, another is to situate these debates within a coherent contextualising framework, and it is Stuart Hall's model which provides that structuring framework here. After the opening section – with its representation of the different theoretical traditions which contribute to contemporary media studies – Part One is organised into three further sections, dealing in turn with 'Production', 'Text' and 'Reception'. Within these, where appropriate, a further division into sub-sections maps the range and variety, the arguments and debates, within work in these areas. The ordering of the three case studies which comprise Part Two mirrors this central organising principle, so that within each one, work in the areas of production, text and reception has been included. Here again, however, debates and differences should be noted. Work on 'News', for example, has been largely concerned with issues of public knowledge and information and has focused chiefly on the study of news production and organisation; while the study of 'Soap Opera' has had as its focus the analysis of popular pleasures, and has centred far more on the text–reader relationship. This difference is reflected in the balance of pieces within each case study.

One final point to be made here concerns the range of media referred to in these chapters. Most of the readings collected in this book focus on broadcasting and the press, and this limitation is quite deliberate. Film studies has a well-established critical tradition which must be traced elsewhere; space does not allow us to do more than refer to it here. Popular music, comics and popular fiction might have been given more attention, but a number of readers now exist which have as their focus the analysis of popular media culture, and the reader may turn to those.[5] Broadcasting and the press have been central to the study of the mass media within a range of theoretical traditions, and that centrality is echoed in this reader.

The study of the mass media has expanded rapidly over the last thirty-five years, and during that period has seen its focus challenged and reshaped by a series of theoretical influences and paradigms. The mapping of such a process must always be partial, and in a reader such as this will be challenged from within as well as outside its covers. We hope, however, that both this particular mapping and the debates which are represented within its fifty-four readings will offer a useful tool in the reader's own understanding of the study and the operations of the mass media.

NOTES

1.   Tony Bennett, 'Theories of the Media, Theories of Society', in Michael Gurevitch, Tony Bennett, James Curran and Janet Woollacott (eds), *Culture, Society and the Media* (London Methuen, 1982) p. 31.
2.   The process by which economically dominant groups in society are able, through their exertion of *cultural* leadership and authority, to win the consent of subordinate groups to the *status quo*. See Antonio Gramsci, *Selections from the Prison Notebooks*, ed. and trans. by Quintin Hoare and Geoffrey Nowell-Smith (London: Lawrence & Wishart, 1971) pp. 181–2.
3.   The term is one which forms the title of the 1991 volume on the relationship between feminism and cultural studies edited by Sarah Franklin, Celia Lury and Jackie Stacey, *OffCentre* (London: HarperCollins, 1991).
4.   See, for example, Jim McGuigan's arguments in *Cultural Populism* (London: Routledge, 1992), especially pp. 61–75.
5.   See, for example, Simon During (ed.), *The Cultural Studies Reader* (London: Routledge, 1993), and John Storey (ed.), *Cultural Theory and Popular Culture: A Reader* (Hemel Hempstead: Harvester Wheatsheaf, 1994).

PART ONE
STUDYING THE MEDIA

Some Introductions

Some Introductions

When attempts at sustained and systematic consideration of the media began to be undertaken in the British academic world in the 1960s, there were essentially two relevant streams of thought available: one within social science (sociology, social psychology, political communications), the other within the humanities (notably English literary study). Social science could look to a substantial body of English-language research built up within the United States around the concept of 'mass communication'. In the USA the arrival of radio broadcasting to set alongside the popular press and mass cinema-going had first generated serious discussion about the mass media in society in the 1920s. Initially this had been of a broad general character,[1] but by the late 1930s more detailed individual empirical studies were being carried out by sociologists and social psychologists.[2] So Lazarsfeld and Merton's piece published in 1948, 'Mass Communication, Popular Taste and Organized Social Action' (Chapter 1), stands on the achievement of ten years or so of social scientific research into 'mass communication', and seeks to summarise the broad features of what they felt was then known. Robert K. Merton stands at the heart of American social science of the mid-twentieth century, and was to become acknowledged as amongst the most professionally eminent of American sociologists. His work was within the *functionalist* tradition of sociology, like that of his teacher at Harvard, Talcott Parsons. This approach is evident in the way the first part of the essay proposes a taxonomy of 'social functions of the mass media'. One of these is seen as a 'dysfunction' – the 'narcotizing dysfunction', which renders 'large masses of the population politically apathetic and inert'. Merton's collaborator in this article, Paul Lazarsfeld, had worked in Vienna as a social psychologist specialising in the study of marketing, before he emigrated to the United States in 1933 to avoid the Nazis. In the 1940s he and Merton became colleagues at Columbia University, where Lazarsfeld founded the Bureau of Applied Social Research to carry out quantitative social survey research work. Lazarsfeld is a central figure in the development of 'communication studies' in America, defining issues and methods in ways that were to prove profoundly influential for a quarter of a century. His interests in marketing, political communication and audience measurement meant that attitude change, influence and persuasive power were major preoccupations in his work – and the 'effects' of communication were long seen as consisting in attitude change and behaviour modification of a measurable kind. This theme is taken up in the final part of the joint essay, with its discussion of the best conditions for effective propaganda, which are said to be 'monopolization',[3] 'canalization' and 'supplementation'.[4] The middle passage in the piece, in which the pair 'consider the impact of the mass media upon popular taste', registers the post-war development in the United States of a substantial public debate over the consequences of the rise of the media for culture in general. Were cultural and aesthetic standards being debased, or was a historically unprecedented mass popular culture being developed by the foremost capitalist democracy? Lazarsfeld and Merton do not come down on either side, but at this early stage conclude '[t]he answer can come only from disciplined research'. The debate was to be a significant one amongst American intellectuals during the Cold War until at least the late 1950s.[5]

A sharply distinct position on the social role of the media was developed within America during the 1940s, though it did not become widely known in the United States or Britain before the 1960s. This was the position of the Frankfurt School. The Institute of Social Research had been founded in Frankfurt am Main (Germany) in 1923 as an independent scholarly research institute specialising in sociology, social psychology, philosophy and political economy, with a pronounced affiliation to Marxism. Many of its leading researchers left Germany in the mid-1930s to avoid Fascism, and the Institute was transplanted to New York, under the leadership of Max Horkheimer. The commitment to developing a Marxist understanding of society adequate to the industrial capitalist economies of the mid-twentieth century led the Frankfurt School writers to a consideration of the media. As German-speaking *émigré* intellectuals in America working within social science, Lazarsfeld and the major Frankfurt School figures were known to one another. In 1941 the Institute for Social Research collaborated with Columbia University's Office of Radio Research on a special issue of the Institute's journal, *Studies in Philosophy and Social Science*, devoted to issues in mass communication, which contained contributions by Horkheimer, Adorno and Lazarsfeld. In Lazarsfeld's piece he drew his celebrated distinction between 'administrative' and 'critical' communications research, the former being to serve the knowledge requirements of the paymasters in the mass communications industry, the latter to meet the broader needs of social progress which might not meet the approval of established interests.[6] But the views of Lazarsfeld and the Frankfurt School did not converge. Lazarsfeld wrote to Adorno 'I have great objections against . . . your disregard of evidence and systematic empirical research'.[7] The Frankfurt School remained essentially peripheral and unknown within the mainstream of American social science.

In 1947 Horkheimer and Adorno published a major work, *Dialectic of Enlightenment*, whose chapter entitled 'The Culture Industry: Enlightenment as Mass Deception' set forth a general view of the media in contemporary society.[8] The term which was proposed was 'culture industry', not 'mass communication'. The dialectic expounded in the book is the play of positive and negative outcomes of the application of human reason in the modern era. The eighteenth-century Enlightenment had promised that the power of human reason could banish the forces of superstition and backwardness, end ignorance through the development of scientific knowledge, bring prosperity from a growing technical mastery of nature, and introduce justice and order to human affairs. But, argued Adorno and Horkheimer, the application of human reason within capitalism often stimulated opposing tendencies. The intellectual conquest of small areas of knowledge amounted merely to the development of technical expertises, the expression of 'instrumental' reason divorced from the wider goals of human emancipation. These contributed to the exploitation of people and nature, and made systems of social domination more efficient and effective. A traditional mitigating element had been works of art, the experience of which offered intimations of the human spirit free of domination by instrumental reason. But now, ran the argument, even this zone of human life was becoming subject to the forces of rationalisation and instrumentalisation through the industrialisation of culture. The 'culture industry' (Hollywood, the mass media, the record industry) is increasingly organised like any other commercial sector of manufacture and consumption, and culture has become commoditised. In contrast to the authenticity of folk and popular art and the human insights of genuine high art, the culture industry supplies 'substitute gratification', and promotes the cult of personality and other authoritarian attitudes. Leisure is rationalised like industrial production, and consciousness is integrated smoothly into the cycle of capitalist reproduction and accumulation. Chapter 2, Adorno's 'Culture Industry Reconsidered', usefully summarises many of the themes from *Dialectic of the Enlightenment* that bear on the consideration of the media.[9] The emphasis on the media as part of a capitalist industrialisation of culture which serves to reconcile people to a dominating social order in a totalising way has made the Frankfurt School's arguments a profound exposition of what are often encountered as unsystematised colloquial opinions.

The 1960s witnessed the dramatic ascent to public celebrity of the Canadian scholar Marshall McLuhan. His book *Understanding Media*, from which the extracts that make up Chapter 3 are taken, was published in 1964. He considered that discussion of the media was too narrowly focused on their *contents* – the effect of an advertisement, the meaning of a film, the line of a newspaper editorial. These were thought to be the 'messages' the media conveyed. But for McLuhan media are technologies each of which extends a particular human sense or faculty, and the real ' "message" of any medium or technology is the change of scale or pace or pattern that it introduces into human affairs'. The true significance of any medium is to be found in the overall impact of the generalised employment of that technological system. Hence, his celebrated claim that 'the *medium* is the message'. He considered that the printing press, a mechanical medium, promoted linearity, individualism and sequential rationality, which he linked to the visual. He preferred the new era of electronic media: radio, the telephone, television, and the coming 'automation' or computerisation. He associated these with instantaneity, the abolition of spatial separation, the unified field and simultaneity, and he linked them to the auditory. The global communications network that he foresaw was to be the ultimate 'extension of man', the externalisation of the central nervous system. In a period when the spread of transistor radios, television, and pop records seemed to many to be linked to the emergence of new patterns of youth behaviour, and when early communications satellites and information-processing systems seemed to herald further profound changes, many looked to McLuhan as offering an account of the significance of these developments – and a celebratory one at that. But although he spent his whole career within the academic world, McLuhan's ideas did not take deep root there. His views were rightly characterised as technological determinist, reductively attributing technological causes to social events. For instance, in what is a reference to the rise of mass movements in Europe in the 1920s and 1930s, he asserts that 'the introduction of radio in Europe' 'restore[d] a tribal pattern of intensive involvement'. Many of his preoccupations, however, now seem remarkably prescient of the themes of postmodernism: the coming of postindustrialism, the dissolution of the high culture/popular culture opposition, the eschewal of linear rationality, the information technology revolution, the contraction of time-space. The work of Jean Baudrillard owes much to McLuhan.

The second current of thought available in Britain in the 1960s to be brought to bear on the media was a native one, Leavisism within English literature. F. R. Leavis was the leading figure in a group of intellectuals connected to the Faculty of English at the University of Cambridge, whose central vehicle from 1932 was a quarterly periodical, *Scrutiny*. They were opposed to both the Edwardian belle-lettrisme that had formerly dominated the study of modern English at Cambridge, and the pseudo-aristocratic dilettantism they perceived in the Bloomsbury clique and other metropolitan literary coteries. In contrast they developed a view of the role of literary intellectuals that called for them to undertake serious tasks: above all, to uphold the continuity of culture and train discriminatory sensibilities in the face of modern mass civilisation. The felt need for such a role to be played had its precursors in Coleridge and Arnold in their views on the tasks of the 'clerisy' and the educators respectively. Because of language's important role in expressing the deepest values of a society and preserving the lines of continuity of a culture, the literary critic – and by extension, the literature teacher – comprises the key social grouping most appropriate to fulfil these functions. And a professionalisation of literary criticism is necessary: in contrast to amateurism, dilettantism and impressionism, the development of specialist professional skills in the close 'scrutiny' of literary texts and detailed analysis of how they are organised is called for – 'practical criticism'. On the other hand, the overarching concern with the state of English culture calls for consideration of how these texts are connected with the broader society and history of which they form a part. In his diagnosis of the state of English culture, made around the time of the founding of *Scrutiny*, Leavis saw the media and popular culture as integral to the 'breach in continuity' that now threatened society as a result of the strains between contemporary civilisation and the cultural tradition. In *Mass Civilization and Minority Culture* (1930) and *Culture and Environment* (1933; co-written with Denys Thompson), Leavis castigated the media of the day. Cinema trades in the 'cheapest emotional appeals', rendering it merely 'a means of passive diversion'. The levelling-down and 'standardizing influence of broadcasting hardly admits of doubt'. Advertising's copywriters abuse the language, and advertising's commercial pressures shape the press. The subtitle of *Culture and Environment* is *The Training of Critical Awareness*, and the book is an educational primer to foster the discriminatory awareness amongst pupils and students that 'films, newspapers, publicity in all its forms, commercially catered fiction – all offer satisfaction at the lowest level'.

Three elements in the Leavisite position – close attention to the (literary) text ('practical criticism'), an interest in its connections with the wider social processes, and the notion that the nature of the media's output is indicative of the general state of civilisation – were available for a reconfiguration that would treat the media with seriousness and without automatic hostility. And this reconfiguration occurred in the early 1960s amongst some literary intellectuals partly formed by Leavisism, though with a more explicit affiliation to the left, notably Raymond Williams and Stuart Hall. Raymond Williams' *Communications* (1962) was a topical book that suggested ways both for analysing press and broadcasting output and for reforming arts and media policy to remove some of the commercial pressures. The extract published here as Chapter 4 indicates how Williams is addressing issues rooted in the Leavisite problematic, but not acquiescing in its terms. In the first part he uses the term 'communications' to reconfigure effectively the ideas of 'culture' and 'civilization' and refuse the maintenance of a distinction that assigns the media solely to the latter. In the second part he discusses 'minority culture' and 'mass communications' in a way that throws doubt on the claims of minority culture – 'I see no real evidence that it is a permanent and reliable means of maintaining a living excellence' – and partially optimistic about the possibilities of mass communication – 'we often forget how many facts, how many new opinions, how many new kinds of work and new ways of seeing the world nevertheless get through'. The policy reforms proposed were designed to strengthen the institutional bases in British society for the positive development of communications. In 1964, Stuart Hall and Paddy Whannel published *The Popular Arts*. This book was an educational primer in the tradition of *Culture and Environment*, but with the crucial difference that the authors argued 'the struggle between what is good and worthwhile and what is shoddy and debased is not a struggle *against* the modern forms of communication, but a conflict *within* these media'.[10] The objective was to develop the skills of critical discrimination in young people amongst works drawn from cinema, broadcasting, popular music and other modern media, which allowed for some detailed discussion and analysis of particular examples.

Stuart Hall, however, was to go on to make a much more far-reaching break with Leavisism, as can be seen from his 'Encoding/Decoding' (Chapter 5). The version reprinted here was first published in 1980, but it is the finalised form of a piece that had started life much earlier, as an address to a 1973 conference on 'understanding television', which then appeared as an occasional paper from the Centre for Contemporary Cultural Studies at the University of Birmingham, Hall's academic home in that period. So it is fundamentally a piece from the early seventies, and can be seen as marking the inauguration of the 'cultural studies' stream in media studies, which has since become the most significant current in the academic study of the media in Britain. The paper represents the simultaneous confluence of, and rupture with, the two available relevant bodies of thinking about the media before that time, the 'mass communication' tradition rooted in American social science, and the 'culture and civilisation' tradition of Leavisism in English literary studies, even in the 'left Leavisite' version that Hall himself had inhabited previously. The residual traces of a Leavis-style concern with the particularity of the text are apparent in his denunciation of the impoverished social scientific conception of the media 'message' or 'content'. But these are no longer rich popular artworks about which a discriminatory sensibility must be cultivated. Instead the new-found influence of structural linguistics and semiology can be detected. 'Messages' should be seen as 'sign vehicles of a specific kind organized, like any form of communication or language, through the operation of codes within the syntagmatic chain of a discourse'; they are 'discursive forms' (see Chapters 14 and 15). Since the 1940s, American mass communication research had worked with a broad underlying model of the elements of (mass) communication that can be summarised as: source – message – receiver. In this piece, Hall took the model and fundamentally recast its terms to propose these 'elements' as a set of articulated moments in the circulation of social meaning. He had in mind an analogy with the value cycle set forth in Marx's account of *Capital*, in which value flows through the economy, changing its form from labour power to finished goods to realised capital and so on. The usefulness of this analogy is to illuminate that 'each [moment] has its specific modality and conditions of existence' and 'while each of the moments, in articulation, is necessary to the circuit as a whole, no one moment can fully guarantee the next moment with which it is articulated'. This point was in order to refuse the strong determinism of the Frankfurt School view of the media, in which the modern culture industry efficiently integrated the consciousness of viewers, listeners and readers to fit the reproduction needs of the capitalist social order (see Chapter 2). In its place Hall was proposing the possibility that viewers might not simply accept wholesale the media's messages just because they were exposed to them. They might make a reading according to a 'negotiated' code, or even a wholly 'oppositional' one. Hall has pointed out since that in the paper these 'are decoding positions; they are not sociological groups'.[11] That's because in a celebrated research project, his colleague David Morley did go on to test the idea of readings made according to 'hegemonic', 'negotiated' and 'oppositional' codes against actual readings made by particular groups of people (see Chapter 31).

Hall has since acknowledged a shortcoming in the paper's presentation of his position:

> I want[ed] to get rid of the notion of any originating moment . . . [W]e are in history already; therefore we are in discourse already. So what the media pick up on is already a discursive universe. The encoding moment doesn't come from nowhere. *I made a mistake by drawing that bloody diagram with only the top half.* You see, if you're doing a circuit, you must draw a circuit; so I must show how decoding enters practice and discourses which a reporter is picking up on.[12]

There is, however, a reason why the 'mistake' might have been made. That's because although encoding is not intended to be seen as an 'originating moment', it's not intended either to be seen as having an equivalence or symmetry with the moment of decoding. There is a 'preferred meaning' encoded in media discourses.

> I don't want a model of a circuit which has no power in it. I don't want a model which is determinist, but I don't want a model without determination. And therefore I don't think audiences are in the same positions of power with those who signify the world to them. And preferred reading is simply a way of saying if you have control of the apparatus of signifying the world, if you're in control of the media, you own it, you write the texts – to some extent it has a determining shape.[13]

'Encoding/Decoding' is the text that marks the opening-up in Britain of study of the media to a Marxism informed by the concepts developed in structuralism and semiology. Over the same period, however, another political current was to begin addressing questions related to the media: the twentieth century's second wave of Western feminism. Like Marxism, feminism is in the first instance a politics, its aim not simply to understand but also to change, in Jane Miller's words, 'the unquestioning male possession of the structures of economic and cultural power'.[14] Such change, however, presumes understanding, and like cultural studies, feminism made use of emergent theoretical approaches – from structuralism and semiology, psychoanalysis and Althusserian Marxism, for example – in order to understand not only how and why particular images and representations of women circulate in Western culture, but also how such representations are tied to the patriarchal structure of society and to our individual sense of a gendered identity within that society. But this focus on *gender* as a structuring principle of our social and symbolic worlds could not simply be added on to the class-based model of the emerging field of cultural studies. In challenging dominant 'knowledges' of, or 'truths' about women and the feminine, feminist theory also questioned the bases of such knowledge, asking how and where knowledge is produced and by whom, what counts as knowledge and whose interests it serves. Stuart Hall has described the 'painful exercise' through which the Birmingham Centre for Contemporary Cultural Studies attempted in the late 1970s to come to terms with feminism's challenge to 'the male-oriented models and assumptions and the heavily masculine subject-matter and topics' which had until then characterised its work.[15] But this effort has not always been matched by similar adjustments within other media research traditions, and feminist theory and criticism continue to occupy an uneasy position within media studies. It is this complex relationship which Annette Kuhn's piece (Chapter 6) outlines, in a chapter which originally formed the Introduction to her 1985 book. *The Power of the Image: Essays on Representation and Sexuality.* Beginning from the insistence that 'politics and knowledge are interdependent', and in the case of feminism mutually regenerative, she describes the way in which feminism has 'both used and transformed' existing knowledge and theoretical frameworks, 'drawing strategically on . . . strands of non-feminist or prefeminist thinking', but also exposing their weaknesses, and ultimately 'generating qualitatively new knowledge, . . . constructing a new field'. Within this field, the questions addressed have concerned the relationship between representation, sexuality, spectatorship, knowledge and power. In asking how representations of women both 'speak to' and help to construct our gendered identities, feminist research has also explored the social and cultural contexts within which such representations circulate, and the pleasures, both complicit and resistant, which they generate. Such analysis may itself, argues Kuhn, be regarded as 'strategic practice', 'an act of resistance in itself', but it also represents that struggle over meaning which is a prerequisite for political change.

The final two chapters in 'Some Introductions' can be seen as representing two antagonistic poles in debates over the media in the late 1980s and 1990s. Jürgen Habermas is a German philosopher and social scientist who stands in the intellectual tradition of the Frankfurt School. Like Adorno and Horkheimer before him, he is concerned with the legacy of the eighteenth-century European Enlightenment and all that it promised for human progress and emancipation. He identifies as a key feature of that period the formation of a 'public sphere', the (immaterial) place – not within the state or the market or private households – where public opinion can be formed. This zone is characterised by the commitment to the values of open rational debate, the public good, and the formal equality of participants. Irrationality and arbitrary or hieratic authority are in principle alien to it; argument based upon evidence is the appropriate discursive mode. One of the major institutional sites of the public sphere in the late eighteenth century was the newspaper press (along with museums and galleries, learned and debating societies, etc.), while '[t]oday, newspapers and periodicals, radio and television are the media of the public sphere'. But in the meantime, argues Habermas, the public sphere has been 'refeudalized', returned to the state of a mere display of public authority, characteristic of 'publicness' in the pre-Enlightenment 'feudal' era. Broadcasting and the press are adulterated by consumer advertising and the public relations industry: the public sphere is thus corrupted and decaying. Habermas wishes to see the fulfilment of the Enlightenment idea of the public sphere, though nowadays the participation of a 'public of private persons acting as individuals would be replaced by a public of organized private persons' in democratically based political parties, campaign groups and other civil associations. There is sometimes said to be an element of retrospective idealisation in Habermas' portrait of the public sphere. His critics point out that the eighteenth-century public sphere was for gentlemen only; artisans, waged workers and most women were excluded.[16] But this criticism overlooks Habermas' intention to register that the development of the idea itself represented a historical progress, like the ideas of 'liberty, equality, solidarity', even though the emergence of these philosophical tenets marked the inauguration of an enormous unfinished struggle to realise them. To many nowadays the concept of the public sphere is another manifestation of the false universalism of the European Enlightenment. However, Habermas' ideas have proved a rallying point for those concerned with democracy and the media, the extension of freedom of information and the curbing of commercial interests in the press and broadcasting. For instance, in the late 1980s a defence of British public-service broadcasting was mounted around the concept of the public sphere.[17]

In Chapter 8, the French philosopher Jean Baudrillard discusses a similar area of concern – the contemporary media and political and social representation – and he too acknowledges that Enlightenment ideals have not been realised, either in society at large or in the role played by the media. His is a position often called 'postmodernist' (though he is rather coy about accepting the term). In contrast to the modern era commencing with the Enlightenment – when scientific reason sought to construct an accurate account of nature, society and history, and thus produce a truthful representation of the world – the postmodern period of today is characterised by the end of representation. For contemporary culture is a culture of 'simulation', 'the generation by models of a real without origin or reality: a hyperreal'.[18] No longer is it a case of an external real reflected or represented by scholarship or the arts; culture is dominated by the media, which exercise a fascination for the masses through the ceaseless play of hyperreal spectacle. 'Reality' becomes inseparably bound up with the media and is increasingly constituted by them. 'The situation no longer permits us to isolate reality ... as a fundamental variable. ... [B]ecause we will never in future be able to separate reality from its statistical, simulative projection in the media, [the result is] a state of suspense and of definitive uncertainty about reality.' The media, far from furnishing a public sphere in which to make social and political representations (in both senses), increasingly fill the space of that politics and society, indeed constitute the hyperreal spectacle that *is* society and politics today. This is 'the implosion of the social in the media'. Baudrillard does not mourn this development or depict it as manipulation by the media causing 'alienation' of the masses from true democratic politics. Instead he suggests it leads to a 'secret strategy' of resistance by the masses to refuse to adopt the part assigned to them by Enlightenment philosophers or power politicians, and derisively allow the rulers to assume the burdens of political responsibility while themselves remaining unknowable behind the spectacle.

These eight chapters are written from a variety of standpoints: classic American social science; Frankfurt critical theory; technological determinism; British 'culturalism' and 'cultural studies; feminism; Habermasian 'public sphere' theory; and postmodernism. Together they form a representative and rich selection of the most significant traditions of thought since the mid-twentieth century on the overall place of the media in society.

NOTES

1. See, for example, Walter Lippmann, *Public Opinion* (New York: Harcourt Brace, 1922); John Dewey, *The Public and its Problems* (Chicago: Swallow Press, 1927); Harold D. Lasswell, *Propaganda Techniques in the World War* (New York: Knopf, 1927); Edward Bernays, *Propaganda* (New York: Horace Liveright, 1928).

2. See, for example, Hadley Cantril, Hazel Gaudet, Herta Herzog, *The Invasion from Mars: A Study in the Psychology of Panic* (Princeton, NJ: Princeton University Press, 1940); Paul F. Lazarsfeld and Frank N. Stanton (eds), *Radio Research: 1942–3* (New York: Duell, Sloan & Pearce, 1944); Carl I. Hovland, Arthur A. Lumsdaine, Fred D. Sheffield, *Experiments in Mass Communication* (Princeton, NJ: Princeton University Press, 1949).

3. The mention of the radio artiste Kate Smith in this section draws on the study Robert Merton and colleagues had made of the reasons for the success of the performer's marathon radio campaign to sell US war bonds: Robert K. Merton, Marjorie Fiske, Alberta Curtis, *Mass Persuasion: The Social Psychology of a War Bond Drive* (New York: Harper, 1946).

4. The idea of 'supplementation' – 'the enhanced effectiveness of th[e] joining of mass media and direct personal contact' – anticipates to some degree one of Lazarsfeld's most famous concepts, the 'two-step flow' of communication influence. This was developed through reflection on the findings of a study of mass media influence on voting in the 1940 US Presidential Election campaign (Paul F. Lazarsfeld, Bernard Berelson, Hazel Gaudet, *The People's Choice* (New York: Columbia University Press, 1944), and set forth in Elihu Katz and Paul F. Lazarsfeld, *Personal Influence: The Part Played by People in the Flow of Mass Communications* (Glencoe, Ill. The Free Press, 1955).

5. For a sense of the range of the American post-war 'mass culture' debate, a useful anthology from the period is: Bernard Rosenberg and David Manning White (eds), *Mass Culture: The Popular Arts in America* (New York: Macmillan, 1957).

6. Paul F. Lazarsfeld, 'Remarks on Administrative and Critical Communications Research', *Studies in Philosophy and Social Science* 9:1 (1941) pp. 2–16.

7. Paul F. Lazarsfeld, unpublished letter to Theodor Adorno, n.d. [1938]. Cited in Hanno Hardt, *Critical Communication Studies: Communication, History and Theory in America* (London: Routledge, 1992).

8. 'The Culture Industry: Enlightenment as Mass Deception' is available in abridged form in James Curran, Michael Gurevitch, Janet Woollacott (eds), *Mass Communication and Society* (London: Edward Arnold, 1977).

9. In his introduction to a published translation of this essay, Andreas Huyssen detects a 'shift of emphasis' in Adorno's position towards a slightly less totalised conception of the culture industry's perpetration of mass deception, but it is for its synoptic reprise of Adorno and Horkheimer's major themes that the

piece is reprinted here. (Andreas Huyssen, 'Introduction to Adorno', *New German Critique* 6 (Fall 1975) pp. 3–11).

10.   Stuart Hall and Paddy Whannel, *The Popular Arts* (London: Hutchinson, 1964) p. 15.

11.   'Reflections upon the Encoding/Decoding Model: An Interview with Stuart Hall', in Jon Cruz and Justin Lewis (eds), *Viewing, Reading, Listening: Audiences and Cultural Reception* (Boulder, Col.: Westview Press, 1994) p. 256.

12.   Ibid., p. 260, editors' italics.

13.   Ibid., p. 261.

14.   Jane Miller, *Seductions: Studies in Reading and Culture* (London: Virago, 1990) p. 10.

15.   Stuart Hall, 'Cultural Studies and the Centre: Some Problematics and Problems', in Stuart Hall, Dorothy Hobson, Andrew Lowe, Paul Willis (eds), *Culture, Media, Language* (London: Hutchinson, 1980) pp. 35–6.

16.   Nancy Fraser, 'What's Critical about Critical Theory? The Case of Habermas and Gender', in Seyla Benhabib and Drucilla Cornell (eds), *Feminism as Critique: On the Politics of Gender* (Minneapois: University of Minnesota Press, 1987); Oskar Negt and Alexander Kluge, 'The Proletarian Public Sphere', in Armand Mattelart and Seth Sieglaub (eds), *Communication and Class Struggle*, vol. 1, (New York: International General, 1979).

17.   See especially Nicholas Garnham, 'The Media and the Public Sphere', in Peter Golding, Graham Murdock, Philip Schlesinger (eds), *Communicating Politics: Mass Communications and the Political Process* (Leicester: Leicester University Press, 1986); and Paddy Scannell, 'Public Service Broadcasting and Modern Public Life', *Media, Culture and Society* 11:2, (1989).

18.   Jean Baudrillard, *Simulations* (New York: Semiotext(e), 1983) p. 2.

1

MASS COMMUNICATION, POPULAR TASTE AND ORGANIZED SOCIAL ACTION

Paul F. Lazarsfeld and Robert K. Merton

A review of the current state of actual knowledge concerning the social role of the mass media of communication and their effects upon the contemporary American community is an ungrateful task, for certified knowledge of this kind is impressively slight. Little more can be done than to explore the nature of the problems by methods which, in the course of many decades, will ultimately provide the knowledge we seek. Although this is anything but an encouraging preamble, it provides a necessary context for assessing the research and tentative conclusions of those of us professionally concerned with the study of mass media. A reconnaissance will suggest what we know, what we need to know, and will locate the strategic points requiring further inquiry.

[. . .]

THE SOCIAL ROLE OF THE MACHINERY OF MASS MEDIA

What role can be assigned to the mass media by virtue of the fact that they exist? What are the implications of a Hollywood, a Radio City, and a Time-Life-Fortune enterprise for our society? These questions can of course be discussed only in grossly speculative terms, since no experimentation or rigorous comparative study is possible. Comparisons with other societies lacking these mass media would be too crude to yield decisive results, and comparisons with an earlier day in American society would still involve gross assertions rather than precise demonstrations. In such an instance, brevity is clearly indicated. And opinions should be leavened with caution. It is our tentative judgment that the social role played by the very existence of the mass media has been commonly overestimated. What are the grounds for this judgment?

From Paul F. Lazarsfeld and Robert K. Merton, 'Mass Communication, Popular Taste and Organized Social Action', in Lyman Bryson (ed.), *The Communication of Ideas* (New York: Harper & Bros., 1948). Also available in Wilbur Schramm (ed.), *Mass Communications* (Urbana: University of Illinois Press, 1960).

It is clear that the mass media reach enormous audiences. Approximately forty-five million Americans attend the movies every week; our daily newspaper circulation is about fifty-four million, and some forty-six million American homes are equipped with television, and in these homes the average American watches television for about three hours a day. These are formidable figures. But they are merely supply and consumption figures, not figures registering the effect of mass media. They bear only upon what people do, not upon the social and psychological impact of the media. To know the number of hours people keep the radio turned on gives no indication of the effect upon them of what they hear. Knowledge of consumption data in the field of mass media remains far from a demonstration of their net effect upon behavior and attitude and outlook.

As was indicated a moment ago, we cannot resort to experiment by comparing contemporary American society with and without mass media. But, however tentatively, we can compare their social effect with, say, that of the automobile. It is not unlikely that the invention of the automobile and its development into a mass-owned commodity has had a significantly greater effect upon society than the invention of the radio and its development into a medium of mass communication. Consider the social complexes into which the automobile has entered. Its sheer existence has exerted pressure for vastly improved roads and with these, mobility has increased enormously. The shape of metropolitan agglomerations has been significantly affected by the automobile. And, it may be submitted, the inventions which enlarge the radius of movement and action exert a greater influence upon social outlook and daily routines than inventions which provide avenues for ideas – ideas which can be avoided by withdrawal, deflected by resistance and transformed by assimilation.

Granted, for a moment, that the mass media play a comparatively minor role in shaping our society, why are they the object of so much popular concern and criticism? Why do so many become exercised by the 'problems' of the radio and film and press and so few by the problems of, say, the automobile and the airplane? In addition to the sources of this concern which we have noted previously, there is an unwitting psychological basis for concern which derives from a socio-historical context.

Many make the mass media targets for hostile criticism because they feel themselves duped by the turn of events.

The social changes ascribable to 'reform movements' may be slow and slight, but they do cumulate. The surface facts are familiar enough. The sixty-hour week has given way to the forty-hour week. Child labor has been progressively curtailed. With all its deficiencies, free universal education has become progressively institutionalized. These and other gains register a series of reform victories. And now, people have more leisure time. They have, ostensibly, greater access to the cultural heritage. And what use do they make of this unmortgaged time so painfully acquired for them? They listen to the radio and go to the movies. These mass media seem somehow to have cheated reformers of the fruits of their victories. The struggle for freedom for leisure and popular education and social security was carried on in the hope that, once freed of cramping shackles, people would avail themselves of major cultural products of our society, Shakespeare or Beethoven or perhaps Kant. Instead, they turn to Faith Baldwin or Johnny Mercer or Edgar Guest.

[. . .]

However little this sense of betrayal may account for prevailing attitudes toward the mass media, it may again be noted that the sheer presence of these media may not affect our society so profoundly as it is widely supposed.

SOME SOCIAL FUNCTIONS OF THE MASS MEDIA

In continuing our examination of the social role which can be ascribed to the mass media by virtue of their 'sheer existence,' we temporarily abstract from the social structure in which the media find their place. We do not, for example, consider the diverse effects of the mass media under varying systems of ownership and control, an important structural factor which will be discussed subsequently.

The mass media undoubtedly serve many social functions which might well become the object of sustained research. Of these functions, we have occasion to notice only three.

The Status Conferral Function

The mass media *confer* status on public issues, persons, organizations, and social movements.

Common experience as well as research testifies that the social standing of persons or social policies is raised when these command favorable attention in the mass media. In many quarters, for example, the support of a political candidate or a public policy by *The Times* is taken as significant, and this support is regarded as a distinct asset for the candidate or the policy. Why?

For some, the editorial views of *The Times* represent the considered judgment of a group of experts, thus calling for the respect of laymen. But this is only one element in the status conferral function of the mass media, for enhanced status accrues to those who merely receive attention in the media, quite apart from any editorial support.

The mass media bestow prestige and enhance the authority of individuals and groups by *legitimizing their status.* Recognition by the press or radio or magazines or newsreels testifies that one has arrived, that one is important enough to have been singled out from the large anonymous masses, that one's behavior and opinions are significant enough to require public notice. The operation of this status conferral function may be witnessed most vividly in the advertising pattern of testimonials to a product by 'prominent people.' Within wide circles of the population (though not within certain selected social strata), such testimonials not only enhance the prestige of the product but also reflect prestige on the person who provides the testimonials. They give public notice that the large and powerful world of commerce regards him as possessing sufficiently high status for his opinion to count with many people. In a word, his testimonial is a testimonial to his own status.

[. . .]

This status conferral function thus enters into organized social action by legitimizing selected policies, persons, and groups which receive the support of mass media. We shall have occasion to note the detailed operation of this function in connection with the conditions making for the maximal utilization of mass media for designated social ends. At the moment, having considered the 'status conferral' function, we shall consider a second: the enforced application of social norms through the mass media.

The Enforcement of Social Norms

Such catch phrases as 'the power of the press' (and other mass media) or 'the bright glare of publicity' presumably refer to this function. The mass media may initiate organized social action by 'exposing' conditions which are at variance with public moralities. But it need not be prematurely assumed that this pattern consists *simply* in making these deviations widely known. We have something to learn in this connection from Malinowski's observations among his beloved Trobriand Islanders. There, he reports, no organized social action is taken with respect to behavior deviant from a social norm unless there is *public* announcement of the deviation. This is not merely a matter of acquainting the individuals in the group with the facts of the case. Many may have known privately of these deviations – e.g., incest among the Trobrianders, as with political or business corruption, prostitution, gambling among ourselves – but they will not have pressed for public action. But once the behavioral deviations are made simultaneously public for all, this sets in train tensions between the 'privately tolerable' and the 'publicly acknowledgeable.'

The mechanism of public exposure would seem to operate somewhat as follows. Many social norms prove inconvenient for individuals in the society. They militate against the gratification of wants and impulses. Since many find the norms burdensome, there is some measure of leniency in applying them, both to oneself and to others. Hence, the emergence of deviant behavior and private toleration in these deviations. But this can continue only so long as one is not in a situation where one must take a public stand for or against the norms. Publicity, the enforced acknowledgment by members of the group that these deviations have occurred, requires each individual to take such a stand. He must either range himself with the non-conformists, thus proclaiming his repudiation of the group norms, and thus asserting that he, too, is outside the moral framework or, regardless of his private predilections, he must fall into line by supporting the norm. *Publicity closes the gap between 'private attitudes' and 'public morality.'* Publicity exerts pressure for a single rather than a dual morality by preventing continued evasion of the issue. It calls forth public reaffirmation and (however sporadic) application of the social norm.

In a mass society, this function of public exposure is institutionalized in the mass media of communication. Press, radio, and journals expose fairly well-known deviations to public view, and as a rule, this exposure forces some degree of public action against what has been privately tolerated. The mass media may, for example, introduce severe strains upon 'polite ethnic discrimination' by calling public attention to these practices which are at odds with the norms of non-discrimination. At times, the media may organize exposure activities into a 'crusade.'

[. . .]

[M]ass media clearly serve to reaffirm social norms by exposing deviations from these norms to public view. Study of the particular range of norms thus reaffirmed would provide a clear index of the extent to which these media deal with peripheral or central problems of the structure of our society.

The Narcotizing Dysfunction

A third social consequence of the mass media has gone largely unnoticed. At least, it has received little explicit comment and, apparently, has not been systematically put to use for furthering planned objectives. This may be called the narcotizing dysfunction of the mass media. It is termed *dysfunctional* rather than functional on the assumption that it is not in the interest of modern complex society to have large masses of the population politically apathetic and inert. How does this unplanned mechanism operate?

Scattered studies have shown that an increasing proportion of the time of Americans is devoted to the products of the mass media. With distinct variations in different regions and among different social strata, the outpourings of the media presumably enable the twentieth-century American to 'keep abreast of the world.' Yet, it is suggested, this vast supply of communications may elicit only a superficial concern with the problems of society, and this superficiality often cloaks mass apathy.

Exposure to this flood of information may serve to narcotize rather than to energize the average reader or listener. As an increasing meed of time is devoted to reading and listening, a decreasing share is available for organized action. The individual reads accounts of issues and problems and may even discuss alternative lines of action. But this rather intellectualized, rather remote connection with organized social action is not activated. The interested and informed citizen can congratulate himself on his lofty state of interest and information and neglect to see that he has abstained from decision and action. In short, he takes his secondary contact with the world of political reality, his reading and listening and thinking, as a vicarious performance. He comes to mistake *knowing* about problems of the day for *doing* something about them. His social conscience remains spotlessly clean. He *is* concerned. He *is* informed. And he has all sorts of ideas as to what should be done. But, after he has gotten through his dinner and after he has listened to his favored radio programs and after he has read his second newspaper of the day, it is really time for bed.

In this peculiar respect, mass communications may be included among the most respectable and efficient of social narcotics. They may be so fully effective as to keep the addict from recognizing his own malady.

That the mass media have lifted the level of information of large populations is evident. Yet, quite apart from intent, increasing dosages of mass communications may be inadvertently transforming the energies of men from active participation into passive knowledge.

The occurrence of this narcotizing dysfunction can scarcely be doubted, but the extent to which it operates has yet to be determined. Research on this problem remains one of the many tasks still confronting the student of mass communications.

THE STRUCTURE OF OWNERSHIP AND OPERATION

To this point we have considered the mass media quite apart from their incorporation within a particular social and economic structure. But clearly, the social effects of the media will vary as the system of ownership and control varies. Thus to consider the social effects of American mass media is to deal only with the effects of these media as privately owned enterprises under profit-oriented management. It is general knowledge that this circumstance is not inherent in the technological nature of the mass media. In England, for example, to say nothing of Russia, the radio is to all intents and purposes owned, controlled, and operated by government.

The structure of control is altogether different in this country. Its salient characteristic stems from the fact that except for movies and books, it is not the magazine reader nor the radio listener nor, in large part, the reader of newspapers who supports the enterprise, but the advertiser. Big business finances the production and distribution of mass media. And, all intent aside, he who pays the piper generally calls the tune.

SOCIAL CONFORMISM

Since the mass media are supported by great business concerns geared into the current social and economic system, the media contribute to the maintenance of that system. This contribution is not found merely in the effective advertisement of the sponsor's product. It arises, rather, from the typical presence in magazine stories, radio programs, and newspaper columns of some element of confirmation, some element of approval of the present structure of society. And this continuing reaffirmation underscores the duty to accept.

To the extent that the media of mass communication have had an influence upon their audiences, it has stemmed not only from what is said, but more significantly from what is not said. For these media not only continue to affirm the status quo but, in the same measure, they fail to raise essential questions about the structure of society. Hence by leading toward conformism and by providing little basis for a critical appraisal of society, the commercially sponsored mass media indirectly but effectively restrain the cogent development of a genuinely critical outlook.

This is not to ignore the occasionally critical journal article or radio program. But these exceptions are so few that they are lost in the overwhelming flood of conformist materials. . . .

Since our commercially sponsored mass media promote a largely unthinking allegiance to our social structure, they cannot be relied upon to work for changes, even minor changes, in that structure. It is possible to list some developments to the contrary, but upon close inspection they prove illusory. A community group, such as the PTA, may request the producer of a radio serial to inject the theme of tolerant race attitudes into the program. Should the producer feel that this theme is safe, that it will not antagonize any substantial part of his audience, he may agree, but at the first indication that it is a dangerous theme which may alienate potential consumers, he will refuse, or will soon abandon the experiment. Social objectives are consistently surrendered by commercialized media when they clash with economic gains. Minor tokens of 'progressive' views are of slight importance since they are included only by the grace of the sponsors and only on the condition that they be sufficiently acceptable as not to alienate any appreciable part of the audience. Economic pressure makes for conformism by omission of sensitive issues.

IMPACT UPON POPULAR TASTE

Since the largest part of our radio, movies, magazines, and a considerable part of our books and newspapers are devoted to 'entertainment,' this clearly requires us to consider the impact of the mass media upon popular taste.

Were we to ask the average American with some pretension to literary or esthetic cultivation if mass communications have had any effect upon popular taste, he would doubtlessly answer with a resounding affirmative. And more, citing abundant instances, he would insist that esthetic and intellectual tastes have been depraved by the flow of trivial formula products from printing presses, radio stations, and movie studios. The columns of criticism abound with these complaints.

In one sense, this requires no further discussion. There can be no doubt that the women who are daily entranced for three or four hours by some twelve consecutive 'soap operas,' all cut to the same dismal pattern, exhibit an appalling lack of esthetic judgment. Nor is this impression altered by the contents of pulp and slick magazines, or by the depressing abundance of formula motion pictures replete with hero, heroine, and villain moving through a contrived atmosphere of sex, sin, and success.

Yet unless we locate these patterns in historical and sociological terms, we may find ourselves confusedly engaged in condemning without understanding, in criticism which is sound but largely irrelevant. What is the historical status of this notoriously low level of popular taste? Is it the poor remains of standards which were once significantly higher, a relatively new birth in the world of values, largely unrelated to the higher standards from which it has allegedly fallen, or a poor substitute blocking the way to the development of superior standards and the expression of high esthetic purpose?

If esthetic tastes are to be considered in their social setting, we must recognize that the effective audience for the arts has become historically transformed. Some centuries back, this audience was largely confined to a selected aristocratic elite. Relatively few were literate. And very few possessed the means to buy books, attend theaters, and travel to the urban centers of the arts. Not more than a slight fraction, possibly not more than one or two per cent, of the population composed the effective audience for the arts. These happy few cultivated their esthetic tastes, and their selective demand left its mark in the form of relatively high artistic standards.

With the widesweeping spread of popular education and with the emergence of the new technologies of mass communication, there developed an enormously enlarged market for the arts. Some forms of music, drama, and literature now reach virtually everyone in our society. This is why, of course, we speak of *mass* media and of *mass* art. And the great audiences for the mass media, though in the main literate, are not highly cultivated. About half the population, in fact, have halted their formal education upon leaving grammar school.

[. . .]

Our formulation of the problem should now be plain. It is misleading to speak simply of the decline of esthetic tastes. Mass audiences probably include a larger number of persons with cultivated esthetic standards, but these are swallowed up by the large masses who constitute the new and untutored audience for the arts. Whereas yesterday the elite constituted virtually the whole of the audience, they are today a minute fraction of the whole. In consequence, the average level of esthetic standards and tastes of audiences has been depressed, although the tastes of some sectors of the population have undoubtedly been raised and the total number of people exposed to communication contents has been vastly increased.

But this analysis does not directly answer the question of the effects of the mass media upon public taste, a question which is as complex as it is unexplored. The answer can come only from disciplined research. One would want to know, for example, whether mass media have robbed the intellectual and artistic elite of the art forms which might otherwise have been accessible to them. And this involves inquiry into the pressure exerted by the mass audience upon creative individuals to cater to mass tastes. Literary hacks have existed in every age. But it would be important to learn if the electrification of the arts supplies power for a significantly greater proportion of dim literary lights. And, above all, it would be essential to determine if mass media and mass tastes are necessarily linked in a vicious circle of deteriorating standards or if appropriate action on the part of the directors of mass media could initiate a virtuous circle of cumulatively improving tastes among their audiences. More concretely, are the operators of commercialized mass media caught up in a situation in which they cannot, whatever their private preferences, radically raise the esthetic standards of their products?

In passing, it should be noted that much remains to be learned concerning standards appropriate for mass art. It is possible that standards for art forms produced by a small band of creative talents for a small and selective audience are not applicable to art forms produced by a gigantic industry for the population at large. The beginnings of investigation on this problem are sufficiently suggestive to warrant further study.

Sporadic and consequently inconclusive experiments in the raising of standards have met with profound resistance from mass audiences. On occasion, radio stations and networks have attempted to supplant a soap opera with a program of classical music, or formula comedy skits with discussions of public issues. In general, the people supposed to benefit by this reformation of program have simply refused to be benefited. They cease listening. The audience dwindles. Researches have shown, for example, that radio programs of classical music tend to preserve rather than to create interest in classical music and that newly emerging interests are typically superficial. Most listeners to these programs have previously acquired an interest in classical music; the few whose interest is initiated by the programs are caught up by melodic compositions and come to think of classical music exclusively in terms of Tschaikowsky or Rimsky-Korsakow or Dvorak.

[. . .]

We turn now to the third and last aspect of the social role of the mass media: the possibilities of utilizing them for moving toward designated types of social objectives.

PROPAGANDA FOR SOCIAL OBJECTIVES

This final question is perhaps of more direct interest to you than the other questions we have discussed. It represents something of a challenge to us since it provides the means of resolving the apparent paradox to which we referred previously: the seeming paradox arising from the assertion that the significance of the sheer existence of the mass media has been exaggerated and the multiple indications that the media do exert influences upon their audiences.

What are the conditions for the effective use of mass media for what might be called 'propaganda for social objectives' – the promotion, let us say, of non-discriminatory race relations, or of educational reforms, or of positive attitudes toward organized labor? Research indicates that, at least, one or more of three conditions must be satisfied if this propaganda is to prove effective. These conditions may be briefly designated as (1) monopolization, (2) canalization rather than change of basic values, and (3) supplementary face-to-face contact. Each of these conditions merits some discussion.

MONOPOLIZATION

This situation obtains when there is little or no opposition in the mass media to the diffusion of values, policies, or public images. That is to say, monopolization of the mass media occurs in the absence of counterpropaganda.

In this restricted sense, monopolization of the mass media is found in diverse circumstances. It is, of course, indigenous to the political structure of authoritarian society, where access to the media of communication is wholly closed to those who oppose the official ideology. The evidence suggests that this monopoly played some part in enabling the Nazis to maintain their control of the German people.

But this same situation is approximated in other social systems. During the war, for example, our government utilized the radio, with some success, to promote and to maintain identification with the war effort. The effectiveness of these morale building efforts was in large measure due to the virtually complete absence of counterpropaganda.

Similar situations arise in the world of commercialized propaganda. The mass media create popular idols. The public images of the radio performer, Kate Smith, for example, picture her as a woman with unparalleled understanding of other American women, deeply sympathetic with ordinary men and women, a spiritual guide and mentor, a patriot whose views on public affairs should be taken seriously. Linked with the cardinal American virtues, the public images of Kate Smith are at no point subject to a counterpropaganda. Not that she has no competitors in the market of radio advertising. But there are none who set themselves systematically to question what she has said. In consequence, an unmarried radio entertainer with an annual income in six figures may be visualized by millions of American women as a hard-working mother who knows the recipe for managing life on fifteen hundred a year.

This image of a popular idol would have far less currency were it subjected to counterpropaganda. Such neutralization occurs, for example, as a result of preelection campaigns by

Republicans and Democrats. By and large, as a recent study has shown, the propaganda issued by each of these parties neutralizes the effect of the other's propaganda. Were both parties to forgo their campaigning through the mass media entirely, it is altogether likely that the net effect would be to reproduce the present distribution of votes.

[. . .]

To the extent that opposing political propaganda in the mass media are balanced, the net effect is negligible. The virtual monopolization of the media for given social objectives, however, will produce discernible effects upon audiences.

CANALIZATION

Prevailing beliefs in the enormous power of mass communications appear to stem from successful cases of monopolistic propaganda or from advertising. But the leap from the efficacy of advertising to the assumed efficacy of propaganda aimed at deep-rooted attitudes and ego involved behavior is as unwarranted as it is dangerous. Advertising is typically directed toward the canalizing of preexisting behavior patterns or attitudes. It seldom seeks to instil new attitudes or to create significantly new behavior patterns. 'Advertising pays' because it generally deals with a simple psychological situation. For Americans who have been socialized in the use of a toothbrush, it makes relatively little difference which brand of toothbrush they use. Once the gross pattern of behavior or the generic attitude has been established, it can be canalized in one direction or another. Resistance is slight. But mass propaganda typically meets a more complex situation. It may seek objectives which are at odds with deep-lying attitudes. It may seek to reshape rather than to canalize current systems of values. And the successes of advertising may only highlight the failures of propaganda. Much of the current propaganda which is aimed at abolishing deep-seated and racial prejudices, for example, seems to have had little effectiveness.

Media of mass communication, then, have been effectively used to canalize basic attitudes but there is little evidence of their having served to change these attitudes.

SUPPLEMENTATION

Mass propaganda which is neither monopolistic nor canalizing in character may, nonetheless, prove effective if it meets a third condition: supplementation through face-to-face contacts.

[. . .]

Students of mass movements have come to repudiate the view that mass propaganda in and of itself creates or maintains the movement. Naziism did not attain its brief moment of hegemony by capturing the mass media of communication. The media played an ancillary role, supplementing the use of organized violence, organized distribution of rewards for conformity, and organized centers of local indoctrination. The Soviet Union has also made large and impressive use of mass media for indoctrinating enormous populations with appropriate ideologies. But the organizers of indoctrination saw to it that the mass media did not operate alone. 'Red corners,' 'reading huts,' and 'listening stations' comprised meeting places in which groups of citizens were exposed to the mass media in common. The 55,000 reading rooms and clubs which had come into being by 1933 enabled the local ideological elite to talk over with rank-and-file readers the content of what they read. The relative scarcity of radios in private homes again made for group listening and group discussions of what had been heard.

In these instances, the machinery of mass persuasion included face-to-face contact in local organizations as an adjunct to the mass media. The privatized individual response to the materials presented through the channels of mass communication was considered inadequate for transforming exposure to propaganda into effectiveness of propaganda. In a society such as our own, where the pattern of bureaucratization has not yet become so pervasive or, at least, not so clearly crystallized, it has likewise been found that mass media prove most effective in conjunction with local centers of organized face-to-face contact.

Several factors contribute to the enhanced effectiveness of this joining of mass media and direct personal contact. Most clearly, the local discussions serve to reinforce the content of mass propaganda. Such mutual confirmation produces a 'clinching effect.' Secondly, the central media lessen the task of the local organizer, and the personnel requirements for such subalterns need not be as rigorous in a popular movement. The subalterns need not set forth the propaganda content for themselves, but need only pilot potential converts to the radio where the doctrine is being expounded. Thirdly, the appearance of a representative of the movement on a nation-wide network, or his mention in the national press, serves to symbolize the legitimacy and significance of the movement. It is no powerless, inconsequential enterprise. The mass media, as we have seen, confer status. And the status of the national movement reflects back on the status of the local cells, thus consolidating the tentative decisions of its members. In this interlocking arrangement, the local organizer ensures an audience for the national speaker and the national speaker validates the status of the local organizer.

This brief summary of the situations in which the mass media achieve their maximum propaganda effect may resolve the seeming contradiction which arose at the outset of our discussion. The mass media prove most effective when they operate in a situation of virtual 'psychological monopoly,' or when the objective is one of canalizing rather than modifying basic attitudes or when they operate in conjunction with face-to-face contacts.

But these three conditions are rarely satisfied conjointly in propaganda for social objectives. To the degree that monopolization of attention is rare, opposing propagandas have free play in a democracy. And, by and large, basic social issues involve more than a mere canalizing of preexistent basic attitudes; they call, rather, for substantial changes in attitude and behavior. Finally, for the most obvious of reasons, the close collaboration of mass media and locally organized centers for face-to-face contact has seldom been achieved in groups striving for planned social change. Such programs are expensive. And it is precisely these groups which seldom have the large resources needed for these expensive programs. The forward looking groups at the edges of the power structure do not ordinarily have the large financial means of the contented groups at the center.

As a result of this threefold situation, the present role of media is largely confined to peripheral social concerns and the media do not exhibit the degree of social power commonly attributed to them.

By the same token, and in view of the present organization of business ownership and control of the mass media, they have served to cement the structure of our society. Organized business does approach a virtual 'psychological monopoly' of the mass media. Radio commercials and newspaper advertisements are, of course, premised on a system which has been termed free enterprise. Moreover, the world of commerce is primarily concerned with canalizing rather than radically changing basic attitudes; it seeks only to create preferences for one rather than another brand of product. Face-to-face contacts with those who have been socialized in our culture serve primarily to reinforce the prevailing culture patterns.

Thus, the very conditions which make for the maximum effectiveness of the mass media of communication operate toward the maintenance of the going social and cultural structure rather than toward its change.

2

CULTURE INDUSTRY RECONSIDERED

Theodor W. Adorno

The term culture industry was perhaps used for the first time in the book *Dialectic of Enlightenment*, which Horkheimer and I published in Amsterdam in 1947. In our drafts we spoke of 'mass culture'. We replaced that expression with 'culture industry' in order to exclude from the outset the interpretation agreeable to its advocates: that it is a matter of something like a culture that arises spontaneously from the masses themselves, the contemporary form of popular art. From the latter the culture industry must be distinguished in the extreme. The culture industry fuses the old and familiar into a new quality. In all its branches, products which are tailored for consumption by masses, and which to a great extent determine the nature of that consumption, are manufactured more or less according to plan. The individual branches are similar in structure or at least fit into each other, ordering themselves into a system almost without a gap. This is made possible by contemporary technical capabilities as well as by economic and administrative concentration. The culture industry intentionally integrates its consumers from above. To the detriment of both it forces together the spheres of high and low art, separated for thousands of years. The seriousness of high art is destroyed in speculation about its efficacy; the seriousness of the lower perishes with the civilizational constraints imposed on the rebellious resistance inherent within it as long as social control was not yet total. Thus, although the culture industry undeniably speculates on the conscious and unconscious state of the millions towards which it is directed, the masses are not primary, but secondary, they are an object of calculation; an appendage of the machinery. The customer is not king, as the culture industry would have us believe, not its subject but its object. The very word mass-media, specially honed for the culture industry, already shifts the accents onto harmless terrain. Neither is it a question of primary concern for the masses, nor of the techniques of communication as such, but of the spirit which sufflates them, their master's voice. The culture industry misuses its concern for the masses in order to duplicate, reinforce and strengthen their mentality, which it presumes

Originally a broadcast talk given on the Hessian Broadcasting System, Federal Republic of Germany in spring 1963, this piece was published in this translation by Anson G. Rabinbach, *New German Critique* no. 6 (Fall 1975) pp. 12–19; repr. as ch. 3 of Theodor W. Adorno, *The Culture Industry: Selected Essays on Mass Culture*, ed. with an introduction by J. M. Bernstein (London: Routledge, 1991) pp. 85–92.

is given and unchangeable. How this mentality might be changed is excluded throughout. The masses are not the measure but the ideology of the culture industry, even though the culture industry itself could scarcely exist without adapting to the masses.

The cultural commodities of the industry are governed, as Brecht and Suhrkamp expressed it thirty years ago, by the principle of their realization as value, and not by their own specific content and harmonious formation. The entire practice of the culture industry transfers the profit motive naked onto cultural forms. Ever since these cultural forms first began to earn a living for their creators as commodities in the market-place they had already possessed something of this quality. But then they sought after profit only indirectly, over and above their autonomous essence. New on the part of the culture industry is the direct and undisguised primacy of a precisely and thoroughly calculated efficacy in its most typical products. The autonomy of works of art, which of course rarely ever predominated in an entirely pure form, and was always permeated by a constellation of effects, is tendentially eliminated by the culture industry, with or without the conscious will of those in control. The latter include both those who carry out directives as well as those who hold the power. In economic terms they are or were in search of new opportunities for the realization of capital in the most economically developed countries. The old opportunities became increasingly more precarious as a result of the same concentration process which alone makes the culture industry possible as an omnipresent phenomenon. Culture, in the true sense, did not simply accommodate itself to human beings; but it always simultaneously raised a protest against the petrified relations under which they lived, thereby honouring them. In so far as culture becomes wholly assimilated to and integrated in those petrified relations, human beings are once more debased. Cultural entities typical of the culture industry are no longer *also* commodities, they are commodities through and through. This quantitative shift is so great that it calls forth entirely new phenomena. Ultimately, the culture industry no longer even needs to directly pursue everywhere the profit interests from which it originated. These interests have become objectified in its ideology and have even made themselves independent of the compulsion to sell the cultural commodities which must be swallowed anyway. The culture industry turns into public relations, the manufacturing of 'goodwill' per se, without regard for particular firms or saleable objects. Brought to bear is a general uncritical consensus, advertisements produced for the world, so that each product of the culture industry becomes its own advertisement.

Nevertheless, those characteristics which originally stamped the transformation of literature into a commodity are maintained in this process. More than anything in the world, the culture industry has its ontology, a scaffolding of rigidly conservative basic categories which can be gleaned, for example, from the commercial English novels of the late seventeenth and early eighteenth centuries. What parades as progress in the culture industry, as the incessantly new which it offers up, remains the disguise for an eternal sameness; everywhere the changes mask a skeleton which has changed just as little as the profit motive itself since the time it first gained its predominance over culture.

Thus, the expression 'industry' is not to be taken too literally. It refers to the standardization of the thing itself – such as that of the Western, familiar to every movie-goer – and to the rationalization of distribution techniques, but not strictly to the production process. Although in film, the central sector of the culture industry, the production process resembles technical modes of operation in the extensive division of labour, the employment of machines and the separation of the labourers from the means of production – expressed in the perennial conflict between artists active in the culture industry and those who control it – individual forms of production are nevertheless maintained. Each product affects an individual air;

individuality itself serves to reinforce ideology, in so far as the illusion is conjured up that the completely reified and mediated is a sanctuary from immediacy and life. Now, as ever, the culture industry exists in the 'service' of third persons, maintaining its affinity to the declining circulation process of capital, to the commerce from which it came into being. Its ideology above all makes use of the star system, borrowed from individualistic art and its commercial exploitation. The more dehumanized its methods of operation and content, the more diligently and successfully the culture industry propagates supposedly great personalities and operates with heart-throbs. It is industrial more in a sociological sense, in the incorporation of industrial forms of organization even when nothing is manufactured – as in the rationalization of office work – rather than in the sense of anything really and actually produced by technological rationality. Accordingly, the misinvestments of the culture industry are considerable, throwing those branches rendered obsolete by new techniques into crises, which seldom lead to changes for the better.

The concept of technique in the culture industry is only in name identical with technique in works of art. In the latter, technique is concerned with the internal organization of the object itself, with its inner logic. In contrast, the technique of the culture industry is, from the beginning, one of distribution and mechanical reproduction, and therefore always remains external to its object. The culture industry finds ideological support precisely in so far as it carefully shields itself from the full potential of the techniques contained in its products. It lives parasitically from the extra-artistic technique of the material production of goods, without regard for the obligation to the internal artistic whole implied by its functionality (*Sachlichkeit*), but also without concern for the laws of form demanded by aesthetic autonomy. The result for the physiognomy of the culture industry is essentially a mixture of streamlining, photographic hardness and precision on the one hand, and individualistic residues, sentimentality and an already rationally disposed and adapted romanticism on the other. Adopting Benjamin's designation of the traditional work of art by the concept of aura, the presence of that which is not present, the culture industry is defined by the fact that it does not strictly counterpose another principle to that of aura, but rather by the fact that it conserves the decaying aura as a foggy mist. By this means the culture industry betrays its own ideological abuses.

It has recently become customary among cultural officials as well as sociologists to warn against underestimating the culture industry while pointing to its great importance for the development of the consciousness of its consumers. It is to be taken seriously, without cultured snobbism. In actuality the culture industry is important as a moment of the spirit which dominates today. Whoever ignores its influence out of scepticism for what it stuffs into people would be naive. Yet there is a deceptive glitter about the admonition to take it seriously. Because of its social role, disturbing questions about its quality, about truth or untruth, and about the aesthetic niveau of the culture industry's emissions are repressed, or at least excluded from the so-called sociology of communications. The critic is accused of taking refuge in arrogant esoterica. It would be advisable first to indicate the double meaning of importance that slowly worms its way in unnoticed. Even if it touches the lives of innumerable people, the function of something is no guarantee of its particular quality. The blending of aesthetics with its residual communicative aspects leads art, as a social phenomenon, not to its rightful position in opposition to alleged artistic snobbism, but rather in a variety of ways to the defence of its baneful social consequences. The importance of the culture industry in the spiritual constitution of the masses is no dispensation for reflection on its objective legitimation, its essential being, least of all by a science which thinks itself pragmatic. On the contrary: such reflection becomes necessary precisely for this reason. To take the culture industry as seriously as its unquestioned role demands, means to take it seriously critically, and not to cower in the face of its monopolistic character.

Among those intellectuals anxious to reconcile themselves with the phenomenon and eager to find a common formula to express both their reservations against it and their respect for its power, a tone of ironic toleration prevails unless they have already created a new mythos of the twentieth century from the imposed regression. After all, those intellectuals maintain, everyone knows what pocket novels, films off the rack, family television shows rolled out into serials and hit parades, advice to the lovelorn and horoscope columns are all about. All of this, however, is harmless and, according to them, even democratic since it responds to a demand, albeit a stimulated one. It also bestows all kinds of blessings, they point out, for example, through the dissemination of information, advice and stress reducing patterns of behaviour. Of course, as every sociological study measuring something as elementary as how politically informed the public is has proven, the information is meagre or indifferent. Moreover, the advice to be gained from manifestations of the culture industry is vacuous, banal or worse, and the behaviour patterns are shamelessly conformist.

The two-faced irony in the relationship of servile intellectuals to the culture industry is not restricted to them alone. It may also be supposed that the consciousness of the consumers themselves is split between the prescribed fun which is supplied to them by the culture industry and a not particularly well-hidden doubt about its blessings. The phrase, the world wants to be deceived, has become truer than had ever been intended. People are not only, as the saying goes, falling for the swindle; if it guarantees them even the most fleeting gratification they desire a deception which is nonetheless transparent to them. They force their eyes shut and voice approval, in a kind of self-loathing, for what is meted out to them, knowing fully the purpose for which it is manufactured. Without admitting it they sense that their lives would be completely intolerable as soon as they no longer clung to satisfactions which are none at all.

The most ambitious defence of the culture industry today celebrates its spirit, which might be safely called ideology, as an ordering factor. In a supposedly chaotic world it provides human beings with something like standards for orientation, and that alone seems worthy of approval. However, what its defenders imagine is preserved by the culture industry is in fact all the more thoroughly destroyed by it. The colour film demolishes the genial old tavern to a greater extent than bombs ever could: the film exterminates its imago. No homeland can survive being processed by the films which celebrate it, and which thereby turn the unique character on which it thrives into an interchangeable sameness.

That which legitimately could be called culture attempted, as an expression of suffering and contradiction, to maintain a grasp on the idea of the good life. Culture cannot represent either that which merely exists or the conventional and no longer binding categories of order which the culture industry drapes over the idea of the good life as if existing reality were the good life, and as if those categories were its true measure. If the response of the culture industry's representatives is that it does not deliver art at all, this is itself the ideology with which they evade responsibility for that from which the business lives. No misdeed is ever righted by explaining it as such.

The appeal to order alone, without concrete specificity, is futile; the appeal to the dissemination of norms, without these ever proving themselves in reality or before consciousness, is equally futile. The idea of an objectively binding order, huckstered to people because it is so lacking for them, has no claims if it does not prove itself internally and in confrontation with human beings. But this is precisely what no product of the culture industry would engage in. The concepts of order which it hammers into human beings are always those of the status quo. They remain unquestioned, unanalysed and undialectically presupposed, even if they no longer have any substance for those who accept them. In contrast to the Kantian, the categorical imperative of the culture industry no longer has anything in common with freedom. It proclaims: you shall conform, without instruction as to what; conform to that which exists anyway, and to that which everyone thinks anyway as a reflex of this power and omnipresence. The power of the culture industry's ideology is such that conformity has replaced consciousness. The order that springs from it is never confronted with what it claims to be or with the real interests of human beings. Order, however, is not good in itself. It would be so only as a good order. The fact that the culture industry is oblivious to this and extols order *in abstracto*, bears witness to the impotence and untruth of the messages it conveys. While it claims to lead the perplexed, it deludes them with false conflicts which they are to exchange for their own. It solves conflicts for them only in appearance, in a way that they can hardly be solved in their real lives. In the products of the culture industry human beings get into trouble only so that they can be rescued unharmed, usually by representatives of a benevolent collective; and then in empty harmony, they are reconciled with the general, whose demands they had experienced at the outset as irreconcileable with their interests. For this purpose the culture industry has developed formulas which even reach into such non-conceptual areas as light musical entertainment. Here too one gets into a 'jam', into rhythmic problems, which can be instantly disentangled by the triumph of the basic beat.

Even its defenders, however, would hardly contradict Plato openly who maintained that what is objectively and intrinsically untrue cannot also be subjectively good and true for human beings. The concoctions of the culture industry are neither guides for a blissful life, nor a new art of moral responsibility, but rather exhortations to toe the line, behind which stand the most powerful interests. The consensus which it propagates strengthens blind, opaque authority. If the culture industry is measured not by its own substance and logic, but by its efficacy, by its position in reality and its explicit pretensions; if the focus of serious concern is with the efficacy to which it always appeals, the potential of its effect becomes twice as weigthy. This potential, however, lies in the promotion and exploitation of the ego-weakness to which the powerless members of contemporary society, with its concentration of power, are condemned. Their consciousness is further developed retrogressively. It is no coincidence that cynical American film producers are heard to say that their pictures must take into consideration the level of eleven-year-olds. In doing so they would very much like to make adults into eleven-year-olds.

It is true that thorough research has not, for the time being, produced an airtight case proving the regressive effects of particular products of the culture industry. No doubt an imaginatively designed experiment could achieve this more successfully than the powerful financial interests concerned would find comfortable. In any case, it can be assumed without hesitation that steady drops hollow the stone, especially since the system of the culture industry that surrounds the masses tolerates hardly any deviation and incessantly drills the same formulas on behaviour. Only their deep unconscious mistrust, the last residue of the difference between art and empirical reality in the spiritual make-up of the masses explains why they have not, to a person long since perceived and accepted the world as it is constructed for them by the culture industry. Even if its messages were as harmless as they are made out to be – on countless occasions they are obviously not harmless, like the movies which chime in with currently popular hate campaigns against intellectuals by portraying them with the usual stereotypes – the attitudes which the culture industry calls forth are anything but harmless. If an astrologer urges his readers to drive carefully on a particular day, that certainly hurts no one; they will, however, be harmed indeed by the stupefication which lies in the claim that advice which is valid every day and which is therefore idiotic, needs the approval of the stars.

Human dependence and servitude, the vanishing point of the culture industry, could scarcely be more faithfully described than by the American interviewee who was of the opinion that the dilemmas of the contemporary epoch would end if people would simply follow the lead of prominent personalities. In so far as the culture industry arouses a feeling of well-being that the world is precisely in that order suggested by the culture industry, the substitute gratification which it prepares for human beings cheats them out of the same happiness which it deceitfully projects. The total effect of the culture industry is one of anti-enlightenment, in which, as Horkheimer and I have noted, enlightenment, that is the progressive technical domination of nature, becomes mass deception and is turned into a means for fettering consciousness. It impedes the development of autonomous, independent individuals who judge and decide consciously for themselves. These, however, would be the precondition for a democratic society which needs adults who have come of age in order to sustain itself and develop. If the masses have been unjustly reviled from above as masses, the culture industry is not among the least responsible for making them into masses and then despising them, while obstructing the emancipation for which human beings are as ripe as the productive forces of the epoch permit.

3

THE MEDIUM IS THE MESSAGE

Marshall McLuhan

In a culture like ours, long accustomed to splitting and dividing all things as a means of control, it is sometimes a bit of a shock to be reminded that, in operational practical fact, the medium is the message. This is merely to say that the personal and social consequences of any medium – that is, of any extension of ourselves – result from the new scale that is introduced into our affairs by each extension of ourselves, or by any new technology. Thus, with automation,* for example, the new patterns of human association tend to eliminate jobs, it is true. That is the negative result. Positively, automation creates roles for people, which is to say depth of involvement in their work and human association that our preceding mechanical technology had destroyed. Many people would be disposed to say that it was not the machine, but what one did with the machine, that was its meaning or message. In terms of the ways in which the machine altered our relations to one another and to ourselves, it mattered not in the least whether it turned out cornflakes or Cadillacs. The restructuring of human work and association was shaped by the technique of fragmentation that is the essence of machine technology. The essence of automation technology is the opposite. It is integral and decentralist in depth, just as the machine was fragmentary, centralist, and superficial in its patterning of human relationships.

The instance of the electric light may prove illuminating in this connection. The electric light is pure information. It is a medium without a message, as it were, unless it is used to spell out some verbal ad or name. This fact, characteristic of all media, means that the 'content' of any medium is always another medium. The content of writing is speech, just as the written word is the content of print, and print is the content of the telegraph. If it is asked, 'What is the content of speech?' it is necessary to say, 'It is an actual process of thought, which is in itself nonverbal.' An abstract painting represents direct manifestation of creative thought processes as they might appear in computer designs. What we are considering here, however,

From Marshall McLuhan, *Understanding Media: the Extensions of Man* (London: Routledge & Kegan Paul, 1964) pp. 11, 15–21, 31–3, 68–9.

are the psychic and social consequences of the designs or patterns as they amplify or accelerate existing processes. For the 'message' of any medium or technology is the change of scale or pace or pattern that it introduces into human affairs. The railway did not introduce movement or transportation or wheel or road into human society, but it accelerated and enlarged the scale of previous human functions, creating totally new kinds of cities and new kinds of work and leisure. This happened whether the railway functioned in a tropical or a northern environment, and is quite independent of the freight or content of the railway medium. The airplane, on the other hand, by accelerating the rate of transportation, tends to dissolve the railway form of city, politics, and association, quite independently of what the airplane is used for.

Let us return to the electric light. Whether the light is being used for brain surgery or night baseball is a matter of indifference. It could be argued that these activities are in some way the 'content' of the electric light, since they could not exist without the electric light. This fact merely underlines the point that 'the medium is the message' because it is the medium that shapes and controls the scale and form of human association and action. The content or uses of such media are as diverse as they are ineffectual in shaping the form of human association. Indeed, it is only too typical that the 'content' of any medium blinds us to the character of the medium. It is only today that industries have become aware of the various kinds of business in which they are engaged. When IBM discovered that it was not in the business of making office equipment or business machines, but that it was in the business of processing information, then it began to navigate with clear vision. The General Electric Company makes a considerable portion of its profits from electric light bulbs and lighting systems. It has not yet discovered that, quite as much as A.T. & T, it is in the business of moving information.

The electric light escapes attention as a communication medium just because it has no 'content.' And this makes it an invaluable instance of how people fail to study media at all. For it is not till the electric light is used to spell out some brand name that it is noticed as a medium. Then it is not the light but the 'content' (or what is really another medium) that is noticed. The message of the electric light is like the message of electric power in industry, totally radical, pervasive, and decentralized. For electric light and power are separate from their uses, yet they eliminate time and space factors in human association exactly as do radio, telegraph, telephone, and TV, creating involvement in depth.

[. . .]

In accepting an honorary degree from the University of Notre Dame a few years ago. General David Sarnoff† made this statement: 'We are too prone to make technological instruments the scapegoats for the sins of those who wield them. The products of modern science are not in themselves good or bad; it is the way they are used that determines their value.' That is the voice of the current somnambulism. Suppose we were to say, 'Apple pie is in itself neither good nor bad; it is the way it is used that determines its value.' Or, 'The smallpox virus is in itself neither good nor bad; it is the way it is used that determines its value.' Again. 'Firearms are in themselves neither good nor bad; it is the way they are used that determines their value.' That is, if the slugs reach the right people firearms are good. If the TV tube fires the right ammunition at the right people it is good. I am not being perverse. There is simply nothing in the Sarnoff statement that will bear scrutiny, for it ignores the nature of the medium, of any and all media, in the true Narcissus style of one hypnotized by the amputation and extension of his own being in a new technical form. General Sarnoff went on to explain his attitude to the technology

3776

of print, saying that it was true that print caused much trash to circulate, but it had also disseminated the Bible and the thoughts of seers and philosophers. It has never occurred to General Sarnoff that any technology could do anything but *add* itself on to what we already are.

[. . .]

[M]echanization is achieved by fragmentation of any process and by putting the fragmented parts in a series. Yet, as David Hume showed in the eighteenth century, there is no principle of causality in a mere sequence. That one thing follows another accounts for nothing. Nothing follows from following, except change. So the greatest of all reversals occurred with electricity, that ended sequence by making things instant. With instant speed the causes of things began to emerge to awareness again, as they had not done with things in sequence and in concatenation accordingly. Instead of asking which came first, the chicken or the egg, it suddenly seemed that a chicken was an egg's idea for getting more eggs.

Just before an airplane breaks the sound barrier, sound waves become visible on the wings of the plane. The sudden visibility of sound just as sound ends is an apt instance of that great pattern of being that reveals new and opposite forms just as the earlier forms reach their peak performance. Mechanization was never so vividly fragmented or sequential as in the birth of the movies, the moment that translated us beyond mechanism into the world of growth and organic interrelation. The movie, by sheer speeding up the mechanical, carried us from the world of sequence and connections into the world of creative configuration and structure. The message of the movie medium is that of transition from lineal connections to configurations. It is the transition that produced the now quite correct observation: 'If it works, it's obsolete.' When electric speed further takes over from mechanical movie sequences, then the lines of force in structures and in media become loud and clear. We return to the inclusive form of the icon.

To a highly literate and mechanized culture the movie appeared as a world of triumphant illusions and dreams that money could buy. It was at this moment of the movie that cubism occurred, and it has been described by E. H. Gombrich (*Art and Illusion*) as 'the most radical attempt to stamp out ambiguity and to enforce one reading of the picture – that of a man-made construction, a colored canvas.' For cubism substitutes all facets of an object simultaneously for the 'point of view' or facet of perspective illusion. Instead of the specialized illusion of the third dimension on canvas, cubism sets up an interplay of planes and contradiction or dramatic conflict of patterns, lights, textures that 'drives home the message' by involvement. This is held by many to be an exercise in painting, not in illusion.

In other words, cubism, by giving the inside and outside, the top, bottom, back, and front and the rest, in two dimensions, drops the illusion of perspective in favor of instant sensory awareness of the whole. Cubism, by seizing on instant total awareness, suddenly announced that *the medium is the message*. Is it not evident that the moment that sequence yields to the simultaneous, one is in the world of the structure and of configuration? Is that not what has happened in physics as in painting, poetry, and in communication? Specialized segments of attention have shifted to total field, and we can now say, 'The medium is the message' quite naturally. Before the electric speed and total field, it was not obvious that the medium is the message. The message, it seemed, was the 'content,' as people used to ask what a painting was *about*. Yet they never thought to ask what a melody was about, nor what a house or a dress was about. In such matters, people retained some sense of the whole pattern, of form and function as a unity. But in the electric age this integral idea of structure and configuration has become [. . .] prevalent [. . .].

[. . .]

HOT AND COLD

[. . .]

There is a basic principle that distinguishes a hot medium like radio from a cool one like the telephone, or a hot medium like the movie from a cool one like TV. A hot medium is one that extends one single sense in 'high definition.' High definition is the state of being well filled with data. A photograph is, visually, 'high definition.' A cartoon is 'low definition,' simply because very little visual information is provided. Telephone is a cool medium, or one of low definition, because the ear is given a meager amount of information. And speech is a cool medium of low definition, because so little is given and so much has to be filled in by the listener. On the other hand, hot media do not leave so much to be filled in or completed by the audience. Hot media are, therefore, low in participation, and cool media are high in participation or completion by the audience. Naturally, therefore, a hot medium like radio has very different effects on the user from a cool medium like the telephone.

A cool medium like hieroglyphic or ideogrammic written characters has very different effects from the hot and explosive medium of the phonetic alphabet. The alphabet, when pushed to a high degree of abstract visual intensity, became typography. The printed word with its specialist intensity burst the bonds of medieval corporate guilds and monasteries, creating extreme individualist patterns of enterprise and monopoly. But the typical reversal occurred when extremes of monopoly brought back the corporation, with its impersonal empire over many lives. The hotting-up of the medium of writing to repeatable print intensity led to nationalism and the religious wars of the sixteenth century. The heavy and unwieldy media, such as stone, are time binders. Used for writing, they are very cool indeed, and serve to unify the ages; whereas paper is a hot medium that serves to unify spaces horizontally, both in political and entertainment empires.

Any hot medium allows of less participation than a cool one, as a lecture makes for less participation than a seminar, and a book for less than dialogue. With print many earlier forms were excluded from life and art, and many were given strange new intensity.

[. . .]

A tribal and feudal hierarchy of traditional kind collapses quickly when it meets any hot medium of the mechanical, uniform, and repetitive kind. The medium of money or wheel or writing, or any other form of specialist speed-up of exchange and information, will serve to fragment a tribal structure. Similarly, a very much greater speed-up, such as occurs with electricity, may serve to restore a tribal pattern of intense involvement such as took place with the introduction of radio in Europe, and is now tending to happen as a result of TV in America. Specialist technologies detribalize. The non-specialist electric technology retribalizes.

[. . .]

By putting our physical bodies inside our extended nervous systems, by means of electric media, we set up a dynamic by which all previous technologies that are mere extensions of hands and feet and teeth and bodily heat-controls – all such extensions of our bodies, including cities – will be translated into information systems. Electromagnetic technology requires utter human docility and quiescence of meditation such as benefits an organism that now wears its brain outside its skull and its nerves outside its hide. Man must serve his electric technology with the same servomechanistic fidelity with which he served his coracle, his canoe, his typography, and all other extensions of his physical organs. But there is this difference, that previous technologies were partial and fragmentary, and the electric is total and inclusive. An external consensus or conscience is now as necessary as private consciousness. With the new media, however, it is also possible to store and to translate everything; and, as for speed, that is no problem. No further acceleration is possible this side of the light barrier.

Just as when information levels rise in physics and chemistry, it is possible to use anything for fuel or fabric or building material, so with electric technology all solid goods can be summoned to appear as solid commodities by means of information circuits set up in the organic patterns that we call 'automation' and information retrieval. Under electric technology the entire business of man becomes learning and knowing.

[. . .]

After three thousand years of explosion, by means of fragmentary and mechanical technologies, the Western world is imploding. During the mechanical ages we had extended our bodies in space. Today, after more than a century of electric technology, we have extended our central nervous system itself in a global embrace, abolishing both space and time as far as our planet is concerned. Rapidly, we approach the final phase of the extensions of man – the technological simulation of consciousness, when the creative process of knowing will be collectively and corporately extended to the whole of human society, much as we have already extended our senses and our nerves by the various media.

Editors' Notes

*Automation: the 1960s term for the introduction of new information technologies; computerisation.
† David Sarnoff (1891–1971). As a young employee of the Marconi radio company, Sarnoff is often credited with having 'invented' broadcasting as an application of the new wireless technology. He founded the first American broadcasting network, NBC, in 1926, and was head of the Radio Corporation of America from 1930 to 1966.

4

'MASS COMMUNICATION' AND 'MINORITY CULTURE'

Raymond Williams

[. . .]

In our own generation, there has been a dramatic tightening of interest in this world of communications. The development of powerful new means of communication has coincided, historically, with the extension of democracy and with the attempts, by many kinds of ruling group, to control and manage democracy. The development has also coincided with important changes in the nature of work and in education, which have given many people new kinds of social opportunity. There has been a great expansion in the scale of ordinary society, both through the new communications systems and through the growth of many kinds of large-scale organization. Acting together, these developments have created social problems which seem to be of a quite new kind.

The growth of interest in communications is an important response to this new situation. It came, really, as a break-through in experience, cutting across our usual categories. Already some of our basic ideas of society are being changed by this new emphasis. From one familiar approach, through traditional politics, we have seen the central facts of society as power and government. From another familiar approach, through traditional economics, we have seen the central concerns of society as property, production, and trade. These approaches remain important, but they are now joined by a new emphasis: that society is a form of communication, through which experience is described, shared, modified, and preserved. We are used to descriptions of our whole common life in political and economic terms. The emphasis on communications asserts, as a matter of experience, that men and societies are not confined to relationships of power, property, and production. Their relationships in describing, learning, persuading, and exchanging experiences are seen as equally fundamental. This emphasis is exceptionally important in the long crisis of twentieth-century society. Many people, starting from older versions of society, have seen the growth of modern communications not as an expansion of men's powers to learn and to exchange ideas and experiences, but as a new

From R. Williams, *Communications* (Harmondsworth: Penguin Special, 1962) pp. 9–12, 68–75.

method of government or a new opportunity for trade. All the new means of communication have been abused, for political control (as in propaganda) or for commercial profit (as in advertising). We can protest against such uses, but unless we have a clear alternative version of human society we are not likely to make our protests effective.

My own view is that we have been wrong in taking communication as secondary. Many people seem to assume as a matter of course that there is, first, reality, and then, second, communication about it. We degrade art and learning by supposing that they are always second-hand activities: that there is life, and then afterwards there are these accounts of it. Our commonest political error is the assumption that power – the capacity to govern other men – is the reality of the whole social process, and so the only context of politics. Our commonest economic error is the assumption that production and trade are our only practical activities, and that they require no other human justification or scrutiny. We need to say what many of us know in experience: that the life of man, and the business of society, cannot be confined to these ends; that the struggle to learn, to describe, to understand, to educate, is a central and necessary part of our humanity. This struggle is not begun, at second hand, after reality has occurred. It is, in itself, a major way in which reality is continually formed and changed. What we call society is not only a network of political and economic arrangements, but also a process of learning and communication.

Communication begins in the struggle to learn and to describe. To start this process in our minds, and to pass on its results to others, we depend on certain communication models, certain rules or conventions through which we can make contact. We can change these models, when they become inadequate, or we can modify and extend them. Our efforts to do so, and to use the existing models successfully, take up a large part of our living energy. The history of a language is a record of efforts of this kind, and is as central a part of the history of a people as its changing political and economic institutions. Moreover, many of our communication models become, in themselves, social institutions. Certain attitudes to others, certain forms of address, certain tones and styles, become embodied in institutions which are then very powerful in social effect. The crisis in modern communications has been caused by the speed of invention and by the difficulty of finding the right institutions in which these technical means are to be used. In modern Britain, we have a whole range of uses of printing, of photography, of television, which do not necessarily follow from the technical means themselves. Many have been shaped by changing political and economic forces. Many, also, have been shaped by what are really particular communication models: the idea that speaking or writing to many people at once is speaking or writing to 'the masses'; the idea that there are clear types of people and interest – 'Third Programme', 'Home Service' and 'Light'*; 'quality' and 'popular' – that we can separate and label. These arguable assumptions are often embodied in solid practical institutions, which then teach the models from which they start. We cannot examine the process of general communication in modern society without examining the shapes of these institutions. Further, if we understand the importance of communication, in all our social activities, we find that in examining the process and the institutions we are also looking at our society – at some of our characteristic relationships – in new ways.

[. . .]

HIGH AND LOW

Men differ in their capacities for excellence. Yet democracy insists that everyone has an equal right to judge. Aren't we seeing, in our own time, the results of this contradiction? Isn't there great danger of the tradition of high culture being overwhelmed by mass culture, which expresses the tastes and standards of the ordinary man? Isn't it really our first duty to defend minority culture, which in its actual works is the highest achievement of humanity?

The difficulty here is that 'minority culture' can mean two things. It can mean the work of the great artists and thinkers, and of the many lesser but still important figures who sustain them. It can mean also the work of these men as received and used by a particular social minority, which will indeed, often add to it certain works and habits of its own.

The great tradition is in many ways a common inheritance, and it has been the purpose of modern education to make it as widely available as possible. Certainly this extension is never as easy as some people expect. Certainly it often happens that in the attempt to make difficult work more widely available, part of the value of the work is lost. Perhaps the whole attempt is wrongly conceived, and we should concentrate instead on maintaining the high tradition in its own terms.

The question is, however, can this in any case be done? The work of the great artists and thinkers has never been confined to their own company; it has always been made available to some others. And doesn't it often happen that those to whom it has been made available identify the tradition with themselves, grafting it into their own way of life?

[. . .]

Again and again, particular minorities confuse the superiority of the tradition which has been made available to them with their own superiority, an association which the passing of time or of frontiers can make suddenly ludicrous. We must always be careful to distinguish the great works of the past from the social minority which at a particular place and time identifies itself with them.

The great tradition very often continues itself in quite unexpected ways. Much new work, in the past, has been called 'low', in terms of the 'high' standards of the day. This happened to much of our Elizabethan drama, and to the novel in the eighteenth century. Looking back, we can understand this, because the society was changing in fundamental ways. The minorities which assumed that they alone had the inheritance and guardianship of the great tradition in fact turned out to be wrong. This mistake can happen at any time. In our own century, there are such new forms as the film, the musical, and jazz. Each of these has been seen as 'low', a threat to 'our' standards. Yet during the period in which films have been made, there have been as many major contributions, in film, to the world's dramatic tradition, as there have been major plays. Of course most films are nowhere near this level. But from the past we have only the best work, and we can properly compare with this only our own best work. Some forms may well be better than others, in that they contain much greater possibilities for the artist, but this cannot be settled until there has been time for development. The great period of the novel came more than a century after the form had become popular and had been dismised as 'low'. It realized possibilities which nobody could then have foreseen. The prestige of an old form is never decisive. There is no reason, today, why a science-fiction story should be thought less serious than a historical novel, or a new musical than a naturalist play. 'Low' equals 'unfamiliar' is one of the perennial cultural traps, and it is fallen into most easily by those who assume that in their own persons, in their own learned tastes and habits, they are the high tradition.

This might be agreed, but does it go to the real issue? These mistakes are made, but new minorities set them right. Still, however, they are minorities. Most people are not interested in the great tradition, old or new. Most people are not interested in art, but merely in entertainment. Actual popular taste is for such things as variety, the circus, sport, and processions. Why force art on such people, especially since you will be in danger of reducing art to that level, mixing it up with the popular and commercial worlds? Wouldn't your effort be better spent on maintaining real art for those who value it?

This distinction between art and entertainment may be much more difficult to maintain than it looks. At its extremes, of course, it is obvious. But over the whole range, is there any easy and absolute distinction? Great art can give us deep and lasting experiences, but the experience we get from many things that we rightly call art is quite often light and temporary. The excitement of the circus, the procession, the variety sketch, can be quite easily forgotten, but at the time it is often intense. Sport, in our century, has become a popular spectacle: its excitements again are intense and often temporary. There may be a difference between such things and the minor decorative arts, the passing comedies, the fashionable artistic performers, but can it really be seen as a difference between 'high' and 'low'? And even where the difference seems absolute, what follows from this? What has to be shown, to sustain the argument that 'high culture' is in danger of being overwhelmed by 'mass culture', is that there is not only difference but conflict. Most of us can test this in our own experience. For, in fact, we do not live in these neatly separated worlds. Many of us go one day to a circus, one day to a theatre; one day to the football, one day to a concert. The experiences are different, and vary widely in quality both between and within themselves. Do we in fact feel that our capacity for any one of these things is affected by our use of the others?

But perhaps this is not the main point. Isn't the real threat of 'mass culture' – of things like television rather than things like football or the circus – that it reduces us to an endlessly mixed, undiscriminating, fundamentally bored reaction? The spirit of everything, art and entertainment, can become so standardized that we have no absorbed interest in anything, but simply an indifferent acceptance, bringing together what Coleridge called 'indulgence of sloth and hatred of vacancy'. You're not exactly enjoying it, or paying any particular attention, but it's passing the time. And in so deadly an atmosphere the great tradition simply cannot live.

Most of us, I think, have experienced this atmosphere. At times, even, we take it as a kind of drug: in periods of tiredness or convalescence, or during tension and anxiety when we have to wait and when almost anything can help us to wait. Certainly as a normal habit of mind this would be enervating and dangerous; there is a good deal of reality that we cannot afford to be cut off from, however much we may want some temporary relief.

The challenge of work that is really in the great tradition is that in many different ways it can get through with an intensity, a closeness, a concentration that in fact moves us to respond. It can be the reporter breaking through our prejudice to the facts; the dramatist reaching so deeply into our experience that we find it difficult, in the first shock, even to breathe; the painter suddenly showing us the shape of a street so clearly that we ask how we could ever have walked down it indifferently. It is sometimes a disturbing challenge to what we have always believed and done, and sometimes a way to new experience, new ways of seeing and feeling. Or again, in unexpected ways, it can confirm and strengthen us, giving new energy to what we already know is important, or what we knew but couldn't express.

Is this living world threatened by the routines of 'mass culture'? The threat is real, but it does not come only from 'mass culture'; it comes also from many kinds of routine art and routine thinking. There are many sources for the formula or routine which insulates us from reality. There is the weakness in ourselves, or at best the insufficient strength. There is also the intention of others, that we should be kept out of touch. Many interests are served by this kind of insulation: old forms of society, old and discredited beliefs, a wish to keep people quiet and uncritical. Such interests, based on power, habit, or privilege, are often served by, often actively seek, formulas and routines that insulate men from reality.

If we look at what we call 'mass culture' and 'minority culture', I am not sure that we invariably find one on the side of reality and one against it. Certainly the great works always challenge us with their own reality, and can stimulate us to active attention. But when these works are embedded in a particular minority culture, which adds to them not only its own local habits but also the facts and feelings which spring from its minority position, the effect can be very different. At best, a minority culture, in keeping the works available, offers the best that has been done and said in the world. At worst, it translates the best into its own accents, and confuses it with many other inferior things. I see no real evidence that it is a permanent and reliable means of maintaining a living excellence.

But even if it isn't permanent and reliable, isn't it bound to be better than the ordinary world of mass communications? There the construction of formulas seems almost built in. It is perhaps the only easy way of getting through quickly to a very large number of people, and the system seems to depend on this. Certainly we can only understand large-scale communications if we acknowledge the importance of formulas which can be fairly quickly and widely learned and used. Yet, in fact, formulas are necessary for all communication. What is at worst a formula for processing an experience is at best a convention for transmitting it in a widely available form. We have seen so much falsification, glamorization, and real vulgarization that we often forget how many facts, how many new opinions, how many new kinds of work and new ways of seeing the world nevertheless get through. By comparison with times when there was no highly organized communications system these are dramatic gains. We have then to adjust the balance much more carefully than a simple contrast of 'minority' and 'mass', 'high' and 'low' would suggest.

There is one further argument, that can very easily be overlooked. The great tradition is itself always in danger of being vulgarized when it is confined to a minority culture. Just because it is a mixed inheritance, from many societies and many times as well as from many kinds of men, it cannot easily be contained within one limited social form. Further, if it is so contained, there can be deep and unnecessary hostility to it from those outside the social minority. If the great tradition is not made generally available, there is often this frightening combination of hostility and a vacuum. What then usually happens is that this is penetrated and exploited from outside. In the worst cultural products of our time, we find little that is genuinely popular, developed from the life of actual communities. We find instead a synthetic culture, or anti-culture, which is alien to almost everybody, persistently hostile to art and intellectual activity, which it spends much of its time in misrepresenting, and given over to exploiting indifference, lack of feeling, frustration, and hatred. It finds such common human interests as sex, and turns them into crude caricatures or glossy facsimiles. It plays repeatedly around hatred and aggression, which it never discharges but continually feeds. This is not the culture of 'the ordinary man'; it is the culture of the disinherited. It seems to me that those who have contrived the disinheritance, by artificially isolating the great tradition, bear as heavy a responsibility for these destructive elements as their actual providers.

In Britain, we have to notice that much of this bad work is American in origin. At certain levels, we are culturally an American colony. But of course it is not the best American culture that we are getting, and the import and imitation of the worst has been done, again and again, by some of our own people, significantly often driven by hatred or envy of the English minority which has associated the great tradition with itself. To go pseudo-American is a way out of the English complex of class and culture, but of course it solves nothing; it merely ritualizes the emptiness and despair. Most bad culture is the result of this kind of social collapse. The genuinely popular tradition is despised, the great tradition is kept exclusive, and into the gap pour the speculators who know how to exploit disinheritance because they themselves are rooted in nothing.

The general situation is very difficult to understand. In part, now, the great tradition is being responsibly extended, and is finding an excellent response, both in the real increase of audiences, and in the answering vitality of new contributions to it from new kinds of experience. The purely destructive exploitation of the vacuum is also very powerful, in part because the control of our cultural organization has passed very largely into the hands of men who know no other definitions. At the same time, against all the apparent odds, elements of the really popular tradition persist, especially in variety, sport, some kinds of spectacle, and the impulse to make our own entertainment, especially in music. It seems impossible to understand this many-sided and constantly changing situation through the old formulas of 'minority' and 'mass', which are the symptoms of the collapse rather than keys to understanding it. We have to look at a new situation in new ways.

Editors' Note

* The 'Third Programme', 'Home Service' and 'Light' were the names of the BBC's domestic wireless networks from 1945/6 to 1967, providing distinct services that in contemporary terms broadly correspond to Radio 3, Radio 4 and Radio 2 respectively.

5

ENCODING/DECODING

Stuart Hall

Traditionally, mass-communications research has conceptualized the process of communication in terms of a circulation circuit or loop. This model has been criticized for its linearity – sender/message/receiver – for its concentration on the level of message exchange and for the absence of a structured conception of the different moments as a complex structure of relations. But it is also possible (and useful) to think of this process in terms of a structure produced and sustained through the articulation of linked but distinctive moments – production, circulation, distribution/consumption, reproduction. This would be to think of the process as a 'complex structure in dominance', sustained through the articulation of connected practices, each of which, however, retains its distinctiveness and has its own specific modality, its own forms and conditions of existence. This second approach, homologous to that which forms the skeleton of commodity production offered in Marx's *Grundrisse* and in *Capital*, has the added advantage of bringing out more sharply how a continuous circuit – production–distribution–production – can be sustained through a 'passage of forms'.[1] It also highlights the specificity of the forms in which the product of the process 'appears' in each ' moment, and thus what distinguishes discursive 'production' from other types of production in our society and in modern media systems.

The 'object' of these practices is meanings and messages in the form of sign-vehicles of a specific kind organized, like any form of communication or language, through the operation of codes within the syntagmatic chain of a discourse. The apparatuses, relations and practices of production thus issue, at a certain moment (the moment of 'production/circulation') in the form of symbolic vehicles constituted within the rules of 'language'. It is in this discursive form that the circulation of the 'product' takes place. The process thus requires, at the production end, its material instruments – its 'means' – as well as its own sets of social (production)

From S. Hall, 'Encoding/Decoding', ch. 10 in Stuart Hall, Dorothy Hobson, Andrew Lowe and Paul Willis (eds), *Culture, Media, Language* (London: Hutchinson, 1980), pp. 128–38; an edited extract from S. Hall, 'Encoding and Decoding in the Television Discourse', CCCS stencilled paper no. 7 (Birminngham: Centre for Contemporary Cultural Studies, 1973).

relations – the organization and combination of practices within media apparatuses. But it is in the *discursive* form that the circulation of the product takes place, as well as its distribution to different audiences. Once accomplished, the discourse must then be translated – transformed, again – into social practices if the circuit is to be both completed and effective. If no 'meaning' is taken, there can be no 'consumption'. If the meaning is not articulated in practice, it has no effect. The value of this approach is that while each of the moments, in articulation, is necessary to the circuit as a whole, no one moment can fully guarantee the next moment with which it is articulated. Since each has its specific modality and conditions of existence, each can constitute its own break or interruption of the 'passage of forms' on whose continuity the flow of effective production (that is, 'reproduction') depends.

Thus while in no way wanting to limit research to 'following only those leads which emerge from content analysis'[2] we must recognize that the discursive form of the message has a privileged position in the communicative exchange (from the viewpoint of circulation), and that the moments of 'encoding' and 'decoding', though only 'relatively autonomous' in relation to the communicative process as a whole, are *determinate* moments. A 'raw' historical event cannot, *in that form*, be transmitted by, say, a television newscast. Events can only be signified within the aural–visual forms of the televisual discourse. In the moment when a historical event passes under the sign of discourse, it is subject to all the complex formal 'rules' by which language signifies. To put it paradoxically, the event must become a 'story' before it can become a *communicative event*. In that moment the formal sub-rules of discourse are 'in dominance', without, of course, subordinating out of existence the historical event so signified, the social relations in which the rules are set to work or the social and political consequences of the event having been signified in this way. The 'message form' is the necessary 'form of appearance' of the event in its passage from source to receiver. Thus the transposition into and out of the 'message form' (or the mode of symbolic exchange) is not a random 'moment', which we can take up or ignore at our convenience. The 'message form' is a determinate moment; though, at another level, it comprises the surface movements of the communications system only and requires, at another stage, to be integrated into the social relations of the communication process as a whole, of which it forms only a part.

From this general perspective, we may crudely characterize the television communicative process as follows. The institutional structures of broadcasting, with their practices and networks of production, their organized relations and technical infrastructures, are required to produce a programme. Using the analogy of *Capital*, this is the 'labour process' in the discursive mode. Production, here, constructs the message. In one sense, then, the circuit begins here. Of course, the production process is not without its 'discursive' aspect: it, too, is framed throughout by meanings and ideas: knowledge-in-use concerning the routines of production, historically defined technical skills, professional ideologies, institutional knowledge, definitions and assumptions, assumptions about the audience and so on frame the constitution of the programme through this production structure. Further, though the production structures of television originate the television discourse, they do not constitute a closed system. They draw topics, treatments, agendas, events, personnel, images of the audience, 'definitions of the situation' from other sources and other discursive formations within the wider socio-cultural and political structure of which they are a differentiated part. Philip Elliott has expressed this point succinctly, within a more traditional framework, in his discussion of the way in which the audience is both the 'source' and the 'receiver' of the television message. Thus – to borrow Marx's terms – circulation and reception are, indeed, 'moments' of the production process in television and are reincorporated, via a number of skewed and structured 'feedbacks', into the production process itself. The consumption or reception of the television message is thus also itself a 'moment' of the production process in its larger sense, though the latter is 'predominant' because it is the 'point of departure for the realization' of the message. Production and reception of the television message are not, therefore, identical, but they are related: they are differentiated moments within the totality formed by the social relations of the communicative process as a whole.

At a certain point, however, the broadcasting structures must yield encoded messages in the form of a meaningful discourse. The institution-societal relations of production must pass under the discursive rules of language for its product to be 'realized'. This initiates a further differentiated moment, in which the formal rules of discourse and language are in dominance. Before this message can have an 'effect' (however defined), satisfy a 'need' or be put to a 'use', it must first be appropriated as a meaningful discourse and be meaningfully decoded. It is this set of decoded meanings which 'have an effect', influence, entertain, instruct or persuade, with very complex perceptual, cognitive, emotional, ideological or behavioural consequences. In a 'determinate' moment the structure employs a code and yields a 'message': at another determinate moment the 'message', via its decodings, issues into the structure of social practices. We are now fully aware that this re-entry into the practices of audience reception and 'use' cannot be understood in simple behavioural terms. The typical processes identified in positivistic research on isolated elements – effects, uses, 'gratifications' – are themselves framed by structures of understanding, as well as being produced by social and economic relations, which shape their 'realization' at the reception end of the chain and which permit the meanings signified in the discourse to be transposed into practice or consciousness (to acquire social use value or political effectivity).

Clearly, what we have labelled in the diagram 'meaning structures 1' and 'meaning structures 2' may not be the same. They do not constitute an 'immediate identity'. The codes of encoding and decoding may not be perfectly symmetrical. The degrees of symmetry – that is, the degrees of 'understanding' and 'misunderstanding' in the communicative exchange – depend on the degrees of symmetry/asymmetry (relations of equivalence) established between the positions of the 'personifications', encoder–producer and decoder–receiver. But this in turn depends on

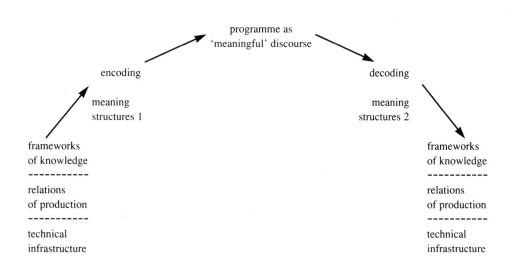

the degrees of identity/non-identity between the codes which perfectly or imperfectly transmit, interrupt or systematically distort what has been transmitted. The lack of fit between the codes has a great deal to do with the structural differences of relation and position between broadcasters and audiences, but it also has something to do with the asymmetry between the codes of 'source' and 'receiver' at the moment of transformation into and out of the discursive form. What are called 'distortions' or 'misunderstandings' arise precisely from the *lack of equivalence* between the two sides in the communicative exchange. Once again, this defines the 'relative autonomy', but 'determinateness', of the entry and exit of the message in its discursive moments.

The application of this rudimentary paradigm has already begun to transform our understanding of the older term, television 'content'. We are just beginning to see how it might also transform our understanding of audience reception, 'reading' and response as well. Beginnings and endings have been announced in communications research before, so we must be cautious. But there seems some ground for thinking that a new and exciting phase in so-called audience research, of a quite new kind, may be opening up. At either end of the communicative chain the use of the semiotic paradigm promises to dispel the lingering behaviourism which has dogged mass-media research for so long, especially in its approach to content. Though we know the television programme is not a behavioural input, like a tap on the knee cap, it seems to have been almost impossible for traditional researchers to conceptualize the communicative process without lapsing into one or other variant of low-flying behaviourism. We know, as Gerbner has remarked, that representations of violence on the TV screen 'are not violence but messages about violence':[3] but we have continued to research the question of violence, for example, as if we were unable to comprehend this epistemological distinction.

The television sign is a complex one. It is itself constituted by the combination of two types of discourse, visual and aural. Moreover, it is an iconic sign, in Peirce's terminology, because 'it posseses some of the properties of the thing represented'.[4] This is a point which has led to a great deal of confusion and has provided the site of intense controversy in the study of visual language. Since the visual discourse translates a three-dimensional world into two-dimensional planes, it cannot, of course, *be* the referent or concept it signifies. The dog in the film can bark but it cannot bite! Reality exists outside language, but it is constantly mediated by and through language: and what we can know and say has to be produced in and through discourse. Discursive 'knowledge' is the product not of the transparent representation of the 'real' in language but of the articulation of language on real relations and conditions. Thus there is no intelligible discourse without the operation of a code. Iconic signs are therefore coded signs too – even if the codes here work differently from those of other signs. There is no degree zero in language. Naturalism and 'realism' – the apparent fidelity of the representation to the thing or concept represented – is the result, the effect, of a certain specific articulation of language on the 'real'. It is the result of a discursive practice.

Certain codes may, of course, be so widely distributed in a specific language community or culture, and be learned at so early an age, that they appear not to be constructed – the effect of an articulation between sign and referent – but to be 'naturally' given. Simple visual signs appear to have achieved a 'near-universality' in this sense: though evidence remains that even apparently 'natural' visual codes are culture-specific. However, this does not mean that no codes have intervened; rather, that the codes have been profoundly *naturalized*. The operation of naturalized codes reveals not the transparency and 'naturalness' of language but the depth, the habituation and the near-universality of the codes in use. They produce apparently 'natural' recognitions. This has the (ideological) effect of concealing the practices of coding which are present. But we must not be fooled by appearances. Actually, what naturalized codes demonstrate is the degree of habituation produced when there is a fundamental alignment and reciprocity – an achieved equivalence – between the encoding and decoding sides of an exchange of meanings. The functioning of the codes on the decoding side will frequently assume the status of naturalized perceptions. This leads us to think that the visual sign for 'cow' actually is (rather than *represents*) the animal, cow. But if we think of the visual representation of a cow in a manual on animal husbandry – and, even more, of the linguistic sign 'cow' – we can see that both, in different degrees, are *arbitrary* with respect to the concept of the animal they represent. The articulation of an arbitrary sign – whether visual or verbal – with the concept of a referent is the product not of nature but of convention, and the conventionalism of discourses requires the intervention, the support, of codes. Thus Eco has argued that iconic signs 'look like objects in the real world because they reproduce the conditions (that is, the codes) of perception in the viewer'.[5] These 'conditions of perception' are, however, the result of a highly coded, even if virtually unconscious, set of operations – decodings. This is as true of the photographic or televisual image as it is of any other sign. Iconic signs are, however, particularly vulnerable to being 'read' as natural because visual codes of perception are very widely distributed and because this type of sign is less arbitrary than a linguistic sign: the linguistic sign, 'cow' possesses *none* of the properties of the thing represented, whereas the visual sign appears to possess *some* of those properties.

[. . .]

The level of connotation of the visual sign, of its contextual reference and positioning in different discursive fields of meaning and association, is the point where *already coded* signs intersect with the deep semantic codes of a culture and take on additional, more active ideological dimensions. We might take an example from advertising discourse. Here, too, there is no 'purely denotative', and certainly no 'natural', representation. Every visual sign in advertising connotes a quality, situation, value or inference, which is present as an implication or implied meaning, depending on the connotational positioning. In Barthes's example, the sweater always signifies a 'warm garment' (denotation) and thus the activity/value of 'keeping warm'. But it is also possible, at its more connotative levels, to signify 'the coming of winter' or 'a cold day'. And, in the specialized sub-codes of fashion, sweater may also connote a fashionable style of *haute couture* or, alternatively, an informal style of dress. But set against the right visual background and positioned by the romantic sub-code, it may connote 'long autumn walk in the woods'.[6] Codes of this order clearly contract relations for the sign with the wider universe of ideologies in a society. These codes are the means by which power and ideology are made to signify in particular discourses. They refer signs to the 'maps of meaning' into which any culture is classified; and those 'maps of social reality' have the whole range of social meanings, practices, and usages, power and interest 'written in' to them. The connotative levels of signifiers, Barthes remarked, 'have a close communication with culture, knowledge, history, and it is through them, so to speak, that the environmental world invades the linguistic and semantic system. They are, if you like, the fragments of ideology'.[7]

The so-called denotative *level* of the televisual sign is fixed by certain, very complex (but limited or 'closed') codes. But its connotative *level*, though also bounded, is more open, subject to more active *transformations*, which exploit its polysemic values. Any such already constituted sign is potentially transformable into more than one connotative configuration. Polysemy must not, however, be confused with pluralism. Connotative codes are *not* equal among themselves. Any society/culture tends, with varying degrees of closure, to impose its classifications of the social and cultural and political world. These constitute a *dominant cultural order*, though it is neither univocal nor uncontested. This question of the 'structure of discourses in dominance' is a crucial point. The different areas of social life appear to be mapped out into discursive domains, hierarchically organized into *dominant or preferred meanings*. New, problematic or troubling events, which breach our expectancies and run counter to our 'common-sense constructs', to our 'taken-for-granted' knowledge of social structures, must be assigned to their discursive domains before they can be said to 'make sense'. The most common way of 'mapping' them is to assign the new to some domain or other of the existing 'maps of problematic social reality'. We say *dominant*, not 'determined', because it is always possible to order, classify, assign and decode an event within more than one 'mapping'. But we say 'dominant' because there exists a pattern of 'preferred readings'; and these both have the institutional/political/ideological order imprinted in them and have themselves become institutionalized.[8] The domains of 'preferred meanings' have the whole social order embedded in them as a set of meanings, practices and beliefs: the everyday knowledge of social structures, of 'how things work for all practical purposes in this culture', the rank order of power and interest and the structure of legitimations, limits and sanctions. Thus to clarify a 'misunderstanding' at the connotative level, we must refer, *through* the codes, to the orders of social life, of economic and political power and of ideology. Further, since these mappings are 'structured in dominance' but not closed, the communicative process consists not in the unproblematic assignment of every visual item to its given position within a set of prearranged codes, but of *performative rules* – rules of competence and use, of logics-in-use – which seek actively to *enforce* or *pre-fer* one semantic domain over another and rule items into and out of their appropriate meaning-sets. Formal semiology has too often neglected this practice of *interpretative work*, though this constitutes, in fact, the real relations of broadcast practices in television.

In speaking of *dominant meanings*, then, we are not talking about a one-sided process which governs how all events will be signified. It consists of the 'work' required to enforce, win plausibility for and command as legitimate a *decoding* of the event within the limit of dominant definitions in which it has been connotatively signified. Terni has remarked:

> By the word *reading* we mean not only the capacity to identify and decode a certain number of signs, but also the subjective capacity to put them into a creative relation between themselves and with other signs: a capacity which is, by itself, the condition for a complete awareness of one's total environment.[9]

Our quarrel here is with the notion of 'subjective capacity', as if the referent of a televisional discourse were an objective fact but the interpretative level were an individualized and private matter. Quite the opposite seems to be the case. The televisual practice takes 'objective' (that is, systemic) responsibility precisely for the relations which disparate signs contract with one another in any discursive instance, and thus continually rearranges, delimits and prescribes into what 'awareness of one's total environment' these items are arranged.

This brings us to the question of misunderstandings. Television producers who find their message 'failing to get across' are frequently concerned to straighten out the kinks in the communication chain, thus facilitating the 'effectiveness' of their communication. Much research which claims the objectivity of 'policy-oriented analysis' reproduces this administrative goal by attempting to discover how much of a message the audience recalls and to improve the extent of understanding. No doubt misunderstandings of a literal kind do exist. The viewer does not know the terms employed, cannot follow the complex logic of argument or exposition, is unfamiliar with the language, finds the concepts too alien or difficult or is foxed by the expository narrative. But more often broadcasters are concerned that the audience has failed to take the meaning as they – the broadcasters – intended. What they really mean to say is that viewers are not operating within the 'dominant' or 'preferred' code. Their ideal is 'perfectly transparent communication'. Instead, what they have to confront is 'systematically distorted communication'.[10]

In recent years discrepancies of this kind have usually been explained by reference to 'selective perception'. This is the door via which a residual pluralism evades the compulsions of a highly structured, asymmetrical and non-equivalent process. Of course, there will always be private, individual, variant readings. But 'selective perception' is almost never as selective, random or privatized as the concept suggests. The patterns exhibit, across individual variants, significant clusterings. Any new approach to audience studies will therefore have to begin with a critique of 'selective perception' theory.

It was argued earlier that since there is no necessary correspondence between encoding and decoding, the former can attempt to 'pre-fer' but cannot prescribe or guarantee the latter, which has its own conditions of existence. Unless they are wildly aberrant, encoding will have the effect of constructing some of the limits and parameters within which decodings will operate. If there were no limits, audiences could simply read whatever they liked into any message. No doubt some total misunderstandings of this kind do exist. But the vast range must contain *some* degree of reciprocity between encoding and decoding moments, otherwise we could not speak of an effective communicative exchange at all. Nevertheless, this 'correspondence' is not given but constructed. It is not 'natural' but the product of an articulation between two distinct moments. And the former cannot determine or guarantee, in a simple sense, which decoding codes will be employed. Otherwise communication would be a perfectly equivalent circuit, and every message would be an instance of 'perfectly transparent communication'. We must think, then, of the variant articulations in which encoding/decoding can be combined. To elaborate on this, we offer a hypothetical analysis of some possible decoding positions, in order to reinforce the point of 'no necessary correspondence'.[11]

We identify *three* hypothetical positions from which decodings of a televisual discourse may be constructed. These need to be empirically tested and refined. But the argument that decodings do not follow inevitably from encodings, that they are not identical, reinforces the argument of 'no necessary correspondence'. It also helps to deconstruct the common-sense meaning of 'misunderstanding' in terms of a theory of 'systematically distorted communication'.

The first hypothetical position is that of the *dominant-hegemonic position*. When the viewer takes the connoted meaning from, say, a television newscast or current affairs programme full and straight, and decodes the message in terms of the reference code in which it has been encoded, we might say that the viewer *is operating inside the dominant code*. This is the ideal-typical case of 'perfectly transparent communication' – or as close as we are likely to come to it 'for all practical purposes'. Within this we can distinguish the positions produced by the *professional code*. This is the position (produced by what we perhaps ought to identify as the operation of a 'metacode') which the professional broadcasters assume when encoding a message which has *already* been signified in a hegemonic manner. The professional code is 'relatively independent' of the dominant code, in that it applies criteria and transformational operations of its own, especially those of a technico-practical nature. The professional code, however, operates *within* the 'hegemony' of the dominant code. Indeed, it serves to reproduce the dominant definitions precisely by bracketing their hegemonic quality and operating instead with displaced professional codings which foreground such apparently neutral-technical questions as visual quality, news and presentational values, televisual quality, 'professionalism' and so on. The hegemonic interpretations of, say, the politics of Northern Ireland, or the Chilean *coup* or the Industrial Relations Bill are principally generated by political and military elites: the particular choice of presentational occasions and formats, the selection of personnel, the choice of images, the staging of debates are selected and combined through the operation of the professional code. How the broadcasting professionals are able *both* to operate with 'relatively autonomous' codes of their own *and* to act in such a way as to reproduce (not without contradiction) the hegemonic signification of events is a complex matter which cannot be further spelled out here. It must suffice to say that the professionals are linked with the defining elites not only by the institutional position of broadcasting itself as an 'ideological apparatus',[12] but also by the structure of *access* (that is, the systematic 'over-accessing' of selective elite personnel and their 'definition of the situation' in television). It may even be said that the professional codes serve to reproduce hegemonic definitions specifically by *not overtly* biasing their operations in a dominant direction: ideological reproduction therefore takes place here inadvertently, unconsciously, 'behind men's backs'.[13] Of course, conflicts, contradictions and even misunderstandings regularly arise between the dominant and the professional significations and their signifying agencies.

The second position we would identify is that of the *negotiated code* or position. Majority audiences probably understand quite adequately what has been dominantly defined and professionally signified. The dominant definitions, however, are hegemonic precisely because they represent definitions of situations and events which are 'in dominance', (*global*). Dominant definitions connect events, implicitly or explicitly, to grand totalizations, to the great syntagmatic views-of-the-world: they take 'large views' of issues: they relate events to the 'national interest' or to the level of geo-politics, even if they make these connections in truncated, inverted or mystified ways. The definition of a hegemonic viewpoint is (a) that it defines within its terms the mental horizon, the universe, of possible meanings, of a whole sector of relations in a society or culture; and (b) that it carries with it the stamp of legitimacy – it appears coterminous with what is 'natural', 'inevitable', 'taken for granted' about the social order. Decoding within the *negotiated version* contains a mixture of adaptive and oppositional elements: it acknowledges the legitimacy of the hegemonic definitions to make the grand significations (abstract), while, at a more restricted, situational (situated) level, it makes its own ground rules – it operates with exceptions to the rule. It accords the privileged position to the dominant definitions of events while reserving the right to make a more negotiated application to 'local conditions', to its own more *corporate* positions. This negotiated version of the dominant ideology is thus shot through with contradictions, though these are only on certain occasions brought to full visibility. Negotiated codes operate through what we might call particular or situated logics: and these logics are sustained by their differential and unequal relation to the discourses and logics of power. The simplest example of a negotiated code is that which governs the response of a worker to the notion of an Industrial Relations Bill limiting the right to strike or to arguments for a wages freeze. At the level of the 'national interest' economic debate the decoder may adopt the hegemonic definition, agreeing that 'we must all pay ourselves less in order to combat inflation'. This, however, may have little or no relation to his/her willingness to go on strike for better pay and conditions or to oppose the Industrial Relations Bill at the level of shop-floor or union organization. We suspect that the great majority of so-called 'misunderstandings' arise from the contradictions and disjunctures between hegemonic–dominant encodings and negotiated–corporate decodings. It is just these mismatches in the levels which most provoke defining elites and professionals to identify a 'failure in communications'.

Finally, it is possible for a viewer perfectly to understand both the literal and the connotative inflection given by a discourse but to decode the message in a *globally* contrary way. He/she detotalizes the message in the preferred code in order to retotalize the message within some alternative framework of reference. This is the case of the viewer who listens to a debate on the need to limit wages but 'reads' every mention of the 'national interest' as 'class interest'. He/she is operating with what we must call an *oppositional code*. One of the most significant political moments (they also coincide with crisis points within the broadcasting organizations themselves, for obvious reasons) is the point when events which are normally signified and decoded in a negotiated way begin to be given an oppositional reading. Here the 'politics of signification' – the struggle in discourse – is joined.

NOTES

1.   For an explication and commentary on the methodological implications of Marx's argument, see S. Hall, 'A reading of Marx's 1857 *Introduction to the Grundrisse*', in WPCS 6 (1974).

2.   J. D. Halloran, 'Understanding television', Paper for the Council of Europe Colloquy on 'Understanding Television' (University of Leicester 1973).

3.   G. Gerbner *et al.*, *Violence in TV Drama: A Study of Trends and Symbolic Functions* (The Annenberg School, University of Pennsylvania 1970).

4.   Charles Peirce, *Speculative Grammar*, in *Collected Papers* (Cambridge, Mass.: Harvard University Press 1931–58).

5.   Umberto Eco, 'Articulations of the cinematic code', in *Cinemantics*, no. 1.

6.   Roland Barthes, 'Rhetoric of the image', in WPCS 1 (1971).

7.   Roland Barthes, *Elements of Semiology* (Cape 1967).

8.   For an extended critique of 'preferred reading', see Alan O'Shea, 'Preferred reading' (unpublished paper, CCCS, University of Birmingham).

9.   P. Terni, 'Memorandum', Council of Europe Colloquy on 'Understanding Television' (University of Leicester 1973).

10.   The phrase is Habermas's, in 'Systematically distorted communications', in P. Dretzel (ed.), *Recent Sociology 2* (Collier-Macmillan 1970). It is used here, however, in a different way.

11.   For a sociological formulation which is close, in some ways, to the positions outlined here but which does not parallel the argument about the theory of discourse, see Frank Parkin, *Class Inequality and Political Order* (Macgibbon and Kee 1971).

12.   See Louis Althusser, 'Ideology and ideological state apparatuses', in *Lenin and Philosophy and Other Essays* (New Left Books 1971).

13.   For an expansion of this argument, see Stuart Hall, 'The external/internal dialectic in broadcasting', *4th Symposium on Broadcasting* (University of Manchester 1972), and 'Broadcasting and the state: the independence/impartiality couplet', AMCR Symposium, University of Leicester 1976 (CCCS unpublished paper).

6

THE POWER OF THE IMAGE

Annette Kuhn

The twentieth century's second wave of Western feminism has distinguished itself from other social and political movements in several important respects. Its espousal of non-hierarchical approaches to organisation and action have lent themselves particularly well to issue-oriented politics – campaigns around abortion legislation and direct action on peace and disarmament, for example. The movement's insistence on bringing to centre stage areas of life hitherto considered secondary, even irrelevant, to 'serious' politics – the division of labour in the household, relations between men and women at home and in the workplace, emotions, sexuality, even the Unconscious – also sets it apart, giving ground to a conviction that the women's movement is opening up and beginning to explore a whole new country. In this process, new maps have had to be drawn, concepts constructed, systems of thought developed, in the effort to order the apparent chaos of a neglected other side of patriarchal culture. To take just one example of the effects of all this: trade union campaigns to combat sexual harassment at work would have been inconceivable before the middle or late 1970s, if only because the phenomenon simply did not have a name before that time. One can scarcely organise around a non-existent concept.

In other words, politics and knowledge are interdependent. In the ordinary way, the link between them will often go unnoticed or be taken for granted: where feminism is concerned, however, this is impossible, precisely because knowledge has had to be self-consciously produced alongside political activity. Each has regenerated the other. This is not to imply that the relationship is always a harmonious and uncontradictory one: mutual dependency always involves difficulty and struggle. Feminists may disagree, for example, on the extent to which producing knowledge is in itself a political activity. Are theory and practice in the final instance separate categories? Or is it acceptable to posit (to use a currently rather unfashionable term) a 'theoretical practice' of feminism?

Knowledge of the kind likely to be useful to the women's movement – knowledge, that is, which increases our understanding of women's lives and the institutions and structures of

From A. Kuhn, *The Power of the Image* (London: Routledge & Kegan Paul, 1985) pp. 1–8.

power which impinge on those lives in varying degrees and in different ways, structures which construct woman as 'other' in a patriarchal society – much of this knowledge is being produced under the banner of women's studies. The fact that women's studies has come to assume an existence in the Academy, apparently independent of the women's movement, may present some problems for the relationship between a body of knowledge and the movement which was its initial *raison d'être*. However, precisely because it so evidently eschews the 'neutrality' demanded by the Academy, the status of women's studies as a subject, researched and taught in universities, polytechnics and colleges, is marginal and precarious and its future uncertain: women's studies, therefore, needs the women's movement as much as *vice versa*. Women's studies also needs an institutional space to develop, and it needs, as well, the opportunity to draw on other areas of intellectual endeavour where these promise to be useful and relevant to its project. The saying that knowledge does not come from nowhere has more than one meaning.

[. . .]

From its beginnings, feminism has regarded ideas, language and images as crucial in shaping women's (and men's) lives. In the USA in 1968, feminists staged a demonstration against the Miss America contest, protesting the event on grounds that it promoted an impossible image of ideal womanhood, and was complicit in the widespread idea that all women – not only participants in beauty contests – are reducible to a set of bodily attributes. From this beginning there followed critiques of stereotypical representations of women in advertisements and in films, and studies of the ways in which language – both vocabulary and linguistic usage – defines and confines women. From the point of view of its politics, then, the women's movement has always been interested in images, meanings, representations – and especially in challenging representations which, while questionable or offensive from a feminist standpoint, are from other points of view – if they are noticed at all – perfectly acceptable.

This interest is in part responsible for the chapters in the present book [*The Power of the Image*]. I say responsible, because without the women's movement a desire to question representation in this way could not be articulated, nor would the public or even the private space to do so exist. I say in part, however, because since the early days feminist interest in images and representations has taken a variety of forms and directions. These have been determined largely by different ways in which representation has been thought about and analysed – that is, by the theories and methods brought to bear on the question. The question, I would argue, is a feminist one: the theories and methods not exclusively so. These come, at least to begin with, from elsewhere, and are appropriated and adapted to the feminist project. Knowledge does not come from nowhere, then: just as in this instance new knowledge is generated through the desire of feminist politics, so existing knowledge is both used and transformed in the service of this desire. The use and transformation of existing knowledge also partly motivates this book, then. It does not pretend to offer a comprehensive account of feminist thought on representation, however, but rather limits itself to an in-depth exploration of certain theoretical and methodological paths, hopefully opening up one or two new byways in the process. Which paths, though, and why?

The emergence of a new feminist movement in the late 1960s coincided with a renewed interest in marxist thought on 'the superstructure' – ideas, culture, ideology – and the place and effectivity of the superstructure within the social formation.[1] The different terms used here to describe the contents of the superstructure reflect a range of tendencies within marxist theory. Certain developments around the concept of ideology, for instance, were embodied in the work of the French philosopher Louis Althusser, work which – alongside that of other intellectuals,

Roland Barthes and Claude Lévi-Strauss, for instance – was associated with structuralism. Barthes had written an introduction to semiotics – the study of signification, or meaning production, in society – and his book *Mythologies* comprised a series of short semiotically informed essays on specific images and representations, and on signification in general: which elements in images produce meaning, how the process operates, and so on.[2]

In the early 1970s, art historian John Berger made a series of programmes for BBC Television called *Ways of Seeing*. In these, Berger also considered how images make meaning, though in this instance without explicit recourse to semiotic concepts. Into this effectively semiotic project Berger injected a more orthodoxly marxist concern with the status of images as commodities – artifacts which are bought and sold, which have exchange value. One particularly influential programme dealt with the female nude, both in the European high art tradition and in mass-produced pinup photographs. Analysis dealt not only with the formal qualities of these images *per se*, but also with the relationship between images and their consumers – who as well as being spectators are often buyers/owners of images too.

Althusserian thought had a certain relevance to feminism because it contained a notion that human beings are constructed by ideology, that our ways of thinking about the world, of representing it to ourselves, becomes so 'naturalised' that we take our conception of that world for granted. If ideology effaces itself, the process by which this takes place could, for instance, explain (though Althusser did not in fact attempt to do so) the taken-for-granted nature of social constructs of femininity. Barthes's work on images suggested, moreover, that meanings are produced through the codes at work in representations, and that while meanings might appear to be natural, obvious, immanent, they are in fact produced: they are constructed through identifiable processes of signification at work in all representations. Finally, *Ways of Seeing* showed that meaning production takes place within social and historical contexts, and that in a capitalist society representations are no more exempt than any other products from considerations of the marketplace.

It is not difficult to see a potential for crossfertilisation between these ideas and feminist concerns with representation: indeed, the work I have described forms a backcloth to the chapters in this book [*The Power of the Image*]. It is really no more than a backcloth, though. Since the early 1970s, the study of images, particularly of cinematic images, as signifying systems has taken up and developed these 'prefeminist' concerns, bringing to the fore the issue of the spectator as subject addressed, positioned, even formed, by representations. To semiotic and structuralist approaches to representation has been added psychoanalysis, whose object is precisely the processes by which human subjectivity is formed.[3] In work on the image, the cinematic image particularly, an emphasis on subjectivity has foregrounded the question of spectatorship in new ways. This, too, informs the writing in this book.

But again, that is by no means the whole story: for feminist thought has long since entered the field of representation in its own right. These chapters may be read as inhabiting a tradition of feminist work on representation which draws strategically on the strands of non-feminist or prefeminist thinking I have described, if only because their objects (images, meanings, ideologies) and their objectives (analysis, deconstruction) have something in common with feminist concerns. At the same time, though, the very process of appropriation has exposed crucial weaknesses in these systems of thought – notably gender-blindness, formalism, and certain methodological shortcomings.[4] Not only, though, has the appropriation of pre-existing theory necessarily – fruitfully – produced criticisms of it: the particular concerns of feminism, when mapped onto that theory, have been instrumental in generating qualitatively new knowledge, in constructing a new field.

Inevitably, the[se] questions [. . .] traverse both feminist concerns and knowledge-in-process. What relation, for instance, does spectatorship have to representations of women? What sort of activity is looking? What does looking have to do with sexuality? With masculinity and femininity? With power? With knowledge? How do images, of women in particular, 'speak to' the spectator? Is the spectator addressed as male/female, masculine/feminine? Is femininity constructed in specific ways through representation? Why are images of women's bodies so prevalent in our society? Such questions may sometimes be answered by looking at and analysing actual images. But although such analysis must be regarded as necessary to an understanding of the relationship between representation and sexuality, it is not always sufficient. For, in practice, images are always seen in context: they always have a specific use value in the particular time and place of their consumption. This together with their formal characteristics, conditions and limits the meanings available from them at any one moment. But if representations always have use value, then more often than not they also have exchange value: they circulate as commodities in a social/economic system. This further conditions, or overdetermines, the meanings available from representations.

Meanings do not reside in images, then: they are circulated between representation, spectator and social formation. All of the chapters in this book [*The Power of the Image*] are concerned in one way or another with images – with films as well as still photographs of various kinds. Each chapter places a slightly different emphasis on each of the terms defining the representation–spectator–social formation triangle: though, given the central place accorded the instance of looking, the spectator undoubtedly sits at the apex. Nevertheless, each chapter marks a move further away from the model of the image/text as an isolated object of analysis, and closer to a conception of the image as inhabiting various contexts: cultural contexts of spectatorship, institutional and social/historical contexts of production and consumption. At the same time, conceptualising texts as embedded within a series of contextual layers, and trying to do this without losing sight of texts as productive of meaning in their own right, does produce certain theoretical and methodological difficulties.

[. . .]

All of the texts/images discussed [. . .] may, in a broad sense, be regarded as 'culturally dominant'. Most of them – Hollywood films and softcore pornography, for example – are produced commercially for mass audiences. Where this is not the case they strive to slot into hegemonic 'high art' institutions. Hegemony is never without contradiction, however, which is one reason why analysing culturally dominant representations can be very productive. Contextual overdetermination notwithstanding, meaning can never be finally guaranteed. In practice, the operations of texts and various levels of context are rarely in harmony, and there is always some space for 'aberrant' reception of dominant representations.

[. . .]

More generally, the very existence of a book like this one is testimony to the fact that readings 'against the grain' are not only available, but often compelling. The activity of deconstruction sets loose an array of 'unintended' meanings, by their nature subversive of the apparently transparent meanings which texts offer us.

But why spend time and effort analysing images of a kind often considered questionable, even objectionable, by feminists? Why not try instead to create alternatives to culturally dominant representations? As I have argued, politics and knowledge are interdependent: the women's movement is not, I believe, faced here with a choice between two mutually exclusive alternatives, though individual feminists – if only because one person's life is too short to encompass everything – often experience their own politics in such a way. Theory and practice inform one another. At one level, analysing and deconstructing dominant representations may be regarded as a strategic practice. It produces understanding, and understanding is necessary to action.

It may also be considered an act of resistance in itself. Politics is often thought of as one of life's more serious undertakings, allowing little room for pleasure. At the same time, feminists may feel secretly guilty about their enjoyment of images they are convinced ought to be rejected as politically unsound. In analysing such images, though, it is possible, indeed necessary, to acknowledge their pleasurable qualities, precisely because pleasure is an area of analysis in its own right. 'Naive' pleasure, then, becomes admissible. And the acts of analysis, of deconstruction and of reading 'against the grain' offer an additional pleasure – the pleasure of resistance, of saying 'no': not to 'unsophisticated' enjoyment, by ourselves and others, of culturally dominant images, but to the structures of power which ask us to consume them uncritically and in highly circumscribed ways.

NOTES

1. See, for example, Robin Blackburn (ed.), *Ideology in Social Science*, London, Fontana, 1972; Raymond Williams, 'Base and superstructure in marxist cultural theory', *New Left Review*, no. 32, 1973, pp. 3–16; Louis Althusser, 'Ideology and ideological state apparatuses', *Lenin and Philosophy and Other Essays*, London, New Left Books, 1971, pp. 121–73.
2. *Elements of Semiology*, London, Jonathan Cape, 1967; *Mythologies*, London, Paladin, 1973.
3. These developments are traced in Rosalind Coward and John Ellis, *Language and Materialism*, London, Routledge & Kegan Paul, 1978.
4. See, for example, Mary Ann Doane et al., 'Feminist film criticism: an introduction', *Re-Vision: Essays in Feminist Film Criticism*, Los Angeles, American Film Institute, 1984, pp. 1–17; Annette Kuhn, 'Women's genres', *Screen*, vol. 25, no. 1, 1984, pp. 18–28.

7

THE PUBLIC SPHERE

Jürgen Habermas

CONCEPT

By 'public sphere' we mean first of all a domain of our social life in which such a thing as public opinion can be formed. Access to the public sphere is open in principle to all citizens. A portion of the public sphere is constituted in every conversation in which private persons come together to form a public. They are then acting neither as business or professional people conducting their private affairs, nor as legal consociates subject to the legal regulations of a state bureaucracy and obligated to obedience. Citizens act as a public when they deal with matters of general interest without being subject to coercion; thus with the guarantee that they may assemble and unite freely, and express and publicize their opinions freely. When the public is large, this kind of communication requires certain means of dissemination and influence; today, newspapers and periodicals, radio and television are the media of the public sphere. We speak of a political public sphere (as distinguished from a literary one, for instance) when the public discussions concern objects connected with the practice of the state. The coercive power of the state is the counterpart, as it were, of the political public sphere, but it is not a part of it. State power is, to be sure, considered 'public' power, but it owes the attribute of publicness to its task of caring for the public, that is, providing for the common good of all legal consociates. Only when the exercise of public authority has actually been subordinated to the requirement of democratic publicness does the political public sphere acquire an institutionalized influence on the government, by the way of the legislative body. The term 'public opinion' refers to the functions of criticism and control of organized state authority that the public exercises informally, as well as formally during periodic elections. Regulations concerning the publicness (or publicity [*Publizität* in its original meaning) of state-related activities, as, for instance, the public accessibility required of legal proceedings, are also connected with this function of public

From S. Seidman (ed.), *Jürgen Habermas on Society and Politics: A Reader*, trans. S. W. Nicholson (Boston: Beacon Press, 1989); originally published as 'Öffentlichkeit', in J. Habermas, *Kultur and Kritik* (Frankfurt ain Main: Suhrkamp Verlag, 1973).

opinion. To the public sphere as a sphere mediating between state and society, a sphere in which the public as the vehicle of public opinion is formed, there corresponds the principle of publicness – the publicness that once had to win out against the secret politics of monarchs and that since then has permitted democratic control of state activity.

It is no accident that these concepts of the public sphere and public opinion were not formed until the eighteenth century. They derive their specific meaning from a concrete historical situation. It was then that one learned to distinguish between opinion and public opinion, or *opinion publique*. Whereas mere opinions (things taken for granted as part of a culture, normative convictions, collective prejudices and judgments) seem to persist unchanged in their quasi-natural structure as a kind of sediment of history, public opinion, in terms of its very idea, can be formed only if a public that engages in rational discussion exists. Public discussions that are institutionally protected and that take, with critical intent, the exercise of political authority as their theme have not existed since time immemorial – they developed only in a specific phase of bourgeois society, and only by virtue of a specific constellation of interests could they be incorporated into the order of the bourgeois constitutional state.

HISTORY

It is not possible to demonstrate the existence of a public sphere in its own right, separate from the private sphere, in the European society of the High Middle Ages. At the same time, however, it is not a coincidence that the attributes of authority at that time were called 'public'. For a public representation of authority existed at that time. At all levels of the pyramid established by feudal law, the status of the feudal lord is neutral with respect to the categories 'public' and 'private'; but the person possessing that status represents it publicly; he displays himself, represents himself as the embodiment of a 'higher' power, in whatever degree. This concept of representation has survived into recent constitutional history. Even today the power of political authority on its highest level, however much it has become detached from its former basis, requires representation through the head of state. But such elements derive from a pre-bourgeois social structure. Representation in the sense of the bourgeois public sphere, as in 'representing' the nation or specific clients, has nothing to do with *representative publicness*, which inheres in the concrete existence of a lord. As long as the prince and the estates of his realm 'are' the land, rather than merely 'representing' it, they are capable of this kind of representation; they represent their authority 'before' the people rather than for the people.

The feudal powers (the church, the prince, and the nobility) to which this representative publicness adheres disintegrated in the course of a long process of polarization; by the end of the eighteenth century they had decomposed into private elements on the one side and public on the other. The position of the church changed in connection with the Reformation; the tie to divine authority that the church represented, that is, religion, became a private matter. Historically, what is called the freedom of religion safeguarded the first domain of private autonomy; the church itself continued its existence as one corporate body under public law among others. The corresponding polarization of princely power acquired visible form in the separation of the public budget from the private household property of the feudal lord. In the bureaucracy and the military (and in part also in the administration of justice), institutions of public power became autonomous vis-à-vis the privatized sphere of the princely court. In terms of the estates, finally, elements from the ruling groups developed into organs of public power, into parliament (and in part also into judicial organs); elements from the occupational status groups, insofar as they had become established in urban corporations and in certain differentiations within the estates of the land, developed into the sphere of bourgeois society, which would confront the state as a genuine domain of private autonomy.

Representative publicness gave way to the new sphere of 'public power' that came into being with the national and territorial states. Ongoing state activity (permanent administration, a standing army) had its counterpart in the permanence of relationships that had developed in the meantime with the stock market and the press, through traffic in goods and news. Public power became consolidated as something tangible confronting those who were subject to it and who at first found themselves only negatively defined by it. These are the 'private persons' who are excluded from public power because they hold no office. 'Public' no longer refers to the representative court of a person vested with authority; instead, it now refers to the competence-regulated activity of an apparatus furnished with a monopoly on the legitimate use of force. As those to whom this public power is addressed, private persons subsumed under the state form the public.

As a private domain, society, which has come to confront the state, as it were, is on the one hand clearly differentiated from public power; on the other hand, society becomes a matter of public interest insofar as with the rise of a market economy the reproduction of life extends beyond the confines of private domestic power. The *bourgeois public sphere* can be understood as the sphere of private persons assembled to form a public. They soon began to make use of the public sphere of informational newspapers, which was officially regulated, against the public power itself, using those papers, along with the morally and critically oriented weeklies, to engage in debate about the general rules governing relations in their own essentially privatized but publicly relevant sphere of commodity exchange and labor.

THE LIBERAL MODEL OF THE PUBLIC SPHERE

The medium in which this debate takes place – public discussion – is unique and without historical prototype. Previously the estates had negotiated contracts with their princes in which claims to power were defined on a case-by-case basis. As we know, this development followed a different course in England, where princely power was relativized through parliament, than on the Continent, where the estates were mediatized by the monarch. The 'third estate' then broke with this mode of equalizing power, for it could no longer establish itself as a ruling estate. Given a commercial economy, a division of authority accomplished through differentiation of the rights of those possessing feudal authority (liberties belonging to the estates) was no longer possible – the power under private law of disposition of capitalist property is nonpolitical. The bourgeois are private persons; as such, they do not 'rule.' Thus their claims to power in opposition to public power are directed not against a concentration of authority that should be 'divided' but rather against the principle of established authority. The principle of control, namely publicness, that the bourgeois public opposes to the principle of established authority aims at a transformation of authority as such, not merely the exchange of one basis of legitimation for another.

In the first modern constitutions the sections listing basic rights provide an image of the liberal model of the public sphere: they guarantee society as a sphere of private autonomy; opposite it stands a public power limited to a few functions; between the two spheres, as it were, stands the domain of private persons who have come together to form a public and who, as citizens of the state, mediate the state with the needs of bourgeois society, in order, as the idea goes, to thus convert political authority to 'rational' authority in the medium of this public sphere. Under the presuppositions of a society based on the free exchange of commodities, it seemed that the general interest, which served as the criterion by which this kind of rationality was to be evaluated, would be assured if the dealings of private persons in the marketplace were emancipated from social forces and their dealings in the public sphere were emancipated from political coercion.

The political daily press came to have an important role during this same period. In the second half of the eighteenth century, serious competition to the older form of news writing as the compiling of items of information arose in the form of literary journalism. Karl Bücher describes the main outlines of this development: 'From mere institutions for the publication of news, newspapers became the vehicles and guides of public opinion as well, weapons of party politics. The consequence of this for the internal organization of the newspaper enterprise was the insertion of a new function between the gathering of news and its publication: the editorial function. For the newspaper publisher, however, the significance of this development was that from a seller of new information he became a dealer in public opinion.' Publishers provided the commercial basis for the newspaper without, however, commercializing it as such. The press remained an institution of the public itself, operating to provide and intensify public discussion, no longer a mere organ for the conveyance of information, but not yet a medium of consumer culture.

This type of press can be observed especially in revolutionary periods, when papers associated with the tiniest political coalitions and groups spring up, as in Paris in 1789. In the Paris of 1848 every halfway prominent politician still formed his own club, and every other one founded his own *journal*: over 450 clubs and more than 200 papers came into being there between February and May alone. Until the permanent legalization of a public sphere that functioned politically, the appearance of a political newspaper was equivalent to engagement in the struggle for a zone of freedom for public opinion, for publicness as a principle. Not until the establishment of the bourgeois constitutional state was a press engaged in the public use of reason relieved of the pressure of ideological viewpoints. Since then it has been able to abandon its polemical stance and take advantage of the earning potential of commercial activity. The ground was cleared for this development from a press of viewpoints to a commercial press at about the same time in England, France, and the United States, during the 1830s. In the course of this transformation from the journalism of writers who were private persons to the consumer services of the mass media, the sphere of publicness was changed by an influx of private interests that achieved privileged representation within it.

THE PUBLIC SPHERE IN MASS WELFARE-STATE DEMOCRACIES

The liberal model of the public sphere remains instructive in regard to the normative claim embodied in institutionalized requirements of publicness; but it is not applicable to actual relationships within a mass democracy that is industrially advanced and constituted as a social-welfare state. In part, the liberal model had always contained ideological aspects; in part, the social presuppositions to which those aspects were linked have undergone fundamental changes. Even the forms in which the public sphere was manifested, forms which made its idea seem to a certain extent obvious, began to change with the Chartist movement in England and the February Revolution in France. With the spread of the press and propaganda, the public expanded beyond the confines of the bourgeoisie. Along with its social exclusivity the public lost the cohesion given it by institutions of convivial social intercourse and by a relatively high standard of education. Accordingly, conflicts which in the past were pushed off into the private sphere now enter the public sphere. Group needs, which cannot expect satisfaction from a self-regulating market, tend toward state regulation. The public sphere, which must now mediate these demands, becomes a field for competition among interests in the cruder form of forcible confrontation. Laws that have obviously originated under the 'pressure of the streets' can scarcely continue to be understood in terms of a consensus achieved by private persons in public discussion; they correspond, in more or less undisguised form, to compromises between conflicting private interests. Today it is social organizations that act in relation to the state in the political public sphere, whether through the mediation of political parties or directly, in interplay with public administration. With the interlocking of the public and private domains, not only do political agencies take over certain functions in the sphere of commodity exchange and social labor; societal powers also take over political functions. This leads to a kind of 'refeudalization' of the public sphere. Large-scale organizations strive for political compromises with the state and with one another, behind closed doors if possible; but at the same time they have to secure at least plebiscitarian approval from the mass of the population through the deployment of a staged form of publicity.

The political public sphere in the welfare state is characterized by a singular weakening of its critical functions. Whereas at one time publicness was intended to subject persons or things to the public use of reason and to make political decisions susceptible to revision before the tribunal of public opinion, today it has often enough already been enlisted in the aid of the secret policies of interest groups; in the form of 'publicity' it now acquires public prestige for persons or things and renders them capable of acclamation in a climate of nonpublic opinion. The term 'public relations' itself indicates how a public sphere that formerly emerged from the structure of society must now be produced circumstantially on a case-by-case basis. The central relationship of the public, political parties, and parliament is also affected by this change in function.

This existing trend toward the weakening of the public sphere, as a principle, is opposed, however, by a welfare state transformation of the functioning of basic rights: the requirement of publicness is extended by state organs to all organizations acting in relation to the state. To the extent to which this becomes a reality, a no longer intact public of private persons acting as individuals would be replaced by a public of organized private persons. Under current circumstances, only the latter could participate effectively in a process of public communication using the channels of intra-party and intra-organizational public spheres, on the basis of a publicness enforced for the dealings of organizations with the state. It is in this process of public communication that the formation of political compromises would have to achieve legitimation. The idea of the public sphere itself, which signified a rationalization of authority in the medium of public discussions among private persons, and which has been preserved in mass welfare-state democracy, threatens to disintegrate with the structural transformation of the public sphere. Today it could be realized only on a different basis, as a rationalization of the exercise of social and political power under the mutual control of rival organizations committed to publicness in their internal structure as well as in their dealings with the state and with one another.

8

THE MASSES: THE IMPLOSION OF THE SOCIAL IN THE MEDIA

Jean Baudrillard

Up to now there have been two great versions of the analysis of the media (as indeed that of the masses), one optimistic and one pessimistic. The optimistic one has assumed two major tonalities, very different from one another. There is the technological optimism of Marshall McLuhan: for him the electronic media inaugurate a generalized planetary communication and should conduct us, by the mental effect alone of new technologies, beyond the atomizing rationality of the Gutenberg galaxy to the global village, to the new electronic tribalism – an achieved transparency of information and communication. The other version, more traditional, is that of dialectical optimism inspired by progressivist and Marxist thought: the media constitute a new, gigantic productive force and obey the dialectic of productive forces. Momentarily alienated and submitted to the law of capitalism, their intensive development can only eventually explode this monopoly. 'For the first time in history,' writes Hans Enzensberger, 'the media make possible a mass participation in a productive process at once social and socialized, a participation whose practical means are in the hands of the masses themselves.'[1] These two positions more or less, the one technological, the other ideological, inspire the whole analysis and the present practice of the media.[2]

It is more particularly to the optimism of Enzensberger that I formerly opposed a resolutely pessimist vision in 'Requiem for the Media.' In that I described the mass media as a 'speech without response.' What characterizes the mass media is that they are opposed to mediation, intransitive, that they fabricate noncommunication – if one accepts the definition of communication as an exchange, as the reciprocal space of speech and response, and thus of *responsibility*. In other words, if one defines it as anything other than the simple emission/reception of information. Now the whole present architecture of the media is founded on this last definition: they are what finally forbids response, what renders impossible any process of exchange

A lecture delivered at the University of Melbourne; trans. Marie MacLean, *New Literary History*, 16:3 (Spring 1985) pp. 577–89; reprinted as ch. 9 in Jean Baudrillard, *Selected Writings*, ed. Mark Poster (Cambridge: Polity Press, 1988) pp. 207–19.

(except in the shape of a simulation of a response which is itself integrated into the process of emission, and this changes nothing in the unilaterality of communication). That is their true abstraction. And it is in this abstraction that is founded the system of social control and power. To understand properly the term *response*, one must appreciate it in a meaning at once strong, symbolic, and primitive: power belongs to him who gives and to whom no return can be made. To give, and to do it in such a way that no return can be made, is to break exchange to one's own profit and to institute a monopoly: the social process is out of balance. To make a return, on the contrary, is to break this power relationship and to restore on the basis of an antagonistic reciprocity the circuit of symbolic exchange. The same applies in the sphere of the media: there speech occurs in such a way that there is no possibility of a return. The restitution of this possibility of response entails upsetting the whole present structure; even better (as started to occur in 1968 and the 70s), it entails an 'antimedia' struggle.

In reality, even if I did not share the technological optimism of McLuhan, I always recognized and considered as a gain the true revolution which he brought about in media analysis (this has been mostly ignored in France). On the other hand, though I also did not share the dialectical hopes of Enzensberger, I was not truly pessimistic, since I believed in a possible subversion of the code of the media and in the possibility of an alternate speech and a radical reciprocity of symbolic exchange.

Today all that has changed. I would no longer interpret in the same way the forced silence of the masses in the mass media. I would no longer see in it a sign of passivity and of alienation, but to the contrary an original strategy, an original response in the form of a challenge; and on the basis of this reversal I suggest to you a vision of things which is no longer optimistic or pessimistic, but ironic and antagonistic.

I will take the example of opinion polls, which are themselves a mass medium. It is said that opinion polls constitute a manipulation of democracy. This is certainly no more the case than that publicity is a manipulation of need and of consumption. It too produces demand (or so it claims) and invokes needs just as opinion polls produce answers and induce future behavior. All this would be serious if there were an objective truth of needs, an objective truth of public opinion. It is obvious that here we need to exercise extreme care. The influence of publicity, of opinion polls, of all the media, and of information in general would be dramatic if we were certain that there exists in opposition to it an authentic human nature, an authentic essence of the social, with its needs, its own will, its own values, its finalities. For this would set up the problem of its radical alienation. And indeed it is in this form that traditional critiques are expressed.

Now the matter is at once less serious and more serious than this. The uncertainty which surrounds the social and political effect of opinion polls (do they or do they not manipulate opinion?), like that which surrounds the real economic efficacy of publicity, will never be completely relieved – and it is just as well! This results from the fact that there is a compound, a mixture of two heterogeneous systems whose data cannot be transferred from one to the other. An operational system which is statistical, information-based, and simulational is projected onto a traditional values system, onto a system of representation, will, and opinion. This collage, this collusion between the two, gives rise to an indefinite and useless polemic. We should agree neither with those who praise the beneficial use of the media, nor with those who scream about manipulation, for the simple reason that there is no relationship between a system of meaning and a system of simulation. Publicity and opinion polls would be incapable, even if they wished and claimed to do so, of alienating the will or the opinion of anybody at all, for the reason that they do not act in the time–space of will and of representation where judgement is formed.

For the same reason, though reversed, it is quite impossible for them to throw any light at all on public opinion or individual will, since they do not act in a public space, on the stage of a public space. They are strangers to it, and indeed they wish to dismantle it. Publicity and opinion polls and the media in general can only be imagined; they only exist on the basis of a disappearance, the disappearance from the public space, from the scene of politics, of public opinion in a form at once theatrical and representative as it was enacted in earlier epochs. Thus we can be reassured: they cannot destroy it. But we should not have any illusions: they cannot restore it either.

It is this lack of relationship between the two systems which today plunges us into a state of stupor. That is what I said: stupor. To be more objective one would have to say: a radical uncertainty as to our own desire, our own choice, our own opinion, our own will. This is the clearest result of the whole media environment, of the information which makes demands on us from all sides and which is as good as blackmail.

We will never know if an advertisement or opinion poll has had a real influence on individual or collective wills, but we will never know either what would have happened if there had been no opinion poll or advertisement.

The situation no longer permits us to isolate reality or human nature as a fundamental variable. The result is therefore not to provide any additional information or to shed any light on reality, but on the contrary, because we will never in future be able to separate reality from its statistical, simulative projection in the media, a state of suspense and of definitive uncertainty about reality. And I repeat: it is a question here of a completely new species of uncertainty, which results not from the *lack* of information but from information itself and even from an *excess* of information. It is information itself which produces uncertainty, and so this uncertainty, unlike the traditional uncertainty which could always be resolved, is irreparable.

This is our destiny: subject to opinion polls, information, publicity, statistics; constantly confronted with the anticipated statistical verification of our behavior, and absorbed by this permanent refraction of our least movements, we are no longer confronted with our own will. We are no longer even alienated, because for that it is necessary for the subject to be divided in itself, confronted with the other, to be contradictory. Now, where there is no other, the scene of the other, like that of politics and of society, has disappeared. Each individual is forced despite himself or herself into the undivided coherency of statistics. There is in this a positive absorption into the transparency of computers, which is something worse than alienation.

There is an obscenity in the functioning and the omnipresence of opinion polls as in that of publicity. Not because they might betray the secret of an opinion, the intimacy of a will, or because they might violate some unwritten law of the private being, but because they exhibit this redundancy of the social, this sort of continual voyeurism of the group in relation to itself: it must at all times know what it wants, know what it thinks, be told about its least needs, its least quivers, *see* itself continually on the videoscreen of statistics, constantly watch its own temperature chart, in a sort of hypochondriacal madness. The social becomes obsessed with itself; through this auto-information, this permanent autointoxication, it becomes its own vice, its own perversion. This is the real obscenity. Through this feedback, this incessant anticipated accounting, the social loses its own scene. It no longer enacts itself; it has no more time to enact itself; it no longer occupies a particular space, public or political; it becomes confused with its own control screen. Overinformed, it develops ingrowing obesity. For everything which loses its *scene* (like the obese body) becomes for that very reason *ob-scene.*

The silence of the masses is also in a sense obscene. For the masses are also made of this useless hyperinformation which claims to enlighten them, when all it does is clutter up the space of the representable and annul itself in a silent equivalence. And we cannot do much against this obscene circularity of the masses and of information. The two phenomena fit one another: the masses have no opinion and information does not inform them. Both of them, lacking a scene where the meaning of the social can be enacted, continue to feed one another monstrously – as the speed with which information revolves increases continually the weight of the masses as such, and not their self-awareness.

So if one takes opinion polls, and the uncertainty which they induce about the principle of social reality, and the type of obscenity, of statistical pornography to which they attract us – if we take all that seriously, if we confront all that with the claimed finalities of information and of the social itself, then it all seems very dramatic. But there is another way of taking things. It does not shed much more credit on opinion polls, but it restores a sort of status to them, in terms of derision and of play. In effect we can consider the indecisiveness of their results, the uncertainty of their effects, and their unconscious humor, which is rather similar to that of meteorology (for example, the possibility of verifying at the same time contradictory facts or tendencies); or again the casual way in which everybody uses them, disagreeing with them privately and especially if they verify exactly one's own behavior (no one accepts a perfect statistical evaluation of his chances). That is the real problem of the credibility accorded to them.

Statistics, as an objective computation of probabilities, obviously eliminate any elective chance and any personal destiny. That is why, deep down, none of us believes in them, any more than the gambler believes in chance, but only in Luck (with a capital, the equivalent of Grace, not with lower case, which is the equivalent of probability). An amusing example of this obstinate denial of statistical chance is given by this news item: 'If this will reassure you, we have calculated that, of every 50 people who catch the metro twice a day for 60 years, only one is in danger of being attacked. Now there is no reason why it should be *you*!' The beauty of statistics is never in their objectivity but in their involuntary humor.

So if one takes opinion polls in this way, one can conceive that they could work for the masses themselves as a game, as a spectacle, as a means of deriding both the social and the political. The fact that opinion polls do their best to destroy the political as will and representation, the political as meaning, precisely through the effect of simulation and uncertainty – this fact can only give pleasure to the ironic unconscious of the masses (and to our individual political unconscious, if I may use this expression), whose deepest drive remains the symbolic murder of the political class, the symbolic murder of political *reality*, and this murder is produced by opinion polls in their own way. That is why I wrote in *Silent Majorities* that the masses, which have always provided an alibi for political representation, take their revenge by allowing themselves the theatrical representation of the political scene.[3] The people have become *public*. They even allow themselves the luxury of enjoying day by day, as in a home cinema, the fluctuations of their own opinion in the daily reading of the opinion polls.

It is only to this extent that they believe in them, that we all believe in them, as we believe in a game of malicious foretelling, a double or quits on the green baize of the political scene. It is, paradoxically, as a game that the opinion polls recover a sort of legitimacy. A game of the undecidable; a game of chance; a game of the undecidability of the political scene, of the equifinality of all tendencies; a game of truth effects in the circularity of questions and answers. Perhaps we can see here the apparition of one of these collective forms of game which Caillois called *aléa*[4] – an irruption into the polls themselves of a ludic, aleatory process, an ironic mirror for the use of the masses (and we all belong to the masses) of a political scene which is caught in its own trap (for the politicians are the only ones to believe in the polls, along with the pollsters obviously, as the only ones to believe in publicity are the publicity agents).

In this regard, one may restore to them a sort of positive meaning: they would be part of a contemporary cultural mutation, part of the era of simulation.

In view of this type of consequence, we are forced to congratulate ourselves on the very failure of polls, and on the distortions which make them undecidable and chancy. Far from regretting this, we must consider that there is a sort of fate or evil genius (the evil genius of the social itself?) which throws this too beautiful machine out of gear and prevents it from achieving the objectives which it claims. We must also ask if these distortions, far from being the consequence of a bad angle of refraction of information onto an inert and opaque matter, are not rather the consequence of an offensive resistance of the social itself to its investigation, the shape taken by an occult duel between the pollsters and the object polled, between information and the people who receive it?

This is fundamental: people are always supposed to be willing partners in the game of truth, in the game of information. It is agreed that the object can always be persuaded of its truth; it is inconceivable that the object of the investigation, the object of the poll, should not adopt, generally speaking, the strategy of the subject of the analysis, of the pollster. There may certainly be some difficulties (for instance, the object does not understand the question; it's not its business; it's undecided; it replies in terms of the interviewer and not of the question, and so on), but it is admitted that the poll analyst is capable of rectifying what is basically only a lack of adaptation to the analytic apparatus. The hypothesis is never suggested that all this, far from being a marginal, archaic residue, is the effect of an offensive (not defensive) counterstrategy by the object; that, all in all, there exists somewhere an original, positive, possibly victorious strategy of the object opposed to the strategy of the subject (in this case, the pollster or any other producer of messages).

This is what one could call the evil genius of the object, the evil genius of the masses, the evil genius of the social itself, constantly producing failure in the truth of the social and in its analysis, and for that reason unacceptable, and even unimaginable, to the tenants of this analysis.

To reflect the other's desire, to reflect its demand like a mirror, even to anticipate it: it is hard to imagine what powers of deception, of absorption, of deviation – in a word, of subtle revenge – there is in this type of response. This is the way the masses escape as reality, in this very mirror, in those simulative devices which are designed to capture them. Or again, the way in which events themselves disappear behind the television screen, or the more general screen of information (for it is true that events have no probable existence except on this deflective screen, which is no longer a mirror). While the mirror and screen of alienation was a mode of production (the imaginary subject), this new screen is simply its mode of disappearance. But disappearance is a very complex mode: the object, the individual, is not only condemned to disappearance, but *disappearance is also its strategy*; it is its way of response to this device for capture, for networking, and for forced identification. To this *cathodic* surface of recording, the individual or the mass reply by a *parodic* behavior of disappearance. What are they; what do they do; what do they become behind this screen? They turn themselves into an impenetrable and meaningless surface, which is a method of disappearing. They eclipse themselves; they melt into the superficial screen in such a way that their reality and that of their movement, just like that of particles of matter, may be radically questioned without making any fundamental change to the probabilistic analysis of their behavior. In fact, behind this 'objective' fortification of networks and models which believe they can capture them, and where the whole population of analysts and expert observers believe that they capture them, there passes a wave of derision, of reversal, and of parody which is the active exploitation, the parodic enactment by the object itself of its mode of disappearance.

There is and there always will be major difficulties in analyzing the media and the whole sphere of information through the traditional categories of the philosophy of the subject: will, representation, choice, liberty, deliberation, knowledge, and desire. For it is quite obvious that they are absolutely contradicted by the media; that the subject is absolutely alienated in its sovereignty. There is a distortion of principle between the sphere of information, and the moral law which still dominates us and whose decree is: you shall know yourself, you shall know what is your will and your desire. In this respect the media and even technics and science teach us nothing at all; they have rather restricted the limits of will and representation; they have muddled the cards and deprived any subject of the disposal of his or her own body, desire, choice, and liberty.

But this idea of alienation has probably never been anything but a philosopher's ideal perspective for the use of hypothetical masses. It has probably never expressed anything but the alienation of the philosopher himself; in other words, the one who *thinks himself or herself other*. On this subject Hegel is very clear in his judgement of the *Aufklärer*, of the *philosophe* of the Enlightenment, the one who denounces the 'empire of error' and despises it.

Reason wants to enlighten the superstitious mass by revealing trickery. It seeks to make it understand that it is *itself*, the mass, which enables the despot to live and not the despot which makes it live, as it believes when it obeys him. For the demystifier, credulous consciousness is mistaken *about itself*.

> The Enlightenment speaks as if juggling priests had, by sleight of hand, spirited away the being of consciousness for which they substituted something absolutely *foreign* and *other*; and, at the same time, the Enlightenment says that this foreign thing is a being of consciousness, which believes in consciousness, which trusts it, which seeks to please it.[5]

There is obviously a contradiction, says Hegel: one cannot confide oneself to an other than oneself and be mistaken about oneself, since when one confides in another, one demonstrates the certainty that one is safe with the other; in consequence, consciousness, which is said to be mystified, knows very well where it is safe and where it is not. Thus there is no need to correct a mistake which only exists in the *Aufklärer* himself. It is not *consciousness*, concludes Hegel, which takes itself for another, but it is the *Aufklärer* who takes himself for another, another than this common man whom he endeavors to make aware of his own stupidity. 'When the question is asked if it is allowable to deceive a people, one must reply that the question is worthless, because it is impossible to deceive a people about itself.'[6]

So it is enough to reverse the idea of a mass alienated by the media to evaluate how much the whole universe of the media, and perhaps the whole technical universe, is the result of a secret strategy of this mass which is claimed to be alienated, of *a secret form of the refusal of will*, of an in-voluntary challenge to everything which was demanded of the subject by philosophy – that is to say, to all rationality of choice and to all exercise of will, of knowledge, and of liberty.

In one way it would be no longer a question of revolution but of massive *devolution*, of a massive delegation of the power of desire, of choice, of responsibility, a delegation to apparatuses either political or intellectual, either technical or operational, to whom has devolved the duty of taking care of all of these things. A massive de-volition, a massive desisting from will, but not through alienation or voluntary servitude (whose mystery, which is the modern enigma of politics, is unchanged since La Boétie because the problem is put in terms of the consent of the subject to his own slavery, which fact no philosophy will ever be able to explain). We might argue that there exists another philosophy of lack of will, a sort of radical antimetaphysics whose secret is that the masses are deeply aware that they do not have to make a decision about themselves and the world; that they do not have to wish; that they do not have to know; that they do not have to desire.

The deepest desire is perhaps to give the responsibility for one's desire to someone else. A strategy of ironic investment in the other, in the others; a strategy toward others not of appropriation but, on the contrary, of expulsion, of philosophers and people in power, an expulsion of the obligation of being responsible, of enduring philosophical, moral, and political categories. Clerks are there for that, so are professionals, the representative holders of concept and desire. Publicity, information, technics, the whole intellectual and political class are there to tell us what we want, to tell the masses what they want – and basically we thoroughly enjoy this massive transfer of responsibility because perhaps, very simply, it is not easy to want what we want; because perhaps, very simply, it is not very interesting to know what we want to decide, to desire. Who has imposed all this on us, even the need to desire, unless it be the philosophers?

Choice is a strange imperative. Any philosophy which assigns man to the exercise of his will can only plunge him in despair. For if nothing is more flattering to consciousness than to know what it wants, on the contrary nothing is more seductive to the other consciousness (the unconscious?) – the obscure and vital one which makes happiness depend on the despair of will – than not to know what it wants, to be relieved of choice and diverted from its own objective will. It is much better to rely on some insignificant or powerful instance than to be dependent on one's own will or the necessity of choice. Beau Brummel had a servant for that purpose. Before a splendid landscape dotted with beautiful lakes, he turns toward his valet to ask him: 'Which lake do I prefer?'

Even publicity would find an advantage in discarding the weak hypothesis of personal will and desire. Not only do people certainly not want to be *told* what they wish, but they certainly do not want to *know* it, and it is not even sure that they want to *wish* at all. Faced with such inducements, it is their evil genius who tells them not to want anything and to rely finally on the apparatus of publicity or of information to 'persuade' them, to construct a choice for them (or to rely on the political class to order things) – just as Brummel did with his servant.

Whom does this trap close on? The mass knows that it knows nothing, and it does not want to know. The mass knows that it can do nothing, and it does not want to achieve anything. It is violently reproached with this mark of stupidity and passivity. But not at all: the mass is very snobbish; it acts as Brummel did and delegates in a sovereign manner the faculty of choice to someone else by a sort of game of irresponsibility, of ironic challenge, of sovereign lack of will, of secret ruse. All the mediators (people of the media, politicians, intellectuals, all the heirs of the *philosophes* of the Enlightenment in contempt for the masses) are really only adapted to this purpose: to manage by delegation, by procuration, this tedious matter of power and of will, to unburden the masses of this transcendence for their greater pleasure and to turn it into a show for their benefit. *Vicarious*: this would be, to repeat Thorstein Veblen's concept, the status of these so-called privileged classes, whose will would be, in a way, diverted against themselves, toward the secret ends of the very masses whom they despise.

We live all that, subjectively, in the most paradoxical mode, since in us, in everyone, this mass coexists with the intelligent and voluntary being who condemns it and despises it. Nobody knows what is truly opposed to consciousness, unless it may be the repressive unconscious which psychoanalysis has imposed on us. But our true unconscious is perhaps in this ironic power of nonparticipation of nondesire, of nonknowledge, of silence, of absorption of all powers, of *expulsion* of all powers of all wills, of all knowledge, of all meaning onto representatives surrounded by a halo of derision. Our unconscious would not then consist of drives, of *pulsions*, whose destiny is sad repression; it would not be repressed at all; it would be made of this joyful *expulsion* of all the encumbering superstructures of being and of will.

We have always had a sad vision of the masses (alienated), a sad vision of the unconscious (repressed). On all our philosophy weighs this sad correlation. Even if only for a change, it would be interesting to conceive the mass, the object-mass, as the repository of a finally delusive, illusive, and allusive strategy, the correlative of an ironic, joyful, and seductive unconscious.

About the media you can sustain two opposing hypotheses: they are the strategy of power, which finds in them the means of mystifying the masses and of imposing its own truth. Or else they are the strategic territory of the ruse of the masses, who exercise in them their concrete power of the refusal of truth, of the denial of reality. Now the media are nothing else than a marvellous instrument for destabilizing the real and the true, all historical or political truth (there is thus no possible political strategy of the media: it is a contradiction in terms). And the addiction that we have for the media, the impossibility of doing without them, is a deep result of this phenomenon: it is not a result of a desire for culture, communication, and information, but of this perversion of truth and falsehood, of this destruction of meaning in the operation of the medium. The desire for a show, the desire for simulation, which is at the same time a desire for dissimulation. This is a vital reaction. It is a spontaneous, total resistance to the ultimatum of historical and political reason.

It is essential today to evaluate this double challenge: the challenge to meaning by the masses and their silence (which is not at all a passive resistance), and the challenge to meaning which comes from the media and their fascination. All the marginal alternative endeavors to resuscitate meaning are secondary to this.

Obviously there is a paradox in the inextricable entanglement of the masses and the media: is it the media that neutralize meaning and that produce the 'formless' (or informed) mass; or is it the mass which victoriously resists the media by diverting or by absorbing without reply all the messages which they produce? Are the mass media on the side of power in the manipulation of the masses, or are they on the side of the masses in the liquidation of meaning, in the violence done to meaning? Is it the media that fascinate the masses, or is it the masses who divert the media into showmanship? The media toss around sense and nonsense; they manipulate in every sense at once. No one can control this process: the media are the vehicle for the simulation which belongs to the system and for the simulation which destroys the system, according to a circular logic, exactly like a Möbius strip – and it is just as well. There is no alternative to this, no logical resolution. Only a logical *exacerbation* and a catastrophic resolution. That is to say, this process has no return.

In conclusion, however, I must make one reservation. Our relationship to this system is an insoluble 'double bind' – exactly that of children in their relationship to the demands of the adult world. They are at the same time told to constitute themselves as autonomous subjects, responsible, free, and conscious, and to constitute themselves as submissive objects, inert, obedient, and conformist. The child resists on all levels, and to these contradictory demands he or she replies by a double strategy. When we ask the child to be object, he or she opposes all the practices of disobedience, of revolt, of emancipation; in short, the strategy of a subject. When we ask the child to be subject, he or she opposes just as obstinately and successfully resistance as object; that is to say, exactly the opposite: infantilism, hyperconformity, total dependance, passivity, idiocy. Neither of the two strategies has more objective value than the other. Subject resistance is today given a unilateral value and considered to be positive – in the same way as in the political sphere only the practices of liberation, of emancipation, of expression, of self-constitution as a political subject are considered worthwhile and subversive. This is take no account of the equal and probably superior impact of all the practices of the object, the renunciation of the position of subject and of meaning – exactly the practices of the mass – which we bury with the disdainful terms *alienation* and *passivity*. The liberating practices correspond to *one* of the aspects of the system, to the constant ultimatum we are given to constitute ourselves as pure objects; but they do not correspond at all to the other demand to constitute ourselves as subjects, to liberate, to express ourselves at any price, to vote, to produce, to decide, to speak, to participate, to play the game: blackmail and ultimatum just as serious as the other, probably more serious today. To a system whose argument is oppression and repression, the strategic resistance is to demand the liberating rights of the subject. But this seems rather to reflect an earlier phase of the system; and even if we are still confronted with it, it is no longer a strategic territory: the present argument of the system is to maximize speech, to maximize the production of meaning, of participation. And so the strategic resistance is that of the refusal of meaning and the refusal of speech; or of the hyperconformist simulation of the very mechanisms of the system, which is another form of refusal by overacceptance. It is the actual strategy of the masses. This strategy does not exclude the other, but it is the winning one today, because it is the most adapted to the present phase of the system.

NOTES

1. Hans Magnus Enzensberger, 'Constituents of a Theory of the Media,' *New Left Review* 64 (1970) 13–36.
2. Armand Mattelart, *De l'usage des média en temps de crise* (Paris, 1979).
3. Jean Baudrillard, *A l'ombre des majorités silencieuses* (Paris, 1978).
4. Roger Caillois, *Man, Play and Games*, trans. Meyer Barash (London, 1962), ch. 8.
5. Georg Wilhelm Friedrich Hegel, *Phänomenologie des Geistes*, ed. Johannes Hoffmeister, trans. M. M. (Hamburg, 1952) pp. 391–2.
6. Hegel, ibid., p. 392.

FURTHER READING

American Mass Communication Theory

Berelson, B. and Janowitz, M., *Reader in Public Opinion and Communication*, (Glencoe, Illinois: Free Press, 1953).
Bryson, L. (ed.), *The Communication of Ideas*. (New York: Harper, 1948).
De Fleur, M., *Theories of Mass Communication* (New York: David McKay Co. Inc., 1966); 5th edn, with Ball-Rokeach, S. (New York: Longman, 1989).
Dexter, L. and White, D. M. (eds), *People, Society and Mass Communications*. (New York: Free Press, 1964).
Gitlin, T., 'Media Sociology: The Dominant Paradigm', *Theory and Society* 6:2 (1978) pp. 205–53.
Hardt, H., *Critical Communication Studies: Communication, History and Theory in America*. (London and New York: Routledge, 1992).
Lazarsfeld, P., Berelson, B. and Gaudet, H., *The People's Choice: How the Voter Makes up his Mind in a Presidential Campaign* (New York: Duell, Sloan & Pearce, 1944).
Merton, R., *Social Theory and Social Structure*, Part III (Glencoe, Illinois: Free Press, 1957).
Morrison, D., 'The Beginnings of Modern Mass Communication Research', *European Journal of Sociology* 19:2 (1978) pp. 347–59.
Rosenberg, D. and White, D. M., *Mass Culture: The Popular Arts in America* (New York: Free Press, 1957).
Schramm, W. (ed.), *Communications in Modern Society* (Urbana: University of Illinois Press, 1948).
Schramm, W. (ed.) *Mass Communications* (Urbana: University of Illinois Press, 1960; 2nd edn, 1975).
Wright, C. R., *Mass Communications: A Sociological Perspective* (New York: Random House Inc., 1959).

Frankfurt School

Adorno, T., *The Culture Industry: Selected Essays on Mass Culture*, Ed. with an introduction by J. M. Bernstein (London: Routledge, 1991).
Adorno, T. and Horkheimer, M., 'The Culture Industry: Enlightenment as Mass Deception', in Curran, J., Gurevitch, M. and Woollacott, J. (eds), *Mass Communication and Society* (London: Open University/Edward Arnold, 1977).
Arato, A. and Gebhardt, E. (eds), *The Essential Frankfurt School Reader* (Oxford: Basil Blackwell, 1978).
Jay, M., *The Dialectical Imagination: A History of the Frankfurt School and the Institute of Social Research 1923–1950* (London: Heinemann, 1973).
Rose, G., *The Melancholy Science: An Introduction to the Thought of T. W. Adorno* (London: Macmillan, 1978).
Slater, P., *Origin and Significance of the Frankfurt School: A Marxist Perspective* (London: Routledge & Kegan Paul, 1977).
Tar, Z., *The Frankfurt School: The Critical Theories of Max Horkheimer and Theodor W. Adorno* (New York: Wiley, 1977).

Marshall McLuhan and Technological Determinism

Ferguson, M., 'Marshall McLuhan Revisited: 1960s Zeitgeist Victim or Pioneer Postmodernist?' *Media, Culture and Society* 13:1 (1991) pp. 71–90.
Kroker, A., *Technology and the Canadian Mind: Innis, McLuhan, Grant* (New York: St Martin's Press, 1984).
McLuhan, M., *Understanding Media: The Extensions of Man* (London: Routledge & Kegan Paul, 1964).
McLuhan, M. and Fiore, Q. *The Medium is the Massage: An Inventory of Effects*. (New York: Bantam Books, 1967).
Marchand, P., *Marshall McLuhan: The Medium and the Messenger* (New York: Tichnenor & Fields, 1989.
Miller, J., *McLuhan* (London: Fontana/William Collins, 1971).
Stearn, G. (ed.), *McLuhan: Hot and Cool* (London: Penguin Books, 1967).
Williams, R. *Television: Technology and Cultural Form* (London: Fontana/William Collins, 1974).
Winston, B., *Misunderstanding Media* (London: Routledge, 1986).

Leavisism to Culturalism

Hall, S. and Whannel, P., *The Popular Arts* (London: Hutchinson, 1964).
Hunter, W. *Scrutiny of Cinema* (London: Wishart, 1932); Reprinted (New York: Arno Press, 1972).

Leavis, F. R., *Mass Civilisation and Minority Culture* (Cambridge: Minority Press, 1930).
Leavis, F. R. and Thompson, D., *Culture and Environment: The Training of Critical Awareness* (London: Chatto & Windus, 1933); reprinted (Westport, Connecticut: Greenwood Press, 1977).
O'Connor, A., *Raymond Williams: Writing, Culture, Politics* (Oxford: Basil Blackwell, 1989).
Storey, J., *An Introductory Guide to Cultural Theory and Popular Culture*, chaps 2 and 3 (Hemel Hempstead: Harvester Wheatsheaf, 1993).
Thompson, D. (ed.), *Discrimination and Popular Culture* (Hardmondsworth: Penguin Books, 1964); 2nd edn, 1973.
Williams, R., *The Long Revolution* (London: Chatto & Windus, 1961).
Williams, R., *Communications* (Harmondsworth: Penguin Special, 1962).

CULTURAL STUDIES

Fiske, J., 'British Cultural Studies and Television', in Allen, R. C. (ed.), *Channels of Discourse: Television and Contemporary Criticism* (London: Methuen, 1987); also *Channels of Discourse, Reassembled* (London: Routledge, 1992).
Hall, S., 'Introduction' to Smith, A. C. H. et al., *Paper Voices: The Popular Press and Social Change 1935–1965* (London: Chatto & Windus, 1975).
Hall, S., 'Culture, the Media and the "Ideological Effect" ', in Curran, J., Gurevitch, M. and Woollacott, J. (eds), *Mass Communication and Society* (London: Open University/Edward Arnold, 1977).
Hall, S., 'The Rediscovery of "Ideology": Return of the Repressed in Media Studies', in Gurevitch, M., Bennett, T., Curran, J. and Woollacott, J. (eds), *Culture, Society and the Media* (London: Methuen, 1982).
Hall, S., Hobson, D., Lowe, A. and Willis, P. (eds), *Culture, Media, Language*, pt three, chaps 8–13, 'Media Studies' (London: Hutchinson, 1980).
Turner, G., *British Cultural Studies: An Introduction* (London: Unwin Hyman, 1990).

FEMINISM

Butcher, H., Coward, R. et al., 'Images of Women in the Media', CCC stencilled paper no. 31 (University of Birmingham, 1974).
Coward, R., *Female Desire* (London: Paladin, 1984).
Doane, M. A., Mellencamp, P., Williams, L. (eds), *Re-Visions: Essays in Feminist Film Criticism* (Los Angeles: American Film Institute, 1984).
Friedan, B., *The Feminine Mystique* (New York: Norton & Co. Inc., 1963).
Kaplan, E. A., 'Feminist Criticism and Television', in Allen, R. C. (ed.), *Channels of Discourse* (London: Methuen, 1987); also *Channels of Discourse, Reassembled* (London: Routledge, 1992).
Kuhn, A., *Women's Pictures* (London: Routledge & Kegan Paul, 1982).
Kuhn, A., 'Women's Genres', *Screen* 25:1 (1984) pp. 18–28.
Mulvey, L., 'Visual Pleasure and Narrative Cinema', *Screen* 16:3 (1975) pp. 6–18.
Tuchman, G. et al. (eds), *Hearth and Home: Images of Women in the Media* (New York: Oxford University Press, 1978).
Women's Studies Group, *Women Take Issue* (London: CCCS/Hutchinson, 1978).
Zoonen, L. van, 'Feminist Perspectives on the Media', in Curran, J. and Gurevitch, M. (eds), *Mass Media and Society* (London: Edward Arnold, 1991).
Zoonen, L. van, *Feminist Media Studies* (London: Sage, 1994).
    See also 'Further Reading' for 'Feminist Readings' below.

THE PUBLIC SPHERE

Calhoun, C., *Habermas and the Public Sphere* (Cambridge, Mass.: MIT Press, 1992).
Curran, J., 'Rethinking the Media as a Public Sphere', in Dahlgren, P. and Sparks, C. (eds), *Communication and Citizenship* (London: Routledge, 1991).
Garnham, N., 'The Media and the Public Sphere', in Golding, P., Murdock, G. and Schlesinger, P. (eds), *Communicating Politics: Mass Communications and the Political Process* (Leicester: Leicester University Press, 1986); also available in Garnham, N., *Capitalism and Communications: Global Culture and the Economics of Information*, ed F. Inglis (London: Sage, 1990).
Habermas, J., *The Structural Transformation of the Public Sphere*, transl. T. Burger (Cambridge: Polity Press, 1989); originally publ. as *Strukturwandel der Öffentlichkeit* (Frankfurt am Main: Suhrkamp-Verlag, 1962).
Keane, J., ' "Liberty of the Press" in the 1990s', *New Formations* no. 8 (1989).
McCarthy, T., *The Critical Theory of Jürgen Habermas*, (Cambridge: Polity Press, 1978).
Scannell, P., 'Public Service Broadcasting and Modern Public Life', *Media, Culture and Society* 11: 2 (1989) pp. 134–66.
Thompson, J. B. and Held, D. (eds), *Habermas: Critical Debates* (London: Macmillan. 1982).

POSTMODERNISM

Baudrillard, J., *Simulations*, transl. P. Foss, P. Patton and P. Beithman, (New York: Semiotext(e), 1983).
Baudrillard, J., 'The Ecstasy of Communication', in Foster, H. (ed.), *Postmodern Culture* (London: Pluto Press, 1985).

Baudrillard, J., *Selected Writings*, ed. and introduced by M. Poster, (Cambridge: Polity Press, 1988).

Best. S. and Kellner, D., *Postmodern Theory: Critical Interrogations* (London: Macmillan, 1991).

Collins, J., 'Postmodernism and Television', in Allen, R. C. (ed.), *Channels of Discourse, Reassembled* (London: Routledge, 1992).

Connor, S., *Postmodernist Culture: An Introduction to Theories of the Contemporary* (Oxford: Basil Blackwell, 1989).

Fiske, J., 'Postmodernism and Television', in Curran, J. and Gurevitch, M. (eds), *Mass Media and Society* (London: Edward Arnold, 1991).

Harvey, D., *The Condition of Postmodernity* (Oxford: Basil Blackwell, 1989).

Jameson, F., 'Postmodernism, or the Cultural Logic of Late Capitalism', *New Left Review* 146: (1984) pp. 53–92.

Production

PRODUCTION

The prevailing tradition in thinking about cultural production, since at least the Romantic period, has been to focus on the individual artist, writer or composer. The mainstream of literary studies, for instance, is notoriously indifferent to the realities of the publishing industry in the various periods when its authors wrote or were read. But in media studies attention has persistently been paid to the economic, sociological, industrial and political factors contributing to and shaping media production. In part this is because – although individual talented journalists, performers and technicians can sometimes command high salaries and acquire celebrity – the work of assembling a newspaper or a broadcast programme more apparently requires teams of people. In addition, the very scale of the investment and turnover involved makes it harder to overlook the economic dimension, and the very nature of much of journalism's material makes obvious a connection with political affairs. But it is also because much of the research has been carried out by scholars in the Marxist tradition, concerned to link the political economy of capitalism with an understanding of the nature and role of the symbolic realm in the maintenance and reproduction of the social order. The first three chapters in this section can be said to fall broadly within that tradition.

The Frankfurt School coined the term 'the culture industry' to refer to the mass media, and Nicholas Garnham is prominent among the scholars who have found this a suggestive formulation. He has sought to pursue the implications of the industrialisation of culture for the nature of cultural production. In Chapter 9 he analyses the economic trends at work within the cultural industries that derive from the commodification of labour power and cultural goods and services within a capitalist economy. Although some individual points of fact have changed since the mid-1980s when the paper from which this piece is extracted was originally written,[1] the account remains a penetrating explanatory overview, allowing us to understand certain fundamental features of the media industry. Garnham's final observation here on the course of development of the cultural market ('a complex hegemonic dialectic of liberation and control') indicates that he does not fully accept the wider Frankfurt School pessimism about media culture in the twentieth century, but takes a more Gramscian view.

In Chapter 10, whose original core readership was composed of trade-unionists in the media industry, Colin Sparks examines the various ways in which the state influences the mass media. He writes from a classical Marxist position and thus regards the state in capitalist society as the ultimate guarantor of the interests of capital, not the disinterested and neutral guardian of the interests of all the people equally that it purports to be. The government is not coterminous with the state, which is fundamentally committed to defending the interests of capital, rather than those of any particular government. The social personification of capital comprises the rich and powerful at the apex of society, amongst whom can be numbered the press barons and broadcasting chiefs. Therefore, as powerful social institutions – most of them private businesses – all the mainstream media fundamentally support the capitalist state, even though they may clash politically with particular governments.

Graham Murdock is a leading critical political economist of the media and communications. Chapter 11 begins from the contradiction between the ownership of the major means of communication by private interests and the need for unfettered circulation of a diversity of information and opinion in a democracy in the public interest. Murdock proceeds to trace the increasing penetration of private business interests within the media sector during the 1980s, and points to a corresponding diminution and weakening of 'the countervailing power of public cultural institutions'. He writes in the conviction that – provided the fact that it 'largely excluded the working class, women and ethnic minorities' can be remedied – 'the idea of the public sphere is worth retaining'[2] (see Chapter 7). Further developments within the media business sector and its relations with public institutions have occurred since those charted in the essay. For instance, in 1994 Silvio Berlusconi – owner of Fininvest, the controlling company of an Italian services conglomerate with substantial media interests including 'effective monopoly control of Italian commercial television'[3] – was elected prime minister of his country after a dazzling campaign run largely through his own networks. This development took to a new stage in Europe the role of private media interests in the relationship between business and the institutions of public authority. Developments such as these continue to confirm the relevance of the themes explored in Chapter 11. Underlying Murdock's piece is a concern for what he has called elsewhere 'the limiting (but not completely determining) impact of cultural production on the range of cultural consumption'[4]

Another line of approach to exploring the range of production determinants shaping media output is to look within the media institutions, at their labour processes, management practices, divisions of labour, work routines and occupational patterns. This is to examine in detail the implications of the fact that media products are made by teams; the subject of the media 'message' is a collective one. Much of the research in British sociology with this focus was carried out in the 1970s. An example is the study of the daily newsroom cycle in the production of broadcast news in Chapter 43. The sociologist Jeremy Tunstall has carried out studies of a number of groups of media workers, including advertisers, parliamentary lobby correspondents, and journalists. Chapter 12 is drawn from a recent investigation of his into the occupational group television producers. This group is pivotal for the television industry, being the lynchpin between the creative and technical staff on the one hand, and the industry's controlling and managerial layers on the other. Tunstall's study draws out how the changing regulation and business practices of the television industry in the 1990s are sustaining this pivotal role of producers, while worsening their conditions of remuneration and security within the occupation.

Chapter 13 is a case study of a particular clash between a broadcasting institution and the government. The occasion was the Suez crisis of 1956 when the Egyptian state took control of the Suez canal from the Anglo-French company that had previously owned it. This was to prove a turning-point in the history of British imperialism. The Eden Government made a military response, with British (and French) planes carrying out bombing raids over Egypt for several days. The United Nations demanded a cessation, and the British government reluctantly complied. The Suez canal remained in Egyptian hands. Imperial interests had been directly challenged, and the government had proved politically unable to defend them. Subsequently, the process of decolonisation was accelerated. Political crises such as these can also generate crises in relations between the government and the regulated broadcasters, particularly the BBC because of its semi-official character. Subsequent examples would include the reporting of the Falklands conflict of 1982 and numerous instances in the Irish war 1969–94. Briggs is a social historian who pioneered detailed archival work on the history of broadcasting institutions, writing a multi-volume history of the BBC. Here he constructs a narrative of the relations between the BBC and the political authorities during the Suez crisis, using a variety of published sources and unpublished internal BBC documents. He refrains, however, from drawing any conclusions. Viewed from within the perspective of liberal political discourse, the incident vindicates the independent status of the BBC in its role of gathering and circulating news and information. From within the perspective of Chapter 10, the incident perhaps confirms the explanatory power of the distinction between the government and the state: though the government was committed to one approach, the military one, the state as a whole was temporarily divided over whether this was the wisest course in pursuit of its interests. This made for the circumstances in which the BBC resisted the government's pressures against the reporting of dissent and domestic opposition to its actions.

NOTES

1.   For instance: the Association of Cinematograph, Television and Allied Technicians no longer exists as a separate organisation, having merged with another media workers' union to form the Broadcasting, Entertainment and Cinematograph Union (thereby contributing to the trend to unification of industrial bargaining organisation to match the conditions of an increasingly unified labour market within the cultural industries); the growth of the Maxwell Communications Corporation ceased abruptly following the sudden death of its founder Robert Maxwell in 1991.
2.   Peter Golding and Graham Murdock, 'Culture, Communication and Political Economy', in James Curran and Michael Gurevitch (eds), *Mass Media and Society* (London: Edward Arnold, 1991) p. 22.
3.   Jeremy Tunstall and Michael Palmer, *Media Moguls* (London: Routledge, 1991) p. 169.
4.   Golding and Murdock, 'Culture', p. 22.

9

ON THE CULTURAL INDUSTRIES

Nicholas Garnham

[. . .]

An analysis of culture structured around the concept of the cultural industries [. . .] sees culture, defined as the production and circulation of symbolic meaning, as a material process of production and exchange, part of, and in significant ways determined by, the wider economic processes of society with which it shares many common features.

Thus, as a descriptive term, 'cultural industries' refers to those institutions in our society which employ the characteristic modes of production and organization of industrial corporations to produce and disseminate symbols in the form of cultural goods and services, generally, although not exclusively, as commodities. These include newspapers, periodical and book publishing, record companies, music publishers, commercial sports organizations, etc. In all these cultural processes, we characteristically find at some point the use of capital-intensive, technological means of mass production and distribution, highly developed divisions of labour and hierarchical modes of managerial organization, with the goal, if not of profit maximization, at least of efficiency. I refer to this as a descriptive use of the term 'cultural industries because it describes characteristics common to the cultural process in all industrial societies, whether capitalist or socialist. Within the descriptive usage we need to note a further distinction made by Adorno, who originally coined the term, between those cultural industries which employ industrial technology and modes of organization to produce and distribute cultural goods or services which are themselves produced by largely traditional or preindustrial means (for example, books and records) and those where the cultural form itself is industrial (such as newspapers, films and TV programmes). We need to remember this distinction because the two forms tend to give rise to different relations of production and types of economic organization.

From N. Garnham, 'Public Policy and the Cultural Industries', Ch. 10 in Nicholas Garnham, *Capitalism and Communication: Global Culture and the Economics of Information* (London: Sage, 1990) pp. 154–68.

But the term 'cultural industries' can also be used analytically to focus upon the effects on the cultural process within the capitalist mode of production of cultural goods and services produced and distributed as commodities by labour, which is itself a commodity.

A key point here is that the cultural sector operates as an integrated economic whole because industries and companies within it compete:

1. for a limited pool of disposable consumer income;
2. for a limited pool of advertising revenue;
3. for a limited amount of consumption time;
4. For skilled labour.

[1]

Consumer expenditure on cultural goods and services has been rising slowly as a proportion of total expenditure, as consumption of basic essentials, such as food and clothing, reaches saturation point. However, this movement has been within limits, and studies have shown this expenditure to be inelastic not only in general but also in the sense that for individuals and families expenditure does not rise in line with income. This is probably linked to the question of limited consumption time.

[2]

[There is a] close relationship between total advertising expenditure and both consumer expenditure and GNP. From 1952 to 1982 it [. . .] varied between 1.94 and 1.15 per cent of consumer expenditure, and between 1.43 and 0.89 per cent of GNP. Moreover, in real terms, total advertising expenditure has remained remarkably stable. [. . .] Against a background of a high level of advertising in the UK in relation to GNP compared with other European economies, the limits of the advertising revenue pool are plain.

[3]

For most people, cultural consumption is confined to a so-called free time, the extension of which is limited by the material necessities of work and sleep. If we assume a working week including travel of 45 hours and sleep time of 48 hours per week, that leaves 75 hours per week in which all other activities have to be fitted. On average, 20 hours per week are taken up by TV viewing.

Cultural consumption is particularly time-consuming in the sense that the most common and popular form of culture, namely narrative and its musical equivalent, are based upon manipulation of time itself, and thus they offer deep resistances to attempts to raise the productivity of consumption time. This scarcity of consumption time explains:

1. the acute competition for audiences in the cultural sector;
2. the tendency to concentrate cultural consumption in the home, thus cutting out travel time;
3. as [. . .] Swedish studies have shown, a sharp rise in the unit cost of each minute of consumption time, in particular as investment on domestic hardware increases while the time for using such hardware does not. Thus in Sweden between 1970 and 1979 time spent listening to music rose by 20 per cent while the cost rose by 86 per cent, with each hour of listening costing 55 per cent more.

[4]

The various cultural industries compete in the same market for labour. Individual film-makers, writers, musicians or electricians may move in their work from film, to television, to live theatre. The electronic engineer may work in manufacturing or broadcasting. The journalist may work in newspapers, periodicals, radio or television.

This unified labour market is reflected in trade-union organizations. The Association of Cinematograph, Television and Allied Technicians (ACTT) organizes across film, television and radio, the National Union of Journalists (NUJ) across newspapers, books, magazines, radio and television. The Musicians' Union members work in film, radio, television and records as well as live performances, and so on.

As a result of these levels of integration within the cultural sector, a shift in one new television channel, such as Channel 4, restructures the broadcasting, film and advertising market in specific ways. Even more, of course, will this be the case with cable and satellite services. The introduction of a new colour supplement has repercussions upon the finances of other publications, but may well also have cross-effects on broadcasting revenue.

[. . .]

[5]

The particular economic nature of the cultural industries can be explained in terms of the general tendencies of commodity production within the capitalist mode of production as modified by the special characteristics of the cultural commodity. Thus we find competition driving the search for profits via increased productivity, but it takes specific forms.

There is a contradiction at the heart of the cultural commodity. On the one hand, there is a very marked drive towards expanding the market share or the form this takes in the cultural sector, audiences. This is explained by the fact that in general, because one of the use-values of culture is novelty or difference, there is a constant need to create new products which are all in a sense prototypes. That is to say, the cultural commodity resists that homogenization process which is one of the material results of the abstract equivalence of exchange to which the commodity form aspires. This drive for novelty within cultural production means that in general the costs of reproduction are marginal in relation to the costs of production (the cost of each record pressing is infinitesimal compared to the cost of recording, for instance). Thus the marginal returns from each extra sale tend to grow, leading in turn to a powerful thrust towards audience maximization as the preferred profit maximization strategy.

On the other hand, the cultural commodity is not destroyed in the process of consumption. My reading of a book or watching of a film does not make it any less available to you. Moreover, the products of the past live on and can be relatively easily and cheaply reproduced anew. Thus it has been difficult to establish the scarcity on which price is based. And thus cultural goods (and some services, such as broadcasting, for technical reasons) tend towards the condition of a public good. Indeed, one can observe a marked tendency, where they are not *de jure* so treated, for consumers to so treat them *de facto* through high levels of piracy, as is now the case with records, video cassettes and books. (It should be noted that this in its turn relates to another contradiction in the cultural sphere, on which I shall comment shortly, between the producers of cultural hardware and software. It is the development of a market in cheap reproduction technology that makes piracy so difficult to control.) In contradiction, then, to the drive to maximize audiences, a number of strategies have had to be developed for artificially limiting access in order to create scarcity.

The drive to audience maximization leads to the observed tendency towards a high level of concentration, internationalization and cross-media ownership in the cultural industries. The strategies to limit access have taken a variety of forms:

1. Monopoly or oligopolistic controls over distribution channels, sometimes, as in broadcasting, linked to the state. One often finds here a close relationship between commercial interests and those of state control.
2. An attempt to concentrate the accumulation process on the provision of cultural hardware – e.g. radio and television receivers, hi-fi, VCRs, etc. – with the programmes, as in the early days of British broadcasting, as necessary loss-leaders. The rationale for the introduction of cable in the UK is an example of this.
3. The creation of the audience as a commodity for sale to advertisers, where the cultural software merely acts as a free lunch. This has proved itself the most successful solution; both the increased proportion of advertising to sales revenue in the press and periodicals market, culminating in the growth of free newspapers and magazines, and the steady expansion of wholly advertising-financed broadcasting services, are indications of this.
4. The creation of commodities, of which news is the classic example, which require constant reconsumption.

[6]

The third key characteristic of the cultural commodity lies in the nature of its use-values. These have proved difficult if not impossible to pin down in any precise terms, and demand for them appears to be similarly volatile. As I have already remarked, culture is above all the sphere for the expression of difference. Indeed, some analysts would claim that cultural goods are pure positional goods, their use-value being as markers of social and individual difference. While this aspect of culture merits much deeper and more extended analysis, it is only necessary here to draw one key conclusion, namely that demand for any single cultural product is impossible to predict. Thus the cultural industries, if they are to establish a stable market, are forced to create a relationship with an audience or public to whom they offer not a single cultural good, but a cultural repertoire across which the risks can be spread. For instance, in the record industry only one in nine singles and one in sixteen LPs makes a profit, and 3 per cent of the output can account for up to 50 per cent of turnover. Similarly, in films the top ten films out of 119 in the UK market in 1979 took 32 per cent of the box-office receipts and the top forty took 80 per cent.

Thus the drive to audience maximization, the need to create artificial scarcity by controlling access and the need for a repertoire bring us to the central point in this analysis. *It is cultural distribution, not cultural production, that is the key locus of power and profit.* It is access to distribution which is the key to cultural plurality. The cultural process is as much, if not more, about creating audiences or publics as it is about producing cultural artefacts and performances. [. . .]

We need to recognize the importance, within the cultural industries and within the cultural process in general, of the function which I shall call, for want of a better word, editorial: the function not just of creating a cultural repertoire matched to a given audience or audiences but at the same time of matching the cost of production of that repertoire to the spending powers of that audience. These functions may be filled by somebody or some institution referred to variously as a publisher, a television channel controller, a film distributor, etc. It is a vital function totally ignored by many cultural analysts, a function as creative as writing a novel or directing a film. It is a function, moreover, which will exist centrally within the cultural process of any geographically dispersed society with complex division of labour.

Taking these various factors into account, we are now in a position to understand why our dominant cultural processes and their modes of organization are the way they are. The newspaper and the television and radio schedule are montages of elements to appeal to as wide a range of readers, viewers and listeners as possible. The high levels of concentration in the international film, record and publishing industries are responses to the problem of repertoire. The dominance of broadcast television stems from its huge efficiency as a distribution medium, with its associated economies of scale.

For this reason, the notion that the new technologies of cable and VCR are fragmenting the market rather than shifting the locus of oligopolistic power needs to be treated with caution, since there are strict limits to how far such fragmentation can go economically.

[7]

As I have noted, power in the cultural sector clusters around distribution, the channel of access to audiences. It is here that we typically find the highest levels of capital intensity, ownership concentration and multinationalization, the operation of classic industrial labour processes and relations of production with related forms of trade-union organization. These characteristics are exhibited to their highest degree in the manufacture of the hardware of cultural distribution, especially domestic hardware. This is a sub-sector increasingly dominated by a few Japanese corporations such as Matsushita, Sony, Sanyo, Toshiba and Hitachi, together with Eastman Kodak, Philips and RCA.

[. . .]

Then there are the major controllers of channels of software distribution, often closely linked to specific modes of reproduction, such as record pressing or newspaper printing. In non-print media there is again a high level of concentration and internationalization, and US firms dominate, owing to the large size of the domestic US market. Here we find some of the same firms as in hardware, e.g. RCA, Thorn-EMI and Philips joined by firms such as Warner, CBS, Time-Life, Gulf-Western and MCA. The multinationalization of print media has been limited by barriers of language. None the less, apart from the high levels of concentration in the national UK market, with three groups controlling 74 per cent of daily newspaper circulation, two of these groups – News International and Reed International (now owned by Maxwell) – have extensive foreign interests.

The increasing tendency in this field, as an extension of the principle of repertoire, is the formation of multi-media conglomerates. Examples are Pearson-Longman and Robert Maxwell in the UK, who own interests across a number of media, thus enabling them both to exploit the same product, be it a film, a book or a piece of music, across several media, and also to expand the principles of risk-spreading not only across a range of consumer choice in one medium but also across consumers' entire range of cultural choice. The development of such centres of cultural powers also, of course, raises barriers to entry.

Around these centres of power cluster groups of satellites. These satellites can be either small companies, for instance independent production companies in relation to Channel 4, or individual cultural workers such as freelance journalists, writers, actors and film directors. In these satellite sectors we find high levels of insecurity, low levels of profitability, low levels of unionization and, where they exist, weak trade-union organizations. Often labour is not waged at all, but labour power is rented out for a royalty.

The existence of this dependent satellite sector fulfils a very important function for the cultural industries because it enables them to shift much of the cost and risk of cultural research and development off their own shoulders and on to this exploited sector, some of which is then [. . .] supported from the public purse. It also enables them to maintain a consistently high turnover of creative cultural labour without running the risk of labour unrest, or bearing the cost of redundancy or pension payments. Their cup brimmeth over when, as is often the case, the workers themselves willingly don this yoke in the name of freedom.

[8]

[. . .]

What should be our attitude to the relation between the market and the cultural process? There is that general tradition which regards culture and the market as inherently inimical. This view is powerfully reinforced within the socialist tradition by opposition to the capitalist mode of production. I think it is crucial, however, to separate the concept of the market from the concept of the capitalist mode of production, that is to say from a given structure of ownership and from the special features derived from labour as a market commodity. In terms of this relationship between consumers, distributors and producers of cultural goods and services, the market has much to recommend it, provided that consumers enter that market with equal endowments and that concentration of ownership power is reduced, controlled or removed. However, we must be clear that removal of the power vested in private or unaccountable public ownership will not remove the need for the function I have described as editorial, whether such a function is exercised individually or collectively. It also has to be stressed that even within the capitalist mode of production the market has, at crucial historical junctures, acted as a liberating cultural force. One thinks of the creation of both the novel and the newspaper by the rising bourgeoisie in the eighteenth century and of working-men's clubs and the working-class seaside holiday in the late nineteenth century.

Indeed, the cultural market, as it has developed in the past 150 years in the UK as a substitute for patronage in all its forms, cannot be read either as a destruction of high culture by vulgar commercialism or as a suppression of authentic working-class culture, but should be read as a complex hegemonic dialectic of liberation and control.

[. . .]

10

THE MEDIA AND THE STATE

Colin Sparks

There is no question but that the government influences the way in which the media reports events. However, the government is not the state, and the influence of the state is a slightly different question.

The government is a fairly small, although very influential, body of people. The state, on the other hand, is very large indeed. It is staffed by 'professional' people who owe their position not to any election, popular or otherwise, but to the allegedly rational internal bureaucratic norms of the sector of the state for which they happen to work. Although in theory the government is supposed to direct and control the state, the fact that they are two such different organizations, one small and transitory, the other large and permanent, means that any such direction will, in practice, be difficult. Indeed, there are substantial sections of the state machine, for example the judiciary, which are even formally independent of the government, and others, like the social services departments, whose first responsibility is to local rather than national government. There is plenty of scope for differences of strategy or opinion between the state and the government.

The row over the *Real Lives* programme illustrates that very clearly.* The BBC is, on any rational account, a state broadcasting institution. The government has legal powers which enable it to direct the BBC, but much more important are the facts that they finance the institution and appoint its Board of Governors. However, the employees of the BBC have an integrated hierarchy (modelled on the civil service and vetted by the secret service) and a professional ideology which continue to operate whether the government is Tory, Labour or whatever.

[. . .]

Nobody would wish to deny that governments do exercise some direction over the state (the example I have just cited clearly shows that they *can*), but it would be naive to imagine that

From Colin Sparks, 'The Media and the State' Ch. 8 in James Curran, Jake Ecclestone, Giles Oakley and Alan Richardson (eds), *Bending Reality: The State of the Media* (London: Campaign for Press and Broadcasting Freedom/Pluto Press, 1986) pp. 76–86.

this is either complete and permanent or entirely one-way. The state in this instance was able to stand up to the government and to defy its wishes.

The state and government acting either in unison or at cross-purposes can be said to influence the mass media in six roles: the patron; the censor; the actor; the masseur; the ideologue; and the conspirator. Let us look at each of them in turn.

The role of patron is one that is often overlooked. There are a number of important ways in which the state acts as the direct economic benefactor of the media. In the case of the BBC it simply hands over the cash to keep the institution running. In the case of the other cable and broadcasting activities it regulates the field to ensure that there is only limited competition, extracting some tax revenue in return. The functioning of this may be compared to the monopolistic corporations beloved of the early Stuarts, in that private individuals pay the state for the privilege of exploiting a resource. The state provides the press with negative economic patronage by exempting it from VAT, but it also provides some positive patronage through the placing of government advertising. This has, in general, been used as a selective instrument. The most notable victim has been the *Morning Star*, denied most state advertising for fairly obvious political reasons.†

The role of censor is much better known. There are a number of ways in which the state can directly determine what does and does not appear in the media. The most obvious of these is positive censorship, in which the state intervenes to prevent the publication or transmission of a particular item. In modern Britain the exercise of this power is relatively rare in peacetime and causes a huge row when it is discovered. However, negative censorship is a much more important factor. The publication of a piece of information can most effectively be prevented if those likely to publish it never become aware of it. The state has a wide discretion over this, notably by means of the definition of something as an official secret. Since, in so far as these measures are effective, there is little prospect of there being any serious row over them until the state papers eventually get released perhaps a century later, this pre-emptive censorship is by far the most effective kind.

Negative censorship is silent and routine in its operation and it suggests that the major ways in which the state influences the media are not the ones which command the most obvious public odium. Perhaps the most effective avenues of influence open to the state are those which proceed by means of the normal functioning of the state machine itself.

The most sensitive area of censorship in the last 18 years has been the war in Northern Ireland. There we have seen both positive and negative censorship playing a prominent role.

[. . .]

The influence of the state as actor is largely routine in its effect. The model of journalism dominant in Britain is one which stresses changes and sudden developments as the centre of news reporting rather than more gradual processes. Consequently the state is bound to provide a major source for the media. The more dramatic the development, the more likely it is to be reported; some of the activities of the state, for example wars, are very dramatic indeed. Thus there is a convergence between the actions of the state and the norms of modern journalism.

From the point of view of the journalist, the existence of a major bureaucracy as the source of a great deal of the news which forms the raw material of their daily working lives has important consequences. A journalist is forced to establish a working relationship with his or her sources and therefore builds up over time a relationship which is hardly likely to be adversarial. It requires no great credulity or venality on the part of a journalist to have a closer relationship with, say, the local police chief than with an unemployed youth who charges the police with brutality; indeed such a relationship is the condition for doing an effective job. Consequently, the official version of events is one which habit, let alone training, teaches the journalist to take seriously. Reviewing the relationship between the relatively feeble local state machine and the media, one commentator argued that there were structural factors which privileged the state as a provider of news:

> These factors are: the built-in dependence of the local press on the local authority as a source of regular news coverage which given individuals can cut off as a form of punishment; the need for speed in creating versions of events by local newspapers, which means that regular suppliers of information have power over the newspapermen [*sic*] that the supplier of one story or isolated piece of information does not have; the endemic secrecy of local government . . . ;the commercial nature of the newspaper enterprise, with the consequent reluctance of the editor to touch 'risky' material; and the libel laws.[1]

All these factors apply even more strongly to the central state and the national media.

The fourth role of the state, that of masseur, follows directly from its role as provider of material for the media. Material can either be raw or, to alter the metaphor, it can be cooked. No doubt some of the material which appears in the media is the result of activities akin to the traditional fictional representation of journalistic practice, but a great deal of it emerges from the state itself in a form which has already been calculated to make it news of a certain sort. The state employs quite a large number of public relations officers. In the recent past the most publicly visible example of this was Ian MacDonald, whose delivery of government press statements on the Falklands/Malvinas War suggested that criteria other than a smooth media image are thought appropriate for the senior levels of this arcane activity. Normally, professional etiquette means that they are much less visible, since their job is to present the actions of the state in such a way as to make it appear that a journalist is the source of the material.

According to a recent account by Cockerell and others, the government information services issue 'over 10,000' press releases each year.[2] Obviously, a great deal of such work will be purely routine. However, it would be silly to assume that this process does not also involve what is termed 'news management'. The same study remarked that: 'All governments seek to manage the news: to trumpet the good, to supress the bad and to polish up the image of the Prime Minister.' The most obvious example of this is the timing of particular press releases to ensure maximum exposure but there are numerous others of which the 'lobby system' is the best known. This is a system by which privileged journalists are treated to private chats by senior members of the government or state. They are allowed to use some of the material they get but not to reveal how they got it. Cockerell and his collaborators devote most of their book to examples of the lobby system in practice. They reveal, not surprisingly, that in this as in so much else that is manipulative and anti-democratic the Thatcher government has set new records. However, as in so much else, they also show that she was building upon solid foundations laid by others:

> Despite the abolition of the regular briefings for the lobby by his press secretary, Sir Harold demonstrated during his second tenure at Downing Street that he had lost none of his old skills at media manipulation. While he was attending the 1975 Commonwealth Prime Ministers' Conference in Jamaica, he summoned the *Daily Telegraph* lobby correspondent, Mr Harry Boyne (later knighted on Sir Harold's recommendation) to see him.

The Prime Minister told Boyne that he was intending to demote Mr Tony Benn in the Cabinet hierarchy. 'Mr Wilson gave me permission to write a story about it, which I duly did. I said: "Of course I won't put any by-line on this story. I think I'll just send it as *Daily Telegraph* reporter." "Well no," he says, "you can make it 'By our political staff'." This was typical of his knowledge, his quite intimate knowledge of how things worked in Fleet Street and in the lobby too.'

The suspension of lobby briefings by Mr Joe Haines had no lasting effect. On Sir Harold's resignation the machine cranked back into gear. Mr Callaghan's regime soon provided a notorious example of the lobby system being used through the non-attribution rule not merely to manipulate the news in the prime minister's favour but, in this case, to blacken the name of a diplomat. Mr Peter Jay, a *Times* journalist, was appointed British ambassador to the United States; Mr Jay was then married to Mr Callaghan's daughter. Mr Jay replaced an experienced and respected career diplomat, Sir Peter Ramsbotham, whose abrupt transfer was bound to cause controversy in Parliament and provoke cries of nepotism. Through the lobby a pre-emptive strike was organized on Mr Callaghan's behalf. Mr (later Sir) Tom McCaffrey, the Number Ten press secretary, briefed correspondents along the lines that Sir Peter was not entirely suited to the special needs of the *Washington Post*, and had to be replaced by a bright young man. Eventually the bottom line was revealed. Mr Christopher Moncrieff says, 'At the end of the meeting Tom McCaffrey privately ventured to one or two ears, accidentally I'm quite sure, that Ramsbotham, the man who was leaving the post, was a snob.' Within hours the *Evening Standard* and *Evening News* carried exactly the same story. 'SNOB ENVOY HAD TO GO' said the *Standard*; 'SNOB ENVOY HAD TO GO' said the *News*. No sources were given for these stories – picked up the next day in the daily papers – except 'the Callaghan camp' and 'governmental circles'.[3]

However, at this point we start to shade into a much more contentious area: that of the state as ideologue. It is commonly believed among academic students of the media that to give any weight to the notion that people, whether politicians, state officials or journalists, give conscious thought to what to present as news and how to present it in a light most favourable to their interests, is to hold to a crude and exploded set of ideas called 'conspiracy theory'.

Personally, I have always believed that such people give just as much thought to their actions and the consequences thereof as do the rest of us: we conspire to change the world and they conspire to keep us in our places. In this instance, there seems to me no reason to doubt that just as politicians employ people to package them so they, and the state as a whole, employ people to package their policies and actions.

Obviously a great deal of this activity takes place at the level of the unconscious or the semi-conscious. Those who people the state and those who people the media hold many of the same beliefs. This common ideology is an important part of the way in which the state influences the media. In modern society the state claims to represent the whole against the parts. It is the universal agency which permits, limits and controls the activities of partial sectoral interests. This 'universality' can be seen most clearly at the points when the state is threatened from outside. However, it also operates in other areas, for example industrial relations. Studying the media reporting of strikes in 1973, one writer observed that:

> The unions are basically presented as being motivated by a narrow-minded concern for their own sectional interest, while the government is presented as being motivated, in a

non-sectarian way, by concern for the 'national interest' . . . The state is presented as the representative of the 'majority of people' – not of any particular class interest.[4]

The notion, true or not, that the state speaks for all of us means that state definitions are often reproduced in the media, without any conscious process of 'conspiracy' taking place. This happens in two ways. The first is that the media adopt the definitions made by the state. At some point considerations of state policy, rather than media concerns, meant that Archbishop Makarios and Menachem Begin stopped being 'terrorists' and became 'statesmen'. No doubt a similar process will occur with Gerry Adams and Martin McGuinness. So, too, the 'Russians' became a 'threat' to the 'Free World': these are definitions dreamt up by ideologists in the service of the state, and by politicians, which are simply taken over by the mass media and repeated endlessly.

The second is more complex. It is an established part of the self-image of journalism that there is a strict separation of fact from opinion. No doubt every reader can think of a dozen recent instances in which that has not been the case, but the ideology does have some importance. It means, for instance, that the media rarely offer an independent interpretation of an event: rather they report the opinion of others, very often the spokespeople of the state or, more narrowly, the government. These people define the issues for the media and set the terms for all subsequent debate. Counter-opinions, which are often permitted in internal matters, are defined as sectional concerns which have to plead against the general interest as represented by the view of the state.

It is fair to point out that there is criticism of the state in some areas of media output. Policies believed to be mistaken are often criticized and there is a well-developed strain of populist criticism of individual state servants. However, at this point the identity between state and government starts to break down since much of the press, while supportive of the state, is hostile to non-Tory governments.

The final area is the one in which arguments about conscious belief and action are of the greatest importance. This is the area I have termed: the state as conspirator. The popular image of Macaulay's 'Fourth Estate' is of an institution suspicious of and hostile to state and government, but consider what they have in common. Both the state and the media are organized as hierarchies in which those at the top got there by proving their suitability to the people already at the top. Those at the top give orders which those lower down obey and enforce penalties of various kinds for non-obedience. In other words both are at their very roots deeply undemocratic organizations that are structured to ensure that the minority at the top controls the activities of the majority of those below them.

Further, those at the top of the media and of the state have a surprisingly high degree of shared experiences. They are likely to have had the same sort of education and they earn roughly the same sort of, very large, salaries. Their children go to the same schools. They often shift about between jobs at the same level. One study, looking at the people who own and run the press and comparing them with other groups of bosses, concluded that:

> If we take the chairmen and vice-chairmen of the ten leading press-owning concerns and their newspaper publishing subsidiaries the resulting group educational profile is remarkably similar to the known profile for other segments of contemporary capital. In all, 66 per cent of the press sample attended public school, compared with 71 per cent of the directors of the boards of Britain's top 200 companies and 70 per cent of John Wakeford's cross-section of industrial and other elites. Similarly, 62 per cent of the press sample went to Oxford or Cambridge, as against 60 per cent of the directors of

clearing banks, and 61 per cent of those on the boards of merchant banks and discount houses. These educational communalities are further cemented by shared membership of exclusive social clubs.[5]

White's, apparently, was the top choice.

If we look at the governors of the BBC, we find exactly the same sort of people. Sir William Rees Mogg left the editorship of the *Times* to become chairman of the Arts Council and a governor of the BBC. (I am conscious that this is not entirely fair. There is an ex-trade unionist on that august body. His name is Sir John Boyd. I think it is fair to say that he was one of the most talented right-wingers during his time in the AUEW and he is a self-proclaimed Salvation Army trombonist. I would not wish to deny that outsiders get admitted to the class I am describing, but it seems that they have to do a great deal of hard work to prove their loyalty first.)

The people who call the shots in the state and the media are indistinguishable. Their relatives and friends people the boardrooms of industry and finance, both public and private. These people take all the important decisions about what is going to happen, how it is going to be reported and what will be done with anyone who objects. They are the ruling class.

We know from recent example that miners and their families fight hard to save their jobs, their communities and their way of life. It is not too difficult, then, to accept that the denizens of Mayfair and Guildford fight to defend their jobs, their communities and their way of life. The major differences appear to be that they are much more united, do it more consciously, more aggressively and, so far, with much more success than we.

The state and the media are two of the weapons that the people who rule us use to ensure their continuation in power. The state is an instrument of coercion, the media are instruments of persuasion. They influence each other as if they were the two arches of a bridge. (Of course the state also persuades, through, for example, the education system. The media also coerce: you get sacked if you get out of line.)

It is at this point that the differences between state and government become of some importance. If the state were the neutral and efficient servant of the government then it might be possible to improve the media by changing the government. The evidence suggests that changes of government leave unaltered the massive concentrations of unelected and irresponsible power concentrated in the hands of the various arms of the state.

[. . .]

The people who run the state, the media, industry and the banks will not just let us get on with changing the world because a temporary majority in the House of Commons tells them to.

[. . .]

Fortunately, just as their armies are made up of the sons of the poor conscripted by unemployment into the service of the rich, so their media are written, filmed, printed and broadcast by working people. The evidence of all great social upheavals is that it is these people who can change the state and change the media, not the elite few who act on our behalf. Changing the state and changing the media have much in common: in both the only way it can and will be done is by the people whose labour makes these institutions work. A socialist society means a quite different state and quite different media.

NOTES

1. David Murphy, *The Silent Watchdog*, London: Constable 1976, p. 62.
2. M. Cockerell, P. Hennessy and D. Walker, *Sources Close to the Prime Minister*, London: Macmillan 1984, p. 9
3. *Ibid*, pp. 126–7
4. D. Morley, 'Industrial Conflict and the Mass Media', in *The Sociological Review*, New Series May 1976, p. 250–51.

5.   G. Murdock, 'Class, Power, and the Press: Problems of Conceptualization and Evidence' in H. Christian (ed.), *The Sociology of Journalism and the Press*, Keele University Press 1980, p. 48.

Editors' Notes

* In 1985 Home Secretary Leon Brittan, the minister responsible for broadcasting in the Thatcher Government, put pressure on the BBC Board of Governors to withdraw from transmission an upcoming edition in the television documentary series *Real Lives* that portrayed two Northern Irish politicians, Loyalist Gregory Campbell and Republican Martin McGuiness, on the grounds that McGuiness was an apologist for terrorism. After previewing the programme, the Governors withdrew it from its scheduled slot, precipitating a storm of protest and a one-day strike by BBC journalists. The contentious edition, *At the Edge of the Union*, was then broadcast with one or two minor modifications a few weeks later.

† The *Morning Star* is a daily newspaper published in London by the Communist Party of Great Britain.

11

CONCENTRATION AND OWNERSHIP IN THE ERA OF PRIVATIZATION

Graham Murdock

At the outset of the modern media age, in the first half of the nineteenth century, most commentators generally saw no contradiction between the private ownership of the press (the major medium of the time) and its public, political roles as a channel for strategic information and a forum for political debate. Freedom of the press was synonymous with the absence of government censorship and licensing and the freedom to operate unhindered in the market-place. Newspapers were viewed as a voice on a par with individual voices, and the advocation of press freedom was seen as a logical extension of the general defence of free speech. This was plausible so long as most proprietors owned only one title and the costs of entering the market were relatively low. As the century wore on, however, and newspaper production became more sophisticated both technologically and operationally, rising costs increasingly restricted entry to major markets and drove smaller titles out of business, while the larger, wealthier concerns expanded their operations. By the beginning of this century the age of chain ownership and the press barons had arrived, prompting liberal democratic commentators to acknowledge a growing contradiction between the idealized role of the press as a key resource for citizenship and its economic base in private ownership. As the American writer, Delos Wilcox, author of one of the earlier systematic analyses of press content, observed in 1900:

> The newspaper is pre-eminently a public and not a private institution, the principal organ of society for distributing what we might call working information. . . . The vital question is, from the social standpoint, the question of control. Who shall be responsible for the newspaper? It is rationally absurd that an intelligent, self-governing community should be the helpless victim of the caprice of newspapers managed solely for individual profit. (Wilcox, 1900: 86–9)

From G. Murdock, 'Redrawing the Map of the Communications Industries: Concentration and Ownership in the Era of Privatization', Ch. 1 in Marjorie Ferguson (ed.), *Public Communication: The New Imperatives* (Beverly Hills: Sage, 1990) pp. 1–15.

Wilcox's concern is more pertinent than ever as we move into an era where the combination of technological change and privatization policies are creating massive communications conglomerates with an unrivalled capacity to shape the symbolic environment which we all inhabit.

OLD PROBLEMS, NEW CONTEXTS

The last two years or so have seen a series of major acquisitions and mergers in the communications industries in Europe, North America and around the world. They include: Sony's acquisition of CBS's record division; General Electric's take-over of the US television network, NBC; the German multi-media group, Bertelsmann's, purchase of the Doubleday book company and RCA records; the Maxwell Communications Corporation's take-over of the New York publisher, Macmillan; and Rupert Murdoch's acquisition of a string of important communications concerns. These include the Twentieth Century Fox film interests; the major British publisher, Collins; Australia's biggest media company, the Herald and Weekly Times, and the Triangle Group of publications, which includes America's best-selling weekly magazine, *TV Guide*. By extending the activities of the leading media groups in such a visible way, these moves have breathed new life into long-standing concerns about concentration and ownership in the communications industries. To assess the significance of these developments, however, we must go beyond the immediate activity of bids, deals and buy-out, and analyse the longer-term movements which underpin them. As a first step we need to identify the key changes in the operating environment of the leading corporations that are facilitating the current wave of expansion and shaping its direction.

Two processes have been particularly important in restructuring the corporate playing field: technological innovation and 'privatization'. The 'digital revolution' which allows voice, sound, text, data and images to be stored and transmitted using the same basic technologies opens up a range of possibilities for new kinds of activity and for novel forms of convergence and interplay between media sectors. At the same time, we must be careful not to overstress the importance of technological innovation or to assign it an autonomous and determining role in the process of corporate development. New technologies create new opportunities, but before corporations can take full advantage of them there has to be a change in the political context which extends their freedom of action. And here the major force has undoubtedly been the growing momentum of privatization initiatives over the last decade. Before we examine the implications of this movement for corporate structures and strategies in more detail, however, we need to answer the prior question of why these changes matter.

MEDIA OWNERSHIP AND SOCIAL THEORY

Part of the answer is that investigation of the emerging patterns of media enterprise and ownership, and the tracing of their consequences for the range and direction of cultural production, is not just a specialized topic in communications enquiry. It also helps to illuminate the general relations between structure, culture and agency in the modern world. This classic problem lies at the heart not just of media research but also of the human sciences more generally, and presents both the greatest challenge to anyone specializing in the social investigation of communications and the best opportunity to reconnect our particular concerns to general developments in the social sciences to the mutual benefit of both. The relations between structure and action have moved steadily up the agenda for debate within social theory, to the extent that they now constitute its central problem (for example, Bourdieu, 1977: Giddens, 1984). More recently, theorists have begun to examine the parallel issue of culture and agency (for example, Archer, 1988), but as yet there has been no systematic attempt to link these general concerns to a detailed investigation of the media system. This is a double loss, to social theory and to communications research.

The question of mass media ownership provides a particularly pertinent point of entry into the structure–culture–agency triangle for two reasons. First, the power accruing to ownership entails both action and structural components (see Layder, 1985). The potential control it bestows over production does not arise solely from specific exercises of power within the corporations directly owned or influenced. It is also a function of pre-existing and enduring asymmetries in the structure of particular markets or sectors, which deliver cumulative advantages to the leading corporations, and enables them to set the terms on which competitors or suppliers relate to them (see Mintz and Schwartz, 1985). Consequently, a close study of the interplay between the structural and action components of control within media industries helps considerably in illuminating the core issues at stake in current debates about the nature of power.

The second theoretical pay-off of analysing media ownership arises from the pivotal role that the communications industries play in organizing the symbolic world of modern capitalist societies and hence in linking economic structures to cultural formations. More particularly, they connect a productive system rooted in private ownership to a political system that pre-supposes a citizenry whose full social participation depends in part on access to the maximum possible range of information and analysis and to open debate on contentious issues. Since this dual formation of liberal democratic capitalism first emerged, sceptics have been asking how far a communications system dominated by private ownership can guarantee the diversity of information and argument required for effective citizenship.

This question is more pertinent than ever today when the modal form of media enterprise is no longer a company specializing in one particular activity, but a conglomerate with interests in a wide range of communications industries, often linked to other key economic sectors through shareholdings, joint ventures and interlocking directorships. Before we examine the ways in which this structure facilitates certain kinds of control over cultural production, however, we need to distinguish between different types of conglomerate.

VARIETIES OF CONGLOMERATE

On the basis of their core activities we can distinguish three basic kinds of conglomerates operating in the communications field: industrial conglomerates; service conglomerates; and communications conglomerates.

Industrial conglomerates are companies which own media facilities but whose major operations are centred on industrial sectors. The Italian press provides a particularly good example of this pattern. The country's leading industrial group, Fiat, controls two major dailies: *La Stampa*, which it owns outright, and *Corriere della Sera* which it controls through its strategic stake in the paper's publisher, Rizzoli. The second largest group, the Ferruzzi-Montedison food and chemicals giant, controls *Il Messageror* and *Italia Oggi* in Milan, while the third main group, which is run through Carlo de Benedetti's master holding company, Cofide, has a controlling interest in the country's second largest publishing house, Editore Mondadori, which own 50 per cent of the best-selling daily, *La Repubblica*. Altogether it is estimated that over 70 per cent of the Italian press is controlled or significantly influenced by these three groups, with other major industrial companies accounting for significant parts of the balance. The widely read paper, *Il Giorno*, for example, is owned by the state energy company, ENI. Not surprisingly, this situation has led to allegations that press coverage is coloured by the owners' corporate interests. Critics include the broadcasting magnate, Silvio Berlusconi, who recently complained that 'Our newspapers are not written by journalists but by industrial competitors with special interests' (Friedman, 1988a: 32).

Berlusconi's own master company, Fininvest, is a good example of the second main type of comglomerate, which is centred on service sectors such as real estate, financial services, and retailing. In addition to owning a national newspaper, a major cinema chain and Italy's three main commercial television networks, Berlusconi's interests include the country's leading property company; a substantial insurance and financial services division; a major chain of department stores, La Standa; and an advertising operation which accounts for around 30 per cent of the nation's billings.

In contrast to this highly diversified structure, the major interests of communications conglomerates are centred mainly or wholly in the media and information industries. Well-known examples include Rupert Murdoch's News International; the Maxwell Communications Corporation; and Bertelsmann. Until recently it was not unusual for communications conglomerates to own companies in unrelated industries. But lately there have been signs that the leading players are shedding these marginal subsidiaries in order to concentrate on expanding their core interests. In 1988, for example, Robert Maxwell disposed of his engineering interests, Associated Newspapers sold their North Sea oil division, and Reed International shed the paper and packaging division which had been their original base.

At the same time, the major communications companies have been making strenuous efforts to expand their core interests. These moves take several forms. First, there is a growing integration between hardware and software, prompted by a desire to ensure a supply of programming to service the new distribution technologies. Sony, for example, recently acquired the CBS record division, giving it a major stake in the international music industry to add to its already dominant position in the world market for compact disc players through its partnership with Philips. Second, there is a growing interpenetration between old and new media markets as major players in established sectors move into emerging areas which offer additional opportunities to exploit their resources. Newspaper and journal publishers, for example, have moved into the provision of on-line data services and broadcasting networks have branched out into cable programming. The rationale behind these moves is the desire for greater 'synergy' between the companies' various divisions so that activity in one sector can facilitate activity in another.

The rise of conglomerates as the modal form of media enterprise considerably increases the major players' potential reach over the communications and information system and makes the old questions of ownership and control more pertinent than ever.

PERSONAL AND IMPERSONAL POSSESSION

Changes in the organization of corporate enterprise have also been accompanied by shifts in ownership, though these are by no means uni-directional. Although there is a discernible trend towards the forms of impersonal possession outlined by John Scott (1986) in which the controlling interests in major corporations are held by other companies and financial institutions, older patterns of personal ownership, where effective control remains in the hands of the founding family or group, have also proved remarkably resilient within the communications industries. According to one recent estimate, for example, sixteen of the top twenty-four media groups in the United States 'are either closely held or still controlled by members of the originating family'

(Herman and Chomsky, 1988: 8). They include both old-established companies such as the *New York Times* (the Sulzbergers) and Dow Jones and Co. (the Bancroft and Cox families) and newer arrivals such as Turner Broadcasting. At the same time, as the recent battles for control of the Springer press empire in West Germany and the Fairfax publishing interests in Australia clearly show, maintaining family or founder control can be a precarious and often expensive business.

The form of ownership is important since in combination with the structure and size of the company, it has an important bearing on the forms of control that proprietors want and are able to exercise. Although concern about the ways in which owner power may operate to curtail the diversity of publicly available information and debate can be traced back to the beginning of the modern media system in the second half of the nineteenth century, they are arguably more important than ever now, for three main reasons.

First, the fact that many of the leading communications companies command interests that span a range of key media sectors and operate across the major world markets gives them an unprecedented degree of potential control over contemporary cultural life. Second, as we shall see presently, the process of privatization has eroded the countervailing power of public cultural institutions. This is a significant loss, since at their best they embodied a genuine commitment to diversity and open argument, and at their minimum they filled a number of important gaps in commercially organized provision. Third, the privately owned media are becoming both more concentrated and more homogenized at a time when a range of new social concerns and movements, around ecological issues, women's rights and racial, regional and religious identities, are emerging in a number of countries. As a consequence, 'there is a growing gap between the number of voices in society and the number heard in the media' (Bagdikian, 1985: 98). What then are the powers of ownership? In what ways are proprietors able to shape the range and direction of cultural production?

THE POWERS OF OWNERSHIP

Owners possess two basic kinds of potential control over the symbolic environment. First and most obviously, they are able to regulate the output of the divisions they own directly, either by intervening in day-to-day operations, or by establishing general goals and understandings and appointing managerial and editorial staff to implement them within the constraints set by the overall allocation of resources (see Murdock, 1982). Second, they may also be able to influence the strategies of companies they do not own in their roles as competitors or suppliers.

In the area of direct intervention, attention has mostly been focused on proprietor's efforts to use the media outlets under their control as megaphones for their social and political ambitions. As the more perceptive commentators recognized when the trend first became apparent at the turn of the century, the movement towards conglomeration offered additional opportunities for the abuse of power. It was no longer simply a question of an individual owner giving himself and his views free publicity. As Edward Ross noted in 1910, the growing integration of newspapers into the core sectors of capital threatened to create new 'no-go' areas for critical reporting on corporate affairs and to undermine the press's role as a Fourth Estate, keeping watch over all those institutions – whether governmental or corporate – with significant power over people's lives. As he pointed out:

> newspapers are subject to the tendency of diverse businesses to become tied together by the cross-investments of their owners. But naturally, when the shares of a newspaper lie in a safe-deposit box cheek by jowl with gas, telephone, and pipe-line stock, a tenderness for these collateral interests is likely to affect the news columns'. (Ross, 1910: 305)

Contemporary cases of such 'instrumental' abuses of power are not hard to find. In the summer of 1988, for example, Toshiba, one of Japan's leading contractors for nuclear power plants, withdrew a record protesting against the country's nuclear programme commissioned by its Toshiba–EMI music subsidiary. As is often the case in these situations, a political judgment was presented as a disinterested commercial decision, with a company spokesman claiming that 'this music is just too good to put before the market right now' (*Marketing Week*, 1988: 18). Direct interventions are also used to denigrate the activities of competitors. In March 1988, for example, the Fiat-controlled daily, *Corriere della Sera*, carried an abusive front-page story and editorial ridiculing the attempts of one of the company's main business rivals, Carlo de Benedetti, to take control of the leading Belgian holding company, Société Générale de Belgique. Although Fiat intervention was denied, it was clear that, however engineered, the story was designed to boost the company's position, and no one in Italy was surprised when the magazine *L'Expresso* produced a mock version of the paper's front page with the title altered to *Corriere della Fiat* (Friedman, 1988b: 115–16).

In both these cases we are dealing with industrial conglomerates defending their corporate interests. With service and communications conglomerates the dynamics of influence are somewhat different. Here the major impetus comes from commercial initiatives designed to maximize the 'synergy' between the company's various operations. When Silvio Berlusconi bought the Standa department store chain in July 1988, he immediately announced a pro-gramme of cross-promotion whereby his television stations would carry daily slots featuring the bargains on offer in the stores, thereby reducing the space available for other kinds of programming. When the publishing group Reed International acquired Octopus Books in 1987, it made no secret of the fact that it was looking to develop titles based on its substantial stable of magazines. Other publishing companies are actively exploring ways of making television programming for satellite distribution using the same editorial resources employed to produce newspapers and magazines (Handley, 1988). These are purely commercial decisions, but by promoting multiplicity over diversity they have a pertinent effect on the range of information and imagery in the public domain. In a cultural system built around 'synergy', more does not mean different; it means the same basic commodity appearing in different markets and in a variety of packages. But owner power does not end with these kinds of interventions.

As we noted earlier, as well as determining the actions of the companies they control directly, the strategies pursued by the major media owners also have a considerable knock-on effect on smaller competitors operating in the same markets and on potential take-over targets. The deeper their corporate pockets, the greater their potential influence. In the autumn of 1988, for example, in an effort to strengthen its defences against the hostile attentions of Rupert Murdoch who had built up a 20 per cent stake in the company, the Pearson group (whose interests include Penguin Books and the *Financial Times*) entered into an alliance with the Dutch publisher, Elsevier, who had been the target of another major media mogul, Robert Maxwell. Whether this tie-up is in the best long-term interests of Pearson or whether another partner would have been more advantageous is open to debate, but there is no doubt that this link will materially affect the company's future options.

The leading corporations' extensive power to shape the future of the communications and information system both directly and indirectly is not in itself new, of course. What is new is the rapid enlargement of these powers produced by a decade of privatization initiatives.

DIMENSIONS OF PRIVATIZATION

Since the term 'privatization' has acquired a variety of meanings in recent debates, I should make it clear that I am using it here in its most general sense to describe all forms of public intervention that increase the size of the market sector within the communication and information industries and give entrepreneurs operating within it increased freedom of manœuvre. Two general features of this process are particularly worth noting. First, although such initiatives are usually associated with conservative administrations – most notably, the three Thatcher governments in Britain and Reagan's terms of office in the United States – they are by no means confined to them. The socialist government of Spain, for example, recently used its majority in the lower house to push through legislation authorizing three new commercial television franchises in the face of strong opposition from both conservative and left parties. More significantly, both the Soviet Union and the People's Republic of China have recently allowed commercial programme providers from overseas into their broadcasting systems. The second, and equally important, feature of privatization is its relative irreversibility. Although the popularity of specific initiatives may decline in the future and the original almost messianic impetus wane somewhat, there is little doubt that the previous balance between public and private enterprise has been tipped permanently in favour of the market in a growing number of societies. It is difficult, for example, to imagine any socialist or social democratic government capable of being elected in Western Europe in the near future, successfully renationalizing the key communications companies that have been sold off to private investors.

Privatization as I am defining it here is a multi-dimensional movement with four distinct components: de-nationalization; liberalization; the commercialization of the public sector; and the regearing of the regulatory environment. Each has important implications for the overall structure of the communications industries, for patterns of ownership, and for corporate strategies, which we need to trace, but it is important to separate them since they are not always pursued together.

DENATIONALIZATION: FROM PUBLIC TO PRIVATE OWNERSHIP

Because denationalization involves selling shares in public companies to private investors, its most significant impact is on patterns of ownership. However, this varies depending on how the shares are placed. Where they are put out to competitive tender and awarded to a particular consortium, as in France under the conservative administration of Chirac, the advantage clearly lies with companies which are already well financed and positioned and who can use the opportunity to extend their interests into areas from which they were previously locked out. For example, the group that took over TF1, which had been France's major public broadcasting network, included the Maxwell media conglomerate, the Bouygues construction group and the major banking group, Société Générale (which also had important stakes in two other denationalized communications concerns: the Havas advertising agency, and the telecommunications and engineering group, Companie Générale d'Electricité).

In contrast, the British strategy of public flotation was expressly designed to create a 'popular capitalism' in which shareholding would be widely dispersed. To this end, shares in the most important communications utility to be sold to date, British Telecom, were underpriced in order to attract first-time investors. Not surprisingly, their value rose sharply as soon as they were traded on the Stock Exchange, and many small shareholders opted to sell and pocket the profit. In the two years between December 1984 and the end of November 1986, the total number of BT shareholders fell by almost 30 per cent from 2.1 million to 1.48 million, reducing the public's overall share to less than 12 per cent and leaving the bulk of BT's equity in the hands of financial institutions, many based overseas.

Overall, then, denationalization has operated to reinforce and extend the power of the leading communications, service and industrial conglomerates rather than to disperse it, or to create new sources of countervailing power. By the same token, liberalization has enabled them to extend their reach into new markets.

LIBERALIZATION

Liberalization policies are designed to introduce competition into markets that were previously served solely by public enterprise. Here the impact depends on the terms on which this competition is allowed to proceed. Broadcasting provides a good example. Britain was the first major European country to introduce a commercial television service in competition with the public broadcasting system, when the ITV network was launched in 1954. However, the private sector was carefully regulated to ensure a reasonable spread of ownership and to limit foreign programming to 14 per cent of the total output. Without these safeguards, moves to liberalize broadcasting serve to open up national markets to the major international corporations. The major shareholders in the new French commercial channels, for example, include the Italian television magnate, Silvio Berlusconi, who has a 25 per cent stake in La Cinq, and Companie Luxembourgeoise de Télédiffusion (which operates the Luxembourg based television service RTL-Plus), which owns 25 per cent of the sixth channel, M6. In addition, the rapid expansion of commercial television paved the way for a sharp rise in the amount of foreign programming imported into the system since the proliferation of new distribution systems outstripped the supply of nationally originated material by a very considerable margin. This effect is noticeable even where broadcasting remains a public monopoly, as in Norway, where the decision to allow local cable systems to take advertising-supported pan-European satellite channels has already acted as a stalking horse for full liberalization by deepening the crisis of public broadcasting.

COMMERCIALIZING THE PUBLIC SECTOR

One response to this crisis is to commercialize the public sector itself. Faced with rising costs and government ceilings imposed on the income they derive from the public purse, this has become an imperative for many public institutions, but it is one which a number are now embracing with enthusiasm. It takes several forms. The first is to allow broadcasters to supplement their income by taking spot advertising, as the state broadcasting network RAI does in Italy. So far this option has been resisted in Britain, but as recent developments at the BBC show, audiences and indeed resources can be opened up to private enterprise in other ways.

In the spring of 1988, the BBC offered two new services to the corporate sector. The first provided for 100 new data channels for use by retailers and other service companies wishing to advertise to their customers. The second allowed a private company, British Medical Television, to use time after regular broadcasts had finished for the night to relay a programme with advertising from the major pharmaceutical companies to VCRs in doctors' homes and surgeries for later viewing. In return, the Corporation will receive a £1 million fee in the first year. As well as gaining access to transmission resources for the first time, private corporations are also gaining a foothold in programme production as a result of the Government's decision that the BBC should move rapidly towards a situation in which at least 25 per cent of its programming is obtained from independent producers. Although the independent sector has only been established for a few years in Britain, prompted by the launch of Channel Four, which buys in almost all its programming, there is already a movement towards concentration which senior figures in the industry expect to continue. As Charles Denton, the Chief Executive of Zenith Productions, one of the country's most successful television independents, told an interviewer: 'I think there will be a move to agglomeration, and to cope with the economic realities there will be some very complex cross-holding. When this industry matures, you will find maybe half a dozen, even fewer, large independents. And we intend to be one of them' (Fiddick, 1988: 21). Recent examples of this trend include Robert Maxwell's takeover of the creative consortium Witzend; the purchase of Goldcrest Films and Elstree Studios by the leisure group Brent Walker; and the acquisition of Zenith itself by Carlton Communications, one of Britain's leading facilities houses. These movements, coupled with the partial relaxation of the rules governing corporate underwriting and sponsorship for programming (particularly on cable), open the way for greater corporate influence over what appears on the domestic screen. This erosion of the traditional 'Chinese walls', separating programming from product or corporate promotion, which we now see in a number of countries, is part of a much wider re-gearing of the regulatory environment in which the communications industries operate.

RE-REGULATION: FROM PUBLIC TO CORPORATE INTERESTS

This process is often called de-regulation. This is a misnomer. What is at stake is not so much the number of rules but the shift in their overall rationale, away from a defence of the public interest (however that was conceived) and towards the promotion of corporate interests. Communications corporations benefit from this shift at two levels. They not only gain from changes to the general laws governing corporate activity in areas such as trade-union rights but, more importantly, they have also gained considerably from the relaxation of the additional rules designed to prevent undue concentration in the market-place of ideas and to ensure diversity of expression.

One of the most important changes has been the general loosening of the restrictions on concentration of ownership. In Britain, for example, Rupert Murdoch's bid for the mid-market daily *Today*, was judged not to be against the public interest on the grounds that, although he owned the country's most popular tabloid paper, the *Sun*, and one of the leading quality titles, *The Times*, he did not have an interest in the middle range and that his acquisition would not therefore increase concentration – a judgment that conveniently leaves aside the question of concentration in the national daily market as a whole.

In the broadcasting field, changes to the rules limiting the number of stations a single owner can possess have led to a significant increase in concentration in both the United States and Australia. In America, in April 1985, the old 7–7–7 limit which had operated since 1953 was replaced by a new 12–12–12 rule which allowed one company to own up to twelve AM and FM radio stations plus twelve television stations, providing that their total audience did not exceed 25 per cent of the country's television households. This made network ownership a more attractive proposition (despite the steady erosion of their overall audience share by cable and independent stations), and all three became the subject of bids. ABC was merged with Capital Cities; NBC was acquired by General Electric; and CBS narrowly fought off a bid from Ted Turner. A similar relaxation occurred in Australia in November 1986 when Bob Hawke's Labour Government replaced the old two-station rule with a new arrangement which allows owners to have as many stations as they like as long as they do not reach more than 60 per cent of the national audience. Here again, the result has been a marked movement towards greater concentration of ownership as companies in the two major markets – Sydney and Melbourne – have branched out to build national networks. Between December 1986 and September 1988, twelve out of the fifteen stations in capital cities changed hands, leaving the commercial television system as a virtual duopoly divided between the media wing of Alan Bond's industrial conglomerate and Christopher Skase's Quintex Group (Brown, 1988)

Changes to the regulatory regime are not uni-directional, however. At the same time as they relaxed the rule on the number of television stations that could be owned, the Australian government imposed new restrictions forbidding cross-ownership of radio stations, television stations or newspapers in the same markets. This accelerated the shake-up in newspaper ownership already under way, though here again the major beneficiaries were the leading groups. At the beginning of 1987, Rupert Murdoch successfully bid for the country's largest press concern, the Herald and Weekly Times, bringing his total share of the Australian newspaper market to 59 per cent. In the United States, in contrast, the rules on crossownership have recently been relaxed, though not without a struggle. Senator Edward Kennedy, for example, appended a clause to the Federal government's spending authorization for 1988, tightening the restrictions on owning television stations and newspapers in the same city. This was directed expressly at Murdoch whose *Boston Herald* had been consistently hostile to Kennedy. Murdoch contested it, and in the spring of 1988 it was overturned by the Circuit Court of Appeals in Washington on the grounds that since it was clearly aimed at one person it violated constitutional guarantees of equal treatment. This ruling was in line with the general trend of recent regulatory thinking typified by the Federal Communication Commission's decision to lift the ban on local telephone companies owning cable systems.

The FCC has also been in the forefront of the drive to loosen the public service requirements governing commercial broadcasting so as to give station owners maximum freedom to make profits. One of the bitterest rows in this area has been over children's television, which during the Reagan years had become one more or less continuous advertisement for toys and other products both in and around the programmes. After a concerted campaign, a citizens' lobby was successful in getting a Bill passed in both the House of Representatives and the Senate, limiting advertising time during children's programmes to twelve minutes in the hour and requiring franchisees to show a commitment to education. However, in one of his last acts as President, Ronald Reagan killed the measure by the simple expedient of omitting to sign it, declaring that its provisions 'simply cannot be reconciled with the freedom of expression secured by our constitution' (*The Economist*, 1988: 50). This statement exemplifies the general view which sees corporate promotion as continuous with individual speech, a position neatly encapsulated in the description of advertising as 'commercial speech'. The cumulative result of these shifts, and the other dimensions of the privatization process I have outlined here, has been to strengthen and extend the power of the leading corporations and to pose more sharply than ever the dilemma that faces a liberal democratic society in which most key communications facilities are held in private hands.

Detailing the way in which our existing maps of the cultural industries are being redrawn by the twin processes of technological changes and privatization policies and tracing their consequences for the range and nature of cultural production is a key task for future research. By the same token, anyone interested in formulating alternative policies for communications urgently needs to grapple with ways of regulating the new multi-media concerns, both nationally and internationally, and with the problem of developing novel forms of public initiative and institution which avoid the overcentralized, unresponsive structures of the past and are capable of responding creatively to the new poly-cultural formations now emerging. This is perhaps the major issue facing those of us interested in the future of communications as an essential resource for developing and deepening democracy.

REFERENCES

Archer, M. S. (1988) *Culture and Agency: the Place of Culture in Social Theory*, Cambridge: Cambridge University Press.

Bagdikian, B. (1985) 'The US Media: Supermarket or Assembly Line?', *Journal of Communication* 35:3, pp. 97–109.

Bourdieu, P. (1977) *Outline of a Theory of Practice*, Cambridge: Cambridge University Press.

Brown, A. (1988) 'Restructure of Australian Commercial Television', paper presented to Oz Media National Conference, Brisbane, 24 Sept.

Economist, The (1988) 'Pocket Vetoes: Licence to Kill', 19 Nov., p. 50.

Fiddick, P. (1988) 'Risk-risk at the Top-top', *Guardian*, 15 Feb., p. 21.

Friedman, A. (1988a) 'Putting Himself in the Picture', *Financial Times*, 1 Aug., p. 32.

Friedman, A. (1988b) *Agnelli and the Network of Italian Power*, London: Harrap.

Giddens, A. (1984) *The Constitution of Society: Outline of a Theory of Structuration* Cambridge: Polity Press.

Handley, N. (1988) 'Multiple Choices in the Single Market', *Marketing Week*, 25 Nov., pp. 73–7.

Herman, E. and Chomsky, N. (1988) *Manufacturing Consent: the Political Economy of the Mass Media*, New York: Pantheon Books.

Layder, D. (1985) *Structure, Interaction and Social Theory*, London: Routledge & Kegan Paul.

Marketing Week (1988) 'Toshiba Forced to Turn Down Music', 15 July, p. 18.

Mintz, B. and Schwartz, M. (1985) *The Power Structure of American Business*, Chicago: University of Chicago Press.

Murdock, G. (1982) 'Large corporations and the control of the communications industries', pp. 118–50 in Michael Gurevitch, Tony Bennett, James Curran and Janet Woollacott (eds), *Culture, Society and the Media*, London: Methuen.

Ross, E. (1910) 'The Suppression of Important News', *Atlantic Monthly* 105, pp. 303–11.

Scott, J. (1986) *Capitalist Property and Financial Power: A Comparative Study of Britain, the United States and Japan*, Brighton: Wheatsheaf.

Wilcox, D. (1900) 'The American Newspaper: A Study of Political and Social Science', *Annals of the American Academy of Political and Social Science* 16, July, pp. 56–92.

12

PRODUCERS IN BRITISH TELEVISION

Jeremy Tunstall

[. . .]

An important characteristic of British television is its tradition of covering a wide range of different programme types, and of carrying this range within the high-audience hours of the evening. Part of the traditional 'public-service broadcasting' project is that both popular and less-popular programming should be scheduled in the most popular hours on the main channels. It is also characteristic of British television that several of the genres are factual – including not only news, current affairs and sport, but also documentary and mixed-goal or 'edinfotainment' programming.

[. . .]

Each specific genre has its particular requirements and working cycles, which tend to cut its producers off from producers and others working in different fields with different timetables. Most British producers spend between 4 and 6 months each year locked into the intensive effort involved in meeting deadlines for a series of programmes; during this intensive phase they may well work 7 days a week for many weeks in succession. The other half of the year includes vacation time and perhaps 5 months of less intensive work. During these other months the producer may be supervising writing, casting supporting roles, engaging in research, looking at locations, seeing possible interviewees, talking to actors' agents, and so on. Producers spend much of the time out of their offices – in the studio, at the location, viewing the raw rushes and, later, the rough edited film or tape.

Even at the quieter times of the year most producers do not arrive home until after the London rush-hour. They often take home with them scripts and programme outlines to read, as well as cassettes of programmes submitted by available writers, directors or performers. Much of their domestic TV viewing is of programming in their own genre. Thus producers tend to be locked into a genre-specific world even when at home.

Each of the genres is located within a department or departments; and even independent

From Jeremy Tunstall, *Television Producers* (London: Routledge, 1993) pp. 2–13, 202–7, 212–16.

production companies specialize, so that here also producers are locked into the private world of a single genre. Each genre has its own specific goal or goals; it has a characteristic style of production – location film, or live studio, or the 'outside broadcasts' of sport. Each genre has its own internal system of status and prestige, its own values and its own world-view.

Departments and genres also function as career-ladders. There is continuing movement between organizations: many producers have started in the BBC, moved to ITV, then back to the BBC, only finally to go freelance or to set up as independent producers; but such job-moves all take place within one small world which shares one broad career-ladder. It is common for a producer's career to have involved several job-moves, each move following one particular senior colleague. Producers also in turn tend to be surrounded by production team-members with whom they have worked on several previous programmes and projects.

Thus the producer's own work-career advances within the private world of a particular genre whose peculiar work-mix of timetables, goals, production schedules and world-view largely shuts its members off from the members of other private genre-worlds.

WHERE THE PRODUCER CAME FROM

The producer role (like television itself) has multiple origins. The British TV producer historically is derived from the civil servant, the radio producer and the film producer, as well as from show business and the stage.

The BBC in the 1920s emerged from the Post Office, which was a department of government. The producer role in the BBC and in advertising-financed television derives from an inter-war civil service which still had colonial responsibilities; there are echoes of the district officer, gallantly attempting to administer one small corner of a vast empire. There is also a military element in this history: the BBC was set up in the 1920s by men who had served in and survived the first world war. British television in the 1940s and 1950s was built by men who had served in the second war or had done two years of post-1945 military service. Many young producers of the 1950s had been 'national-service' officers, and the television producer was seen as a leader of men (not women).

Political neutrality was a key element. The producer, like the civil servant and the army officer, avoided partisanship. In contrast to France or Germany, the British producer role was not, and still has not been, politicized. In Britain the BBC gradually evolved the tradition of being non-partisan while quietly patriotic. This non-partisanship has also been supported by the BBC's early reliance on neutral news agencies as a model for radio news. The non-partisan tradition acquired in 1955 a non-commercial element; when advertising was introduced with ITV, the relevant legislation and regulatory authority required producers to be sheltered from any direct advertising connections.

The BBC, modelled on the Post Office with its monopoly of post and telephone, was a vertically integrated monopoly. This conception of vertical integration was only modified by the ITV and its cartel of fifteen regional companies. The British TV-producer role developed within a pattern of two large systems – BBC and ITV – both of which made the bulk of their own programming and also transmitted it to a national audience.

This pattern, which reached maturity in the 1970s, involved two large cultural bureaucracies with an occupational hierarchy. Like the civil service, television had three main occupational categories. At the top were the managers, amongst whom former and current programme producers were the largest subgroup; producers mingled with general administrators, accountants and senior engineers, constituting a managerial elite. In the middle was a large category of TV skills and crafts; there were the men (and a few women) who operated TV studios and the outside broadcasts, the outdoor filming, the post-production and editing functions and other craft skills. Third and last were the clerical and lower service functions, in which women predominated. These latter two groupings were again reminiscent of the civil-service executive and clerical levels.

Another crucial civil-service-style feature in the 1970s was job security. It was required by the trade unions, and accepted by both BBC and ITV, that 70 per cent or more of the employees were in permanent and pensionable employment. In the 1970s a substantial minority of producers and directors were freelances; but many of these had been in staff positions previously and had chosen to go freelance. At the skilled levels and above in both the BBC and ITV there were very low rates of employee turnover, and 86 per cent of BBC employees in 1989 had been in the BBC for all their broadcasting work-careers. The numbers of producers and other personnel employed in British television expanded steadily – buoyed up by expanding revenue – in almost every single year from 1946 to 1988.

Producers were integrated into general management. Within this broad category, several levels of programme decision-making can be identified in 1990s terms:

Channel Heads
Departmental Head (BBC); Director of Programmes (ITV)
Executive Producer (BBC); Department Head (ITV)
Series Producer; Editor
Producer; Assistant Producer.

In this study we are focusing primarily upon the series producer or editor; this is the highest level of person who is in regular daily editorial or 'hands-on' control of the content of a series of programmes. At the executive-producer levels and above, the responsibility is typically for more than one series and has a lower 'hands-on' component.

Many producers are hesitant about accepting promotion out of the series-producer level; they often express their dilemma by referring to parallel cases of people promoted above the core-activity level – the teacher who is too senior to teach, the sailor who is too senior to go to sea. The tradition in British television is that the producer is part of management. The producer is made aware of what the senior people are thinking; the producer receives a flow of advice and guidance – much of it spoken, some of it written. Words such as 'guidance', 'guidelines' and 'consultation' are heavily used.

The emphasis placed on 'flexibility' and the avoidance of rigid rules in turn reflects the vague collection of goals towards which British broadcasting traditionally strives; each one of the public-service trio 'education, entertainment and information' is fairly vague, and how these can, or should, be mixed together in a particular series of programmes is very uncertain indeed.

There is inevitably a substantial degree of tension in such a system. From time to time conflicts between creative autonomy and organizational hierarchy surface into press publicity and political controversy; this may involve a channel controller vetoing the work of a series producer. However, much more frequently these tensions are managed quietly within the system; often the disciplinary intervention takes the form of a 'Don't do that again' retrospective memo, rather than an actual veto.

Many, or most, difficult decisions for the producer focus, in fact, on logistics and money. If television is an art-form, it is a cumbersome and expensive one. If the producer is an auteur or author, he is an author who needs the active involvement of thirty or forty other people, expensive equipment, studio space and – not least – a network to transmit the end-product.

Few people who have not been involved in television recognize how much work, energy and time in programme preparation go into polishing and refining small details; dotting the 'i's and crossing the 't's is an elaborate undertaking in this thousands-of-pounds-per-minute medium.

The producer role encompasses elements not only of the civil servant but of a latter-day Renaissance Man, capable of playing all the parts. The producer ideally should be good with both words and pictures, the two main building blocks of television. He or she needs some basic grasp of TV technology, of tape against film, of sound, lighting and sets; requires (usually extensive) specialist knowledge of the particular programme genre, such as drama or news; needs to be able to juggle ideas against finance; needs plenty of sheer energy; needs some performance skills – the ability to enthuse and activate others during a long working day; and needs diplomatic skills to smooth ruffled egos and to persuade outsiders to do things at different times and for less money than they would prefer.

This civil servant, macho-military, Renaissance Man, creative manager was in practice usually a man – a white, responsible, British male who could be trusted to do a decent job in difficult circumstances. Some of this tradition has now changed in ways favourable to women – if not to ethnic minorities – but the point remains that the producer role was traditionally conceived as male.

FROM INTEGRATED-FACTORY PRODUCTION

Until 1982 British television consisted of just two vertically integrated organizations (BBC and ITV) which each made the bulk of the programmes in its own factories (or studios), assembled the schedule and transmitted it over a national network. This 'integrated-factory' approach derives from BBC radio, where the radio studios could be tucked quietly away in the basement. In the case of television the studios were larger, but were still placed at the lower levels of buildings; above ground were the programme-makers' offices and on the top floor were the senior managers. British television was vertically integrated both as an industry and within its own buildings.

There are two other possible production systems which in the 1990s are both increasingly important. In 1982 Channel Four introduced the 'publisher' concept to Britain; it 'published' (assembled and transmitted) programming commissioned and acquired from other producers. By the early 1990s, on government direction, this publisher model was also increasingly followed in both ITV and BBC television.

There is also a third model, that of the 'packager', which prevails in cable and satellite systems. Cable did not get far in 1980s Britain, but from 1990 satellite offerings did attract customer-households in increasing numbers. These satellite and cable channels are typically themed to one specific genre such as news, sport or movies. The cable or satellite provider typically packages the channels with programming acquired in bulk from large suppliers of news, sport, movies, and so on.

By 1990 the Channel Four publisher model was well established and, along with it, a distinction between, on the one hand, 'commissioning editors' inside Channel Four, and, on the other hand, outside producers who actually made the programming. The packager model was also starting to become entrenched; the packager, of course, only directly employs very small numbers of producers.

Up to about 1990, however, the integrated-factory system of production remained the normal and dominant pattern. In the 1970s the British TV producer had been largely insulated from fierce head-to-head competition and from harsh financial pressures. For a period of eighteen years (1964–82) there were just three channels, with the audience in effect amicably shared 50/50 between one ITV channel and two BBC channels. The audience was offered large rations of educational and informational programming as well as entertainment. There was plenty of money – with all the booming advertising revenue supporting just one channel, and a steadily growing licence fee (as consumers switched to colour sets) going to the BBC; British television in the 1970s was much more generously funded than was western Europe's television overall.

Television producers lived a sheltered life within a system based on consensus and cartel. There was a consensus between the political parties and between broadcasters schooled in the BBC and ITV versions of public service. The trade unions also played a central role, favouring good-quality British programming, a broad mix of programming genres, and strict quotas of cheap programme imports. The unions got secure employment for their members, with extremely generous levels of manning and overmanning.

The ITV network was a cartel of non-competing regional companies which had a monopoly on TV advertising; the regulatory body, the Independent Broadcasting Authority, required it to carry quotas of non-entertainment, mainly factual, programming. Each of the ITV companies bargained fiercely to keep its share of programming airtime, which meant that even ITV's entertainment programming was supplier-driven and less than 100 per cent market-orientated.

[. . .]

While a few established (popular or prestige) successes might run for 25 or 35 weeks per year, most British TV series conformed to a mini-series pattern of as few as 6, and no more than 13, programmes per year. Popular situation comedies, for example, could take 15 years to accumulate 100 episodes. This mini-series emphasis fitted both ITV cartel-bargaining and BBC deference towards TV writers; it fitted also with the producers' perception that quantity often led to reduced quality.

This mini-series system of short runs – but lengthy preparation and extended filming/recording – reflected producers' interests. The performers (such as actors) were not very highly rewarded in British television; nor were the army of (mainly women) clerical and support staff. The people who did well were the producers and their teams and the highly unionized technicians; they were fairly well paid, securely employed, not over-worked on very long series runs, and provided with interestingly varied work.

[. . .]

British producers, as late as 1990, still lived in a world in which cash and specific sums of money were not the effective currency. A producer in practice worked primarily within a budget, not of money, but of resources. These resources would involve people – such as researchers, reporters, actors, the design people and the studio crew; second, there would be the studio spaces and the use of outdoor film or outside broadcast units; and third, there was the time for which these people and resources were allocated – often very generous by international standards. In addition, the producer would have some cash (for travel, staying in hotels and so on) but knew that the cash element was only a fraction of the total cost. The producer had little idea of the real cost and often suspected, or knew, that the ITV company itself or the BBC also did not know the real cost: so why should the producer bother? Even the concept of 'overspending' the budget was a vague one, because – in these vertically integrated organizations with their permanent facilities and staff – there was no agreed cost that could be attached to, say, one extra day for forty people and a studio.

With many short runs of 6 or 7 programmes, the producer might have only a hazy idea of the intended audience, the real cost, or the real goal (from the company's viewpoint). Given this degree of vagueness, the producer was also likely to be unclear how 'success' could be defined.

In keeping with this traditional lack of concern for financial detail, producers – despite being managers – were given little or no management preparation. Indeed, the recruitment process, which focused broadly on artistic skills and education in the humanities, selected and promoted some people who were not good at arithmetic. Finance was seen by some producers as a tiresome chore which could safely be entrusted to a unit manager or some other member of the production team.

AROUND 1990: BRITAIN'S TV REVOLUTION

[. . .]

The publisher element in British broadcasting gradually expanded in the decade after 1982. Initially, Channel Four only had a few per cent of the British TV audience; by the late 1980s both it and the independent-production sector were getting larger. The Thatcher Government then set a 25 per cent independent-production target for ITV and later (in the 1990 Act) for the BBC. During the early 1990s it became increasingly clear that both the BBC and ITV would contract out more than 25 per cent of the production to outside producers. The four new ITV companies which in 1991 won new franchises from the previous incumbents all began broadcasting in 1993 using the publisher model. By 1993 the four conventional British channels were operating two production systems alongside each other. The two advertising-financed channels – Channel Four and ITV – now operated predominantly the publisher model. The BBC still operated mainly as an integrated factory but was also moving towards the publisher model.

What made the changes around 1990 indeed revolutionary – compared with normal British slow evolution – was that around 1990 not only the second publisher system but also the third system – the packager – was arriving on the British scene. This was a move not just to one additional channel but to multiple additional channels.

[. . .]

[From about 1988 'casualization' became a major trend.]

'Casualization' had several aspects. First, there was a massive reduction in regular employment. In 1987–8 the ITV companies were employing 17,000 people to run a single national channel (with some regional programming); by 1993 ITV employed 6,000 fewer. The BBC – especially from 1990 – began cutting staff, although it favoured many small bites of a hundred or two hundred redundancies rather than the ITV big-bang approach.

Second, there was a marked shift towards employing people on short contracts, usually for a few months. Consequently in the early 1990s some people (mainly aged over 40) were permanently employed on the old life-long basis; some senior people were on contracts of a few years; many producers were on contracts of one year or six months; more junior production personnel were often employed for the few months of the series run. In the technical studio areas there was a similar range.

Third, another major facet was the closing of studio buildings. In their vertical factories both the BBC and ITV companies had too much production capacity, too many buildings and too many studios. With the move towards contracting production out to independents it gradually became evident that this over-capacity was on a massive scale. In late 1991 the BBC announced a 40 per cent cut in its capacity for studios and facilities.

Fourth, there was a quite overt attack on the trade unions. This had been a repeated theme in Thatcher Government rhetoric and policy documents in the 1980s. The broadcasting trade unions – in the 1970s of legendary strength – now saw their power rapidly reduced. There was a spate of trade-union mergers, resulting in one main union, BECTU (its full name – Broadcasting, Entertainment, Cinematograph and Theatre Union – indicates its genealogy).

These numerous changes and forms of casualization had multiple impacts on British TV producers. Many producers interviewed for this study had entered television in the 1960s or 1970s when it offered extremely secure employment:

> If you were any good, they expected and wanted you to stay there for life.

By the early 1990s producers felt themselves to be in a fairly insecure job, which now involved working here for a year or two before moving on to some other organization.

The 1990 changes also involved various forms of slimming-down and speeding-up. The slimming-down affected not only the number of people on a camera-crew but the number of people responsible for researching, filming and editing a programme. Speeding-up took different forms in different genres; but in drama, for instance, a producer who in the mid-1980s might have had 15 days to film an hour's drama would by the early 1990s have been reduced to 10 or 11 days.

[. . .]

LESS SECURE, MORE AUTONOMOUS

During the recent years of turbulence, British TV producers have undergone a paradoxical combination of changes: they have become less secure but more autonomous.

Few British TV producers would deny that producers overall have become less secure in recent years. This study has focused on producers whose names were in the *Radio Times* attached to productions just being transmitted. Many other producers were becoming ex-producers; indeed, a number of the producers we interviewed in 1990 were already ex-producers by 1992.

How, then, can they have become more autonomous at the same time? The paradox derives from a significant shift in the nature of the producer's job. Those producers who are (still) working are being asked to do more things than was the case before 1986. First, producers have been forced to take budgeting more seriously. Second, producers (especially in fields such as documentary and drama) are increasingly expected to take part in raising finance. Third, with the increasing contracting-out of programming by the BBC and ITV, many working producers are not only producing programmes but commissioning them out to other producers.

Fourth, producers are required to make more decisions about resources and encouraged to use outside freelance camera-crews, studios or graphics specialists, instead of the BBC's or the ITV company's own in-house facilities. The BBC in 1992 launched its new effort of this kind called 'Producer Choice'; the BBC made clear that choices would rest with series producers and not with heads of output departments.

All this adds up to more work, more responsibility, more control and more autonomy – for those producers who are still producing.

A PROFESSION?

Television producers do not constitute a profession.

Television producers collectively have some similarities to the many occupations which have been professionalizing in recent decades; but TV producers have not tried very hard to do the classic things normally done by occupations which have a strong urge to professionalize.

Television producers have not tried to control entry; on the contrary, entry has become more open. Television producers have not set up a 'qualifying association' which vets qualifications, establishes standards and the like. Television producers lack 'clients' of the kind that doctors, lawyers, architects or teachers claim to serve. Although TV producers are serving the general public, their 'hands-on' work refers not to clients or patients but to cameras, scripts, editing, performers – the business of TV production, not TV consumption.

There is another simple reason why British TV producers are not likely to go much further in a professional direction. In British television the producers – more than any other occupational category – are, or become, the general managers. Apprentice producers can start as 'researcher' and eventually become chief executive. This occupation of producer is not only a lengthy career-ladder, but also fits closely with the organizational hierarchy from bottom to top.

The TV-producer role covers a very wide horizontal range in terms of genres and types of output. In recent years the producer role has become further fragmented by the introduction of two new industrial systems, each of which introduced new definitions of producer to the British scene. The publisher model introduced the 'commissioning editor' and the 'independent producer'; the satellite or cable channels give weight to the acquisition and packaging of large flows of pre-existing production.

Some associations and organizations of a 'professional' kind do exist. There is the Royal Television Society which holds conferences and awards prizes. There are bodies which lobby on behalf of independent producers. Trade unions, although now weaker, still exist.

There is however, no single body which seeks to preserve, defend and advance the interests of TV producers in Britain. The producers are too involved in their organizations – many devote their 'professional' loyalty to the BBC which they see as preserving the kind of television they believe in; indeed, many ITV and independent producers also express deep loyalty to the BBC and what it stands for.

Producers' deep involvement in their private genre-worlds is also in part both cause and effect of this lack of professional feeling or organization.

AN ELITE OCCUPATION?

Television production is not an elite occupation.

This study indicates that TV production is a well-established occupational category but the term 'elite' certainly does not fit many producers' social backgrounds. The [254] producers interviewed in this study are not a representative sample of all TV producers. Of those interviewed about one-quarter were educated at either Oxford or Cambridge; about another quarter were at one of another small group of institutions (including two London University colleges – the London School of Economics and University College – as well as Bristol, York, East Anglia and Manchester Universities). The majority of these producers did not attend fee-paying schools; more went to grammar schools or comprehensives. In terms of their social and educational origins these producers' backgrounds are broadly middle-class and meritocratic. Despite having lived in London most of their adult lives, many of these producers speak with some trace of a British regional accent. In this respect, and in others, the producers are probably very similar to their presenters whose faces appear on the screen.

These are jobs, however, which many young people would like to do. A number of producers complained about the huge numbers of applicants that a single newspaper advertisement for a 'TV researcher' would attract. This occupation, of course, has no specific entry-qualification.

[. . .]

PRODUCER AS EMPLOYER

In British television, the producer (of various kinds) has taken over some functions previously performed by management and also by trade unions; increasingly, the producer is becoming the effective employer.

'We have removed an entire tier of management' said one senior executive of an ITV company. Some of the functions previously performed by both specialist and general management are now heaped on to the producer.

The same is true of the trade unions, which until about 1986 in practice managed much of what went on in the craft areas. For example, the unions operated penally high overtime rates of pay which greatly affected the entire practice of location filming. The construction of sets, the operation of studios, the outside broadcasting of sporting events – all of these areas of work were partly managed by unions and partly managed by management. When trade-union power radically declined after 1986, these management tasks were not given back to management, which itself was slimming down radically.

The producer of a series run often has one, two or three million pounds to spend; and there are several possible strategic paths which could be followed. Do you do all the location filming first? Do you work alternate weekends? Do you start in the studio when the days are shorter in March? In the past all such decisions were heavily influenced by union rules. Now it is the producer who sits down, maybe for quite a long time, worrying away at the cheapest and most efficient use of the available time, resources and people. The producer makes a management plan, carries it out and is held responsible for it.

Increasingly, the producer is not just a general manager; the producer is also coming to be the effective employer. This latter has happened most obviously in independent production; but it is happening also within the BBC and ITV. With the short series runs so common in British television, employment is very often for a few months; it is the producer who effectively employs the production team, and increasingly also the technical crew, for those weeks or months. The producer who from 'inside' the BBC or an ITV company takes on a production team – via the personnel department – is increasingly likely to be either a freelance producer employed for that short series run, or a producer on a contract of perhaps one year.

British television is no less – probably more – producer-driven today than before 1986. The production systems have changed and the publisher system has become central; but the production culture has remained the same, in focusing on the producer as the person who holds the reins. The overall system has increasingly fragmented into smaller programme-making units. Everyone seems to agree that to the question of who should be in charge, in most cases the answer has to be the producer. If the producers are not driving the system, no other suitable occupational category – under British conditions – is available to do the job.

[. . .]

TOWARDS 2022

In the 1990s the competitive pressures and industrial changes will continue to make for major changes in the working conditions of producers. As the average series size (in hours and episodes) increases – and there are fewer very-short series – the balance between the numbers of 'executive producers' and 'series producers' will shift. The executive producer, instead of being in charge of several short series and their series producers, will increasingly be in charge of just one big series.

The executive producer will be supported by a larger team of fairly senior producers and script editors. It will become more rare for one director or producer-director to direct all the programmes in a series. The typical series will employ not only more producers, but also more writers and more directors. The status of the individual director is likely to decline since he or she will only be directing, say, 4 programmes in a series of 26 programmes. Directors will have less say in the script–filming–editing sequence overall; some directors may cease to be involved in the post-production editing of their 'own' work.

WOMEN PRODUCERS

The proportion of producers who are women will greatly increase, especially in the BBC; in more and more genres within the BBC women will be in the majority. This advance of women producers will have a massive impact across British broadcasting and beyond.

Around 1989–90 the BBC began to take seriously equal opportunities for women (it was slower in the case of ethnic minorities). Even though there was a pause or small falling-back in the early 1990s, this policy has a big head of steam. The proportions of women producers at all levels will increase; and there will be a 'the more, the more' effect. Women tend to promote other women; some men do not want to work for women.

By 1992 the majority of the BBC's science TV programmes were produced by women. This trend will continue most strongly in documentary and edinfotainment areas. Drama will be in a middle position. Bringing up the rear will be sport, entertainment and comedy, although women will advance here also.

Not all producers, male or female, want to become executive producers. Probably a higher proportion of women producers prefer to stay in their present working-niche. Nevertheless, the proportions of women producers will increase for several reasons.

First, within the private worlds of the separate genres the promotion of even one or two women producers can have a big impact. When a success like *One Foot in the Grave* was produced by a woman, who could any longer say that women could not produce comedy?

Second, the BBC is especially attractive to women because of its vigorous equal-opportunities policy. There are large numbers of women in the BBC in the junior-producer ranks. They appear more willing than men to accept the BBC's lower rates of pay; although some women do become independent producers, they may be less inclined than men to go independent. As the independent sector continues to be so insecure and stressful, it looks increasingly a better bet for a woman – especially with children – to remain in the some what less insecure BBC.

Third, there may be a tendency for men to occupy BBC executive-producer jobs, employing a team of mainly women producers; but the BBC is committed to equality at all levels.

ITV can be expected to follow the BBC – as it often has – but at something of a distance. A number of men, as well as women, producers denounced the whole of ITV as 'male-chauvinist'. This was somewhat sweeping; but the ITC, although proclaiming its equal-opportunities loyalty, wasted a unique moment in the 1991 franchise round. However, the ITC will doubtless focus its attention on this issue in due course. There may also be anxiety within ITV that the BBC has an advantage in its greater proportion of women producers. The argument will be made that ITV depends on advertising aimed primarily at women consumers. This argument will eventually prove compelling, especially combined with the point that you may be able to pay women slightly less.

Increasingly in the later 1990s it will become apparent that the BBC is going to be the first major organization in Britain in which around half the senior management are women.

This in turn will have consequences, not all of which can easily be predicted. One probable consequence is that still-stronger flows of well-qualified young women will be attracted to the BBC; it will be interesting to see how young men react.

This advance of women may not hugely change the programming output. BBC1 and ITV are already strongly ratings-driven and will get more so. However, the advance of women will finally remove those earlier conceptions of the TV producer as an ex-military man in charge of men.

[. . .]

PRODUCER-DRIVEN TELEVISION

British television during the 1990s will continue to be producer-driven.

The extent to which British television has fragmented, and will fragment, can be exaggerated. However, in so far as further fragmentation does occur in the 1990s, it will be producers who are in charge of the fragments. In this, as in much else, the new independent producers of the 1980s were showing the way which others would follow.

Increasingly sharp distinctions will be made between different categories of producers. One important distinction will be between buyers and sellers – the commissioning editor in the network who buys and the seller, who will be an independent production company or a freelance.

Executive Producers will be distinguished more sharply from the working, or line, producer. Increasingly, EP could as appropriately stand for 'Entrepreneur Producer'. The range of skills and knowledge ideally required of the senior producer will not be found in any single human being. Some producers will focus more on the creative side and still think of themselves as producer-directors or producer-writers; such creative producers may need especially strong support in finance and management. Other producers will be strongest on the financial and deal-making side of things; the packager, or deal-maker, or more finance-orientated producer may require stronger support on the creative side. Producers who combine both artistic and managerial creativity will be highly regarded and more highly paid than today's producers. British television will throughout the 1990s continue to be producer-driven.

[. . .]

So long as a mix of in-house production and the publisher system continues to predominate, then the broad producer-driven style of television [. . .] will prevail; but if, or when, the themed channels become the predominant, and no longer the minority, pattern, then the driving forces will be the operators of batches of themed channels and the operators of delivery systems. British producer-driven television will then be a thing of the past.

13

THE BBC AND THE 1956 SUEZ CRISIS

Asa Briggs

The most serious threat to the BBC as an institution occurred a year after the start of commercial television. But it came from the Government of Sir Anthony Eden, not from the competitor. On 26 July 1956, President Gamal Abdel Nasser nationalised the Anglo-French Suez Canal Company, one of whose directors was Sir Alexander Cadogan, the BBC Chairman, who had also served long and faithfully as Eden's right-hand man at the Foreign Office.

The immediate reaction of the Labour Party was sharply anti-Nasser. Thus, Hugh Gaitskell, the Leader of the Opposition, denounced the Egyptian President as another Hitler, and Herbert Morrison called him the 'pocket dictator in Cairo.'[1] On 8 August, during this period of political harmony, Eden made what then was only the second Ministerial broadcast on television. It was delayed twenty-four hours so that it could also be relayed by ITV. It was simultaneously broadcast by domestic radio and on shortwave by the General Overseas Service. It was also relayed by all four radio networks in the United States, in all Dominions and in many Colonies.[2] The Prime Minister warned the world against appeasing dictators and said that Nasser had created 'a very grave situation'.

Thereafter, for a number of reasons, the Labour Opposition became increasingly critical of the Eden Government's stand, and the changing political situation was reflected by a special balanced discussion on Suez broadcast on 10 August by the Television Service. Radio, however, made no immediate comparable effort to include anti-Government views.[3] Meanwhile, Eden was strongly backed by Robert Menzies, the Prime Minister of Australia, who arrived in London, and at lunch with Eden agreed to a suggestion that he should broadcast on the BBC about Australia's support for the British Government.[4]

Menzies was surprised, and Eden angry, when this offer to broadcast was declined by John Green, Controller of Talks (Sound), on grounds of political imbalance.[5] Green was acting for Harman Grisewood (who was in hospital) as the BBC's liaison with the political parties. He felt that Menzies would make another 'semi-ministerial' broadcast, and noted that Selwyn

From Asa Briggs, *Governing the BBC* (London: BBC Publications, 1979) pp. 209–17.

Lloyd, the Foreign Secretary, had claimed a radio Ministerial for about the same time. Green was concerned that radio appeared to be presenting a one-sided account of the Government's position.[6] He ignored what was happening on television.

The Prime Minister then telephoned his old friend the Chairman, taking strong exception to Green's rejection of the Menzies offer, and Cadogan agreed that it was absurd.[7] This is really nonsense', he recorded in his diary, and telephoned Sir Ian Jacob to say that Menzies must be allowed to speak 'no matter what our traditions and inhibitions might be'.[8] The Menzies broadcast was accordingly accommodated in the Television Service.[9]

The incident disturbed Harman Grisewood, the Chief Assistant to the Director-General, on his return from hospital. He was worried not so much by the contact between the Prime Minister and the Chairman, as by the danger that, influenced by the Prime Minister, Cadogan would assume more of an executive responsibility inside the BBC than seemed to Grisewood practical or constitutionally proper.[10]

Meanwhile, the Board as a whole was concerned about political balance at the top level. By agreement between the Parties Ministerial broadcasts were 'meant' to be confined to non-controversial measures: they were to be used to make factual pronouncements, to explain legislation approved by Parliament, or to appeal to the public to co-operate in national policies. If the Opposition considered that a Ministerial broadcast had transgressed into party controversy, it could claim a reply through the 'usual channels', the Chief Whips, and if after three days the Government would not yield a reply, the Opposition could appeal to the BBC Board to arbitrate.[11] In such circumstances the Board would then be faced with an essentially political decision which the Governors did not welcome.

By mid-September the Suez question had become highly controversial, and there were sharp differences of approach on the part of Government and Opposition. The House of Commons had been recalled, and Gaitskell was demanding an opportunity to present the Labour Party's viewpoint on television.[12] Cadogan and Jacob doubted whether Ministers or Opposition leaders would wish to broadcast about Suez in a party political context, and expected that there might be a request from Downing Street for a further television Ministerial which could hardly fail to raise further controversy.[13] The Board was thus being steadily driven into a difficult political position in which existing machinery would not work. As Jacob put it later, 'the procedures which govern political broadcasting were designed for domestic controversy of the kind that normally accompanies political life; a national emergency when Government action was not nationally supported presented a new problem'.[14]

The Board accordingly authorised Cadogan and Jacob to discuss this problem with both Government and Opposition,[15] and a meeting was held on 14 September 1956 with R. A. Butler (Lord Privy Seal) and Gaitskell. This resulted in an invitation to Gaitskell to appear in *Press Conference* on 21 September, in other words in a normal BBC television programme rather than in the context of a Party Political or a Ministerial Reply. A similar invitation went to Selwyn Lloyd to be interviewed in *Panorama* on 24 September.

After secret Anglo–French–Israeli consultations near Paris, suspected but hotly denied at the time, and now admitted,[16] Israeli forces entered Egypt on 29 October, and attacked positions in the Sinai desert. The next day Britain and France sent an ultimatum both to Egypt and Israel to cease hostilities and withdraw, and on 31 October the RAF and the French Air Force began to attack Egyptian airfields. This was military action, but there had been no declaration either of war or of a state of emergency.

As often happens in such circumstances, leading personalities were missing. Jacob was by then on his way to a Commonwealth Broadcasting Conference in Australia, and Cadogan was not immediately available. It was the Vice-Chairman, Sir Philip Morris, therefore, who after a long conversation with Grisewood agreed that there should be 'no changes as regards programmes, editorial objectivity or relationships between staff and normal contact outside'. In Morris's words this 'occasioned surprised reactions outside the BBC, particularly at No. 10 and the Foreign Office and to some extent, within the BBC'.[17]

A further request for a television Ministerial then came from Eden's public relations adviser, William Clark, who was told that if Gaitskell went on to request a right of reply the Board would probably concede it. Clark said this was understood and expected by the Prime Minister.[18] Eden duly broadcast from 10 Downing Street, therefore, on the evening of Saturday 3 November, explaining why the Government had decided to bombard Egypt: 'What we did do, was to take police action at once.' The broadcast was also carried by ITV. Gaitskell immediately telephoned the BBC demanding the right to reply the next day. There was some delay while the formalities were observed and the request was forwarded through the 'usual channels' of Opposition Chief Whip (Herbert Bowden) to Government Chief Whip (Edward Heath).[19] Heath told Bowden that Eden's broadcast had been the least controversial it could be in the circumstances, adding that though the Government felt that no reply should be conceded, if the Board of Governors decided to allow Labour to reply no objection would be made.[20] By then it was after midnight and Grisewood refused to awaken Cadogan. It was not until the following morning that Cadogan granted Gaitskell a television reply that evening, Sunday 4 November. The Board unanimously endorsed the Chairman's action.[21]

The House of Commons earlier that week had reflected the mood of a country which was far from united. As the Deputy Editor of *The Times* later recalled: 'At each word the whole of the Labour benches rose like a wall, no longer shouting. They were howling with anger and real anguish ... The Speaker could no longer be heard ... I just saw him wave as a sign that the sitting was suspended, and out the Members trooped, still shouting and shaking their fists.'[22]

In this atmosphere Gaitskell's television reply intensified the passionate divisions, particularly when he appealed to 'those Conservatives who, like us, are shocked and troubled by what is happening' and undertook to 'support a new Prime Minister in halting the invasion of Egypt, in ordering the ceasefire and complying with the decisions and recommendations of the United Nations'.

From No. 10 Clark telephoned the BBC urging that the more inflammatory parts of Gaitskell's broadcast should not be transmitted in the BBC's Arabic Service,[23] and later he passed on an informal but strongly worded request that not too much prominence should be given to the domestic opposition to the Prime Minister's policy merely because the *Manchester Guardian* expressed it well.[24]

Clark was to resign, quietly, from his Downing Street service as soon as the Suez action ended. When he came to write 'an inside story' of Suez in *The Observer* twenty years later, he mentioned that Eden was worried that the BBC's overseas services, extensively heard in Egypt, gave 'comfort to the enemy by reporting domestic divisions, thus weakening the credibility of our threats'. He then added 'These worries resulted in innumerable schemes to discipline the BBC,' without attempting to specify what these 'schemes' were.[25] Clark had been encouraged by Eden to take a holiday in the second half of October 1956 and was in Spain when he received an urgent message to return on 29 October, the day of the Israeli attack on Sinai.[26] His more specific statement, made soon after his return, that the Prime Minister had actually instructed the Lord Chancellor, Lord Kilmuir, to prepare an instrument which would take over the BBC altogether and subject it wholly to the will of the Government[27] has been widely discussed, and even debated in the House of Commons.[28] But it lacks any independent confirmation and relates to a time when Clark himself was abroad.

The Board had indeed been facing exceptionally heavy pressure from Whitehall on the External Services based in Bush House. Between Munich and Suez, Great Britain had not been divided by any fundamental issue in foreign affairs. Eden in 1956 expected the BBC to rally to a nation virtually at war, as it had rallied in 1939; indeed, he saw striking parallels between the two situations. For many Governors, however, there was a conflict between what seemed to be the Government's immediate interests and the long-term credibility of BBC broadcasting. There had to be both veracity and consistency. Eight years earlier Haley had defined the problem thus: 'The BBC does not attempt to have one story for its own people and another for the rest of the world . . . That has been our policy all through. In some ways, curiously enough, it is an easier policy to sustain in war than in peace. In war, the perils are so great that you dare to tell the truth and everyone applauds. In peacetime . . . specious arguments are sometimes put forward to prove that it is in the long-term interest to be not quite so meticulous.' [29]

Such an argument was put forward by the Foreign Office in relation to the Bush House daily summary of press opinion which had continued to include extracts from editorials critical of Government policy. Just before his departure for Australia Jacob had been summoned to the Foreign Office and told that it was proposed to reduce the Government Grant-in-Aid which financed the External Services by one million pounds and to divert the money to other overseas information purposes. It was made clear that this was a punitive action.[30]

Cadogan and Jacob saw R. A. Butler the next day, and as a result of the meeting the threatened cut was reduced by one half. Yet at both these meetings it was proposed that a special Foreign Office liaison officer should be stationed at Bush House as a watchdog.[31] On 31 October, the day the Anglo-French bombardment began, the Foreign Office decided the time had come to place this liaison officer in Bush House. He was to be Lanham Titchener, an ex-BBC television producer, then *en poste* in Teheran. Pending his return Duncan Wilson[32] was installed. He immediately let it be known that his task was to vet BBC news bulletins in Arabic to see whether they were suitable for rebroadcasting by a radio station in Cyprus which the Governor had just requisitioned for British Government purposes and which had been renamed 'The Voice of Britain'.[33]

After Jacob's departure for Australia the Director of Administration, Sir Norman Bottomley, was the Acting Director-General during the more acute stages of the Suez crisis. Bottomley was then 65, and in the last weeks of his BBC career. He had previously been Deputy Chief of the Air Staff, Air Officer Commanding-in-Chief Bomber Command, under 'Bomber' Harris, and Inspector-General of the RAF. He proved nonetheless to be a stalwart proponent of BBC independence throughout a period of heavy pressure from Whitehall and of continuing debate, often bitter debate, in the country.

The *Manchester Guardian* had denounced the Anglo-French action as soon as it took place as 'an act of folly without justification in any terms but brief expediency',[34] and J. B. Clark, the Director of External Broadcasting, with a long record of dedication to accurate reporting, pointed out that no honest press review could ignore the *Guardian* leader. Bottomley referred the matter to Cadogan, who ruled that scheduled press reviews should continue in the normal manner. The Board subsequently endorsed the Chairman's action.[35] The Foreign Office, however, took strong exception to the BBC following its normal policy. Paul Grey, the Under-Secretary concerned, stated vehemently to Bottomley that in such a situation as the military action against Egypt it was not necessary to tell the whole truth, and argued that certain news items should be suppressed in Arabic bulletins. The Acting Director-General and the Chairman spoke separately to the Paymaster-General, Sir Walter Monckton, recalling the Government's proclaimed long-term policy that treatment of an item in an Overseas news bulletin must never differ materially from its treatment in domestic news,[36] and the Chairman told the Board he believed the Paymaster-General would support the BBC in the matter of news objectivity.[37]

Meanwhile, BBC news objectivity was being attacked from another quarter. On 7 November Peter Rawlinson, Conservative MP for Epsom, telegraphed Bottomley demanding an immediate enquiry into the selection of news during the Suez crisis, and in an adjournment debate a week later he and Charles Ian Orr-Ewing, Conservative MP for North Hendon, charged the BBC with making deliberate distortions in news bulletins, press reviews and other current affairs programmes, and with partial presentation by omission, exaggeration or the use of voice tone and an unrepresentative choice of people for interview. Bottomley told the Board these criticisms were probably unprecedented.[38] They made a great many specific allegations against the competence of BBC news and impugned the integrity of BBC parliamentary correspondents.[39]

The BBC staff prepared lengthy reports examining each charge which had been made in the adjournment debate, and on 22 November the Board inspected in great detail the evidence, side by side with the allegations.[40] It concluded, with minor reservations, that in the field of news bulletins and press reviews 'a successful and creditable result had been generally achieved' during a period of great difficulty, 'and that this result fulfilled the BBC's obligation for impartiality, objectivity and for telling the truth'.[41]

By that time, however, the international situation had changed; there had been a serious run on the pound and the British Government had had to accept the United Nations' demand for a cease-fire. There was a crisis in Eastern Europe also, and the Russians had sent tanks into Budapest. Eisenhower had been re-elected for a second term as President and Eden was flying to Jamaica to recuperate from a serious illness. The Suez crisis was over. As the Vice-Chairman of the BBC put it: 'The action of the United Nations brought relief all round and it remained only for the Governors to deal with various reports on what had happened during the crisis. The discussion was considerable, as it was bound to be between eight/nine people with no common view on the events themselves as distinct from the BBC's behaviour in relation to them.' [42] The role of broadcasting during the crisis continued to provoke argument. There was a sense, indeed, in which it was never resolved even after the Suez crisis itself had passed into history.

NOTES

1. Anthony Nutting, *No End of a Lesson* (1967), p. 47.
2. G. Mosley, 'The Suez Crisis and the BBC', July 1961.
3. G. Wyndham Goldie, *Facing the Nation* (1977), p. 178.
4. R. Menzies, *Afternoon Light* (1967), p. 151.
5. Wyndham Goldie, op. cit., pp. 178–81.
6. J. Green to L. Wellington, 13 Aug. 1956.
7. A. Eden, *Full Circle* (1960), p. 448.
8. D. Dilks (ed.), *The Diaries of Sir Alexander Cadogan* (1971), p. 797.
9. In *Highlight*, 13 Aug. 1956.
10. H. Grisewood, *One Thing at a Time* (1968), pp. 196–7.
11. Aide-Memoire on Political Broadcasting, 6 Feb. 1947, revised July 1948.
12. Board of Governors, Minutes, 13 Sept. 1956.
13. Ibid.
14. Sir Ian Jacob, 'The Suez Crisis and the BBC', Ariel, Jan. 1957.
15. Board of Governors, *Minutes*, 13 Sept. 1956.
16. Selwyn Lloyd, *Suez 1956: a Personal Account* (1978), pp. 180–7.
17. Sir Philip Morris to Sir Hugh Greene, 26 Dec. 1975.
18. Mosley, loc. cit.

19.   Grisewood, op. cit., p. 202.

20.   Ibid.

21.   Board of Governors, *Minutes*, 8 Nov. 1956.

22.   Iverach McDonald, *Tonight*, 'The Suez Affair Part III', 10 Nov. 1976.

23.   Mosley, loc. cit.

24.   Ibid.

25.   William Clark, 'Suez: an Inside Story' in *The Observer*, 3 Oct. 1976.

26.   Record of Conversation between Clark and Miall, 10 April 1976.

27.   Grisewood, op. cit., p. 199.

28.   Hansard, vol. 764, cols 173–82, 6 May 1968.

29.   W. Haley, 'The Responsibilities of Broadcasting', *Lewis Fry Memorial Lecture*, Bristol University, May 1948.

30.   Mosley, loc. cit.

31.   Ibid.

32.   Later British Ambassador to Moscow and Master of Corpus Christi College, Cambridge.

33.   Mosley, loc. cit. See also E. Watrous, 'Report on the Near East Arab Broadcasting Station, Sharq al Adna', 23 Oct. 1956.

34.   *Manchester Guardian*, 31 Oct. 1956.

35.   Board of Governors, *Minutes*, 22 Nov. 1956.

36.   Cmd 6852 (1946), *Broadcasting Policy*, para. 59.

37.   Board of Governors, *Minutes*, 8 Nov. 1956.

38.   Bottomley, 'Debate in the House of Commons, Nov. 14th, BBC Broadcasts: Political Balance', 28 Nov. 1956 (posted on all BBC noticeboards).

39.   Board of Governors, *Papers*, 'Debate in the House of Commons, 14 Nov. 1956, BBC News Broadcasts', 21 Nov. 1956.

40.   Bottomley, loc. cit.

41.   Board of Governors, *Minutes*, 22 Nov. 1956.

42.   Morris to Greene, 26 Dec. 1975.

FURTHER READING

Boyce, G., Curran, J. and Wingate, P. (eds), *Newspaper History from the Seventeenth Century to the Present Day* (London: Constable, 1978).

Briggs, A., *The History of Broadcasting in the United Kingdom*, vols 1–5 (London: Oxford University Press, 1961–95).

Burns, T., *The BBC: Public Institution and Private World* (London: Macmillan, 1977).

Collins, R., *Television: Policy and Culture* (London: Unwin Hyman, 1990).

Collins, R., Curran, J., Garnham, N., Scannell, P., Schlesinger, P. and Sparks, C. (eds), *Media, Culture and Society: A Critical Reader* (London: Sage, 1989).

Collins, R., Garnham, N. and Locksley, G., *The Economics of Television: The UK Case* (London: Sage, 1988).

Curran, J. and Seaton, J., *Power without Responsibility: The Press and Broadcasting in Britain* (London: Routledge, 1992).

Drummond, P. and Paterson, R. (eds), *Television in Transition* (London: BFI, 1985).

Elliott, P., *The Making of a Television Series: A Case Study in the Sociology of Culture* (London: Constable, 1972).

Garnham, N., *Capitalism and Communication: Global Culture and the Economics of Information* (London: Sage, 1990).

Golding, P. and Murdock, G., 'Culture, Communications and Political Economy', in Curran, J. and Gurevitch, M. (eds), *Mass Media and Society* (London: Edward Arnold, 1991).

Halmos, P. (ed.), *The Sociology of Mass Media Communicators*, Sociological Review Monographs 13 (Keele: University of Keele, 1969).

Harvey, S., 'Deregulation, Innovation and Channel Four', *Screen* 30:1/2 (1989) pp. 60–78.

Koss, S., *The Rise and Fall of the Political Press in Britain*, 2 vols (London: Hamish Hamilton, 1981 and 1984).

Lee, A. J., *The Origins of the Popular Press* (London: Croom Helm, 1976).

Lewis, P. M. and Booth, J., *The Invisible Medium: Public, Commercial and Community Radio* (London: Macmillan, 1989).

MacCabe, C. and Stewart, O. (eds), *The BBC and Public Service Broadcasting* (Manchester: Manchester University Press, 1986).

Murdock, G., 'Large Corporations and the Control of the Communications Industries', in Gurevitch, M., Bennett, T., Curran, J. and Woollacott, J. (eds), *Culture, Society and the Media* (London: Methuen, 1982).

O'Malley, T., *Closedown? The BBC and Government Broadcasting Policy 1979–92* (London: Pluto Press, 1994).

Potter, J., *Independent Television in Britain*, vols 3 and 4 (London: Macmillan, 1987 and 1990).

Scannell, P., 'Public Service Broadcasting: The History of a Concept', in Goodwin, A. and Whannel, G. (eds), *Understanding Television* (London: Routledge, 1990).

Scannell, P. and Cardiff, D., *A Social History of British Broadcasting*, vol. 1, *1922–1939: Serving the Nation* (Oxford: Basil Blackwell, 1991).

Schlesinger, P., *Media, State and Nation* (London: Sage, 1991).

Sendall, B., *Independent Television in Britain*, vols 1 and 2 (London: Macmillan, 1982 and 1985).

Seymour-Ure, C., *The British Press and Broadcasting since 1945* (Oxford: Blackwell, 1991).

Tracey, M., *The Production of Political Television* (London: Routledge & Kegan Paul, 1978).

Tunstall, J., *Journalists at Work* (London: Constable, 1971).

Tunstall, J., *The Media in Britain* (London: Constable, 1983).

Tunstall, J., *Television Producers* (London: Routledge, 1993).

Tunstall, J. and Palmer, M., *Media Moguls* (London: Routledge, 1991).

Text
Codes and Structures

TEXT: CODES AND STRUCTURES

The 'mass communication' tradition of investigating the media was part of the American social-scientific project of the 1940s and 1950s, whose predominant character was scientistic, functionalist and quantitative. This approach had an impoverished conception of the 'message' in mass communication; the most sophisticated thinking was 'content analysis', counting the number of column inches devoted to a particular topic or the frequency of certain key words.[1] But in Britain this thin legacy was to be counteracted from the direction of the humanities, where in English Literature there was a rich Leavisite tradition of close consideration of literary texts in all their complexity. Some of those influenced by this tradition – notably Richard Hoggart, Raymond Williams, and Stuart Hall and Paddy Whannel – turned to the consideration of the texts of the media and popular culture. Thus, in an important conceptual shift, the 'message' was to become seen as a 'text'. The elaboration of detailed attention to media texts – to the forms, structures and meanings of newspapers or broadcast programmes – came to assume an important place in the study of the media from the 1960s.

Film studies in this period drew on the ideas of semiology to examine the workings of meaning-making in films,[2] and the study of other media began to follow suit in the 1970s. (Semiology is the study of signs and their processes of generating meaning.) The development of semiology – originating in a suggestion by the Swiss linguist Ferdinand de Saussure[3] – had accelerated in the 1960s through the work of the French critic Barthes. 'A sign has three essential characteristics: it must have a physical form, it must refer to something other than itself, and it must be used and recognised by people as a sign.'[4] Media texts are composed of signs (images, words, sounds) from which meaning or significance is derived. In 'Radio Signs' (Chapter 14), Andrew Crisell classifies and discusses the kinds of signs that are to be found in radio broadcasts. At one level, radio sets simply emit sound waves that make a variety of noises, yet listeners derive information, emotions and understandings from these; so at another level, radio broadcasts consist of complicated sequences of signs.

Collections of signs are organised in certain rule-governed ways that are called 'codes'. In Chapter 15 John Fiske selects as an example two scenes from the 1980s American television series *Hart to Hart* in order to anatomise the codes at work in a programme. For each element of the programme, the programme-makers have made a choice from among possible options, and each of these elements carries a meaning in accordance with socially established (though rarely spelt out) codes – some of which are specific to television, many of which are not. Fiske brings out the connection between the term 'code' and the concept of 'ideology'. Ideologies are interlinked groups of ideas that circulate socially, and the possibility of understanding the elements of a text – of 'decoding' them – requires the mental mobilisation, consciously or unconsciously, of particular ideologies. Codes are not given by Nature, nor are they invariantly meaningful throughout time or across cultures. Semiology's historic – and persisting – value lies in the way it compels a close regard for how meanings are made by a text, which thereby 'de-naturalises' these meanings and highlights their socially produced character. (Further material on ideology is available in the section 'Ideology and Genre'.)

The next two chapters are also concerned with formal properties of media texts, in both cases those which derive from the particular social institutionalisation of a specific media technology. Chapter 16 is an extract from Raymond Williams' book *Television: Technology and Cultural Form*, whose title signals a concern with this relationship. The ideas of Marshall McLuhan about media technologies, though widely popularised, did not gain many adherents in the academic development of media studies in Britain, and Williams' book is in many ways an explicit refutation of McLuhan's claims for the strong determining role of technologies, taking television as a specific instance. But Williams does not argue that the technological nature of television has no effectivity; here he suggests that the technical character of broadcasting as the continuous emission of a signal for domestic reception, combined with its institutionalisation within a fundamentally commercial system that aims to retain audiences' attention maximally, makes for an output whose 'characteristic organisation . . . is one of sequence or flow'. The continuous availability of television, the heterogeneity of programme types, the intermixing of commercials and programme chunks, the constant station announcements, promotions and trailers, the ceaseless flux, the remorseless onward drive through time: taken together, these features mean that 'both internally, in its immediate organisation, and as a generally available experience, this characteristic as flow seems central'.

In his study of the contrasting characters of cinema and broadcast television, John Ellis builds on Williams' insight. Both writers suggest that the best definition of the broadcast text should not necessarily be taken to be the individual programme; instead the 'text' might usefully be seen as both greater and lesser than that. Perhaps, Williams implies, the text for analysis should be an evening's viewing (though that transmutes nowadays imperceptibly into night-time broadcasting, rather than exhibiting sharp boundaries). Ellis points in two other directions as well. First, to the micro-unit: there is the reliance by broadcast television on the unit of the 'segment' to organise and present (or 'narrate') its material. In the domestic setting of its reception, broadcast television cannot be sure of commanding unbroken attention, so it proceeds segment by segment, often with loose connections between them and a stress on sound as the principal track. Secondly, there are the connections that are made across time – a day, a week – within series and serials and long-running magazine shows, which adopt a pattern of repetition and novelty. Chapter 17 contributes to an illuminating exploration of certain general formal features of the broadcast television text.

NOTES

1. See, for example, Nathan Leites and Ithiel de Sola Pool, *On Content Analysis* (Washington, DC: Library of Congress, 1942); Bernard Berelson, *Content Analysis in Communication Research* (Glencoe, Ill.: Free Press, 1952).
2. Peter Wollen, 'Cinema and Semiology: Some Points of Contact', *Form*, no. 7 (1968); id., *Signs and Meaning in the Cinema* (London: Secker & Warburg, 1969).
3. 'A science that studies the life of signs within society is conceivable . . . I shall call it semiology.' Ferdinand de Saussure, *Course in General Linguistics* (London: Fontana, 1974); orig. pub. 1916.
4. Tim O'Sullivan, John Hartley, Danny Saunders, John Fiske, *Key Concepts in Communications*, 1st edn (London: Methuen, 1983).

14

RADIO SIGNS

Andrew Crisell

[. . .]

[I shall here examine] the raw material of radio, [. . .] the signs which its codes make use of in order to convey messages, and for this purpose I shall borrow some rudimentary distinctions from what is in fact a highly sophisticated classification of signs devised by the American philosopher, C. S. Peirce (1839–1914). Peirce, who is commonly regarded as a founding father of semiotics or semiology, the study of signs, distinguishes between the *icon* – a sign which resembles the object which it represents, such as a photograph; the *index* – a sign which is directly linked to its object, usually in a causal or sequential way: smoke, for instance, is an index of fire; and the *symbol* – a sign which bears no resemblance or connection to its object, for example the Union Jack as a symbol of Great Britain (Peirce, 1960, I, 196; II, 143, 161, 165, 168–9; Hawkes, 1977, 127–30; Fiske, 1982, 50). In radio all the signs are auditory: they consist simply of noises and silence, and therefore use *time*, not space, as their major structuring agent (Hawkes, 1977, 135). The noises of radio can be subdivided into words, sounds and music, and we will look at each of these in turn and also at the nature and functions of silence [. . .].

WORDS

Since words are signs which do not resemble what they represent (we may represent a canine quadruped by the word 'dog' but we may equally refer to it as 'chien', 'hund' or 'cur' or even invent a private word of our own), they are symbolic in character. Their symbolism is the basis of radio's imaginative appeal, for if the word-sign does not resemble its object the listener must visualize, picture or *imagine* that object. But there is an important difference between words which are written or printed on a page and words on the radio, and that is that words on the radio are always and unavoidably *spoken*. They therefore constitute a binary code in which the words themselves are symbols of what they represent, while the voice in which they are

From Andrew Crisell, *Understanding, Radio*, 1st edn (London: Methuen, 1986) pp. 45–56.

heard is an index of the person or 'character' who is speaking – a fact which was perceived and researched fairly early in the medium's history (Pear, 1931). In other words such factors as accent and stress have semiotic functions, or at least effects (O'Donnell and Todd, 1980, 95). Almost irrespective of what is said in a French accent, for example, the listener may automatically ascribe a romantic personality to its speaker. In fact, voice can be so powerful an expression of personality that merely by virtue of some well-delivered links a presenter or disc jockey can impose a unifying and congenial presence on the most miscellaneous of magazine or record programmes. Moreover, the voice of a continuity announcer is an index not only of herself, whom she may identify by name from time to time, but of the whole station or network. As a matter of deliberate policy she will give a kind of composite unity to its various programmes, set the tone or style of the whole network (Kumar, 1977, 240–1). Indeed an announcement such as 'You're listening to Radio 4' is ambivalent, for it means not only 'The programmes you're presently hearing are the output of Radio 4' but 'Since the network has no other self-conscious means of expression, *I* am Radio 4'. The ambivalence can be seen rather more clearly, and is taken even further, in the name of the USA's world service where at intervals we can hear 'You're listening to the Voice of America' in which the 'voice' is an index not only of the continuity announcer and the radio station, but of the entire nation.

By now it will be clear that signification is not static or rigid, but a highly fluid or elastic process which varies according to context and the preconceptions we bring to it – a fact which is not sufficiently acknowledged by some semioticians. A voice may be interpreted merely as the index of a human presence; or on another level as the index of a personality (a country bumpkin, seductive French woman, and so on); or on yet a third level as the index of a programme, broadcasting institution or entire nation. It might be useful to see the latter two levels as examples of *extended* signification.

SOUNDS

Unlike words, which are a human invention, sound is 'natural' – a form of signification which exists 'out there' in the real world. It seems never to exist as an isolated phenomenon, always to manifest the presence of something else. Consequently we can say that sounds, whether in the world or on the radio, are generally indexical. We could of course say that recorded sound on the radio is iconic in the elementary sense that it is an icon or image of the original sound or that a sound in a radio play is an icon of a sound in the real world, but if we do we are still faced with the question of what the sound *signifies*, what it is that is *making* the sound. Thus sounds such as the ringing of a door-bell or the grating of a key in a lock are indexical in signifying someone's presence. Shut your eyes for a moment and listen. The chances are that you will become aware of sounds which you have been hearing for some time but which you have not been aware of before. You have not been aware of them because you are reading such a fascinating book that you have ignored the messages coming from your ears. Suppose, however, that your desire for a cup of coffee is almost equal to your absorption in this book and that a friend has agreed to bring one to you about now. You will be quite capable of picking out from the welter of unimportant noises which surround you the keenly awaited sounds of rattling cup and turning door-handle. But the radio medium is such that the listener cannot select his own area of attention in this way: the broadcasters must prioritize sounds for him, foregrounding the most important ones and eliminating the irrelevant ones, or if this is not possible reducing them to the level of the less important ones. This has been illustrated in respect of radio drama by Erving Goffman (1980, 162–5). Taking a conversation at a party as his scenario Goffman points out that whereas in real life we would be able to distinguish the important from the less important strand of sound, this has to be done for us on the radio by certain conventions. Among the possibilities he instances

1. Fading in party chatter then fading it down and holding it under the conversation, or even fading it out altogether.
2. Allowing one or two low sounds to stand for what would actually be a stream of background noise.

What Goffman is concerned to stress about these conventions is their artificiality, which is aptly conveyed in the stock phrase 'sound *effects*': 'the audience is not upset by listening in on a world in which many sounds are not sounded and a few are made to stand out momentarily; yet if these conditions suddenly appeared in the off-stage world, consternation would abound' (ibid., 163). Nevertheless it is important to realize that such conventions are indispensable even in radio which deals with real life. In a location interview, for instance, the interviewer will set the recording-level on her portable tape-machine so that the sound of her voice and that of the person she is interviewing will be foregrounded against all the other noises of the location. Let us imagine an interview which takes place against a background of traffic noise. If the interview is with a superintendent of highways about noise pollution the traffic noise, while of less importance – and therefore less loud – than the interview, will still be of relevance to it. If, however, the interview is with the Chancellor of the Exchequer about his Budget proposals the noise of traffic will be quite irrelevant, an unavoidable evil, and the listener will be fully capable of distinguishing between these positive and negative functions of background noise. This second type of location interview is, of course, a *faute de mieux*: it brings a broadcasting facility to an interviewee who cannot be brought into the studio, for an important function of the studio with its sound-proofing is that it eliminates irrelevant noise altogether. My point, then, is that radio does not seek to reproduce the chaotic, complex and continuous sounds of actual life: it may tolerate them to a degree, but seeks to convey only those sounds which are relevant to its messages and to arrange them in their order of relevance. Nevertheless the ultimate test of relevance is the verbal context: it is the subject under discussion in the interview which will tell us whether we should be paying any attention to the traffic noise.

Yet even when the relevant sounds have been distinguished from the irrelevant, the *level* of that relevance often needs to be determined. Let us imagine a programme which begins with an owl-hoot. The 'relevance' or importance of the sound is not in doubt since we can hear virtually nothing else. But what does that relevance consist in? Are we to take the sound simply as an index of the bird, as we would in a documentary about wild-life or the countryside? Or does it carry what I have termed an extended signification in evoking not merely a solitary owl but an entire setting – an eerie, nocturnal atmosphere, as it would in a radio melodrama or a programme about the occult? In the first place, how do such sounds as owl-hoots acquire an extended signification? A crowing, sound, for instance, frequently signifies not only 'a cock' but 'daybreak', while the sound of strumming may suggest not only a guitar but a Spanish setting. Because radio broadcasters seldom walk while broadcasting, the sound of footsteps, frequently heard – and ignored – in real life, acquires a peculiar suggestiveness on the radio. Drama producers will use it sparingly, and to convey not only that a person is moving but also that an atmosphere of tension or solitude is developing. This extended signification seems to be established through a process of custom and habit. It is likely that such sounds were originally chosen as an effective way of reinforcing particular pieces of dialogue or description. But since they *are* effective and part of what is a rather limited range of resources open to the radio producer they were chosen again and again and came to acquire the status of a convention, an acoustic shorthand, in that they could *replace* or absorb much of the adjacent language. In hearing the hoot of the owl the listener would begin to brace himself for darkness and mystery before a word had been uttered. Nevertheless, while such conventions may be useful in replacing *much* of adjacent language they cannot *wholly* replace it, for ultimately it is only the words which follow upon our owl-hoot which will tell us whether what we are listening to is *Sounds Natural* or *Afternoon Theatre*.

But it is not simply the case that radio broadcasters must discriminate between important and unimportant sounds on their listeners' behalf and that they must also make the *level* of that importance clear: in some cases they must clarify the very *nature* of those sounds. Why? Shut your eyes and listen again to the sounds around you. You may be surprised at how few of them you can identify with any precision. The frequency range of most sounds is narrow and what we often overlook about the way in which we normally recognize them are the clues our other senses afford, notably the visual sense. When we do not actually see what is causing them they often mean nothing at all. Moreover studio simulations of sounds can often sound more 'real' on the radio than the actual sounds themselves would. Among the better known and genuine examples of these studio simulations are the clapping together of coconut shells to convey horses' hooves and the rustle of a bunch of recording tape to convey someone walking through undergrowth (McLeish, 1978, 252). These are not straightforwardly indexical, since the sounds made by coconut shells and recording tape have no *direct* connections with horses and people in undergrowth. They are 'images' of the sounds made by horses and people and are therefore best described as iconic indexes. They might also be described as 'non-literal signifiers' analogous to an actor in the theatre who represents a table by kneeling on all fours (Elam, 1980, 8); but in radio such signifiers must approximate rather more closely to that which they signify than signifiers in the visual media. Yet however carefully selected and 'realistic' the sounds may be, the listener may still be unclear as to what aspect of reality they are meant to signify. The rustle of recording tape may sound like someone walking through undergrowth, but it also sounds like the swish of a lady's gown and remarkably like the rustle of recording tape. In a radio play which of these things would it signify?

Accompanied by 'Damn! I don't often hit it off the fairway': a golfer searching for his ball in the rough.

Accompanied by 'Darling, you'll be the belle of the ball tonight': a lady in an evening gown.

Accompanied by 'This studio's a pig-sty. Throw this old tape out': a bunch of recording tape.

In other words, sounds require textual pointing – support from the dialogue or narrative. The ear will believe what is led to believe. This pointing might be termed 'anchorage', which is how Roland Barthes describes the function of words used as captions for photographs. Visual images, he argues, are polysemous. But so are sounds. Hence words help '*Fix* the floating chain of signifieds in such a way as to counter the terror of uncertain signs' (Barthes, 1977, 39).

Music

Music on the radio, as on television, seems to perform two main functions. It is an object of aesthetic pleasure in its own right, in record shows, concerts, recitals, and so on; and either by itself or in combination with words and/or sounds it performs an ancillary function in signifying something outside itself.

As an object of pleasure in its own right, music is quite simply the mainstay of radio's output. Some stations offer little or nothing else. Even on the four BBC networks, one of which – Radio 4 – devotes over three-fifths of its output to news and current affairs, music accounted for 61.3 per cent of total radio output in 1983–4 (BBC *Annual Report and Handbook 1985*, 1984, 145). The difficulty is to define such music in semiotic terms since there is some doubt as to the sense in which music can be said to signify. Broadly speaking, words and images refer to something outside themselves but the assertion cannot be quite so confidently made about music. Music with lyrics seems to present less of a difficulty since we could say that the significance or meaning of the music means one thing and the lyrics mean another and that they are quite capable of counterpointing as well as complementing each other. Quite apart from this, the question of what meaning (if any) attaches to wordless music is a formidable one. It can of course be seen as an index of the instruments and musicians that are playing it. When we hear a record on the radio but miss the disc jockey's introduction to it, we may still be able to identify which group is playing by the characteristic sound it has evolved. But to leave the matter there is rather like saying that spoken words are signs of nothing but the identity of their speaker. Dictionary definitions of music generally ascribe an emotional significance to it, and some compositions (for example Tchaikovsky's *1812 Overture*) evoke historical events: but while acknowledging this we would have to point out that music does not convey these emotions or events with anything like the precision that words do. Indeed there is room for disagreement about the emotional significance of certain compositions with unrevealing titles like 'Opus No. 3' or 'Study in E Flat' – and who could tell merely from hearing it that Chopin's *Minute Waltz* is about a dog chasing its tail? This means that written commentaries which point to particular features of a piece of music as referring to particular emotional or historical conditions tend to rely consciously or unconsciously on circumstantial evidence – the title of the piece and/or the famous legend which it 'narrates', the situation in which it was composed, the biographical and psychological details of the composer, and so on. Hence our very difficulty in discerning what music refers to means that if it does signify, then apart from its local imitations of 'natural' sounds its mode of signification will be almost entirely symbolic.

This virtual absence, or at any rate imprecision, of meaning in music makes it at once highly suited to the radio medium and somewhat unilluminating as to its nature. It is highly suited because in being largely free of signification it allows us to listen without making strenuous efforts to imagine what is being referred to, but to assimilate it, if we wish, to our own thoughts and moods – a fact which helps to explain why music has become even more popular since radio's rebirth as a secondary medium. But it is unilluminating in the sense that in its fully realized form (that is, not as a written score) it consists almost purely of sound, refers scarcely at all to anything outside itself, and is therefore one code which is not distinctively shaped by radio since radio is itself a purely acoustic medium. This was recognized fairly early in broadcasting history by a features producer who wished to dismiss the idea that there was anything especially 'radiogenic' about music:

> There is no such thing as radio music. Composers go on composing music just as if wireless had never been invented, and the music of all periods is played before microphones in exactly the same way as it has always been played. It does not have to be 'adapted'.   (Sieveking, 1934, 24)

Apart from the fact that radio allowed the listener to hear music without visual distractions (and even in this was anticipated by the gramophone), the point is that music is rather less revealing about the nature and possibilities of the medium than, say, news, drama and light entertainment:

for whereas we can compare radio versions of the latter with their corresponding forms on the stage, screen or in newspapers and see the distinctive way in which the medium has adapted them, music in its essential form is always and everywhere the same. Not modified by radio, it does not particularly illuminate it.

Nevertheless the broad emotive power of music enables it to be combined with words and/or sounds as a way of signifying something outside itself, and some of these forms of signification are worth considering in detail.

1. Music as a 'framing' or 'boundary' mechanism. Musical jingles (sometimes known as 'IDs') identify or 'frame' radio stations just as signature or theme music frames an individual programme by announcing its beginning and/or end. Station IDs are similar in function to the voice of the continuity announcer, they set the style or tone of the station and could be seen as both index and symbol. It is interesting to speculate why musical IDs are more closely associated with 'popular' and verbal IDs with 'quality' networks; but it is certainly the case that the work done by continuity announcers on Radios 3 and 4 is performed largely by jingles on Radios 1 and 2!

    As a way of framing individual items theme music is also common in film and television, but it is of particular significance in radio because of the blindness of the medium. Silence, a pause, can also be used as a framing mechanism, but unlike that of film and television it is *total*, devoid of images. To give the programmes connotations, an overall style or mood, music is therefore an especially useful resource on radio – less bald, more indefinitely suggestive, than mere announcements. Let us take a formal but lively piece of eighteenth-century music played on a harpsichord – a gavotte or bourrée composed by Bach, perhaps – and consider its possibilities for the radio producer. It is highly structured and symmetrical in form and therefore commonly regarded as more cerebral or 'intellectual' than the Romantic compositions of the following century. She might therefore regard it as ideal theme music for a brains trust or quiz programme. But its characteristics have other possibilities. The 'period' quality of both the harpsichord and the music is unmistakable and might lend itself to a programme about history or antiques. Alternatively the 'tinny' tone of the instrument combined with the rhythmic nature of the piece might introduce a children's programme about toys or music boxes or with a faery or fantasy theme. You can doubtless imagine other possibilities for yourself, and I would simply make two further points. The first is that depending on the specific contents of the programmes I have suggested, it would be possible to discern all three modes of signification in such theme music – the symbolic, the indexical and the iconic. Secondly I would stress that these are *extrinsic* meanings of the music: we could not say that it is 'about' cerebration or history or toys. Another way we might describe them is as 'associative' meanings: in a serial, for instance, the theme music will bring to the listener's mind what he already knows about the story-line; even more than this, it is a 'paradigm' of that *genre* of programme (Fiske and Hartley, 1978, 169). This function of music as a framing mechanism and the two following functions are noticed by Goffman (1980, 164–5).

2. Music as a link between the scenes of a radio play or the items of a programme. Such links are analogous to curtain drops in the theatre, since they keep certain aspects of the programme apart and may additionally signal advertising breaks. But as well as keeping apart they bridge the changes of scene or subject, thus providing a kind of continuity.

3. 'Mood' music during a play, a background enhancement which is understood not to be heard by the characters, but is heard by the listeners as a clue to the characters' feelings or

thoughts. These last two functions of music could be seen as symbolic, but there is another which Goffman appears to overlook:

4. Music as a kind of stylized replacement for naturalistic sound effects in a play, for example musical simulations of storms or battles. It has an imitative function and is a sort of iconic index. It is heard by the characters in the play, but not in that form.
5. Music in an indexical function, as part of the ordinary sounds of the world which radio portrays. These sounds are usually known collectively as 'actuality'. Here is a typical example from a news programme:

> FADE IN SOUND OF BAGPIPES AND DRUMS
> *Presenter:*The Band of the Argyll and Sutherland Highlanders, who were today granted the freedom of Aldershot.

The semiotic function of the music would be much the same whether it were live actuality from the freedom ceremony, or a recording of the actuality, or simply taken from a gramophone record (radio producers often 'cheat'). In the first instance the music would be indexical and in the other two instances the recordings would simply be acting as icons of the sounds the band was making at the ceremony – sounds which are an index of its presence. They would therefore be iconic indexes.

SILENCE

Though it is natural for us to speak of radio as a sound medium we should remember that the *absence* of sound can also be heard. It is therefore important to consider silence as a form of signification. It has both negative and positive functions which seem to be indexical. Its negative function is to signify that for the moment at least, nothing is happening on the medium: there is a void, what broadcasters sometimes refer to as 'dead air'. In this function silence can resemble noise (that is, sounds, words and music) in acting as a framing mechanism, for it can signify the integrity of a programme or item by making a space around it. But if the silence persists for more than a few seconds it signifies the dysfunction or non-functioning of the medium: either transmitter or receiver has broken down or been switched off.

The positive function of silence is to signify that something is happening which for one reason or another cannot be expressed in noise. Because radio silence is total (unlike film and theatrical silences, which are visually filled) it can be a potent stimulus to the listener, providing a gap in the noise for his imagination to work: 'Pass me the bottle. Cheers . . . Ah, that's better!' But such silences or pauses can suggest not only physical actions but abstract, dramatic qualities, generate pathos or irony by confirming or countering the words which surround them. They can also generate humour, as in a famous radio skit which featured Jack Benny, a comedian with a reputation for extreme miserliness:

> The skit consists of a confrontation between Benny and a mugger on the street. Says the mugger: 'Your money or your life'. Prolonged pause: growing laughter; then applause as the audience gradually realises what Benny *must* be thinking, and eventually responds to the information communicated by the silence and to its comic implications.   (Fink, 1981, 202)

How, then, does the listener discriminate among these various negative and positive functions of silence? His guide is clearly the context – in the first instance whether any noise frames the silence and in the second, what that noise signifies.

REFERENCES

Barthes, R. (1977) *Image – Music – Text* (trans. S. Heath) Glasgow: Fontana.

BBC Annual Report and Handbook 1985 (1984) London: British Broadcasting Corporation.

Elam, K. (1980) *The Semiotics of Theatre and Drama*, London: Methuen.

Fink, H. (1981) 'The sponsor's v. the nation's choice: North American radio drama', in P. Lewis (ed.) *Radio Drama*, London and New York: Longman.

Fiske, J. (1982) *An Introduction to Communication Studies*, London: Methuen.

Fiske, J. and J. Hartley (1978) *Reading Television*, London: Methuen.

Goffman, E. (1980) 'The radio drama frame' in Corner, J. and Hawthorn, J. (eds) *Communication Studies*, London: Edward Arnold.

Hawkes, T. (1977) *Structuralism and Semiotics*, London: Methuen.

Kumar, K. (1977) 'Holding the middle ground: the BBC, the public and the professional broadcaster' in Curran, J., Gurevitch M., and Woollacott J. (eds) *Mass Communication and Society*, London: Edward Arnold.

McLeish, R. (1978) *The Technique of Radio Production*, London: Focal Press.

O'Donnell, W. and Todd, L. (1980) *Variety in Contemporary English*, London: George Allen & Unwin.

Pear, T. H. (1931) *Voice and Personality*, London: Chapman & Hall.

Peirce, C. S. (1960) *Collected Papers*, vols I and II, (eds) Hartshorne, C. and Weiss, P., Cambridge, Mass: Harvard University Press.

Sieveking, L. (1934) *The Stuff of Radio*, London: Cassell.

15

THE CODES OF TELEVISION

John Fiske

[. . .]

[To demonstrate] a traditional semiotic account of how television makes, or attempts to make, meanings that serve the dominant interests in society, [. . . I shall analyse . . .] a short segment of two scenes from a typical, prime-time, long-running series, *Hart to Hart*

[. . .]

The Harts are a wealthy, high-living husband and wife detective team. In this particular episode they are posing as passengers on a cruise ship on which there has been a jewel robbery. In scene 1 they are getting ready for a dance during which they plan to tempt the thief to rob them, and are discussing how the robbery may have been effected. In scene 2 we meet the villain and villainess, who have already noticed Jennifer Hart's ostentatiously displayed jewels.

SCENE 1

HERO: He knew what he was doing to get into this safe.

HEROINE: Did you try the numbers that Granville gave you?

HERO: Yeh. I tried those earlier. They worked perfectly.

HEROINE: Well you said it was an inside job, maybe they had the combination all the time.

HERO: Just trying to eliminate all the possibilities. Can you check this out for me. (*He gestures to his bow tie.*)

HEROINE: Mm. Yes I can. (*He hugs her.*) Mm. Light fingers. Oh, Jonathon.

HERO: Just trying to keep my touch in shape.

HEROINE: What about the keys to the door.

HERO: Those keys can't be duplicated because of the code numbers. You have to have the right machines.

HEROINE: Well, that leaves the window.

From John Fiske, *Television Culture* (London and New York: Methuen, 1987) pp. 1–13.

HERO: The porthole.

HEROINE: Oh yes. The porthole. I know they are supposed to be charming, but they always remind me of a laundromat.

HERO: I took a peek out of there a while ago. It's about all you can do. It's thirty feet up to the deck even if you could make it down to the window, porthole. You'd have to be the thin man to squeeze through.

HEROINE: What do you think? (*She shows her jewelry.*) Enough honey to attract the bees?

HERO: Who knows? They may not be able to see the honey for the flowers.

HEROINE: Oh, that's the cutest thing you've ever said to me, sugar. Well, shall we? (*Gestures towards the door.*)

SCENE 2

VILLAIN: I suppose you noticed some of the icing on Chamberlain's cup cake. I didn't have my jeweler's glass, but that bracelet's got to be worth at least fifty thousand. Wholesale.

VILLAINESS: Patrick, if you're thinking what I know you're thinking, forget it. We've made our quota one hit on each ship. We said we weren't going to get greedy, remember.

VILLAIN: But darling, it's you I'm thinking of. And I don't like you taking all those chances. But if we could get enough maybe we wouldn't have to go back to the Riviera circuit for years.

VILLAINESS: That's what you said when we were there.

VILLAIN: Well maybe a few good investments and we can pitch the whole bloody business. But we are going to need a bit more for our retirement fund.

Figure 1 shows the main codes that television uses and their relationship. A code is a rule-governed system of signs, whose rules and conventions are shared amongst members of a culture, and which is used to generate and circulate meanings in and for that culture. (For a fuller discussion of codes in semiotics see Fiske 1983 or O'Sullivan et al. 1983.) Codes are links between producers, texts, and audiences, and are the agents of intertextuality through which texts interrelate in a network of meanings that constitutes our cultural world. These codes work in a complex hierarchical structure that Figure 1 oversimplifies for the sake of clarity. In particular, the categories of codes are arbitrary and slippery, as is their classification into levels in the hierarchy; for instance, I have put speech as a social code, and dialogue (i.e. scripted speech) as a technical one, but in practice the two are almost indistinguishable: social psychologists such as Berne (1964) have shown us how dialogue in 'real life' is frequently scripted for us by the interactional conventions of our culture. Similarly, I have called casting a conventional representational code, and appearance a social one, but the two differ only in intentionality and explicitness. People's appearance in 'real life' is already encoded: in so far as we make sense of people by their appearance we do so according to conventional codes in our culture. The casting director is merely using these codes more consciously and more conventionally, which means more stereotypically.

The point is that 'reality' is already encoded, or rather the only way we can perceive and make sense of reality is by the codes of our culture. There may be an objective, empiricist reality out there, but there is no universal, objective way of perceiving and making sense of it. What passes for reality in any culture is the product of that culture's codes, so 'reality' is always already encoded, it is never 'raw.' If this piece of encoded reality is televised, the technical codes and representational conventions of the medium are brought to bear upon it so as to make it (a) transmittable technologically and (b) an appropriate cultural text for its audiences.

Figure 1 The codes of Television

An event to be televised is already encoded
by *social codes* such as those of:

Level one:
'REALITY'

appearance, dress, make-up, environment, behavior, speech,
gesture, expression, sound, etc.

these are encoded electronically by
technical codes such as those of:

Level two:
REPRESENTATION

camera, lighting, editing, music, sound

which transmit the
conventional representational codes, which shape the
representations of, for example:
narrative, conflict, character, action, dialogue, setting,
casting, etc.

Level three:
IDEOLOGY

which are organised into coherence and social acceptability by
the *ideological codes*, such as those of:
individualism, partriarchy, race, class, materialism,
capitalism, etc.

Some of the social codes which constitute our reality are relatively precisely definable in terms of the medium through which they are expressed – skin color, dress, hair, facial expression, and so on.

Others, such as those that make up a landscape, for example, may be less easy to specify systematically, but they are still present and working hard. Different sorts of trees have different connotative meanings encoded into them, so do rocks and birds. So a tree reflected in a lake, for example, is fully encoded even before it is photographed and turned into the setting for a romantic narrative.

Similarly the technical codes of television can be precisely identified and analyzed. The choices available to the camera person, for example, to give meaning to what is being photographed are limited and specifiable: they consist of framing, focus, distance, movement (of the camera or the lens), camera placing, or angle and lens choice. But the conventional and ideological codes and the relationship between them are much more elusive and much harder to specify, though it is the task of criticism to do just that. For instance, the conventions that govern the representation of speech as 'realistic dialogue' in scene 1 result in the heroine asking questions while the hero provides the answers. The representational convention by which women are shown to lack knowledge which men possess and give to them is an example of the ideological code of patriarchy. Similarly the conventional representation of crime as theft of personal property is an encoding of the ideology of capitalism. The 'naturalness' with which the two fit together in the scene is evidence of how these ideological codes work to organize the other codes into producing a congruent and coherent set of meanings that constitute the *common sense* of a society. The process of making sense involves a constant movement up and down through the levels of the diagram, for sense can only be produced when 'reality,' representations, and ideology merge into a coherent, seemingly natural unity. Semiotic or cultural criticism deconstructs this unity and exposes its 'naturalness' as a highly ideological construct.

A semiotic analysis attempts to reveal how these layers of encoded meanings are structured into television programs, even in as small a segment as the one we are working with. The small size of the segment encourages us to perform a detailed analytical reading of it, but prevents us talking about larger-scale codes, such as those of the narrative. But it does provide a good starting point for our work.

CAMERA WORK

The camera is used through angle and deep focus to give us a perfect view of the scene, and thus a complete understanding of it. Much of the pleasure of television realism comes from this sense of omniscience that it gives us. Camera distance is used to swing our sympathies away from the villain and villainess, and towards the hero and heroine. The normal camera distance in television is mid-shot to close-up, which brings the viewer into an intimate, comfortable relationship with the characters on the screen. But the villain and villainess are also shown in extreme close-up (ECU). Throughout this whole episode of *Hart to Hart* there are only three scenes in which ECUs are used: they are used only to represent hero/ine and villain/ess, and of the twenty-one ECUs, eighteen are of the villain/ess and only three of the hero/ine. Extreme close-ups become a codified way for representing villainy.

This encoding convention is not confined to fictional television, where we might think that its work upon the alignment of our sympathies, and thus on our moral judgment, is justified. It is also used in news and current affairs programs which present themselves as bringing reality to us 'objectively.' The court action resulting from General Westmoreland's libel suit against the CBS in 1985 revealed these codes more questionably at work in television reporting. Alex Jones recounts their use in his report of the trial for the *New York Times*:

> Among the more controversial techniques is placing an interviewee in partial shadow in order to lend drama to what is being said. Also debated is the use of extreme close-ups that tend to emphasize the tension felt by a person being interviewed; viewers may associate the appearance of tension with lying or guilt.
>
> The extreme close-up can be especially damaging when an interview is carefully scripted and a cameraman is instructed to focus tightly on the person's face at the point when the toughest question is to be asked. Some documentary makers will not use such close-ups at all in interviews because they can be so misleading.
>
> The CBS documentary contained both a shadowed interview of a friendly witness

and 'tight shots' of General Westmoreland. Such techniques have been used in documentaries by other networks as well.

Even the wariest viewer is likely to find it difficult to detect some other common techniques. 'I can't imagine a general viewer getting so sophisticated with techniques that they could discount them,' said Reuven Frank, a former president at NBC News who has been making documentaries for about 30 years. (*NYT*, February 17, 1985: 8E)

There are two possible sources of the conventions that govern the meanings generated by this code of camera distance. One is the social code of interpersonal distance: in western cultures the space within about 24 inches (60 cm) of us is encoded as private. Anyone entering it is being either hostile, when the entry is unwelcome, or intimate, when it is invited. ECUs replicate this, and are used for moments of televisual intimacy or hostility, and which meanings they convey depends on the other social and technical codes by which they are contextualized, and by the ideological codes brought to bear upon them. Here, they are used to convey hostility. The other source lies in the technical codes which imply that seeing closely means seeing better – the viewer can see *into* the villain, see *through* his words, and thus gains power over him, the power and the pleasure of 'dominant specularity.'

These technical and social codes manifest the ideological encoding of villainy.

Most of the other technical codes can be dealt with more quickly, with only brief comments.

LIGHTING

The hero's cabin is lit in a soft, yellowish light, that of the villains in a harsh, whiter one. (I am reminded of Hogben's (1982) anecdote about the occasion when he was given a hostile treatment in a television interview. He did, however, manage to convince the interviewer that his point of view deserved more sympathy, whereupon the interviewer insisted they record the interview again, but this time without the greenish-white studio lighting.)

EDITING

The heroes are given more time (72 secs) than the villains (49), and more shots (10 as against 7), though both have an average shot length of 7 seconds. It is remarkable how consistent this is across different modes of television (see Fiske 1986): it has become a conventional rhythm of television common to news, drama, and sport.

MUSIC

The music linking the two scenes started in a major key, and changed to minor as the scene changed to the villains.

CASTING

This technical code requires a little more discussion. The actors and actresses who are cast to play hero/ines, villain/esses and supporting roles are real people whose appearance is already encoded by our social codes. But they are equally media people, who exist for the viewer intertextually, and whose meanings are also intertextual. They bring with them not only residues of the meanings of other roles that they have played, but also their meanings from other texts such as fan magazines, showbiz gossip columns, and television criticism. Later on in the book [*Television Culture*] we will discuss intertextuality and character portrayal in greater depth: here we need to note that these dimensions of meaning are vital in the code of casting, and that they are more important in the casting of hero/ines than of villain/esses.

Characters on television are not just representations of individual people but are encodings of ideology, 'embodiments of ideological values' (Fiske 1987a). Gerbner's (1970) work showed that viewers were clear about the different characteristics of television heroes and villains on two dimensions only: heroes were more attractive and more successful than villains. Their attractiveness, or lack of it, is partly the result of the way they are encoded in the technical and social codes – camera work, lighting, setting, casting, etc., but the ideological codes are also important, for it is these that make sense out of the relationship between the technical code of casting and the social code of appearance, and that also relate their televisual use to their broader use in the culture at large. In his analysis of violence on television, Gerbner (1970) found that heroes and villains are equally likely to use violence and to initiate it, but that heroes were successful in their violence, whereas villains finally were not. Gerbner worked out a killers-to-killed ratio according to different categories of age, sex, class, and race. The killers category included heroes and villains, but the killed category included villains only. He found that a character who was white, male, middle class (or classless) and in the prime of life was very likely, if not certain, to be alive at the end of the program. Conversely characters who deviated from these norms were likely to be killed during the program in proportion to the extent of their deviance. We may use Gerbner's findings to theorize that heroes are socially central types who embody the dominant ideology, whereas villains and victims are members of deviant or subordinate subcultures who thus embody the dominant ideology less completely, and may, in the case of villains, embody ideologies that oppose it. The textual opposition between hero/ine and villain/ess, and the violence by which this opposition is commonly dramatized, become metaphors for power relationships in society and thus a material practice through which the dominant ideology works. (This theory is discussed more fully in Fiske and Hartley 1978 and in Fiske 1982.)

The villain in this segment has hints of non-Americanness; some viewers have classed his accent, manner, and speech as British, for others his appearance has seemed Hispanic. But the hero and heroine are both clearly middle-class, white Americans, at home among the WASPs (White Anglo-Saxon Protestants). The villainess is Aryan, blonde, pretty, and younger than the villain. Gerbner's work would lead us to predict that his chances of surviving the episode are slim, whereas hers are much better. The prediction is correct. She finally changes sides and helps the hero/ine, whereas he is killed; hints of this are contained in her condemnation of the villain's greed, which positions her more centrally in the ideological discourse of economics (see below).

These technical codes of television transmit, and in some cases merge into, the social codes of level 1. Let us look at how some of them are working to generate meanings and how they embody the ideological codes of level 3.

SETTING AND COSTUME

The hero/ine's cabin is larger than that of the villain/ess: it is humanized, made more attractive by drapes and flowers, whereas the other is all sharp angles and hard lines. The villain wears a uniform that places him as a servant or employee and the villainess's dress is less tasteful, less expensive than the heroine's. These physical differences in the social codes of setting and dress are also bearers of the ideological codes of class, of heroism and villainy, of morality, and of attractiveness. These abstract ideological codes are condensed into a set of material social ones, and the materiality of the differences of the social codes is used to guarantee the truth and naturalness of the ideological. We must note, too, how some ideological codes are more explicit than others: the codes of heroism, villainy, and attractiveness are working fairly openly and acceptably. But under them the codes of class, race, and morality are working less openly and more questionably: their ideological work is to naturalize the correlation of lower-class, non-American with the less attractive, less moral, and therefore villainous. Conversely, the middle and the white American is correlated with the more attractive, the more moral and the heroic. This displacement of morality onto class is a common feature of our popular culture: Dorfman and Mattelart (1975) have shown how Walt Disney cartoons consistently express villainy through characteristics of working-class appearance and manner; indeed they argue that the only time the working class appear in the middle-class world of Ducksville it is as villains. Fiske (1984) has found the same textual strategy in the *Dr Who* television series.

MAKE-UP

The same merging of the ideological codes of morality, attractiveness, and heroism/villainy, and their condensation into a material social code, can be seen in something as apparently insignificant as lipstick. The villainess has a number of signs that contradict her villainy (she is blonde, white American, pretty, and more moral than the villain). These predict her eventual conversion to the side of the hero and heroine, but she cannot look too like them at this early stage of the narrative, so her lips are made up to be thinner and less sexually attractive than the fuller lips of the heroine. The ideology of lipstick may seem a stretched concept, but it is in the aggregate of apparently insignificant encodings that ideology works most effectively.

ACTION

There are a number of significant similarities and differences between the actions of the hero/ine and the villain/ess. In both cabins the women are prettying themselves, the men are planning. This naturalizes the man's executive role (Goffman 1979) of instigating action and the woman's role as object of the male gaze – notice the mirror in each cabin which enables her to see herself as 'bearer of her own image' (Berger 1972): the fact that this is common to both hero/ine and villain/ess puts it beyond the realm of conflict in the narrative and into the realm of everyday common sense within which the narrative is enacted. The other action common to both is the getting and keeping of wealth as a motive for action, and as a motor for the narrative: this also is not part of the conflict-to-be-resolved, but part of the ideological framework through which that conflict is viewed and made sense of.

A difference between the two is that of cooperation and closeness. The hero and heroine co-operate and come physically closer together, the villain and villainess, on the other hand, disagree and pull apart physically. In a society that places a high value on a man and woman being a close couple this is another bearer of the dominant ideology.

DIALOGUE

The dialogue also is used to affect our sympathy. That of the villain and villainess is restricted to their nefarious plans and their mutual disagreement, whereas the hero and heroine are allowed a joke (window/porthole/laundromat), an extended metaphor (honey and the bees), and the narrative time to establish a warm, co-operative relationship. Both the hero/ine and villain/ess are allowed irony.

IDEOLOGICAL CODES

These codes and the televisual codes which bring them to the viewer are both deeply embedded in the ideological codes of which they are themselves the bearers. If we adopt the same ideological practice in the decoding as the encoding we are drawn into the position of a white, male, middle-class American (or westerner) of conventional morality. The reading position is the social point at which the mix of televisual, social, and ideological codes comes together to make coherent, unified sense: in making sense of the program in this way we are indulging in an ideological practice ourselves, we are maintaining and legitimating the dominant ideology, and our reward for this is the easy pleasure of the recognition of the familiar and of its adequacy. We have already become a 'reading subject' constructed by the text, and, according to Althusser (1971), the construction of subjects-in-ideology is the major ideological practice in capitalist societies.

This ideological practice is working at its hardest in three narrative devices in this segment. The first is the window/porthole/laundromat joke, which, as we have seen, is used to marshal the viewer's affective sympathy on the side of the hero/ine. But it does more than that. Freud tells us that jokes are used to relieve the anxiety caused by repressed, unwelcome, or taboo meanings. This joke revolves around the 'feminine' (as defined by our dominant culture) inability to understand or use technical language, and the equally 'feminine' tendency to make sense of everything through a domestic discourse. 'Porthole' is technical discourse – masculine: 'window-laundromat' is domestic-nurturing discourse – feminine. The anxiety that the joke relieves is that caused by the fact that the heroine is a detective, is involved in the catching of criminals – activities that are part of the technical world of men in patriarchy. The joke is used to recuperate contradictory signs back into the dominant system, and to smooth over any contradictions that might disrupt the ideological homogeneity of the narrative. The attractiveness of the heroine must not be put at risk by allowing her challenge to patriarchy to be too stark – for attractiveness is always ideological, never merely physical or natural.

The metaphor that expresses the sexual attractiveness of women for men in terms of the attraction of honey and flowers for the bees works in a similar way. It naturalizes this attraction, masking its ideological dimension, and then extends this naturalness to its explanation of the attractiveness of other people's jewelry for lower-class non-American villains! The metaphor is working to naturalize cultural constructions of gender, class, and race.

The third device is that of jewelry itself. As we have seen, the getting and keeping of wealth is the major motor of the narrative, and jewelry is its material signifier. Three ideological codes intersect in the use of jewelry in this narrative: they are the codes of economics, gender, and class.

In the code of economics, the villain and villainess stress the jewelry's investment/exchange function: it is 'worth at least fifty thousand wholesale,' it forms 'a retirement fund.' For the hero and heroine and for the class they represent this function is left unstated: jewelry, if it is an investment, is one to hold, not cash in. It is used rather as a sign of class, of wealth, and of aesthetic taste.

The aesthetic sense, or good taste, is typically used as a bearer and naturalizer of class differences. The heroine deliberately overdoes the jewelry, making it vulgar and tasteless in order to attract the lower-class villain and villainess. They, in their turn, show their debased taste, their aesthetic insensitivity, by likening it to the icing on a cupcake. As Bourdieu (1968) has shown us, the function of aesthetics in our society is to make class-based and culture-specific differences of taste appear universal and therefore natural. The taste of the dominant classes is universalized by aesthetic theory out of its class origin; the metaphor of 'taste' works in a similar way by displacing class differences onto the physical, and therefore natural, senses of the body.

The meaning of jewelry in the code of gender is clear. Jewels are the coins by which the female-as-patriarchal-commodity is bought, and wearing them is the sign both of her possession by a man, and of his economic and social status. Interestingly, in the code of gender, there is no class difference between hero/ine and villain/ess: the economics of patriarchy are the same for all classes, thus making it appear universal and natural that man provides for his woman.

This analysis has not only revealed the complexity of meanings encoded in what is frequently taken to be shallow and superficial, but it also implies that this complexity and subtlety has a powerful effect upon the audience. It implies that the wide variety of codes all cohere to present a unified set of meanings that work to maintain, legitimate, and naturalize the dominant ideology of patriarchal capitalism. Their ideological effectivity appears irresistible, [although I do not think it is, and argue elsewhere why it is not (Fiske 1987b, chs. 5 and 6).] For the moment, however, it serves to demonstrate that popular television is both complex and deeply infused with ideology.

REFERENCES

Althusser, L. (1971) 'Ideology and Ideological State Apparatuses' in *Lenin and Philosophy and Other Essays*, New York and London: Monthly Review Press, 127–86.
Berger, J. (1972) *Ways of Seeing*, Harmondsworth: Penguin.
Berne, E. (1964) *Games People Play: the Psychology of Human Relationships*, Harmondsworth: Penguin.
Bourdieu, P. (1968) 'Outline of a Sociological Theory of Art Perception', *International Social Sciences Journal* 2: 225–54.
Dorfman, A. and Mattelart, A. (1975) *How to Read Donald Duck*, New York: International General.
Fiske, J. (1982) *Introduction to Communication Studies*, London: Methuen.
Fiske, J. (1983) 'The Discourses of TV Quiz Shows or School + Luck = Success + Sex, *Central States Speech Journal* 34, 139–50.
Fiske, J. (1984) 'Popularity and ideology: A Structuralist Reading of Dr Who' in W. Rowland and B. Watkins (eds) (1984) *Interpreting Television: Current Research Perspectives*, Beverley Hills: Sage, 165–98.
Fiske, J. (1986) 'Television: Polysemy and Popularity,' *Critical Studies in Mass Communication* 3:4, 391–408.
Fiske, J. (1987a) 'British Cultural Studies' in R. Allen (ed.) (1987) *Channels of Discourse: Television and Contemporary Criticism*, Chapel Hill: University of North Carolina Press, 254–89.
Fiske, J. (1987b) *Television Culture*, London and New York: Methuen.
Fiske, J. and Hartley, J. (1978) *Reading Television*, London: Methuen.
Gerbner, G. (1970) 'Cultural Indicators: the Case of Violence in Television Drama,' *Annals of the American Association of Political and Social Science* 338, 69–81.
Goffman, E. (1979) *Gender Advertisements*, London: Macmillan.
Hogben, A. (1982) 'Journalists as Bad Apples,' *Quadrant*, January/February, 38–43.
O'Sullivan, T., Hartley, J., Saunders, D., and Fiske, J. (1983) *Key Concepts in Communication*, London: Methuen.

16

PROGRAMMING AS SEQUENCE OR FLOW

Raymond Williams

[. . .]

In all developed broadcasting systems the characteristic organisation, and therefore the characteristic experience, is one of sequence or flow. This phenomenon, of planned flow, is then perhaps the defining characteristic of broadcasting, simultaneously as a technology and as a cultural form.

In all communications systems before broadcasting the essential items were discrete. A book or a pamphlet was taken and read as a specific item. A meeting occurred at a particular date and place. A play was performed in a particular theatre at a set hour. The difference in broadcasting is not only that these events, or events resembling them, are available inside the home, by the operation of a switch. It is that the real programme that is offered is a *sequence* or set of alternative sequences of these and other similar events, which are then available in a single dimension and in a single operation.

Yet we have become so used to this that in a way we do not see it. Most of our habitual vocabulary of response and description has been shaped by the experience of discrete events. We have developed ways of responding to a particular book or a particular play, drawing on our experience of other books and plays. When we go out to a meeting or a concert or a game we take other experience with us and we return to other experience, but the specific event is ordinarily an occasion, setting up its own internal conditions and responses. Our most general modes of comprehension and judgment are then closely linked to these kinds of specific and isolated, temporary, forms of attention.

Some earlier kinds of communication contained, it is true, internal variation and at times miscellaneity. Dramatic performances included musical interludes, or the main play was preceded by a curtain-raiser. In print there are such characteristic forms as the almanac and the chapbook, which include items relating to very different kinds of interest and involving quite different kinds of response. The magazine, invented as a specific form in the early

From Raymond Williams, *Television: Technology and Cultural Form* (London: Fontana, 1974) pp. 86–96.

eighteenth century, was designed as a miscellany, mainly for a new and expanding and culturally inexperienced middle-class audience. The modern newspaper, from the eighteenth century but very much more markedly from the nineteenth century, became a miscellany, not only of news items that were often essentially unrelated, but of features, anecdotes, drawings, photographs and advertisements. From the late nineteenth century this came to be reflected in formal layout, culminating in the characteristic jigsaw effect of the modern newspaper page. Meanwhile, sporting events, especially football matches, as they became increasingly important public occasions, included entertainment such as music or marching in their intervals.

This general trend, towards an increasing variability and miscellaneity of public communications, is evidently part of a whole social experience. It has profound connections with the growth and development of greater physical and social mobility, in conditions both of cultural expansion and of consumer rather than community cultural organisation. Yet until the coming of broadcasting the normal expectation was still of a discrete event or of a succession of discrete events. People took a book or a pamphlet or a newspaper, went out to a play or a concert or a meeting or a match, with a single predominant expectation and attitude. The social relationships set up in these various cultural events were specific and in some degree temporary.

Broadcasting, in its earliest stages, inherited this tradition and worked mainly within it. Broadcasters discovered the kinds of thing they could do or, as some of them would still normally say, transmit. The musical concert could be broadcast or arranged for broadcasting. The public address – the lecture or the sermon, the speech at a meeting – could be broadcast as a talk. The sports match could be described and shown. The play could be performed, in this new theatre of the air. Then as the service extended, these items, still considered as discrete units, were assembled into programmes. The word 'programme' is characteristic, with its traditional bases in theatre and music-hall. With increasing organisation, as the service extended, this 'programme' became a series of timed units. Each unit could be thought of discretely, and the work of programming was a serial assembly of these units. Problems of mix and proportion became predominant in broadcasting policy. Characteristically, as most clearly in the development of British sound broadcasting, there was a steady evolution from a general service, with its internal criteria of mix and proportion and what was called 'balance', to contrasting types of service, alternative programmes. 'Home', 'Light' and 'Third', in British radio, were the eventual names for what were privately described and indeed generally understood as 'general', 'popular' and 'educated' broadcasting. Problems of mix and proportion, formerly considered within a single service, were then basically transferred to a range of alternative programmes, corresponding to assumed social and educational levels. This tendency was taken further in later forms of reorganisation, as in the present specialised British radio services One to Four. In an American radio programme listing, which is before me as I write, there is a further specialisation: the predominantly musical programmes are briefly characterised, by wavelength, as 'rock', 'country', 'classical', 'nostalgic' and so on. In one sense this can be traced as a development of programming: extensions of the service have brought further degrees of rationalisation and specialisation.

But the development can also be seen, and in my view needs to be seen, in quite other ways. There has been a significant shift from the concept of sequence as *programming* to the concept of sequence as *flow*. Yet this is difficult to see because the older concept of programming – the temporal sequence within which mix and proportion and balance operate – is still active and still to some extent real.

What is it then that has been decisively altered? A broadcasting programme, on sound or television, is still formally a series of timed units. What is published as information about the broadcasting services is still of this kind: we can look up the time of a particular 'show' or 'programme'; we can turn on for that item; we can select and respond to it discretely.

Yet for all the familiarity of this model, the normal experience of broadcasting, when we really consider it, is different. And indeed this is recognised in the ways we speak of 'watching television', 'listening to the radio', picking on the general rather than the specific experience. This has been true of all broadcasting, but some significant internal developments have greatly reinforced it. These developments can be indicated in one simple way. In earlier phases of the broadcasting service, both in sound and television, there were *intervals* between programme units: true intervals, usually marked by some conventional sound or picture to show that the general service was still active. There was the sound of bells or the sight of waves breaking, and these marked the intervals between discrete programme units. There is still a residual example of this type in the turning globe which functions as an interval signal in BBC television.

But in most television services, as they are currently operated, the concept of the interval – though still, for certain purposes, retained as a concept – has been fundamentally revalued. This change came about in two ways, which are still unevenly represented in different services. The decisive innovation was in services financed by commercial television. There was a specific and formal undertaking that 'programmes' should not be interrupted by advertising; this could take place only in 'natural breaks': between the movements of a symphony, or between the acts in *Hamlet*, as the Government spokesman said in the House of Lords! In practice, of course, this was never complied with, nor was it ever intended that it should be. A 'natural break' became any moment of convenient insertion. News programmes, plays, even films that had been shown in cinemas as specific whole performances, began to be interrupted for commercials. On American television this development was different; the sponsored programmes incorporated the advertising from the outset, from the initial conception, as part of the whole package. But it is now obvious, in both British and American commercial television, that the notion of 'interruption', while it has still some residual force from an older model, has become inadequate. What is being offered is not, in older terms, a programme of discrete units with particular insertions, but a planned flow, in which the true series is not the published sequence of programme items but this sequence transformed by the inclusion of another kind of sequence, so that these sequences together compose the real flow, the real 'broadcasting'. Increasingly, in both commercial and public-service television, a further sequence was added: trailers of programmes to be shown at some later time or on some later day, or more itemised programme news. This was intensified in conditions of competition, when it became important to broadcasting planners to retain viewers – or as they put it, to 'capture' them – for a whole evening's sequence. And with the eventual unification of these two or three sequences, a new kind of communication phenomenon has to be recognised.

Of course many people who watch television still register some of these items as 'interruptions'. I remember first noticing the problem while watching films on British commercial television. For even in an institution as wholeheartedly commercial in production and distribution as the cinema, it had been possible, and indeed remains normal, to watch a film as a whole, in an undisturbed sequence. All films were originally made and distributed in this way, though the inclusion of supporting 'B' films and short features in a package, with appropriate intervals for advertising and for the planned selling of refreshments, began to develop the cinema towards the new kind of planned flow. Watching the same films on commercial television made the new situation quite evident. We are normally given some twenty or twenty-five minutes of the film, to get us interested in it; then four minutes of commercials, then about fifteen more minutes of the film; some commercials again; and so on to steadily decreasing lengths of the film, with commercials between them, or them between the commercials, since by this time it is assumed that we are interested and will watch the film to the end. Yet even this had not prepared me for the characteristic American sequence. One night in Miami, still dazed from a week on an Atlantic liner, I began watching a film and at first had some difficulty in adjusting to a much greater frequency of commercial 'breaks'. Yet this was a minor problem compared to what eventually happened. Two other films, which were due to be shown on the same channel on other nights, began to be inserted as trailers. A crime in San Francisco (the subject of the original film) began to operate in an extraordinary counterpoint not only with the deodorant and cereal commercials but with a romance in Paris and the eruption of a prehistoric monster who laid waste New York. Moreover, this was sequence in a new sense. Even in commercial British television there is a visual signal – the residual sign of an interval – before and after the commercial sequences, and 'programme' trailers only occur between 'programmes'. Here there was something quite different, since the transitions from film to commercial and from film A to films B and C were in effect unmarked. There is in any case enough similarity between certain kinds of films, and between several kinds of film and the 'situation' commercials which often consciously imitate them, to make a sequence of this kind a very difficult experience to interpret. I can still not be sure what I took from that whole flow. I believe I registered some incidents as happening in the wrong film, and some characters in the commercials as involved in the film episodes, in what came to seem – for all the occasional bizarre disparities – a single irresponsible flow of images and feelings.

Of course the films were not made to be 'interrupted' in this way. But this flow is planned: not only in itself, but at an early stage in all original television production for commercial systems. Indeed most commercial television 'programmes' are made, from the planning stage, with this real sequence in mind. In quite short plays there is a rationalised division into 'acts'. In features there is a similar rationalised division into 'parts'. But the effect goes deeper. There is a characteristic kind of opening sequence, meant to excite interest, which is in effect a kind of trailer for itself. In American television, after two or three minutes, this is succeeded by commericals. The technique has an early precedent in the dumbshows which preceded plays or scenes in early Elizabethan theatre. But there what followed dumbshow was the play or the scene. Here what follows is apparently quite unconnected material. It is then not surprising that so many of these opening moments are violent or bizarre: the interest aroused must be strong enough to initiate the expectation of (interrupted but sustainable) sequence. Thus a quality of the external sequence becomes a mode of definition of an internal method.

At whatever stage of development this process has reached – and it is still highly variable between different broadcasting systems – it can still be residually seen as 'interruption' of a 'programme'. Indeed it is often important to see it as this, both for one's own true sense of place and event, and as a matter of reasonable concern in broadcasting policy. Yet it may be even more important to see the true process as flow: the replacement of a programme series of timed sequential units by a flow series of differently related units in which the timing, though real, is undeclared, and in which the real internal organisation is something other than the declared organisation.

For the 'interruptions' are in one way only the most visible characteristic of a process which at some levels has come to define the television experience. Even when, as on the BBC, there are no interruptions of specific 'programme units', there is a quality of flow which our received vocabulary of discrete response and description cannot easily acknowledge. It is evident that what is now called 'an evening's viewing' is in some ways planned, by providers and then by viewers, *as a whole*; that it is in any event planned in discernible sequences which in this sense override particular programme units. Whenever there is competition between television channels, this becomes a matter of conscious concern: to get viewers in at the beginning of a flow. Thus in Britain there is intense competition between BBC and IBA in the early evening programmes, in the belief – which some statistics support – that viewers will stay with whatever channel they begin watching. There are of course many cases in which this does not happen: people can consciously select another channel or another programme, or switch off altogether. But the flow effect is sufficiently widespread to be a major element in programming policy. And this is the immediate reason for the increasing frequency of programming trailers: to sustain that evening flow. In conditions of more intense competition, as between the American channels, there is even more frequent trailing, and the process is specifically referred to as 'moving along', to sustain what is thought of as a kind of brand-loyalty to the channel being watched. Some part of the flow offered is then directly traceable to conditions of controlled competition, just as some of its specific original elements are traceable to the financing of television by commercial advertising.

Yet this is clearly not the whole explanation. The flow offered can also, and perhaps more fundamentally, be related to the television experience itself. Two common observations bear on this. As has already been noted, most of us say, in describing the experience, that we have been 'watching television', rather than that we have watched 'the news' or 'a play' or 'the football' 'on television'. Certainly we sometimes say both, but the fact that we say the former at all is already significant. Then again it is a widely if often ruefully admitted experience that many of us find television very difficult to switch off; that again and again, even when we have switched on for a particular 'programme', we find ourselves watching the one after it and the one after that. The way in which the flow is now organised, without definite intervals, in any case encourages this. We can be 'into' something else before we have summoned the energy to get out of the chair, and many programmes are made with this situation in mind: the grabbing of attention in the early moments; the reiterated promise of exciting things to come, if we stay.

But the impulse to go on watching seems more widespread than this kind of organisation would alone explain. It is significant that there has been steady pressure, not only from the television providers but from many viewers, for an extension of viewing hours. In Britain, until recently, television was basically an evening experience, with some brief offerings in the middle of the day, and with morning and afternoon hours, except at weekends, used for schools and similar broadcasting. There is now a rapid development of morning and afternoon 'programmes' of a general kind. In the United States it is already possible to begin watching at six o'clock in the morning, see one's first movie at eight-thirty, and so on in a continuous flow, with the screen never blank, until the late movie begins at one o'clock the following morning. It is scarcely possible that many people watch a flow of that length, over more than twenty hours of the day. But the flow is always accessible, in several alternative sequences, at the flick of a switch. Thus, both internally, in its immediate organisation, and as a generally available experience, this characteristic of flow seems central.

Yet it is a characteristic for which hardly any of our received modes of observation and description prepare us. The reviewing of television programmes is of course of uneven quality, but in most even of the best reviews there is a conventional persistence from earlier models. Reviewers pick out this play or that feature, this discussion programme or that documentary. I reviewed television once a month over four years, and I know how much more settling, more straightforward, it is to do that. For most of the items there are some received procedures, and the method, the vocabulary, for a specific kind of description and response exists or can be adapted. Yet while that kind of reviewing can be useful, it is always at some distance from what seems to me the central television experience: the fact of flow. It is not only that many particular items – given our ordinary organisation of response, memory and persistence of attitude and mood – are affected by those preceding and those following them, unless we watch in an artificially timed way which seems to be quite rare (though it exists in the special viewings put on for regular Reviewers). It is also that though useful things may be said about all the separable items (though often with conscious exclusion of the commercials which 'interrupt' at least half of them) hardly anything is ever said about the characteristic experience of the flow sequence itself. It is indeed very difficult to say anything about this. It would be like trying to describe having read two plays, three newspapers, three or four magazines, on the same day that one has been to a variety show and a lecture and a football match. And yet in another way it is not like that at all, for though the items may be various the television experience has in some important ways unified them. To break this experience back into units, and to write about the units for which there are readily available procedures, is understandable but often misleading, even when we defend it by the gesture that we are discriminating and experienced viewers and don't just sit there hour after hour goggling at the box.

For the fact is that many of us do sit there, and much of the critical significance of television must be related to this fact. I know that whenever I tried, in reviewing, to describe the experience of flow, on a particular evening or more generally, what I could say was unfinished and tentative, yet I learned from correspondence that I was engaging with an experience which many viewers were aware of and were trying to understand. There can be 'classical' kinds of response, at many different levels, to some though not all of the discrete units. But we are only just beginning to recognise, let alone solve, the problems of description and response to the facts of flow.

17

BROADCAST TV NARRATION

John Ellis

Commercial entertainment cinema is overwhelmingly a narrative fiction medium. Non-fiction films have always had a precarious place in the commercial cinema, and nowadays they are practically non-existent. Broadcast TV on the other hand carries large amounts of non-fiction: news, documentaries, announcements, weather forecasts, various kinds of segments that are purely televisual in their characteristic forms. It could be argued, therefore, that any model of televisual narration would have to give pride of place to this division of TV products between fiction and non-fiction. Whereas the classical narrative model, basically a fiction model, still underlies our assumptions about the entertainment film, it would seem that no such generalised conception of TV narration would be possible. In fact, this does not seem to be the case. Quite the reverse, the non-fiction and fiction modes of exposition of meanings seem to have converged within TV, under the impulsion of the characteristic broadcast TV forms of the segment and the series, and the pervasive sense of the TV image as live. This has produced a distinctive regime of fictional narration on TV which owes much to its non-fictional modes. After all, the first true use of the open-ended series format would seem to be the news bulletin, endlessly updating events and never synthesising them.

The mode of narration on TV does not have to be divided into two distinct models, one appropriate to fiction, the other to non-fiction. Instead, one model seems to be enough, a model that is capable of inflection by fictional or non-fictional concerns. This explains the case that TV has long since had of producing programmes that are ambiguous in their status: the documentary-drama, or the drama-documentary, forms that seem to have existed in the late 1950s at least on the BBC. The divisions between fiction and non-fiction exist at another level to that of narration; they are chiefly concerned with the origin of material used in the programme.

Any model of narration on broadcast TV therefore has to be based on the particular institutional and material nature of that TV as we now know it. It depends on the conception of the broadcast output as that of segment following segment, segments which by no means

From John Ellis, *Visible Fictions: Cinema, Television, Video* (London: Rentledge & Kegan Paul, 1982) ch. 9.

always have any connection between them. It depends on the counterpart to this segmental process, the programme series with its distinctive forms of repetition and favoured forms of problematic. It depends on the conception of TV as a casual, domestic form, watched without great intensity or continuity of attention. It assumes the ideology of TV as a medium which transmits events as they happen, even though (especially in Britain) this is virtually never the case. It is worth repeating in this connection that, although the overwhelming mass of TV output is recorded, it still carries a different sense of immediacy from the cinematic image. Broadcast TV is capable of adopting a filmic mode of narration as a kind of borrowing from an already established medium. This will almost always be announced as such: by the form of the TV movie (often a 'pilot' for a series), or by the designation of a programme as a prestigious cultural event. This tends to mean that the programme will not so much have been made on film as made within a cinematic mode of narration. In this sense, TV acknowledges a certain inferiority to cinema. Cinema, for TV, means the culturally respectable, the artistic text. The designation 'film' for a TV transmission indicates that this transmission is to be viewed despite TV; it is not to be segmented, interruptions in terms of advertisements breaks or viewer attention 'at home' are to be kept to a minimum. The 'film' transmission on TV will then proceed to construct a more cinematic narration. The vast majority of such events, indeed, are cinema films which have already been exhibited in a cinematic context. Cinema is currently not capable of a similar borrowing of broadcast TV forms, however: the collective exhibition of TV material is still a novelty or an aberration.

Cinema narration has a strong internal dynamic, a movement from an initial equilibrium that is disrupted towards a new harmony that is the end of the fiction. Broadcast TV narration has a more dispersed narrational form: it is extensive rather than sequential. Its characteristic mode is not one of final closure or totalising vision; rather, it offers a continuous refiguration of events. Like the news bulletin series, the broadcast TV narrative (fiction and non-fiction) is open-ended, providing a continuous update, a perpetual return to the present. Since closure and finality is not a central feature of TV narration (though it does occur in specific major ways), it follows that the hermetic nature of the cinema narrative, with its patterns of repetition and novelty, is also absent. Repetition in the TV narrative occurs at the level of the series: formats are repeated, situations return week after week. Each time there is novelty. The characters of the situation comedy encounter a new dilemma; the documentary reveals a new problem; the news gives us a fresh strike, a new government, another earthquake, the first panda born in captivity. This form of repetition is different from that offered by the classic cinema narrative, as it provides a kind of groundbase, a constant basis for events, rather than an economy of reuse directed towards a final totalisation.

The series is composed of segments. The recognition of the series format tends to hold segments together and to provide them with an element of continuity and narrative progression from one to the next. The segment form itself has a strong internal coherence. Certain forms of segments are free-standing: the spot advertisement and the item in the news bulletin are both examples. They occur alongside similar segments which have no connection with them except a similarity of class. Other segments, those in a documentary exposition of a particular situation, or a frictional depiction of characters, will have definite connections of a narrative kind. But again, the movement from event to event is not as concentrated and causal as it tends to be in classic cinema narration. Broadcast TV's fictional segments tend to explore states and incidents in real time, avoiding the abbreviation that is characteristic of cinema. Hence a certain sense of intimacy in TV drama, a different pace and attention from entertainment cinema.

The segment is self-contained in TV production partly because of the fragmentary nature of much broadcast TV (especially if it carries spot advertising), but also because of the attention span that TV assumes of its audience, and the fact that memory of the particular series in all its detail cannot be assumed. People switch on in the middle and get hooked; they miss an episode or two; someone phones up in the middle. The TV production cannot be hermetic in the way that the film text is, otherwise the audience for a long-running soap opera like *Coronation Street* would now consist of half a dozen ageing addicts. The segment and the series are the repository of memory, and thus of the possibility of repetition and coherence.

The segment is a relatively self-contained scene which conveys an incident, a mood or a particular meaning. Coherence is provided by a continuity of character through the segment, or, more occasionally, a continuity of place. Hence many fictional segments consist of conversations between two or three characters, an encounter which produces a particular mood (embarrassment, relief, anger, love-at-first-sight, insults, anxiety) and tends to deliver a particular meaning which is often encapsulated in a final line. The segment ends and, in conventional TV fiction, is succeeded by another which deals with a different set of (related) characters in a different place, or the same characters at a different time. There is a marked break between segments. The aspect of break, of end and beginning, tends to outweigh the aspect of continuity and consequence. The non-fiction segment tends to operate in the same way, though in the expository or investigatory documentary it is a series of fragments (interviews, stills, captions, studio presenters, reporter-to-camera in locations) which are held together as a segment by the fact that they all combine to deliver a particular message. Each segment then represents a 'move' in the argument of the overall programme. In both drama and investigatory documentary, the segment is relatively self-contained and usually does not last longer than five minutes.

Being self-contained, the segment tends to exhaust its material, providing its own climax which is the culmination of the material of the segment. It is a characteristic of soap operas that they withhold the climactic revelation or action to the end of the segment and the end of the episode. [. . .] This process of climaxing directly followed by a break to other forms of segments (title sequences, advertisements, programme announcements, etc.) generates a series of segments in the next episode which effectively chart the repercussions of the climactic event. A series of conversations and actions exhaustively explores and, in the process, re-capitulates the climactic action or revelation. The discovery of a husband's affair is followed by a rush of disconnected segments, adverts and so on; a week's wait produces a series of conversations: wife to friend, children, neighbours; husband to lover, colleague; and perhaps even The Couple themselves. Each depicts a certain attitude and mood, produces subsidiary revelations and mulls over the situation. These segments are self-exhausting: enough is said, done and shown to convey a particular meaning. This completion and internal coherence means that movement from one segment to the next is a matter of succession rather than consequence.

This effect of the self-containedness of the segment is intensified, especially in fiction and observational documentary work, by the use of real time. Where cinema elides actions within a scene by cutting out 'dead time' (a character's movement across a room that has no directly narrative function, for example), TV tends to leave this 'dead time' in. This stems directly from the studio multiple camera technique, where events are staged in temporal sequence and picked up by a number of cameras one of whose images is selected at any one moment by the director. Where cinema stages events in a very fragmentary way (sometimes just a gesture, a look), TV will stage much more like a theatrical scene. The result is that events unroll in real time for the audience, in the time that they took. A segment will tend to hold to temporal unity, especially if it is a conversation. This produces a sense of intimacy within the segment, and a sharp break between segments.

[. . .]

The narrative movement between segments does not follow the cinematic pattern of a relatively rapid transition from event to event in causal sequence. The movement from event to event is more circumspect. This circumspection shows itself in two ways. The first is the multiplication of incidents whose consequences and conclusion are suspended. This is a characteristic of the TV action series like the cop saga *Starsky and Hutch*. Our heroes perpetually encounter fresh incidents, and equally often find themselves suspended in an ambiguous position at the end of a segment (cue for commercial break). The second form of circumspect movement from event to event is that characterised by the soap opera and the drama alike. Events are at a premium: when they occur they generate tidal waves of verbiage, of gossip, discussion, speculation, recrimination. Guilt, jealousy, worry and an immense curiosity about people is generated by this form. The action series tends to generate car journeys, car chases, interrogations and the segment that reveals the furtive goings-on that the action-heroes will head off.

In each form, the events that take place are anticipated. For the soap opera/drama, the deliciousness of the anticipation is worth in many instances more than the event itself. Speculation abounds; the event is perfunctory; the mulling over of the repercussions is extended. But it is a characteristic of the action series too that it carries few surprises. Its form of suspense is more incidental. Rather than proposing a central 'whodunnit' problem, it is more characteristic to find the central mystery revealed fairly early in the programme. Suspense then becomes a serial affair: the heroes and villains become entangled in a series of different situations, each of which involves escape, chase, shoot-out, etc. Narration in the cinematic sense is relatively perfunctory. Little play is made with the fact that the solution to the 'whodunnit' has been revealed to audience before it has to the heroes. This differential knowledge and analytic attitude to the actions of the heroes, characteristic of a cinema director like Fritz Lang (who usually reveals the narrative enigma to the audience), is relatively absent.

[. . .]

The unifying principle behind TV programmes is not as it is in cinema (significant patterns of repetition and innovation of meanings; narrative sequence; central problematic); it is the series which provides coherence between segments. The series provides the unity of a particular programme, pulling together segments into a sense of connection which enables a level of narrative progression to take place between them. The series is the major point of repetition in TV, matching the innovation that takes place within each segment. This pattern of repetition and innovation is very different from the cinematic model. Where the cinematic form is a closed system which aims to reuse as much material as possible and to balance kinds of repetition and innovation against each other, the TV form is more open-ended. It is a pattern of repetition that is far more centred on the narrative problematic than in cinema. Cinema's single texts tend to inaugurate a novel problematic, a new story subject, for each film. The TV series repeats a problematic. It therefore provides no resolution of the problematic at the end of each episode, nor, often, even at the end of the run of a series. Hence again the reduction of onward narrative progression. The TV series proposes a problematic that is not resolved; narrative resolution takes place at a less fundamental level, at the level of the particular incidents (clinches, confrontations, conversations) that are offered each week (in the case of situation comedies) or between one week and the next (with the cliff-hanger serial ending). Fundamentally, the series implies the form of the dilemma rather than that of resolution and closure. This perhaps is the central contribution that broadcast TV has made to the long history of narrative forms and narrativised perception of the world.

The series is based on the repetition of a problematic. It repeats a situation, a situation which can be fictional or non-fictional. Hence the news series and the current affairs series both present a certain inquiring, fact-finding vision: the situation of reporters observing and collating information, then organising it for presentation to an uninformed public. This is as much a situation as a father and son running a scrap business with a totter's horse and cart and a crowded London yard (*Steptoe and Son*). The news and current affairs series present a problematic of vision and of explanation. Specific characters encounter a specific set of circumstances every week. But across the specificity of the week's circumstances runs the generality of the same problematic: that of how to see, how to understand. The terms of the understanding are always specified by the programme format. It will be 'we go behind the scenes' (*Panorama*), 'we ask the awkward questions' (*World in Action*), 'we update and see how this affects London' (*The London Programme*), 'we glance around' (*Nationwide*). In addition to these specific forms of understanding, there are the terms in which these understandings are cast: 'moderate/extremist', 'the housewife', 'But surely you don't think that . . . ?' The role of presenter is fundamental to these operations. The characters who investigate and explain for us are a loose group remarkably similar to the cast of a soap opera: some are central, long-running figures (presenters, anchor-persons); others come and go (reporters). In some areas of current affairs, the soap opera aspect becomes more or less explicit. *Nationwide* and *That's Life* are specific examples. The series format constitutes a stable basis of repetition in the programme format, its cast of characters, and its particular kind of reporting attention. Novelty in each edition is provided by the specific circumstances that these characters and their vision run up against. It is often explicit that the particular focus of attention for the characters is provided by outside forces over which they have no control, the world of current events. This world tends to be constituted as a place where problems occur. The political actions that the current events series is constituted to explain thus become a particular modality of action: they are problems, troubles, disturbances. The current events series provides a security against these disturbances. The result is that the political arena tends to be given the same status as the emotional problems encountered by soap opera characters. This is one effect of the series format, and one aspect of it.

The fictional series, too, repeats a basic problematic or situation week after week. Like the news and current affairs series, the situation comedy, the crime drama and the hospital series all return to the stability of the basic dilemma at the end of the week's episode. There is no development at all across the series. The serial marks a long slow narrative movement towards a conclusion, but often that conclusion is tentative (allowing a second series) or incidental (the dispersion of the characters). The situation that provides the steady core is a state of permanent or semi-permanent relationships between a stable but antagonistic group of characters. This is most fully developed in the situation comedy. *Steptoe and Son* may well hate each other, but they also love each other, and Harold's repeated threats to leave his father were never serious. This is exactly the dilemma that situation comedy deals with: it presents conflicting forces or emotions that can never be resolved. Hence the series situation is highly suited to present a particular static vision of the family and of work relations. What is particularly marked about the situation series is that the characters lose all memory of the previous week's incidents. They never learn.

[. . .]

Repetition across the series is one of problematic, of both characters and the situation (or dilemma) in which they find themselves. These situations provide a steady state to which audience and fiction return each week. Specific incidents are fed into this steady state, to provide fresh ammunition for our embattled family to fire at each other and the world, or for our reporters to look into and arrange for our inspection and concern. The incidental problems are solved, but the series format provides no real place for its own resolution. There is no final closure to the series' own recurring problematic. The run of a series ends without resolving its basic dilemma. This marks a basic difference between the cinema narrative and the TV series narrative. The film text aims for a final coherent totalising vision, which sets everything back into order. The series does not share this movement from stable state to stable state. The basic problematic of the series, with all its conflicts, is itself a stable state.

[. . .]

Further Reading

Barthes, R., *Elements of Semiology*, transl. A. Lavers and C. Smith (London: Jonathan Cape, 1967); Orig. 1964.

Barthes, R., *Image–Music–Text*, transl. S. Heath (Glasgow: Fontana/William Collins, 1977).

Burgelin, O., 'Structural Analysis and Mass Communication', in McQuail, D. (ed.), *Sociology of Mass Communications* (Harmondsworth: Penguin Books, 1972).

Eco, U., 'Towards a Semiotic Inquiry into the Television Message', WPCS no. 3 (1972); and Corner, J. and Hawthorn, J. (eds), *Communication Studies: An Introductory Reader* (London: Edward Arnold, 1980).

Ellis, J., *Visible Fictions: Cinema, Television, Video* (London: Routledge & Kegan Paul, 1982).

Fiske, J., *Introduction to Communication Studies* (London: Methuen, 1982).

Fiske, J. and Hartley, J., *Reading Television* (London: Methuen, 1978).

Hartley, J., *Understanding News* (London: Metheun, 1982).

Hawkes, T., *Structuralism and Semiotics* (London: Methuen, 1977).

Heath, S. and Skirrow, G., 'Television: A World in Action', *Screen* 18:2 (1977) pp. 7–59.

Screen Education no. 20 (1976). Special issue on '*The Sweeney*': TV Crime Series'.

Woollacott, J., 'Messages and Meanings', in Gurevitch, M., Bennett, T., Curran, J. and Woollacott, J. (eds), *Culture, Society and the Media* (London: Methuen, 1982).

Text
Ideology and Genre

TEXT: IDEOLOGY AND GENRE

Much of the thinking about the media has concerned itself with the connection between the media as institutions with social power and the ideas that they circulate. In the tradition that has developed in Britain, the term 'ideology' has come to play a substantial role in articulating this relationship. The concept of ideology, taken generally from Marxism, was given an influential inflection by the French philosopher Louis Althusser, and although his use of the term has not survived unmodified, it still underlies most of the ways in which it is employed.[1] 'Ideologies' rather than 'ideas' is used to bring out several significant aspects. It loses the association of individually generated notions that can adhere to 'ideas', in order to stress the social, transindividual nature of the thinking that circulates. It carries the consideration that *clusters* of *interlinked* ideas are being referred to: 'ideologies do not consist of isolated and separate concepts, but in the articulation of different elements into a distinctive set or chain of meanings', as Stuart Hall expresses it in Chapter 18. And most importantly, it is intended to convey the fact that in an unequal society ideas and clusters of ideas are inevitably implicated in the differential allocation and operation of social power and the struggles over this, even though it may not be their manifest focus.

Stuart Hall's abridged essay (Chapter 18) begins with some useful general points about ideologies and the media, and then discusses racist ideology in the British media in particular. He discerns two major streams of racist ideology, which he calls the 'overt' and the 'inferential'. These roughly correspond to the right-wing and the liberal. He points to the fact that British imperial culture has provided a capacious repertoire of racist elements available for remobilisation, reworking and recombining by the media. Not surprisingly, the essay bears the traces of the historical moment of its composition (1979–81), and it provokes consideration of how racist ideology has evolved over the intervening period, of the nature of the ideologies operative in a changed political conjuncture.

Hall's essay ranges over a number of media (popular literature, films, newspapers, television), but also refers to several 'genres': news, situation comedy, current affairs. 'Genre' is literally French for kind or type; in the study of media and popular culture it refers to the subsets into which the output can be classified, the various kinds or types of content or material. Thus amongst magazines there are women's magazines, current affairs magazines, computer magazines; television genres include police series, sports programmes, game shows and documentaries. Discussion of two further genres – soap operas and news bulletins – appears in Part Two of this book. Janet Woollacott's Chapter 19 is devoted to the television genre of situation comedy. She is partly concerned to develop a view of how sitcoms differ from other genres, and finds a distinct kind of narrative, that lacks 'progression' and tends towards a different kind of resolution or (temporary) closure. Given this tendency to return to the 'situation', combined with the use of stereotyping, leads to the question of whether the humour is necessarily ideologically reactionary. Does it serve to reconcile people to their conditions of social existence? Or is it a cultural vehicle for resisting grim conformism and symbolically defying social power? Woollacott's response is that examination of the text alone cannot reveal the answer to this, and suggests that it will partly depend on the nature of the connections between the ideology of the particular sitcom and the conjuncturally important ideologies circulating elsewhere in society, including in other media and other genres. This question, and its answer, can be seen to be underpinned by the Gramscian version of Marxism that Stuart Hall has done so much to introduce within British cultural studies. Indeed, Woollacott explicitly references a collaborative work (*Policing the Crisis*, 1978) in which Hall had participated, and from which 'The Social Production of News' in Part Two is taken (Chapter 44). The other part of her answer – that it will depend on the 'reading formations' which viewers inhabit – has affinities with the work of David Morley (see Chapter 31) as well as drawing explicitly on the work of Tony Bennett.[2]

John Caughie (Chapter 20) takes for discussion a genre in which British television produced artistically acclaimed work in the 1960s and 1970s, the documentary drama. Because of the prestige – borrowed from the British theatre – accorded to the authorial figure of the dramatist, and the prestige – borrowed from the British 'quality' film tradition – accorded to realism and documentary, it was the production and availability of these works that gave the study of television some of its initial footholds within formal education. Caughie is writing in the wake of a notorious debate between Colin McArthur and Colin McCabe[3] over the documentary drama *Days of Hope*,[4] which pivoted on whether the realist mode of the series mitigated against its political progressiveness or not. Through his discussion of naturalist aesthetics, and of the play of looks within the documentary drama, Caughie explores the issues for the genre in detail. The chapter illustrates how many of the questions and approaches for media studies regarding the interrelationship of style, genre and ideology were influenced by work in film studies.

Broadcast TV has areas which tend towards the cinematic, especially the areas of serious drama or of various kinds of TV film. But many of TV's characteristic broadcast forms rely upon sound as the major carrier of information . . .[5] Whereas Chapter 20 deals with a genre that tends towards the cinematic, Chapter 21 is concerned with a broadcast genre that reflects television's love of talk, the chat show. Andrew Tolson's (Chapter 21) illustrates how, for television talk, detailed analysis of the verbal track is highly illuminating.[6] Tolson demonstrates that in a genre centred on personality, the *performance* of personality has increasingly become the manifest content. The former kind of chat show that probed for the authentic personality has tended to be replaced by one that proffers the display of the synthetic personality. The piece usefully draws attention to a generic shift, one which seems consonant with some characterisations of the postmodern (though Tolson eschews this conclusion).[7]

NOTES

1.   Louis Althusser, 'Ideology and Ideological State Apparatusses', in id., *Lenin and Philosophy and Other Essays*, trans. Ben Brewster (London: New Left Books, 1971).

2.   Tony Bennett, 'Text, Readers, Reading Formations', *Literature and History* 9:2 (1983) pp. 214–27.

3.   Colin McArthur, 'Days of Hope', *Screen* 16:4 (1975–6) pp. 139–44; Colin MacCabe, 'Days of Hope – a Response to Colin McArthur', *Screen* 17:1 (1976) pp. 98–101. The debate is available in Tony Bennett, Susan Boyd-Bowman, Colin Mercer, Janet Woollacott (eds), *Popular Television and Film* (London: British Film Institute/The Open University Press, 1981).

4. *Days of Hope* (BBC, 1975, 4 episodes), prod. Tony Garnett, sc. Jim Allen, dir. Ken Loach. The series dramatised the related stories of three fictional English working-class characters from the imposition of wartime conscription in 1916 to the General Strike of 1926.

5. John Ellis, *Visible Fictions: Cinema, Television, Video*, 1st edn (London: Routledge & Kegan Paul, 1982).

6. An early example of this is Stuart Hall, Ian Connell, Lidia Curti, 'The "Unity" of Current Affairs Television', *Working Papers in Cultural Studies* 9 (1976) which examines a 1974 edition of *Panorama*.

7. In the full version of the article from which Chapter 21 is extracted, Tolson writes 'I am not going to argue here that . . . we have moved into some kind of "postmodern" world where people no longer speak honestly or sincerely, or where experience is no longer taken to be a source of truth.'

18

RACIST IDEOLOGIES AND THE MEDIA

Stuart Hall

[. . .]

'Racism and the media' touches directly the problem of *ideology*, since the media's main sphere of operations is the production and transformation of ideologies. An intervention in the media's construction of race is an intervention in the *ideological* terrain of struggle. [. . .] I am using the term [ideology] to refer to those images, concepts and premises which provide the frameworks through which we represent, interpret, understand and 'make sense' of some aspect of social existence. Language and ideology are not the same – since the same linguistic term ('democracy' for example, or 'freedom') can be deployed within different ideological discourses. But language, broadly conceived, is by definition the principal medium in which we find different ideological discourses elaborated.

Three important things need to be said about ideology in order to make what follows intelligible. First, ideologies do not consist of isolated and separate concepts, but in the articulation of different elements into a distinctive set or chain of meanings. In liberal ideology, 'freedom' is connected (articulated) with individualism and the free market; in socialist ideology, 'freedom' is a collective condition, dependent on, not counterposed to, 'equality of condition', as it is in liberal ideology. The same concept is differently positioned within the logic of different ideological discourses. One of the ways in which ideological struggle takes place and ideologies are transformed is by articulating the elements differently, thereby producing a different meaning: breaking the chain in which they are currently fixed (e.g. 'democratic' = the 'Free' West) and establishing a new articulation (e.g. 'democratic' = deepening the democratic content of political life). This 'breaking of the chain' is not, of course, confined to the head: it takes place through social practice and political struggle.

From S. Hall, 'The Whites of Their Eyes: Racist Ideologies and the Media', in George Bridges and Rosalind Brunt (eds), *Silver Linings* (London: Lawrence & Wishart, 1981); also available in Manuel Alvarado and John O. Thompson (eds), *The Media Reader* (London: British Film Institute, 1990).

Second, ideological statements are made by individuals: but ideologies are not the product of individual consciousness or intention. Rather we formulate our intentions *within ideology*. They pre-date individuals, and form part of the determinate social formations and conditions in which individuals are born. We have to 'speak through' the ideologies which are active in our society and which provide us with the means of 'making sense' of social relations and our place in them. The transformation of ideologies is thus a collective process and practice, not an individual one. Largely, the processes work *unconsciously*, rather than by conscious intention. Ideologies produce different forms of social consciousness, rather than being produced by them. They work most effectively when we are not aware that how we formulate and construct a statement about the world is underpinned by ideological premises; when our formations seem to be simply descriptive statements about how things are (i.e. must be), or of what we can 'take-for-granted'. 'Little boys like playing rough games; little girls, however, are full of sugar and spice' is predicated on a whole set of ideological premises, though it seems to be an aphorism which is grounded, not in how masculinity and femininity have been historically and culturally constructed in society, but in Nature itself. Ideologies tend to disappear from view into the taken-for-granted 'naturalised' world of common sense. Since (like gender) race appears to be 'given' by Nature, racism is one of the most profoundly 'naturalised' of existing ideologies.

Third, ideologies 'work' by constructing for their subjects (individual and collective) positions of identification and knowledge which allow them to 'utter' ideological truths as if they were their authentic authors. This is not because they emanate from our innermost, authentic and unified experience, but because we find ourselves mirrored in the positions at the centre of the discourses from which the statements we formulate 'make sense'. Thus the same 'subjects' (e.g. economic classes or ethnic groups) can be differently constructed in different ideologies.

[. . .]

Ideologies therefore work by the transformation of discourses (the disarticulation and re-articulation of ideological elements) and the transformation (the fracturing and recomposition) of subjects-for-action. How we 'see' ourselves and our social relations *matters*, because it enters into and informs our actions and practices. Ideologies are therefore a site of a distinct type of social struggle. This site does not exist on its own, separate from other relations, since ideas are not free-floating in people's heads. The ideological construction of black people as a 'problem population' and the police practice of containment in the black communities mutually reinforce and support one another. Nevertheless, ideology is a practice. It has its own specific way of working. And it is generated, produced and reproduced in specific settings (sites) – especially, in the apparatuses of ideological production which 'produce' social meanings and distribute them throughout society, like the media.

[. . .]

Amongst other kinds of ideological labour, the media construct for us a definition of what *race* is, what meaning the imagery of race carries, and what the 'problem of race' is understood to be. They help to classify out the world in terms of the categories of race.

The media are not only a powerful source of ideas about race. They are also one place where these ideas are articulated, worked on, transformed and elaborated. We have said 'ideas' and 'ideologies' in the plural. For it would be wrong and misleading to see the media as uniformly and conspiratorially harnessed to a single, racist conception of the world. Liberal and humane ideas about 'good relations' between the races, based on open-mindedness and tolerance, operate inside the world of the media – among, for example, many television journalists and newspapers like the *Guardian* – alongside the more explicit racism of other journalists and newspapers like the *Express* or the *Mail*. In some respects, the line which separates the latter from the extreme right on policies, such as, for example, guided repatriation for blacks, is very thin indeed.

[. . .]

[An] important distinction is between what we might call 'overt' racism and 'inferential' racism. By *overt* racism, I mean those many occasions when open and favourable coverage is given to arguments, positions and spokespersons who are in the business of elaborating an openly racist argument or advancing a racist policy or view. Many such occasions exist; they have become more frequent in recent years – more often in the press, which has become openly partisan to extremist right-wing arguments, than in television, where the regulations of 'balance', 'impartiality and neutrality' operate.

By *inferential* racism I mean those apparently naturalised representations of events and situations relating to race, whether 'factual' or 'fictional', which have racist premisses and propositions inscribed in them as a set of *unquestioned assumptions*. These enable racist statements to be formulated without ever bringing into awareness the racist predicates on which the statements are grounded.

Both types of racism are to be found, in different combinations, in the British media. Open or overt racism is, of course, politically dangerous as well as socially offensive. The open partisanship of sections of the popular press on this front is an extremely serious development. It is not only that they circulate and popularise openly racist policies and ideas, and translate them into the vivid populist vernacular (e.g. in the tabloids, with their large working-class readership) it is the very fact that such things can now be openly said and advocated which *legitimates* their public expression and increases the threshold of the public acceptability of racism. Racism becomes 'acceptable' – and thus, not too long after, 'true' – just common sense: what everyone knows and is openly saying. But *inferential racism* is more widespread – and in many ways, more insidious, because it is largely *invisible* even to those who formulate the world in its terms.

An example of *this* type of racist ideology is the sort of television programme which deals with some 'problem' in race relations. It is probably made by a good and honest liberal broadcaster, who hopes to do some good in the world for 'race relations' and who maintains a scrupulous balance and neutrality when questioning people interviewed for the programme. The programme will end with a homily on how, if only the 'extremists' on *either side* would go away, 'normal blacks and whites' would be better able to get on with learning to live in harmony together. Yet every word and image of such programmes are impregnated with unconscious racism because they are all predicated on the unstated and unrecognized assumption that the *blacks* are the *source of the problem*. Yet virtually the whole of 'social problem' television about race and immigration – often made, no doubt, by well-intentioned and liberal-minded broadcasters – is precisely predicated on racist premisses of this kind. This was the criticism we made in the CARM programme, *It Ain't Half Racist, Mum** and it was the one which most cut the broadcasters to their professional quick. It undermined their professional credentials by suggesting that they had been partisan where they are supposed to be balanced and impartial. It was an affront to the liberal consensus and self-image which prevails within broadcasting. Both responses were, in fact, founded on the profound misunderstanding that racism is, by definition, mutually exclusive of the liberal consensus – whereas, in inferential racism, the two can quite easily cohabit – and on the assumption that if the television discourse could be shown to be racist, it must be because the individual broadcasters were intentionally and deliberately racist. In fact, an ideological discourse does *not* depend on the conscious intentions of those who formulate statements within it.

[. . .]

[There is a] rich vocabulary and syntax of race on which the media have to draw. Racism has a long and distinguished history in British culture. It is grounded in the relations of slavery, colonial conquest, economic exploitation and imperialism in which the European races have stood in relation to the 'native peoples' of the colonised and exploited periphery.

Three characteristics provided the discursive and power-coordinates of the discourses in which these relations were historically constructed. (1) Their imagery and themes were polarised around fixed relations of subordination and domination. (2) Their stereotypes were grouped around the poles of 'superior' and 'inferior' natural species. (3) Both were displaced from the 'language' of history into the language of Nature. Natural physical signs and racial characteristics became the unalterable signifiers of inferiority. Subordinate ethnic groups and classes appeared, not as the objects of particular historical relations (the slave trade, European colonisation, the active underdevelopment of the 'underdeveloped' societies), but as the given qualities of an inferior *breed*. Relations, secured by economic, social, political and military domination were transformed and 'naturalised' into an order of *rank*, ascribed by Nature. Thus, Edward Long, an acute English observer of Jamaica in the period of slavery wrote (in his *History of Jamaica*, 1774) – much in the way the Elizabethans might have spoken of 'the Great Chain Of Being' – of 'Three ranks of men [sic], (white, mulatto and black), dependent on each other, and rising in a proper climax of subordination, in which the whites hold the highest place'.

[Often it is] 'forgotten' [the] degree to which in the period of slavery and imperialism popular literature is saturated with these fixed, negative attributes of the colonised races. We find them in the diaries, observations and accounts, the notebooks, ethnographic records and commentaries, of visitors, explorers, missionaries and administrators in Africa, India, the Far East and the Americas. And also something else: the 'absent' but imperialising 'white eye'; the unmarked position from which all these 'observations' are made and from which, alone, they make sense. This is the history of slavery and conquest, written, seen, drawn and photographed by The Winners. They cannot be *read* and made sense of from any other position. The 'white eye' is always outside the frame – but seeing and positioning everything within it.

[T]elling sequences [can be found in] early film of the British Raj in India – the source of endless radio 'reminiscences' and television historical show-pieces today. The assumption of effortless superiority structures every image – even the positioning in the frame: the foregrounding of colonial life (tea-time on the plantation), the background of native bearers. . . . In the later stages of High Imperialism, this discourse proliferates through the new media of popular culture and information – newspapers and journals, cartoons, drawings and advertisements and the popular novel. Recent critics of the literature of imperialism have argued that, if we simply extend our definition of nineteenth-century fiction from one branch of 'serious fiction' to embrace popular literature, we will find a second, powerful strand of the English literary imagination to set beside the *domestic* novel: the male-dominated world of imperial adventure, which takes *empire*, rather than *Middlemarch*, as its microcosm. I remember a graduate student, working on the construction of race in popular literature and culture at the end of the Nineteenth Century, coming to me in despair – racism was so *ubiquitous*, and at the same time so *unconscious* – simply assumed to be the case – that it was impossible to get any critical purchase on it. In this period, the very idea of *adventure* became synonymous with the demonstration of the moral, social and physical mastery of the colonisers over the colonised.

Later, this concept of 'adventure' – one of the principal categories of modern *entertainment* – moved straight off the printed page into the literature of crime and espionage, children's books, the great Hollywood extravaganzas and comics. There, with recurring persistence, they still remain. Many of these older versions have had their edge somewhat blunted by time. They have been distanced from us, apparently, by our superior wisdom and liberalism. But they still reappear on the television screen, especially in the form of 'old movies' (some 'old movies', of course, continue to be made). But we can grasp their recurring resonance better if we identify some of the base-images of the 'grammar of race'.

There is, for example, the familiar *slave-figure*: dependable, loving in a simple childlike way – the devoted 'Mammy' with the rolling eyes, or the faithful field-hand or retainer, attached and devoted to 'his' Master. The best known extravaganza of all – *Gone With The Wind* – contains rich viriants of both. The 'slave-figure' is by no means limited to films and programmes *about* slavery. Some 'Injuns' and many Asians have come on to the screen in this disguise. A deep and unconscious ambivalence pervades this stereotype. Devoted and childlike, the 'slave' is also un-reliable, unpredictable and undependable – capable of 'turning nasty', or of plotting in a treach-erous way, secretive, cunning, cut-throat once his or her Master's or Mistress's back is turned: and inexplicably given to running way into the bush at the slightest opportunity. The whites can never be sure that this childish simpleton – 'Sambo' – is not mocking his master's white manners behind his hand, even when giving an exaggerated caricature of white refinement.

Another base-image is that of the 'native'. The good side of this figure is portrayed in a certain primitive nobility and simple dignity. The bad side is portrayed in terms of cheating and cunning, and, further out, savagery and barbarism. Popular culture is still full today of countless savage and restless 'natives', and sound-tracks constantly repeat the threatening sound of drumming in the night, the hint of primitive rites and cults. Cannibals, whirling dervishes, Indian tribesmen, garishly got up, are constantly threatening to over-run the screen. They are likely to appear at any moment out of the darkness to decapitate the beautiful heroine, kidnap the children, burn the encampment or threatening to boil, cook and eat the innocent explorer or colonial administrator and his lady-wife. These 'natives' always move as an anonymous collective mass – in tribes or hordes. And against them is always counterposed the isolated white figure, alone 'out there', confronting his Destiny or shouldering his Burden in the 'heart of darkness', displaying coolness under fire and an unshakeable authority – exerting mastery over the rebellious natives or quelling the threatened uprising with a single glance of his steel-blue eyes.

A third variant is that of the 'clown' or 'entertainer'. This captures the 'innate' humour, as well as the physical grace, of the licensed entertainer – putting on a show for The Others. It is never quite clear whether we are laughing with or at this figure: admiring the physical and rhythmic grace, the open expressivity and emotionality of the 'entertainer', or put off by the 'clown's' stupidity.

One noticeable fact about all these images is their deep *ambivalence* – the double vision of the white eye through which they are seen. The primitive nobility of the ageing tribesman or chief, and the native's rhythmic grace, always contain both a nostalgia for an innocence lost forever to the civilised, and the threat of civilisation being over-run or undermined by the recurrence of savagery, which is always lurking just below the surface; or by an untutored sexuality, threatening to 'break out'. Both are aspects – the good and the bad sides – of *primitivism*. In these images, 'primitivism' is defined by the fixed proximity of such people to Nature.

Is all this so far away as we sometimes suppose from the representation of race which fill the screens today? These *particular* versions may have faded. But their *traces* are still to be observed, reworked in many of the modern and up-dated images. And though they may appear to carry a different meaning, they are often still constructed on a very ancient grammar. Today's restless native hordes are still alive and well and living, as guerilla armies and freedom fighters in the Angola, Zimbabwe or Namibian 'bush'. Blacks are still the most frightening, cunning and glamorous crooks (and policemen) in New York cop series. They are the fleet-footed, crazy-talking under-men who connect Starsky and Hutch to the drug-saturated ghetto. The scheming villains and their giant-sized bully boys in the world of James Bond and his progeny are still, unusually, recruited from 'out there' in Jamaica, where savagery lingers on. The sexually-available 'slave girl' is alive and kicking, smouldering away on some exotic TV set or on the covers of paperbacks, though she is now the centre of a special admiration, covered in a sequinned gown and supported by a white chorus line. Primitivism, savagery, guile and unreliability – all 'just below the surface' – can still be identified in the faces of black political leaders around the world, cunningly plotting the overthrow of 'civilisation': Mr Mugabé,† for example, up to the point where he happened to win both a war and an election and became, temporarily at any rate, the best (because the most politically credible) friend Britain had left in that last outpost of the Edwardian dream.

The 'Old Country' – white version – is still often the subject of nostalgic documentaries: 'Old Rhodesia', whose reliable servants, as was only to be expected, plotted treason in the outhouse and silently stole away to join ZAPU in the bush . . . Tribal Man in green khaki. Black stand-up comics still ape their ambiguous incorporation into British entertainment by being the first to tell a racist joke. No Royal Tour is complete without its troupe of swaying bodies, or its mounted tribesmen, paying homage. Blacks are such 'good movers', so *rhythmic*, so *natural*. And the dependent peoples, who couldn't manage for a day without the protection and know-how of their white masters, reappear as the starving victims of the Third World, passive and waiting for the technology or the Aid to arrive, objects of our pity or of a *Blue Peter* appeal. They are not represented as the subjects of a continuing exploitation or dependency, or the global division of wealth and labour. They are the Victims of Fate.

These modern, glossed and up-dated images seem to have put the old world of Sambo behind them. Many of them, indeed, are the focus of a secret, illicit, pleasurable-but-taboo admiration. Many have a more active and energetic quality – some black athletes, for example, and of course the entertainers. But the connotations and echoes which they carry reverberate back a very long way. They continue to shape the ways whites see blacks today – even when the white adventurer sailing up the jungle stream is not *Sanders Of The River*,‡ but historical drama-reconstructions of Stanley and Livingstone; and the intention is to show, not the savagery, but the serenity of African village life – ways of an ancient people 'unchanged even down to modern times' (in other words, still preserved in economic backwardness and frozen in history for our anthropological eye by forces unknown to them and, apparently, unshowable on the screen).

'Adventure' is one way in which we *encounter* race without having to *confront* the racism of the perspectives in use. Another, even more complex one is 'entertainment'. In television, there is a strong counterposition between 'serious', informational television, which we watch because it is good for us, and 'entertainment', which we watch because it is pleasurable. And the purest form of pleasure in entertainment television is *comedy*. By definition, comedy is a licensed zone, disconnected from the serious. It's all 'good, clean fun'. In the area of fun and pleasure it is forbidden to pose a serious question, partly because it seems so puritanical and destroys the pleasure by switching registers. Yet race is one of the most significant themes in situation comedies – from the early Alf Garnett to *Mind Your Language, On The Buses, Love Thy Neighbour* and *It Ain't Half Hot, Mum*. These are defended on good 'anti-racist' grounds: the appearance of blacks, alongside whites, in situation comedies, it is argued, will help to naturalise and normalise their presence in British society. And no doubt, in some examples, it does function in this way. But, if you examine these fun occasions more closely, you will often find, as we did in our two programmes, that the comedies do not simply include blacks: they are *about race*. That is, the same old categories of racially defined characteristics and qualities, and the same relations of superior and inferior, provide the pivots on which the jokes actually turn, the tension-points which move and motivate the situations in situation comedies. The comic register in which they are set, however, protects and defends viewers from acknowledging their incipient racism. It creates disavowal.

This is even more so with the television stand-up comics, whose repertoire in recent years has come to be dominated, in about equal parts, by sexist and racist jokes. It's sometimes said, again in their defence, that this must be a sign of black acceptibility. But it *may* just be that racism has become more normal: it's hard to tell. It's also said that the best teller of anti-Jewish jokes are Jews themselves, just as blacks tell the best 'white' jokes against themselves. But this is to argue as if jokes exist in a vacuum separate from the contexts and situations of their telling. Jewish jokes told by Jews among themselves are part of the self-awareness of the community. They are unlikely to function by 'putting down' the race, because both teller and audience belong on equal terms to the same group. Telling racist jokes across the racial line, in conditions where relations of racial inferiority and superiority prevail, reinforces the *difference* and reproduces the unequal relations because, in those situations, the point of the joke depends on the existence of racism. Thus they reproduce the categories and relations of racism, even while normalizing them through laughter. The stated good intentions of the joke-makers do not resolve the problem here, because they are not in control of the circumstances – conditions of continuing racism – in which their joke discourse will be read and heard. The time *may* come when blacks and whites can tell jokes about each other in ways which do not reproduce the racial categories of the world in which they are told. The time, in Britain, is certainly *not yet arrived*.

Two other arenas [. . .] relate to the 'harder' end of television production – news and current affairs. This is where race is constructed as *problem* and the site of *conflict* and debate. There have been good examples of programmes where blacks have not exclusively appeared as the source of the 'problem' (ATV's *Breaking Point* is one example) and where they have not been exclusively saddled with being the aggressive agent in conflict (the London Weekend Television *London Programme* and the Southall Defence Committee's *Open Door* programme on the Southall events are examples). But the general tendency of the run of programmes in this area is to see blacks – especially the mere fact of their existence (their 'numbers') – as constituting a problem for English white society. They appear as law-breakers, prone to crime; as 'trouble'; as the collective agent of civil disorder.

In the numerous incidents where black communities have reacted to racist provocation (as at Southall) or to police harrassment and provocation (as in Bristol)§ the media have tended to assume that 'right' lay on the side of the law, and have fallen into the language of 'riot' and 'race warfare' which simply feeds existing stereotypes and prejudices. The precipitating conditions of conflict are usually *absent* – the scandalous provocation of a National Front march through one of the biggest black areas, Southall, and the saturation police raiding of the last refuge for black youth which triggered off Bristol – to take only two recent examples. They are either missing, or introduced so late in the process of signification, that they fail to dislodge the dominant definition of these events. So they testify, once again, to the disruptive nature of black and Asian people *as such*.

The analysis of the media coverage of Southall contained in the NCCL Unofficial Committee of Inquiry *Report*, for example, shows how rapidly, in both the television and press, the official definitions of the police – Sir David McNee's statement on the evening of 23 April, and the ubiquitous James Jardine, speaking for the Police Federation on the succeeding day – provided the media with the authoritative definition of the event. These, in turn, shaped and focused what the media reported and how it explained what transpired. In taking their cue from these authoritative sources, the media reproduced an account of the event which, with certain significant exceptions, translated the conflict between racism and anti-racism into (a) a contest between Asians and the police, and (b) a contest between two kinds of extremism – the so-called '*fascism*' of left and right alike.

This had the effect of downgrading the two problems at the centre of the Southall affair – the growth of and growing legitimacy of the extreme right and its blatantly provocative anti-black politics of the street; and the racism and brutality of the police. Both issues had to be *forced* on to the agenda of the media by a militant and organized protest. Most press reports of Southall were so obsessed by embroidering the lurid details of 'roaming hoardes of coloured youths' chasing young whites 'with a carving knife' – a touch straight out of *Sanders Of The River*, though so far uncorroborated – that they failed even to mention the death of Blair Peach. This is selective or tunnel-vision with a vengeance.

A good example of how the real causes of racial conflict can be absorbed and transformed by the framework which the media employ can be found in the *Nationwide* coverage of Southall on the day following the events. Two interlocking frameworks of explanation governed this programme. In the first, conflict is seen in the conspiratorial terms of far-left against extreme-right – the Anti-Nazi League against the National Front. This is the classic logic of television, where the medium identifies itself with the moderate, consensual, middle-road, Average viewer, and sets off, in contrast, extremism on both sides, which it then equates with each other. In this particular exercise in 'balance', fascism and anti-fascism are represented as *the same* – both equally *bad*, because the Middle Way enshrines the Common Good under all circumstances. This balancing exercise provided an opportunity for Martin Webster of the National Front to gain access to the screen, to help set the terms of the debate, and to spread his smears across the screen under the freedom of the airwaves: 'Well,' he said, 'let's talk about Trotskyists, extreme Communists of various sorts, raving Marxists and other assorted left-wing cranks.' Good knockabout stuff. Then, after a linking passage – 'Southall, the day after' – to the second framework: rioting Asians *vs* the police. 'I watched television as well last night,' Mr Jardine argued, 'and I certainly didn't see any police throwing bricks . . . So don't start making those arguments.' The growth of organised political racism and the circumstances which have precipitated it were simply not visible to *Nationwide* as an alternative way of setting up the problem.

In the CARM programme *It Ain't Half Racist, Mum*, we tried to illustrate the inferential logic at work in another area of programming: the BBC's 'Great Debate' on Immigration. It was not necessary here to start with any preconceived notions, least of all speculation as to the personal views on race by the broadcasters involved – though one can't expect either the BBC hierarchy or Robin Day to believe that. You have simply to look at the programme with one set of questions in mind: Here is a problem, defined as 'the problem of immigration'. What is it? How is it defined and constructed through the programme? What logic governs its definition? And where does that logic derive from? I believe the answers are clear. The problem of immigration is that 'there are too many blacks over here', to put it crudely. It is *defined* in terms of *numbers of blacks* and what to do about them. The *logic* of the argument is 'immigrants = blacks = too many of them = send them home'. That is a racist logic. And it comes from a chain of reasoning whose representative, in respectable public debate and in person, on this occasion, was Enoch Powell. Powellism set the agenda for the media. Every time (and on many more occasions than the five or six we show in the programme) the presenter wanted to define the base-line of the programme which others should address, Mr Powell's views were indicated as representing it. And every time anyone strayed from the 'logic' to question the underlying premiss, it was back to 'as Mr Powell would say . . . ' that they were drawn.

It certainly does not follow (and I know of no evidence to suggest) that Robin Day subscribes to this line or agrees with Mr Powell on anything to do with race. I know absolutely nothing about his views on race and immigration. And we made no judgment on his views, which are irrelevant to the argument. If the media function in a systematically racist manner, it is not because they are run and organised exclusively by active racists; this is a category mistake. This would be equivalent to saying that you could change the character of the capitalist state by replacing its personnel. Whereas the media, like the state, have a *structure*, a set of *practices* which are *not* reducible to the individuals who staff them. What defines how the media function is the result of a set of complex, often contradictory, social relations; not the personal inclinations of its members. What is significant is not that they produce a racist ideology, from some single-minded and unified conception of the world, but that they are so powerfully constrained – 'spoken by' – a particular set of ideological discourses. The power of this discourse is its capacity to constrain a very great variety of individuals: racist, anti-racist, liberals, radicals, conservatives, anarchists, know-nothings and silent majoritarians.

What we said, however, about the *discourse* of problem television was true, despite the hurt feelings of particular individuals: and demonstrably so. The premiss on which the Great Immigration Debate was built and the chain of reasoning it predicated was a racist one. The evidence for this is in what was said and how it was formulated – how the argument unfolded. If you establish the topic as 'the numbers of blacks are too high' or '*they* are breeding too fast', the opposition is obliged or constrained to argue that 'the numbers are not as high as they are represented to be'. This view is opposed to the first two: but it is also imprisoned by the same logic – the logic of the 'numbers game'. Liberals, anti-racists, indeed raging revolutionaries can contribute 'freely' to this debate, and indeed are often obliged to do so, so as not to let the case go by default: without breaking for a moment the chain of assumptions which holds the racist proposition in place. However, changing the terms of the argument, questioning the assumptions and starting points, breaking the logic – this is a quite different, longer, more difficult task.

[. . .]

Editors' Notes

* Stuart Hall worked with colleagues in the Campaign Against Racism in the Media (CARM) to make a programme for the BBC TV Community Programmes Unit *Open Door* slot about racism on television. *It Ain't Half Racist, Mum* was transmitted on 1 March 1979. For an account of the resistance encountered in the production of the programme, see Carl Gardner, *It Ain't Half Racist Mum: Fighting Racism in the Media* (London: Comedia, 1982) pp. 85–9.
† Robert Mugabe, leader of ZANU, one of the two main armed political movements which fought against white minority rule in Rhodesia. (The other movement was ZAPU.) In 1979 free elections were held, and Mugabe became the first president of the new Zimbabwe.
‡ *Sanders of the River* (prod. Alexander Korda, 1935), a British feature film based on Edgar Wallace's stories about a white district commissioner in West Africa.
§ In April 1979 the Metropolitan Police attacked Anti-Nazi League (ANL) supporters who had gathered in the Southall district of London to protest against a public parade being held by the racist National Front. ANL supporter Blair Peach died as a result. On 2–3 April 1980, provoked by months of saturation policing, black youth in the St Paul's district of Bristol fought with the police.

19

FICTIONS AND IDEOLOGIES: THE CASE OF SITUATION COMEDY

Janet Woollacott

Escapist fiction, that which purportedly allows its viewers or readers to 'escape' from the problems of the real world, was the category within which situation comedies found their home in terms of television criticism. Whereas some popular genres show obvious connections with the more general ideological formations in play at the time of their popularity (the spy thriller during the 1960s, for example, or the television crime series during the seventies), situation comedies could be held to have a more general grip on their audience. Over a longer period of time, at least for the last three decades, they have been a consistent part of the flow of the evening's television entertainment, a necessary and vital ingredient in the television controller's strategy for keeping the audience 'tuned in'. Moreover, the popularity of situation comedies has remained, throughout major shifts in more general ideological configurations in the period, and through the rise and decline of other popular genres such as the crime series. It is the aim of this article to outline some of the general characteristics of situation comedies, their narrative and comic strategies, use of character and performance; to consider some of the 'pleasures' of situation comedies and to suggest some of the issues raised by the role of situation comedies in considering the relations betweeen fictions and other ideologies.

Despite the very wide range of targets for joking and humour in situation comedies, the programmes do conform to relatively strict conventions. Clearly some aspects of their formal organisation are related to institutional constraints; the weekly half-hour slot, the limited number of characters and the cheap sets. In this respect and others they can be considered as a television genre. Ryall suggests in relation to film genres that 'genres may be defined as patterns/forms/styles/structures which transcend individual films and which supervise both their construction by the film-maker and their reading by an audience'.[1] In the mutual expectations of television producers and audiences, genre conventions are constantly varied but rarely totally exceeded or broken. Generally situation comedies are pre-eminently texts

From T. Bennett, C. Mercer and J. Woollacott (eds), *Popular Culture and Social Relations* (Milton Keynes: Open University Press, 1986) pp. 196–218.

which are linked to a comfortable practice of reading. As Stephen Neale remarks of all popular genres, 'the existence of genres means that the spectator, precisely, will always know that everything will be made right in the end, that everything will cohere, that any threat or danger in the narrative process itself will always be contained.' [2]

[. . .]

In Eaton's attempt to outline a typology of situation comedy, he suggests that the two basic 'situations' of situation comedy are those of home and work. [. . .] Within these parameters, he argues that the narrative form of situation comedies is organised around an 'inside/outside' dichotomy. Moreover, the dichotomy 'affects every aspect of production down to its finest budgetary details'.[3] In plot terms, this means that events or characters from the outside can be allowed to enter the situation but only in such a way that the outsiders don't affect the situation which can be maintained for future weekly episodes. [. . .] In Eaton's typology, the inscription of the viewer within situation comedies is made manifest rather than being rendered invisible as in so many forms of novelistic fiction. However, this particular form of inscription is not typical of [. . .] many [. . .] situation comedies. Moreover, as Eaton acknowledges, he pays little attention to the pleasures of situation comedy, suggesting only that an analysis of such pleasures would not be incompatible with his typology. One of the problems of Eaton's analysis is the extent to which it relies on simply listing the typical characteristics of situation comedies. For example, the circumstances which Eaton perceptively categorises as 'typical', the small number of characters 'stuck with one another' at work or at home, or in some other boundaried setting, may occur in other genres. The situation of *Blake's Seven*, for example, in which the characters are confined to their spaceship, with fleeting teleported trips to other worlds, is not markedly dissimilar to that described by Eaton as a feature of situation comedies, and for rather similar institutional reasons. Even jokes or comic situations are not limited to situation comedies. Soap operas usually have their comic characters and situations. Regan's wit, in a crime series like *The Sweeney* is one much quoted reason for his popularity, while part of the format of a James Bond film is to follow an exciting 'action' sequence with a one-like joke from the hero. Indeed, the generic specificity of situation comedy is not really a question of certain exclusive elements ('situation', jokes, etc.) but of particular combination of elements. In Neale's terms, it's a matter of 'the exclusive and particular weight given in any one genre to elements which in fact it shares with other genres'.[4]

NARRATIVE AND SITUATION COMEDY

Most forms of popular fiction involve a narrative which is initiated through the signification of a disruption, a disturbance, which the narrative proceeds to resolve. The narrative offers to the readers or the viewers a transformation of the initial equilibrium through a disruption and then a reordering of its components. Hence, it could be argued that one of the pleasures of reading a Bond novel rests on the simultaneous existence within the Bond novels of a disturbance both in a discourse of sexuality and in a discourse of imperialism and a progression towards the resolution of those disturbances through the activities of the hero. It is possible to suggest that all genres play with a disturbance, process and closure within the narrative, although in different ways. In so doing, genres construct particular temporal sequences. In the detective story, for example, the enigma with which the narrative begins structures suspense not simply by organising the narrative as a puzzle, but also by setting up a particular temporal sequence. The enigma or disturbance involves separate times; the time of the story behind the crime and the time of its reconstruction in the narrative. Closure is effected through the bringing together of the two times. Thus detective films construct a memory from instances of the story of the crime, from the story of its investigation and from the process of the text itself so that the 'memory constructed within the film duplicates the memory constructed by the film'. The temporal tension produced is the main characteristic of the suspense of a detective story.

The suspense of the thriller form is achieved slightly differently, but one common structure is that of the playing of the protagonist against a grouping of apparently disparate threats. In the Bond novels, the symbolic phallic threat takes a number of forms, that of Bond's substitute father M, that of the villains and that of the heroine. In a crime series programme such as *The Sweeney*, Jack Regan is threatened by criminals and by bureaucratic elements in the law and on occasion by problems with his family or private life. This doubling and occasionally trebling of threats to the hero not only increases the danger to him, but also sets up a temporal sequence involving both the number and complexity of the tasks which have to be performed for an effective and coherent closure to the narrative, for the story to 'end satisfactorily'. Suspense resides in the tension between the viewer's desire for the narrative to progress, although this involves a degree of risk for the hero, and the viewer's desire for the narrative to end, although this requires the full working out of the complex interconnections of the threats to the hero or heroine.[5]

Situation comedies also order the narrative and effect a particular closure, setting up a temporal sequence and positioning the subject, not in suspense but amusement and laughter. Eaton's argument suggests one aspect of the narrative of situation comedies, the lack of 'progression' involved in many situation comedies. In a sense, this lack of progression can only be identified in comparison with other genres, in which the progressive aspect of the narrative, that is the impetus towards the resolution of the initial disturbance, is more strongly weighted. In the opening episode of *Steptoe and Son*, the disturbance from the 'outside', the 'offer' does not lead to an obvious resolution in which either Harold takes the offer and leaves or rejects the offer and stays, but to Harold's inability to take the offer and his remaining without acceptance. In situation comedies, the viewer's pleasure does not lie in the suspense of puzzle solving nor in the suspense surrounding the hero's ability to cope through action with various tasks and threats. Rather the tension of the narrative to which the viewer responds revolves around the economy or wit with which two or more discourses are brought together in the narrative. The pleasure of situation comedy is linked to the release of that tension through laughter.

Eaton's account of the 'inside/outside' dichotomy in situation comedies indicates the narrative structuring of many situation comedies around an intersection of two discourses. The resolution of the disturbance, the contradictions and resistances of the bringing together of the two discourses has to be accomplished with economy and wit, with conscious and overt fictional manipulation. The 'circularity' of many situation comedy plots is precisely an indication of that formally articulated wit. In Tony Hancock's 'The Blood Donor', you may remember the narrative follows this type of economic circularity. The episode begins with Hancock's entry into the Blood Donor Department of a hospital.

[. . .]

The two discourses are present from the beginning. On the one hand there is Hancock's discourse, in which the hero constantly and ineffectively seeks higher status, from his name ('Anthony Aloysius St John Hancock' rather than Tony Hancock), his conviction that he has aristocratic connections, to his desire to be given a badge for giving blood. [. . .] On the other hand, there is the discourse of the hospital and the older blood donors, the resisting world against which Hancock's delusions normally clash. The intersection of the two discourses is finally marked in the text of 'The Blood Donor', by Hancock's return to the hospital to be given the pint of blood he had donated earlier. He has cut himself with a kitchen knife.

[. . .]

The pleasure and coherence of this ending is partly one of Hancock's triumph over the hospital and blood donorship. Hancock overcomes the resistance of the hospital and subordinates it to his personal demands, thus reordering the discourses in another relationship to that of the beginning, from one of altruism to one of self-interest. But our amusement is also linked to the way in which Hancock's mixture of self-interest and would-be altruism comes full circle.

The narratives of most popular situation comedies within each episode tend to follow this pattern, although over a whole series the narrative sometimes develops beyond a constant return to square one. *Whatever Happened to the Likely Lads?* sees Terry's return from the army, the re-establishment of his friendship with Bob and the events leading up to Bob's wedding to Thelma and his removal to the Elm Lodge housing estate. The three series of *Agony* see the breakup of agony aunt, Jane Luca's marriage to Laurence, her living alone, her affair with Vincent Fish and with Laurence, her pregnancy, return to Laurence and the birth of her child.[6] At the same time, although events happen, the discursive relationships often remain the same. In *Whatever Happened to the Likely Lads?* the clash between Bob and Terry's long-established friendship and common interests and Bob's new relationship with Thelma remains at the centre of the narrative of each episode. Similarly, in *Agony*, the contradiction between Jane's public image of helping others and her private difficulties in helping herself, her husband and friends, continues to provide the mainspring for the comic strategies of each episode.

In one sense, it is quite clear that while watching situation comedies we already know the likely outcome, just as we know the likely outcome of a detective story or a thriller. This does not, however, eradicate a sense of narrative tension. The tension and suspense of situation comedy is produced through a particular organisation of narrative time. A simple internal example of this is the use in situation comedies of the 'anticipation of the inevitable'. The joke is telegraphed in advance and the pleasurable effects are achieved through the viewer's foreknowledge of it. The comedy stems from the timing and economy with which a scene or a series of scenes are treated.

[. . .]

IDEOLOGY AND [STEREOTYPES]

One of the recurring interests in the study of comedy is the issue of its 'subversive' nature. In the British Film Institute's Dossier on situation comedy, the question of whether situation comedy is ideologically incorporative or ideologically subversive is broached time and again and with conclusions varying from seeing situation comedy as essentially conservative despite its reputation for subversion to seeing it as a fictional form which is capable of both inflections.[7]

[. . .]

In the case of situation comedies, one characteristic mode of identifying ideological 'bias' has been that concerned with the use of stereotypes. Stereotypes are forms of characterisation which are simple, memorable, widely recognised and frequently repeated. 'Dumb blondes', for example, are a recognisable type through a range of texts from Judy Holliday in *Born Yesterday*, to Marilyn Monroe in *Some Like It Hot*, to Lucy in the *I Love Lucy* show, to Wendy Craig in situation comedies such as *And Mother Makes Five*. The notion of stereotype assumes, not altogether unjustifiably, that there are important consequences stemming from the repetition of character types.

Stereotyping is not simply a 'neutral' exercise. Forms of stereotyping in the media have been identified as part of the way in which the media define and reinforce the deviant status of particular groups. Pearce sums up news coverage of homosexuality as 'How to be immoral, and ill, pathetic and dangerous, all at the same time'.[8] In a monograph on *Gays and Films*, Sheldon suggests the difficulties for homosexuals of responding to films with negative stereotypes: 'I remember being depressed for days after seeing *Sister George*, feeling "Sure, such a relationship may exist, but what a miserable one, and what's it doing on film to pervert young minds about lesbians" '.[9] Particular stereotypes are often attacked for their failure adequately to convey the 'real', either in terms of the complexity of any one individual or in terms of the range of real concrete individuals, homosexuals, blacks or women, who make up the membership of any particular stereotyped group. Criticism of the characterisation offered in stereotypes often explicitly demands more 'realism', in the sense of being truer to the real individuals outside the text, but it may also, of course, implicitly endorse some forms of signification at the expense of others. The typical characterisation of the nineteenth-century bourgeois novel, for example, is normally seen to be more adequate than that of a popular, contemporary situation comedy. Stereotypes are also attacked, however, for their failure to offer an ideal, a positive rather than a negative image.

Richard Dyer attempts to theorise the positive and negative aspects of stereotypes, by taking up Klapp's distinction between social types and stereotypes:

> stereotypes refer to things outside one's social world, whereas social types refer to things with which one is familiar; stereotypes tend to be conceived of as functionless or disfunctional (or, if functional, serving prejudice and conflict mainly), whereas social types serve the structure of society at many points.[10]

As Dyer makes clear, most social types turn out to be white, middle class, heterosexual and male, and the distinction between social type and stereotype refers to those characters or types who are to be seen within and outside the boundaries of normal acceptability. Stereotypes in this formulation are inevitably negative. Indeed, Dyer suggests that they form part of a wider strategy of social control.

> The establishment of normalcy through social and stereotypes is one aspect of the habit of ruling groups – a habit of such enormous political consequences that we tend to think of it as far more premeditated than it actually is – to attempt to fashion the whole of society according to their own world-view, value system, sensibility and ideology. So right is the worldview for the ruling groups that they make it appear (as it does to them) as 'natural' and 'inevitable' – and for everyone – and insofar as they succeed, they establish their hegemony.[11]

There are one or two problems with this outline of the ideological functions of social types and stereotypes. One problem is simply the extent to which a focus on stereotypes and on their repetition leads to the neglect of differences between characters in situation comedies. Wendy Craig's Ria in the BBC2 series *Butterflies*, for example, undoubtedly plays upon certain aspects of the 'dumb blonde' stereotype, but it also differs substantially from the earlier version. Moreover, any analysis which works on the assumption of relatively unambiguous identification between the viewer or reader and the stereotype, ignores the way in which identification works through textual and inter-textual formations. Identification with a character in a situation comedy follows both from the articulation of a character within a text and from the spectator's position within a particular reading formation. Neale suggests in relation to film that identification situation with character depends upon identification with the text itself. 'It is this primary identification that provides the basis of the spectator's relationship to the text and its characters and so requires initial attention and analysis.'[12] In one sense, this simply appears as understanding the function of the character in the text. Hence, the appearance of homosexual characters in *Whatever Happened to the Likely Lads?* appears to function simply to reinforce the 'healthy' heterosexuality of Bob and Terry, despite their intimate friendship. In 'Strangers on a Train' after Bob and Terry have re-established their friendship, they quarrel in the train buffet over Bob's marriage to Thelma. As Bob leaves, full of affronted dignity, Terry orders a Scotch and remarks to the barman that he gave the best years of his life for that man (an implicit reference to his stint in the army). The barman, however, who has been listening sympathetically, puts a comforting hand over Terry's and remarks, 'Never mind, sailor, lots of other pebbles on the beach'. The camera focuses on Terry's aghast reaction to this. The typical and dominant response of the viewer is with Bob and Terry and the camera ensures that it remains with Terry in this case rather than with the barman.

Yet to a large extent, the 'reading' relationships or 'viewing' relationships have to be conceived of in terms of an interrelationship between the reading formations of the viewers and the internal characteristics of the situation comedy. Questions about the subversive or incorporative qualities of stereotypes in situation comedy are fraught with problems, but particularly so when dependent simply on a textual analysis of a situation comedy. Medhurst and Tuck, for example, argue that situation comedies such as *Butterflies* or *Solo* lie outside the main pattern of situation comedy, moving towards melodrama because they involve themes untypical of situation comedy, that the woman rather than the male is seen as the victim of marriage and domesticity. To a certain extent this is seen as an explanation of differing views of these two series.

> They are controversial series, liable to cause radical disagreements (not least between the two writers of this essay). Does *Butterflies*, for example, represent any kind of break-through in representations of women in comedy, or does it stand as the most insidious example of the method of innoculation? Ria is shown to be unable to cook; do we read this as a positive rejection of the housewifely role or a tired revival of the old jokes about female incompetence? Similarly, in the last episode of the first series of *Solo*, Gemma remarks of her relationship with Danny, 'If only the world hadn't changed and shown me things I really didn't want to see.' This can be taken as a positive acknowledgement of the impact of contemporary feminism, or as a glibly innoculatory gesture towards such an acknowledgement.[13]

But many 'non-controversial' situation comedies allow for different strategies of identification. In *Whatever Happened to the Likely Lads?*, the dominant critical reading undoubtedly involved identification with the 'lads'. Clive James summarises this 'male' view.

> Back from forces, Terry has spent the last couple of months trying to pull the birds. Bob, however, is on the verge of the ultimate step with the dreaded Thelma, and last week felt obliged to get rid of his boyhood encumbrances. Out of the old tea chest came the golden stuff: Dinky toys, Rupert and Picturegoer Annuals, all the frisson inducing junk that Thelma would never let weigh down the shelf units. 'I need those for reference', whined Bob with his arms full of cardboard covered books. There were Buddy Holly 78s – never called singles in those days, as Terry observed with the fantastic pedantry typical of the show. Obviously Bob will have a terrible time with Thelma.[14]

But discussions with Open University Summer School students showed a substantial proportion of them, predominantly women, who identified with Thelma as a strong maternal
figure, similar to those in soap operas such as *Coronation Street*, against which the activities of
Bob and Terry are simply the amusing antics of children. Clearly, this does not show that
Whatever Happened to the Likely Lads? is a subversive text, but it does indicate that there can
be very different readings of a situation comedy depending upon the operations of gendered
reading formations and it itself suggests that any judgement about ideological subversion or
incorporation can only be made in relation to the analysis of reading formations or viewing
formations over time.

Of course, stereotypes are one attempt to bridge the gap between individual readings and
more general ideological formations, but they tend to work in terms of a view in which ruling
class ideas are handed down to the masses. Dyer, for example; suggests that stereotypes are one
way through which ruling class groups project their own worldview. If however, the sphere
of popular fiction is viewed as occupying an area of exchange and negotiation between ruling
groups and subordinate classes, it could still be said to be the case that stereotypes play a
particular role in establishing elements of the ideologies of dominant groups. Homosexuals,
blacks and women could all be said to have negative images in contrast with white heterosexual
males but it can also be argued that there is considerable negotiation around the use of
stereotypes, indicated by the shifts and differences in one stereotype across a range of texts
and by the way in which social subjects established in different reading formations negotiate
identification with a stereotyped character. Thus, the use of stereotypes in popular fictional
forms such as situation comedies may be rather less unambiguously a reflection of dominant
group views than Dyer suggests.

POPULAR FICTION AND CONSENT

Mick Eaton in a recent article quotes a Tony Allen routine in which the comic is approached by
the Anti-Nazi League to perform at one of their benefits. He is questioned over the phone by
the organiser over whether his humour is 'anti-black' and replies that it isn't. He is then asked
whether his humour is 'anti-women' – he thinks that it isn't. Allen then warns the organiser that
his humour has a broader span, 'it's anti-life'. 'That's all right', says the organiser, 'that's not
an area of current concern'. Eaton uses the joke to argue that discussions of comedy cannot
be separated from the ideological/political positions available in a class society. One way of
conceiving the relationships between ideologies and situation comedies is to focus rather less
on the 'progressive' or 'non-progressive', 'subversive' or 'non-subversive' polarities of situation
comedies and more on the way in which situation comedies perform alongside and in relation
to other ideologies.

Traditionally, Marxist theories of ideology were centrally concerned with determination.
Indeed, the preoccupation with questions of determination, with the determining relationship
between economic base and ideological superstructures, led to the problems of reductionism
referred to earlier. Changes in Marxist theories of ideology, initiated largely through the
work of Althusser, involved some crucial reformulations in this area. Althusser's 'structuralist'
reworking of Marxist theory stressed not the view of ideology as distortion, involving false
consciousness, but the notion that ideology constituted the forms and representations through
which men and women 'live' in an imaginary relation, their relationship to their real conditions
of existence. Althusser's work generally, with its conceptualisation of ideology as determined
only 'in the last instance' by the economic base, and in conjunction with developments in

semiology, refocused attention on the autonomy and materiality of the ideological and on the notion of articulation, on the relationships between parts within a structure rather than solely on determination. Theories of hegemony make use of the idea of articulation in a particular way to suggest that within a given mode of hegemony, popular consent is won and secured around an articulating principle, which ensures the establishment and reproduction of the interests of ruling groups while at the same time winning popular consent. The success of hegemonic ideological dominance can then be judged by the degree to which the articulating principle secures an ordering of different and potentially oppositional ideological discourses.

The area of popular fiction and popular culture generally works to shift and secure subject positions with the active consent of its readers and viewers. It constitutes a crucial area of negotiation of consent. When forms of popular fiction such as situation comedy rework the subject positions available to viewers they move their viewers on into different ideological frameworks. For example, regardless of whether a series like *Butterflies* truly 'subverts' or really 'incorporates', it does move its viewers on to a different set of ideological coordinates in relation to extramarital sex on the woman's part in terms of past handlings of this theme in situation comedies. In a reading framework of feminist criticism, of course, this move to a new set of ideological coordinates may not appear to be an improvement but it does occur. The popularity of a particular situation comedy or other fictional forms is an indicator of the success of that securing or shifting of subject positions.

In *Policing the Crisis*,[15] the authors outline a number of changes which have taken place in the ideological configurations of post-war Britain. *Policing the Crisis* takes as its starting point the orchestration by the media of mugging as a 'moral panic' and seeks to establish that this represents a movement from a 'consensual' to a more 'coercive' management of the class struggle, which in itself stems from the declining international competitiveness of the British economy following the post-war period, the erosion of which led to attempts to secure 'consent' by more coercive although legitimate means. The immediate post-war period saw the construction of a consensus based on the politics of affluence. Economic decline triggered the disintegration of the 'miracle of spontaneous consent' based on these politics and there was an attempt to put forward a Labourist variant of consent to replace it. The exhaustion of this form of consent, however, combined with the rise of social and political conflict, the deepening of the economic crisis and the resumption of more explicit class struggle, culminated in the 'exceptional' form of class domination through the state in the 1970s, in which the ideological articulating principle was a discourse of 'law and order'.

The media play a central part in this analysis. They are described as a 'key terrain where "consent" is won or lost', as 'a field of ideological struggle'.[16] The key to the media's involvement in the construction of consent lies in the authors' analysis of news as performing a crucial transformative but secondary role in defining social events. The primary definers are those to whom the media turn, their accredited sources in government and other institutions. Although *Policing the Crisis* emphasises the transformative nature of media news reporting, in the selection and structuring of themes and topics, the conception of the media role is one of 'structured subordination' to the primary definers. Further, the creative media role serves to reinforce a consensual viewpoint, by using public idioms and by claiming to voice public opinion. Thus, in the 'crisis' described, the media have endorsed and enforced primary definitions of industrial militancy, troublesome youth cultures, mugging, student protest movements, as part of a 'law and order' problem.

Policing the Crisis confines its account of the media largely to the area of news coverage and only touches upon the area of popular culture tangentially. Yet clearly the idea of the dominant articulating principle of ideological hegemony, a principle which structures ideological discourses and which involves the media in the construction of that articulation, could and should be extended beyond the confines of news coverage. One obvious area for development is in establishing the relationship between the dominant articulating principle and particular popular fictional genres. Given that genres themselves constitute specific articulations of ideological and formal elements, it would seem to follow that shifts in the dominant articulating principle would be registered in the area of popular fiction by the increased popularity of appropriate genre articulations. The police crime series, for example, became popular at a time when there were major shifts in the dominant articulating principle, from the terrain of ideologies of 'affluence' to that of 'law and order'. The television crime series was a form in which both arguments for and reservations about current 'law and order' issues could be put into play in terms of the subject positions produced by the genre.

Similarly the thriller format developed around notions of Britain's internal and external security in programmes such as *The Professionals* and *Sandbaggers*. *The Professionals* stands at one end of a range of programmes which focus directly on themes of 'law and order' and which extend the notion of policing quite radically. Where programmes such as *The Sweeney* suggested the dissatisfactions of a working policeman in the Flying Squad in terms of the barriers placed by bureaucratic police procedures on the arrest of criminals, *The Professionals* begins from the premise that the ordinary police cannot handle certain problems. One of the books derived from the programmes describes the heroes as the 'hard men'. 'They're the hard men. The Professionals. Doing society's dirty work in the ever more bloody war against violence and destruction . . .'[17]

The process of articulation with a hegemonic principle may help explain one of the continuing problems of the study of genre – why particular genres are popular at any one historical moment and why they may increase or decrease in popularity over time. Works of fiction and specific genres are popular precisely because they articulate, work upon and attempt in different ways to resolve contemporary ideological tensions. The case of situation comedies raises two important issues in relation to this, however. In the first place any comparison of situation comedies and television crime series will indicate something of the complexities of the process whereby popular genres both organise ideological themes differently and interpellate their subjects differently. Thus the episode of *Till Death Us Do Part*, 'If we want a proper democracy we've got to start shooting a few people' (transmission October 1972), constructs one version of the 'law and order' discourse with Garnett 'pulling in' a range of problems into the same problem of law and order.

Alf	. . . Enoch's wrong, having a go at the coons.
Mike and Ria	(astonished) Oh!!!
Alf	Yes! He ain't seen the real danger. It's not the coons. We don't want 'em over here stinking the country out with their curries and making a row on their dustbin lids. But they're bloody harmless – not like yer bloody Russian Unions and yer Chinese *Take-Aways* . . . Hot beds of bloody fifth column they are. But we're on to 'em, don't worry. You'll see the next time one of them commy shop stewards goes in the nick he'll rot there. All they organise them bloody strikes for is so they can get on the bleedin' telly. I blame the BBC for encouraging 'em. They'll put anyone on the bloody telly, they will. Rock an' roll vicars . . . and sex maniacs, an' bloody Irish gunmen. Admit they put stockings over their heads first, but still. They only let the Queen go on for one show at Christmas – I

don't know what they've got against that woman. She should have her own series, 'cos she's better'n Lulu. (*Rita giggles.*) Blimey, she's the best thing on at Christmas.

Garnett's mad logic takes the argument on to cover both prison conditions and the unions and the solution to it all.

Alf	And why shouldn't they get bloody slops? Prisons supposed to be a bloody deterrent annit? They ain't supposed to sit about all day scoffing and shagging! (*Else is shocked.*) I mean, blimey, they'll be putting yer Billy Butlin in charge of the prisons soon, and have bloody red-coats for warders! I mean in the old days, they used to put 'em in bloody chains and ship 'em out to the Colonies. But we can't do that now, 'cos your bloody Labour Party gave all the Colonies away. So we have to keep 'em here and feed 'em out of our taxes. And what if five of their ring leaders [of the prison officer's union] defy the law, eh? They can't bung them in prison, 'cos they're already in there.
Else	They'll have to fine their union.
Alf	Don't be so bloody daft. What are they gonna fine them? Eighty gallons of porridge? A hundredweight of hardtack? And another thing what would yer Russians have done, eh? They wouldn't have put them in prison, would they, eh? And your Chinese, eh? If five of their dockers had defied their laws, eh? They wouldn't have put them in prison, would they? Eh? No. They'd have bloody shot 'em.
Mike	And I suppose you'd like to see 'em shoot our dockers, eh?
Alf	We wouldn't! That's the trouble with this country. That's our weakness! If we want a proper democracy here, we've got to start shooting a few people . . . like yer Russians do.[18]

Till Death Us Do Part quite clearly registers a political concern with the ideological themes which were the focal point of other popular genres, notably the television crime series. At the same time, it could be argued that *Till Death Us Do Part* handles those themes rather differently. Garnett's suggestion that 'we've got to start shooting a few people' may sound more than reminiscent of the solution that is found in most episodes of *The Professionals*, but it is also a conclusion that we are supposed to laugh at rather than applaud. Moreover while *Till Death Us Do Part* was relatively unusual amongst the popular situation comedies of its period in its direct concern with political issues, it was also organised like many other situation comedies to pull the right-wing views of the inimitable Alf Garnett into a family narrative, playing off his position outside a liberal consensus against his position within the family. Later situation comedies such as *Shelley, Citizen Smith* or *Agony* dealt with characters and problems relevant to 'law and order' issues (unemployment in *Shelley*, political radicalism in *Citizen Smith* and sexual permissiveness in *Agony*) in a manner which also tended to pull 'deviance' into a familiar sitcom world of 'universal' problems of family, sexuality and class. The crime series, however, tended to place those same problems and characters as threatening to and outside the parameters of the family, class and 'normal' sexuality. In important ways then situation comedies and the crime series in the 1970s work against one another rendering their themes and subjectivities in opposed directions and in so doing indicating something of the complexity of the relationship between a hegemonic principle and the fictional field.

In the second place, popular and controversial situation comedies such as *Till Death Us Do Part* raise certain questions about the relationship between specific fictional forms and more general ideological formations. It is clearly the case that some fictions are not simply popular but also play a particular part in relation to the ordering of other ideologies. Such fictions have a place in the public arena above and beyond their immediate textual base. The public outcry which surrounded *Till Death Us Do Part* and the way in which Alf Garnett became a figure in the popular imagination even for people who didn't watch television indicates this process at work. At specific historical moments, some fictions, rather than working alongside and in relation to other ideologies, come to provide a nexus through which ideologies may be actively reorganised, shifting the subjectivities at their core, while other fictions work precisely to stabilise existing subjectivities. It is in this area that it is possible to establish in historical rather than formal terms the subversive or incorporative qualities of situation comedies. Without work of this order, the discussion of situation comedies in terms of their potentially subversive effects is simply an exercise in criticism, an attempt to organise situation comedies to mean some things and not others, to establish the protocols of viewing: a perfectly legitimate but rather different exercise.

NOTES

1. T. Ryall, 'Teaching through Genre', *Screen Education*, 1976, p. 27.
2. S. Neale, *Genre*, British Film Institute, London, 1980, p. 28.
3. M. Eaton, 'Laughter in the Dark', *Screen Education*, 1981, p. 33.
4. Neale, *Genre*, p. 9.
5. Ibid., p. 27.
6. G. Hickman, *Agony*, Arrow Books, London, 1980.
7. *Television Sitcom*, BFI Dossier no. 17, British Film Institute, London, 1982.
8. F. Peace, 'How to be immoral and ill, pathetic and dangerous, all at the same time: mass media and the homosexual' in S. Cohen and J. Young (eds), *The Manufacture of News*, Constable, London, 1973, p. 284.
9. Sheldon quoted in R. Dyer (ed.), *Gays and Films*, British Film Institute, London, 1977, p. 16.
10. Klapp quoted in ibid., p. 29.
11. Ibid., p. 30.
12. S. Neale, 'Stereotypes', *Screen Education*, 1979, p. 35.
13. A. Medhurst and L. Tuck, 'The Gender Game' in *British Film Institute Dossier, Television Sitcom*, p. 52.
14. C. James, *The Observer*, 11 March 1972.
15. S. Hall, C. Critcher, T. Jefferson, J. Clarke and B. Roberts, *Policing the Crisis: Mugging, the State and Law and Order*, Macmillan, London, 1978.
16. Ibid., p. 220.
17. K. Blake, *The Professionals 4: Hunter Hunted*, Sphere, London, 1978.
18. J. Speight, *Till Death Us Do Part*, The Woburn Press, London, 1973, pp. 136–7.

20

PROGRESSIVE TELEVISION AND DOCUMENTARY DRAMA

John Caughie

[. . .]

TELEVISION AND THE SINGLE PLAY

It is not uncommon for the majority of viewers to see, regularly, as much as two or three hours of drama, of various kinds, every day. The implications of this have scarcely begun to be considered.

Raymond Williams[1]

The importance of drama for television hardly needs restating. Not only, as Williams indicates, is it massively there, regularly, in its various kinds, but it is also, as a general characteristic of television, everywhere: 'the dramatic', spilling over the edges of programming categories, ordering the viewer's attention: the 'little dramas' which Stephen Heath and Gillian Skirrow expose and 'make strange' in their *World in Action* analysis.[2] Given this importance, the lack of rigorous attention to television drama itself and to the television play is surprising. At a formal level, there are questions of the mechanisms of the look and of the subject of television drama which have barely begun to be asked; questions which are important not only for television itself, bringing to it work which has been done in film, but also for theory: television in its different specificity, offers a resistance to universalised theories of representation, and to essentialisms of vision.

More centrally here, television drama raises difficult political questions. Part of the hesitancy in engaging with drama production may come from a reasonable suspicion of the way in which the cultural prestige of 'serious drama' is used by television and television reviewing. Or it may come from an assessment of the increasingly marginal place which theatre and theatrical forms occupy in present culture. Either way, what is clear is that the vast majority of politically engaged attention has been directed towards the forms of representation of actuality (current affairs, documentary, news), or to popular genres (soap opera, situation comedy, light entertainment).

From *Screen*, 21: 3 (1980) pp. 9–35.

I want to offer here an argument for the importance of 'serious drama' within a political understanding of television.

Firstly, and somewhat tentatively, within certain areas of social and/or sexual unease, the single play or play series seems to function for television as some kind of cutting edge, working to extend television's social or sexual discourse. Drama tests, and occasionally extends, what it is possible not only to say, but also, and more perilously, to show.

[. . .]

Secondly, and more assertively, drama's extension of the television discourse becomes politically important in a concrete way at the point at which it confronts censorship. It is precisely the extension of what can be said and shown that concerns the National Viewers' and Listeners' Association, and, more importantly, it is an uncertainty as to what can and cannot be shown which creates nervous reactions within institutional control. Explicit censorship is always a problem for broadcasting which claims public responsibility, since it exposes the tensions within that claim, opens up contradictions between broadcasting's declared principles and the determinations of its practice, and disturbs its view of itself: a confusion arises between the role of guardian and the role of public servant. Thus the censorship of current affairs programmes on Ireland throws into question again and again television's claim to be an independent, and hence objective, reporter. Clearly, broadcasting has developed a vocabulary to deal with such a confusion of roles, and, in suppressing current affairs material, can offer apparently clear criteria in terms of 'national security', 'civic responsibility', 'objectivity', or simple 'truth to fact'; criteria, that is, which may throw a shadow over notions of 'independence' and 'the public's right to know', but which carry with them the appearance of reasonable authority which will seriously divide the audience only along already established political lines. The censorship of drama, on the other hand, relies on a much less secure language: 'taste', 'public sensibility', 'the little gap between fact and fiction'; and it treads on a substantial area of the liberal consensus involving assumptions about the relationship of art and society, and about the creative artist's right to express him- or herself. Assumptions which broadcasting shares and supports in its insistence on the 'seriousness' of drama ('Drama is the most deeply penetrating way of knowing what it is to be human.' – *Radio Times*, 4th April, 1968) and on the necessary encouragement of creative freedom ('These twenty plays are the result of an invitation to authors of fame or promise to write for television without being subject to dictation on the kind of play required'. – *Radio Times*, 23rd September, 1960). Within the context of its pronouncements, it is never comfortable for the institution to impose limits on what may be penetrated by 'serious drama', or to accept the role of curtailing the freedom of the artist.

[. . .]

The single play or play series is not essential to television. It has been virtually absent from American television for some time, and its expense and awkwardness within the schedules have made it perpetually precarious in Britain: bulletins on the ill health and imminent death of the single play were appearing in *The Radio Times* and *The Listener* in the early 1960s. It has been preserved on British television because it confers a certain cultural prestige, a 'seriousness', on television as a whole. But in order to function in this way, in order to be 'serious', drama occasionally has to appear to overstep limits, to show what has not been shown before. The tension surrounding this is politically important within the institutions, and is an important factor in determining the movements of forces within television. The nature of its political importance within the programmes is more uncertain: I propose to come back to that uncertainty in its particular relationship to documentary drama.

[. . .]

DOCUMENTARY DRAMA

Drama or documentary? – the 'Scotland Yard' programmes fall uneasily between. Basically these are documentary, each dealing with some different aspect of the extremely complex activities of Scotland Yard. Unfortunately it seems to have been felt, quite wrongly, that this would be insufficiently interesting in itself, so little shots of drama are injected and these give the impression, I am sure the quite unfair impression, that the police are incompetent or venal or both.

Hilary Corke, Listener, *2nd June*, 1960.

Writing, apparently without irony in 1960, Hilary Corke anticipates precisely the 'little gap between fact and fiction' which worried William Deedes (editor of the *Telegraph*) in the discussion which followed the transmission of *Days of Hope*, or dismays Lord Carrington over *Death of a Princess*: in a speech to the Anglo-Arab Middle East Association, he says, 'The new formula of mixing fact with fiction, dramatisation masquerading as documentary, can be dangerous and misleading'.

The formula is not, in fact, new and forms of dramatised documentary have been occupying an uneasy place on television for more than twenty years. Before that, dramatic reconstructions of actuality have a history in cinema as old as cinema itself, beginning with Meliès' reconstructions of coronations and assassinations, and continuing with the Soviet cinema's celebrations of the Revolution. For British television the important cinematic antecedent could be found in the various ideologies and practices which were circulating in the documentary movement in the 1930s and 1940s – from *Fires Were Started* to Ralph Bond and the Cooperative Society films. In American theatre during the Depression, the Federal Theatre Project had developed the Living Newspaper to dramatise documentation about urban housing, farm-workers' struggles for unionisation, the power industry; and some of this was picked up by left-wing theatre groups in Britain, and subsequently developed by Joan Littlewood in the 1950s and 1960s. On radio, a crucial source of early television genres, dramatised documetaries were a commonplace, and had been given a certain left-wing inflection in the 'radio ballads' devised by Charles Parker and Ewan McColl (who was also associated with Joan Littlewoods's theatre) which dramatised areas of working-class life and history. Far from being new, there are a number of histories and traditions which can be followed through from film, theatre, and radio into television.

Two ideas can be identified in this for an understanding of the development of television documentary drama: one, the 'documentary idea', can be associated with Grierson and Walter Lippman and the extension of democracy through social education and the presentation of information in its most accessible form; the other, to the left of this, attemps to recover lost histories and dramatise repressed documents. Television, in its dramatised documentaries of the 1950s and early 1960s, seems to have accepted the form fairly unproblematically within the terms of its social responsibility to inform and educate: there were dramatised documentaries on Scotland Yard, on bankruptcy, on the town vet, on regional symphony orchestras, on a doctor struck off the medical list, on the immigration service. Interestingly, in the light of the subsequent history of the form, these early programmes were as likely to be dismissed for their complicity, as regretted for their unease:

I don't suppose the series will dare suggest an immigration officer can ever behave unreasonably, can abuse his alarming power, can ever become anything less than a sagacious and trustworthy protector of society.

Derek Hill, Listener, 6th *September*, 1962

These information programmes appeared regularly on BBC until the end of 1962, and then disappeared as a clearly marked form. After 1962 there are isolated events of considerable importance – Peter Watkins' *Culloden* in 1964, the Loach/McTaggart *Up the Junction* in 1965, Peter Watkins' suppressed *The War Game* in 1966 – and the Loach/Garnett *Cathy Come Home* which appears at the end of 1966. It is the line which develops from *Cathy Come Home*, the line associated with the Loach/Garnett label – with the recovery of lost histories, with the exposure of social injustice, with 'progressive realism' – that I am primarily concerned with here.

Something further should be added to separate this line from other forms of dramatised documentary which have become current. On one side of the line, there are American 'factions' like *Holocaust* or *Washington: Behind Closed Doors:* on the other side there are documentary reconstructions like *Three Days in Szczecin*, or *Invasion*. 'Factions' are constructed along firm dramatic, or melodramatic lines, their 'documentariness' coming from the actuality of their historical referent, rather than from any mixture of forms: there is in fact very little stylistic or narrative distinction between, say, *Holocaust* and the American television serialisation of *From Here to Eternity*. 'Dramadoc', on the other hand, is identified by Leslie Woodhead, producer of *Three Days in Szczecin* for Granada, as 'dramatised journalism':

Our priorities, disciplines, sources and basic motivations are journalistic, and where there is a clash with dramatic values, journalism wins. We make bad plays – not a slogan, just a declaration of priorities.

Listener, 23rd September, 1976

This dramatised journalism is the aggressive development of the earlier innocuous information programmes, dramatising socially important events and documented facts which the cameras were not there to record at the time, the dramatic reconstruction is made necessary by television's need to show.

Each of these forms has its own interest and its own problems, and there is an obvious overlap within all forms of dramatised documentary, particularly between dramatised journalism and documentary drama, the one exploiting the visual rhetoric of the other. For the sake of particularity, however, I am interested here in the relation of documentary drama to drama, rather than its relation to journalism, and while the two forms share the possibility of a confusion between fact and fiction which gives them both an uneasy place within television, each has a formal and functional specificity which needs to be considered separately. Here I am concerned with the particular articulation of the dramatic and the documentary within fictional dramatic narrative, with the way in which the one functions for the other, and with the nature of the unease which the articulation seems to produce.

Within fictional dramatic narrative, it would clearly be a mistake to constitute documentary drama as a homogeneous category, and there are important shifts and developments between, say, *Cathy Come Home* or *The Big Flame* on the one hand, and *Days of Hope* and *Law and Order* on the other. Nor is it simply a process of evolutionary change: *The Spongers* probably has more in common with *Cathy Come Home* than it has with *Law and Order*. The variations – in narrative construction, in camera technique, in lighting, in acting – are important, but it seems more useful here to establish the consistencies: it is, in fact, one of the defining characteristics of documentary drama that it has a consistent televisual style, a visual appearance and a relationship to narrative space which is particular to it, which is recognisable, which circulates its own meanings. This consistency and specificity can be elaborated in terms of *mise en scène*, or more precisely in terms of the articulation of two looks – the look of the documentary, and the look of the dramatic fiction.

By the 'dramatic look' I mean the system of looks and glances which is familiar from fictional film, and which works to produce the consistency and movement of the narrative, placing the spectator in relation to it – the rhetoric, that is, of narrative realist film: eye-line match, field/reverse-field, point-of-view. This rhetoric centres the narrative: it establishes, within a world of events, scenes, characters, and little narratives, the line and the connections which are to be privileged. It orders the world into a readable hierarchy. It is worth noting that, made on film, documentary drama tends, within the articulation of its dramatic look, to have a more highly elaborated narrative rhetoric, with a more cinematic deployment of field/reverse-field or point-of-view, than the television drama which has its roots in the multi-camera techniques of the studio.

By the 'documentary look' I mean the system of looks which constructs the social space of the fiction, a social space which is more than simply a background, but which, in a sense, constitutes what the documentary drama wishes to be about, the 'document' which is to be dramatised. Thus, *Cathy Come Home* and *The Spongers* wish to be about the social environment of sections of the community and the bureaucracy which oppresses them; *Days of Hope* claims as its subject the whole of the labour movement from rural community to organised labour. This attention to the social environment and to the community is what connects documentary drama with the ideology of naturalism:

We are looking for the cause of social evil; we study the anatomy of classes and individuals to explain the derangements which are produced in society and in man . . . No work can be more moralising than ours, then, because it is upon it that law should be based.
Zola, To the Young People of France [in *The Experimental Novel & Other Essays*, trans. Sheridan,
New York, Haskell House, 1964]

This connection with naturalism can be extended to the level of method: Zola's 'experimental method' consisted of observing the material world closely and then analysing it 'scientifically' by setting in motion an 'experiment', a narrative situation, to see what would happen. In a similar way, documentary drama seems to produce its analysis by setting in motion a dramatic experiment within the world observed and constructed by the documentary look.

Observed *and constructed*. The documentary look is not the perfect vision of an actual world, but operates, as does the dramatic, within a specific rhetoric which is not innocent, offering an objective, true social space, but which works within rules and strategies to produce a social space which is also a narrative, fictional space. What seems specific to documentary drama as compared with narrative realist film is that, whereas classical realist film depends to a greater or lesser extent on the illusion of unmediated vision, on a transparency of form and style, documentary drama operates a rhetoric of mediated style which is clearly marked, but which has a prior association with truth and neutrality. If classical realist film depends on a certain invisibility of form, and on a spectator who forgets the camera, the documentary look takes its appearance of objectivity from its place within the conventions of documentary: thus, the hand-held camera, the cramped shot, natural lighting, inaudible sound. The appearance in the fiction of the documentary look, easily visible but unsteady and apparently unpremeditated, establishes the impression of a basis of unproblematic fact on which the dramatic 'experiment' can be conducted, and which will guarantee its validity.

In one sense, the documentary look takes different forms, finding its guarantee in different sources, different documentary conventions. While black and white film was still acceptable for television, *The War Game* could rely on hand-held camera and grainy film, the conventions of immediacy, reportage, and *cinéma verité*. *Law and Order*, particularly in the early episodes, works with the rhetoric of a concealed, investigative camera, spying on its object behind cover (cf *Rome Open City*): it also depends on the illusion that, where sound is inaudible and language incomprehensible, they cannot have been created but must simply have been captured (cf Altman). [. . .] The point of interest is that all of these strategies of the documentary look rely less on the guarantees of their own reflection of the real world and more on a reference to other formal conventions which are associated with reflection.

At another, and I think more fundamental level, the documentary look finds its consistency in the rhetoric of the 'unplanned' or 'unpremeditated' shot: the camera surprised by the action.

If you are making a documentary and there was just a cameraman in the room and he was following the conversation, he would never be at somebody when they started to speak. He would follow the conversation. That's what we tried to do really, to let the conversation call for the cuts, rather than the camera knowing who was going to speak next and, therefore, always being in at the start of a sentence.

Ken Loach interview in Cinema Papers, April 1976

[. . .]

Now this could easily degenerate into a naïve critique of deception and cheating; or into the equally naïve assumption that the film-makers are not aware of what they are doing. Clearly they know, and, fairly reasonably, expect us to know that they are producing fictions, and exploiting certain conventions. My point is not to expose trickery, but to try to point to the bases and the determinations of conventions which are not innocent instruments, simply available for any use, but which come to documentary drama already weighted with significances and associations. More immediately, and more concretely, I am interested in what the articulation of the dramatic look and the documentary look does within the fiction.

I have already suggested that the dramatic look gives the narrative a centre, orders the heterogeneity of the world 'captured' by the documentary look, and establishes the privileged figures and events. Thus there is an easily discernible story running through the history of the working class in *Days of Hope* and in *Law* and *Order* we have no difficulty in picking out the figures of the Detective, the Villain, and the Brief from the total system of the institutions of the law. The problem is that, in the end, though documentary drama within its naturalist project wishes to be about the community and the social environment, there is always the risk that the balance will fail, the dramatic narrative will impose its resolutions on the documentary disorder, and the drama will end up being about the privileged, centred individuals. Thus, at the end of *Days of Hope*, we are as likely to be interested in whether Sarah and Philip will patch up the problems of their marriage, as to be interested in the future of the Party and its relationship to the working class. Within the terms of narrative resolutions this is an inevitable risk.

More than this, the rhetoric of the dramatic look inscribes the document into experience. Eye-line match, field/reverse-field, point-of-view are mechanisms which work within film and television to articulate the look of the viewing subject, and to construct a system of viewing places for the spectator within the fiction. The viewing subject identifies with the fictional world through identifying with the looks of the dramatic figures within it. By deploying this rhetoric of looks, documentary drama produces systems of identification which are specific to it as a televisual form and cannot simply be homogenised into a monolithic narrative system, but which nevertheless set in motion a play of sympathetic involvement for the spectator. The spectator experiences the drama. What documentary drama offers (like naturalism) is the experience of the drama, rather than the analysis of (or 'scientific experiment' on) the document. It is therefore vulnerable to the critique of Lukács that it is a 'subjective protest', or to the critique of Brecht that it fails to expose the spectator to the contradictions which have to be worked out. Thus *Days of Hope* offers the experience of history – memory – rather than its analysis; *The Spongers* or *Cathy Come Home* offers the experience of social injustice – bad conscience. The issue of experience and analysis is clearly part of a wider debate, which will have to be picked up again in discussing documentary drama's 'progressiveness.'

If the rhetoric of the drama inscribes the document within narrative and experience, the rhetoric of the documentary establishes the experience of the real, and places it within a system of guarantees and confirmations. The look of the documentary is qualitatively different, lacking the reverse field of the dramatic look, its 'reversibility'.[3] The documentary look is a look at its object rather than putting its look into play, the object looked at but only itself looking on: the figures of the drama exchange and reverse looks, the figures of the documentary are looked at and look on.

Within the conventions of documetary, the objectifying look is part of the support of truth and neutrality. For documentary drama, however, two looks are in play, and they come to constitute a hierarchy: the rhetoric of the drama operates an exchange of looks between the characters, dramatising their relationship, activating divisions between them and within them, putting them in doubt, giving them an incompleteness which can only be filled by the eventual plentitude of the narrative. The rhetoric of documentary, the fixed and fixing look, constitutes its object – the community, the social environment, the working class – as simply there, unproblematic, already completed, 'extras'. The working class, the community appears as a simple unquestioned presence, functioning to locate the dramas of others, but not themselves dramatised.

[. . .]

The problem, then, is one of integration. The two discourses, of documentary and of drama, are integrated to produce a movement of confirmations, guarantees and narrativisations back and forth between them. Each functions to support the other rather than to call the other into question; there is no contradiction for the spectator between the drama and the document, but only a confirmation; the tensions are all within the drama, rather than between it and its referent. The discourse is ultimately one of unproblematic truth. This is reinforced by the hierarchies established within the narrative, a narrative which, although it digresses to bring in the life of the community (the club scene in *The Spongers*, or the extended celebration dance at the end of the second episode of *Days of Hope*), nevertheless re-centres itself, pulling attention back towards narrative and resolution.

DOCUMENTARY DRAMA AND 'PROGRESSIVENESS'

All this, however, does not close off the question of documentary drama's progressiveness. On one level, the important question is not what the form has been, but what it could be. In this respect, there is a clear model of a potential development of documentary drama in the television production of *The Cheviot, The Stag, and the Black, Black Oil.*

[. . .]

For the development of the formal effectiveness of documentary drama, *The Cheviot . . .* represents a radical separation of the discourses of the drama and the discourses of the documentary: the television production is at the same time a drama, a documentary on the way in which the theatrical performance circulated in the Highlands, a historical reconstruction, and a documentary on working conditions in the North Sea oil industry. The elements are not integrated to confirm and support each other, but are clearly separated out and allowed to play against each other. The risk which the theatrical production always ran of being overwhelmed by the exuberance of its own performance is tempered by the possibility which the separation of discourses allows of continually unsettling the spectator's postion. The documentary on the present oil industry produces a contemporaneity of history which both undercuts the romanticism of a 'Celtic twilight', and offers a way of seeing this struggle in terms of other struggles. It is the possibility of this collision of documentary and drama, of the refusal of integration, which makes the documentary drama a potentially interesting political form. It also has to be said that, whereas *Cathy Come Home* started a tradition, the model of *The Cheviot* . . . has not yet been followed up.

At another level, progressiveness on television is not ultimately a question of form, of integration or separation, because television occupies a particular social space which makes its progressiveness or regressiveness more difficult to calculate. Thus, however much the ideology within which it operates may be characterised as reformist, the screening of *Cathy Come Home* is an event with material effects within the history of British social work; *Law and Order* is an event within the history of the relations between the police and one of the major media; the screening of *The Big Flame*, coinciding with the Devlin Report on the docks and the Upper Clyde Shipyard sit-in, occurs within a particular conjuncture of events and forces which makes the identification of its political effectivity more complex. Unlike films or plays, television programmes are seen all at once (and reacted to all at once) by a national audience. Because of this, it becomes difficult, and unrewarding, to establish the final conditions for the progressiveness of television. The conjuncture in which programmes are screened has to be critically identified; and because the programmes are made within basically conservative institutions which are both highly determined and highly determining, their place within the politics of the institutions has also to be brought into consideration. The political analysis of a television programme such as *Law and Order* or *The Big Flame* has to go beyond the identification of the politics which it speaks, towards an analysis of the place which it occupies within the political forces and contradictions which are current at the time of its screening, and towards an understanding of its relationship to the other representations which television predominantly circulates and supports.

Also, to argue for the need to develop forms which will produce the spectator in contradiction implies a position within a wider political debate against the political effectiveness of notions of experience and solidarity. For television, I am less confident of this position. Under certain conditions, of which the present may be one, I want to be able to say that, *for television*, in its specific conditions, it may be politically progressive to confirm an identity (of sexuality or class), to recover repressed experience or history, to contest the dominant image with an alternative identity. Documentary drama seems to me to have occupied a progressive role within television insofar as it has introduced into the discourses of television a repressed political, social discourse which may contribute to an audience's political formation, and may increase its scepticism of the other representations which television offers. I want to be able to say this at the same time as arguing for different ways of looking.

This, in a sense, is to collapse the whole notion of 'the progressive text', whose progressiveness can be measured against some scale of correctness. Within the social space of television, within the politics of its institutions, and within the way it circulates, television programmes have the capacity to be events as much as to be texts. But simply to leave it at that, is to accept a relativism, which can only determine progressiveness after the event, and cannot influence the development of progressive forms of representation.

[. . .]

It is in this sense that I am arguing for the importance of documentary drama in particular, and drama in general: in the sense, that is, in which drama and documentary drama represent areas of tension and uncertainty for television, areas in which debate could be effective and in which institutional debates already exist. The question is one of privileging those areas as sites of critical and theoretical engagement: a question of how to respect those areas for their political progressiveness for television; a question, at the same time, of how to argue against them, for an extension of television's discourse in forms which will contest easy images, unsettle its conventional patterns, and break up the homogeneity of its representations.

NOTES

1. Williams, *Television: Technology and Cultural Form*, London, Fontana Collins, 1974.
2. See Stephen Heath and Gillian Skirrow. 'Television: a world in action', *Screen,* vol. 18, no. 2. Summer 1977.
3. In the sense in which Serge Daney uses the term when he criticises Antonioni's documentary on China as the work of a *'contrabandier'*, smuggling out in images the 'properties' of the Chinese people: see, *'La rémise en scene', Cahiers du Cinéma*, no. 268–9, July–August, 1976, p. 23.

21

TELEVISED CHAT AND THE SYNTHETIC PERSONALITY

Andrew Tolson

Just as television, and broadcasting more generally, has developed its own particular dramatic genres (e.g. situation comedy), so too it has developed certain forms of broadcast talk which have identifiable generic structures. These forms of talk are, in general terms, 'informal and conversational' (Scannell, 1988), but more precisely, they should be seen as institutionalized variants of 'conversation' as such. Moreover, these forms of talk occur across the different programme formats within which 'talk' predominates. For instance, it would be interesting to undertake a study of the art of 'live commentary' as a speech genre which clearly takes different forms on radio and television, but which occurs across sports programmes, state occasions, live political events and, sometimes, disasters. Live commentary is one broadcast speech genre; and 'chat', I am suggesting, is another. Chat is a form of studio talk, which can be found in all types of interviews, panel discussions, game shows and human interest programmes (e.g. *That's Life!*) – wherever in fact there is a studio.

What then characterizes 'chat' as a broadcast speech genre? In many contexts [. . .] chat is apparent in a clear shift of *register* within the programme format where it occurs, such that the primary business of the format is temporarily delayed or suspended. Thus in the context of a game show, chat between participants delays the actual playing of the game (a prime example would be *Blankety Blank* [a celebrity quiz show]); whereas in the context of a current affairs interview chat introduces a suspension within the 'main' discourse, whilst a 'subsidiary' discourse (an aside, a metadiscursive comment) is briefly formulated (cf. Montgomery, 1977). It is this functional contrast between main and subsidiary levels of discourse which frequently allows us to recognize chat when we hear it:

Robin Day.	Mrs Thatcher do you intend to lead the Conservative Party into the next election in say '87?
Mrs Thatcher.	I hope so.

From Andrew Tolson, 'Televised Chat and the Synthetic Personality', Ch. 9 in Paddy Scannell (ed.), *Broadcast Talk* (London: Sage, 1991) pp. 179–87.

Day.	Because if you do that and let's say that the next is in the autumn of 1987 do you realise then that you would have been, held the office of Prime Minister for a longer, for the longest continuous period this century and possibly long before that?
Thatcher.	Yes.
Day.	Eight-and-a-half-years, and you'll be six . . .
Thatcher.	Not very long.
Day.	Eight-and-a-half-years.
Thatcher.	Yes it's not very long if you look back to other times.
Day.	And you'll be sixty-two. You still think you want to go ahead at the next election?
Thatcher.	Yes. I shall be a very fit sixty-two. You might be a little bit nearer that than I am, but you feel all right?
Day.	*(chuckles)* Forgive me if I don't answer that question Prime Minister, towards the end of this interesting interview. (*Panorama*, April 1984).

Actually, I think Brown and Yule [1983] have overestimated the difficulties in arriving at a formal definition of 'chat'. There are at least three main identifying features of this speech genre, not all of which may be operating at once. First, there is often a topical shift towards the 'personal' (as opposed to the institutional), or towards the 'private' (as opposed to the public). Secondly, this shift may be accompanied by displays of wit (e.g. foregrounding lexical ambiguities) or humour (double entendres, etc.). But thirdly, and this is the vital point, in any context 'chat' always works by opening up the possibility of transgression. Chat does not simply reproduce norms and conventions, rather it flirts with them, for instance, it opens up the possibility of the interviewee putting questions to the interviewer. Certainly, in the context of a *Panorama* interview, Robin Day must appear to 'manage' this behaviour; but at the same time (as this example shows) it is not simply disavowed. For in this momentary transgression of convention, both Mrs Thatcher, and in his response Day himself, are constructed as 'television personalities'.

Defined in these terms, I would suggest that 'chat' is a central feature of televised public discourse, and I shall return to a discussion of its effects. For not only is chat a ubiquitous and constant possibility for nearly every kind of televised studio talk; it is also, because of the studio's pivotal location in the regime of broadcasting, in a certain position of dominance. However, from a discursive point of view, perhaps the most interesting of all programme formats is the contemporary 'chat' or 'talk' show (I will use the American term 'talk show' to emphasize that 'chat' is a genre which occurs in several formats). In the 1980s, the talk show attained new heights of sophistication, both in Britain and in the USA. In America, David Letterman might be compared and contrasted to the earlier format personified by Johnny Carson; whilst in Britain, the genre dominated in the 1970s by Michael Parkinson (previously, a journalist) was taken over and developed by Terry Wogan (previously, a disc jockey). The talk show is, by definition, devoted to the production of 'chat'; but by the mid-1980s the BBC's prime-time Saturday night show *Wogan* had developed 'chat' to the point where it was virtually an art form.

TELEVISION CHAT AND THE 'PERSONALITY EFFECT'

Consider for example the following exchange between Terry Wogan and Shelley Winters (*Wogan*, 10 March 1984):

Winters.	You had to give away my age, huh?
Wogan.	No no.
Winters.	You had to say how old I was. When was it, 1939?
Wogan.	1957 or something, wasn't it?
Winters.	When was *Gone With The Wind* done?
Wogan.	I'm not sure.
Winters.	The only reason I didn't get the part was that I had a Brooklyn accent. Vivien Leigh spoke better otherwise I would have got it.
Wogan.	You would have walked that.
Winters.	* What was that accent, that man, who just talked for fifteen minutes?
Wogan.	What, Terry Venables?
Winters.	Yes.
Wogan.	I'm not sure, a type of East End accent I think. I think he makes it up as he goes along.
Winters.	I did a picture with Michael Caine a while ago called *Alfie* which was sort of a good picture but I never knew what he was saying. Whenever he took a breath I said my line, it was like that.
Wogan.	Many of us have difficulty with Michael Caine, yes.
Winters.	It seems like the same language but it isn't. I mean sometimes you get in a lot of trouble.
Wogan.	What sort of trouble have you been in?
Winters.	I'm not discussing it.
Wogan.	Come on.
Winters.	There are millions of people watching I mean you say anything on your television . . .
Wogan.	That's what you think.
Winters.	I know er, but you know, no there's nothing. Well you say anything. Last night I watched something on BBC2 about sex.
Wogan.	Yes we have that over here. What do you call that in America?
Winters.	You don't talk about it you do it *(laughter)*. I mean, I never saw a show *Sex Education for Adults*. That's what it was.
Wogan.	Yes, I saw it myself. I learned quite a lot.
Winters.	* It was slides and pictures and diagrams and er, I was, did it shock you?
Wogan.	No, because I know where I'm going wrong now.
Winters.	* Well, listen how long have you done this show, three years?
Wogan.	Feels like it. Only a year.
Winters.	No, you don't.
Wogan.	Still a boy, still a boy at the game. Yes, before I did this there was a very old man who used to do it called Dartington or something.
Winters.	Have you thought, now Saturday nights because of inflation and everything, I learned from the crew – I've just been doing a picture called *Always*, and I think it will be done always. It's all about, I play a Russian psychic lesbian I think, I'm not sure.
Wogan.	I'm glad you looked at that sex instruction film.
Winters.	I know er.
Wogan.	I can see the problems you'd have with that part.

Winters.	Well, anyway, it was a sort of weird love story that takes place between 1936 and now and the people they have trouble making out. Do you say making out?
Wogan.	No. Making up? Making it?
Winters.	No, when you do it.
Wogan.	Doing it?
Winters.	Yeah, do you say making out?
Wogan.	No, we say doing it.
Winters.	Well, in the still of the night if you can't sleep do you ever wonder, because people don't go out much on Saturday nights as they used to, it used to be a regular thing.
Wogan.	They do now, look they usen't to, but they do now since we started.
Wingers.	* This interview. OK. Now have you ever wondered sort of if people are at home Saturday nights and they're watching you and its warm and they stretch out in the bedroom or the living room wherever the telly is (*TW:* steady, yes). Have you ever thought how many babies you're responsible for?
Wogan.	No, I'm responsible for no babies whatsoever.
Winters.	Well you are though.
Wogan.	No I'm not (*SW:* Yes you are) No, people nod off to me.
Winters.	I didn't nod off last week when Joan Rivers said all those terrible things.
Wogan.	Didn't she, didn't she say some shocking . . . You talk about us saying some shocking things, I mean she really does.
Winters.	No we don't let her say those things on television in America.
Wogan.	Yes you do.
Winters.	No we don't. We laugh at night clubs and then we are ashamed we laughed. I mean I'm not exactly a Women's Libber but I mean I get so angry when I laugh at her (. . .)
Wogan.	* You've been a bit of a shocker yourself though, haven't you?
Winters.	Yes, but I put it in print I don't do it on television.

I will begin my formal analysis of this exchange by recognizing that as a species of interviewing, it contains some peculiar, and in other contexts abnormal, features. Just in straight quantitative terms Winters (interviewee) puts nine questions to Wogan, whilst he (interviewer) puts seven questions to his guest. Furthermore, at least four of Winters' questions (marked by asterisks in the transcript) can be counted as major topical initiations, requiring developed responses from Wogan, which Winters then follows up with supplementary questions and comments. Wogan himself makes three such topical initiations, the first of which is rejected by the interviewee ('I'm not discussing it'). Equally, many of the utterances in this exchange are hearable neither as questions nor as answers, but rather as initiating propositions or as contributions to sequences of argument.

Nor is this exactly the intimate and cosy 'fireside chat', casting the audience in the position of 'eavesdroppers' to a private conversation, which some previous forms of the talk show have attempted to simulate (Greatbatch, 1987: 35). Rather, the Wogan/Winters dialogue seems to be much more aware of itself as a public performance: at times it is a kind of double act, with mock pantomimic arguments ('Oh yes you do'; 'Oh no I don't') and with Wogan playing the straight man to Winters' humorous lines. In a word, the talk show interview is now dedicated to *banter*. It is as if the conventions of interviewing have now become a pretext for the development of clever and complex forms of verbal improvisation in which both parties more or less equally participate. Within this space, Winters in particular stretches her position as interviewee to the limit: not only does she ask most of the questions and introduce most of the topics; as she comments on Wogan's introduction and interrogates his career as a talk show host she seems to be highlighting the artificiality of his role.

However, my principal reason for reproducing this extract here is because it provides a particularly rich illustration of my three defining features of 'chat' as a speech genre. First then, in terms of content, there is the characteristic focus on the 'personal', which in *Wogan* was often equated with the sexual, but also was more generally articulated in terms of gossip – both about other stars/personalities (Leigh, Caine) and previous performances on the programme (Rivers). Also at this level a common cultural knowledge is invoked (e.g. the date of *Gone With The Wind*, the joke about 'Dartington' i.e. Parkinson, the BBC's best-known talk show interviewer before Wogan). This is the kind of mass-mediated cultural knowledge which is classified in many contexts today as 'trivia'.

Secondly, and building on this foundation, there is a sustained and highly self-reflexive metadiscourse about television as a cultural institution. Here participants not only invoke the cultural knowledge of the viewer, they also draw attention to the construction of their own performances. It is assumed for instance, that the viewer has a knowledge of the history of television, of its genres and is reflexively aware of the domestic conditions of its reception. Indeed, when Winters refers to these, in her speculations about viewers and babies, she comes very close to transgressing the formal distance between television and its audience – the next step would be to address the viewer directly. It is certainly very far from a realistic simulation, where disbelief is 'suspended', because here the reflexive nature of the talk assumes a viewer who is consciously aware of the forms as well as the contents of television.

In my view, however, it is at a third level that this kind of talk becomes really clever. There is a level at which the dialogic improvisation is somewhat similar to a jazz performance, not only because it is apparently unrehearsed, but also in so far as it involves a play of thematic repetition and variation. In this dialogue the metadiscursive level ('Here we are on television'/'How are people watching this at home?') is articulated to a repetition of two topics (both introduced by the interviewee): i.e. language/cultural difference and sex/the limits of public discourse. A form of *wit* is demonstrated by interweaving these various topics, so that each is inflected in terms of the other. Thus the topic of linguistic difference is inflected into the terminology of sex ('Do you say making out?'), whilst the topic of sexual discourse is inflected into cultural differences in the publicly sayable ('We don't let her say those things on television'). Two or three topics are in the air at once and the skill of the participants consists in their ability to manipulate the dialogue to ensure that the verbal juggling act continues.

And the performance is of course given added impetus by the fact that it is apparently 'live'. Will the participants be able to sustain this spontaneous flow of wit and repartee? In fact, in this case, the programme was recorded, the 'liveness' is an illusion; but an effect of liveness and immediacy is constructed in a number of ways. In this context, with its 'live' studio audience, liveness is an effect of the studio location; but it is also reinforced by deictic features of the reflexive metadiscourse: 'What was that accent that just talked?', 'How long have you been doing this show?' When Shelley Winters talks about the viewer's domestic situation she indirectly refers to immediate conditions of viewing. My point here is that whilst the metadiscourse does, on one level, 'demystify' the institution of television, it also simultaneously contributes to a 'liveness' effect which helps to sustain it. At this level then, the metadiscourse *re-mystifies*: it reaffirms a bond between television performers, studio audience and, by extension, the domestic viewer which implicates all parties in a common and immediate situation.

All of which serves to reproduce a particular kind of 'personality effect'. It is instructive at this point to refer to the discussion of 'personality' in television studies which, in some accounts, has made reference to the effects of televised 'chat'. For instance, John Langer (1981) has defined television's 'personality system' in terms of a 'complex unity [of] heterogenous and multi-faceted codes', amounting to a 'systematic tendency' across many forms of television (Langer, 1981: 352). But after talking in general terms about the effects of 'speaking for oneself' in television interviews, and in close-up, Langer comes to focus specifically on a notion of 'disclosure':

> In the context of the talk-show's carefully orchestrated informality, with its illusion of lounge-room casualness and leisurely pace, the host and guest engage in 'chat'. During the course of this chat, with suitable questions and tactful encouragement from the host, the guest is predictably 'drawn in' to making certain 'personal' disclosures, revealing aspects of what may be generally regarded as the private self, in fact becoming incorporated into television's personality system by disclosing for the purposes of television, one's 'personality'.
>
> . . . What prevails in the end is not the talk show's diluted hucksterism and commercial 'hype' but its capacity to provide a special setting for personal disclosure where guests appear to be showing us their 'real' selves, where they can discuss how they 'feel' and reflect on their private lives with impunity. If these guests are among the great and powerful or are well-known celebrities, which is most frequently the case, this is the place where the cares and burdens of high office or public life can be set aside, where we can see them as they 'really are', which in the end after all, as these programmes set out to illustrate, is just like us, 'ordinary folks'. (Langer, 1981: 360–1)

On this basis, Langer goes on to attribute an ideological effect to this discourse of personality, in so far as it displaces social and political criteria. But perhaps his frequent recourse to inverted commas ('real' selves, etc.) already begins to suggest some doubts about the sincerity of personal disclosure in the contemporary talk show. In fact, what Langer really seems to be describing here is an earlier form of 'human interest' interview programme, of which John Freeman's *Face to Face* (BBC, 1959–62) would be an exemplary instance, where indeed a populist personality discourse was frequently reflected in the open and apparently sincere disclosure of 'real feelings'. In these programmes, Freeman's interviewing technique might certainly be characterized as a strategy of 'tactful encouragement', allied to a rigorous, probing use of the camera. But today, I would suggest, this kind of transparent populism appears old-fashioned. Although its rhetorical structure (i.e. public/private persons; apparent/real selves, etc.) persists as a generic formula for the talk show, it seems to me that a fundamental shift has taken place in the way this formula is reproduced.

Increasingly, as the Winters interview illustrates, 'personality' now appears not in transparent revelation, but in the interviewee's capacity to negotiate the terms of 'disclosure'. This is precisely not the context for a 'true confession' (as Winters herself indicates) and so part of the pleasure for the audience in this speech genre consists in working out the different degrees of truth/untruth in what is then spoken. A certain level of complexity, which implicates the 'knowingness' of the viewer, is related to a form of speaking from 'experience' where *the experiences may or may not be real.* [. . .] [C]learly at this level 'personality' is no longer reducible to 'people as they really are'. Rather, it seems to me that the personality effect now consists in the willingness of stars and celebrities, like Winters, to take the risk of playing this kind of public verbal game. In the contemporary talk show the interview is explicitly and transparently a *performance* of 'chat' – that is its *raison d'être* – and there are moments in this performance when the very concept of 'personality' is up for discussion.

PERSONALITY AS PERFORMANCE

In the *Wogan* series, regularly and in various ways, the whole notion of 'personality' was called into question. But it was not that the populist personality discourse, with its emphasis on sincerity and authenticity, was entirely redundant; rather the earlier formula was now explicitly interrogated, and other rhetorics of 'authenticity' were on display. Consider, first of all, the following dialogue between two established television 'personalities':

(Terry Wogan interviewing Bob Monkhouse, 10 March 1984.)

Wogan. You've done your chat show series for BBC 2. How do you like being an interviewee rather than an interviewer?

Monkhouse. I found being an interviewer very very difficult. I have watched this series of course I have, and the last one and the previous one. And I think you are, I hate to do this, I think you're very good *(laughter)*. I really do . . . I found it very difficult. I find the biggest problem for me is, that my admiration for my guests, because they were all comedians, is so considerable that I can't disguise it, I can't hide it, and therefore it's possible to appear erm obsequious and er over enthusiastic about a guest when that is a genuine emotion, and that's been criticised. I noticed er *(W: Yes)*. Well I should develop the same contempt that you obviously have for your guests.

Wogan. No, only for some of them.

Monkhouse. *(Laughs)* Adsum.

Wogan. Do you think then that erm, being honest or showing honest emotions on television is not a good idea, if they could be misinterpreted, as they have been in your case, they're called smarm which is genuine admiration?

Monkhouse. *(Laughs)* Yes, er I don't think er, television is a place for me to show my genuine emotions. I think it's a place for, I would rather, I'm much happier, er Joan Rivers when you interviewed her the other week so, so excellently said the cabaret stage was her psychiatrist er that she regarded her job as to entertain, to get laughs. And that's the way I feel I, I came into the business in eighteen hundred and forty five in order to get laughs but that meant inventing a persona, offering something which is not necessarily me, it's an invention, it's a construction.

I, I've known you long enough to know that there are er, inconceivably deeper parts of you than are actually visible on the TV screen. There are parts of you which have never been seen on the TV screen *(audience laughter)*. I for one hope that they will never be seen.

| Wogan. | You nearly got into a compliment there. And you decide to duck out of it. Because a little bit of the real Bob came out there and you quickly shoved it back again. |
| Monkhouse. | Yes, yes I don't really want to, no, exposing myself on the TV screen is not my idea of fun. |

In a previous article (Tolson, 1985) I have analysed another extract from this interview in which Monkhouse tells a couple of very funny anecdotes about a television programme he used to compere, *The Golden Shot*. The aim of that article was to highlight certain similarities between the formal structure of the anecdote and the regime of broadcast television – arguing that the rhetoric of much contemporary television can be characterized as 'anecdotal'. However, that discussion also makes a further point which is more immediately relevant to this extract, where Monkhouse and Wogan are directly discussing the activity in which they are simultaneously engaged. This point is again that increasingly, talk on television is self-reflexive. It is not only talk, but also talk about talk: that is 'metatalk', and talk about television in general (Tolson, 1985: 23).

Moreover, I think it is very significant that some of the talk about television in the contemporary talk show, now extends to the notion of 'television personality' as such. There now seems to be a space for Monkhouse to engage in what is effectively a *critique* of his own television personality. In the light of Langer's account this is a very interesting discussion: for Monkhouse is now saying that his television personality is a 'construction' – and that the same point applies to our host, Wogan himself. Not that this critique is particularly disturbing, however – for somehow Monkhouse appears as an even more authentic and sincere personality ('the real Bob') in so far as he admits that his television personality is a sham.

Also, of course, Monkhouse is making an attempt to inject some (not very subtle) humour into the discussion. Again, in comparison with *Face to Face* (recall Freeman's interview with Tony Hancock) the rhetoric of personality has changed. The terms of an acceptable talk show performance now extend to an ability to play with conventions of sincerity and personal disclosure, and to develop jokes at their expense. Joan Rivers herself is particularly adept at this kind of strategy:

(Terry Wogan interviewing Joan Rivers, 3 March 1984.)

Wogan.	You do chat shows yourself I know in the States. You sit in for the biggest chat show they have there, *Johnny Carson*, and he hates you because you're more popular than he is.
Rivers.	No no he loves me. He found me, he found me. He's my mentor.
Wogan.	So you're his protegee.
Rivers.	I'm his protegee.
Wogan.	Mm. And when you hosted that show you had a bit of a run in with one of our own lovely ladies Joan Collins, didn't you?
Rivers.	The best, she's the best. She's the best because she's bitchy back. Do you know what fun it is, Joan Collins is so . . . 'Cause that's what television should be, it should be fun. And she gets on, and I'll be bitchy to her. It's like a tennis match and she goes whack back. I said to her, you know 'cause we call her the British Open, I mean she's just had everybody, so but *(laughter, applause)*
Wogan.	But did you say that to her face?

Rivers.   Yes, so I said to her, you know 'who is the best man you ever had?'
And she said to me 'your husband'. (*laughter*) Well, that's great. You
just want to say that's what television should be.

Of course, not everyone tells them like Joan Rivers, and in fact when the Rivers talk show was
shown subsequently on British television it was not particularly successful. But in both content
and form I think this exchange with Wogan is indicative of a transformation in the talk show
genre, and its attendant concept of 'good television', as compared for instance to the kind of
talk show interview which Langer has described. Two essential points can be made. First, the
grounds for speaking from 'experience' have changed. In so far as personal experiences still
remain the focus for such interviews, and in so far as they are 'disclosed', they may be recounted
sincerely (Monkhouse), but equally they may be represented as constructions, even fabrications
(Rivers) for the 'game' which is 'good television'. But, secondly, the reason why the grounds
for disclosure have shifted is that a key generic development has taken place in the history of
the talk show interview. The Rivers interview (and there were several similar interviews in the
1984 series of *Wogan*) is in fact indicative of an institutional 'mixing' of genres, where the talk
show interview meets stand-up comedy. The interview provides a vehicle and the interviewer
poses as the straight-man, for an established and rehearsed comedy routine. Thus 'chat' may
still be serious, or it may be comic; but more often than not it has now become a complex and
entertaining mixture of the two.

REFERENCES

Brown, G. and G. Yule (1983) *Discourse Analysis* Cambridge: Cambridge University Press.
Greatbatch, D. (1987) 'A Turn Taking System for British News Interviews', Warwick Working Papers in
Sociology, University of Warwick, Department of Sociology
Langer, J. (1981) 'Television's "Personality System" ' *Media, Culture and Society* 3:351–65.
Montgomery, M. (1977) 'Discourse Structure and Cohesion in Selected Science Lectures', MA thesis, University
of Birmingham.
Scannell, P. (1988) 'The Communicative Ethos of Broadcasting'. Paper presented at the International
Television Studies Conference, London (BFI).
Tolson, A. (1985) 'Anecdotal Television' *Screen* 26(2): 18–27.

FURTHER READING

Allen, R. C. (ed.), *Channels of Discourse* (Chapel Hill: University of North Carolina Press, 1987).

Allen, R. C. (ed.), *Channels of Discourse, Reassembled* (London: Routledge, 1992).

Alvarado, M. and Stewart, J. (eds), *Made for Television: Euston Films Limited* (London: BFI, 1985).

Alvarado, M. and Thompson, J. O. (eds), *The Media Reader* (London: BFI, 1990).

Barthes, R., *Mythologies* (London: Paladin, 1973).

Bennett, T., Boyd-Bowman, S., Mercer, C. and Woollacott, J. (eds), *Popular Television and Film* (London: BFI, 1981).

Bennett, T., Martin, G., Mercer, C. and Woollacott, J. (eds), *Culture, Ideology and Social Process* (London: Batsford Academic and Educational Ltd., 1981).

Bennett, T., Mercer, C. and Woollacott, J. (eds), *Popular Culture and Social Relations* (Milton Keynes: Open University Press, 1986).

Bennett, T. and Woollacott, J., *Bond and Beyond: The Political Career of a Popular Hero* (London: Macmillan Education, 1987).

Boys from the Blackstuff, British Film Institute Dossier 20 (1984).

Brandt, G. W. (ed.), *British Television Drama* (Cambridge: Cambridge University Press, 1981).

Brunsdon, C. and Morley, D., *Everyday Television: 'Nationwide'* (London: BFI, 1978).

Caughie, J. (ed.), *Television, Ideology and Exchange* (London: BFI, 1978).

Caughie, J., 'Rhetoric, Pleasure, and "Art Television" – *Dreams of Leaving*', *Screen* 22: (1981) pp. 9–31.

Corner, J. (ed.), *Documentary and the Mass Media* (London: Edward Arnold, 1986).

Corner, J. (ed.), *Popular Television in Britain* (London: BFI, 1991).

Curran, J., Ecclestone, J., Oakley, G. and Richardson, A. (eds), *Bending Reality: The State of the Media* (London: Pluto Press, 1986).

Curran, J., Smith, A. and Wingate, P. (eds), *Impacts and Influences: Essays on Media Power in the Twentieth Century* (London: Methuen, 1987).

Davis, H. and Walton, P. (eds), *Language, Image, Media* (Oxford: Blackwell, 1983).

Drama-Documentary, British Film Institute Dossier 19 (1984).

Elliott, P., Murdock, G. and Schlesinger, P., '"Terrorism" and the State: A Case Study of the Discourses of Television', *Media, Culture and Society* 5:2 (1983) MTM: pp. 155–77.

Feuer, J., 'Narrative Form in Television', in C. MacCabe (ed.), *High Theory/Low Culture: Analysing Popular Television and Film* (Manchester: Manchester University Press, 1986).

Feuer, J., Kerr, P. and Vahimagi, T., *'Quality Television'* (London: BFI, 1984).

Fiske, J., *Television Culture* (London: Methuen, 1987).

Fiske, J. and Hartley, J., *Reading Television* (London: Methuen, 1978).

Gilbert, W. S., 'The TV Play: Outside the Consensus' *Screen Education* 35 (1980) pp. 35–44.

Gitlin, T., *Inside Prime Time* (New York: Pantheon, 1985).

Goodwin, A. and Whannel, G. (eds), *Understanding Television* (London: Routledge, 1990).

Hall, S., Hobson, D., Lowe, A. and Willis, P. (eds), *Culture, Media, Language* (London: Hutchinson, 1980).

Hartley, J., *Tele-Ology: Studies in Televison* (London: Routledge, 1992).

Heath, S. and Skirrow, G., 'Television: A World in Action', *Screen* 18:2 (1977) pp. 7–59.

Kaplan, E. A. (ed.), *Regarding Television: Critical Approaches – An Anthology* (Frederick, Md.: University Publications of America, 1983).

McArthur, C., *Television and History* (London: BFI, 1978).

MacCabe, C. (ed.), *High Theory Low Culture: Analysing Popular Film and Television* (Manchester: Manchester University Press, 1986).

McGrath, J., 'TV Drama: The Case Against Naturalism', *Sight and Sound* 46:2 (1977) pp. 100–5.

Masterman, L. (ed.), *Television Mythologies: Stars, Shows and Signs* (London: Comedia, 1984).

Mellencamp, P. (ed.), *Logics of Television* (Bloomington and London: Indiana University Press and BFI, 1990).

Millington, B. and Nelson, R., *'Boys from the Blackstuff': The Making of TV Drama* (London: Comedia, 1986).

Modleski, T. (ed.), *Studies in Entertainment: Critical Approaches to Mass Culture* (Bloomington: Indiana University Press, 1986).

Morse, M., 'Talk, Talk, Talk – the Space of Discourse in Television', *Screen* 26:2 (1985) pp. 2–15.

Murdock, G., 'Authorship and Organization', *Screen Education* 35 (1980) pp. 19–34.

Neale, S., *Genre* (London: BFI, 1980).

Neale, S. and Krutnik, F., *Popular Film and Television Comedy* (London: Routledge, 1990).

Nichols, B., *Representing Reality: Issues and Concepts in Documentary* (Bloomington: Indiana University Press, 1991).

Silverstone, R., 'Narrative Strategies in Television Science – A Case Study', *Media, Culture and Society* 6:4 (1984) pp. 377–410.

Skovmand, M. and Schroder, K. C. (eds), *Media Cultures: Reappraising Transnational Media* (London: Routledge, 1992).

Strinati, D. and Wagg, S. (eds), *Come on Down? Popular Media Culture* (London: Routledge, 1992).

Television Sitcom, British Film Institute Dossier 17 (1982).

Tulloch, J., *Television Drama: Agency, Audience, and Myth* (London: Routledge, 1990).

Tulloch, J. and Alvarado, M., '*Doctor Who': The Unfolding Text* (London: Macmillan, 1983).

White, M., 'Television Genres: Intertextuality', *Journal of Film and Video* 37: (1985) pp. 41–47.

Williams, R., 'A Lecture on Realism', *Screen* (Spring 1977).

Williams, R., *Raymond Williams on Television*, ed. A. O'Connor (London: Routledge, 1989).

EUP: Media Studies: A Reader (revises)
Monotype Garamond, 47 lines/page, 10/12pt
Running Heads: Univers-Bold caps/small caps, 10pt

Text
Feminist Readings

Text: Feminist Readings

Feminist textual readings should not be seen as constituting a homogeneous body of work. They do, however, share a common politics, in what Liesbet van Zoonen describes as their 'unconditional focus on analysing *gender* as a mechanism that structures material and symbolic worlds and our experiences of them'.[1] In this, they also share an uneasy position within media studies, at once extending and radically challenging its preoccupations. In particular, feminist readings of television texts have usefully drawn on the insights gained from feminist film theory and criticism, where work on the visual construction of women as spectacle and the gendering of visual pleasure has been developed in relation both to mainstream Hollywood film and to melodrama, or 'the woman's film'. Yet feminist media theory and criticism have not played the central role in the development of the whole field of media studies which they have in film studies.

Instead, the focus of feminist work on the mass media has tended to reproduce the public/private, knowledge/pleasure, masculine/feminine split which characterises its field of study – though the extent of the challenge posed by the insistence on *taking seriously* popular media forms for women to a field of study often focused on issues of public information and knowledge should not be underestimated. Much feminist research, then, has focused on what Charlotte Brunsdon calls 'mass cultural fictions of femininity',[2] popular forms for women such as soap opera, mass-produced romantic fiction and girls' and women's magazines, and on the (often contradictory) pleasures and ideological positionings which they offer. This research has in its turn raised issues around the theorising of pleasure, the relationship of gender to genre, to narrative modes and patterns of address, and the relationship of the 'ideal' spectator addressed by the text to the real social subject who responds to that address.

The first extract in this section (Chapter 22) is taken from Janice Winship's *Inside Women's Magazines* (1987). Winship begins by addressing the public/private split described above. 'As TV soap opera is to news and current affairs,' she writes, 'so women's magazines are the soaps of journalism', disparaged within both critical and popular discourse. The 'Woman's World' which they claim to offer us is both an affirmation of women's interests and identity, and an indication of women's marginality: 'Men do not have or need magazines for "A Man's World"; it *is* their world, out there, beyond the shelves.' This ambiguity characterises the magazines: the 'gaze between cover model and women readers' marks the extent to which women see themselves 'in the image which a masculine culture has defined'; at the same time the model is 'centre stage and powerful', affirming the importance of 'women's territory'. The magazines, then, offer us 'survival skills' to deal with the real dilemmas of femininity, and 'daydreams' that these strategies might actually work.

Danae Clark's '*Cagney & Lacey*: Feminist Strategies of Detection' (Chapter 23) addresses the separation between public and private worlds in a different way. The 1980s series *Cagney & Lacey* is a hybrid text, mixing the police drama series – whose episodes end in narrative closure, – with an 'open and fragmented' central narrative, – which centres on the lives of the two major characters. It is a text, argues Clark, which both addresses women and 'challenges the boundaries of patriarchal discourse'. First, it centres on women's active control over *decision-making*, in situations where this process is facilitated through female bonding: female viewers are thus invited to consider their own demands and how they might articulate them, within a context of female support. Second, as a detective series, *Cagney & Lacey* assigns to its female characters the traditionally male role of investigation and judgement. In this investigation public and private are merged: it is the institution of the family which is frequently the object of investigation, and the personal may become political in the form of a 'social issue'. Third, the series challenges male control of the 'gaze' in a number of ways. In giving its female characters 'possession of the look', it privileges the woman's point of view without reducing its male characters to 'fetishised objects of female desire and power'. In establishing relations of looking *between* women it also permits women to 'interact as *subjects*', in relationship with each other. Its privileging of women's *voices*, too, in the characters' frequent 'rest room' conversations, undercuts the power of the gaze to determine meaning. Finally, in the disguises adopted by its detectives, *Cagney & Lacey* comments on the issue of female representation, sometimes critically and sometimes playfully. While the series' overt politics might belong to liberal feminism, therefore, its textual strategies are far more radical.

The final chapter of this section (Chapter 24) examines a text not usually identified with female pleasure: the *Sun*'s Page Three. Newspapers, argues Patricia Holland, are composed of an interweaving of 'multiple fractured narratives' which we, the readers, work to structure and render coherent. In the case of the *Sun*, these narratives – whether news, features or question-naires – are centred upon sexual dramas. Her article asks how *women* are invited to participate in these narratives. Features, she finds, are often addressed to both sexes simultaneously, but where they are gender-specific, it is women who are spoken to directly. Men, however, are 'the implied . . . addressees': 'Women are spoken to directly, but it is men who share the joke'. Page Three is no exception. Its fetishised image dominates the meaning of 'woman' in the *Sun*, but it also invites women to aspire to the role it offers, with that role's particular construction of sexual enjoyment and sexual freedom. Within the narrative of Page Three, therefore, the status of model which it holds out to its women readers promises simultaneously achievement and defeat, autonomy and containment. Within the wider range of the *Sun*'s narratives, Page Three confirms for its male readers that 'the Page Three principle is present in all women', even as, in the distance revealed between the role and 'the model's real-life persona', we can see femininity revealed as performance, or masquerade. Yet millions of women continue to read the *Sun*. The reason, Holland concludes, lies in the fact that its organisation of gender roles operates in the name of a working class which is 'defined by its modes of consumption rather than its place in production'. In this context, '[s]ex is fun, a leisure activity', and the *Sun*'s organisation of gender roles is legitimated by its identification with a working class 'which takes its pleasures when they can because they're only too fleeting'.

NOTES

1.   Liesbet Van Zoonen, *Feminist Media Studies* (London: Sage, 1994) p. 3
2.   Charlotte Brunsdon, 'Pedagogies of the Feminine: Feminist Teaching and Women's Genres', *Screen* 32:4 (1991) p. 365.

22

SURVIVAL SKILLS AND DAYDREAMS

Janice Winship

[. . .]

'. . . A STORY ABOUT MEN; AND WOMEN'

Women's magazines, perhaps especially *Woman* and *Woman Own*, have become as well known nationally in Britain as any of the daily or Sunday newspapers. Yet though a million of *Woman's* 5 to 6 million readers and around one-third of *Cosmopolitan*'s, for example, are men, magazines are very specifically associated with femininity and *women's* culture. Indeed, it is impossible to think about femininity and women without considering, among other things, motherhood and family life, beauty and fashion, love and romance, cooking and knitting – and therefore romantic novels, cookery books and women's magazines. It is difficult to envisage a masculine culture without contemplating work and careers, brawls in the boxing ring or on the 'real' battlefields of war, train spotting and messing around with cars, the pub and pulling girls – and therefore newspapers, hobby journals and 'girlie' magazines. No matter that not all women are mothers or read women's magazines, and that many men loathe boxing and have rarely glanced at a 'girlie' magazine; no matter either that feminism has chipped away at the stereotypes of femininity and masculinity, those versions of two genders are still profoundly influential in our experiences of growing up. Our lives as women and men continue to be culturally defined in markedly different ways, and both what we read and how it is presented to us reflects, and is part of, that difference.

The cultural image of father-reading-newspaper-at-breakfast, mother-busy-on-the-domestic-front may have been starkly present in my family thirty years ago. But it has not yet disappeared, either literally or symbolically.

The same cultural gap can be seen at any local newsstand. There on the rack marked 'Woman's

---

From J. Winship, *Inside Women's Magazines* (London: Pandora Press, 1987) pp. 5–14.

World' are the women's magazines which women are glancing through and buying. A short distance away is another stand marked 'Leisure' or 'Hobbies'. There are all the 'girlie' magazines, the photography, computing and do-it-yourself magazines (crochet, cooking and sewing magazines are, of course, with the women's magazines), and *their* voyeurs and purchasers are almost exclusively men. All this we take for granted as we amble or scurry through the shop for our own purchase. Yet those labels and that separation between a 'woman's world' and 'leisure' or 'hobbies' reveal much about our gendered culture. Men do not have or need magazines for 'A Man's World'; it *is* their world, out there, beyond the shelves: the culture of the workplace, of politics and public life, the world of business, property and technology, there they are all 'boys' together. Women have no culture and world out there other than the one which is controlled and mediated by men. The 'girls' are drawn in to support the masculine quest: 'boys will be boys' whatever the game being played.

Women tend to be isolated from one another, gathering together briefly and in small huddles, stealing their pleasures in the interstices of masculine culture so graciously allowed them: family gatherings, rushed coffee mornings or the children's events, and the occasional night out with the 'girls'. The tasks they immerse themselves in, the priorities they believe in, constantly take second place to the concerns of men. In men's presence women are continually silenced, or they are ridiculed, scolded or humiliatingly ignored. Thus the 'woman's world' which women's magazines represent is created precisely because it does not exist outside their pages. In their isolation on the margins of the men's world, in their uneasiness about their feminine accomplishments, women need support – desperately. As Jane Reed, long-time editor of *Woman's Own* and then editor-in-chief of *Woman*, put it, 'a magazine is like a club. Its first function is to provide readers with a comfortable sense of community and pride in their identity' (Hughes-Hallett 1982, p. 21).

Yet such is the power of masculine wisdom that women's magazines and their millions of readers are perenially belittled – by many women no less than by most men. As TV soap opera is to news and current affairs, so women's magazines are the soaps of journalism, sadly maligned and grossly misunderstood. Over the years critics have disparagingly opined that women's magazines are 'a journalism for squaws . . . you find yourself in a cosy twilit world' (1965); it is a world of 'the happy ever after trail' (1976); 'cooking and sewing – the woman's world' (1977); 'kitchen think' (1982). They lament that women's magazines do not present a true and real picture of women's lives: 'Why . . . does the image deny the world?' (1965). Worse, magazines are 'completely schizophrenic' (1958); 'experience and make-believe merge in a manner conductive to the reader's utter bewilderment' (1971).

But if the focus of women's magazines *is* predominantly home and hearth, if the world they present *is* a happy-ever-after one, if they *do* refuse the reality of most women's lives, if they *do* offer a schizophrenic mix – and none of these characteristics is quite accurate – then there are pertinent cultural reasons why this is so. I want[. . .]to delve beneath this simple and dismissive description in order both to explain the appeal of the magazine formula and to critically consider its limitations and potential for change.

HIDDEN COVER LINES: TALKING TO 'YOU'

If the profile of women's magazines is partly determined by the state of play between women and men, it is also (as indeed is the 'game' between women and men) shaped by a consumer culture geared to selling and making a profit from commodities, and whose sales are boosted (it's firmly believed) through the medium of advertising. As commodities, women's magazines sell their weekly or monthly wares not only by advertising proper but also by the 'advertisement' of their own covers.

On any magazine stand each women's magazine attempts to differentiate itself from others also vying for attention. Each does so by a variety of means: the title and its print type, size and texture of paper, design and lay-out of image and sell-lines (the term the magazine trade aptly uses for the cover captions), and the style of model image – but without paying much attention to *how* a regular reader will quickly be able to pick out her favourite from others nestling competitively by it. Cover images and sell lines, however, also reveal a wealth of knowledge about the cultural place of women's magazines. The woman's face which is their hallmark is usually white, usually young, usually smoothly attractive and immaculately groomed, and usually smiling or seductive. The various magazines inflect the image to convey their respective styles – domestic or girl-about-town, cheeky or staid, upmarket or downmarket – by subtle changes of hairstyle, neckline and facial pose. They waver from it occasionally rather than regularly with royals and male celebrities, mothers-and-babies and couples. Only magazines on the fringes of women's magazines, like *Ideal Home* (concentratedly home-oriented and with a high male readership) never use the female model. It is no profundity to say that as the sign of 'woman' this cover image affirms and sells those qualities of white skin, youth, beauty, charm and sexuality as valuable attributes of femininity. In marked contrast *Spare Rib* covers break sharply with the stereotyped plasticity of the model face, and communicate immediately how far that magazine distances itself from such an evaluation of femininity.

There is one other important and defining characteristic of this cover image: the woman's gaze. It intimately holds the attention of 'you', the reader and viewer. Such an image and gaze also has a wide currency in ads directed at women and men, has a daily venue on page 3 of the *Sun* and *Star*, and appears on the cover of 'girlie' magazines like *Mayfair* and *Fiesta*. The woman's image in these latter is obviously caught up in a provocatively sexual significance. Her partially revealed body speaks the sexuality about which the facial expression often equivocates. Her gaze holds that of the male voyeur; but it is he who has the controlling look: to look or not to bother, to choose to be sexually aroused or to turn over the page. She is the object and toy for his sexual play. It would be pushing it to suggest that the covers of women's magazines work in quite this way. For one thing many completely play down the 'come-on' look, for another the covers are primarily addressed to women. Nevertheless, what I would argue is that the gaze between cover model and women readers marks the complicity between women that we see ourselves in the image which a masculine culture has defined. It indicates symbolically too, the extent to which we relate to each other as women through absent men: it is 'the man' who, in a manner of speaking, occupies the space between model image and woman reader.

In fact few women readers will make an immediate identification with these cover images: they are too polished and perfect, so *un*like us. Paradoxically, though, we do respond to them. Selling us an image to aspire to, they persuade us that we, like the model, can succeed. For the image is a carefully constructed one, albeit that it sometimes apes a 'natural look'. The model is only the cipher, the (often) anonymous face for others' skills and a range of commodities to fill. As *Company* puts it: 'Cover photograph of Joanne Russell by Tony McGee. Vest dress by Sheridan Barnett; necklace by Pellini. Hair by Harry Cole at Trevor Sorbie. Make-up by Philippe at Sessions' (April 1983). Easy then, 'you' too can create the look – given the ready cash. *Company* continues, 'Our cover girl look can be achieved by using Charles of the Ritz signature Collection for spring: complexion, Amboise Ritz Mat Hydro-Protective Make-up; cheeks, Cinnamon Glow Revenescence Cheekglow; eyes, Country Plums Perfect

Finish Powder, Eyecolour Trio, Black, Ritz Eye Pencil, Black Perfect Lash Mascara; lips, Pink Carnation Perfect Finish Lip Colour; nails, Champagne Rose Superior Nail Lacquer.' Phew! Etched though the final image is here by the combined talents of men and the myriad make-up offerings of consumer culture, it also offers 'you' hope – of sorts: she is 'successful'; why not 'you'? It is a seductive appeal.

There is however, a counterthread to this image which perhaps provides the stonger attraction for women. Woman is placed first here; she is centre stage and powerful. The gaze is not simply a *sexual* look between woman and man, it is the steady, selfcontained, calm look of unruffled temper. She is the woman who can manage her emotions and her life. She is the woman whom 'you' as reader can trust as friend; she looks as one woman to another speaking about what women share: the intimate knowledge of being a woman. Thus the focus on the face and the eyes – aspects which most obviously characterise the person, the woman – suggests that inside the magazine is a world of personal life, of emotions and relationships, clearly involving men and heterosexuality, but a world largely shunned by men. This is all women's territory.

More than that, the careful construction of the model's appearance not only points to the purchase of certain commodities but also covertly acknowledges the *creative work* involved in producing it, a work executed in everyday life not by the 'experts' but by women themselves.

The cover image shouts that this woman's world of personal life and feminine expressivity is one worth bothering about, engendering a feel for the reader that such pursuits are successful, and moreover bring happiness: the model smiles. Idealistic as all this is (some would say oppressive), it is less a denial of the 'real world' than an affirmation of how much women and feminine concerns are neglected in that 'real world'.

With the model's gaze on 'you', the magazine invites 'you' into its world. It may address you directly: 'Self-esteem': a little more will take you a long way' declares *Company*; or (You) 'Win a speed boat worth £4000' urges *Options*, the magazine 'For your way of living'. Like the language of advertising, these sell-lines for that issue's inside delights ambiguously address 'you' as an individual. There is the suggestion that the relationship being struck up is the intimate one between the magazine and 'you' – just one reader. The same is implied in the title *My Weekly*. This address to the individual [. . .] heightens the sense of, on the one hand, the magazine speaking to the 'lonely woman', and, on the other, the strength of the support the magazine provides for its readers.

What 'you' are also offered on the cover is a careful balance between practical items linked to daily life and those which draw you, dreamily, into another world. Regarded by some critics as 'conducive to the readers' utter bewilderment', this mixture of entertainment and advice has been consciously promoted by editors since the inception of women's magazines. For example, *The Lady's Magazine* of 1770 aimed to combine 'amusement with instruction'; *The Englishwoman's Domestic Magazine*, published in 1852 by Samuel Beeton (husband of that doyenne of cookery Mrs Isabella Beeton) and one of the forerunners of modern middle-class home magazines, combined 'practical utility, instruction and amusement'. More contemporarily, in 1976 Beatrix Miller, then editor of *Vogue*, remarked, 'We are 60% selling a dream and 40% offering practical advice.' And in the launch issue of *options* in April 1982 its editor Penny Radford hopefully declared, 'We want *Options* to be a lot of information, a lot of help and a lot of fun. So enjoy it.'

Why should women's magazines offer this mix? Men's magazines seem to settle for one or the other: 'entertainment' ('girlie' magazines) or 'information' (all the hobby journals). But then men's lives tend to be more clearly compartmentalised and – often thanks to women's hidden labour – men are singular about their activities: they are at work *or* at leisure; they are watching

TV *or* engaged in their hobby. Many of the activities women carry out – often several at once – cut across categories: at work they can find themselves 'being mother', entertaining visitors or giving the feminine (sensitive) ear to others' work problems; lunch breaks are devoted to the 'work' or 'pleasure' of shopping; running a home can be both 'work' and a 'hobby' – cooking and sewing are tasks which can eat up leisure time, while ironing can be done in front of the TV.

After my father had glanced through the newspaper at breakfast he would go out to work and my brother and I would rush off to school, but my mother would stay put. Working mainly in the house, she often had to take 'time off' there too. When we all came home she had to cater to our needs, switching hats according to our various moods, and moving from one thing to another as we each in turn wanted this – a clean collar (my father rushing out to a meeting) – or that – a hem of a dress pinned up (me) – even as she was baking, tidying up or doing her own sewing.

At odd moments in this many-faceted and disrupted routine she would snatch the time to escape into her *Woman's Weekly*. At other times *Woman's Weekly* would deliver 'the recipe' or the answer to a stubborn stain. Women's magazines provide for these rhythms and routines of women's lives in which private time and space are precious, work and leisure merge, activities overlap, and dreams and escape often feed on a modest vocabulary of everyday possibilities: modest partly because the horizons of women's lives are still limited and partly because women's desires are constantly forestalled. The predominantly masculine world neither welcomes women nor women's ways of doing things. Notwithstanding its (often empty) tributes to mothers and wives and page 3 pin-ups, it will do its damnedest to exclude them from certain domains, frighten them on the streets, hassle them in the pub, or stamp on their hopes and ambitions.

No wonder that women need the 'refuge' of women's magazines.

For their part most women tolerate these harassments because, whatever the costs of being a woman, there are also compensations. The balance sheet of feminine qualities far outweighs that of masculinity. Women do not want to be the kind of people men are and it is difficult to envisage *other* ways of being women (and men). Women's magazines provide a combination of (sometimes wholly inadequate) survival skills to cope with the dilemmas of femininity, and daydreams which offer glimpses that these survival strategies *do* work. They are dreams of a better and different life, but one that remains well within a spectrum of familiar possibilities.

The survival skills offered by feminist magazines like *Spare Rib* and *Everywoman* may be more political, aimed at getting women off the 'desert island' of femininity and encouraging their daydreams of a radical future. Yet the formula is similar. They offer help and, above all, hope. They present a catalogue, both sad and heartening, of women's ability to survive in a world where the odds are stacked against them.

[. . .]

REFERENCES

Adams, Carol and Laurikietis, Rae (1980), *The Gender Trap 3: Messages and Images*, Virago, London.
Adamson, Lesley (1977), 'Cooking and sewing – the woman's world', *Guardian*, 3 November.
Berger, John (1972), *Ways of Seeing*, Penguin, Harmondsworth.
Braithwaite, Brian and Barrel, Joan (1979), *The Business of Women's Magazines*, Associated Business Press, London.
Connell, Myra (1981), 'Reading Romance', MA thesis, University of Birmingham.
Coward, Rosalind (1983), *Female Desire*, Paladin, London.
Curran, Charles (1965), 'Journalism for squaws', *Spectator*, 19 November.
Ferguson, Marjorie (1978), 'Imagery and ideology: the cover photographs of traditional women's magazines', in Gay Tuchman, Arlene Kaplan Daniels and James Benet (eds), *Hearth and Home*, Oxford University Press, New York.

Ferguson, Marjorie (1983), 'Learning to be a woman's woman', *New Society*, 21 April.

Greer, Germaine (1972), *The Female Eunuch*, Paladin, London.

Hall, Stuart, Hobson, Dorothy, Lowe, Andy and Willis, Paul (eds) (1980), *Culture, Media, Language*, Hutchinson, London.

Hughes-Hallett, Lucy (1982) 'The cosy secret of a jolly good Reed', *The Standard*, 8 February.

King, Josephine and Stott, Mary (1977), *Is This Your Life?*, Virago, London.

Lefebvre, Henri (1971), *Everyday Life in the Modern World*, Allen Lane, London.

McRobbie, Angela (1977), '*Jackie*', stencilled paper, Centre for Contemporary Cultural Studies, University of Birmingham.

McRobbie, Angela and McCabe, (1982) Trisha, *Feminism is Fun: An Adventure Story for Girls*, Routledge & Kegan Paul, London.

Reed, Jane (1982), 'The story so far', *Guardian*, 20 October.

Root, Jane (1983), *Pictures of Women: Sexuality*, Pandora, London.

Sharpe, Sue (1976), *Just Like a Girl*, Penguin, Harmondsworth.

Tolson, Andrew (1977), *The Limits of Masculinity*, Tavistock, London.

Toynbee, Polly (1977), 'At the end of the happy ever after trail', *Guardian*, 21 June.

White, Cynthia (1977), *Royal Commission on the Press, the Women's Periodical Press in Britain 1946–76*, Working Paper 4, HMSO, London.

23

CAGNEY & LACEY: FEMINIST STRATEGIES OF DETECTION

Danae Clark

The connection between *Cagney & Lacey* and feminism can be traced back to 1974 when Barbara Corday, one of the show's creators, made her husband, producer Barney Rosenzweig, read Molly Haskell's feminist attack on the film industry, *From Reverence to Rape: The Treatment of Women in the Movies.* According to Corday, Rosenzweig became 'enlightened' when he encountered Haskell's point that women had never been portrayed as buddies in film or television, and thereafter he was committed to producing a female buddy movie[1]. Unfortunately, executives in the entertainment industry had still not attained enlightenment. Corday developed a movie script of *Cagney & Lacey* along with Barbara Avedon in 1974, but it was not until 1981 that CBS finally produced it as a TV-movie and (based on its high ratings) subsequently developed *Cagney & Lacey* into a weekly series.

While *Cagney & Lacey* may have been inspired by feminist film criticism, its continued existence has been attributed to its predominantly female viewing audience. When the show was cancelled during its first season, executive producer Rosenzweig managed to keep it on the air. But when *Cagney & Lacey* was cancelled again after its second season (1982–83), thousands of letters sent in by viewers convinced CBS that *Cagney & Lacey* had a dedicated and sizeable audience. According to Rosenzweig, 'a lot of women, especially younger women, had been identifying almost fiercely with the show'.[2] They were not the traditional starstruck fans, he added. 'They were affluent, well-educated people . . . working women [and] college students'.[3] Overwhelmingly, women responded to *Cagney & Lacey's* 'complex, real women characters' and 'honestly portrayed women's friendships'.[4] This held true even among women who tended not to care for 'the usual cop shows'.

Cagney & Lacey has certainly challenged the stereotypes found in earlier police dramas such as *Police Woman*, in which a highly sexualised Angie Dickinson was put into dangerous, suggestive situations only to be rescued by her male partners. But the importance of *Cagney & Lacey* to

From M. E. Brown (ed), *Television and Women's Culture* (London: Sage, 1990) pp. 117–133.

feminism lies beyond its presentation of a new or 'better' image of women. As a text that specifically addresses women and women's issues, *Cagney & Lacey* potentially challenges the boundaries of patriarchal discourse at the same time as it allows viewers to actively enter into the process of its meaning construction. Thus, as I hope to demonstrate in this essay, the 'fierce identification' experienced by the show's female viewers may derive from their participation in and empowerment by the show's discursive strategies. In particular, I will argue that *Cagney & Lacey* empowers women and encourages women-identified constructions of meaning through a combination of its narrative form, its representational codes, and its structures of looking.

NARRATIVE STRATEGIES/FEMINIST STRATEGIES

Barney Rosenzweig summarises *Cagney & Lacey*'s narrative construction when he says '[t]his is not a show about two cops who happen to be women; it's about two women who happen to be cops'.[5] While *Cagney & Lacey* is categorised as a police drama, this aspect assumes only minor significance. The major aspect, or real drama of the show, revolves around the personal lives of Christine Cagney (Sharon Gless) and Mary Beth Lacey (Tyne Daly) both inside and outside the 14th Precinct. Although these two aspects are interwoven in any given episode, they differ significantly in their narrative structure. As in other police dramas, the protagonists of *Cagney & Lacey* are presented with a case to solve, the criminal is apprehended or outwitted, and a sense of order is restored at the end when the case is either solved or dismissed. But the drama of Cagney and Lacey's lives continues beyond a single episode. Unlike the linear, cause and effect progression of the police subplot, the main plot is open and fragmented. We don't know from any cause and effect structure what Chris will decide about marriage or how Mary Beth will cope with having breast cancer. More importantly, we eventually learn about their decisions and feelings through dialogue, not action. Because of this, the narrative structure of *Cagney & Lacey*'s major plotline seems more characteristic of the soap opera than the classical realist text.

According to Tania Modleski, one of the chief differences between these types of texts is that the soap opera appears to be participatory in a way that the realist text almost never is. In soap operas, 'action is less important than *re*action and *inter*action', and this is one reason, she says, that fans insist on the soap opera's 'realism':

> Despite the numerous murders, kidnappings, blackmail attempts, emergency operations, amnesia attacks, etc., . . . [one] knows that these events are not important in themselves; they merely serve as occasions for characters to get together and have prolonged, involved, intensely emotional discussions with each other.[6]

Cagney & Lacey differs from soap operas in relegating the more outrageous events to the police drama subplot, while the more 'realistic' events of the two women's lives provide the occasions for intense, ongoing discussion. Yet, like the soap opera, *Cagney & Lacey* contains a combined narrative structure that permits closure on a subsidiary level while remaining open on a another level.

[. . .]

Another major difference between the soap-like structure of *Cagney & Lacey* and soap operas themselves, is the way that viewers are invited to participate in the problem-solving process of characters' lives. According to Modleski, soap operas provide the spectator with training in 'reading' other people, in being sensitive to their needs and desires. She equates this skill in reading with the function of the woman in the home who must be attuned to the effects of the world upon her family.

[. . .]

In relation to *Cagney & Lacey*, however, a viewer's active reading is potentially influenced by two important factors: the experience of female bonding that is strengthened and explored through Cagney and Lacey's interaction, and the emphasis that their interaction places on decision-making – a skill not generally associated with traditionally feminine competencies.

Various strategies are used in emphasising the decision-making process in *Cagney & Lacey*. In some cases, viewers are not presented with the outcome or immediate effects of the characters' decisions. For example, [. . .] when Mary Beth learns that she has breast cancer, textual emphasis is placed on her deliberation over the options available to her rather than the treatment she decides to receive. In a soap opera, her medical treatment would have become the object of spectacle as well as an occasion for other characters to engage in prolonged, involved discussion. The absence of this occasion in *Cagney & Lacey*, however, serves to emphasise women's active control over the decision-making process.

From time to time, other female characters are brought into the decision-making process. In the two-part episode on sexual harassment, for example, Chris decides to press charges against a superior officer who threatens to withhold a job promotion if she refuses to comply with his sexual demands. To ensure his conviction, she seeks the testimony of a woman who has been also harassed by him. But because the woman had succumbed to his threats, she is afraid that her co-operation will result in the loss of her job and the promotion she had been promised. Although Chris' statements about the need for women to speak out against sexual harassment in the workplace are met with resistance, the woman finally comes forward. But the episode concludes *before* she delivers her testimony. The outcome of her decision (winning or losing the case) thus becomes less important than the decision-making process itself. In this way textual emphasis is placed on the difficulties and risks that such decisions pose for women within patriarchy. Or, more significantly, emphasis is placed on the need to reach effective and empowering decisions on such matters.

[. . .]

In other situations, the follow-up action becomes an integral part of the decision-making process. When Chris finally admits to having an alcohol problem, for example, her realisation is not in itself constituted as a solution. The process also includes her decision to attend Alcoholics Anonymous and announce publicly: 'My name is Christine, and I am an alcoholic'.

When the decision process is represented in terms of reaction and interaction, rather than action, *Cagney & Lacey* invites the participation of the spectator to complete the process of meaning construction in ways that are meaningful to her. Cagney, Lacey, and the show's other characters, provide a 'concert of voices' that interchangeably listen to and provide feminist as well as non-feminist options to problems that affect women and women's autonomy (e.g., rape, sexual harassment, pregnancy, and breast cancer).[7] While not all women have had the same experience of these situations, the knowledge and experience they do have *as women* allow them to identify with discussions of what options are available, what decisions might put them in control, and what discursive strategies are appropriate for arriving at these decisions. When the characters' subsequent actions are represented, viewers may additionally identify with the desire and courage to follow through on such decisions.

Above all, viewers are encouraged to identify with the role that female bonding plays in decision-making. Although the relationship between Chris and Mary Beth has been strained and challenged over the six years of the show's existence, the two women depend upon each other for support and constantly reaffirm their friendship. The text thus acknowledges women's need to talk to each other (without male intervention) and also suggests to the female viewer that the positive support of women can help her in coping with the problems encountered under patriarchy.

[. . .]

When decisions involve the issue of female bonding itself, additional strategies come into play. These strategies are less compromising in the sense that divisions among women are not easily tolerated. For example, after Chris is made sergeant, she occasionally pulls rank on Mary Beth and insists on a plan of action that her partner opposes. Mary Beth's confrontation with Chris on this issue often produces heated accusations and threats (including the dissolution of their partnership). But, ultimately, Chris recognises that her attempt to establish a hierarchical relationship is an improper and intolerable option that only serves to weaken their collective power. In other instances, patience and silence are shown to be necessary correlatives to verbal confrontation. When Chris is struggling with alcoholism, Mary Beth aggressively confronts her with the truth of her situation, but thereafter quietly stands vigil at her bedside. When the two women are shown together, clasping hands at the AA meeting, the unspoken and unquestioning support between them makes the issue of female bonding as important as the issue of alcoholism.

The viewer's relation to *Cagney & Lacey* thus contrasts markedly with the viewer-text relation Modleski suggests for the soap opera. Although both texts provide women with multiple points of view, the *Cagney & Lacey* viewer is not addressed as an 'ideal mother' with no demands of her own. On the contrary, *Cagney & Lacey* calls upon women to examine what their demands might be and how they might articulate them. This relation between textual strategies and reading practices most closely resembles the framework and goals of feminist consciousness-raising groups in the sense that women are encouraged to join in the discussion of women's issues and find answers that will empower them. The aspect of female bonding, which privileges trust among women and assumes a crucial, supportive role in the process of women's decision-making, has prompted one critic to suggest that *Cagney & Lacey* offers 'a nascent feminist ideology within the context of mass art'.[8]

CODES OF DETECTION

At the risk of contradicting the points made in the previous section, I would now like to suggest that no discernible separation exists between the police drama subplot of *Cagney & Lacey* and the drama of the main characters' lives, and that the show can also be read in relation to certain textual strategies found in the detective genre.

It is commonly thought, for example, that the detective undertakes two simultaneous investigations – one involving the world of crime, and the other the sphere of sexuality. In the process of detecting the truth, the former precipitates the latter and, ultimately, the question of sexuality assumes primary importance. The typical male hero of such texts is forced to encounter his own sexual anxieties in relation to another (usually female) character. Annette Kuhn explains it thus:

> It is often the woman . . . who constitutes the motivator of the narrative, the 'trouble' that sets the plot in motion, [and] the film's resolution depends on [his] resolution of the particular 'woman question'.[9]

Cagney & Lacey works against the generic boundaries of traditional detective fiction by usurping the male's privileged role as representative of the (patriarchal) Law. Yet, significantly, the text continues to centre on the 'woman question'. This focus challenges and often reverses the relations of power that structure traditional (male-defined) detective genres such as *film noir*. Within *film noir*, for example, the woman question is generally resolved by determining the guilt or innocence of women, and guilty women (by virtue of their independence or expression of sexual desire) are killed, punished, or otherwise eradicated from the text. But within *Cagney & Lacey*, women (i.e. Chris and Mary Beth) assume the voice(s) of judgement concerning female sexuality while attempting to resolve the trouble that patriarchal structures create for women. Resolution of the woman question thus becomes a resolution of the issues that affect women's autonomy and expression.

The power and credibility of Cagney and Lacey as heroines derive from the text's refusal to separate the public and private aspects of their lives. In other words, Cagney and Lacey are not defined solely by a private (sexual and familial) identity, but also in relation to a public (professional) role. According to Jane Tompkins, '[The] public-private dichotomy, which is to say the public-private *hierarchy*, is a founding condition of female oppression'.[10] This dichotomy, in other words, results in women's objectification and confinement, privatising their functions within the home while privileging the role of men as decision-makers in the public sphere. The dissolution of this distinction in *Cagney & Lacey* can thus be read as an attempt to represent women in more empowering social relations. As women engaged in a demanding profession, work forms an integral part of Cagney's and Lacey's experiences and provides a context outside the home in which decisions are discussed and acted upon.

[. . .]

The representation of the institution of the family may, on the other hand, serve as a vehicle for the expression of frustration and non-fulfilment of desire. According to Sylvia Harvey, 'one of the defining characteristics of *film noir* is to be found in its treatment of the family and family relations'.[11] While the presence of the family may appear to legitimate and naturalise the dominant social values embodied in the patriarchal nuclear family, it may also serve to expose the 'intolerable contradictions' and suppression of desires that this institution sustains. If, as I am suggesting, *Cagney & Lacey* can be read according to certain textual strategies found in the detective genre (which finds its most exaggerated interpretation in *film noir*), then the show's representation of 'broken, perverted, peripheral' family relations may actually be founded upon the *absence* of the family.[12]

[. . .]

The institution of the family also provides a context in which other issues, such as racial and economic differences, can be explored. Differences between Cagney and Lacey, for example, are defined as much by class standing as by marital status. While Cagney claims the working-class background of her father, she more obviously embraces the upper-class interests of her (deceased) mother. Chris regards Mary Beth's 'low culture' tastes with some disdain, and Mary Beth often feels impelled to defend her latch-key childhood and working-class husband against Chris' more economically-privileged existence. While these conflicts are never resolved, neither are they erased. The exploration of class differences within the context of the family rather serves to create greater awareness of the family's social and economic effects on women.

This awareness is heightened through Cagney and Lacey's contacts with other women. Welfare mothers, for example, are not represented simply as women without husbands, but as economically-disadvantaged women who are victimised by a variety of patriarchal, capitalist institutions. During one investigation, Cagney and Lacey encounter a woman who is sleeping with her slum tenement landlord. When Cagney tells her that she does not have to exchange sexual favours for a place to live, the woman replies, 'You mean *you* don't'. This exchange foregrounds the experience of a woman (or class of woman) who is ordinarily absent from televisual representation; at the same time it foregrounds differences between women. Thus, far from being a commentary on family life, such an exchange points to the larger issues of women's oppression and offers a 're-visioning' of women's social relations. Within this context, the traditional family loses its force. *Cagney & Lacey* challenges a unified concept of the family by exposing its internal strife, by exploring the economic and political conflicts that exist *between* families, and by insisting on establishing a connection among women across family lines in spite of – or, rather, because of – their differences. As Teresa de Lauretis notes, textual representations of feminism succeed to the extent that they can generate an understanding of how women are 'constructed and defined in gender across multiple representations of class, race, language and social relations'.[13]

As these examples suggest, the lack of separation between public and private in *Cagney & Lacey* works as a narrative strategy to highlight social issues while reinforcing the idea that the personal is political. The investigative structure can translate personal conflict into public concerns and anchor viewer identification to a specific political stance, especially when the police subplot and the drama of characters' lives are integrally connected in an episode. For example, at a time when Mary Beth is trying to cope with her son's decision to enlist in the military, her police work brings her into contact with a WW II veteran who proudly shows off his war decorations. The man becomes a target for Mary Beth's displaced frustrations (since she feels she cannot interfere with Harv Jr.'s decision). But the fact that this man turns out to be a murderer in civilian life substantiates her outrage towards the stupidity and false pride of war. Harvey, Mary Beth's husband, occupies an important position in relation to this issue. He not only shares his wife's views about the military, but explicitly critiques Reagan's Central American policies. In this particular case, then, the personal and the political coincide to reinforce viewer sympathy with a pacifist stance and to discourage identification with militarism.

Aside from Harvey's supportive role as husband in *Cagney & Lacey*, his character is often used to signify opinions or positions that the show's stars do not articulate. Other minor characters who take up controversial stances are also featured in episodes – especially when the social issue in question is not explicitly feminist. In addition to Harvey's liberal (sometimes bordering on socialist) working-class position, for example, Detective Marcus Petrie repeatedly takes a stand against racism, insisting on the recognition of his racial difference as a way of confronting the racist attitudes of others. [. . .] The positions assumed by minor characters may be seen by some as a diversion tactic or safe method of keeping a more conservative representation of Cagney and Lacey intact. On the other hand, it could be argued that these additional voices work in concert with the women's own political agendas to suggest a broad based approach to social problems.

The investigative structure of *Cagney & Lacey* can be summarised as a 'struggle between different voices for control over telling the story'.[14] Working in conjunction with its soap opera strategies to provide multiple points of view and identification, *Cagney & Lacey* uses codes of detection to uncover the 'truth' of women's social relations. While the show departs from the traditional detective genre in significant ways, and its investigative structure might work just as well if Cagney and Lacey were members of a different profession (e.g., medicine), the authority invested in these women as representatives of the Law makes its comparison with the detective genre both profitable and unavoidable. According to *Cagney & Lacey's* newly-emerging law governing crime and sexuality, women are presumed innocent, the voices of many different women are examined, and women's struggle to assert control over their own lives is legitimised.

RECLAIMING THE LOOK

One final way in which *Cagney & Lacey* challenges patriarchal discourse and encourages women-identified constructions of meaning is through its economy of vision. In fact, it is this aspect, more than any other, that most clearly distinguishes *Cagney & Lacey* from other texts. Dominant theories of spectatorship maintain that traditional (male-governed) texts are founded on a subject/object dichotomy that places a male subject in control of the 'gaze' and positions the woman as object of his look. Since the woman becomes the passive raw material for the active gaze and visual pleasure of the male, the female viewer's possibilities for identification become extremely limited; she must choose between adopting the voyeuristic (sadistic) position of the male subject or the masochistic position of the female object.[15] But this model of spectatorship does not describe the viewer's relation to *Cagney & Lacey*. As I have pointed out in the previous sections, female viewers are more likely to feel empowered by their identifications with Cagney and Lacey. Thus they experience a pleasure in viewing that cannot be explained in masochistic terms.

Cagney & Lacey provides an alternative viewer-text relation that breaks up traditional structures of looking in several different ways. First of all, the show's female characters are in possession of the look. By virtue of their authority to control the process of detection and narrative action, Cagney and Lacey define the text's point of view and vision of social relations. Thus, they not only act as subjects of narration, but rarely become the objects of a male gaze. It could be argued that it is precisely because Cagney and Lacey are not the fetishised objects of male desire that they are able to assert control [. . .]. However, this control is not necessarily a control *over* men. Instead of reversing the traditional relations of looking and objectifying men as the fetishised objects of female desire and power, *Cagney & Lacey* attempts to break the pattern of dominance and submission altogether. Even though the text privileges the woman's point of view, reverse discrimination is not seen as the answer to women's empowerment.

Cagney & Lacey actively works to frustrate the traditional relations of voyeurism and fetishism by avoiding scenes which would ordinarily result in an objectification of women. For example, in episodes on spouse abuse and child abuse, viewers are not privy to scenes in which women or female children are physically assaulted, thus discouraging a sadistic and voyeuristic identification with violence against women.

[. . .]

The relations of looking established between women in *Cagney & Lacey* also challenge traditional economies of vision. Since women are not isolated from each other as objects for male consumption, women have more freedom to initiate and act upon relations with each other. The de-eroticised images of women, in other words, permit women to interact as *subjects*. This sort of re-visioning requires women to look beyond the surface level of a woman's image and to place into question male-defined images of women. Thus, women are perceived by other women not as sexual objects, but as the victimised subjects of patriarchal desire. *Cagney & Lacey* does not foreclose the possibility of erotic identification – a point that lesbian viewers can substantiate – but the female viewer's *objectification* of female characters is discouraged. Since *Cagney & Lacey* looks behind the image to examine women's oppression and encourages identification with the various struggles that women encounter, viewers are less likely to identify these women as fetish objects. In this way, *Cagney & Lacey* offers a vision of female bonding that simultaneously threatens patriarchal definitions of sexual relations and offers female viewers a point of identification that is neither sadistic nor masochistic. This results in more empowering (rather than power-filled) social relations for and among women.

Another way that *Cagney & Lacey* avoids the objectification of women is by shifting the viewer's attention from sight to sound. In other words, greater emphasis is placed on the voice (what women say) than on the image (how women look). As Mary Ann Doane notes, '[the] voice displays what is inaccessible to the image, what exceeds the visible: the "inner life" of the character'.[16] Thus the voice can be seen as 'a potentially viable means whereby the woman can make herself heard'.[17] *Cagney & Lacey* provides 'an isolated haven' for the voice of women within patriarchy, through the creation of woman's space. Within the enclosed space of the police car or the rest room at the 14th Precinct House (spaces which are both public and private), Cagney and Lacey speak to each other without male intervention and are free to explore and affirm the dimensions of female partnership. The importance of this woman's space (and the female bonding that occurs within it) is underscored by the fact that the show includes at least one such scene in every episode.

Other textual strategies in *Cagney & Lacey* rely on the voice (e.g., the reaction and interaction evident in the process of women's decision-making). But when examined in relation to the gaze, strategies involving the voice take on added significance. The voice is sometimes placed in counterpoint to the gaze – a strategy that allows *Cagney & Lacey* to play with the conventions of voyeurism. For instance, when Cagney and Lacey are in the precinct house rest room, the camera often focuses on their reflections as they primp themselves in front of the mirror. But within this woman's space, the role of the image becomes undermined. Either the woman's concern with her image is shown to be a diversionary tactic (a way to avoid discussing the real issues at hand), or the image itself turns out to be a false or incomplete source of information (it is, after all, only a reflection). Viewers are thus discouraged from investing any identification or voyeuristic pleasure in the image. To gain access to the character's inner feelings we must actively look beyond the image and listen to rather than look at the characters.

In other instances, the voice and the image combine in ways that explicitly usurp male privilege. In the episode on spouse abuse, for example, Chris' ACLU boyfriend, David, is the trial lawyer who gets the accused husband convicted. But instead of showing the actual courtroom scene, the site of David's authority and expertise, the event is recounted verbally in the women's rest room. Mary Beth performs for Chris the details of the trial by playing David's role and speaking in his place. In this way, the woman's voice is privileged and Mary Beth, instead of David, receives recognition for all the hard work she put in on the case. Although Mary Beth makes a 'spectacle' of herself during this scene, the woman's space provides a safe environment for her performance while it, once again, allows a woman to speak and to be heard.

Finally, *Cagney & Lacey* tampers with the conventions of voyeurism through the use of masquerade. As Mary Ann Doane notes, '[t]here is always a certain excessiveness, a difficulty associated with women who appropriate the gaze, who insist on looking'.[18] In order to maintain control – over the narrative, the look, and her own body – a woman must destabilise the image and confound the masculine structure of the look. One option is to give (male) viewers more than they bargain for. Thus, instead of refusing the familiar trappings of femininity, a woman might *flaunt* her femininity, play the game of femininity, by using her own body as a disguise. This masquerade allows a woman to distance herself from the image (to refuse complicity with objectification) while she demonstrates and controls the representation of her body.

In *Cagney & Lacey*, the detectives often adopt disguises in the service of their undercover work. While these disguises generally connote a power of action that extends beyond a woman's sexualised form, the occasions of feminine masquerade provide a direct commentary on the issue of female representation. In a 1987 episode, for example, Cagney and Lacey go undercover as hookers to catch a mugger. In their role as women dressed up as women, they display an excess of femininity – mounds of makeup and hair (wigs of unnatural color), revealing dresses, feathers, jewellery – that creates a ridiculous image of the female form. The masquerade allows Cagney and Lacey to expose the sadism of male desire, i.e., 'those "ogling" eyes that turn women into pieces of meat', as Cagney remarks. Moreover, when the detectives change into their street clothes and assume a different identity, they deconstruct this fetishised image of woman and expose male-defined femininity as a mask that can be worn or simply removed. At the end of the episode (after they have successfully closed the case), Cagney and Lacey return to the privacy of the woman's rest room and conduct a ceremonial ritual in which they burn their costumes. Once free of the burden of their feminised images, Cagney remarks, 'We are better cops now, Mary Beth'. 'And smarter', replies her partner.

[. . .]

Other uses of masquerade are more celebratory than pedagogical. When Cagney and Lacey dress up as fruits for a game show, and when they perform a Rockettes number for a police awards banquet, their disguises invite laughter rather than critical reflection. In circumstances such as these, masquerade provides an occasion for play and the detectives do not comment directly on the conventions of female representation. Nonetheless, their disguises act as a visual statement on the fluid, potentially subversive quality of the female image and women's ability to change and control the parameters of its representation. And this is finally what *Cagney & Lacey* is all about: the empowerment and pleasure that women gain from representing themselves (to themselves). If the makers of *Cagney & Lacey* occasionally celebrate and flaunt this pleasure, many female viewers, including myself, feel that they have earned the right to do so.

Visual playfulness and other disruptions of conventional representation do not automatically mark *Cagney & Lacey* as a radical text however.[19] As Julie D'Acci has noted, the show's representations are often rooted in liberal notions of feminist politics which perceive 'social change and difference for women (as) simply a matter of equal rules, equal jobs and equal representation'.[20] Its liberal politics thus tend to promote individual accomplishment (i.e., representations of women who have 'made it') and pluralism (i.e., many different types of successful women) as a means to correct the social imbalance of a white male dominated culture.[21] Yet, *Cagney & Lacey*'s pluralism of representation should not be confused or equated with the show's discursive strategies of detection. In spite of its apparent liberalism, the text opens up the possibility of a reading practice that goes beyond a mere identification with certain stereotypes or roles and engages its female viewers in a process of locating and (re)articulating women's positioning within social practices. This becomes possible because *Cagney & Lacey* actively works to create viewing positions which empower the text's female viewers as political subjects.

NOTES

1. *American Film*, July–August 1985, pp. 11–12.
2. O'Connor, J. 1984.
3. Farber, S. 1984.
4. Reilly, S. 1985, p. 14.
5. McHenry, S. 1984, p. 23.
6. Modleski, T. 1983, p. 68.
7. White, M. 1987, p. 158.
8. Ibid.

9. Kuhn, A. 1982, p. 34.
10. Tompkins, J. 1987, p. 169. This quotation occurs slightly out of context. Tompkins is referring to the public-private dichotomy within the academy that berates women for combining emotionality (personal response) with rationality (scholarly discourse). This said, I would add that the form this paper takes, and the positive reading of the text that I argue for here, emerges out of my own 'fierce identification' with and sense of empowerment by *Cagney & Lacey*.
11. Harvey, S. 1980, p. 23.
12. Ibid. p. 25.
13. DeLauretis, T. 1985, pp. 167–168.
14. Gledhill, C. 1980, p. 16.
15. Mulvey, L. 1975, p. 17.
16. Doane, M. A. 1980, p. 41.
17. Ibid. p. 49.
18. Doane, M. A. 1982, p. 83.
19. Brower states that *Cagney & Lacey* is 'by no means a radical show', even though its aesthetic and political marginalisation has been equated with 'quality' (i.e. progressive) television programming (p. 28).
20. D'Acci, 1987, p. 222.
21. Ibid. p. 205.

REFERENCES

Brower, S. TV "Trash" and "Treasure": Marketing *Dallas* and *Cagney & Lacey*', *Wide Angle* 11.1, 1989: pp. 18–31.
D'Acci, J. 'The Case of Cagney and Lacey'. *Boxed In: Women and Television*. Baehr, H., and Dyer, G. (eds). Pandora Press, London. 1987.
De Lauretis, T. 'Aesthetic and Feminist Theory: Rethinking Women's Cinema'. *New German Critique*. 34. Winter 1985, pp. 154–175.
Doane, M. A. 'The Voice in the Cinema: The Articulation of Body and Space'. *Yale French Studies* 60, 1980: pp. 33–50.
Doane, M. A. 'Film and the Masquerade: Theorising the Female Spectator'. *Screen* 23, 3–4, 1982, pp. 74–88.
Farber, Stephen. 'A New Chance for *Cagney & Lacey*'. *New York Times* 14 March 1984, Sec. C: 26.
Gledhill, C. '*Klute* 1: A Contemporary Film Noir and Feminist Criticism'. *Women in Film Noir*. Kaplan, E. A. (ed). British Film Institute, London. 1980.
Harvey, S. 'Woman's Place: The Absent Family in Film Noir'. *Women in Film Noir*. Kaplan, E. A. (ed). British Film Institute, London. 1980.
Kuhn, A. *Women's Pictures: Feminism and Cinema*. Routledge & Kegan Paul, London. 1982.
McHenry, S. 'The Rise and Fall – And Rise of TV's *Cagney & Lacey*'. *Ms*, April 1984. pp. 23–26.
Modleski, T. 'The Rhythms of Reception: Daytime Television and Women's Work'. *Regarding Television*. Kaplan, E. A. (ed). American Film Institute, Los Angeles. 1983.
Mulvey, L. 'Visual Pleasure and Narrative Cinema'. *Screen* 16. 3. Autumn 1975. pp. 6–18.
O'Connor, J. *Cagney & Lacey*, Police Series on CBS. *New York Times* 2 July 1984.
Reilly, S. 'The Double Lives of Cagney and Lacey'. *McCall's*. April 1985: pp. 14, 204.
Tompkins, J. 'Me and My Shadow'. *New Literary History* 19. 1. Autumn 1987, pp. 169–78.
White, M. 'Ideological Analysis and Television'. *Channels of Discourse*. Allen, R. C. (ed). University of North Carolina Press, Chapel Hill. 1987.

24

THE PAGE THREE GIRL SPEAKS TO WOMEN, TOO

Patricia Holland

First: Sizzling Sauciness . . .

Are you a flirt?
Try the Sun's *sizzling sauciness test.*
Some people just can't help it. Every time they come face to face with a member of the opposite sex they start flirting like crazy.
It is all harmless good fun. There is nothing like a flirty encounter to brighten your day.

(September 17)[1]

A vocabulary of emotional arousal summons laughter, thrills, shocks, desire, on every page of the *Sun*. But no sooner do they surge into being than these unmanageable forces find themselves tamed, re-expressed as fun, enjoyment, sparkle. 'It's all in your soaraway *Sun* today'; 'Your pow-packed *Sun*'; 'Life's more fun with your Number One *Sun*'. Fun organises and contains emotion.

The tone is exclamatory, celebratory, laced with a self-congratulation which verges on self-parody ('We're out of this world'). Everything in the *Sun* is subordinated to enjoyment presented with self-conscious relish – there is a continuous commentary in the *Sun* on the *Sun*.

Pleasure is organised across the pages of the paper through its photographs, layout, language, and beyond that two-dimensional surface there's an explicit address outwards to the reader, an address which is personal and direct. The reader is continuously invited to go beyond mere spectatorship and partake in the universal jollity. This is *your* pow-packed *Sun*, the flirty encounter brightened *your/my* day, *I* could be this week's Bingo winner . . . and indeed I could, for, as I read this paper, *I* am the reader addressed, I am the one invited, tempted to make myself a *Sun*lover.

From *Screen*, 24:3 (1983) pp. 84–102.

A purveyor of pleasures, an organiser of your pleasures, my pleasures . . . But are they my pleasures? Am I not, rather, repelled by those pleasures called on by the *Sun*, by its appeal to a trivial sexuality, by its insults to the female body, by its jokes at the expense of women, its flippancy . . . 'Relatively few readers of the *Observer* can be close students of the *Sun*,' began an article by Charles Wintour on Sunday October 3. Locating myself an *Observer* reader, I, too, reject the appeal of the *Sun*, understand it is not for me, turn away from its address. To put it bluntly, I know the *Sun* does not want me.

The *Sun* does not want spoilsports, killjoys, those who are not prepared to join in the high jinks, the sauciness, to allow a flirty encounter to brighten their day. Labour party critics are a 'dreary and embittered band' (leader, October 2). The *Sun's* readers are different from those of the 'ageing *Daily Express*, the pompous *Daily Mail* and the boring *Guardian*'. It frankly warns us off, then celebrates its own rising circulation: 'Your super *Sun* has gone out of this world and set new circulation records for the galaxy. Last month we sold an amazing 4,249,000 copies every single day' (October 5).

So the *Sun* does not want people like me and I want nothing to do with the *Sun*. But, pause. . . . Many things about the *Sun* repel me, but surely one of the things I find most unpleasant is its presentation of *women*. Yet when I read more closely I find that the *Sun* is not rejecting me as a *woman*. When it attempted to advertise in student newspapers with a 'Nudie-Varsity Challenge' it was, unsurprisingly, attacked by the National Union of Students: 'Page Three is grossly sexist, insulting to women and debasing.' But the *Sun* was sure of its ground. It called on a woman to speak to women. 'Luscious Linda Lusardi', the Page Three of the day, 'hopes that Britain's college cuties will ignore the spoilsports and try their luck on the nation's favourite glamour page' (October 15). The *Sun* rejects pomposity, boring analysis, critical thought, and it can confidently invite women students to reject those things, too, to ignore the spoilsports and join in the saucy fun. The *Sun* speaks directly to women readers.

This article is an attempt to put aside my initial feeling of repulsion, and my social knowledge that the *Sun* is not for me. It is an attempt to make some sort of sense of that address.

NEXT: DROOLING AT BREAKFAST TIME

The *Sun* has openly located its pleasure around sexuality – heterosexual sexuality. Its features and its presentation of 'news' are organised around forms of arousal ranging from shock and disgust to thrills or celebration, but sexual stimulus is a constant underlying theme, with the Page Three 'girls' – that particular, styled presentation of the female body as spectacle – 'those luscious ladies you drool over at breakfast' (September 20) as a central image.

Like all newspapers, the *Sun* constructs on the surface of its pages a series of narrative structures with similarities to the narratives we meet in feature films and novels: not the shaped and moulded narratives usual in those forms, but narratives nevertheless, organised in a temporal sequence with a range of characters who relate to each other in particular ways and whose stories develop in sequential episodes through both words and pictures. The narratives of a newspaper operate at different levels of abstraction, ranging from major structuring threads to close particularities. The narrative threads involve the setting up of conflicts, moves to new alignments, aims, resolutions of conflict, surprise twists, key characters and so on.[2]

The narrative flow of a daily newspaper has its own particular form. Its forward movement is structured by its regular recurrence, but each morning there is a pause, as the mosaic presentation of that day's edition cuts across the forward flow. Each day the reader gains a certain freedom of reading, can organise the paper at will – begin at the back with the sport or in the middle with the TV or the feature – guided by certain principles. The main eye-catcher is on the front, Page Three is on page three, and the sports news – male bodies in action – is at the back, the only part of the paper in which the discourse of sex is not made explicit. Within the pages of a newspaper multiple fractured narratives intertwine, interweave. Unlike the traditional narrative there is no final climax, no closure, for we never arrive at the last page. But the search for closure is there, both in the work of the newspaper itself and in the efforts of the reader. Thus, news and feature items are constructed into the flow of the narrative over time. New events and characters are brought in to fill the well-known roles. The different narratives influence each other and are cross-referenced. So, each day's edition is not a random collection of items: moreover, we readers work at it, make efforts to structure it and give it coherence. For we already know what Barthes has put into words – 'a narrative is never made up of anything other than functions: in differing degrees, everything in it signifies. This is not a matter of art (on the part of the narrator), but of structure; in the realm of discourse, what is noted is by definition notable.'[3] And the *Sun* itself directly calls on us to make sense of its stories, gives us indications and reminds us of what is notable. After all we know the plot so far and we have a good idea of the expected outcome.

In the *Sun* the news stories are dominated by sexual dramas, and features are dominated either by sex spectaculars or by invitations to sexual, or more precisely heterosexual, games. Characters who make front page headlines include football players like 'love tangle soccer star Andy Gray', who starred in 'secret baby for Andy Gray, soccer star shock' (September 28) which went through several daily episodes; entertainers like Liberace, sued by an ex-lover ('a liar and a junkie: Liberace blasts lover boy,' October 16); and, of course Royalty. Prince Andrew's holiday with 'sexy actress', 'soft porn starlet', 'sizzling actress' Koo Stark reverberated through its pages for several weeks. 'Is that courageous young man going to be corrupted and depraved – or is he just going to have a bit of fun under the palms?' asked a defence counsel at a pornography trial, reported as a '*Sun* exclusive' under the heading 'Randy Andy's legal laugh-in' (October 12). Less well known performers are confined to the inner pages under headlines like 'Girls slam sexy sirs at school of scandal' (August 16); 'Love-in newly weds miss the jet' (March 22); 'Wonderbra! The mayoress strips off to a German band' (October 23). And this news, which is news of sex, is backed up by the sexualisation of public events. The *Sun* reported the return of the QE2 from the Falklands with 'Liner of love. Buxom blonde Jane Broomfield yesterday spilled the beans on the saucy antics that turned the QE2 into a floating lovenest on the voyage home from the Falklands' (June 12).

The sexual activities on the news pages are paralleled by, and often indistinguishable from, the sexual games on the feature pages, which range from sex spectaculars featuring show-biz or other celebrities – 'How I saved my marriage by Bjorn Borg: inside the love nest of the world's top tennis star' (August 19); 'Romeo Julio: beauties are begging to get into his bed' (October 22) – to questionnaires and participation games played by *you* – 'Total loving: train your body to tell him I love you' (July 26); 'The mating game. Ten sexy steps to help you win a new love' (February 6); 'Sex and the newly single girl: the *Sun's* special report on how to cope with a love crisis' (October 14). Sometimes they mix show-biz with the everyday: under the headline 'Who are the naughtiest girls in Britain', *Sun* reporter Judy Wade asked various (male) touring performers to 'tell us which town served up the hottest receptions' (May 6 '77).

The features addressed to 'you' tread a delicate line between what is accepted and what is possible. A base line of heterosexual monogamy is assumed, but beyond that, hints at saucy antics range from: 'Are you a cheating lover? A questionnaire to discover if you are in danger, by Wendy Leigh, author of "What makes a man good in bed" ' (August 24), to 'Giggles galore at the naughty bring and buy' (an October 4 story about housewives' tea parties for selling sex aids).

> *The function of narrative is not to 'represent', it is to constitute a spectacle still very enigmatic for us but in any case not of a mimetic order. The 'reality' of a sequence lies not in the 'natural' succession of the actions composing it but in the logic there exposed, risked, satisfied.*[4]

Yes, yes. We know all about that: that was written sixteen years ago. But does it work for *newspapers*? I will argue that to read the *Sun* as a collection of narratives and to see the people constructed in its pages not as 'beings' but as 'participants', to use Barthes' terms again, is the only way to make sense of what it is up to.

The all-important question which then arises is: how is the reader . . . are the readers . . . are different groups of readers . . . included in, addressed by these narratives? The verbal address of the features is often directed to both sexes simultaneously: you could say it was double-sexed:

> *We all know lovers who cheat – and even some who get away with it. But are you sure it could never happen to you? How confident are you that you could never be tempted into a one-night stand? And that you would spot the signs immediately if your partner was having an affair?*

'Partner' is a useful word. It assumes stability regardless of legal status and is not gender-specific. The questions in 'Are you a cheating lover?' also have a 'double-sexed' address, referring to 'the person you cheated with' and using 'they' and 'them' as singular pronouns. 'Have you ever suspected your partner of cheating? What did you do when you suspected them?' But despite the dual address of the words, the accompanying pictures show a high degree of differentiation between the sexes.

However, when verbal address does become gender specific, it is women who are spoken to directly. Almost all the features on sex are written under women's names, and in almost all of them when they speak to 'you', 'you' turns out to be a woman. Thus it is the newly single *girl* for whom sex is a problem: 'total loving' teaches women how to woo a man, and insists that we should 'never accept frigidity'.

Men by contrast are the implied, rather than the direct, addressees. They are almost never 'you'. Male attitudes to women are openly presented as predatory or contemptuous: Julio Iglesias says, 'Women are beautiful, I love them all and why shouldn't I?' (October 22); Kenny Everett says, 'People seem to like lots of nubile, scantily dressed girls on my shows. . . . I said go and find some fresh talent, rub in a bit of body oil and throw 'em on the set' (August 12). So even when the tone shifts to 'the greatest moment in any woman's life is when sex and love blend perfectly', certain assumptions about the male reader lie behind the address to his female counterpart, and those are the assumptions which provoke the knowing wink and permit the salacious joke. Women are spoken to directly, but it is men who share the joke. It is men who drool at breakfast time, but meanwhile the invitation is out to women to come and join the fun.

AND THEN YOU TOO CAN BE A PAGE THREE GIRL

> * *Aim for a look which is full of allure. A flirty smile in your eyes should not be difficult – especially with your favourite man behind the camera. And please, please relax.*
> * *Try to avoid a toothy grin or a Bardot pout. this sort of expression can make you look self-conscious. it's Best not to copy anyone – just be yourself.*
>
> *(October 27 '81)*

Every morning millions of readers/viewers of the *Sun* newspaper turn from the front page bearing today's latest thrill, and instantly meet the gaze, exchange looks with, find their own gaze absorbed by, that of the Page Three 'girl'. The daily turn of the page uncovers her flirty smile above the aggressive breasts that define her – a two dimensional striptease, performed on our behalf as often as we want. Her look of allure is always directed at us, her eyes always engage with ours, her favourite man behind the camera is, miraculously, replaced by . . . every one of those millions – men, women, children and old people – who make the gesture of turning.

[. . .]

Page Three is a direct address by the newspaper to its audience. It organises that audience, sorts it into groups, addressing itself separately both to men and to women. It presents itself as a source of pleasure to both men and women. Page Three condenses within itself the newspaper's view of itself and its audience: it declares how the paper wants to be seen, how it should be appreciated, used and enjoyed. It is the pivotal point of the *Sun's* address to its audience. It is central to its marketing and thus to its very existence.

But does Page Three really address *women*? Surely this pictured woman is no more than a fetishised image, designed for male gratification? Surely she tells us about the nature of male, not female, eroticism? Surely she is in the tradition of the pin-up, for male eyes only, to be overlooked or tactfully ignored by women viewers? Yet, although it does not exhaust it, Page Three dominates the meaning of 'woman' in the *Sun*, and women readers must cope with this meaning – a meaning which both does and does not refer to them, does and does not offer them back a sense of themselves. They look over it and through it when reading the newspaper in search of what is addressed to them *as women* . . . or do they?

In fact, as in the rest of the paper, there are important ways in which Page Three is addressed directly to women. It is part of the *Sun's* discourse on female sexuality which invites sexual enjoyment, sexual freedom and active participation in heterosexual activity: 'Never accept frigidity'.

In order to understand Page Three's address to women, we need to look at its position within the newspaper's narratives: first at the narrative of Page Three itself, and then at the position of Page Three within the multiple narratives of the *Sun*. First, Page Three: its central character, the model girl, is only one of the roles in the drama. Other characters are the photographer (always a man), the male viewers, who appear both as a group and as named individuals, and the female viewers, including other potential Page Three girls. Various peripheral characters make an appearance from time to time: the model's mother, her boyfriend, her boss. Finally there is the Voice of the *Sun*, the authorial voice which speaks directly to us, endlessly jokes with its audience.

Like Saussure's famous 8.25 from Geneva to Paris, the Page Three girl is every day different yet every day the same. Regardless of who plays her part, she occupies the same central position in the plot, for this is her drama. Like a character in any narrative construction she is not a 'being' but a 'participant'. There is one action that defines her – she bares her breasts for the delight of male viewers.

Among the obvious differences between the narrative of newspapers and that of, say, most plays or feature films, is that the individuals who get to play the parts, to perform the roles, are plucked, so it seems, from 'real life'. This is so even when, as is often the case in the *Sun*, these individuals are in fact professional actors: or when the parts they are called on to play do not masquerade as 'news'. Because of the special relation of the newspaper narrative to real events, all of the characters bring into their roles something of this 'real life' quality. Thus a newspaper character like a Page Three girl is present in the narrative on a double level, she has a double presence. She is there in her capacity as Page Three, but she is also there in her capacity as a 'real life woman'. Such a double presence is much stronger in newspapers than it is in, say, the film star/fictional character duality in a cinema because it participates in the ideology of truth which underpins all newspaper discourse including that of the *Sun* ('We shall go on reporting the truth, the whole truth' – leader, October 8). A newspaper is about what 'is'. The concept of 'fiction' which makes possible the construction of a novel or a feature film is alien to it. It makes its judgements by appealing to a clear opposition between 'truth' and 'falsehood'. So it is with the Page Three model: although she *becomes* Page Three, although she totally fills that role, that is not all there is to her. She has a 'real life' role in the newspaper, too, but it is more fragmented, more difficult to grasp. It comes and goes, surfaces in different parts of the newspaper. Yet its very reality remains as a constant resource both for writers and readers.

A sense of *performance* is central to an understanding of Page Three, and the performance is there to be observed in the concurrent presence *in the narrative* of both performer and role. Alongside the visible construction of the role is a constant commentary on the act of construction itself, a constant self-reference. The newspaper 'contains' and visibly places its own particular narrative style in a way similar to that noted by Stephen Heath in regard to classic cinema: 'Classic cinema does not efface the signs of production, it contains them, according to the narrativisation described above.[5]

Much of the *Sun* is written in terms of show business and many of those who people its pages are 'personalities'. And within the paper there is a continuous discourse on acting and on the meaning of performance. Dolly Parton, introduced as 'Hollywood's bustiest blonde', tells us: 'I'm not ashamed of the way I look. I have to live with it, so I might as well have fun … I look one way but I'm really another, and I look on the Dolly image just like a ventriloquist looks on his dummy.' Dolly clearly has the right attitude as far as the *Sun* is concerned. Writer Alex Harvey comments approvingly: 'What Dolly Parton has above all is a sense of good humour about herself and the way she looks' (October 1). Similarly many Page Three stories direct our attention simultaneously to the role (a bit of fun, a game, a joke at the lady's expense) and to the person who is playing the role ('I look one way but I'm really another'), in effect to a second, simultaneous role. Thus the act of playing a part itself becomes part of the celebratory tone of Page Three, for this is no ordinary role, but a star role, coveted by many women. So the *Sun* invites all those aspirants to try their luck. 'The hunt is on for girls beautiful enough to make their debut on Page Three' (October 28 '81); 'Girls, do you do an unusual job and want to appear on Page Three? Send a picture and details of yourself' (September 21); 'College girls, ignore the spoilsports and try your luck on the nation's favourite glamour page' (October 15). And it offers advice on how to do it. From the lesson on how to be a Page Three girl (October 27 '81) we learn that this involves at least two people, the model herself and the photographer, her favourite man behind the camera. Models are told how to pose (body three-quarters on to the camera), what sort of look to adopt (flirty smile in the eye) and what to avoid (heavy make up, fussy jewellery, toothy grin). The photographer is told to look out for his backgrounds (avoid heavily patterned wallpapers) how to arrange the lighting (avoid ugly shadows) and generally how to imitate 'the *Sun*'s top glamour photographer Beverley Goodway'. He constructs her picture and she takes a willing part in the reconstruction of her self. An essential quality of the Page Three role is the willing and eager participation of the pictured woman, epitomising the *Sun*'s construction across its pages of a willing and eager female sexuality. Page Three is 'the world's top glamour spot' (October 4) and to reach it is an achievement – for a woman – overshadowing other achievements, to be greeted with pride.

[. . .]

It seems that despite the never forgotten presence of the men in the story, the tension, the essential drama, is for women. It has to do with the aspiration to the status of model (autonomous femininity) and the jockeying for position between that aspiration and other modes of femininity – between the marriageable Jacqui and the 'delicious 36–24–36' Jacqui. For women like Jacqui the search for autonomy on these terms involves both an achievement and a defeat. The Voice of the *Sun*, while pressing its version of the achievement, is nevertheless constantly working to turn it into a defeat. It must present this 'excess of femininity' as its own creation and work to keep it under its control and that of the male audience. Once more, the work is done by means of jokes, and for the Voice of the *Sun* and its complicitous male chorus the joke is always on the woman.[6] Hence its search for the most extreme expression of the tension, and its triumph in casting a policewoman in the role, turning her policewoman's hat from a symbol of authority into a provocative garment [. . .] – something to relieve the unsexy nature of total nudity. After all, 'who would hesitate to be handcuffed by such a beautiful bobby?'

The crucial mediator in the transformation from working woman to model girl is, of course, the photographer. He literally stands in the position of the drooling millions and offers his view to them. But he has the privilege of creating the spectacle they merely yearn for. He witnesses the completion of Lesley's gesture, he organises the removal of Merlita's uniform and the redirection of her eyes. He awakens, brings out, the model girl latent in all women. It was Beverley Goodway who 'gave Merlita a taste of the model world'. Just as a certain sort of sex manual invites men to awaken the desire of their female partners, so we expect the expert Beverley, the prime ravisher, to advise male readers on how to draw out the Page Three girl concealed in their wives and girlfriends. Yet at the same time the feature on 'Do you want to be a Page Three girl' takes its place among the *Sun*'s frequent articles on sexual games, and, like them – though perhaps unlike sex manuals – addresses itself more to women than to men. In 'How to be a Page Three girl' women are not invited merely to respond to the photographer. No, it is up to them to prepare themselves, to work on themselves, to rehearse, to create their own autonomy. In this scenario the photographer is not the all-powerful creator, but the collaborator, adviser, technician. The Page Three girl must learn to ravish him.

So the Page Three role is clearly seen as a role, and is placed against the model's real-life persona which is anchored in normality. Even the professional models have had fairly ordinary jobs: 'Carole-Ann worked as a sea front waitress in Weymouth before she became a tasty dish herself' (August 16). Peripheral characters are introduced from this world of normality, most often parents and other relations who express pride at their daughter's achievement: 'My mother's very excited and terribly proud of me' says Merlita (September 23); 'I'm very proud of her and her Dad's thrilled to bits' says Ellan's mother (October 4); Pepita's thirteen-year-old nephew will be 'pleased as punch' and her boss 'thinks it's great' (October 13).

This act, this double performance of Page Three, is close to what Mary Ann Doane, after Joan Riviere, has described as 'the masquerade': 'The masquerade doubles representation; it is constituted by the hyperbolisation of the accoutrements of femininity.'[7] It is not recuperable 'precisely because it constitutes an acknowledgement that it is femininity itself which is constructed as a mask – as the decorative layer which conceals a non-identity'.[8] In recognising the role *as* a role both the viewer and the actor have already distanced themselves from it and have put themselves into a position to manipulate it.

The action of Page Three takes place at a number of levels, and at each level there is a struggle going on, a struggle to define and contain, a struggle for autonomy and resistance:

1. The level of the pin-up: Page Three as a picture.
    The three-dimensional flesh-and-blood men in the British Leyland spares department cut
    out a two-dimensional black-and-white picture from a newspaper for their own use. At
    this level the story is one of a relationship between real men and some meaningful marks
    on a flimsy sheet of paper. The woman is nothing but that picture, confined to the frame
    which surrounds it. The male spectators are the only actors. From time to time this real life
    drama is re-enacted in the paper, reminding us that this is the paradigmatic relationship
    which justifies the very existence of Page Three.

2. The narratives of Page Three: Page Three girl as double presence.
    At this level, as we have seen, the characters work out their plots and subplots within the
    frame of Page Three itself. Male readers can follow the *Sun's* attempts to win new recruits,
    can watch its attempts to overcome different sorts of resistance and can chortle at its
    jokes. Female readers can take part in the drama. Who will be Page Three tomorrow? It
    could be *you.*

3. The other narratives of the newspaper: Page Three as model, as real life persona, and the
    introduction of the Page Three principle.
    At this level the model is not confined to her frame. She appears as a character in the
    sexual dramas which thread through the daily pages of the *Sun.* Professional Page Threes
    appear in the news and on the feature pages. One has a baby, another gets a part in a film;
    a feature on 'Page Three pioneers' (October 26) traces the lives of Page Three models
    from ten years ago; a news story on the sexual harassment of baby sitters is illustrated by
    an account from a Page Three girl. Amateur Page Threes appear in their real-life personae.
    After all there's a story here, we want to know what happened to them.
    [. . .]
    Other amateur Page Threes force themselves into the role, confirming the *Sun's* convic-
    tion that the Page Three principle is present in all women. 'Naughty Erica' runs topless
    onto a football pitch; the fleet comes home, and is greeted with the Page Three principle,
    the baring of breasts for male gaze. ('I wish I could meet her,' said the man who sold
    me the paper.)

4. Life: Page Three girl as a real person
    The women we were introduced to as 'Merlita' and 'Erica' also exist out of print, unspoken
    by newspapers. There too for all of us the struggle between femininity and autonomy
    must be worked out.

FINALLY: PLAYFUL PAULINE'S FROLIC OR THIS IS NOT THE SORT OF BEHAVIOUR ONE EXPECTS FROM CIVIC LEADERS

Yes, but. . . . Millions of women read the *Sun* and, what is more, they go on reading it. But all
that analysis has not changed my own attitude. My rejection of the *Sun* remains as violent as
ever, I have not argued it away. And of course I do not want to argue it away, for I believe it
to be grounded in justifiable reasons. However, I cannot fail to note that my rejection, too, is
constructed by the *Sun.* The paper calls down on its head uninhibited abuse from the rest of the
press – abuse, it may be noted, often couched in sexual terms ('The harlot of Fleet Street', *Daily
Mirror* May 8). But it has incorporated that abuse into its very image of itself. The *Sun* is what it is,
its vast circulation is what it is, precisely because it is not like the rest. The *Daily Express* is ageing,
the *Daily Mail* is pompous, the *Guardian* is boring. The *Mirror* is losing readers because it did
not support Our Boys in the Falklands, Labour Party critics are a 'dreary and embittered crew'.

At the 1982 Labour Party conference MP Frank Allaun described the *Sun* as 'the most reactionary, jingoistic and anti-working class paper of them all'. But the *Sun* knows that it compels unswerving loyalty from many of its readers – 'There's no *Sun* today, and I don't bother with the other papers,' replied a station paper vendor when I asked about the news. 'Our readers will see right through this hysterical charge that the *Sun* is anti-working class. No newspaper has a better record in defending the real interests of working class men and women' (leader, October 2). And, when censured by the Press Council for its reporting of the black people's day of action,[9] the *Sun* answered, 'We have more coloured readers than any other newspaper' (October 8).

What the *Sun* is rejecting is moralism of any sort, bureaucratic power disguised as moral and cultural values, the whole range of attempts to put something over on you, to push you around, re-expressed in terms of elevation, education, propriety. The *Sun* rejects all that in the name of a working class whose rise to prosperity is still a live memory. Those who talk of a decline in that prosperity are the dreary and embittered who resent enjoyment, who attack the right to have fun, to be entertained. The *Sun* addresses a working class defined by its modes of consumption rather than its place in production. It unifies and organises its readers in terms of their forms of entertainment, by cultural attitudes rather than by class solidarity. The fact that these forms of entertainment are actually provided by advanced capitalism disappears from view. Traditions of working-class discipline and organisation are rejected along with the middle-class bureaucrats, social workers and cultural moralists. Rejected, too, are those who threaten this precarious position in a disorderly way: the immigrants, the muggers, the social security scroungers who snatch scarce resources and thus imperil the rest of the working class. The police are the allies of the working class in this scenario, defending them against attacks from below.

The *Sun*'s call for a particular kind of sexual liberation fits into this pattern. Sex is fun, a leisure activity, one of the rights of the consumer. Thus the organisation of gender roles takes place in terms of class identification. It is the moralists, the educators, the social workers who are the spoilsports, condemning Page Three as sexist and degrading. The *Sun*'s values are those which organise a working class – not the working class of labour histories, a class defined by self-help and hard work, but a working class which takes its pleasures when it can because they're only too fleeting. This is a working class that cannot be represented by the Labour Party. When Mayoress Pauline Duval demonstrated her acceptance of the Page Three principle, 'the attractive brunette stunningly shed the cares of office. Playful Pauline's frolic won roars of approval from her true-blue audience.' But her po-faced Labour opponents replied: 'It's not the sort of behaviour one expects from civic leaders.'

NOTES

1. Unless otherwise stated newspaper references are all to the *Sun*, 1982.
2. See Patricia Holland, 'The Invisible and the Obvious', *Lunatic Ideas*, London, Corner House Books, 1978, pp. 47–64, for a close look at the interweaving of narratives over a period of time in the *Daily Mirror*.
3. Roland Barthes, 'Introduction to the Structural Analysis of Narratives', *Image-Music Text*, London Fontana, 1977, p. 89
4. Ibid., p. 123
5. Stephen Heath, 'Narrative Space' *Screen* Autumn. 1976, vol. 17 no. 3, p. 97.
6. See Mary Ann Doane, 'Film and the Masquerade: Theorising the Female Spectator', *Screen* Sept. Oct. 1982 vol. 23 no. 3/4, p. 85. In her analysis of a still photograph '*Un Regard Oblique*' she points out that, 'The woman is there as the butt of a joke – a "dirty joke" which, as Freud has demonstrated, is always constructed at the expense of a woman.'
7. Ibid., p.82.
8. Ibid., p.81.
9. For a look at the way the popular press treated the black people's Day of Action see Patricia Holland, 'The New Cross Fire and the Popular Press', *Multiracial Education* Summer 1981, vol. 9 no. 3, pp. 61–80.

FURTHER READING

Ang, I., 'Feminist Desire and Female Pleasure', *Camera Obscura* 16 (1988) pp. 179–91.

Baehr, H. and Dyer, G. (eds), *Boxed In: Women and Television* (London: Pandora, 1987).

Ballaster, R., Beetham, M., Frazer, E. and Hebron, S., *Women's Worlds: Ideology, Femininity and the Woman's Magazine* (London: Macmillan, 1991).

Betterton, R. (ed.), *Looking On: Images of Femininity in the Visual Arts and Media* (London: Pandora, 1987).

Brown, M. E. (ed.), *Television and Women's Culture* (London: Sage, 1990).

Brunsdon, C., 'Pedagogies of the Feminine: Feminist Teaching and Women's Genres', *Screen* 32:4 (1991) pp. 364–81.

Brunsdon, C., 'Identity in Feminist Television Criticism', *Media, Culture and Society* 15:2 (1993) pp. 309–20.

Brunt, R. and Rowan, C. (eds), *Feminism, Culture and Politics* (London: Lawrence & Wishart, 1982).

Butcher, H. et al., 'Images of Women in the Media', CCCS stencilled paper (University of Birmingham, 1974).

Byars, J., 'Gazes/Voices/Power: Expanding Psychoanalysis for Feminist Film and Television Theory', in Pribram, E. D. (ed.), *Female Spectators* (London: Verso, 1988).

Coward R., *Female Desire* (London: Paladin, 1984).

Creedon, P. (ed.), *Women in Mass Communication: Challenging Gender Values* (London: Sage, 1989).

D'Acci, J., *Defining Women: Television and the Case of* Cagney and Lacey (Chapel Hill: University of North Carolina Press, 1993).

Davies, K., Dickey, J. and Stratford, T. (eds), *Out of Focus: Writing on Women and the Media* (London: The Women's Press, 1987).

Ferguson, M., *Forever Feminine: Women's Magazines and the Cult of Femininity* (London: Heinemann, 1983).

Feuer, J., 'Melodrama, Serial Form and Television Today', *Screen* 25:1 (1984) pp. 4–16.

Gamman, L. and Marshment, M. (eds), *The Female Gaze: Women as Viewers of Popular Culture* (London: The Women's Press, 1988).

Gledhill, C., 'Pleasurable Negotiations', in Pribram, E. D. (ed.), *Female Spectators* (London: Verso, 1988).

hooks, b., *Black Looks: Race and Representation* (London: Turnaround, 1992).

Kaplan, E. A. (ed.), *Regarding Television* (Los Angeles: American Film Institute, 1983).

Kaplan, E. A., 'Feminist Criticism and Television', in Allen, R. C. (ed.), *Channels of Discourse, Reassembled* (London: Routledge, 1992).

McCracken, E., *Decoding Women's Magazines* (London: Macmillan, 1993).

McRobbie, A., '*Jackie*: An Ideology of Adolescent Femininity', in Waites, B., Bennett, T. and Martin, G. (eds), *Popular Culture: Past and Present* (London: Croom Helm, 1982).

McRobbie, A., *Feminism and Youth Culture: From 'Jackie' to 'Just Seventeen'* (London: Macmillan, 1991).

Mattelart, M., *Women, Media, Crisis: Femininity and Disorder* (London: Comedia, 1986).

Mellencamp, P. (ed.), *Logics of Television* (Bloomington and London: Indiana University Press and BFI, 1990).

Modleski, T., *Loving with a Vengeance: Mass-Produced Fantasies for Women* (London: Methuen, 1984).

Modleski, T. (ed.), *Studies in Entertainment: Critical Approaches to Mass Culture* (Bloomington: Indiana University Press, 1986).

Modleski, T., 'Femininity as Mas(s)querade: A Feminist Approach to Mass Culture', in MacCabe, C. (ed.), *High Theory/Low Culture: Analysing Popular Television and Film* (Manchester: Manchester University Press, 1986).

Modleski, T., *Feminism without Women* (London: Routledge, 1991).

Pribram, E. D., *Female Spectators: Looking at Film and Television* (London: Verso, 1988).

Skirrow, G., '*Widows*', in Alvarado, M. and Stewart, J. (eds), *Made for Television: Euston Films Limited* (London: BFI, 1985).

Steeves, L., 'Feminist Theories and Media Studies', *Critical Studies in Mass Communication* 4:2 (1987) 11. 95–135.

Tuchman, G. et al. (eds), *Hearth and Home: Images of Women in the Media* (New York: Oxford University Press, 1978).

Winship, J., *Inside Women's Magazines* (London: Pandora Press, 1987).

Women's Studies Group (eds), Centre for Contemporary Cultural Studies, *Women Take Issue* (London: Hutchinson, 1978).

Zoonen, L. van, 'Feminist Perspectives on the Media', in Curran, J. and Gurevitch, M. (eds), *Mass Media and Society* (London: Edward Arnold, 1991).

Zoonen, L. van, *Feminist Media Studies* (London: Sage, 1994).

Text
'Postmodern' Media

Text: 'Postmodern' Media

Television, video and rock music have attracted increasing attention from theorists of the postmodern. In particular, television's multiplicity of narratives, its emphasis on the 'now', its interreferentiality and intercutting of images, and its technical reproducibility, all lend themselves to such interpretations, as does its increasingly fragmented pattern of use, particularly among the young. For Jean Baudrillard, indeed, television and its technologies become a metaphor for the universe of simulation which Western culture has become, in which the 'screen and network' collapse old distinctions between public and private and replace both with 'the ecstasy of communication'.[1]

Quite what the implications of such an identification of 'postmodern' media forms might be is less certain. The elimination of boundaries which characterises the postmodern may be read as negative, as the absorption and neutralisation of resistant strategies; or as positive, offering liberating possibilities of difference, multiplicity and de-centredness. Alternatively, it may be read as poised ambiguously between the two.

E. Ann Kaplan's study of MTV (Chapter 25) picks up Baudrillard's characterisation of television as postmodern, arguing that 'the phenomena he outlines seem to apply particularly to [MTV]', with its twenty-four-hour flow of constantly changing, four-minute segments.[2] If MTV, then, 'embodies and then further develops major cultural changes', producing an endless play of representations, what, she asks, are the implications for a left, and particularly for a feminist, cultural critique? Kaplan argues that television is a very different 'apparatus' to that of film, on which feminist analysis has largely concentrated, both in its textual characteristics and in its modes of reception. Its continuous fragmented texts mean that closure is forever deferred, and that across its segments we are presented with a range of addresses or 'gazes' which offer a multiplicity of identifications. Within these, particularly in MTV, gender address is often blurred and ambiguous, and where positions *appear* to be offered they may be merely pastiche, an empty quoting of earlier film or television texts. Despite this apparent fluidity, however, few of the videos shown on MTV have central figures who are female; of those which do, most, like those of Madonna, offer an ambiguous 'post-feminist heroine'. Finally, then, Kaplan is pessimistic about the implications of MTV. Its endless play of images and surfaces in a context of consumption 'co-opts any possible critical position by the very incorporation of what were previously "dissenting" images'.

Chapter 26 by Angela McRobbie challenges the pessimism of this account. Recent debates on postmodernism, argues McRobbie, possess 'both a positive attraction and a usefulness to the analyst of popular culture'. Postmodernism, in its insistence on the collapse of boundaries between image and lived reality, challenges the narrowness of structuralism's focus on the text as its object of study. Moreover, the phenomena which it describes – the 'frenzied expansion of the mass media', the intertwining of image and reality, media and society, the self-referentiality and endless cross-referencing of media output, the inescapability of images from popular culture – are not, as Kaplan suggests, themselves without critical potential. Postmodernism's collapsing of boundaries challenges old dualisms – between the 'self' and 'other', between 'the West' and its postcolonial 'other' – and forges new alliances. The outburst of energy released can produce new resistances and a 'vibrant critique' through its use of pastiche, its 'ransacking and recycling of culture'. As an example, McRobbie points to black urban culture, which thrives on its 'assertive re-assembling of bits and pieces' and 'fake, forged identities'. Black women writers, too, she argues, have produced an 'explosion of the written word' whose rhythms approximate 'the jazz sounds of the city'. Postmodernism's emphasis on fragmentation, she concludes, describes the experience of many groups of young people, and far from being its victims, they are 'putting it to work for them'.

NOTES

1. Jean Baudrillard, 'The Ecstasy of Communication', in H. Foster (ed.), *Postmodern Culture* (London: Pluto Press, 1985), p. 126.
2. See also Kaplan's longer study of MTV, *Rocking Around the Clock: Music Television, Postmodernism and Consumer Culture* (London: Methuen, 1987).

25

WHOSE IMAGINARY? THE TELEVISUAL APPARATUS, THE FEMALE BODY AND TEXTUAL STRATEGIES IN SELECT ROCK VIDEOS ON MTV

E. Ann Kaplan

The social Imaginary that I shall explore in Music Television (MTV)[1] has been constructed through the contradictory post-1960s historical moment in which rock videos arise as a mass popular culture form. It is the mapping in the 1980s of the new 1960s discourses about politics, sex and romance on to the increasingly high-tech stage of an already advanced capitalism that partly produces the extraordinary MTV Imaginary.

A symptom of the new high-tech stage of advanced capitalism is the deployment of television as itself a unique kind of apparatus, very different from the filmic one. Since MTV embodies in extreme form the characteristics of this apparatus, it is worth dwelling briefly on it, particularly as it has been described by Jean Baudrillard. Baudrillard points to television's cultural role in developing what he calls the new 'cold' universe of communication.[2] The universe involves marked changes in the relationship of subject to image; for while the movie screen harnesses the subject's desire through appearing momentarily to provide a longed for plenitude,[3] the television screen keeps the subject in a position of alienation. The television screen's constantly changing 'texts', of whatever kind, provide the constant *promise* of plenitude, but this is for ever *deferred*. Instead of the illusory and temporary plenitude of the cinema, the television screen–spectator relationship mimics the subject's original discovery of split subjectivity before the mirror. The decentred, fragmented self that becomes the subject's human condition (although masked in daily life by the illusory construction of a permanent 'self') is duplicated in the processes of television watching; the crucial difference from daily life is the constant *expectation* of unity, oneness, in the *next* text-segment.

Baudrillard takes things a step further, arguing that the television screen symbolizes a new era in which 'The Faustian, Promethean (perhaps Oedipal) period of production and consumption' has given way to 'the narcissistic and protean era of connections, contact, continuity, feedback

From E. Deidre Pribram (ed.), *Female Spectators: Looking at Film and Television* (Verso: 1988) pp. 132–55.

and generalized interface that goes with the universe of communication.' By this, Baudrillard means that the whole earlier 'intimate' universe (in his words, 'projective, imaginary and symbolic'), with its domestic scene, interiority, private space–time correlative to a public space, is all disappearing. 'Instead,' he says, 'there is a screen and a network. In place of the reflexive transcendence of mirror and scene, there is the nonreflecting surface, an immanent surface where operations unfold – the smooth operational surface of communication.' He concludes that 'with the television image – the television being the ultimate and perfect object for this era – our own body and the whole surrounding universe become a control screen.' (See Chart 1.)

For Baudrillard, this entails a dramatically different relationship of the subject to objects; people, for him, no longer project themselves into their objects in the old ways of getting psychological gratification out of them. If the psychological dimension can still be marked out, one has the sense that this is no longer actually the terrain in which things take place; we have instead usage of things (Baudrillard has the automobile in mind, but what he says applies equally to the television set), and a range of potentialities that we can produce through operating the machine. We are thus in the position of mastery and control, and can play with various possibilities. This is far different from relating to the object (car, television set) as a psychological sanctuary.

Baudrillard's idea are significant enough to warrant examination in relation to MTV, since the phenomena he outlines seem to apply particularly to that channel. How true is it that 'we no longer live in the drama of alienation' (Marx's world) but rather in that of 'the ecstasy of communication'? How true is it that the old 'hot, sexual obscenity' (the world of Freud) has been succeeded by 'the cold and communicational, contactual and motivational obscenity of today'? Does MTV offer an example of such a universe?

To begin with, it does seem that, in line with Baudrillard's theory, MTV partly exploits the imaginary desires allowed free play through the various 1960s liberation movements, divesting them, for commercial reasons, of their originally revolutionary implications, reducing them to the 'radical chic' and the pornographic. But at the same time its chosen non-stop, twenty-four-hour format of short, four-minute texts inevitably enables expression of positions critical of the status quo not necessarily favoured by the institution. Given Baudrillard's conceptualizations, however, we need to analyse how far these 'alternate' positions in fact have anything behind them – any ongoing alternative politics in the realm of the social formation. How far do the left/humanist positions have referents? How far are they, like much else on MTV, mere simulacra, with nothing behind, mere representations, images?[4]

I am, then, interested in the myths, images and representations evident in the rock videos played on MTV as these might be seen as both reflecting unconscious changes in young people's

Chart 1: Summary of Baudrillard's Scheme

Old 'hot' universe			*New 'cold' universe*		
Investment			Hazard		Ecstasy
Desire		Expression	Chance		Obscenity
Passion		Competition	Vertigo		Fascination
Seduction					Communication
Processes of hysteria (female) and paranoia (male)			Processes of schizophrenia, elimination of boundaries, exteriorization of the interior		

'real conditions of existence'[5] and as tapping into the unsatisfied desire remaining in the psyche from the Lacanian mirror-phase, in the manner suggested above. MTV at once embodies and then further develops major cultural changes. I shall extend these arguments by looking at how the televisual apparatus functions, and at the psychic processes it involves. I will then discuss the implications of the televisual imaginary specifically for women before undertaking some textual analyses of female representation in select rock videos by female stars.

By 'televisual apparatus,' I mean the complex of elements including the machine itself – its technological features (the way it produces and presents images); its various 'texts', including ads, commentaries, displays; the central relationship of programming to the sponsors, whose own texts – the ads – are arguably the real television texts;[6] the now various sites of reception from the living-room to the bathroom. Scholars may focus on problems of enunciation, that is of who speaks a text, and to whom it is addressed, which includes looking at the manner in which we watch television, its presence in the home, the so-called 'flow' of the programmes, the fragmentation of the viewing experience even within any one given programme, the unusual phenomenon of endlessly serialized programmes; or they may study the ideology embedded in the forms of production and reception, which are not 'neutral' or 'accidental,' but a crucial result of television's overarching commercial framework.

One of the still unresolved issues that work in this area has to address (whether explicitly or implicitly) is that of the degree to which theories of film are applicable to the very different 'televisual' apparatus. Since feminist film theory evolved very much in relation to the classic Hollywood cinema, it is particularly important for women approaching television to consider how far that theory is relevant to the different apparatus that television is; for example, do theories about the 'male gaze' apply to watching television, when usually there is no darkened room, where there is a small screen, and where viewing is often interrupted by commercials, people coming in, or by the viewer switching channels? To what extent is the television spectator addressed in the same manner as the film spectator? Do the same psychoanalytic processes of subject construction apply? Will semiotics aid in illuminating the processes at work? Is there a different form of interaction between the television text and the female viewer than between the cinema screen and the female spectator? What might that relation then be?

Much recent film theory has argued that one cannot make any distinction between the apparatus and the narrative, since it is the apparatus itself that produces certain inevitable 'narrative' effects (such as, in the film, the forced identification with the look of the camera). Thus, we need to know how the televisual apparatus is used in any one television genre to represent the female body – to see what possibilities there are for different kinds of female representation, and how bound by the limits of the apparatus are images of woman on television.

Let me first say something about the construction of what I have elsewhere called the 'decentred' spectator through the very rapid flow of what are comparatively short segments within a continuous, twenty-four-hour channel.[7] Here MTV carries to an extreme elements present in other TV programmes in the United States, particularly those that are also twenty-four-hour stations like continuous weather and news channels; but also those that are daily 'serials' in some form or another, for instance, game shows, talk shows, the soaps, and also the news (which is regularly slotted and so highly stylized as to be 'drama'[8]).

All of these programmes exist on a kind of horizontal axis that is never ending, rather than consisting of discrete units consumed within a fixed two-hour limit, like the Hollywood movie, or other forms such as the novel, which also have a fixed, and clearly defined 'frame'. Television in a certain sense is not so bounded. Rather television texts resemble an endless film strip, turned on its side, in which the frames are replaced by episodes. Or, as Peggy Phelan has argued, perhaps a better model is that of Foucault's Panopticon, in which the guard surveys a series of prisoners through their windows.[9] Phelan is interested in setting up the television producer as the 'guard' and the individual television viewer as the 'prisoner' who watches in a 'sequestered and observed solitude'. But I think the guard metaphor works well also for the spectator's relationship to the various episodes that represent in Foucault's words, 'a multiplicity that can be numbered and supervised': in fact, for the television viewer, that desire for plenitude, for complete knowledge is of course forever delayed, forever deferred. The television is seductive precisely because it speaks to a desire that is insatiable – it promises complete knowledge in some far distant and never-to-be-experienced future; its strategy is to keep us endlessly consuming in the hopes of fulfiling our desire; it hypnotizes us through addressing this desire, keeps us returning for more.

This strategy is particularly evident in MTV since the texts here are only four minutes long and so keep us for ever watching, for ever hoping to fulfil our desire with the next one that comes along. The mechanism of 'Coming Up Next . . . ' that all programmes employ, and that is the staple of the serial, is an intricate aspect of the minute-by-minute watching of MTV. Lured by the seductiveness of the constant promise of immediate plenitude, we endlessly consume.

Now, the question is how does this decentring televisual apparatus position women? Are women necessarily addressed in specific ways by the apparatus, as was argued (at least initially) for the classical Hollywood film? Is there something inherent in the televisual apparatus that addresses woman's social positioning as absence and lack, as again was the case for the Hollywood film?

These questions take me beyond the confines of my topic, but it is possible that what is true for MTV is true also for other television programmes: namely, that instead of a more or less monolithic (and largely male) gaze as was found in the Hollywood film, there is a wide range of gazes with different gender implications. In other words, the apparatus itself, in its modes of functioning, is not gender specific *per se*; but across its 'segments,' be they soap opera segments, crime series segments, news segments, morning show segments, we can find a variety of 'gazes' that indicate an address to a certain kind of male or female Imaginary. If the address in some videos is not exactly genderless, people of both genders are often able to undertake multiple identifications.

What this implies is that the televisual Imaginary is more varied than the cinematic one; it does not involve the same regression to the Lacanian mirror-phase as theorists discovered in the filmic apparatus. In the case of MTV, for example, instead of the channel evoking aspects of the Lacanian mirror-phase Ideal Imago – a process that depends on sustained identification with a central figure in a prolonged narrative – issues to do with split subjectivity, with the alienation that the mirror-image involves, are evoked instead. (See Chart 2.) In other words, filmic processes (at least for the male viewer) heal the painful split in subjectivity instituted during the mirror-phase while MTV rather reproduces the decentred human condition that is especially obvious to the young adolescent.

MTV thus addresses the desires, fantasies and anxieties of young people growing up in a world in which traditional categories and institutions are apparently being questioned. I have elsewhere argued that there are five main types of video on MTV, and that a whole series of gazes replaces the broadly monolithic Hollywood gaze (see Chart 3 for summary of these types and of how the gaze affects female images). The plethora of gender positions on the channel arguably reflects the heterogeneity of current sex-roles, and the androgynous surface of many

Chart 2: Polarized Filmic Categories in Recent Film Theory

The classic text (Hollywood)	The avant-garde text
Realism/narrative	Non-realism/anti-narrative
History	Discourse
Complicit ideology	Rupture of dominant ideology

star-images indicates the blurring of clear lines between genders characteristic of many rock videos.[10]

Because of both the peculiarities of the televisual apparatus and the new phase of youth culture produced by the 1960s, most of the feminist methodologies that have emerged in television research so far are inappropriate for the rock videos on MTV. This is mainly because of the sophisticated, self-conscious and skewed stance that these television texts take toward their own subject matter. It is often difficult to know precisely what a rock video actually means, because its signifiers are not linked along a coherent, logical chain that produces an unambiguous message. The mode, to use Frederic Jameson's contrast, is that of *pastiche* rather than parody. By this Jameson means that whereas modernist texts often took a particular critical position *vis-à-vis* earlier textual models, ridiculing specific stances or attitudes in them, or offering a sympathetic, comic perspective on them, postmodernist works tend to use *pastiche*, a mode that lacks any clear positioning with regard to what it shows, or toward earlier texts that are used.[11]

This has implications for gender first because the source of address of the rock video text is often so unclear – consequently it is also unclear whether the male or female discourse dominates; and second because attitudes toward sex and gender are often ambiguous. One finds oneself not knowing, for instance, whether or not a video like John Parr's 'Naughty Naughty', or John Cougar Mellencamp's 'Hurts So Good',[12] are virulently sexist or merely pastiching an earlier Hollywood sexism. Even in the category that I call 'classical,' where the gaze is clearly voyeuristic and male, there is a studied self-consciousness that makes the result quite different from that in the dominant commercial cinema.

A different but equally problematic ambiguity is just as prevalent in the videos made from lyrics by female stars as in those of white male stars featured on the channel. But, before going into that, let me note that it is precisely here that the cycling of videos featuring female singers across the twenty-four-hour flow is important for understanding first the broad gender address of MTV and, related to this, the kind of Imaginary that predominates. Both issues are further linked to the overarching commercial framework of MTV, in that only those female representations considered the most 'marketable' are frequently cycled: and what is most marketable is obviously connected with dominant ideology, with the social Imaginary discussed above, and with the organization of the symbolic order around the phallus as signifier.

According to a recent quantifying study of MTV, videos featuring white males take up 83 per cent of the twenty-four-hour flow.[13] Only 12 per cent of MTV videos have central figures who are female: 11 per cent white, 1 per cent Black (the figure is 3 per cent for Black males). Brown and Campbell assert that 'white women are often shown in passive and solitary activity or are shown trying to gain the attention of a man who ignores them' (p. 104). Among the 12 per cent of videos featuring women, the only ones frequently cycled are those in which the female star's position is ambiguous, where what we might call a post-feminist stance is evident.

Before discussing what I mean by this 'post-feminist' stance, I want first to note the other kinds of female representations that do appear on the channel, if only rarely. First, there are videos in the 'socially conscious' category that make the kind of statement one could call 'feminist' (for instance, Pat Benatar's 'Love Is a Battlefield', or her more recent 'Sex as a Weapon'; or Donna Summer's 'She Works Hard for the Money'); these have quite conventional narratives, although they do not adhere strictly to Hollywood codes. Second, there are occasional videos that appear to comment upon the objectifying male gaze (as perhaps does Tina Turner's 'Private Dancer') and whose visual strategies creatively embody those deconstructive aims. Finally, some videos attempt to set up a different gaze altogether, or to play with the male gaze, as arguably happens in the recent Aretha Franklin/Annie Lennox video 'Sisters Are Doin' It for Themselves'. Except for Benatar's 'Love Is a Battlefield', these videos remained in circulation for only a short period of time, and then not at a high density rate.

It is important that the channel's format of short, four-minute texts does permit gaps through which a variety of enunciative positions are made possible. I am thus able to 'stop the flow' as it were, in order to concentrate on constructions of the female body other than the prevailing 'post-feminist' or various 'male gaze' ones. But this is with full awareness that these isolated moments are in fact overridden by the plethora of texts presenting other positions. The various possibilities for 'seeing otherwise' in these different figurations of the female body are worth exploring as part of understanding what popular culture *can* do; but the ordinary MTV spectator will get little opportunity for this kind of 'seeing'. For such female images do not fit into the rich sensation of glossy surfaces, bright colours, rapid action, or the parade of bodies in contemporary clothing that the dominant videos offer.

Take, for example, the video, 'Material Girl', featuring madonna, the female star who perhaps more than any other embodies the new post feminist heroine in her odd combination of seductiveness and a gutsy sort of independence. 'Material Girl' is particularly useful as a point of discussion because it exemplifies a common rock-video phenomenon, namely the establishment of a unique kind of intertextual relationship with a specific Hollywood movie. For this reason, and because of difficulty of ensuring the text's stance toward what it shows and the blurring of many conventional boundaries, I would put the video in the 'post-modern' category in my chart, despite its containing more narrative than is usual in this type.

[. . .]

In some sense, then, Madonna represents the post-feminist heroine in that she combines unabashed seductiveness with a gutsy kind of independence. She is neither particularly male nor female identified, and seems mainly to be out for herself. This post-feminism is part of a larger postmodernist phenomenon which her video also embodies in its blurring of hitherto sacrosanct boundaries and polarities of the various kinds discussed. The usual bi-polar categories – male/female, high art/pop art, film/television, fiction/reality, private/public, interior/exterior – no longer apply to many rock videos, including 'Material Girl'.[14] [. . .] [An] analysis of 'Material Girl' [. . .] [shows]the ambiguity of enunciative positions within the video, which is in turn responsible for the ambiguous representation of the female image. The positioning of a video like 'Material Girl', moreover, within the twenty-four-hour flow on the commercial MTV channel, lets us see that it is precisely *this* sort of ambiguous image that appears frequently, as against other possible female images, in videos which are only rarely shown. The post-feminist ambiguous images are clearly the ones sponsors consider 'marketable', since they are those most often cycled and also propagated in the ad texts interspersed among the video texts.

[. . .]

Chart 3: Types of Gaze in Music Television

		MODES (All use avant-garde strategies, especially self-reflexivity, play with the image, etc.)				
		Romantic	*Socially conscious*	*Nihilist*	*Classical*	*Postmodernist*
	Style	Narrative	Elements varied	Performance Anti-narrative	Narrative	Pastiche No linear images
Predominant MTV themes	*Love/sex*	Loss and Reunion (Pre-Oedipal)	Struggle for autonomy: Love as problematic	Sadism/ masochism Homo-eroticism Androgyny (Phallic)	The male gaze (Voyeuristic, Fetishistic)	Play with Oedipal positions
	Authority	Parent figures (positive)	Parent and public figures Cultural critique	Nihilism Anarchy Violence	Male as subject Female as object	Neither for nor against authority (ambiguity)

The televisual apparatus as a whole contributes to the prevalence of the ambiguous female image. To summarize: first, the main force of MTV as a cable channel is consumption on a variety of levels, ranging from the literal (selling the sponsors' goods, the rock stars' records, and MTV itself) to the psychological (selling the image, the 'look,' the style). MTV is more obviously than other channels one nearly continuous advertisement, the flow being broken down merely into different *kinds* of advertisements. More than other channels, then, MTV positions the spectator in the mode of constantly hoping that the next ad segment (of whatever kind) will satisfy the desire for plenitude: the channel keeps the spectator in the consuming mode more intensely because its items are all so short.

Since the mode of address throughout is that of the advertisement, then like the advertisement the channel relies on engaging the spectator on the level of unsatisfied desire; this remains in the psyche from the moment of entry into the Lacanian symbolic, and is available for channelling in various directions. Given the organization of the Lacanian symbolic around the phallus as signifier, it is not surprising that MTV basically address the desire for the phallus remaining in the psyche of both genders. This partly accounts for the dominance on the channel of videos featuring white male stars.

Nevertheless, as Chart 3 shows, the male gaze is not monolithic on the channel: here again, the television apparatus enables the production of a variety of different gazes due to the arrangement of a series of short, constantly changing segments which replace the closure of the two-hour film, the classical novel and the theatrical play. There is no possibility within the four-minute segment for regression to the Freudian Oedipal conflicts in the manner of the classical narrative. What we have rather is a semi-comical play with Oedipal positions as in the postmodern video, or a focus on one particular mode in the Oedipal complex in some of the other video-types outlined in the chart.

The implications of all this for a feminist perspective need close analysis. Feminism, particularly in America, has traditionally relied on a liberal- or left-humanist position. It is these ideologies that provided the stance from which feminists have been able to critique dominant practices and call them 'sexist' or 'patriarchal'. Humanist values, applied specifically to those humans called 'women' who often were not included in humanist cultural projections, formed the basis for arguments to improve women's conditions of existence. If Baudrillard is correct in seeing the television screen and the entire televisual apparatus as symbolizing a new era in which left/liberal humanism no longer has a place, then feminism needs to address the changed situation. Gender has been one of the central organizing categories of what Baudrillard calls the old 'hot' (as against the new 'cold') universe, but this category itself may be in the process of eliminiation, with unclear (and not necessarily progressive) results. It could be that women will no longer have the humanist position from which to critique what is going on; the new postmodern universe arguably makes impossible the critical position itself, making then irrelevant any 'feminist' stance.

Feminists then, in particular, need to explore television's part in the changed, and still changing, relationship of self to image. This change began at the turn of the century with the development of advertising and of the department-store window; it was then further affected by the invention of the cinematic apparatus, and television has, in its turn, produced more changes. The television screen now replaces the cinema screen as the central controlling cultural mode, setting up a new spectator–screen relationship which I have here begun to analyse in relation to MTV. For MTV constantly comments upon the self in relation to image (especially the television image), to such an extent that this may be seen as its main 'content'. The blurring of distinctions between a 'subject' and an 'image' – or the reduction of the old notion of 'self' to 'image' – is something for feminists to explore, even as we fear the coming of Baudrillard's universe of 'simulacra'.[15]

The reduction of the female body to an 'image' is something that women have long endured: the phenomenon has been extensively studied by feminist film critics, who were able to assume a humanist position from which to critique film constructions. From that position the possibility of constructing other representations always existed. The new postmodern universe, however, with its celebration of the look, surfaces, textures, the self-as-commodity, produces an array of images/representations/simulacra that co-opts any possible critical position by the very incorporation of what were previously 'dissenting' images; this makes difficult the processes of foregrounding or exposing gender issues that feminist film-makers have used. As a cultural mode, postmodernism would eliminate gender difference as a significant category, just as sweeps aside other polarities. Television, as a postmodernist apparatus with its decentred address, its flattening out of things into a network or system that is endless, unbounded, unframed and whose parts all rely on each other urgently requires more thorough examination, particularly in relation to its impact on women.

NOTES

1. The term 'social Imaginary' brings together concepts developed by Jacques Lacan, Louis Althusser, Roland Barthes, and others. In particular, it combines Lacan's notions of the subject split at the moment of entry into the Symbolic with Althusser's conception of Ideological State Apparatuses. The two most relevant texts here are Lacan's 'The Mirror Stage as Formative of the I', reprinted in *Ecrits: A Selection*, Alan Sheridan (trans.) London and New York: W. W. Norton and Co., 1979, pp. 1–7; and Louis Althusser, 'Ideology and Ideological State Apparatuses (Notes Towards an Investigation)', in *Lenin and Philosophy and Other Essays* Ben Brewster (trans.), New York and London: Monthly Review Press, 1971, pp. 127–86.

MTV – Music Television – is a twenty-four-hour, non-stop cable station for which subscribers do not pay an extra fee. It is made up of rock video, VJs' ('video jockeys') comments, music news, interviews with rock stars, advertisements by sponsors and advertisements for MTV itself. MTV is beamed across America wherever cable service exists, and latest audience figures are 28 million, ranging in age from twelve to thirty-four.

2.   Jean Baudrillard, 'The Ecstasy of Communication', in *The Anti-Aesthetic: Essays in Postmodern Culture*, Hal Foster (ed.), Port Townsend: Washington Bay Press, 1983, pp. 125–38.

3.   For more discussion of these differences generally, see Sandy Flitterman, 'Fascination in Fragments: Psychoanalysis in Film and Television', in *Channels of Discourse: Television Criticism in the 80's*, Robert Allen (ed.), Chapel Hill: North Carolina University Press, 1987. An expanded version of the present essay, particularly in relation to differences between movie and television screens, can be found in E. Ann Kaplan, *Rocking Around the Clock: Music Television, Postmodernism and Consumer Culture*, London and New York: Methuen, 1987.

4.   By 'simulacra' Baudrillard means a world in which all we have are simulations, there being no 'real' external to them, no 'original' that is being copied. It is as if all were reduced merely to exteriors, there no longer being any 'interiors'. For full development of the notion of 'simulacra' see Jean Baudrillard, *Simulations*, Paul Foss, Paul Patton and Philip Beitchman (trans.), New York: Semiotext(e), 1983.

5.   Althusser, 'Ideology and Ideological State Apparatuses (Notes Towards an Investigation)'; p. 162.

6.   Sandy Flitterman, 'The Real Soap Operas: TV Commercials', in *Regarding Television: A Critical Anthology* E. Ann Kaplan (ed.), Los Angeles: American Film Institute 1983, pp. 84–96. See also my article in *Channels of Discourse*.

7.   For details of these arguments, see Kaplan, *Rocking Around the Clock*.

8.   Robert Stam, 'Television News and Its Spectator', in *Regarding Television*, pp. 23–44.

9. Peggy Phelan, 'Panopticism and the Uncanny: Notes Toward Television's Visual Time', unpublished paper, 1986.

10.   For further discussion of the classic avant-garde film polarity and of Chart 3, see Kaplan, *Rocking Around the Clock*.

11.   Fredric Jameson, 'Postmodernism and Consumer Society', in *The Anti-Aesthetic*, p. 113.

12.   For details of videos referred to in this essay, see the Videography below.

13.   Jane Brown and Kenneth C. Campbell, 'The Same Beat But a Different Drummer: Race and Gender in Music Videos', *Journal of Communication*, vol. 36, no. 1 (1986) pp. 94–106. That the video is directed by a woman, Mary Lambert, does not alter my assessment of the video as post-feminist. I would not want to collapse biological gender with ideological stance.

14.   Madonna has recently offered a dramatically changed image in her new 'Papa Don't Preach' video. While abandoning her trashy bag lady image for a new svelte, gamine-style modern teenager, Madonna nevertheless still combines traditional images (in this case the 'little girl' and the 'whore'). For more discussion of this change, see Kaplan, *Rocking Around the Clock*.

15.   Baudrillard, *Simulations*.

VIDEOGRAPHY

John Parr, 'Naughty Naughty', *John Parr*, Atlantic Records, 1984.

John Congar Mellencamp, 'Hurts so Good', *American Fool*, Riva Polygram Records, 1982.

Pat Benatar, 'Love Is a Battlefield', *Get Nervous*, Chrysalis Records, 1983.

Pat Benatar, 'Sex as a Weapon', *Seven the Hard Way*, Chrysalis Records, 1986.

Donna Summer, 'She Works Hard for the Money', *She Works Hard for the Money*, Mercury/Polygram Records, 1983.

Tina Turner, 'Private Dances', *Private Dances*, Capital Records, 1984.

Aretha Franklin and Annie Lennox, 'Sisters Are Doin' It for Themselves', *Be Yourself Tonight*, RCA Records, 1986.

Madonna, 'Material Girl', *Madonna*, Sire/Warner Brothers Records, 1985.

26

POSTMODERNISM AND POPULAR CULTURE

Angela McRobbie

THE 'SOWETO DASH'

Rather than starting with a definition of postmodernism as referring either to a condition of contemporary life, or a textual, aesthetic practice, I want to begin by suggesting that the recent debates on postmodernism possess both a positive attraction and a usefulness to the analyst of popular culture. This is because they offer a wider, and more dynamic, understanding of contemporary representation than other accounts to date. Unlike the various strands of structuralist criticism, postmodernism considers images as they relate to and across each other. Postmodernism deflects attention away from the singular scrutinizing gaze of the semiologist, and asks that this be replaced by a multiplicity of fragmented, and frequently interrupted, 'looks'.

The exemplary text or the single, richly coded, image, gives way to the textual *thickness* and the visual *density* of everyday life, as though the slow, even languid 'look' of the semiologist is, by the 1980s, out of tempo with the times. The field of postmodernism certainly expresses a frustration, not merely with this seemingly languid pace, but with its increasing inability to make tangible connections between the general conditions of life today and the practice of cultural analysis.

Structuralism has also replaced old orthodoxies with new ones. This is apparent in its re-reading of texts highly placed within an already existing literary or aesthetic hierarchy. Elsewhere it constructs a new hierarchy, with Hollywood classics at the top, followed by selected advertising images, and girls' and women's magazines rounding it off. Other forms of representation, particularly music and dance, are missing altogether. Andreas Huyssen[1] in his recent introduction to postmodernism draws attention to this 'high' structuralist preference for the works of high modernism especially the writing of James Joyce or Mallarmé.

There is no doubt that center stage in critical theory is held by the classical modernists:

From ICA Documents 4: *Postmodernism* (1986) pp. 54–8.

Flaubert . . . in Barthes; . . . Mallarmé and Artaud in Derrida; Magritte . . . in Foucault; . . . Joyce and Artaud in Kristeva . . . and so on *ad infinitum.*

He argues that this reproduces unhelpfully the old distinction between the high arts and the 'low', less serious, popular arts. He goes on to comment,

> Pop in the broadest sense was the context in which a notion of the postmodern first took shape, and . . . and the most significant trends within postmodernism have challenged modernism's relentless hostility to mass culture.

High theory was simply not equipped to deal with multi-layered pop. Nor did it ever show much enthusiasm about this set of forms, perhaps because pop has never signified within one discrete discourse, but instead combines images with performance, music with film, or video, and pin ups with the magazine form itself. As a *Guardian* journalist recently put it, 'Rock and pop performers today have to speak in multi-media tongues' (3.1.86).

With the exception of Barthes, 'heavy weight' criticism has been focussed towards memorable texts, while lightweight cultural analysis is given over to the more forgettable images of everyday life. And the 'purity' of the about-to-be-decoded-image is reflected in the pivotal position occupied by semiology and structuralist criticism in media courses up and down the country. Despite gestures towards intertextuality and interdisciplinarity, this centrality given to *the structualisms* in effect squeezes all the other complex relations which locate the text, or the image, and allow it to produce meaning, out of the picture. These relations include those which mark out its physical place within the world of commodities, its sequencing, and its audience as well as consumers. Such issues are frequently relegated, with some disregard, to the realm of sociology or 'empiricism' as though these were the same thing. And while critics argue that this outside reality is really nothing more than a series of other texts, they are in the meantime happy to treat questions about consumers, readers, audience, and viewers, as intrinsically uninteresting, as though this entails hanging about street corners with a questionnaire and clipboard.

Postmodernism allows what were respectable sociological issues to reappear on the intellectual agenda. It implicitly challenges the narrowness of structuralist vision, by taking the deep interrogation of every breathing aspect of lived experience by media imagery as a starting point. So extensive and inescapable is this process that it becomes conceptually impossible to privilege one simple moment.

[. . .]

Postmodernism has entered into a more diverse number of vocabularies more quickly than most other intellectual categories. It has spread outwards from the realms of art history into political theory and onto the pages of youth culture magazines, record sleeves, and the fashion pages of *Vogue.* This seems to me to indicate something more than the mere vagaries of taste. More also, than the old Marcusian notion of recuperation, where a radical concept which once had purchase, rapidly becomes a commodity, and in the process is washed, laundered, and left out to dry.

[. . .]

Postmodernism certainly appeared in the UK like a breath of fresh air. It captured in a word, a multitude of experiences, particularly what Baudrillard[2] has called the 'instantaneity of communication'. This refers to the incursion of imagery and communication into those spaces that once were private – where the psyche previously had the chance to at least explore the 'other', to explore, for example, alienation. Baudrillard claims this space now to be penetrated by the predatory and globally colonialist media. But as the frontiers of the self are effaced and transformed, so too are the boundaries which mark out separate discourses and separate politics. Baudrillard interprets the new associative possibilities thrown up by 'instantaneity' gloomily. 'Everything is exposed to the harsh and inexorable light of information and communication', which in turn generates only an 'ecstasy of communication' . . . But need Baudrillard be quite so pessimistic? Why must this speeding-up process, this intensification or exchange be greeted with such foreboding?

The remainder of this paper will be given over to arguing the case for postmodernism. It will suggest that the frenzied expansion of the mass media has political consequences which are not so wholly negative. This becomes most apparent when we look at representations of the Third World. No longer can this be confined to the realist documentary, or the exotic televisual voyage. The Third World refuses now, to 'us', in the West, to be reassuringly out of sight. It is as adept at using the global media as the old colonialist powers. Equally the 'we' of the British nation no longer possesses any reliable reality. That spurious unity has been decisively shattered. New alliances and solidarities emerge from within and alongside media imagery. A disenchanted black, inner city population in Britain, can look in an 'ecstasy of communication' as black South Africans use every available resource at hand to put apartheid into crisis. Jokily, and within a kind of postmodern language Dick Hebdige wrote, in *Subculture*,[3] that TV images of Soweto in 1976 taught British youth 'the Soweto dash'. Ten years later this connection has amplified. The image is the trigger and the mechanism for this new identification.

IMPLOSION

Of course it's not quite so simple. The South African government has recently banned journalists from the black townships. And in less politically sensitive arenas, the media continues, relentlessly, to hijack events and offer in their place a series of theatrical spectacles whose points of relevance are only tangentially on what is going on, and whose formal cues came from other, frequently televisual, forms of representation. 1985 was rich in examples. Reagan's illness was relayed to the public, overwhelmingly in the language of soap opera. A *Guardian* correspondent pointed out that nobody would have been convinced if his doctors had not appeared at the press conferences dressed in white coats. A few weeks earlier Shi'ite militiamen took over a TWA airline in Athens. In what was largely a bid for space on Western prime-time television, the captors could afford to appear smiling and jubilant as they offered their victims a Lebanese banquet, against a backdrop of random gunfire at the ceiling, before packing them off to the United States.

This easing out of the real in favour of its most appropriate representation makes it more difficult to talk about the media and society today. It creates even greater difficulties in assessing the relationship between images, or between popular cultural forms, and their consumers. The consciousness industries have changed remarkably over the last ten years, but so have the outlook and the expectations of their audiences.

Against a backdrop of severe economic decline, the mass media continues to capture new outlets, creating fresh markets to absorb its hi-tech commodities. Symbolically the image has assumed a contemporary dominance. It is no longer possible to talk about the image and reality, media and society. Each has become so deeply intertwined that it is difficult to draw the line between the two. Instead of referring to the real world, much media output devotes itself to referring to other images, other narratives. Self-referentiality is all-embracing, although it is rarely taken account of. The Italian critic and writer, Umberto Eco, recently contrasted what TV was (paleo-TV), with what it now is, (neo-TV). 'Its prime characteristic is that it talks less and less about the external world. Whereas paleo-television talked about the external world, or pretended to, neo-television talks about itself and about the contacts it establishes with its own public.[4]

Self-referentiality occurs within and across different media forms. One TV programme might be devoted to the production of another (Paul Gambaccino 'on' the Tube), just as television films based on the making of other large-scale cinema productions are becoming increasingly common. There is a similar dependency for material and content, as well as a relatively recent redefinition of what is interesting, and what readers and viewers want, in the print media's use of *televisual stories*. *The Face* magazine ran a piece on The Tube, and more recently on Michelle, the pregnant schoolgirl, in East Enders . . . The *NME* carried a major feature on Brookside, and *City Limits* sent two journalists to the Coronation Street set, for a week. It's not so much that fiction is being mistaken for fact; more that one set of textual practices (in this case British soap) has become the reference point for another (reading the newspaper or glancing at a headline).

Media interdependency is both an economic and a cultural imperative. Children's TV on a Saturday morning evolves entirely around the pop music industry, offering an exclusive showcase for new 'promo' videos. The contents of these programmes are orchestrated around all the familiar pop business, phone-in to the stars, interviews, the new single, the talent competition for young hopefuls. This shows the feeding-off effect between mass media today. Where once the middle class world of Blue Peter documented children's initiatives for charity, now Capital, in the form of culture and visual communications, penetrates further into the youth marker. In the *classless* world of these programmes this means pushing back the frontiers of young people as consumers by transforming children and even toddlers into fans and thus part of the record-buying public.

The implications of this endless cross-referencing are extensive. They create an ever-increasing, but less diverse verbal and visual landscape. It is these recurring fictions, and the characters who inhabit them which feed into the field of popular knowledge, and which in turn constitute a large part of popular culture. It would be difficult not to know about Victoria Principal, it would be impossible not to know about Dallas.

Texts have always alluded to or connected with others. Simone De Beauvoir's *Memoirs of a Dutiful Daughter* gives up many pages to all the other books she read during her childhood, adolescence and early adult years.[5] Indeed this critical bibliography forms a major strand of the work. The difference now is that the process is less restricted to literature, more widespread, and most apparent in the commercial mass media where there are more spaces to be filled. And such an opening up doesn't necessarily mean an extension of rights of access, only rights of consumption. More often it means a form of cosy, mutual congratulatory, cross-referencing and repetition. (Wogan in Denver, Clive James in Dallas). Baudrillard greets these recent changes with some cynicism. He claims that more media offers less meaning in the guise of more information'. 'All secrets, spaces and scenes abolished in a single dimension of information'.[6] Eco follows this when he describes the scrambling effect of multi-channel choice on TV. 'Switching channels reflects the brevity and speed of other visual forms. Like flicking through a magazine, or driving past a billboard. This means that "our" TV evenings no longer tell us stories, it is all a trailer!'[7]

Images push their way into the fabric of our social lives. They enter into how we look, what we earn, and they are still with us when we worry about bills, housing and bringing up children. They compete for attention through shock tactics, reassurance, sex, mystery and by inviting viewers to participate in series of visual puzzles. Billboard advertisements showing an image without a code, impose themselves, infuriatingly, on the most recalcitrant passer-by.

[. . .]

And, if media forms are so inescapable 'if unreality is now within everyone's grasp' (Eco),[8] then there is no reason to assume that the consumption of pastiche, parody or high camp is, by definition, without subversive or critical potential. Glamour, glitter, and gloss, should not so easily be relegated to the sphere of the insistently apolitical. For the left, necessarily committed to endorsing the real and the material conditions of peoples' lives, there remains still an (understandable) stiffness about Neil Kinnock's appearance in a Tracy Ullman video. This need not be the case.

If, as Jameson suggests, life has been dramatised to the level of soap, if love is always like a *Jackie* story, then yes, the sharp distinction between real life and fictional forms must give way to a deep intermingling, unmeasurable and so far captured most precisely in fictive or cinematic forms. Scorsese's *King of Comedy* traced this 'overdetermination by the image', as did Woody Allen's *Stardust Memories*, as well as his more recent *Zelig* and *The Purple Rose of Cairo*. But Gore Vidals novel *Duluth* outstrips all of these.[9] It is a model of postmodern writing. Gore Vidal has his tongue firmly in his cheek. *Duluth* is a witty multi-layered fiction which moves from the town of the title, to the soap series based on the place, outwards to the novel of the soap, backwards into the historical romances favoured by the town's top woman cop, and forwards into a science fiction setting where Roland Barthes makes a guest appearance. Obligingly Vidal ends the novel by handing over to a word processor.

All of this comes close to what Baudrillard infuriatingly calls implosion.[10] It's a vague but appropriate term. It implies an outburst of energy which is nonetheless controlled and inclining inwards. Baudrillard, Eco and Jameson all see this as a totalising and all-immersing process. But none of them consider the new associations and resistances which have come into prominence by way of these processes in the last fifteen years. Many of these share more in common with the shattered energy of implosion, with Jameson's fragmented schizophrenic consciousness, than with the great narratives of the old left,

> It was especially the art, writing, film-making and criticism of women and minority artists, with their recuperation of buried and mutilated traditions, their emphasis on exploring forms of gender- and race-based subjectivity in aesthetic productions and experiences, and their refusal to be limited to standard canonizations, which added a whole new dimension to the critique of high modernism and to the emergence of alternative forms of culture.[11]

In the British context one would want to append to this formidable production not just the proliferation of pop culture and the challenge it has mounted to the mainstream arts, but also the involvement of youth in the creation of an egalitarian avant-garde. Of course this is no longer an avant-garde proper, since the privileging of the forms have been abandoned in favour of a cross referencing between forms, and notably between pop music and 'art', between aesthetics and commerce, between commitment and the need to make a living. This leads directly to a further failing in Jameson's account. There is no recognition that those elements contained within his diagnosis of postmodernism – including pastiche, the ransacking and recycling of culture, the direct invocation to other texts and other images – can create a vibrant critique rather than an inward-looking, second-hand aesthetic. What else has black urban culture in the last few years been, but an assertive re-assembling of bits and pieces, 'whatever comes to hand', noises, debris, technology, tape, image, rapping, scratching, and other hand me downs? Black urban music has always thrived on fake, forged identities, creating a façade of grand-sounding titles which reflect both the 'otherness' of black culture, the extent to which it is outside that which is legitimate, and the way in which white society has condemned it to be nameless. Who, after all, is Grandmaster Flash or Melle Mel? Or who was Sly and the Family Stone? Who mixed the speech by Malcolm X onto a haunting disco funk backing track? Reggae also parodies this enforced namelessness. Many of its best known musicians suggest a deep irony in their stagenames: Clint Eastwood, Charlie Chaplin, and so on.

In America graffiti remains the best example of fleeting, obsolescent urban aesthetics. It gives its creators fame once they get into the galleries but otherwise only faint notoriety,

> It is a cultural identity which half mocks, half celebrates, the excesses of mainstream white culture. The graffiti painter is the Spiderman of the ghettos, projecting pure fantasy. A terminal vantage point on white consumer culture. Hip hop is a subculture which feeds for its material upon the alien culture which needs make no concession to blacks. The spray paints and comic book images of graffiti painting, to the disco beats and found sounds of rapping, are diverted from their mainstream domestic use and put out on the streets as celebration. For the white middle class kid, the comic heroes occupy a space of boredom. For the black ghetto kid they are transformed by graffiti art into fantastic visions invested with secret meanings.[12]

Alongside these largely male forms, must be placed the writing of black women, the great explosion of the written word which writes a history otherwise condemned to remain only within popular memory. Toni Cade Bambara's[13] prose is closest in rhythm to the jazz sounds of the city. It is breath-taking, agile writing, insisting on the pleasures, the wit and the idiosyncracies of a community more often characterised as monolithic and deprived. All of this is taking place within the cracks of a crumbling culture where progress is in question and society seems to be standing still.

There *is* no going back. For populations transfixed on images which are themselves a reality, there is no return to a mode of representation which politicizes in a kind of straightforward 'worthwhile' way. Dallas is destined to sit alongside images of black revolt. And it is no longer possible, living within postmodernism, to talk about unambiguously negative or positive images. But this need not be seen as the end of the social, or the end of meaning, or for that matter the beginning of the new nihilism. Social agency is employed in the activation of *all* meanings. Audiences or viewers, lookers or users are not simple-minded multitudes. As the media extends its sphere of influence, so also does it come under the critical surveillance *and* usage of its subjects.

The reason why postmodernism appeals to a wider number of young people, and to what might be called the new generation of intellectuals (often black, female, or working class) is that they themselves are experiencing the enforced fragmentation of impermanent work, and low career opportunities. Far from being overwhelmed by media saturation, there is evidence to suggest that these social groups and minorities are putting it to work for them. This alone should prompt the respect and the attention of an older generation who seem at present too eager to embrace a sense of political hopelessness.

NOTES

1.   Andreas Huyssen, 'Mapping the Postmodern', *New German Critique* 1984.
2   Jean Baudrillard, 'The Ecstasy of Communication', *Postmodern Culture* ed. Hal Foster [Pluto Press 1985].
3   Dick Hebdige, *Subculture, The Meaning of Style*, Methuen 1979.
4   Umberto Eco, 'A Guide to the Neo Television of the 1980s', *Framework no. 25*.

5   Simone De Beauvoir, *Memoirs of a Dutiful Daughter*, Penguin 1984.

6   Jean Baudrillard see above.

7   Umberto Eco see above.

8   Umberto Eco see above.

9   Gore Vidal, *Duluth*, Heinemann 1983.

10   Jean Baudrillard [*For a Critique of the Political Economy of the Sign*, trans. C. Levin, St. Louis, MO: Telos Press, 1981].

11   Andreas Huyssen see above.

12   Atlanta and Alexander, 'Wild Style . . . Graffiti Painting', *ZG* no. 6.

13   Toni Cade Bambara, *Gorilla, My Love*, The Women's Press 1983.

Further Reading

Collins, J. *Uncommon Cultures: Popular Culture and Post-modernism* (London: Routledge, 1989).

Collins, J. 'Postmodernism and Television', in Allen, R. C. (ed.), *Channels of Discourse, Reassembled* (London: Routledge, 1992).

Connor, S., *Postmodernist Culture: An Introduction to Theories of the Contemporary* (Oxford: Blackwell, 1989).

Docherty, T., *Postmodernism: A Reader* (Hemel Hempstead: Harvester Wheatsheaf, 1992).

Fiske, J., 'MTV: Post Structural Post Modern', *Journal of Communication Enquiry* 10:1 (1986) pp. 74–9.

Fiske, J., 'Postmodernism and Television', in Curran, J. and Gurevitch, M. (eds), *Mass Media and Society* (London: Edward Arnold, 1991).

Goodwin, A., 'Music Video in the (Post)Modern World', *Screen* 28:3 (1987) pp. 36–55.

Goodwin, A., 'Popular Music and Postmodern Theory', *Cultural Studies* 5:2 (1991) pp. 174–90.

Grossberg, L., 'The In-Difference of Television', *Screen* 28:2 (1987)

Grossberg, L., *We Gotta Get Out of this Place: Popular Conservatism and Postmodern Culture* (London: Routledge, 1992).

Hebdige, D., *Hiding in the Light: On Images and Things* (London: Routledge, 1988).

Huyssen, A., *After the Great Divide: Modernism, Mass Culture, Postmodernism* (London: Macmillan, 1986).

Joyrich, L., 'All that Television Allows: TV Melodrama, Postmodernism, and Consumer Culture', *Camera Obscura*, 16 (1988) pp. 128–53.

Kaplan, E. A., *Rocking Around the Clock: Music Television, Postmodernism and Consumer Culture* (London: Methuen, 1987).

Kaplan, E. A. (ed.), *Postmodernism and its Discontents: Theories, Practices* (London: Verso, 1988).

McRobbie, A., *Postmodernism and Popular Culture* (London: Routledge, 1994).

Mellencamp, P. (ed.), *The Logics of Television* (Bloomington and London: Indiana University Press and BFI, 1990).

Modleski, T. (ed.), *Studies in Entertainment: Critical Approaches to Mass Culture* (Bloomington: Indiana University Press, 1986).

Strinati, D., 'Postmodernism and Popular Culture', *Sociology Review*, April (1992) pp. 2–7.

Wollen, P., 'Ways of Thinking about Music Video (and Post-modernism)', *Critical Quarterly* 28:1.2 (1986) pp. 167–70.

Reception
'Effects' to 'Uses'

Reception: 'Effects' to 'Uses'

When British social science began to give attention to media reception, it turned to the existing American social scientific tradition for its ideas and models. This tradition was marked by a behaviourist psychology and a functionalist sociology, and tended to focus on the search for direct, palpable, short-term effects of media messages.

One of the leading figures in the British psychological establishment, Hans Eysenck, Professor of Psychology at the University of London from 1955, had himself long researched within a behaviourist paradigm, and was thus in tune with the underlying approach of much of the American experimental research when he came to take up the topic of the media. In his book *Sex, Violence and the Media*, co-written with Nias, he draws largely on this American research to sustain a case for the judicious employment of censorship to prevent the ill-effects of the portrayal of violence (and some kinds of sexual conduct) in the media. The experiments cited are noteworthy for the degree to which they aim to screen out – laboratory-style – all other cultural and social factors besides the 'pure' exposure to audiovisual material depicting violence; for the immediate and analogic nature of the effects they expect to capture; and for the incorporation in several instances of even a measurable *physiological* definition of media effects. The reported consequences of exposure to media portrayals of violence include a tendency for viewers to become 'disinhibited' about employing violence themselves, a tendency for some direct 'imitation', and – as covered by chapter 27 – a tendency to become 'desensitized' to 'violent materials', to fail to feel appropriate revulsion from them. Eysenck summarises 'effects' research within a particularly extreme behaviourist paradigm of the human animal, who can be consciously or inadvertently trained or conditioned, so that certain stimulus inputs will generate certain behavioural outputs. The publication in Britain in the late 1970s of this summary account of American behaviouristic research into the 'effects' of media 'violence' was taken by many as implicit endorsement for the main lines of approach of the pro-censorship campaign being mounted by the Christian fundamentalist-led National Viewers' and Listeners' Association and the Festival of Light.

But by then the mainstream of American social science had long been doubtful about the notion of strong, direct, measurable attitude changes attributable to individual mass communication messages. Mass communication was turning out to have very 'limited effects'. A widely read review of the American research, published in 1960, concluded that 'mass communication does not ordinarily serve as a necessary and sufficient cause of audience effects, but rather functions through a nexus of mediating factors'.[1] This was the predominant drift of thinking by the 1960s when the pioneering social scientists of mass communication in Britain began their work – notably Denis McQuail, Jeremy Tunstall, Jay G. Blumler and James Halloran.[2] Since the platform for this work was, not surprisingly, a reading of the American mass communication literature, the objective was to grasp this complex nexus. Chapter 28 comprises two extracts from *The Effects of Television* (1970), edited by James Halloran, head of the Centre for Mass Communication Research at the University of Leicester from 1966. The first extract registers the view that 'attitude change has been over-used as the primary criterion of influence . . . Influence must not be equated with attitude change.' The second extract discusses studies of the reception of particular British television programmes (*Children of Revolution*, *Nature of Prejudice* and *Rainbow City*) that confirmed this view. The need for a more complex and comprehensive conception of the reception of broadcast transmissions had been demonstrated by these native studies. David Morley later remarked that 'The empirical work of the Leicester Centre at this time marked an important shift in research from forms of behavioural analysis to forms of cognitive analysis.'[3]

Denis McQuail took up another, subordinate, strand in the American literature, one which concerned itself with audience 'gratifications'.[4] This inverted the 'effects' approach, and set out 'to concentrate less on what the media do to people than on what people do *with* the media.'[5] What are people's motives in reading a newspaper or listening to a particular radio programme? What are the uses for them of such activities? What needs are gratified, what satisfactions derived? The posing of these questions, and the pursuit of their answers, often within the framework of a functionalist sociology, had become known as the 'uses and gratifications' approach.[6] In the study reported in Chapter 29, McQuail and his colleagues Jay G. Blumler and J. R. Brown investigated what functions the television quiz shows *University Challenge*, *TV Brain of Britain* and *Ask the Family* served for a sample of viewers in Leeds. From the viewers' responses when questioned, they developed a four-part inventory of gratifications and uses, which they suggested might have a general applicability for media use. These four types of 'media-person interaction' are: surveillance (information gathering); personal identity; personal relationships (social integration and interaction); and diversion (entertainment). The attempt to correlate instances of the expression of each of these kinds of satisfaction with social and demographic variables, however, proved rather inconclusive: the results 'were not without ambiguity and left many questions unanswered'. Also, in relation to the various kinds of programmes, it seemed that 'people can look to quite different kinds of material for essentially the same gratification and, correlatively, find alternative satisfactions in the same televised material'.

Two of the commonplace colloquial views on popular media had been to despise them as trivially 'escapist', while regarding them as powerful agents of mental influence. As American empirical research – and the British research that followed in its footsteps – had come to eclipse the latter view, the former threatened to maintain its sway. So it was a gain for British media studies that McQuail and his colleagues simultaneously refused both a one-dimensional view of the irresistible power of the media to impose itself upon passive audiences, *and* the widespread unquestioning disdain for popular media consumption as simply 'escapist'. But the 'uses and gratifications' approach came under attack from within a Marxian sociology hostile to functionalism. Philip Elliott of the University of Leicester Centre for Mass Communication Research, in a paper abridged here as Chapter 30, pointed to a fundamental problem of logic within the exponents' arguments:

> In both variants – use leads to the gratification of need or need leads to satisfaction through functional behaviour – need is the residual factor and yet it is also put forward

as an explanation for the process. . . . [Much uses and gratifications] research invites the accusation that it lacks explanatory power.

McQuail himself was troubled by something similar to this. He had written:

> The guiding assumption of utility can lead the analyst to impute a social function where none may exist, with a resulting circularity of argument: a regularity in the pattern of media content is observed, linked to an assumed configuration of social and individual needs which fit this pattern, and mass communication may then be 'explained' in terms of these needs.[7]

But Elliott's criticism goes further than simply identifying a circularity in the argumentation. 'Uses and gratifications' research findings may add up to generalisations about 'aggregates of individuals, but they cannot be converted in any meaningful way into social structure and process'. To him it is a profound shortcoming, implicit in the functionalist origins of the approach, that '[n]o attempt is made to differentiate between media or people on the basis of the interests they represent or the power they possess'. He sees the approach as fundamentally conservative:

> In themselves, uses and gratifications data can only point in one direction, towards a justification of the present situation. . . . If the media-output audience-satisfaction nexus were explored in uses and gratifications terms, the only possible conclusion would be that the audience was getting something out of it. But that is not in dispute. The issue in dispute is whose interests are being served in the process, and that is an issue which the approach itself is powerless to elucidate.

But Elliott acknowledged that '[t]o reject the idea of a purposive audience out of hand would be to adopt a completely determinist view'. He was reaching towards a similar view to that of Stuart Hall's 'Encoding/Decoding' (Chapter 5). In the mass communication process, production and reception are distinct moments, yet the two moments are not equivalent: there is an asymmetry of power.

NOTES

1. Joseph T. Klapper, *The Effects of Mass Communication* (Glencoe, Ill.: Free Press, 1960).
2. William Belson, Hilde Himmelweit and Joseph Trenaman also carried out significant pioneering research in Britain.
3. David Morley, *The 'Nationwide' Audience* (London: British Film Institute, 1980) p. 7. See especially James D. Halloran, Philip Elliott, Graham Murdock, *Demonstrations and Communication: A Case Study* (Harmondsworth: Penguin, 1970), ch. 7.
4. Examples of 'gratification' studies from the classic period of American mass communication research include: Herta Herzog, '*Professor Quiz*: A Gratification Study', in Paul F. Lazarsfeld (ed.), *Radio and the Printed Page* (New York: Duell, Sloane & Pearce, 1940); Bernard Berelson, 'What "Missing the Newspaper" Means', in Paul F. Lazarsfeld and Frank N. Stanton (eds), *Communication Research 1948–49* (New York: Harper & Bros., 1949); Katherine M. Wolfe and Marjorie Fiske, 'The Children Talk about Comics', in Paul F. Lazarsfeld and Frank N. Stanton (eds), *Communication Research 1948–49* (New York: Harper & Bros., 1949).
5. Denis McQuail, *Towards a Sociology of Mass Communications* (London: Collier Macmillan, 1969) p. 71.
6. From a phrase in Elihu Katz, 'Mass Communication Research and the Study of Culture', *Studies in Public Communication* 2 (1959) pp. 1–60.
7. McQuail, *Towards a Sociology*, p. 88. Also, in Chapter 29, McQuail and his colleagues express certain reservations over adopting functionalism *tout court*: 'However appropriate otherwise, the language of functionalism is so overworked, ambiguous and imprecise that we prefer to avoid it, and to attempt a new start. . . . [W]e propose to use the expression "media–person interaction", to refer to the orientations distinguished in the typology.'

27

DENSENSITIZATION, VIOLENCE AND THE MEDIA

Hans Eysenck and D. K. B. Nias

[. . .]

Civilized man everywhere has erected barriers to the simple expression of sexual and violent impulses in direct action – rape and murder are universally prohibited, and punished by law. These barriers are internalized, probably through some form of conditioning (Eysenck, 1977), although it is quite possible and even likely that innate factors also play some part – even animals tend to act out their intraspecific conflicts in a more or less symbolic way. Lions seldom kill lions, nor do gorillas normally kill gorillas. Humans are almost unique in having ritualized murder by inventing 'war', but even so humans tend on the whole to have some seemingly innate aversion to taking human life. It seems probable that these innate tendencies are strengthened by a process of conditioning, but for the purpose [here . . .] it is not really vital to know the precise provenance of the very obvious barriers to the direct expression of primitive impulses which characterize civilized man (and even primitive man).

Let us now consider how we could weaken these barriers, supposing that we wanted to. Clearly it could be done by using the methods of desensitization. What would be required would be the portrayal, at second hand (i.e. through the written word, or in pictures, or film, or on TV) of acts of violence or abnormal sex which, had they occurred normally in our presence, would have aroused strong negative emotions of disgust, dislike and fear. By viewing them in this second-hand, indirect form we immediately reduce the impact and relegate the images to the lower ranks of our hierarchy. At the same time we view them under conditions of relaxation – in our own homes in the case of TV, or in a comfortable seat in the cinema, in the case of films. Thus the situation combines all the vital elements of desensitization – relaxation and exposure to low-ranking items in the hierarchy of fears and anxieties. We are in fact free to select for ourselves the precise images which are low enough in our own, individual hierarchy to make the viewing tolerable, and not excite too much anxiety – we usually have some information

From H. J. Eysenck and D. K. B. Nias, *Sex, Violence and the Media* (London: Maurice Temple Smith, 1978) pp. 50–1, 178–84.

about the film or play to be seen, or the TV series to be viewed. And if we are wrong in our choice, we can always walk out of the cinema, or turn off the TV, to reduce anxiety. It would not be too much to say that if the Martians had in mind the brutalization of our civilization by incitement to violence and sexual exploitation, they could not have hit upon a better method than making use of the media in their present form to achieve their aims.

Desensitization, then, is a method of changing conduct and emotional reactions which is well documented experimentally, both in animals and in humans; it has been widely used, with considerable success, to cure neurotic fears and anxieties; it seems highly unlikely that under the conditions under which pornographic and violent materials are shown these should have no effect on the viewer whatsoever. Desensitization in this case is the technical term for what many critics of the media call 'brutalization'; the idea is the same. It would need a very powerful argument indeed to persuade anyone familiar with the extensive literature on desensitization (Bergin and Garfield, 1971) to take seriously the proposition that viewing large numbers of scenes of explicit sex and violence on film or TV would leave the viewers completely unaffected. Most writers who favour the view that such scenes have no effect do not in fact argue the point; they simply disregard the evidence and the theory, as if it did not exist. This is a simple way of dealing with the difficulty, but it does not impress the unbiased critic as a good way of disposing of an inconvenient argument. It is true that the conditions of viewing are not scientifically prearranged to produce optimum effects, as could only be done in individual therapy; it is the large number of people exposed to the 'treatment', and the large number of exposures, which create the effect.

Some readers may object that Pavlovian conditioning is a very primitive method which surely does not apply to human beings in the same manner as to dogs, rats and other mammals. The evidence is strong that this is not true; humans follow the same laws of conditioning as do animals.

[. . .]

People, by constant exposure to violence, will eventually become 'desensitized' and no longer be upset or aroused by witnessing violence.

When feeling emotional we tend to sweat, and very slight increases in moisture can be detected electrically by what is known as a 'galvanic skin response' or 'skin conductance' measure. This highly sensitive indicator of emotional arousal, which is used in 'lie detector' tests, was being used in a study in which students were shown a film of an aboriginal ceremony that vividly depicted a sequence of crude operations performed with a piece of flint on several adolescent boys (Lazarus et al., 1962). Skin conductance tended to 'peak' every time there was a particularly gory scene, but these peaks were not as high towards the end of the film as they were at the beginning. This is evidence of desensitization, but, because this demonstration was not the main point of the study, no attempt was made to control for alternative interpretations such as the later scenes being less horrific and so accounting for the decline in emotional responsiveness.

Fortunately this necessary control was incorporated in the design of an experiment by Berger (1962). Galvanic skin responses were monitored in fifteen subjects who either watched a man being given a series of electric shocks in order 'to see what level he could take' or the same man merely having his galvanic skin responses recorded. The 'victim' was in fact a confederate of the experimenter, and the subjects were reassured that it would not be necessary to give them shocks. Skin responses were evident in the experimental subjects each time the victim jerked his arm at the shock, but their emotional response became less with each repetition of the procedure.

Heart rate and self-reported distress were monitored as well as skin conductance in a study of habituation to an industrial accident film (Averill, et al., 1972). Male students were shown twenty repetitions of either a gruesome accident or a benign scene, and then the complete film involving three accidents. This procedure was repeated on three occasions, and each time prior exposure to the accident scene was found to reduce emotional arousal when that same scene was viewed in the context of the whole film. There was, however, little evidence of generalization since emotional responses to the other two accidents were similar for the control and experimental subjects. This lack of desensitization to the new accidents helps explain why the interest of existing TV audiences is maintained if producers provide them with new forms of violence. Nevertheless, generalization is known to occur in other situations and it may not have become apparent in this study simply because it may need more than three days of brief exposure to one type of violence in order to manifest itself. Evidence from a field study does in fact suggest that generalization to TV violence occurs in real life; this study is listed together with the above in Table [27.1].

Boys were shown a sequence, including a brutal boxing scene, from a Kirk Douglas film (Cline et al., 1973). Galvanic skin response and blood volume pulse amplitude were recorded before and during this film for two groups of boys. One group had been selected on the basis of having watched TV for twenty-five hours or more a week over the previous two years, and the other for four hours or less a week. Emotional arousal during the violent scene was less for the 'hardened' viewers than it was for the 'low exposure' controls, whereas before this scene the physiological measures were similar for the two

---

Table [27.1]

Lazarus et al. (1962)   A progressive drop in skin conductance was noted for 70 students while watching a seventeen-minute film of primitive mutilation.

Berger (1962)   Compared with a control group, galvanic skin responses occurred more frequently for subjects who were witnessing a man being shocked, but these responses steadily declined over thirteen trials.

Averill et al. (1972)   For three days, 45 students watched a twenty-five second accident scene twenty times at half-minute intervals before seeing a twelve-minute film in which this was one of three accidents. Compared with 23 control subjects, emotional arousal was significantly reduced only for the accident to which they had been desensitized.

Cline et al. (1973)   Boys aged 5 to 14 years were selected on the basis of high or low exposure to TV. While watching an eight-minute violent scene in a fourteen-minute film, emotional responses were lower for 17 'high exposure' than for 15 'low exposure' boys.

---

groups. Because this was a field study, the results suffer from a weakness inherent in the method, namely that alternative interpretations are always apparent. For example, if boys who are particularly sensitive to violence are less inclined to watch TV, then this alone could be sufficient to account for the results obtained. Because of this limitation we shall return to laboratory studies, which also provide important evidence of desensitization to violence generalizing to another situation.

In one of the few studies in the Surgeon General's Commission to be concerned with desensitization, children were shown either a violent *Peter Gunn* or a neutral *Green Acres TV* episode, and then compared in a test for awareness of violence (Rabinovitch et al., 1972). The test involved a stereoscopic projector by which two slides can be presented simultaneously to each eye so quickly that only one is seen. Nine pairs of slides were used in which one portrayed a violent and the other a neutral scene. For example, a man hitting another over the

Table [27.2] Effects of films on toleration of aggression

	Violent film	No film
Boys	104 seconds	63 seconds
Girls	119 seconds	75 seconds

Time taken before notifying the experimenter of an altercation between two younger children for whom the subject had taken responsibility.

(Based on Drabman and Thomas, 1974)

head with a gun was paired with a picture of a man helping another hit a pole into the ground with a gun butt. The children were asked to write down descriptions of what they saw, and it was the group who had just seen *Peter Gunn* who identified fewer of the violent pictures. This constitutes evidence that the violent programme, by making them temporarily less sensitive to violence, blunted their awareness of the violent pictures. It is difficult to think of an alternative interpretation of this result unless it was catharsis making the violent group think of peaceful rather than violent scenes.

Evidence that attitudes in real life can be influenced by a violent film is provided in an ingenious experiment by Drabman and Thomas (1974). Children who had watched a violent scene from *Hopalong Cassidy* were compared with a control group, who had not seen a film, for tolerance of violent acts. This was done by asking each subject to keep an eye on a couple of children who were playing in another room, and to summon the experimenter if there was any trouble. They were able to watch the children by way of a videotape monitor; by this technique it was possible to arrange for both groups of subjects to see exactly the same sequence of events. After playing peacefully the two children started to abuse each other verbally and then to fight during the course of which the TV camera was knocked over and contact was eventually lost. The measure of attitude to aggression was the time taken before the subject sought help from the experimenter, and these results are presented in Table [27.2].

Just over half the control subjects notified the experimenter of the argument before physical fighting began, whereas only 17 per cent of the film group did so. Whether these results were obtained because of a temporary reduction in emotional responsivity in the film group, or simply because the argument and fighting appeared trivial in comparison with the filmed violence, they constitute strong evidence that violent film can lead to increased tolerance of aggression. One criticism, however, is apparent and this concerns the possibility that the film group took less notice of their responsibility because they were still thinking of the exciting film. It would have been better if the control subjects had been shown an exciting but non-violent film instead of nothing. This was duly done in a replication by Thomas and Drabman (1975) and the result still held; children who had watched an excerpt from *Mannix* took an average of 145 seconds before summoning help, whereas those who had watched an exciting baseball film took only 88 seconds.

Thomas et al. (1977) attempted to produce temporary desensitization by showing children a violent TV police drama, and then assessed the effect in terms of their response to a videotape of two pre-school children fighting. Compared with a control group who were shown an exciting volleyball game, the 'desensitized' children responded with fewer galvanic skin responses when shown the videotape of 'real' aggression. This again provides evidence that the viewing of TV violence can make children inured to real-life violence, only this time there is the additional information that after watching TV they feel less emotional when witnessing scenes of real fighting. The study was repeated with students, except that news films of riots were used instead of the fighting scenes, and similar results were obtained at least for males.

The above studies, which are summarized in Table [27.3] have all provided evidence of desensitization to violence. That desensitization occurs is not really in doubt, although we have noted that generalization to other forms of violence is a very gradual process. It probably requires years of ardent viewing before people become immune to whatever type of violence is next to appear on the screens. According to the reports of cinemas managers, some members of the audience fainted or were sick during the screening of *Soldier Blue* and *A Clockwork Orange*. Presumably these viewers had not been sufficiently 'desensitized' for films of such a violent nature. Carruthers and Taggart (1973) took electrocardiogram recordings and other physiological measures from adult men and women watching these two films. Reactions to the violent scenes were assessed relative to baseline measures taken during pre-film commercials. The interesting observation was made that although there was increased adrenaline excretion, indicating excitement or arousal, there was also a slowing of the heart, indicating horror or revulsion, during the most violent scenes. In some people the heart rate slowed even below forty beats per minute; this provides an explanation for the fainting attacks since with a drastically slowed heart beat insufficient blood may be reaching the brain to retain consciousness. A very interesting extension to this research would be to observe changes in these physiological measures during a process of desensitization. If the aversive reaction habituates more rapidly than the excitment reaction, then we would have the ominous prospect of the 'hardened' viewer responding to such films only with excitement.

Table [27.3]

Rabinovitch et al. (1972)   57 children, aged 11 to 12 years, watched either a violent or a neutral TV programme, and were then shown pictures of violent and neutral scenes flashed momentarily before them. The violent group were less likely than the controls to notice the violent pictures.

Drabman and Thomas (1974)   44 children, aged 8 to 10 years, watched either an eight-minute violent film or nothing, and were then asked to keep an eye on two younger children. The violent group were less likely than the controls to call the experimenter when the children started to fight.

Thomas and Drabman (1975)   In a replication of the above study, 20 children who had just seen a fifteen-minute violent detective film on TV were slower to summon help than were 20 controls who saw an exciting non-violent film. This result was not apparent, however, for younger children aged 6 to 7 years.

Thomas et al. (1977)   28 boys and 16 girls, aged 8 to 10 years, were shown either a violent police drama or an equally emotion-arousing sports film. Subsequently, a videotape of real-life aggression (children fighting) produced less emotional response (skin resistance) in the violent group. Similar results were obtained for 29 male students, but not 30 females, in a replication. In both studies, amount of TV violence normally viewed was negatively related to responsivity while viewing aggression.

In an earlier review of the desensitization evidence, Howitt and Cumberbatch (1975) commented that 'it is very likely that this process of habituation does occur for mass media violence ... but the social consequences of this are unclear'. One such consequence is that desensitization, by reducing anxiety, may make people more likely to carry out acts of aggression in the future. In other words, in order to commit an act of aggression it may be necessary to overcome certain inhibitions, and this is where prior exposure, even if only to acts of a similar nature on the screen, probably helps. The experiment by Drabman and Thomas indicates another social consequence. As people become more and more used to violence, there is the danger that they will come to accept and tolerate it. If witnessed continually, violence may eventually come to be regarded as normal behaviour.

The effects of desensitization to violence have been generally overlooked by theorists in favour of the imitation and disinhibition effects. [. . .] But it seems to us that the consequences of a nation 'desensitized' to violence are just as serious, if not more so, than one which is merely exposed to examples of how to be violent.

REFERENCES

Averill, J. R., Malmstrom, E. J., Koriat, A. and Lazarus, R. S. (1972). Habituation to complex emotional stimuli. *Journal of Abnormal Psychology*, 80, 20–8.
Berger, S. M. (1962). Conditioning through vicarious instigation. *Psychological Review*, 69, 450–66.
Bergin, A. E. and Garfield, S. L. (Eds) (1971). *Handbook of Psychotherapy and Behaviour Change*. London: Wiley.
Carruthers, M. and Taggart, P. (1973). Vagotonicity of violence: Biochemical and cardiac responses to violent films and television programmes. *British Medical Journal*, 3, 384–9.
Cline, V. B., Croft, R. G., and Courrier, S. (1973). Desensitization of children to television violence. *Journal of Personality and Social Psychology*, 27, 360–5.
Drabman, R. S. and Thomas, M. H. (1974). Does media violence increase children's tolerance of real-life aggression? *Developmental Psychology*, 10, 418–21.
Eysenck, H. J. (1977). *Crime and Personality* (3rd Edition). London: Routledge & Kegan Paul.
Howitt, D. and Cumberbatch, G. (1975). *Mass Media Violence and Society*. New York: Halstead.
Lazarus, R. S., Speisman, J. C., Mordkoff, A. M., and Davison, L. A. (1962). A laboratory study of psychological stress produced by a motion picture film. *Psychological Monographs*, 76 (Whole No. 553).
Rabinovitch, M. S., McLean, M. S., Markham, J. W. and Talbot, A. D. (1972). Children's violence perception as a function of television violence. In *TV and Social Behaviour* (Vol. 5). Washington DC: US Government Printing Office.
Thomas, M. H. and Drabman, R. S. (1975). Toleration of real life aggression as a function of exposure to televised violence and age of subject. *Merrill-Palmer Quarterly*, 21, 227–32.
Thomas, M. H., Horton, R. W., Lippincott, E. C. and Drabman, R. S. (1977). Desensitization to portrayals of real-life aggression as a function of exposure to television violence. *Journal of Personality and Social Psychology*, 35, 450–8.

28

ON THE SOCIAL EFFECTS OF TELEVISION

James D. Halloran

[. . .]

The early view of mass communication assumed that people could be persuaded by the media to adopt almost any point of view desired by the communicator. Manipulation, exploitation and vulnerability were the key words. In this crude sense this extreme view is no longer accepted, although some of the implications of this initial position are still with us. In one way or another it has provided a base from which so much of our thinking about mass communication (pessimistic as well as optimistic) has stemmed. Some people still write and talk about television as a powerful direct influence and of its tremendous potential for good or evil. In some quarters the myth of omnipotence dies hard.

Social science has undergone many changes since the days of instinct theory and the early ideas about mass society. Models of society, concepts of human nature and images of man, all change. Learning theory, work on motives and attitudes, the development of personality theory, the emphasis on selectivity in attention and perception, recognition of the importance of individual differences, the formulation of psychodynamic models of persuasion, the use of social categories in surveys and empirical work generally, the 'rediscovery' of the primary group, the acceptance of the influence of informal group ties, the development of such concepts as reference group and the work on diffusion of information and social interaction, have all played their part in producing more refined and elaborate approaches and more developed theories than the one referred to above.

It is sometimes said that one of the dangers today is that so much attention is given to the intervening or associated factors that we are in danger of neglecting what should always be central to our work, namely, the medium itself – television. In general the trend has been away from the idea of exploitation, away from an emphasis on the viewer as tabularasa, as someone wide open just waiting to soak up all that is beamed at him. Now we think more in terms of

From James D. Halloran, 'Studying the Effects of Television' and James D. Halloran, 'The Social Effects of Television', in James D. Halloran (ed.), *The Effects of Television* (London: Panther Books, 1970) pp. 18–20 and 39–43.

interaction or exchange between medium and audience, and it is recognized that the viewer approaches every viewing situation with a complicated piece of filtering equipment. This filter is made up not only of his past and present, but includes his views of and hopes for the future. We should welcome this change in emphasis but there is always a possibility that in making the shift the baby might be thrown out with the bath water. Instead of having the false picture of the all-powerful influence of television presented to us we now run the risk of getting an equally false picture of no influence whatsoever.

Even today despite all the changes and developments the picture should not be regarded as final. Granted the state of our knowledge, we could not afford to let things stay as they are. One of the healthy signs about the current situation is that in research the established ways of doing things are being questioned and challenged. [. . .] There is, of course, plenty of room for change. For example, although we have seen that the viewer is no longer *thought of* as an isolated individual in front of a television set – the importance of his background, experiences and relationships are recognized – he is still frequently researched as though he were an isolated individual. In many research exercises the individual remains the main sampling unit, and *in practice* there would still appear to be a fairly widespread acceptance of the atomistic nature of the audience.[1]

Attitude has been one of the central concepts in both social psychology and mass communication research for a long time, but there is a growing body of opinion which holds that attitude change has been over-used as the primary criterion of influence. [. . .] [T]here is much more to television's influence than can be studied through direct changes in attitude and opinion as these have normally been defined and assessed. Television may provide models for identification, confer status on people and behaviour, spell out norms, define new situations, provide stereotypes, set frameworks of anticipation and indicate levels of acceptability, tolerance and approval. Influence must not be equated with attitude change.

It is neither necessary nor desirable to confine or even to concentrate our research on conventional approaches which seek to study viewer reactions before and after exposure to television programmes. Whilst accepting that quite often a concern with media content, to the exclusion of other factors, has led to misleading predictions about effects, we still cannot afford to ignore content. A *systematic* study of what television provides, whilst not telling us what happens to people, will tell us what is available, what there is for them to use. If we have also studied the patterns of use and the relevant relationships, predispositions and background experience of those who use television, then it is possible for predictions to be made about the consequence of that use.

[. . .]

A study[2] carried out at the Centre for Mass Communication Research at the University of Leicester on a programme which dealt with the lives of young people in Czechoslovakia, in addition to providing further support for the principle that different people get different things from the same programme, indicated that it could be misleading to think of the effects of television solely in terms of visual impact. The effects of this particular programme seemed to follow the commentary. Whilst accepting that any television programme is essentially a complex audio-visual message, it seemed that the clear and unambiguous statements about Czech life made in the programme had considerable impact. Several years ago the late Joe Trenaman also drew attention to the importance of the verbal element in what is sometimes regarded as a purely visual medium.[3]

This research also showed that it might be possible for a programme to produce short-term changes in attitude about certain topics covered by the programme (in this case favourable changes about specific aspects of Czech life) and yet produce no change at the more general or overall level (in this case, favourable change in attitude about Czechoslovakia as a political state).

The programme in question, *Children of Revolution*, was an Intertel programme, and Intertel aims to produce programmes which promote 'a wider knowledge of contemporary world affairs and a better mutual understanding of world problems'. We might ask if this is a realistic policy – can television hope to do this? It would be unwise to rely too much on the results from one small piece of research but this research did show that, after viewing the programme, people not only had more knowledge about life in Czechoslovakia but in general took a more favourable view of life in that country. In a sense then, the objectives of the programme were met. However, we have already seen that the favourable change in attitude did not extend to the government and the state. These were often more negatively evaluated after the programme. It is possible, as Roger Brown suggests, that people had their prior beliefs in the tensions supposedly inherent in a Communist society strengthened by the programme. The favourable shifts in attitude with regard to the parts of the programme (e.g. Czech youth) may have been bought at the price of a less favourable image of the Czech state. In this complex situation is it possible to assess whether or not the programme-makers really achieved their objectives?

What can one hope to achieve by presenting social and political issues on television? Unfortunately, good intentions are no guarantee of success, as the reactions to many a programme (drama, documentary and educational) clearly show. Research on the ATV seven-programme series *Nature of Prejudice*, presented in 1968, showed – like the findings from many other studies – that the same message can be used in different ways by different people. From this study it is possible to argue that audience members saw in the programme what was uppermost in their own minds, rather than what the programme itself stressed most. In general, viewers found a way of avoiding the anti-prejudice message. Different sorts of viewers did see different things in the programmes, and did respond in different ways. This comes out clearly both in the comparison between prejudiced and non-prejudiced respondents, and in that between adolescent and adult viewers. But this is only another way of saying that individuals brought to the viewing situation a range of differing interests, beliefs, concepts and levels of knowledge, and that these acted as filters through which the programmes were viewed. This latter description of the situation, in its turn, raises questions about the 'success' of the programme in penetrating the defences which all of us raise against alien ideas, and about the particular processes which take place between the time our eyes and ears receive a particular sort of stimulation and the time when we arrive at some vision of the original message which fits in as well as possible with our initial needs and predispositions.[4]

In a different genre, the BBC produced a six-episode serial, *Rainbow City*, in 1967. The avowed purpose of these programmes was to contribute to the reduction of inter-racial tensions and to promote a sympathetic understanding of coloured immigrants. The evidence available from a minor research project on these programmes indicates that sympathy was enlisted for particular characters, but that the attitudes of viewers to coloured people or immigrants in general were not modified. Identification or empathy with individual screen personalities belonging to an outgroup or minority group does not necessarily rub off on the group in general.

In view of the American experience over the years (e.g. with musicians, sporting personalities etc.) it might be argued that we do not require research to teach us this lesson. Nevertheless, it is worth emphasizing, with regard to prejudice as with other attitudes, that as far as this form of attitude change is concerned, television can only work within the existing climate.[5] If the general climate is hostile to the message, there is even the possibility of a boomerang effect, i.e. the hostility being increased. Although in this particular case we can say nothing about the overall quality of the series or about the form of presentation, it is possible that – with issues that produce strong reactions – these factors may not be particularly relevant. It seems reasonable to suggest that certain topics in television programmes will produce predictable reactions from given sections of the viewing audience independently of quality and mode of presentation.

In considering the presentation of social issues on television and the effects of such presentations, it is essential to make the distinction between a gain in knowledge or information, and a change in attitude. It is usually easier to convey knowledge than to change attitudes. Research carried out several years ago by the BBC Audience Research Department, on programmes dealing with such topics as crime and the death penalty,[6] showed that although in the latter case attitudes were modified (not changed), the former programme had very little effect on either knowledge or attitudes. Even where there was a considerable increase in knowledge about a particular topic or item covered in the programme, the majority of the viewing audience still remained ignorant on the same topic after viewing. It may be easier to impart knowledge than to change attitudes, but powerful restricting factors, external to the programme itself, would appear to operate in both cases.

Several points can be made about the apparent lack of effects of these programmes which dealt with social and political issues.[7] The first is that even within the limited terms of reference and possibilities of this type of research, it would be quite unreasonable to expect a single programme or even a series of programmes to bring about appreciable changes in attitudes. Change just doesn't take place so easily. The second is that it is a mistake to equate lack of change, in the sense of people not changing from a pro to a con position (or vice versa) after seeing a programme with the overall lack of influence of that programme. The programme may confirm or reinforce the existing attitudinal position or, on the other hand, as we have just seen, the attitude may be modified in intensity. Many researchers have confined their attention to the narrower interpretation of change (from a pro to a con position) and this has undoubtedly contributed to the idea, still widely held in some quarters, that the media have little influence.

There have, of course, been many occasions when the media have been credited with, or accused of having, too much influence. Perhaps television does not have the influence that some people would have us believe but it must be recognized that influence can take several forms. Influence should certainly not be equated with these relatively narrow definitions of change.

NOTES

1. Marten Brouwer, 'Prolegomena to a Theory of Mass Communication', in *Communication Concepts and Perspectives*, Ed. Lee Thayer, Spartan Books, 1967.
2. Roger L. Brown. *Some Effects of the Television Programme 'Children of Revolution'*. A Report prepared for the Television Research Committee, Centre for Mass Communication Research, University of Leicester. 1967. 160 p. & vi p.
3. Joseph Trenaman. 'The Effects of Television', in *Twentieth Century*. Nov. 1959. pp. 332–342.
4. Television Research Committee. *Second Progress Report and Recommendations*. Leicester University Press. 1969. p. 34.

5.   The part played by television in creating the climate remains to be considered.

6.   See B. P. Emmett. 'The Design of Investigations into the Effects of Radio and Television Programmes and other Mass Communications'. *Journal of the Royal Statistical Society*. Vol. 129. 1966.

7.   Some studies have demonstrated that other programmes have been *slightly* more effective.

29

THE TELEVISION AUDIENCE: A REVISED PERSPECTIVE

Denis McQuail, Jay G. Blumler and J. R. Brown

The single concept which seems to have assumed most prominent in discussions of mass media experience has been that of 'escape'

[. . .]

When all due allowance is made for distinctions and reservations, it must be admitted that the escapist hypothesis still occupies much of the central ground in discussion and study of the television audience.

Like several other notions that are deeply entrenched in the vocabulary of discourse about culture and society, the concept of escape is exceptionally potent because it inextricably intermingles what might otherwise be a merely descriptive assertion in the scientific spirit (hypothesizing that most viewers predominantly use television in order to forget stressful and disliked features of their environment) with a strongly held normative standpoint. Deployed in the latter sense, the escapist thesis has helped to precipitate and perpetuate certain derogatory assumptions about the typical relationship between television and the viewer, from which even the qualifications and reservations mentioned above are usually excluded.

Firstly there is the view that popularity is inconsistent with high quality, since the latter is assumed to connote educational attainment, critical standards, sensitivity of judgement, effort and creativity, all of which stand in contrast to the dominant meanings of the escape concept. Second, there is an assumption of homogeneity; the content of a mass medium like television is regarded virtually as a single commodity, in which one programme could stand in quite readily for any other. The audience is unselective because all or most programmes offer essentially the same satisfaction and are watched for broadly the same motive. A third and related point is that the experience of television is uninvolving and, by implication, unimportant according to a widely held scale of values. It is regarded as shallow, undemanding and trivial. Fourth,

From Denis McQuail, Jay G. Blumler and J. R. Brown, 'The Television Audience: A Revised Perspective', ch. 7 in Denis McQuail (ed.), *Sociology of Mass Communications* (Harmondsworth: Penguin, 1972).

television is regarded as a residual category of leisure activity; it is a time-filler, a substitute for doing nothing or something more worthwhile, shaped more by variations in other demands on one's time than by any positive attractions or considered motivations. This view finds some support in the phenomenal *quantity* of time devoted to it. The general bearing of this set of views is to see the experience of watching television as largely lacking in meaning, hardly deserving of serious interest or respect, a chance outcome of a set of market circumstances. The explanatory formula is thus closed and virtually self-validating. So the evidence showing long hours of time spent watching television is not interpreted as pointing to the influence of powerful attraction or strong need, but as indicative instead of a vacancy of outlook, an emptiness of life and a uniformity of response. And when evidence shows that people do actually depend a good deal on television and are upset when it is not available, this is taken more as a sign of their stupidity than of the constructive role which the medium plays in their lives.

[. . .]

The danger is that an uncritical acceptance of the escapist thesis will go hand-in-hand with a simplistic view of the relations between audience and media content and an underestimation of the diversity and complexity of motives that may sustain the mass audience. It could also have undesirable consequences for the organization of television and the evolution of policies that determine its place in society – undesirable, that is, if television is not in fact so constrained as the escapist theory makes out from performing a wider range of social functions than is generally assigned to it in western societies today.

In this essay we aim, then, to advance, on the basis of empirical research evidence, a typology of viewer gratifications which can both enlarge our understanding of what escape implies and help to place it in a context of a number of other equally important orientations, motives and links between people and television. We strive to substantiate the claim that escape does not represent the only, or even the invariably most appropriate, formulation of the needs served by the mass communication process and to direct attention towards several other formulations of what this process may fundamentally involve and signify.

The evidence presented for illustration and support derives from a programme of investigation initiated in 1969 at the Centre for Television Research in the University of Leeds. It was designed to further in a systematic way the tradition of inquiry which has been concerned with audience 'uses and gratifications', and which seeks to explain, usually on the basis of the audience member's own subjective account of the media experience, just what functions a particular kind of content serves in particular circumstance.

[. . .]

Our work was guided by certain presuppositions, which should be briefly outlined. Most fundamentally, we adopted the view that an important part of television viewing is goal-directed. While this premise may seem question-begging, we could not proceed far with our investigation without it, and it does not imply in advance any single kind of motive. Second, we assumed that the goals of television viewing can only be discovered from viewers themselves and that people will be sufficiently self-aware to be able to report their interests and motives in particular cases or at least to recognize them when confronted with them in an intelligible and familiar verbal formulation. Third, we were prepared to find diverse and overlapping patterns of motive and satisfaction; if a viewer was moved by several different concerns to follow the same content, we want our instruments of investigation to disclose, not to ignore, this fact. Fourth, we were prepared to treat as a conceptually independent unit of analysis something which might variously be described as a satisfaction, a motive, a gratification, an interest or a function. These units could be distributed in varying ways amongst a given population of television viewers and also be associated with different programmes and programme types in varying degrees.

Because it stands on the same plane of generality as the assumptions specified above, a final orientation deserves to be mentioned here, even though it only emerged explicitly as evidence was collected and analysed. This is that media use is most suitably characterized as an interactive process, relating media content, individual needs, perceptions, roles and values and the social context in which a person is situated. Our model of this process is that of an open system in which social experience gives rise to certain needs, some of which are directed to the mass media of communication for satisfaction. It is also possible that media content may occasionally help to generate in the audience member an awareness of certain needs in relation to his social situation. The linkage is necessarily a complex one and may take diverse forms; it may involve a process of deprivation-compensation in which the media offer substitute satisfactions for something desired or valued, but relatively unavailable; or it may involve a process of value reinforcement in which salient values, beliefs or attitudes are sustained by attention to certain content forms; or materials taken from the media may contribute to certain processes of social interchange which go with the occupancy of certain roles. The essential point to be stressed is our belief that media use is interactive. That is, it does not conform to the typical lineaments of a subject-object relationship, and should not be treated merely as a one-way tension-reducing mechanism. Such a model would leave out of account the many ways in which, according to our evidence, audience members seem to bring back into their lives, their patterns of activity and their circles of familiar acquaintances some of the broadcast programmes to which they have become attached.

[. . .]

[An] account follows of one programme study, that which was concerned with television quiz programmes. This was the second study carried out and the first in which a group of programmes as a type, rather than a single programme, was examined. The choice was influenced by the fact that quiz programmes form a distinctive and popular category of television content with a seeming diversity of associations. In addition, there existed a link with early research in the form of an interesting study of a small sample of listeners to an American radio quiz programme, providing material for comparison and a source of some hypotheses (Herzog, 1940).

A series of tape-recorded discussions was first held with followers of television quiz programmes, and a questionnaire compiled in the light of the analysis of material thus obtained. This questionnaire was then administered to a quota sample of seventy-three Leeds residents (with controls for sex, age, housing type and social grade), all of whom had designated as among their favourite television programmes one of several quiz programmes from a wider list. The three quiz programmes were *University Challenge, TV Brain of Britain*, and *Ask the Family*, each of them involving genuine tests of knowledge rather than being merely parlour games with big prizes, gimmicks and a prominent element of chance.

The most relevant part of the questionnaire consisted of an inventory of forty-two statements about quiz programmes, divided into three sections, which were presented to respondents for endorsement on a four-point scale. The first section contained statements indicating expected satisfactions and accompanied by the wording: 'When I think of watching a quiz [the statement] applies very much, quite a lot, a little, not at all.' The second referred to experienced satisfactions in the following way: 'When watching quizzes [the experience] has happened very often, quite often, only now and then, never.' In the third section respondents were asked whether certain descriptive phrases applied 'very well', 'slightly', or 'not at all' to quiz programmes.

[. . .]

The pattern of the gratifications viewers seek from quiz programmes emerged from an analysis involving two stages. First, associations between endorsements of the scales were set out in a 42 × 42 matrix of intercorrelations. Second, the statements were re-arranged into sub-sets by means of a cluster analysis (McQuitty's elementary linkage analysis, 1957). This technique is designed to arrange intercorrelated items into clusters which maximize the average internal correlation of the clustered items and minimize the correlation between sub-sets. It is an approximate method, easy to apply, which provides an entirely empirical solution to the problem of ordering interrelated data. Every item is assigned to one and only one cluster, although it may be the case that a particular statement could equally well fit in more than one cluster.

The results of the quiz programme cluster analysis are presented in Table [29–1]. We find four main clusters of items emerging, with several small groups in pairs also separated out.

[. . .]

[T]hey form a strikingly clear and interpretable pattern, or so we can conclude about the four relatively large clusters. The six later clusters add little to the results, partly because most of their meanings have already been covered and partly because two- or three-item groups are inevitably low in reliability.

According to this analysis, then, four main kinds of gratifications are involved in the viewing of quiz programmes. One stems from a *self-rating appeal*, whereby watching a quiz enables the viewer to find out something about himself. Inspection of the individual items in Cluster 1 suggests that it embraces several related elements. There is the possibility of assessing one's ability by comparing one's own responses to the questions with the performance of other contestants. There is the possibility of testing one's judgement by guessing which group of competitors will turn out to be the winners. There is the theme of projection, whereby the viewer can imagine how he would fare if he were on the programme himself. And there is the possibility of being reminded of what one was like as a schoolchild. In the last context it is interesting to note that Herzog also detected a self-rating appeal of quiz programmes and speculated that one of its ingredients was the attraction of 'being taken back to one's own school days' (1940).

The meaning of Cluster 2 seems equally definite. A second major appeal of quiz programmes is their provision of a *basis for social interaction* with other people. Each item in the cluster (with only one exception) bears this interpretation. A quiz programme offers shared family interest; there is the possibility of observing 'what the children get out of it'; the whole family can work together on the answers; alternatively, viewers can compete with each other in trying to answer the questions; and the occasion can form a topic of conversation afterwards. Clearly quiz programmes are well adapted to serving a 'coin of exchange' function.

A third main appeal of TV quizzes arises from the *excitement* they can engender. Many of the items in Cluster 3 convey this emphasis. Quiz programmes apparently offer the excitement of competition itself, guessing who might win and seeing how one's forecast turns out, and the prospect of a close finish. Herzog seemed to have this gratification in mind when referring to the so-called 'sporting appeal' of *Professor Quiz* (1940). Perhaps what is distinctive about the composition of Cluster 3 in this study is its injection of an 'escapist' note into the associated group of items ('I like to forget my worries for a while', and 'I completely forget my worries'). It is as if the various tensions of a quiz programme facilitate its 'escapist' function and help the viewer to shed his everyday cares for a while.

Finally, Cluster 4 picks out an *educational appeal* of quiz programmes. Here, too, several ingredients are involved. It is not just that quizzes can help to stimulate thought ('I think over some of the questions afterwards'). In addition, two of the items sound a note of 'self-improvement' ('I feel I have improved myself', and 'I find I know more than I thought'), in terms which suggest that people who feel insecure in their educational status may use quizzes to reassure themselves about their own knowledgeability. And this suggests yet another way of interpreting Cluster 4 – as expressive of the function of quiz programmes in projecting and reinforcing educational values.

Subsequent analysis involved the testing of relationships between the appeals represented by these main clusters and variables representative of social experience and attitudes. In effect we wished to know what kinds of people were most attracted to quiz programmes for reasons implied in these different clusters

[. . .]

[and] what kinds of social circumstances are associated with, and hence possibly causative of, liking the programme in question for a given type of reason. The results are of interest both as tests of certain hypotheses and as means of validating the distinctiveness of two separate clusters. The findings are complex, but for each of four quiz clusters we can report the sub-group or groups which are maximally involved.

Cluster 1 Self-rating appeal

The analysis separates out as relatively high scorers those members of the sample (thirty-six out of seventy-three) living in council housing. This suggests that the working-class fans of a programme type which in fact had a generally stronger appeal for middle-class people were more concerned to use it to 'learn things about themselves' than were other viewers.

Cluster 2 Basis for social interaction

Here the strongest associations were with social contact variables. The first high-scoring group to emerge from the analysis consisted of those respondents who reported having a very large number of acquaintances in their neighbourhoods. Among the other sample members, those with a large extended family were then distinguished as particularly high-scoring on this cluster. The use of quiz material as a 'coin of exchange' seemed, then, to be directly related to the number of opportunities for interaction available in the individual's immediate social environment.

Cluster 3 Excitement

The highest scoring group consisted of working-class viewers who had measured low on an index of acts of sociability and who were late-born children of large families. While the significance of the role of family background here is not clear, the predominant meaning of the link to low sociability seems to favour an escapist or compensatory explanation of this motive for watching quiz programmes.

Cluster 4 Educational appeal

The strongest and most clearcut association here was with educational background, since the analysis, after first distinguishing Leeds-born respondents from the 'immigrants' to the city,

Table [29.1] Results of cluster analysis of statements relating to television quiz programmes

	Coefficients of homogeneity	reliability
Cluster 1 Self-rating appeal	0.24	0.69
I can compare myself with the experts		
I like to imagine that I am on the programme and doing well		
I feel pleased that the side I favour has actually won		
I imagine that I was on the programme and doing well		
I am reminded of when I was in school		
I laugh at the contestant's mistakes		
Hard to follow		
Cluster 2 Basis for social interaction	0.31	0.79
I look forward to talking about it with others		
I like competing with other people watching with me		
I like working together with the family on the answers		
I hope the children will get a lot out of it		
The children get a lot out of it		
It brings the family together sharing the same interest		
It is a topic of conversation afterwards		
Not really for people like myself		
Cluster 3 Excitement appeal	0.34	0.78
I like the excitement of a close finish		
I like to forget my worries for a while		
I like trying to guess the winner		
Having got the answer right I feel really good		
I completely forget my worries		
I get involved in the competition		
Exciting		

	Coefficients of homogeneity	reliablity
Cluster 4 Educational appeal	0.30	0.68

Cluster 4 Educational appeal

I find I know more than I thought

I feel I have improved myself

I feel respect for the people on the programme

I think over some of the questions afterwards

Educational

Cluster 5

It is nice to see the experts taken down a peg

It is amusing to see the mistakes some of the contestants make

Cluster 6

I like to learn something as well as to be entertained

I like finding out new things

Cluster 7

I like trying to guess the answers

I hope to find that I know some of the answers

Cluster 8

I find out the gaps in what I know

I learn something new

A waste of time

Cluster 9

Entertaining

Something for all the family

Cluster 10

I like the sound of voices in the house

I like seeing really intelligent contestants showing how much they know then split the former into a high-scoring group whose education had finished at the minimum school-leaving age. Thus the educational appeal of quiz programmes was strongest for those individuals with the most limited school experience.

These and other results which related to quiz programmes were not without ambiguity and left many questions unanswered, but they appeared to lend support to some of our basic working assumptions. They also foreshadowed some of the categories that figure in the typology of viewer gratifications which stemmed from our attempt to organize the results of several different studies, of which the quiz investigation was but one example.

The four most successful studies yielded a total of nineteen clusters to which substantive labels could be attached, and when these were regarded as a whole a relatively small number of recurrent categories were found to emerge. It was this striking, and only partly anticipated, degree of overlapping in the gratification clusters which makes it possible, without further de-tailed research, to prepare the outlines of the overall framework of appeals by which television may meet the needs of its audience. A major implication of this phenomenon of overlapping dispositions is that people can look to quite different kinds of material for essentially the same gratification and, correlatively, find alternative satisfactions in the same televised material. Thus an 'escape' motive seemed to feature in the structure of orientations to broadcast materials as diverse as *The Dales* radio serial, *The Saint*, television news and quiz programmes. It should be noted that these types of content are hardly comparable in terms of the degree to which they provide a faithful representation of reality; yet they still offer a recognizably similar kind of satisfaction to audience members. Other gratification types ranged with equal facility across a similarly diverse set of programme areas.

In fact, this repetition of a small number of themes was the starting point for the development of an overall framework of gratification types.

[. . .]

The conceptual status of the typology calls for a brief comment. What, exactly, it may be asked, *are* the sorts of things that we are classifying? However appropriate otherwise, the language of functionalism is so overworked, ambiguous and imprecise that we prefer to avoid it, and to attempt a new start. In keeping with our view of mass media use as being potentially highly involving and also two-way, we propose to use the expression, 'media-person interaction', to refer to the orientations distinguished in the typology. Our clusters of items seem to reveal certain types of relationship between the user and the communicated content that depend on the perceptions of the audience member. A good deal of imprecision remains in the concept, but this stems from the variability inherent in the situation. What we wish to avoid is any specific inference about the presence of a discrete motive or the occurrence of a precise 'effect'. The audience member temporarily occupies a particular position in relation to what he is viewing, a position affected by a large number of factors, including those deriving from his personality, social background, experience, immediate social context, and, of course, from the content itself. He brings certain expectations and responds in line with these, and he derives certain affective, cognitive and instrumental satisfactions.

The typology of media–person interactions is intended to differentiate certain common constellations of disposition and response. It does so only very approximately and at present hypothetically. Its main strength as a heuristic device or source of hypotheses derives from its empirical base and its main weakness from the possibly limited character of this base.

The categories of our typology can first be presented in a summary form and then elaborated and illustrated more fully:

1 Diversion
   (a) Escape from the constraints of routine
   (b) Escape from the burdens of problems
   (c) Emotional release
2. Personal Relationships
   (a) Companionship
   (b) Social utility
3. Personal Identity
   (a) Personal reference
   (b) Reality exploration
   (c) Value reinforcement
4. Surveillance

Diversion

The meaning of the three sub-types listed under this heading can be illustrated from the results of the programme studies mentioned above. The first sub-type of the category labelled 'diversion' is instanced by the first main clustering of responses to *The Saint*. This cluster included the following set of empirically linked items:

> 'It helps you escape from the boredom of everyday life'
> 'It takes you out of yourself'
> 'The stories often have interesting backgrounds'
> 'It does you good to see somebody doing things you can't do yourself'
> '*The Saint* keeps me in suspense'

What a programme of this kind offers is a fantasy world which is attractive in itself, and which the viewer can temporarily occupy.

A somewhat different relationship, justifying a second sub-type, is indicated by one of the clusters concerning quiz programmes where the item 'I completely forgot my worries' is closely linked with two others that refer to the mechanism involved: 'I like the excitement of a close finish', and 'I like trying to guess the winner'. Another expression of this kind of diversion seems implicit in one of the news-viewing clusters which linked the following items:

> 'It helps me to get away from my problems'
> 'It's like having a good gossip'
> 'I like the sound of voices in my house'

Third, the category of media function, which we have labelled 'emotional release' (familiar from Herzog's pioneering study (1944) of radio soap operas of thirty years ago) appeared in connection with *The Dales* radio serial. Only two linked items of response can bear this meaning – 'Sometimes I think "I wish that were me"', and 'Sometimes it makes me want to cry' – and probably it applies to only a minority of the audience for certain limited kinds of media material. Even so, the appropriate content may have been under-represented in the small sample of programmes studied, and additional evidence obtained in a follow-up study of the original sample of *The Dales* listeners seemed to confirm the presence of this kind of response. Thus, when fifty-five members of the sample were reinterviewed and asked directly if *The Dales* did provide an opportunity 'to relieve their feelings', sixteen answered affirmatively. The existence of this kind of reaction to books, films and plays is so familiar that it perhaps needs no further proof. More important is our wish to treat it as a form of 'diversion' and to distinguish it from an escape into a more desirable imaginary world or out of an oppressive reality.

Personal Relationships

Two gratification types have been placed under this heading because they both refer to the viewer's relationships with other poeple – either real-life persons or media personalities. The 'companionship' category stands for a process whereby the audience member enters into a vicarious relationship with media personalities (fictional characters, entertainers, or presenters) as if he was on friendly terms with them, and as if they could stand in for real persons. Two perceptive observers have termed this tendency a 'para-social relationship' (Horton and Wohl, 1956). The clearest expression of the wish to use media in this way is represented in one of *The Dales* clusters, the most frequently endorsed item of which was 'It is good company when you're alone'. Some of the other related items were:

> 'The characters have become like close friends to me'
> 'It gives me something in common with other *Dales* listeners'
> 'I like the sound of the characters' voices in my house'

A familiar assumption about the mass media, and a phenomenon which will be within the experience of most people is attested to by the occurrence of this set of attitudes in relation to a programme which attracted a large number of solitary listeners, *The Dales*. What our evidence about this programme suggested, however, was that the companionship element was even stronger than is often supposed: the characters may become virtually real, knowable and cherished individuals, and their voices are more than just a comforting background which breaks the silence of an empty house. This point can be illustrated by some further data, relating this time to the TV serial, *Coronation Street*. In the course of interviewing the sample of viewers, an opportunity arose of asking respondents how they felt about a road crash which had occurred in the programme. Amongst the many replies demonstrating the ease with which fictional events are integrated into real life were a number relevant to the idea of substitute companionship: 'I'm sorry. I like all of them. Minnie's just like Auntie; you feel you know them. You know you feel as if they had been in a real accident and you'd like to do something for them'; or 'Shattered. I'm very upset. I hope they'll be all right'; and 'My wife was very upset. So was I. I hope they'll be all right.'

The category we have called 'social utility' is a disparate one, but would cover those uses of the media which are instrumental for social interaction with real people in familiar surroundings. Social utility here may refer to media use as a source of conversational material, as a subject of conversation in itself, as a common activity for a family or other group engaging, say, in viewing together, or as something that helps an individual to discharge a definite social role or to meet the membership requirements of one or more of his peer groups. The research literature includes a number of examples describing a 'coin of exchange' function served by the media in conversational and other social situations (Riley and Riley, 1951). One of the clearest illustrations from our own work is provided by many of the items included in the second cluster of responses to television quiz programmes:

> 'I look forward to talking about it with others'
> 'I like competing with other people watching with me'
> 'I like working together with the family on the answers'

'It brings the family together sharing the same interest'
'It is a topic of conversation afterwards'

And a prominent cluster in the analysis of television newsviewing located a somewhat more specific information-relaying use of television, grouping the following items:

'I like to be the first with the news so that I can pass it on to other people'
'It satisfies my sense of curiosity'
'Keeping up with the news give you plenty to talk about'
'Somehow I feel more secure when I know what is going on'

Perhaps this category of media use provides the best support for our contention that the relationship between medium and audience is not one-sided and that the role and social situation of the viewer may help to govern his selection and response. It also serves to make plausible the view that the specific content of the media can be relatively unhelpful in predicting the grounds of audience response; consequently, categorization of content based on overt meaning may have a limited value in mass communications research. The 'meaning' of an example of viewing behaviour is not self-evident from knowledge of content alone, or of the social-demographic parameters of the audience.

Personal Identity

The set of gratification types classified under this heading brings together ways of using programme materials to reflect upon or to give added salience to something important in the viewer's own life or situation. One such disposition – a use of television for what has been termed 'personal reference' – provided perhaps that most novel outcome of the exploratory research, for few previous uses and gratification studies have reported anything like it. This reflected a use of programme content to characterize or highlight for the viewer some feature of his own situation, character or life, past or present. For example, the dominant item of the first *Dales* cluster was worded 'The programme reminds me that I could be worse off than I am', while other items with which this was associated included:

'I can compare the people in the programme with other people I know'
'It reminds me of things that have happened in my own life'
'It sometimes brings back memories of certain people I used to know'

In addition, the first quiz cluster brought together a group of items which reflected the viewer's interest in rating his abilities by responding to the questions asked on the programmes and comparing his achievement with that of the performers. This orientation is reminiscent of the perspective of symbolic interactionism, according to which a central element in the world of every person is some notion of himself, and such a notion is formed in great part by looking at oneself through the eyes of others. Apparently, not only interpersonal exchanges but also mass communications can help some people to form or reassess impressions of their own 'selves'.

A second version of this concern of people to explore their own personal identity was distinguished from the first mainly by the kind of reflection that was evoked. In contrast to the more descriptive activities of classification and labelling subsumed under 'personal reference', the process of 'reality exploration' involved a use of programme content to stimulate ideas about certain problems which the viewer was experiencing, or might at some time experience, in his more immediate social environment. The *Dales* cluster which seemed to express this tendency included such items as: 'The people in *The Dales* sometimes have problems that are like my own', and 'It sometimes helps me to understand my own life'. The emergence of a similar cluster from the *Saint* analysis – centering on the dominant item 'It provides food for thought' – was more surprising, since this series would seem to many observers to provide no more than a succession of wish-fulfilling fantasies. The result suggests that keen 'fans' of almost any kind of fictional content may regard it as a stimulus relevant to their own real-life problems.

Less surprisingly, amongst the appeals of television news, we located a small group of items which together indicated an empathic response to news viewing. This cluster separated out the following: 'It helps me realize my life is not so bad after all'; 'It helps me to understand some of the problems other people have'; 'It sometimes makes me feel sad'. While the allocation of this type of response between the categories of 'personal reference' and 'reality exploration' is uncertain, there is little doubt that news enters into the process of establishing and maintaining identity and of relating the self to the wider society.

The third gratification category under 'personal identity' in the typology, termed 'value re-inforcement', is more or less self-explanatory. It locates the appeal to a viewer of a programme which upholds certain values that he also believes in. This particular mode of media–person interaction is most clearly illustrated by one of the *Dales* clusters, the dominant item of which, worded, 'It's nice to know there are families like the Dales around today', was linked with two others: 'It reminds me of the importance of family ties', and 'It puts over a picture of what family life should be like'. Two other instances of a value-reinforcing relationship involving broadcast material may be noted. One of these emerged from the quiz study where a set of items expressive of a positive attitude to self-improvement and educational values generally was picked out by the analysis. The second was also found in *Dales* study and involved a valuation of the serial as a programme for women, including in this assessment an appreciation of its gentility and moral respectability in contrast to other media content deemed to emphasize sex and violence.

Surveillance

We have no empirical basis for subdividing this category which has been labelled in accordance with Lasswell's original classification of media functions (1948), although further research might make this necessary. As one would expect, our own work shows it to have an important place in news viewing dispositions. One large cluster included the following items:

> 'Television news provides food for thought'
> 'It tells me about the main events of the day'
> 'I like to see how big issues are finally sorted out'
> 'I follow the news so I won't be caught unawares by price increases and that sort of thing'
> 'Watching the news helps me to keep an eye on the mistakes people in authority make'
> 'Television news helps me to make my mind up about things'

Although the meaning of this cluster seems similar to that of the 'reality exploration' category, its main thrust is directed elsewhere – more towards having some information and opinions about events in the wider world of public affairs than towards stimuli for reflecting upon a set of more immediately experienced personal problems. In fact this very distinction was preserved in the analysis itself, since another cluster of attitudes to the news conveyed just such a more personal emphasis.

CONCLUSIONS

[. . .]

[I]t is unlikely that any universally valid structure of media–person interactions could ever be erected on an empirical basis, since the phenomena in question are to some extent variable according to changes in audience experience and perception and also to changes in communication content and differences of social context. But there is no reason why, with further research along the reported lines, a good deal more precision could not be attained. Moreover, we would be surprised if more extensive inquiry, using the same methods, were to necessitate a fundamental revision of the pattern we have located and described.

The main implications for the problems discussed at the outset of this essay are also fairly self-evident. If the typology is accepted as approximating to the true state of affairs, then the escapist formula, as it has often been applied to the television viewing experience, is clearly inadequate. For one thing the motives and satisfactions to which the term 'escape' has customarily been applied are far from exhaustive of audience orientations. Although we have grouped an important set of interactions under the heading of 'diversion' in our typology, it is clear that in many people these coexist with several other very important kinds of expectation and outlook.

[. . .]

Second, the relationship between content categories and audience needs is far less tidy and more complex than most commentators have appreciated. It is not just that most popular programmes are multi-dimensional in appeal. It is also the case that we have no single scale by which we can reliably attach a value to any given content category. Given the heterogeneity of materials transmitted over the broadcast media, not only is one man's meat another man's poison, but one man's source of escape from the real world is a point of anchorage for another man's place in it, defining or underlining certain features of his personality, of the problems he has encountered in daily living, and of the values he adheres to. There is neither a one-to-one correspondence between communication content and audience motivation, nor any such correspondence between the place on a presumed scale of cultural worth to which programme material may be assigned (according to prevailing standards of aesthetic judgement) and the depth of meanings that may be drawn from them by many of their most keen attenders.

And third, the supports of any sweepingly dismissive attitude to the popular viewing experience tend to crumble in so far as the predominently escapist interpretation of its meaning is successfully challenged. Of course mass communications research is still unable to shed much light on the lasting contributions made by time spent viewing television, but at least much of what they look for no longer seems quite so ignoble as depicted in the light of the escapist perspective.

But why should so many of the common assumptions about the television audience [. . .] have proven to be at odds with the evidence? Several explanations suggest themselves. An obvious one is the paucity in the past of the kind of data that might have better informed the views of critics and commentators. In addition, many vocal commentators are culturally disposed to adopt a superior attitude towards a popular medium like television, perhaps supposing that people deprived of the richness and diversity of the communication materials made available by literature, the arts, the specialist press and personal association with educated people, must simply go without altogether. In reality, people who, for whatever reason, lack access to multiple communication sources are much less functionally specific in their use of television; for them it is much more of an all-purpose medium than for the kinds of special population groups from which many critics and students of the mass media tend to be drawn. Finally, one must point to the dominance in television content of material which, on the face of it, is oriented to escape and diversion and which is often represented as such by its presenters because they believe that this will help to attract larger audiences. If one assumes a one-to-one relationship between the overt category of content and the kind of response it elicits, and if one also assumes a determining power in the media to shape audience response beyond what evidence and theory warrants, then the escapist interpretation becomes virtually inevitable. [. . .] The research we have described should pose a challenge to closed ways of thinking about mass communications. The typology which has emerged from it should provide a stimulus to further studies of the place of television in the lives of members of its audience.

REFERENCES

Herzog, H. (1940), 'Professor Quiz: A gratification study', in P. F. Lazarsfeld (ed.) *Radio and the Printed Page*, Duell, Sloan & Pearce.
Herzog, H. (1944), 'What do we really know about daytime serial listeners', in P. F. Lazarsfeld and F. N. Stanton (eds), *Radio Research, 1942–1943*, Duell, Sloan & Pearce.
Horton, D., and Wohl, R. (1956) 'Mass communication and para-social interaction', *Psychiat*, vol. 19, pp. 215–219.
Lasswell, H. D. (1948), 'The structure and function of communication in society', in L. Bryson (ed.), 1964, *The Communication of Ideas*, Institute for Religious and Social Studies, New York.
McQuitty, L. L. (1957), 'Elementary linkage analysis', *Educ. Psychol. Measurement*, vol. 17, pp. 207–29.
Riley, J., and Riley, M. W. (1951) 'A sociological approach to communications research', *Pub. Opinion Q.* vol. 15, pp. 445–60.

30

USES AND GRATIFICATIONS RESEARCH: A CRITIQUE

Philip Elliott

[. . .]

[The] distinction between size and satisfaction has dogged broadcast audience research from its infancy. In addition, research using traditional socio-demographic background variables has proved singularly unrevealing when applied to the consumption of the mass media and especially television. Research using such variables as education and social class has established that while people may differ in what they say they do, they differ very little in actual patterns of consumption behavior (Abrams, 1959, 1968; McQuail, 1970; Marplan, 1965; Steiner, 1963; Wilensky, 1964). But the main focus of empirical methods in social research is on explaining differences between groups. This has led to the proposition that there is a set of intervening variables between media output and media consumption that may provide more effective predictors of media behavior differences than crude classifications of output or demographic indicators.

This proposition links the various approaches to be found under the uses and gratifications heading. The proposition is most commonly formulated in psychological terms emphasizing the needs and gratifications experienced by the individual in the mass communication process, but there are also variants that appear to be more sociological and employ the language of functionalism (Rosengren and Windahl, 1972, 1973). There is some uncertainty within the approach about whether these internal states are independent, dependent, or intervening variables. There is also considerable variation in terminology and in whether explicit reference is made to needs as well as gratifications. In general, it seems that whereas the early studies carried out in the United States in the 1940s were content to deal with gratifications, more recent work has made more explicit reference to needs. Even so there are exceptions (Fearing, 1947). The trend, however, seems to be toward identifying general patterns of gratification and

From Philip Elliott, 'Uses and Gratifications Research: A Critique and Sociological Alternative', ch. 12 in Jay G. Blumler and Elihu Katz (eds), *The Uses of Mass Communications: Current Perspectives on Gratifications Research* (Beverly Hills: Sage, 1974).

need and using these as independent variables to explain media consumption (Katz, Blumler and Gurevitch, 1974).

The functional variant also relies on the concept of need (Rosengren and Windahl, 1972, 1973). Individuals experience basic human needs that may be met through media use or by other patterns of behavior. In this case there is less emphasis on the individual purposively using one channel in place of another to find his satisfaction. Rather the frustration of some natural way to satisfy a need will necessarily lead to the substitution of a 'functional alternative' – media consumption.

The concept of need is the source of most of the difficulties to be found in uses and gratifications research in general. In the psychological formulation individuals are allowed to identify their own needs or at least the gratifications from which needs may be inferred. The difficulty of providing independent evidence for the existence and importance of the intervening mental states and processes becomes more acute as they proliferate. The more one aspect of the process has to be used as evidence for another the more the argument becomes circular and unnecessarily complex. In both variants – use leads to the gratification of need or need leads to satisfaction through functional behavior – need is the residual factor and yet it is also put forward as an explanation for the process. As explanatory variables, 'needs' appear to exist outside time and space. In searching for 'basic human needs' the aim is to find needs that are true of human beings qua human beings. The basic concept tends to set the approach off in a direction that is too general, too static, and too asocial for it to be effectively redirected at a later stage by the reintroduction of social or psychological variables. Such variables are unlikely to turn out to be powerful predictors of need distribution and satisfaction if the needs themselves have been selected to represent the general human condition.

[. . .]

The uses and gratifications approach is basically *mentalistic*, relying as it does on intervening mental states and processes. But their introduction only adds to the confusion and circularity of the argument because their existence and importance can only be assessed indirectly. The approach is *individualistic* in the sense that it deals with intra-individual processes. These can then be generalized to aggregates of individuals, but they cannot be converted in any meaningful way into social structure and process. It is *empiricist*. The existence of the intervening states and processes appears to be proved by the methods used, but they may also be an artifact of these methods. Moreover, although there are exceptions in the literature, the methods are usually imposed upon the subjects rather than taken from them. Tests too often contain items that cannot be answered and that no self-respecting researcher would (or should) consider trying to answer himself.[1] As the approach is not informed by any initial social theory, findings have to be explained post hoc. Given an association between variables, the difficulty is to know what they mean.[2]

This lack of social theory contributes to another characteristic of the approach, its *static-abstraction*. The mass communication process is treated in isolation from any other social process. Social variables may be introduced at a late stage in the analysis, but these too are abstracted from the social context, posing once again the problem of meaning. The sampling and analysis techniques used ensure that respondents are wrenched from their social situation, from ongoing social process, from the groups and subcultures that provide a framework of meaning for their activities, especially in a symbolic field like media consumption.

Static-abstraction is largely responsible for another general problem with the approach – its *low explanatory power*. There seems to be an inverse relationship between the level of abstraction and generality of the studies and the interest of the results produced. Although uses and gratifications studies seem to have developed partly because demographic variables proved so ineffective in explaining different patterns of media consumption, uses and gratifications variables themselves have not so far been spectacularly revealing or effective. This may be because they are simply a more cumbersome way of tapping the original demographic variables.

Finally, the approach raises all the problems commonly associated with *functionalism*, and more besides, since it is based on a peculiarly individualistic variant of functionalism. Because of the inferences involved, the argument that use leads to the gratification of needs is at best circular and at worst imprisons research within a stable system of functional interdependencies from which there is no escape. Functionalism at the individual level is matched by a very generalized view of society. No attempt is made to differentiate between media or people on the basis of the interests they represent or the power they possess; no analysis is made in terms of the functions and dysfunctions for different power groups and their ideologies.[3] Dysfunctions, when they appear at all, tend to be negatively labelled phenomena which might prevent society (as a whole) from reaching its ideals, as for example the narcotizing dysfunction identified by Lazarsfeld and Merton (1948).

[. . .]

THEORY AND ASSUMPTIONS

[. . .]

[T]he idea of an active audience consciously selecting its media fare in order to maximize its gratifications, brings out the ideological ambiguities involved in this supposedly value-free approach. The idea of an active audience has its attractions when fitted into a broader model of the communication process. Overarching the stimulus-response model was the fear that the new media had put people and society directly at the mercy of those who controlled them. The idea of an active audience is apparently more optimistic. People are credited with more control over their own activities. [. . .] Active in this case means purposive. The activity of media consumption is directed toward the achievement of certain goals – the gratification of certain needs.

[. . .]

'Needs' are founded on the idea of deficit motivation, but, as Maslow (1964) has pointed out, this is only plausible when applied to basic or deficiency needs, cases where lack of satisfaction produces physiological consequences. Maslow contrasts these needs with the growth needs that motivate healthy people toward 'self-actualization (defined as ongoing actualization of potential capacities and talents, as fulfilment of mission . . . as a fuller knowledge of, and acceptance of, the person's own intrinsic nature, as an unceasing trend toward unity . . . within the person).' If we must talk of needs in relation to media consumption, then, it seems clear that they are growth needs, not deficiency needs, that they are learned, not innate, that media consumption is founded on growth rather than deficiency motivation. But learned needs are a product of social experience. In that case media consumption should be explained as part of a positive process of self-development taking place in a series of social situations.

To reject the idea of an active, purposive audience out of hand would be to adopt a completely determinist view. But the problem lies in the equation of goals and needs. To reinstate man as a conscious actor, it is only necessary to suggest that he orients his behavior toward the external world rather than internal mental states. To translate this into a verstehen perspective, the task then becomes one of identifying the social meaning of different media and their outputs for groups differentially located in society. This also sidesteps another difficulty with the goal-needs equation. Need-goals appear to operate outside time and space. On occasion they are used as if they were once for all properties of individuals forming a basis from which the media consumption behavior of groups with different needs can be assessed. At bottom there is something fundamentally illogical in the claim that basic human needs are differentially distributed through society; that this distribution can be explained by reference to social and psychological factors; and that the needs themselves will explain differences in behavior. What is more, there seems every reason to declare the needs redundant and to go back to social and psychological factors as direct explanations of behavior.

METHOD AND FINDINGS

[. . .]

If it can be shown that the methods of data collection themselves construct reality, and that the new processes identified coincide with and obscure ones that were already known, then the foundations are cut away from the impressive edifices of statistical analysis that are the tour de force of contemporary uses and gratifications researchers. [. . .] The argument that the methods used themselves construct reality rests on the type of questions commonly asked. The aim is to assess the importance of various need-goals to the respondent and the importance he attaches to different media and other types of behavior as means of achieving them. Both the need-goals and the media are selected on the assumption that they are important (Lundberg and Hultén, 1968; Kjellmor, 1973; Katz et al., 1973). In most cases respondents can only be differentiated according to the degree of importance they attach to goals and means.

Given the level of generality at which the questions are aimed, it is not surprising to find that people will subscribe to them. One can hardly reject truisms out of hand. The difficulty is whether they are truisms about the people – whether, for example, some people really have a greater need than others to avoid boredom – or whether they are truisms about the situations in which people find themselves – boredom varies according to situation and also according to the social meaning of the concept. But as soon as this possibility is introduced, it becomes clear that measuring boredom avoidance or indeed any other need-goal is liable to be a way of measuring variance in the social situation, or available social meanings, variance that could be more directly expressed in terms of familiar demographic variables.

For all their methodological ingenuity Rosengren and Windahl (1972, 1973) seem to have run into the same difficulty in their studies of mass media consumption as a functional alternative to actual interaction. Their claim that people less involved in actual interaction will become more involved in media consumption is backed up by data collected around four indices: degree of involvement in mass media output, interaction potential, actual interaction, and amount of mass media consumption. The names given to these indices make the argument sound plausible, but it must be questioned whether the first three indices are such discrete measures of newly identified phenomena as is suggested.

Degree of involvement, for example, is based on whether respondents answer in personal terms when asked what type of media output they like. The authors themselves recognize that the tendency to think in personal terms may be a class phenomenon. More than that, however, when dealing with television output there is more scope for giving a personal answer about entertainment programs which commonly include well-known stars, than about news or information programs. The whole notion of personal involvement has some problems when applied to newspapers, but answers in terms of local people seem much more likely to come from geographically stable, lower-class people with a local orientation to their community.

The construction of the next two indices, interaction potential and actual interaction, seems to confirm these suspicions that what we are really dealing with is a class phenomenon. Among the six indicators of interaction potential are education, car ownership, and leisure time. Actual interaction is based on the number of contacts at work and with friends outside. It seems, therefore, that the association between lack of interaction and degree of involvement can be translated into the more familiar terms that lower-class people tend to say they like entertainment programs (and tend to be locally oriented) more than middle-class.

Such a conclusion is the stock in trade of many uses and gratifications studies (Weiss, 1971).[4] It is also a reason why such research invites the accusation that it lacks explanatory power. The contrast between information and entertainment usually turns up in some guise as a classification both of media output and of audience need-goals. It is then not surprising to find that these differences in tastes, reported consumption behavior, or need-goals can in turn be related to social class and similar variables. It may be questioned, however, whether this is a step forward, since it is already known that, at least so far as television is concerned, it is reported behavior, not actual behavior, which differs along this dimension (Steiner, 1963; Marplan, 1965; Wilensky, 1964). Uses and gratifications researchers often make a virtue out of the fact that they have to rely on their respondents' ability to recognize and verbalize their needs and gratifications. It may be a good thing to trust people, but it is naive to suppose that people can give answers as if they were in a social vacuum. The various media and the consumption behaviors associated with them are already socially stratified (Murdock and McCron, 1973). Their social meaning will be clear to people and so too will the social meaning of the associated need-goals.

[. . .]

CRITIQUE – POLICY IMPLICATIONS

The uses and gratifications approach is commonly put forward as an advance on traditional 'head-counting' techniques of broadcast audience research (Emmett, 1968). The substance of this claim was questioned in the previous section. But the claim also includes the idea that measuring audience gratifications and needs would provide more useful data to guide broadcasting policy. Audience figures have an accepted place in program planning. We may all agree that broadcasters should know more about their audience, but it seems unlikely that they will learn much from uses and gratifications data. The approach is effectively neutered by its assumptions.

The difficulty stems from the basic tautology that use leads to gratification. Different gratifications may be identified independently of use, but there is no way of distinguishing between them according to the level of satisfaction they supply. The difficulty is well illustrated by the few references to dysfunctions that are to be found in the uses and gratifications literature. In most cases dysfunctions are types of gratifications that the researchers suppose will have harmful consequences for society. At the individual level, to label some gratifications functional, others dysfunctional, would clearly be to reintroduce the critical judgments of popular culture theorists by the back door. But the social dysfunctions identified have no firmer basis, especially so long as they are applied to society as a whole or to the general quality of life within it. Thus the only basis for policy is to decide normatively which gratifications should be encouraged, which suppressed.[5]

This problem also underlies Brian Emmett's scheme to replace the maximization of audience size with the maximization of audience satisfaction. If audience satisfaction can be concluded from use, it is just as effective to count heads. If not, then some place will have to be found in the uses and gratifications approach for dissatisfaction. But even if it were, the fundamental difficulty would remain. Different types of gratification are not additive. It may also be questioned how far they are stable entities dependent directly on media content, as Emmett's model would suppose. Taking the view that media consumption is a specifically situated, social process, on the other hand, would suggest that gratification depends on a dynamic relationship between the individual and his whole social environment. Of course the problem could always be sidestepped by throwing the onus on the long-suffering respondents and asking them to provide a general satisfaction score. While the respondent tries to work out what he is being asked, the researcher will have time to pause and wonder what the answer will be worth when he gets it. Uses and gratifications research is effectively hoist with its own petard. Research has led to 'a growing consensus that almost any type of content may serve practically any type of function' (Rosengren and Windahl, 1972), but research cannot produce any criteria for differentiating between them.

Having argued that the approach provides no basis for policy making, it may seem perverse, if not illogical, to go on to argue that if it were used, its effect would be positively harmful. But this follows given the tautological and functional assumptions behind the approach. In themselves, uses and gratifications data can only point in one direction, toward a justification of the present situation. One example is the finding cited above that any content may serve any function (yield a variety of gratifications). In other words, the audience may not be getting what was intended from media output, but at least they are getting something.

Another example may be taken from Katz, Blumler and Gurevitch's (1974) attempt to defuse the radical critique of mass communications as a dysfunctional 'latter-day opiate of the masses' by suggesting that uses and gratifications research would be peculiarly suited to exploring the supposed 'media-output audience-satisfaction nexus.' The implication is that 'dysfunction' as used here is simply a negative evaluation, as it would be in the uses and gratifications approach itself. It rests, however, on a social analysis in which it is seen to be in the interests of those controlling the media to distract others in society from a true recognition of their own interests. If the media-output audience-satisfaction nexus were explored in uses and gratifications terms, the only possible conclusion would be that the audience was getting something out of it. But that is not in dispute. The issue in dispute is whose interests are being served in the process, and that is an issue which the approach itself is powerless to elucidate.

Nordenstreng (1970) raised the same issue when he pointed out that needs develop within the existing social structure and so that any approach based on identifying such needs would inevitably provide support for the status quo. The conclusion to be drawn from this critique is not that individual opinions do not matter, as Katz, Blumler and Gurevitch interpret it, but that some prior analysis of social structure is necessary to know what such opinions are worth. The quest to identify functions for 'society as a whole' or basic underlying human needs must inevitably rule out any consideration of the differential distribution of power and opportunity in society, of the conflict of interests between different groups, and of the development and use of different ideologies to protect them.

[. . .]

NOTES

1.   For example, 'How important is it for you to understand the true quality of our leaders?' or 'How important is it for you to feel satisfied with the way of life in Israel as compared with other countries?' (Katz et al., 1973).

2.   For example, in describing the correlates of a tendency to seek 'excitement' from quiz program viewing, McQuail et al. (1972) state that 'The highest scoring group consisted of working-class viewers who were late-born children of large families. While the significance of the role of family background here is not clear. . . . ' And, in presenting data from a functional study of children's media uses, Brown et al. (1973) write: 'As with the earlier table we cannot attempt to explain many of the findings. Instead we will conclude by offering a few conjectures which might help to integrate and explain the somewhat disjointed data presented.'

3.   Thus 'not all effects of mass communication are germane to functional analysis, only those which are relevant and important if the system under analysis is to continue to function normally' (Wright, 1960).

4.   The same argument, that uses and gratifications concepts only work because class relationships are already built into them, applies especially to Schramm, Lyle and Parker (1961).

5.   Emmett (1968) recognizes this: ' . . . one other matter has to be considered. That is the relative importance, or weight, to be given to the gratification of various needs. The decision about these weights is crucial, since they ultimately determine the solution. It is not too extreme to say that they must encapsulate the philosophy or value system of the organisation. . . . '

REFERENCES

Abrams, M. (1968) Education, Social Class and Readership of Newspapers and Magazines. London: JICNARS.

Abrams, M. (1959) 'The mass media and social class in Great Britain.' Paper presented at the Fourth World Congress of Sociology, Stresa, Italy.

Brown, J. R., J. K. Cramond, and R. J. Wilde (1973) 'Children's use of the mass media: a functional approach.' Paper presented at the Annual Conference of the Social Psychology Section of the British Psychological Society, Bristol.

Emmett, B. P. (1968) 'A new role for research in broadcasting.' Public Opinion Quarterly 32: 654–665.

Fearing, F. (1947) 'Influence of the movies on attitudes and behaviour.' Annals of the American Academy of Political and Social Science 254: 70–80.

Katz, E., J. G. Blumler, and M. Gurevitch (1974) 'Utilization of mass communication by the individual: an overview,' in J. G. Blumler and E. Katz (eds) The Uses of Mass Communications: Current Perspectives on Gratifications Research. Beverly Hills: Sage.

Katz, E., M. Gurevitch, and H. Haas (1973) 'On the use of the mass media for important things.' American Sociological Review 38 (April): 164–181.

Kjellmor, S. (1973) 'Basic subjective broadcasting media functions.' Paper presented to the Stockholm Conference on Uses and Gratifications Studies.

Lazarsfeld, P. F. and R. K. Merton (1948) 'Mass communication, popular taste and organized social action,' [abridged as Chapter 1 of this volume] in B. Rosenberg and D. M. White (eds) Mass Culture – The Popular Arts in America. New York: Free Press, 1957.

Lundberg, D. and O. Hulten (1968) Individen och Mass Media. Stockholm: Norstedts.

McQuail, D. (1970) 'The audience for television plays,' in J. Tunstall (ed.) Media Sociology. London: Constable.

McQuail, D., J. G. Blumler, and J. R. Brown (1972) 'The television audience: a revised perspective,' [abridged as Chapter 29 of this volume] in D. McQuail (ed.) Sociology of Mass Communications. Harmondsworth: Penguin.

Marplan Ltd. (1965) Report on a Study of Television and the Managerial and Professional Classes. London: ITA.

Maslow, A. B. (1964) 'Deficiency motivation and growth motivation,' in R. C. Teevan and R. C. Birney (eds) Theories of Motivation in Personality and Social Psychology. London: Van Norstrand.

Murdock, G. and R. McCron (1973) 'Scoobies, skins and contemporary pop.' New Society (March 29).

Nordenstreng, K. (1970) 'Comments on "gratifications research" in broadcasting.' Public Opinion Quarterly 34: 130–132.

Rosengren, K. E. and S. Windahl (1973) 'Mass media use: causes and effects.' Lund. (mimeo)

Rosengren, K. E. and S. Windahl (1972) 'Mass media consumption as a functional alternative,' in D. McQuail (ed.) Sociology of Mass Communications. Harmondsworth: Penguin.

Schramm, W., J. Lyle, and E. B. Parker (1961) Television in the Lives of Our Children. Stanford: Stanford University Press.

Steiner, G. A. (1963) The People Look at Television. New York: Knopf.

Weiss, W. (1971) 'Mass Communications.' Annual Review of Psychology 22.

Wilensky, H. (1964) 'Mass society and mass culture: interdependence or independence.' American Sociological Review 29, 2: 173–197.

Wright, C. R. (1960) 'Functional analysis and mass communication.' Public Opinion Quarterly 24: 605–620.

Further Reading

Belson, W., *The Impact of Television* (London: Crosby Lockwood, 1967).

Blumler, J. G. and Katz, E., *The Uses of Mass Communications: Current Perspectives on Gratifications Research* (London: Sage, 1974).

Blumler, J. G. and McQuail, D., *Television in Politics: Its Uses and Influence* (London: Faber & Faber, 1968).

Chaney, D., *Processes of Mass Communication* (London: Macmillan, 1972).

Halloran, J. D., *The Effects of Mass Communication; with Special Reference to Television* (Leicester: Leicester University Press, 1964).

Halloran, J. D. (ed.), *The Effects of Television* (London: Panther Books, 1970).

Halloran, J. D., Elliott, P. and Murdock, G., *Demonstrations and Communication: A Case Study* (Harmondsworth: Penguin, 1970).

Himmelweit, H., 'A Theoretical Framework for the Consideration of the Effects of Television – a British Report', *Journal of Social Issues* XVIII: 2 (1962) pp. 16–27.

Himmelweit, H., Oppenheim, A. and Vince, P., *Television and the Child* (London: Oxford University Press, 1958).

Howitt, D. and Cumberbatch, G., *Mass Media, Violence and Society* (New York: John Wiley, 1975).

Klapper, J. T., *The Effects of Mass Communication* (New York: Free Press, 1960).

Lazarsfeld, P. F. and Stanton, F. N. (eds), *Radio Research 1942–3* (New York: Duell, Sloan & Pearce, 1944).

Lazarsfeld, P. F. and Stanton, F. N. (eds), *Communications Research 1948–9* (New York: Harper & Bros., 1949).

McQuail, D., *Towards a Sociology of Mass Communications* (London: Collier Macmillan, 1969).

McQuail, D. (ed.), *Sociology of Mass Communications* (Harmondsworth: Penguin, 1972).

McQuail, D., 'The Influence and Effects of Mass Media', in Curran, J., Gurevitch, M. and Woollacott, J. (eds), *Mass Communication and Society* (London: Edward Arnold, 1977).

McQuail, D., *Mass Communication Theory: An Introduction*, 2nd edn (London: Sage, 1983).

Trenaman, J., 'The Effects of Television', *Twentieth Century*, Nov. (1959) pp. 332–42.

Trenaman, J. and McQuail, D., *Television and the Political Image* (London: Methuen, 1961).

Tunstall, J. (ed.), *Media Sociology: A Reader* (London: Constable, 1970).

Reception
The Politics of Reading

Reception: The Politics of Reading

In Stuart Hall's introduction to the six chapters on media studies included in the 1980 Birmingham CCCS collection, *Culture, Media, Language*, he outlines the 'paradigm break' which differentiates this work from earlier traditions of 'mass-communications research'. Work at the Centre, he writes,

> broke with the models of 'direct influence' – using a sort of stimulus-response model with heavily behaviourist overtones, media content serving as a trigger – into a framework which drew much more on what can broadly be defined as the 'ideological' role of the media. This latter approach defined the media as a major cultural and ideological force, standing in a dominant position with respect to the way in which social relations and political problems were defined and the production and transformation of popular ideologies in the audience addressed.[1]

As a result, this work also 'broke with the passive and undifferentiated conceptions of the "audience"' which had dominated earlier research, replacing them 'with a more active conception of the "audience", of "reading" and of the relation between how media messages were encoded, the "moment" of the encoded text and the variations of audience "decodings"'.[2] This account has been criticised as over-simplistic,[3] but it nevertheless signals a decisively different approach to the study of the audience from those represented in preceding chapters of this book, one which begins from *overtly* theoretical and political concerns.[4] Hall's encoding/decoding model (see Chapter 5), further developed by David Morley in *Reconceptualizing the Audience*,[5] provided the theoretical model, which Morley's empirical research into audience readings of the BBC's early evening magazine programme *Nationwide* would seek to test. The television audience, writes Morley, must be seen as

> clusters of socially situated individual readers, whose individual readings will be framed by shared cultural formations and practices pre-existent to the individual: shared 'orientations' which will in turn be determined by factors derived from the objective position of the individual reader in the class structure.[6]

Chapter 31 is David Morley's (1983) account of the theoretical context, the methods, and the findings of his study of *The 'Nationwide' Audience*. Morley's starting point is the 'potential disjuncture between the codes of those sending and those receiving messages' through the mass media. This 'disjuncture' is a product of power structures within society, and 'the subcultures and codes inhabited by different classes and class fractions within British society'.

The meaning of a text, then, 'cannot be "read off" straight from textual characteristics'; it must be 'interpreted in terms of which set of discourses it encounters in any particular set of circumstances'. Morley's project, therefore, set out to analyse the discourse of 'Nationwide', and then to study the readings made of the programme by 29 groups drawn from different social backgrounds. The framework he used was that proposed by Stuart Hall: audience decodings would fall into the 'preferred/dominant', the 'negotiated' or the 'oppositional' category. Morley's research, however, produced complex results. A 'multiplicity of discourses' was evident in the groups' decodings, and it was clear that 'social position in no way directly, or unproblematically, correlates with decoding'. Nevertheless, Morley concludes, these 'different responses and interpretations' should not be read 'in terms of individual psychologies'; they are the product of 'cultural differences embedded within the structure of society'. With a more complex 'cultural map of the audience', we shall be able to see how textual codes interact with those of audience groupings to produce a range of 'social meanings'.

Chapter 32 comes from Dorothy Hobson's ethnographic study of women's media consumption, published in 1980, which forms part of the feminist challenge to the class-based model of audience decodings developed by Hall and Morley. In her study, Hobson found that her respondents made a clear distinction between programmes which they saw as constituting the 'woman's world' – comedy series, soap operas, American television drama, light entertainment and quiz shows, and films – and those which they saw as constituting the 'man's world' – news, current affairs, scientific programmes and programmes dealing with politics or war, whether documentary or fiction. They were equally firm in their rejection of the latter group, seeing only 'topics which can be regarded as of "domestic" interest' as 'important or interesting'. Despite this, however, the women accepted the 'masculine' programmes as *more important* than their own. Hobson concludes, then, in findings which foreshadow Morley's conclusions in his 1986 *Family Television*, that the 'ideology of femininity' both over-determines the women's choice of programmes and is '*reproduced* and *reinforced*' by the narrative structures of these programmes. In Morley's words, the women 'accept the terms of a masculine hegemony' which the programmes themselves reinforce.[7]

Recent years have seen the increasing use within 'mainstream' uses and gratifications research of the 'qualitative' research methods developed within cultural studies. Against this proposed 'convergence of antagonistic traditions',[8] Ien Ang's 1989 chapter (Chapter 33) offers a forceful reassertion of their fundamental incompatibility. Despite a certain commonality of research questions and methods of enquiry, there are, Ang insists, fundamental differences between the two approaches 'not only in epistemological, but also in theoretical and political attitudes towards the aim and status of doing empirical research'. Uses and gratifications research, she argues, is conceptualised as a 'scientific' enterprise, whose aim is to 'categorize[ ], systematize[ ], and explain[ ]' its object of study, 'the audience'. Its findings aspire to the status of 'total knowledge' and objective 'truth'. The purposes of cultural studies approaches are very different. Cultural studies scholars are concerned with issues of social and cultural power, seeing media consumption as a 'site of struggle' over meanings and pleasures. The cultural studies researcher is therefore engaged in the process of *interpretation*, in a 'dialectic between the empirical and the theoretical' which is always political. What are produced in this encounter between researcher and informants are 'historically and culturally specific' knowledges and interpretations, inevitably incomplete and partial. To interpret recent developments in audience research as a convergence of the two traditions is therefore to 'misconceive the issues at stake'.

NOTES

1. Hall, 'Introduction to Media Studies at the Centre', in S. Hall, D. Hobson, A. Lowe and P. Willis (eds), *Culture, Media, Language* (London: Hutchinson, 1980) p. 117.

2. Ibid. p. 118.

3. See James Curran's criticism of David Morley's 1989 version of this 'history' in 'The New Revisionism in Mass Communication Research: A Reappraisal', *European Journal of Communication* 5 (1990) pp. 146ff.

4. As Curran, Gurevitch and Woollacott point out, 'empirical communications research is based upon theoretical models of society even if these are often unexamined and unstated'. See J. Curran, M. Gurevitch and J. Woollacott, 'The Study of the Media: Theoretical Approaches', in M. Gurevitch, T. Bennett, J. Curran and J. Woollacott (eds), *Culture, Society and the Media* (London: Methuen, 1982) p. 15.

5. D. Morley, *Reconceptualizing the Audience*, CCCS Stencilled Paper, no. 9.

6. D. Morley, *The 'Nationwide' Audience* (London: BFI, 1980) p. 15.

7. D. Morley, *Family Television: Cultural Power and Domestic Leisure* (London: Comedia, 1986) p. 161.

8. This phrase is taken from Kim Christian Schroder, 'Convergence of Antagonistic Traditions? The Case of Audience Research', *European Journal of Communication* 2 (1987) pp. 7–31.

31

CULTURAL TRANSFORMATIONS: THE POLITICS OF RESISTANCE

David Morley

Mattelart has pointed to the fact that forms of popular resistance to, and subversion of, dominant cultures have rarely been studied. The point here, he argues, is that while the 'receiver' of communications is often considered as a passive consumer of information or leisure commodities, it is nonetheless true that the audience does not necessarily read the messages sent to it within the cultural code of the transmitters. The way in which the subaltern groups and classes in a society reinterpret and make sense of these messages is therefore a crucial problem for any theory of communications as a mode of cultural domination. At the macro level of international cultural relations, he argues, the consequences of a message being interpreted in a different way from what its senders intended may be quite radical. He asks:

> In how many countries do the Aryan heroes of the television series, Mission Impossible, fighting against the rebels, undergo a process of identification which is the exact opposite of that intended by the imperialist code, and how often are they viewed as the 'bad guys' in the story? (Mattelart & Siegelaub 1979, p. 27)

Mattelart warns that any notions of ideological domination must be employed with great care and recommends that the idea that imperialism invades different sectors of society in a uniform way be abandoned in favour of an analysis of the particular milieux which favour or resist penetration.

In the domestic context, the argument alerts us to the relation between the dominant ideological forms of the media, and the subcultures and codes inhabited by different classes and class fractions within British society.

[. . .]

This is to argue that the structures of imperialism and of class domination, when introduced into the study of communications, pose the problem of audience responses to and interpretations of the mass media as a critical area of research.

From H. Davis and P. Walton (eds), *Language, Image, Media* (Oxford: Blackwell, 1983) pp. 104–117.

COMMUNICATIONS: A BROKEN CIRCUIT?

We are faced with a situation in which there is a potential disjunction between the codes of those sending and those receiving messages through the circuit of mass communications (cf. Hall 1973, pp. 18–19; Eco 1972, p. 121). The problem of (non-)complementarity of codes at the production and reception ends of the chain of communications is indissolubly linked with the problem of cultural domination and resistance. In a research project on Nationwide (a popular current affairs magazine programme on BBC television), we attempted to pose this as a specific problem about the degree of complementarity between the codes of the programme and the interpretative codes of various sociocultural groups (Brunsdon & Morley 1978; Morley 1980). We were concerned to explore the extent to which decodings take place within the limits of the preferred (or dominant) manner in which the message has been initially encoded. However, there is a complementary aspect to this problem, namely the extent to which these interpretations, or decodings, also reflect, and are inflected by, the codes and discourses which different sections of the audience inhabit, and the ways in which these decodings are determined by the socially governed distribution of cultural codes between and across different sections of the audience – that is, the range of decoding strategies and competencies in the audience.

To raise this as a problem for research is already to argue that the meaning produced by the encounter of text and subject cannot be 'read off' straight from textual characteristics. The text cannot be considered in isolation from its historical conditions of production and consumption. And an analysis of media ideology cannot rest with an analysis of production and text alone.

[. . .]

Thus the meaning of the text must be interpreted in terms of which set of discourses it encounters in any particular set of circumstances, and how this encounter may restructure both the meaning of the text and the discourses which it meets. The meaning of the text will be constructed differently according to the discourses (knowledges, prejudices, resistances etc.) brought to bear by the reader, and the crucial factor in the encounter of audience/subject and text will be the range of discourses at the disposal of the audience. The crucial point here is that individuals in different positions in the social formation defined according to structures of class, race or sex, for example, will tend to inhabit or have at their disposal different codes and subcultures. Thus social position sets parameters to the range of potential readings by structuring access to different codes.

Whether or not a programme succeeds in transmitting the preferred or dominant meaning will depend on whether it encounters readers who inhabit codes and ideologies derived from other institutional areas (e.g. churches or schools) which correspond to and work in parallel with those of the programme or whether it encounters readers who inhabit codes drawn from other areas or institutions (e.g. trade unions or 'deviant' subcultures) which conflict to a greater or lesser extent with those of the programme.

[. . .]

THE MESSAGE: ENCODING AND DECODING

In outline, the premises on which we base our approach are as follows:

a The production of a meaningful message in television discourse is always problematic 'work'. The same event can be encoded in more than one way.

b The message in social communication is always complex in structure and form. It always contains more than one potential 'reading'. Messages propose and prefer certain readings over others, but they cannot be entirely closed around one reading: they remain polysemic.

c The activity of 'getting meaning' from the message is also problematic practice, however transparent and natural it may seem. Messages encoded in one way can also be read in a different way.

Thus, the communicative form and structure of the encoded message can be analysed in terms of its preferred reading: the mechanisms which prefer one, dominant reading over the other readings; the means which the encoder uses to try to win the assent of the audience to his particular reading of the message. Special attention can be given here to the control exercised over meaning, and to 'points of identification' within the message which transmit the preferred reading to the audience.

It is precisely the aim of the presenter to achieve identification with the audience through mechanisms which gain the audience's complicity and 'suggest' preferred readings. If and when these identificatory mechanisms are attenuated or broken, will the message be decoded in a different framework of meaning from that in which it was encoded? Broadcasters undoubtedly make the attempt to establish a relationship of complicity with the audience (Brunsdon & Morley 1978) but there is no justification for assuming that the attempt will always be successful.

THE STRUCTURE OF THE AUDIENCE: DECODINGS IN CULTURAL CONTEXT

We might profitably think of the media audience not so much as an undifferentiated mass of individuals but as a complex structure of socially organized individuals in a number of overlapping subgroups and subcultures, each with its own history and cultural traditions. This is not to see cultural competence as automatically determined or generated by social position but to pose the problem of the relation between, on the one hand, social categories and social structure and, on the other, codes, subcultures and ideologies. In this perspective the primary relationships for analysis are those between linguistic and cultural codes and patterns of class (cf. Bernstein 1971; Rosen 1972), race (cf. Labov 1969) and sex (cf. Lakoff 1976; Spender 1980). We are therefore proposing a model of the audience, not as an atomized mass of individuals, but as composed of a number of subcultural formations or groupings whose members will share a cultural orientation towards decoding messages in particular ways. Individual members' readings will be framed by shared cultural formations and practices. Such shared 'orientations' will in turn be determined by factors derived from the objective position of the individual reader in the social structure. These objective factors must be seen as setting parameters to individual experience although not determining consciousness in a mechanistic way: people understand their situation and react to it by way of subcultures and meaning systems (Critcher 1975).

Bernstein's work on sociolinguistic codes and his hypothesis of a correlation between particular social (class) categories and codes is of obvious relevance to any theory of the media audience, in terms of how different sections of that audience may relate to different kinds of messages – perhaps through the employment of different codes of interpretation. However, Bernstein's scheme is highly simplified: it contains only two classes (working and middle) and two codes (restricted and elaborated), and no attempt is made to differentiate within these classes, nor within their 'corresponding' codes.

[. . .]

Bernstein's oversimplistic formulation of the relation between classes and cultural codes, and his neglect of cultural differentiation within classes, is to some extent paralleled in Parkin's attempt to produce a typology of 'meaning systems' in relation to class structure. Parkin's treatment of class structures as the ground of different meaning systems (1971, ch. 3) is a fruitful if crude point of departure which provided some basic categories for Hall's (1973) hypotheses about typical decoding positions. The key question at issue is that of the nature of the fit between, say, class, socioeconomic or educational position and interpretative codes.

Following, but adapting Parkin, we have suggested three hypothetical-typical positions which the decoder may occupy in relation to the encoded message. He or she may take the meaning fully within the interpretative framework which the message itself proposes and 'prefers': if so, decoding proceeds within, or is aligned with, the dominant or 'hegemonic' code. Second, decoders may take the meaning broadly as encoded; but by relating the message to some concrete, located or situational context which reflects their position and interests, they may modify or partially inflect the meaning. Following Parkin, we would call this a 'negotiated' position. Third, the decoder may recognize how the message has been contextually encoded, but bring to bear an alternative frame of interpretation, which sets aside the encoding framework and superimposes on the message an interpretation which works in a directly oppositional way – an oppositional, or 'counter-hegemonic' decoding.

Parkin elaborated these positions as three possible and typical positions of different classes in relation to a class-based hegemonic ideology. We have transposed them in order to describe possible alternative ways of decoding ideologically constructed messages. Of course, Parkin's conceptual framework is limited in that it provides only a statement of the three logical possibilities: that a given section of the audience may either share, partly share, or not share the dominant code in which the message has been transmitted (Morley 1974). If the three basic decoding positions have any sociological validity it will necessarily be at the very broad level of what one might call class competencies in the reading of ideological messages. Even at this level, further distinctions may have to be made: for example between a version of the negotiated position which reflects a deferential stance towards the use of the hegemonic code, or one which reflects a subordinate stance, as defined by Parkin, where messages cast at a general or abstract level are subject to negotiation when referred to a more limited or sectional interest.

Much of the important work in this respect consists in differentiating Parkin's catch-all category of 'negotiated code' into a set of empirically grounded subvariants of this basic category, which are illustrated in the sociological work on different forms of sectional and corporate consciousness (cf. Parkin 1971; Mann 1973; Nichols & Armstrong 1976). The crucial development from this perspective has been the attempt to translate Parkin's three ideal types (which are themselves a considerable advance on any model which sees the audience as an unstructured aggregate of individuals) into a more sensitive model of actual decoding positions within the media audience.

There remains, however, one critical problem in the attempt to integrate the sociological work of authors such as Parkin into a theory of communications. This is the tendency to directly convert social categories (e.g. class) into meanings (e.g. ideological positions) without attending to the specific factors which govern this conversion. It is simply inadequate to present demographic and sociological factors such as age, sex, race or class position as objective correlates or determinants of differential decoding positions without any attempt to specify *how* they intervene in the process of communication. The relative autonomy of signifying practices means that sociological factors cannot be 'read in' directly as affecting the communication process. These factors can only have effect through the (possibly contradictory) action of the discourses in which they are articulated.

AUDIENCES AND IDEOLOGIES: METHODOLOGICAL AND EMPIRICAL QUESTIONS

I will now attempt to illustrate some of these theoretical arguments by drawing on material from the Nationwide research project (see Brunsdon & Morley 1978 and Morley 1980 for a full account of this project). The research was designed to provide an analysis of the programme discourse and then to ascertain which sections of the programme's audience decoded in line with the preferred/dominant codes, and which sections operated negotiated/oppositional decodings.

Two videotaped Nationwide programmes were shown to 29 groups drawn from different social and cultural backgrounds, and from different levels of the educational system. Our procedure was to gain entry to a situation where the group already had some existence as a social entity – at least for the duration of a course. The videotape showings and the subsequent interviews were arranged to slot into the context of their established institutional settings as far as possible.

The groups usually consisted of between five and ten people. After the viewing session the discussion was taperecorded (usually about 40 mins duration) and this was later transcribed in full to provide the basic data for the analysis. The project used the 'focused interview' method originally developed by Merton and Kendall (1946). Thus the interviews began with non-directive prompting designed to establish the 'working vocabulary' (Mills 1939) and frame of reference of the groups, and the order of priority in which *they* raised issues, before moving on to a more structured set of questions based on our programme analysis.

We were particularly concerned to identify the nature of the groups' 'lexico-referential systems' (Mills 1939) and to examine how these systems related to those employed by the broadcasters. Our questions were designed to reveal whether audiences used the same words in the same ways as the broadcasters, in discussing different topics in the programme; whether the groups ranked issues and topics in the same order of priority as that given in the programme discourse; and whether there were aspects of topics not discussed by the broadcasters that were specifically mentioned by these groups. The decision to work with group rather than individual interviews followed from our desire to explore the extent to which individual 'readings' are shaped by the sociocultural groupings within which they are situated.

We attempted to work as far as possible with the raw data of actual speech instead of trying to convert responses into immediately categorizable forms. Although this choice raised problems which we cannot claim in any sense to have solved, it did allow us to bring into focus the question of the relation between the forms of speech employed by broadcasters and those employed by respondents.

[. . .]

CLASSES, CODES, DECODINGS

The problematic proposed here does not attempt to derive decodings directly from social class position or 'reduce' them to it. It is always a question of how social position, as it is articulated through particular discourses, produces specific kinds of readings or decodings. These readings can then be seen to be patterned by the way in which the structure of access to different discourses is determined by social position. The question is which cultural repertoires and codes are available to which groups, and how do they utilize these symbolic resources in their attempt to make sense of messages coming from the media?

Although the project as a whole investigated decodings made by groups across a range of class positions, I shall, in order to focus the comparisons more sharply, deal here only with the differences between the decodings made by three kinds of groups, all sharing a roughly similar working-class position or background. These groups were, first, young apprentice engineers and metallurgists, second, groups of trade union officials and of shop stewards, and third, young black students at a college of further education.

Of these groups it was the apprentices who most closely inhabited the dominant code of the programme. Their decodings were mostly closely in line with the dominant/preferred meanings of Nationwide. This seemed to be accounted for by the extent to which the lads' use of a form of populist discourse ('damn all politicians – they're all as bad as each other . . . it's all down to the individual in the end, isn't it?') was quite compatible with that of the programme. Although the dominant tone of these groups' responses to Nationwide was one of cynicism, a resistance to anyone 'putting one over' on them, most of the main items in the programme were, in fact, decoded by these groups within the dominant framework or preferred reading established by the programme. They tended to accept the perspectives offered by and through the programme's presenter. The situation here seems to be the converse of that outlined by Parkin: here we have working-class groups who cynically claim to be distanced from the programme at a general level but who accept and reproduce its ideological formulations of specific issues. The 'commonsense' interpretations which the programme's presenters offer seem 'pretty obviously OK' to these groups too, and Nationwide's questions are justified as 'natural' or 'obvious' – and therefore unproblematic: 'They just said the obvious comment didn't they?'

The groups involved in the activities and discourse of trade unionism produced differently inflected versions of negotiated and oppositional decodings, depending on their social position and positioning in educational and political discourses. There is a profound difference between the groups who are non-union, or are simply members of trade unions, and those with an active involvement in and commitment to trade unionism – the latter producing much more negotiated or oppositional readings of Nationwide. So the structure of decoding is not a simple function of class position, but rather the result of differential involvement and positioning in discourse formations.

Further, there are the significant differences between the articulate, fully oppositional readings produced by the shop stewards as compared with the negotiated/oppositional readings produced by the trade union officials. This, we would suggest, is to be accounted for by the greater distancing of the stewards from the pressures of incorporation which full-time officials experience, which thus allows them to inhabit a more 'left-wing' interpretation of trade unionism.

The trade union officials on the whole inhabit a dominant/populist inflected version of negotiated code and espouse a right-wing Labour perspective. They are regular Nationwide watchers and approve both the programme's mode of address and ideological stance – 'I find that quite interesting . . . here's something in that programme for everyone to have a look at . . . '; 'It seems to be a programme acceptable to the vast majority of people.' They accept the individualistic theme of the programme and accept the programme's construction of an undifferentiated national community which is currently suffering economic hardship: to this extent they can be said to identify with the national 'we' which the programme discourse

constructs. However, this is at an abstract and general level: at a more concrete, local level –
that of directly economic 'trade union' issues – they take a more critical stance, and specific
items within this category are then decoded in a more oppositional way (the classic structure
of the negotiated code).

It is the shop stewards who spontaneously produce by far the most articulate, fully
oppositional reading of the programme. They reject the programme's attempt to tell us what
'our grouse' is and its attempt to construct a national 'we' – 'They want "*we*" . . . they want the
average viewer to all think "we" . . .' And they identify this Nationwide form of presentation
as part of a general pattern: 'I mean, take Nationwide, add the *Sun* . . . the *Mirror* and the *Daily
Express* to it . . .' This is a pattern in which: 'Union leaders are always being told "You're ruining
the country!"' '

Finally, the black students made hardly any connection with the discourse of Nationwide.
The concerns and the cultural framework of Nationwide are simply not the concerns of their
world. They do not so much produce an oppositional reading as refuse to 'read' it at all. These
groups are so totally alienated from the discourse of Nationwide that their response is in the
first instance 'a critique of silence'. In a sense they fail, or refuse, to engage with the discourse of
the programme enough to deconstruct or redefine it. They are clear that it's not a programme
for them, it's for 'older people, middle-class people'; it doesn't deal with their specific interests
– 'Why didn't they never interview Bob Marley?' – and it fails to live up to their standards of
'good TV' defined in terms of enjoyment and entertainment (in which terms Today and ITV in
general are preferred to Nationwide and BBC).

To this group Nationwide is 'so boring' it's not interesting at all': they 'don't see how
anyone could watch it'. There is a disjunction between the discourse of their own culture and
that, not simply of Nationwide in particular, but of the whole field of 'serious TV' ('BBC is
definitely boring') and of party politics ('God that's rubbish'). Moreover, these groups reject
the descriptions of their life offered by the programme. They can find no point of identification
within the programme's discourse about the problems of families in Britain today – a discourse
into which, the programme presenters have claimed, 'most people in Britain' should fit. Their
particular experience of family structures among the black, working-class, inner city community
is simply not accounted for. The programme's picture of family life is as inappropriate to them
as that offered in a 'Peter and Jane' reading scheme:

> It didn't show one-parent families . . . the average family in a council estate – all these
> people seemed to have cars, their own home . . . property . . . Don't they ever think of
> the average family?

Now this is precisely what Nationwide would claim to think of: the point here is that the
representation of 'the family' within the discourse of Nationwide has no purchase on the
representation of that field within the discourse and experience of these groups – and is
consequently rejected.

However these are statements at the level of gross differences of orientation between the
groups, and they should not blind us to the differences, divisions and overlaps which occur
within and among these groups. For example, although the apprentice groups were generally
in sympathy with the programme and identified with the perspectives on events offered by
its presenters, they did at times find it hard to relate to the programme's style of presentation
or 'mode of address' (Neale 1977). At this point they frequently invoked Nationwide's ITV
competitor as being 'more of a laugh' or 'better entertainment' and were, to this extent,
alienated from the discourse of the BBC programme.

Moreover, if we are to characterize the apprentice group as decoding in a dominant mode, we must recognize that this is only one version, or inflection, of 'dominant code': within the study there were groups from quite different social positions (bank managers, schoolboys, teacher training students) whose decodings shared some of the dominant characteristics of those made by the apprentice groups, but which diverged from theirs at other points. Thus the category of dominant code would need to be differentiated, in terms of the material in this study, to account for different versions (radical and traditional Conservative, deferential, Leavisite) of the dominant code.

Equally, we must distinguish between different forms and formulations of negotiated and oppositional readings, between the 'critique of silence' offered initially by the black students, the critical reading (from an educational point of view) articulately expressed by some of the higher-education groups (though this itself varied, with topic-critical readings being made by these groups on moral and social issues, but dominant code readings being made by the same groups on economic and trade union issues), and the various forms of 'politicized' negotiated and oppositional readings made by the trade union groups.

These are simply instances of a more general phenomenon of differentiation within and across the basic categories derived from Parkin's scheme which we would need to take account of in developing an adequate model of the media audience. We need to understand the process through which the multiplicity of discourses in play in any social formation intersect with the process of decoding media material. The effect of these discourses is precisely to lend variety to decodings. Thus, in each of the major categories of decoding (dominant, negotiated, oppositional) we can discern a number of varieties and inflections of what, for purposes of gross comparison only, is termed the same 'code'.

CONCLUSIONS

This quick sketch of a large quantity of material at least allows us to see clearly the fundamental point that social position in no way directly, or unproblematically, correlates with decoding. The apprentice groups, the trade union and shop stewards groups and the black college students can all be said to share a common class position, but their decodings of a television programme are inflected in different directions by the discourses and institutions in which they are situated. In one case the framework derives from a tradition of mainstream working-class populism, in another from trade unions and Labour party politics, in another, from black youth subcultures. In each case the discourses in play inflect and organize the groups' responses to and decodings of the media material shown.

Any superficial resemblance between this study of television audience and the 'uses and gratifications' perspective in media research is misleading. In the latter, the focus would be entirely on what individuals 'do with' messages.[1] But the different responses and interpretations reported here are not to be understood simply in terms of individual psychologies. They are founded on cultural differences embedded within the structure of society; cultural clusters which guide and limit the individual's interpretation of messages. To understand the potential meanings of a given message we need a cultural map of the audience to whom that message is addressed – a map showing the various cultural repertoires and symbolic resources available to differently placed subgroups within that audience. Such a map will help to show how the social meanings of a message are produced through the interaction of the codes embedded in the text with the codes inhabited by the different sections of the audience.

NOTES

1. Carey & Kreiling 1974 give an account of the relation between 'cultural studies' and the 'uses and gratifications' approach. The present work owes its main categories and concepts to the cultural studies tradition.

REFERENCES

Bernstein, B. 1971: *Class, codes and control*, vol. 1. London: Routledge & Kegan Paul.

Blumler, J. & Katz, E., editors, 1974: *Uses and gratification studies: theories and methods*. London: Sage.

Brunsdon, C. & Morley, D. 1978: *Everyday television: Nationwide*. London: British Film Institute.

Carey, J. & Kreiling, A. 1974: Cultural studies and uses and gratifications. In Blumler & Katz 1974.

Corner, J. 1980: Codes and cultural analysis. In *Media, Culture and Society* 2, 73–86.

Critcher, C., 1975: Structures, cultures and biographies. *Working Papers in Cultural Studies* 7/8, 167–73.

Eco, U. 1972: Towards a semiotic enquiry into the television message. *Working Papers in Cultural Studies* 3, 103–21.

Giglioli, P. (ed.) (1972) *Language and Social Context*, Harmondsworth, Penguin.

Hall, S. 1973: Encoding and decoding in the television discourse. Stencilled occasional paper, Centre for Contemporary Cultural Studies, University of Birmingham. [See Chapter 5 of this volume.]

Labov, W. 1969: The logic of nonstandard English. In Giglioli 1972.

Lakoff, R. 1976: *Language and woman's place*. New York: Harper & Row.

Mann, M. 1973: *Consciousness and action among the western working class*. London: Macmillan.

Mattelart, A. & Siegelaub, S., editors, 1979: *Communication and class struggle*, vol. 1. New York: International General.

Merton, R. & Kendall, P. 1946: The focused interview. *American Journal of Sociology*, L1, 541–57.

Mills, C. Wright 1939: *Power, politics and people*. London/New York: OUP.

Morley, D. 1974: Reconceptualising the media audience. Stencilled occasional paper, Centre for Contemporary Cultural Studies, University of Birmingham.

Morley, D. 1980: *The 'Nationwide' audience*. London: British Film Institute.

Neale, S. 1977: Propaganda. *Screen* 18, 3, 9–40.

Nichols, T. & Armstrong, P. 1976: *Workers divided*. London: Fontana.

Parkin, F. 1971: *Class inequality and political order*. London: MacGibbon & Kee (also Paladin, 1972).

Rosen, H. 1972: *Language and class*. Bristol: Falling Wall Press.

Spender, D. 1980: *Man made language*. London: Routledge & Kegan Paul.

32

HOUSEWIVES AND THE MASS MEDIA

Dorothy Hobson

[. . .]

TELEVISION – 'TWO WORLDS'

Linda

No, I never watch the news, never!

The ideology of a masculine and a feminine world of activities and interests and the separation of those gender-specific interests is never more explicitly expressed than in the women's reactions and responses to television programmes. Here both class-and gender-specific differences are of vital importance, in terms of both which programmes the women choose to watch or reject and their definition and selection of what are appropriately masculine and feminine programmes and topics. Also, they select television programmes much more consciously than radio programmes. This must partly be a consequence of the fact that they have more freedom during the evenings, and they can make active choices because they are no longer subject to constant interruptions caused by their responsibility for domestic labour and child care. This is in contrast to their listening to the radio during the day, when radio programmes are selected primarily as 'easy listening', a background while they do their housework or look after the children.

There is an *active* choice of programmes which are understood to constitute the 'woman's world', coupled with a complete *rejection* of programmes which are presenting the 'man's world'. However, there is also an acceptance that the 'real' or 'man's world' is important, and the 'right' of their husbands to watch these programmes is respected: but it is not a world with which the women in this study wanted to concern themselves. In fact, the 'world', in terms of what

From S. Hall, D. Hobson, A. Lowe and P. Willis (eds), *Culture, Media, Language* (London: Hutchinson, 1980) pp. 105–14.

is constructed as of 'news' value, is seen as both alien and hostile to the values of the women. For them television programmes appear to fall into two distinct categories. The programmes which they watch and enjoy are: comedy series *(Selwyn Froggitt, Are You Being Served?)*; soap operas *(Emmerdale Farm, The Cedar Tree, Rooms, Crown Court* and, predominantly, *Crossroads* and *Coronation Street)*; American television films *(MacMillan and Wife, Dr Welby, Colombo)*; light entertainment and quiz shows *(Whose Baby?, Mr and Mrs)*; and films. All these programmes could be broadly termed as 'entertaining' rather than 'educational and informative'. The programmes which are actively rejected deal with what the women designate the 'real world' or 'man's world', and these predominantly cluster around the news, current affairs programmes *(Panorama, This Week)*, scientific programmes *(Tomorrow's World)*, the subject-matter of politics or war, including films about war, and, to a lesser extent, documentary programmes. Selected documentaries will be viewed as long as the *subject-matter* is identified as of feminine interest. The following are extracts from responses to questions about television, and it can be seen from these that there is a clear distinction between what men and women watch and what is seen to be the *right* of the husband to watch (news and current affairs programmes).

Anne

D.   What programmes do you watch on television?

A.   Er . . . *Crown Court, Rooms, Cedar Tree, Emmerdale Farm, Mr and Mrs.* What else is there? *Dr Welby.* Then there's a film on on a Friday.

D.   This is all on ITV, isn't it?

A.   (Long pause while she thinks of other programmes) Yes, er . . . yes, that's another programme. *Whose Baby?*

D.   There's a film on on Mondays as well, isn't there?

A.   No, no . . . oh, yes, there is. It's *Mystery Movie*. I don't like, I'm not very interested in them, you know. I sort of half-watch them.

D.   So it's more the short series. ((Yes.)) What do you like about the programmes that you watch?

A.   Something to look forward to the next day 'cos most of them are serials.

D.   Do you like them to . . . Which do you like the best, which type?

A.   Er, I like *The Cedar Tree* more than *Emmerdale Farm*. I'm not really keen on that. I only watch it through habit. Er, more romantic, I think, you know, there's sort of, er, family life, that is, more than *Emmerdale Farm*. I don't know, I . . . something about that isn't so good.

D.   That only really takes you up to tea time, so do you watch the television at night?

A.   Yes, in between half-five and eight, that's me busiest time, feed him, change him, sometimes bath him. I don't bath him very often, erm, get Richard's dinner and I always clean up straight away, the washing up, and then I get everything settled and that takes me up to about 8 o'clock, 'cos I stop at half-past six to watch *Crossroads* (laughs). And then from 8 onwards I just sit and watch the box (laughs).

D.   Why do you like *Crossroads?*

A.   Just that you like to know what's going to happen next, you know. I mean they're terrible actors, I know that, and I just see through that, you know. I just, now and then I think, 'Oh my God, that's silly,' you know, but it's not the acting I'm interested in, it's what's going on. I suppose I'm nosy. . . .

D.   The time then between that – do you watch the news?

A.   I watch a little bit of it, erm (pause). I don't really like the news much because it's all politics, generally and British Leyland out on strike again, and this and that. I like to hear the news things if, er, – if there's been a murder, I know that sounds terrible, but I like to hear – 'Oh what's happening next, what have they found out?' That sort of news I like, you know – gossip. ((Yes.))

D. Do you ever watch documentaries?

A. Now and then I find an interesting one. I watched one the other night about people who'd got diseases.

Lorna

L. We have the radio on all day, you know, from the time we get up till the time the tele comes back on. I usually put it on at 4 o'clock for the kids' tele and they watch all the children's programmes, and it might come back off at 6 and it might not go back on again till half-past seven.

D. So you don't watch the news?

L. No, I never watch the news, never.

D. Why don't you watch it?

L. I don't like it, I don't like to hear about people dying and things like that. I think about it afterwards and I can't sleep at all. Like when I watched that thing, *World at War*, and I watched it once and all I could see were people all over the place, you know, heads and no arms and that and at night I could not sleep. I can't ask him to turn it over 'cos he likes it, so I go in the kitchen till it's finished.

It is clear that the news, current affairs, political programmes and scientific programmes, together with portrayals of war (real or in the guise of war films) are actively rejected by the women. They will leave the room rather than sit there while the news is on. The world as revealed through the news is seen to be (a) depressing, (b) boring, but (c) important. The 'news values', as realized in agendas, are 'accepted', but they have *alternative* values which the women recognize but do not suggest should form an alternative coverage. In fact, the importance of accepted 'news values' is recognized, and although their own world is seen as more interesting and relevant to them, it is also seen as secondary in rank to the 'real' or 'masculine' world. In terms of what the news is seen to present, they only select items which they *do not wish to see*. Comments or judgements are made in terms not only of what the items are but also of the effect which they have on the individual. Thus the items are not judged solely for their 'news value' but also for the way they affect the individual. There would appear to be a model for the programmes which are discussed and then rejected.

The women's interpretation of news and current affairs programmes is an accurate reflection of the news items which are contained in these programmes. They may mis-identify the foci of some news reports, but this perhaps reinforces their claim not to watch these programmes. For

The news

Content	Conceptualization of value of content	Effects on individual
Politics	Boring	Depressing
War	Male-orientated	Causing nightmares and sleeplessness
Industrial troubles		

instance, when Lorraine says 'It's all Vietnam, on the news', she is not necessarily identifying specific examples. In fact, Northern Ireland is much more likely to have been the exact focus of the news at the time. The general point is clear enough: 'Vietnam' has become a generic term for war.

The grouping together of the news and current affairs programmes by the women is a response to the circularity of these programmes, which is determined by the interrelation between the news and current events programmes and the prior selection of news items for their news value. A news 'story' becomes a 'current events topic', and the selection of news items according to the hierarchy of 'news value' puts political and military concerns, industrial relations and economic affairs at the head of topics for inclusion.[1] The editorial selection of these items is premised on their 'news value', and this also reflects a masculine bias in terms of the ideology of the subjects of the items included. The women find little of interest for them in the news except for any 'human interest' items, which are necessarily low in news value and rarely occur. When domestic affairs do reach the news it is often in terms of deviation or murder, and this in turn reinforces the accepted absence of these items from 'normal' news bulletins. This is illustrated when Anne says that she likes to hear news about murders.

[. . .]

It is not the fact that someone has been murdered which she finds interesting in the news but the fact that *there are elements within the situation to which she can relate.*

The ideology of femininity and feminine values over-determines the structures of what interests women. It is topics which can be regarded as of 'domestic' interest which they see as important or interesting, and it is also significant that 'domestic affairs', constructed in terms of 'news values' to include the economy and industrial relations, are not defined as 'domestic' in the categories which the women construct for themselves. 'Domestic' clearly relates to their own interests and not to the definition which is constructed through the hierarchy of 'news values'. It can be said that the majority of items which are included in news, current affairs and documentary programmes have a content which has little or no intrinsic interest for these women, and the way that they are presented means that they exclude these women from 'participation' at the point of identification with the items included. At the same time, the women accept that these are *important*, and this reinforces the split between the masculine values, which are interpreted as being important, and the interests which they see as representing their own feminine values.

THE FEMININE 'WORLD' OF TELEVISION

D.   Do you like programmes that are like your life or that are entirely different?

R.   I think I like things different really, 'cos if it's like me life, it's not very exciting 'cos there's nothing much really ever happens. Something exciting, different. I like watching detectives, anything creepy like ghost stories, I love ghost stories, anything creepy like that.

First, in conjunction with the programmes which women reject, there are programmes which they choose to watch and to which they obviously relate. These can be defined as those which are related to their own lives, the programmes which can loosely be termed 'realistic' – *Coronation Street, Crossroads, Emmerdale Farm, The Cedar Tree.* Secondly, the programmes which can be described as having 'fantasy content' (horror movies, or American movies or television movies), although not seen as representing 'real life' in the women's own terms, are seen as an alternative to the reality of their own lives. Finally, there are the programmes which can be categorized as light entertainment (quizzes, or competitions which often have an 'everyday' or 'domestic' theme, either because the contestants are seen as ordinary people or because of the subject-matter. In *Whose Baby?*, for example, the children of celebrity guests appear and the panel has to guess who is the famous father or mother – a direct link of parenthood between the 'famous' and the 'ordinary' viewer (in this case, the woman).

The programmes which are interpreted by the women as portraying 'everyday' or 'family' life are, in fact, far from portraying anything which has a point of *real* identification with the women's own lives. The programmes may not relate to the everyday lives of the women in the study. Within the programmes which are seen as 'realistic' there are common elements of identification. Many of the characters in the series *Coronation Street* and *Crossroads* are women who themselves have to confront the 'problems' in their 'everyday' lives, and the resolution or negotiation of these problems within the drama provides points of recognition and identification for the women viewers. It is in the 'living out' of problem areas that much of the appeal of the series is located. However, the resolution of areas of conflict, contradiction or confusion within a dramatic situation is double-edged. The woman can be confronted with the problems and also informed of the different elements which have to be considered in any 'living out' or resolution of problems. It is in the forms that the resolutions are made within programmes that the ideological basis of consensual femininity is *reproduced* and *reinforced* for women. As with the problems that are discussed in phone-in programmes and in the chatter of DJs, the very fact of recognition and *seeming* discussion or consideration by some 'outside' or 'independent' authority gives an impression that the problems have been aired. The outcome remains the same. The resolutions within either the soap opera series or the telephone conversations or talks are not revolutionary; what emerges is the reinforcement of the fatality or inevitability of the situation, without the need to change it.

It is impossible to attempt a detailed analysis of the decoding of the programmes which is made by the women because at this stage this would be only supposition.[2] What is clear, however, is that the programmes which the women watch are differentiated specifically in terms of both class and gender. Overall the programmes fall into the categories of popular drama and light entertainment, and although it is obvious that the women reject news and the political content of current affairs programmes, it would be wrong to contend that they do not have access or exposure to news or politics. Within comedy programmes, news and current affairs topics are presented in a mediated form – and often in a more easily accessible or even 'joking' or parodying manner. The news on Radio 1, which is transmitted every hour, is relatively accessible; it is also introduced by music which is recognizable, bright and repetitive and demanding of attention. The women in this study are exposed to news in this form, but they do not mention finding that unacceptable. Clearly, what is important is the definition of specifically feminine interests which women select from media output and the rejection of items which they see as specifically of masculine interest. They combat their own isolation through their interest in radio programmes during the day, and they see television programmes as a form of 'leisure' or relaxation. Radio is integral to their working day, but early-evening television is secondary to the domestic labour which they perform. The programmes which the women watch and listen to, together with the programmes which they reject, reinforce the sexual division of spheres of interest, which is determined both by their location in the home and by the structures of femininity that ensure that feminine values are secondary (or less 'real') than those of the masculine world of work and politics, which the women regard as *alien*, yet *important*.

NOTES

1. I. Connell, L. Curti and S. Hall, 'The "unity" of current affairs television', in *Culture and Domination, WPCS,* no. 9 (CCCS, University of Birmingham, 1976).

2. There has been some early work on the audience responses to radio serials. Hertzog looked at the structure of audiences and their responses to programmes of a similar kind – daytime radio serials. She was predominantly concerned with the psychological responses of the audience to features within the text and relied on the 'uses and gratification' theory. Also, Arnheim looked at the content of daytime radio serials in an attempt to identify features to which the audience responded. Both these works are important starting-points for future research into the possible identification which women may make to radio and television programmes, since many of the features of the programmes analysed in Arnheim are common to the present television series watched by the women in my study. My own work in this study starts at a point where the audience selects from the given range of available programmes. I have not been concerned, in this article, so much with how they decode those programmes as with the structures which have mediated in their choice of programmes. See H. Hertzog, 'What do we really know about daytime serial listeners?', in P. F. Lazersfeld and F. N. Stanton (eds), *Radio Research 1942–43* (New York: Duell, Sloan & Pearce 1944); R. Arnheim, 'The world of the daytime serial', in Lazersfeld and Stanton, *Radio Research 1942–43.*

33

WANTED: AUDIENCES. ON THE POLITICS OF EMPIRICAL AUDIENCE STUDIES

Ien Ang

In his pioneering book *The 'Nationwide' Audience*, David Morley situates his research on which the book reports as follows: 'The relation of an audience to the ideological operations of television remains in principle an empirical question: the challenge is the attempt to develop appropriate methods of empirical investigation of that relation.'[1]

Although this sentence may initially be interpreted as a call for a technical discussion about empirical research methods, its wider meaning should be sought in the theoretical and political context of Morley's work. To me, the importance of *The 'Nationwide' Audience* does not so much reside in the fact that it offers an empirically validated, and thus 'scientific' account of 'the ideological operations of television,' or merely in its demonstration of some of the ways in which the television audience is 'active.' Other, more wide-ranging issues are at stake.

[. . .]

ACADEMIC CONVERGENCE?

The 'Nationwide' Audience has generally been received as an innovative departure within cultural studies, both theoretically and methodologically. If *Screen* theory can be diagnosed as one instance in which critical discourse on television suffered from the problem of the 'disappearing audience,'[2] Morley's project is an indication of a growing acknowledgment within cultural studies that television viewing is a practice that involves the active production of meanings by viewers.

But the book has also been welcomed by some adherents of the influential uses and gratifications approach, who see it as an important step on the part of 'critical' scholars in their direction, that is as an acceptance of, and possible contribution to, a refinement of their own basic axiomatic commitment to 'the active audience.' On the other hand, some uses

From E. Seiter, H. Borchers, G. Kreutzner and E.-M. Warth (eds), *Remote Control: Television, Audiences and Cultural Power* (London: Routledge, 1989) pp. 96–115.

and gratifications researchers, for their part, have begun to take over semiologically informed cultural studies concepts such as 'text' and 'reader,' thereby indicating an acknowledgment of the symbolic nature of negotiations between media texts and their readers which they, in their functionalist interest for the multiple relationships between audience gratifications and media 'uses,' had previously all but ignored.[3]

On top of this conceptual rapprochement, these social scientists have also expressed their delight in noticing a methodological 'concession' among 'critical' scholars: finally, so it is argued, some 'critical' scholars at least have dropped their suspicion of doing empirical research. In a benevolent, rather fatherly tone, three senior ambassadors of the uses and gratifications approach, Blumler, Gurevitch, and Katz, have thus proclaimed a gesture of 'reaching out' to the other 'camp,' calling for incorporating some of the insights developed within the 'critical' perspective into their own paradigm.[4] Evoked then is the prospect of merging the two approaches, to the point that they may ultimately fuse into a happy common project in which the perceived hostility between the two 'camps' will have been unmasked as academic 'pseudo-conflicts.' As one leading gratifications researcher, Rosengren, optimistically predicts: 'To the extent that the same problematics are empirically studied by members of various schools, the present sharp differences of opinion will gradually diminish and be replaced by a growing convergence of perspectives.'[5]

However, to interpret these recent developments in audience studies in terms of such a convergence is to simplify and even misconceive the issues at stake. For one thing, I would argue that the two perspectives only superficially share 'the same problematics,' and that what separates a 'critical' from a 'mainstream' perspective is more than merely some 'differences of opinion,' sharp or otherwise: it concerns fundamental differences not only in epistemological, but also in theoretical and political attitudes toward the aim and status of doing empirical research as such.

The academic idealization of joining forces in pursuit of a supposedly common goal as if it were a neutral, scientific project is a particularly depoliticizing strategy, because it tends to neutralize all difference and disagreement in favor of a forced consensus. If I am cautious about this euphoria around the prospect of academic convergence, it is not my intention to impose a rigid and absolute eternal dichotomy between 'critical' and 'mainstream' research. Nor would I want to assert that Morley's project is entirely 'critical' and the uses and gratifications approach completely 'mainstream.' As I have noted before, the relationship between 'critical' and 'mainstream' is not fixed one; it does not concern two mutually exclusive, antagonistic sets of knowledge, as some observers would imply by talking in terms of 'schools' or 'paradigms.' In fact, many assumptions and ideas do not intrinsically belong to one or the other perspective. For example, the basic assumption that the television audience is 'active' (rather than passive) and that watching television is a social (rather than an individual) practice is currently accepted in both perspectives. There is nothing spectacular about that.[6] Also, I would suggest that the idea that texts can generate multiple meanings, and that the text/reader relationship takes the form of negotiations, is not in itself a sufficient condition for the declared convergence.[7]

In other words, in evaluating whether we can really speak of convergence, it is not enough to establish similar research questions, or to identify a common acknowledgment of the usefulness of certain methods of inquiry. Of course, such commonalities are interesting enough and it would be nonsense to discard them categorically. I do think it is important to get rid of any dogmatism or antagonism-for-the-sake-of-it, and to try to learn from others wherever that is possible. But at the same time we should not lose sight of the fact that any call for convergence itself is not an innocent gesture. It tends to be done from a certain point of view and therefore inevitably involves a selection process in which certain issues and themes are highlighted and others suppressed. And it is my contention that an all too hasty declaration of convergence could lead to neglecting some of the most important distinctive features of cultural studies as a critical intellectual enterprise.

A difference in conceptualizing the object of study is a first issue that needs to be discussed here. Thus, to take the common interest in 'audience activity' as an example in a cultural studies perspective, 'audience activity' cannot and should not be studied in isolation. Rather than dissecting 'audience activity' into variables and categories in order to be able to study them one by one, so that we could ultimately have a complete and generalizable formal 'map' of all dimensions of 'audience activity,' which seems to be the drive behind the uses and gratifications project,[8] the aim of cultural studies, as I see it, is to arrive at a more historicized insight into the ways in which 'audience activity' is related to social and political structures and processes. In other words, what is at stake is not the understanding of 'audience activity' as such as an isolated and isolable phenomenon and object of research, but the embeddness of 'audience activity' in a network of ongoing cultural practices and relationships.

As a result, an audience researcher working within a cultural studies sensibility cannot restrict herself or himself to 'just' studying audiences and their activities (and, for that matter, relating those activities with other variables such as gratifications sought or obtained, dependencies, effects, and so on). She or he will also engage with the structural and cultural processes through which the audiences she or he is studying are constituted and being constituted. Thus, one essential theoretical point of the cultural studies approach to the television audience is its foregrounding of the notion that the dynamics of watching television, no matter how heterogeneous and seemingly free it is, is always related to the operations of forms of social power. It is in this light that we should see Morley's decision to do research on viewers' decodings: it was first of all motivated by an interest in what he – in the quote at the beginning of this chapter – calls 'the ideological operations of television.'

It is important then to emphasize that the term 'active audience' does not occupy the same symbolic status in the two approaches. From a cultural studies point of view, evidence that audiences are 'active' cannot simply be equated with the rather triumphant, liberal-pluralist conclusion, often expressed by gratificationists, that media consumers are 'free' or even 'power-ful' – a conclusion which allegedly undercuts the idea of 'media hegemony.' The question for cultural studies is not simply one of 'where the power lies in media systems' (i.e. with the audience or with the media producers),[9] but rather how relations of power are organized within the heterogeneous practices of media consumption. In other words, rather than constructing an opposition between 'the' media and 'the' audience, as if these were separate ontological entities, and, along with it, the application of a distributional theory of power (that is, power is a property that can be attributed to either side of the opposing entities), cultural studies scholars are interested in understanding media consumption as a site of cultural struggle, in which a variety of forms of power are exercised, with different sorts of effects.[10] Thus if, as Morley's study has shown, viewers can decode a text in different ways and sometimes even give oppositional meanings to it, this should not be conceived as an example of 'audience freedom,' but as a moment in that cultural struggle, an ongoing struggle over meaning and pleasure which is central to the fabric(ation) of everyday life.

I hope to have made clear by now that in evaluating the possibility or even desirability of convergence, it is important to look at how 'audience activity' is theorized or interpreted, and how research 'findings' are placed in a wider theoretical framework. So, if one type of 'audience activity' which has received much attention in both approaches recently has been the interpretative strategies used by audiences to read media texts (conceptualized in terms of decoding structures, interpretative communities, patterns of involvement, and so on), how are we to make sense of those interpretative strategies? The task of the cultural studies researcher, I would suggest, is to develop *strategic interpretations* of them, different not only in form and content, but also in scope and intent, from those offered in more 'mainstream' -oriented accounts.[11] I will return to this central issue of interpretation.

BEYOND METHODOLOGY

A troubling aspect about the idea of (and desire for) convergence, then, is that it tends to be conceptualized as an exclusively 'scientific' enterprise. Echoing the tenets of positivism, its aim seems to be the gradual accumulation of scientifically confirmed 'findings.' It is propelled by the hope that by seeking a shared agreement on what is relevant and by developing shared methodological skills the final scientific account of 'the audience' can eventually be achieved. In this framework, audience studies are defined as just another branch of an academic discipline (i.e. mass communication), in which it is unproblematically assumed that 'the audience' is a proper object of study whose characteristics can be over more accurately observed, described, categorized, systematized, and explained, until the whole picture is 'filled in.' In principle (if not in practice), this scientific project implicitly claims to be able to produce total knowledge, to reveal the full and objective 'truth' about 'the audience.' Audience here is imagined as and turned into an object with researchable attributes and features (be it described in terms of arrays of preferences, decodings, uses, effects, or whatever) that could be definitively established – if only researchers of different breeding would stop quarreling with each other and unite to work harmoniously together to accomplish the task.[12]

From such an academic point of view, the question of methodology becomes a central issue. After all, rigor of method has traditionally been seen as the guarantee *par excellence* for the 'scientific' status of knowledge. In positivist social science, the hypothetico-deductive testing of theory through empirical research, quantitative in form, is cherished as the cornerstone of the production of 'scientific' knowledge. Theory that is not empirically tested, or that is too complex to be molded into empirically testable hypotheses, is dismissed as 'unscientific'. These assumptions, which are central to the dominant version of the uses and gratifications approach as it was established in the 1970s, are now contested by a growing number of researchers who claim that reality cannot be grasped and explained through quantitative methods alone. Furthermore, they forcefully assert that to capture the multidimensionality and complexity of audience activity the use of qualitative methods – and thus a move towards the 'ethnographic' – is desperately called for.[13]

From an academic point of view, it is this methodological challenge that forms the condition of possibility of the perceived convergence. However, although I think that the struggle for legitimization of qualitative research is a very important one, I do believe that it is not the central point for critical cultural studies. This is because the struggle is cast primarily in methodological terms, and therefore its relevance is confined to the development of audience research as an *academic* enterprise. Given the decade-long hegemony of positivism and the quantifying attitude in audience research, this development is a significant one indeed. Unfortunately, however, many discussions about the usefulness of qualitative methods still do not question the epistemological distinction between science and common sense that lies at the heart of positivism. The aim is still the isolation of a body of knowledge that can be recognized as 'scientific' (in its broadest meaning), the orientation is toward the advancement of an academic discipline, and concomitantly, the technical improvement of its instruments of analysis.

A cultural studies perspective on audience research cannot stop short at this level of debate. For a critical cultural studies, it is not questions of methodology or academic struggle as such that prevail. On the contrary, we should relativize the academic commitment to increasing knowledge for its own sake and resist the temptation to what Stuart Hall has called the 'codification' of cultural studies into a stable realm of established theories and canonized methodologies.[14] In this respect, the territorial conflict between 'mainstream' and 'critical,' quantitative and qualitative, humanistic and social scientific, and so on, should perhaps not bother us too much at all in the first place. As James Carey once remarked, 'perhaps all the talk about theory, method, and other such things prevents us from raising or permits us to avoid raising, deeper and disquieting questions about the purposes of our scholarship.'[15] And indeed: why are we so interested in knowing about audiences in the first place? In empirical audience research, especially, it is important to reflect upon the status of the knowledge produced. After all, scrutinizing media audiences is not an innocent practice. It does not take place in a social and political vacuum. Historically, the hidden agenda of audience research, even when it presents itself as pure and objective, has all too often been its commercial or political usefulness. In other words, what we should reflect upon is the *political* interventions we make when talking about audiences – political not only in the sense of some distant societal goal, but, more importantly, in that we cannot afford ignoring the political dimensions of the *process* and practice of knowledge production itself. What does it mean to subject audiences to the researcher's gaze? How can we develop insights that do not reproduce the kind of objectified knowledge served up by, say, market research or empiricist effects research? How is it possible to do audience research which is 'on the side' of the audience?[16] These are nagging political questions which cannot be smoothed out by the comforting canons of epistemology, methodology, and 'science.'

Of course, it is not easy to pin down what such considerations would imply in concrete terms. But it could at least be said that we should try to avoid a stance in which 'the audience' is relegated to the status of exotic 'other' – merely interesting in so far as 'we,' as researchers, can turn 'them' into 'objects' of study, and about whom 'we' have the privileged position to acquire 'objective' knowledge.[17] To begin with, I think, critical audience studies should not strive and pretend to tell 'the truth' about 'the audience.' Its ambitions should be much more modest. As Lawrence Grossberg has suggested, 'the goal of [critical research] is to offer not a polished representation of the truth, but simply a little help in our efforts to better understand the world.'[18] This modesty does not have so much to do with some sort of false humility as with the basic acknowledgment that every research practice unavoidably takes place in a particular historical situation, and is therefore principally of a partial nature. As Hammersley and Atkinson have provocatively put it, 'all social research takes the form of participant observation: it involves participating in the social world, in whatever role, and reflecting on the products of that participation.'[19] The collection of data, either quantitative or qualitative in form, can never be separated from their interpretation; it is only through practices of interpretative theorizing that unruly social experiences and events related to media consumption become established as meaningful 'facts' about audiences. Understanding 'audience activity' is thus caught up in the discursive representation, not the transparent reflection, of realities having to do with audiences.

These considerations lead to another, more politicized conception of doing research. It is not the search for (objective, scientific) knowledge in which the researcher is engaged, but the construction of *interpretations,* of certain ways of understanding the world, always historically located, subjective, and relative. It is the decisive importance of this interpretative moment that I would like to highlight in exploring the possibilities of critical audience studies.[20]

In positivism, interpretation is assigned a marginal place: as a result of its emphasis on the empirical testing of theory, interpretation is assumed to follow rather automatically from the so-called 'findings.' Achieved then is an apparent innocence of interpretation, one that is seemingly grounded in 'objective social reality' itself. In fact, the term 'interpretation' itself would seem to have definite negative connotations for positivists because of its connection with 'subjectivism.' And even within those social science approaches in which the interpretative act of the researcher – not only at the moment of data analysis, but also at that of data collection – is taken more seriously, interpretation is more often than not problematized as a methodical rather than a political matter, defined in terms of careful inference making rather than in terms of discursive constructions of reality.

It should be recognized, however, that because interpretations always inevitably involve the construction of certain representations of reality (and not others), they can never be 'neutral' and merely 'descriptive.' After all, the 'empirical,' captured in either quantitative or qualitative form, does not yield self-evident meanings; it is only through the interpretative framework constructed by the researcher that understandings of the 'empirical' come about. The choice of empirical methods of investigation is only one part of a double venture: it is in the dialectic between the empirical and the theoretical, between experience and explanation, that forms of knowledge, that is interpretations, are constructed. Here then the thoroughly political nature of any research manifests itself. What is at stake is a *politics of interpretation*: 'to advance an interpretation is to insert it into a network of power relations.[21]

This also implies a shift in the position of the researcher. She or he is no longer a bearer of truth, but occupies a 'partial' position in two senses of the word. On the one hand, she or he is no longer the neutral observer, but is someone whose job it is to produce historically and culturally specific knowledges that are the result of equally specific discursive encounters between researcher and informants, in which the subjectivity of the researcher is not separated from the 'object' s/he is studying. The interpretations that are produced in the process can never claim to be definitive: on the contrary, they are necessarily incomplete (for they always involve simplification, selection, and exclusion) and temporary. 'If neither history nor politics ever comes to an end, then theory (as well as research) is never completed and our accounts can never be closed or totalized.' [22] And on the other hand, and even more important, the position of the researcher is also more than that of the professional scholar: beyond a capable interpreter, she or he is also inherently a political and moral subject. She or he is an intellectual who is not only responsible to the Academy, but to the social world she or he lives in as well. It is at the interface of 'ethics' and 'scholarship' that the researcher's interpretations take on their distinctive political edge.[23]

Of course, all this entails a different status for empirical research. Material obtained by ethnographic fieldwork or depth-interviews with audience members cannot simply be treated as natural 'data.' Viewers' statements about their relation to television cannot be regarded as self-evident facts. Nor are they immediate, transparent reflections of those viewers' 'lived realities' that can speak for themselves. What is of critical importance, therefore, is the way in which those statements are made sense of, that is interpreted. Here lies the ultimate political responsibility of the researcher. The comfortable assumption that it is the reliability and accuracy of the methodologies being used that will ascertain the validity of the outcomes of research, thereby reducing the researcher's responsibility to a technical matter, is rejected. In short, to return to Morley's opening statement, audience ethnographies are undertaken because the relation between television and viewers is an empirical *question*. But the empirical is not the privileged domain of the *answers*, as the positivist would have it. Answers (temporary ones, to be sure) are to be constructed, in the form of interpretations.[24]

[. . .]

NOTES

1. David Morley, *The 'Nationwide' Audience: Structure and Decoding* (London: British Film Institute, 1980), p. 162.
2. See Fred Feyes, 'Critical Communications Research and Media Effects: The Problem of the Disappearing Audience,' *Media, Culture, and Society 6 (1984): 219–32.*
3. 'Gratifications researchers, in their paradigmatic personae, have lost sight of what the media are purveying, in part because of an overcommitment to the endless freedom of the audience to reinvent the text, in part because of a too rapid leap to mega-functions, such as surveillance or self-identity.'
   (Jay G. Blumler, Michael Gurevitch, and Elihu Katz, 'Reaching Out: A Future for Gratifications Research,' in K. E. Rosengren, L. A. Wenner, and Ph. Palmgreen (eds) *Media Gratifications Research: Current Perspectives* (Beverly Hills, Calif.: Sage, 1985), p. 272)
4. Ibid.
5. Karl Erik Rosengren, 'Communication Research: One Paradigm, or Four?' *Journal of Communication* 33 (1983): 203; also Tamar Liebes, 'On the Convergence of Theories of Mass Communication and Literature Regarding the Role of the Reader' (paper presented to the Conference on Culture and Communication, 1986); and Kim Christian Schroder, 'Convergence of Antagonistic Traditions? The Case of Audience Research,' *European Journal of Communication* 2 (1987): 7–31. Such an insistence upon convergence is not new among 'mainstream' communication researchers. For example, Jennifer Daryl Slack and Martin Allor have recalled how in the late 1930s Lazarsfeld hired Adorno in the expectation that the latter's critical theory could be used to 'revitalize' American empiricist research by supplying it with 'new research ideas.' The collaboration ended only one year later because it proved to be impossible to translate Adomo's critical analysis into the methods and goals of Lazarsfeld's project. Lazarsfeld has never given up the idea of a convergence, however. See Jennifer Daryl Slack and Martin Allor, 'The Political and Epistemological Constituents of Critical Communication Research,' *Journal of Communication* 33 (1983): 210.
6. Note, for instance, the striking similarities between the following two sentences, one from a uses and gratifications source, the other from a cultural studies one: 'There seems to be growing support for that branch of communications research which asserts that television viewing is an active and social process' (Katz and Liebes, 'Mutual Aid in the Decoding of *Dallas*: Preliminary Notes for a Cross-Cultural Study,' in Phillip Drummond and Richard Paterson (eds) *Television in Transition* (London: British Film Institute, 1985), p. 187); 'Television viewing, the choices which shape it and the many social uses to which we put it, now turn out to be irrevocably active and social processes' (Stuart Hall, 'Introduction,' in David Morley, *Family Television. Cultural Power and Domestic Leisure* (London: Comedia, 1986), p. 8).
7. Tamar Liebes suggests that 'the focus of the convergence is on the idea that the interaction between messages and receivers takes on the form of negotiation, and is not predetermined' ('On the Convergence,' p. 1). However, as I will try to show, what makes all the difference in the theoretical and political thrust of ethnographic audience studies is the way in which 'negotiation' is conceived. Furthermore, 'not predetermined' does not mean 'undertermined,' – and how (complex, structural, conjunctural) determinations should be conceived remains an important point of divergence between 'critical' and 'mainstream' studies. It is also noteworthy to point out that, while uses and gratifications researchers now seem to be 'rediscovering the text,' researchers working within a cultural studies perspective seem to be moving away from the text. This is very clear in Morley's second book, *Family Television*. In fact, it becomes more and more difficult to delineate what 'the television text' is.
8. See, for example, M. R. Levy and S. Windahl, 'Audience Activity and Gratifications: A conceptual Clarification and Exploration,' in Rosengren et al., *Media Gratifications Research*, pp. 109–22.
9. Blumler et al., 'Reaching Out,' p. 260.
10. In stating this I do not want to suggest that cultural studies is a closed paradigm, or that all cultural studies scholars share one – say, Foucaultian – conception of power. Thus, the Birmingham version of cultural studies, with its distinctly Gramscian inflection, is critized by Lawrence Grossberg for its lack of a theory of pleasure. An alternative, postmodernist perspective on cultural studies is developed by Grossberg in his 'Cultural Studies Revisited and Revised,' in Mary S. Mander (ed.) *Communications in Transition* (New York: Praeger, 1983), pp. 39–70.
11. Strategic interpretations, that is interpretations that are 'political' in the sense that they are aware of the fact that interpretations are always concrete interventions into an already existing discursive field. They are therefore always partial in both senses of the word, and involved in making sense of the world in specific, power-laden ways. See Mary Louise Pratt, 'Interpretive Strategic Strategic Interpretations: On Anglo-American Reader-Response Criticism,' in Jonathan Arac (ed.) *Postmodernism and Politics*, (Minneapolis: University of Minnesota Press, 1986), pp. 26–54.

12.   Rosengren expresses this view in very clear cut terms, when he reduces the existence of disagreements between 'critical' and 'mainstream' researchers to 'psychological reasons' ('Communication Research: One Paradigm, or Four?,' p. 191).

13.   Cf. James Lull, 'The Naturalistic Study of Media Use and Youth Culture,' in Rosengren et al., *Media Gratifications Research*, pp. 209–24; Klaus Bruhn Jensen, 'Qualitative Audience Research: Towards an Integrative Approach to Reception,' *Critical Studies in Mass Communication* 4 (1987): 21–36; Thomas R. Lindlof and Timothy P. Meyer, 'Mediated Communications as Ways of Seeing, Acting and Constructing Culture: The Tools and Foundations of Qualitative Research,' in Lindlof, *Natural Audiences: Qualitative Research and Media Uses and Effects* (Norwood NJ: Ablex Publishing Company, 1987), pp. 1–30.

14.   Lawrence Grossberg (ed.) 'On Postmodernism and Articulation: An Interview with Stuart Hall,' *Journal of Communication Inquiry* 10, no. 2 (summer 1986): 59.

15.   James Carey, 'Introduction,' in Mander *Communications in Transition*, p. 5.

16.   I borrowed this formulation from Virginia Nightingale, 'What's Happening to Audience Research?,' *Media Information Australia* 39 (February 1986): 21–2. Nightingale remarks that audience research has generally been 'on the side' of those with vested interests in influencing the organization of the mass media in society, and that it is important to develop a research perspective that is 'on the side' of the audience. However, it is far from simple to work out exactly what such a perspective would mean. The notion of the 'active audience,' for example, often put forward by uses and gratifications researchers to mark the distinctive identity of the 'paradigm,' is not in itself a guarantee for a stance 'on the side of the audience.' In fact, the whole passive/active dichotomy in accounts of audiences has now become so ideologized that it all too often serves as a mystification of the real commitments behind the research at stake.

17.   Reflections on the predicaments and politics of research on and with living historical subjects have already played an important role in, for example, feminist studies and anthropology, particularly ethnography. At least two problems are highlighted in these reflections. First, there is the rather awkward but seldom discussed concrete relation between researcher and researched as human beings occupying certain positions invested with power; second, there is the problem of the discursive form in which the cultures of 'others' can be represented in non-objectifying (or better, less objectifying) ways. See, for example, Angela McRobbie, 'The Politics of Feminist Research,' *Feminist Review* 12 (October 1982): 46–57; James Clifford, 'On Ethnographic Authority,' *Representations* 1, no. 2 (1983): 118–46; James Clifford and George E. Marcus (eds) *Writing Culture. The Poetics and Politics of Ethnography* (Berkeley, Los Angeles, London: University of California Press, 1986). Researchers of media audiences have, as far as I know, generally been silent about these issues. However, for a perceptive and thought-provoking engagement with the problem, see Valerie Wakerdine, 'Video Replay: Families, Films and Fantasy,' in Victor Burgin, James Donald and Cora Kaplan (eds) *Formations of Fantasy* (London and New York: Methuen, 1986), pp. 167–99.

18.   Lawrence Grossberg, 'Critical Theory and the Politics of Empirical Research,' in Michael Gurevitch and Mark R. Levy (eds) *Mass Communication Review Yearbook*, vol. 6 (Newbury Park, Calif.: Sage, 1986), p. 89.

19.   Martyn Hammersley and Paul Atkinson, *Ethnography: Principles in Practice* (London and New York: Tavistock, 1983), p. 16.

20.   For a general overview of the interpretative or hermeneutic turn in the social sciences, see Paul Rabinow and William M. Sullivan (eds) *Interpretive Social Science* (Berkeley, Los Angeles, London: University of California Press, 1979). A more radical conception of what they call interpretive analytics' is developed by Hubert Dreyfuss and Paul Rabinow in their *Michel Foucault: Beyond Structuralism and Hermeneutics* (Chicago, Ill.: University of Chicago Press, 1982).

21.   Pratt, 'Interpretative Strategies/Strategic Interpretations,' p. 52.

22.   Grossberg, 'Critical Theory,' p. 89.

23.   Cf. Paul Rabinow, 'Representations Are Social Facts: Modernity and Post-Modernity in Anthropology,' in Clifford and Marcus, *Writing Culture*, pp. 234–61.

24.   A more general, lucid criticism of empiricist mass communications research is offered by Robert C. Allen in his *Speaking of Soap Operas* (Chapel Hill and London: University of North Carolina Press, 1985), chapter 2.

Further Reading

See 'Further Reading' for 'Beyond Hegemony?'

Reception
Beyond Hegemony?

Reception: Beyond Hegemony?

The three preceding chapters all depend for their theoretical framework on the concept of 'hegemony' as adopted by the Birmingham Centre in the 1970s. As articulated by Stuart Hall in 1980, Gramsci's concept

> refers to all those processes whereby a fundamental social group . . . which has achieved direction over the 'decisive economic nucleus', is able to expand this into a moment of social, political and cultural leadership and authority throughout civil society and the state . . . For Gramsci, 'hegemony' is never a permanent state of affairs and never uncontested. . . . It marks a shift in the dispositions of contending forces in a field of struggle and the articulation of that field into a tendency.[1]

It is this concept which underpins both Hall's encoding/decoding model and Ang's description of media consumption as a 'site of cultural struggle'.

More recently, however, this concept has proved less successful in organising a 'cultural studies' approach to audience study. The model which it proposes has been challenged, in particular, by the influence of the work of two thinkers, Michel Foucault and Pierre Bourdieu. Foucault's view of power as dispersed and decentred – manifest throughout the system of social networks and operating as 'a fundamentally enabling force',[2] while it opens up consideration of power relations other than those of class – fits uneasily with a model of cultural consumption as *struggle*. The influence of Bourdieu's work on the correspondence between socio-economic positioning and patterns of taste, on the other hand, has been to shift emphasis away from the text–reader relationship and towards *contexts* of consumption, and 'the issue of how popular taste and popular pleasures can be understood'.[3] As a result, the media audience has become less easy to conceptualise or even to distinguish. Indeed, John Hartley has suggested that the very idea of the audience is an imaginary construction, an 'invisible fiction', fashioned to serve the needs of the imagining institution, whether that is the advertising industry or the 'institution' of cultural studies research.[4] The two chapters which follow offer two very different examples of these shifts in the field of audience research.

Ann Gray's study of women's use of video recorders in the home focuses on the domestic and family context for video viewing, arguing that the text–reader relationship is one that itself 'has to be negotiated, struggled for, won or lost, in the dynamic and often chaotic processes of family life'. Gray's work, therefore, has links with that of Dorothy Hobson (see Chapters 32 and 41), as well as the later work of David Morley.[5] The domestic sphere, argues Gray, is increasingly becoming women's only leisure space, but it is a space which is structured by gendered power relationships which determine how and when women may make choices in leisure activities. Video technology is itself gendered, with women usually having access to the VCR's most basic functions but not to the operation of the timer or remote control. The hiring of tapes for family viewing, too, is usually done by men. In her study, Gray found two contexts in which women could exercise choice over video viewing; both were in the absence of men. The first is alone, as a 'breathing space' between daytime domestic tasks. The second, which Gray sees as giving more grounds for optimism, is one in which several women meet to watch a video which they have hired jointly. These latter contexts 'give a focus to an almost separate female culture', with pleasures and gratifications which would be derided by the women's male partners. The domestic context, concludes Gray, is not a 'singular and unchanging' one; the domestic use of the VCR demonstrates the way in which its gendered power structures construct and limit women's ability to negotiate their own viewing pleasures.

John Fiske's recent work, while continuing to insist that 'the text [i]s a site of struggle for the power to make meanings', nevertheless demonstrates the collapse of the hegemonic model under the pressure of a Foucauldian concept of a decentred and 'productive' power. For Fiske, then (Chapter 35), the concepts of 'text' and 'audience' should be abandoned, to be replaced by 'textuality' and the 'intertextuality' of 'moments of viewing'. Fiske's model of society is of 'a vast shifting range of subcultures and groups' whose members form shifting alliances and become different viewing subjects at different times, producing a range of meanings and pleasures from the semiotic potential that television offers. Fiske proposes the existence of a 'cultural economy' which operates with 'relative autonomy' from the 'financial economy'. In the latter, audiences are commodities, but in the former, – which Fiske grants 'equal, if not greater, power', – they are free to act as producers – of their own pleasures and meanings. The task of the critic is, then, to 'understand popular pleasures and popular discrimination', not by examining texts, audience readings or the processes of production, but through the 'investigation of instances', 'moments of television' in which the 'variety of cultural activities that take place in front of the screen' can be glimpsed.

NOTES

1.   S. Hall, 'Cultural Studies and the Centre: Some Problematics and Problems', in S. Hall, D. Hobson, A. Lowe and P. Willis (eds), *Culture, Media, Language* (London: Hutchinson, 1980) pp. 35–6.
2.   Lois McNay, *Foucault: A Critical Introduction* (Cambridge: Polity Press, 1994) p. 3.
3.   David Morley, 'Changing Paradigms in Audience Studies', in E. Seiter, H. Borchers, G. Kreutzner and E. -M. Warth (eds), *Remote Control: Television, Audiences and Cultural Power* (London: Routledge, 1989) p. 28.
4.   J. Hartley, 'Invisible Fictions', in J. Hartley, *Tele-Ology: Studies in Television* (London: Routledge, 1992) p. 105.
5.   D. Morley, *Family Television: Cultural Power and Domestic Leisure* (London: Comedia, 1986).

34

BEHIND CLOSED DOORS:
VIDEO RECORDERS IN THE HOME

Ann Gray

The video cassette recorder is arguably the major innovation in home entertainment in Britain since television. When we address questions of how women watch television and video we inevitably raise a complex set of issues which relate to women and their everyday lives. In talking to women about home video cassette recorders (VCR) and television use, I have identified some of the determining factors surrounding these activities which take place within the domestic environment.[1] With the development of VCRs and other products such as home computers and cable services, the 1980s is seeing an ever increasing trend towards home-centred leisure and entertainment. New technology in the home has to be understood within a context of structures of power and authority relationships between household members, with gender emerging as one of the most significant differentiations. This far from neutral environment influences the ways in which women use popular texts in general and television and video in particular, and the pleasures and meanings which these have for them.

[. . .]

VIDEO AND FAMILY LIFE

Although there are many aspects of the video phenomenon which are worthy of study, my research initially focuses on the potential choice which the VCR offers for viewing within the domestic and family context. The major reason for this is that, until recently, attention to the context of viewing seems to have been largely neglected in media and cultural studies.[2] The relationship between the viewer and television, the reader and text, is often a relationship which has to be negotiated, struggled for, won or lost, in the dynamic and often chaotic processes of family life. As video recorders offer, above all, extended choice of content and time management for viewing within the home, research into its use has to be focused within that very context. The context of 'the family' is, for my purposes, conceived of as a site of

From H. Baehr and G. Dyer (eds), *Boxed In: Women and Television* (London: Pandora Press, 1987) pp. 38–54.

constant social negotiation within a highly routinised framework of material dependency and normative constraint,[3] and all these elements enter into the negotiations which surround viewing decisions. This family setting, with its power relationships and authority structures across gender, is an extremely important factor in thinking more generally of 'leisure' and, specifically, home-based leisure. The home has increasingly become the site for entertainment, and we can see VCRs as yet one more commodity which reduces the necessity for household members to seek entertainment outside the home, a situation reinforced by the present economic climate in Britain:

> JS: Well, we can't really afford to go out to the pictures, not any more. If we all go and have ice-creams, you're talking about eight or nine pounds. It's a lot of money.

What is especially important for women is that the domestic sphere is increasingly becoming defined as their only leisure space. Many married women are in paid work outside the home, but women are still largely responsible for the domestic labour in the home. Childcare, food provision, laundry, shopping and cleaning the living space, are ultimately women's responsibility even if their male partners help. While men in paid employment come home to a non-work environment, women who either work in the home all day or go out to paid employment still have to work at home in the evenings and at weekends:

> AS: Him? Oh, he sits on his backside all night, from coming in from work to going to bed.

Indeed, many women do not consider themselves as having any leisure at all. (Deem, 1984). And many certainly would not allow themselves the luxury of sitting down to watch television until the children are fed and put to bed and the household chores have been completed:

> JK: I'd feel guilty, I'd feel I was cheating. It's my job and if I'm sat, I'm not doing my job.

This is a context which, at the most basic and practical level, positions women in relation to the whole area of leisure, but particularly in relation to television and video viewing:

> AS: Like, if he comes in and he's rented a video, straight after tea he wants to put it on. I say 'well let me finish the washing-up first'. I mean, I just wouldn't enjoy it if I knew it was all to do.

VIDEO AS TECHNOLOGY

Women and men have differential access to technology in general and to domestic technology in particular. The relations between domestic technology and gender are relatively unexplored,[4] though there is more work on gender and technology in the workplace where, as Jan Zimmerman notes, new technology is entering existing and traditional sets of relations. Old values in this way become encoded in new technologies (Zimmerman, 1981; Cockburn, 1983, 1985). It is interesting to note that American researchers discovered that in the early 1970s the full-time housewife was spending as much time on housework as her grandmother had done fifty years earlier. Domestic technology may be labour-saving, replacing the drudgery of household work, but it is time-consuming in that each piece of equipment requires work if it is to fulfil its advertised potential. Rothschild argues that far from liberating women from housework, new technology, embedded as it is in ideological assumptions about the sexual division of labour, has further entrenched women in the home and in the role of housewife (Rothschild, 1983).

When a new piece of technology is purchased or rented, it is often already inscribed with gender expectations. The gender specificity of pieces of domestic technology is deeply implanted in the 'commonsense' of households, operating almost at an unconscious level. As such it is difficult for the researcher to unearth. One strategy I have employed which throws the gender of domestic technology into high relief is to ask the women to image pieces of equipment as coloured either pink or blue.[5] This produces almost uniformly pink irons and blue electric drills, with many interesting mixtures along the spectrum. The washing machine, for example, is most usually pink on the outside, but the motor is almost always blue. VCRs and, indeed, all home entertainment technology would seem to be a potentially lilac area, but my research has shown that we must break down the VCR into its different modes in our colour-coding. The 'record', 'rewind' and 'play' modes are usually lilac, but the timer switch is nearly always blue, with women having to depend on their male partners or their children to set the timer for them. The blueness of the timer is exceeded only by the deep indigo of the remote control switch which in all cases is held by the man:

> SW: Oh, yes, that's definitely blue in our house. He flicks from channel to channel, I never know what I'm watching – it drives me mad.

It does appear that the male of the household is generally assumed to have knowledge of this kind of technology when it enters the household, or at least he will quickly gain the knowledge. And certain knowledges can, of course, be withheld and used to maintain authority and control:

> AS: Well, at first he was the only one who knew how to record things, but then me and my young son sat down one day and worked it out. That meant we didn't have to keep asking him to record something for us.

Although women routinely operate extremely sophisticated pieces of domestic technology, often requiring, in the first instance, the study and application of a manual of instructions, they often feel alienated from operating the VCR. The reasons for this are manifold and have been brought about by positioning within the family, the education system and the institutionalised sexism with regard to the division of appropriate activities and knowledges in terms of gender. Or there may be, as I discovered, 'calculated ignorance':

> CH: If I learnt how to do the video it would become my job just like everything else.

If women do not feel confident or easy in approaching and operating the recorders, let alone in setting the timer for advance recording, they are at an immediate and real disadvantage in terms of exercising the apparent choices which the VCR offers. This, combined with constraints in the hiring of video tapes, either financial or simply normative, means that for women the idea of increased freedom and choice of viewing may well be spurious.

GENRE AND GENDER

If women are 'positioned' within the context of consumption, it seems that they are also positioned, or even structured in absence, by the video industry itself in terms of the kind of audience it seems to be addressing. To enter a video library is to be visually bombarded by 'covers' depicting scenes of horror, action adventure, war, westerns and 'soft' pornography, traditionally considered to be 'male' genres.[6] Is it therefore mainly men who are hiring video tapes, and if so, what do women feel about the kinds of tapes they are watching at home? Do women ever hire tapes themselves, or do they feel alienated from both the outlets and what they have to offer? In other words, what are the circumstances surrounding the use of video libraries and what is the sexual division of labour associated with the hiring and viewing of tapes? I have already made reference to the so-called 'male' genres which imply that certain kinds of films address themselves to and are enjoyed by a male audience and the same, of course, could be said for 'female' genres. But why do certain kinds of texts or genres appeal to women and not to men and *vice versa* and how should we conceive of the audience for these texts made up of women and men?

The 'gendered audience' has a theoretical history which, as Annette Kuhn usefully points out, has developed within two different perspectives, one emerging from media studies and the other from film theory (Kuhn, 1984). This has resulted in two quite different notions of the gendered audience. The sociological emphasis of media studies has tended to conceive of a 'social audience', that is, an audience made up of already constituted male and female persons who bring (among other things) maleness or femaleness to a text, and who decode the text within that particular frame of reference. Film theory on the other hand, has conceived of a 'psychological audience', a collection of individual spectators who do not read the text, but rather the text 'reads' them. In other words, the film offers a masculine or feminine subject position and the spectator occupies that position. Of course, this is not automatic and there is nothing to prevent, for example, a female spectator taking up a masculine subject position. However, the construction of masculinity and femininity across the institutions within society is so powerfully aligned to the social categories 'male' and 'female' that the two usually coincide apparently seamlessly. But, as Kuhn points out, what is suggested by these two perspectives is a distinction between femaleness as a social gender and femininity as a subject position. The problem here is that neither of these two perspectives is sufficient in themselves to gain a full understanding of what happens when men and women watch films. In the former case, context is emphasised over text and in the latter text over context. The spectator–text relationship suggested by the psychoanalytic models used in film theory tend to disregard those important factors of social context involved in film and TV watching. Also, they find it difficult to allow for the subject constituted outside the text, across other discourses, such as class, race, age and general social environment. The social audience approach, conversely, sees the response to texts as a socially predetermined one, and in this way does not allow for consideration of how the texts themselves work on the viewers/readers.

There have been some attempts to link text with context by examining the particular features of 'women's genres'. Soap operas, for example, have been looked at in terms of their distinctive narrative pattern, which is open-ended and continuous; their concern with so-called 'female' skills; their scheduling on television which fits into the rhythm of women's work at home, all of which can be seen as specifically addressing a social audience of women (Brunsdon, 1981; Modleski, 1982). However, this would still seem to stress context over text and in this area the film theory perspective has certainly been limited by its implicit assumption of an intense and concentrated relationship between spectator and text in a darkened cinema. For television this relationship is more likely to be characterised by distinction and diversion. As Kuhn points out:

This would suggest that each medium constructs sexual difference through spectatorship in rather different ways: cinema through the look and spectacle, and TV – perhaps less evidently – through a capacity to insert its flow, its characteristic modes of address and the textual operations of different kinds of programmes into the rhythms and routines of domestic activities and sexual divisions of labour in the household at various times of day. (Kuhn, 1984, p. 25)

This distinction is important and useful, but when thinking about the use of VCRs the two media are viewed in the same context. Movies have long been a part of television's nightly 'flow' as well as part of daytime viewing. But in video recording movies off television for watching at a later date, and in hiring movies, we have a discrete 'event' which disrupts the flow of television and its insertive scheduling:

AC: Oh yes, we all sit down and watch – 'we've got a video, let's sit down' – TV's different, that's just on.

Concepts of the psychological audience and the social audience are not sufficient in themselves to explore the whole complexity of text, subject and context and the ways in which they intersect. But both are necessary, representing as they do different instances within the process of consumption of popular texts. While the psychological model posits an unacceptably homogeneous and 'universal' audience, it does allow us to consider the importance of how texts work, not only in terms of subject positioning and interpellation, but also in terms of pleasure and desire. The social model demands that the audience is heterogeneous and requires us to explore those other differences and contexts which, to a greater or lesser extent, determine the ways in which women and men read those texts. It seems clear that the problem of the relationship between text and gendered audience cannot be resolved at the theoretical level, but rather must be kept in play and, if possible, problematised throughout the research enterprise.

VIEWING CONTEXTS

It would seem that women do have certain preconceptions about what constitutes a 'film for men' as against a 'film for women', and furthermore, a typology of viewing contexts is beginning to emerge, along with appropriate associated texts (see Table [34.1]).

I wish to focus mainly on Context (Female alone), but before I do it is worth mentioning the difference between the negotiations around Contexts (Male alone) and (Female alone). For the latter to exist, the male partner must normally be out of the house, either at work or at leisure, whereas, Context (Male alone) would be likely to exist when both male and female were in the house together. The women simply wouldn't watch:

BA: If he's watching something I'm not enjoying, I'll either knit or read.
JS: Well, I can read when the telly's on if it's something I don't like.
DS: I usually go to bed with a book, or sometimes I'll watch the portable in the kitchen, but it's damned uncomfortable in there.
CH: Well, when he's in, Father has priority over what's on. Yes, he does, but I can go in the other room if I don't want to watch it.

WOMEN ONLY

For women who are at home all day, either with very small children or children of school age, and whose husbands are out at work, there are obvious opportunities for them to view alone. However, most of the women I have talked to are constrained by guilt, often referring to daytime viewing as some kind of drug:

> SW: No, I've got too many things to do during the daytime, I couldn't do it to myself, I'd be a total addict.
>
> JK: Well, I watch *Falcon Crest* – it's a treat, when I've done my work, then I sit down and it's my treat. But I'm not one to get videos during the day because I think you can get really addicted, then everything else suffers.

The second woman quoted indicates what is a fairly common strategy – that of using daytime television programmes to establish some time for herself as a reward to which completion of household tasks will lead. This assuages the guilt to a certain extent and the pleasure afforded by this particular viewing context seems to go far beyond the pleasures of the text itself. What it represents is a breathing space when the busy mother can resist the demands of her children and domestic labour for a brief period of time. One of the most popular daytime programmes cited was *Sons & Daughters*, an Australian imported soap opera, transmitted three afternoons a week in the Yorkshire region. Most of the women preferred to watch this alone, some taking the telephone off the hook to ensure uninterrupted concentration, but they would watch it with a friend if they happened to be in each other's houses at the time. Janice Radway in her study of women and romantic fiction talks with regret of the isolated context within which popular romances are consumed by women (Radway, 1984). The next viewing context I wish to discuss reveals a more optimistic state of affairs for women.

This context is again female only, but is one in which several women get together to watch a video which they have hired jointly. This would normally happen during the day when their

Table [34.1] *Typology of viewing contexts*[7]

Context	Film	TV
1　Family together	*Superman* Walt Disney *Jaws* Comedy	Children's TV Quiz shows Comedy *EastEnders*
2　Male and female partners together	*An Officer and a Gentleman* *Kramer v. Kramer* The Rockys Any Clint Eastwood	*Aufweidersehen Pet* *Minder* Shows *Coronation Street* *EastEnders*
3　Male alone	War Action adventure* Horror* Adults*	Sport News Documentaries
4　Female alone	*Who Will Love My Children?* *Evergreen* Romance	*Coronation Street* *Crossroads* *Dallas* *Dynasty* *A Woman of Substance* *Princess Daisy*

* These are the category headings used by many video libraries

children are at school. Far from being instrumental in isolating women, it would seem that there is a tendency to communal use of hired videos, mainly on economic grounds, but also on the grounds that the women can watch what they want together without the guilt or the distraction of children:

BS: There are three of us, and we hire two or three films a week and watch them together, usually at Joyce's house when the kids are at school. We can choose what we want then.

JK: Yes, if there's something we want to see we wait 'til the kids have gone back to school so's we can sit and watch it without them coming in saying 'can I have . . . can I have . . . ' it makes it difficult.

The idea of viewing together during the day for this particular network of women living on the same street came when one of them found herself continually returning the video tapes which her husband had hired the night before. She discovered that there were films which she would like to watch but which her husband never hired. A good relationship was established with the woman who worked in the video library who would look out for good films:

BS: She comes into the shop where I work and I go 'have any new videos come out?' She tells me. She knows what we like.

One favoured form for this viewing network is that of the long family saga, often running to two or three tapes:

JK: We like something in two or three parts; something with a really good story to it so's you can get involved.

BS: Mm . . . the other week we had a Clint Eastwood and Burt Reynolds film because she [MD] likes Clint Eastwood but we talked all the way through that, didn't we?

When the group views sagas which extend over two or three tapes there is obvious pleasure in anticipating both the outcome of the narrative and the viewing of the following tape. A considerable amount of discussion and speculation ensues and a day for the next viewing is fixed:

MD: We like to spread them out – every other day, it helps to break the week up. Sometimes we have them on an evening, if our husbands are away or out. We'll have a bottle of wine then, then we don't even have to get up to make a cup of tea.

These women are also devotees of the American soap operas and operate a 'failsafe' network of video recording for each other, refusing to discuss each episode until they have all seen it. These popular texts form an important part of their friendship and association in their everyday lives and give a focus to an almost separate female culture which they can share together within the constraints of their positions as wives and mothers. Furthermore, they are able to take up the feminine subject positions offered by these texts comfortably and pleasurably. In contrast, the films which their husbands hire for viewing Context (Male & female partners together) mainly offer a masculine subject position which the women seem to take up through their male partners, who in turn give their approval to such texts.

The major impetus for a viewing group like this is that films which women enjoy watching are rarely, if ever, hired by their male partners for viewing together because they consider such films to be 'trivial' and 'silly' and women are laughed at for enjoying them:

BA: I sit there with tears running down my face and he comes in and says 'you daft thing.'

This derision also applies to soap operas, and is reproduced in male children:

JK: Oh, my son thinks I'm stupid because I won't miss *Dallas* – perhaps I am.

It is the most powerful member within the household who defines this hierarchy of 'serious' and 'silly', 'important' and 'trivial'. This leaves women and their pleasures in films downgraded, objects and subjects of fun and derision, having to consume them almost in secret. But the kinds of films and television soap operas which women enjoy watching alone deal with things of importance to them, highlighting so-called 'female' concerns – care of children, concern for members of one's own family, consideration for one's own sexual partner, selflessness in characters – all of which are the skills of competence, the thought and caring which husbands and children expect of women and assume as a matter of natural course.[8] This is a deeply contradictory position for women, lying between the realities of their day to day lives and the pleasures and gratifications that they seek to find in texts that their partners and very often their children, look upon as so much rubbish:

JS: I think a lot of storylines in soap operas are very weak and I think a man needs something to keep his interest more than a woman. That makes a man sound more intelligent, but that's not what I mean. It's got to be something worth watching before he'll sit down and actually watch it, but I'd watch anything. I think he thinks its unmanly to watch them.

SW: All the soap operas are rubbish for men, fantasy for women.

AG: *Do you think men need fantasy?*

SW: They need fantasy in a different way, detectives and wars, that's their fantasy world, and science fiction, a tough, strong world. Not sloppy, who's fallen in love with who, who's shot JR – it's rubbish. Men know it's rubbish, that's the difference.

Here are two women talking about a genre they love in relation to their male partners, giving us a sense of the 'power of definition' within the partnerships, but also the ways in which the women themselves think of their own pleasures.

CONCLUSION

Theories of the gendered audience as they have been developed are useful, but when women and men watch movies and television they become that hybrid, the *social spectator* (Kuhn, *ibid.*) and, in understanding the subject–text–context relationship, the social and the psychological have to be kept in play to a proportionately greater or lesser degree. This allows us to consider how texts and contexts (both the specific and the wider social context) combine together in producing the gendered reading subject. Charlotte Brunsdon, writing on *Crossroads*, has attempted to resolve this dualism and suggests that, 'The relation of the audience to the text will not be determined solely by that text, but also by positionalities in relation to a whole range of other discourses – discourses of motherhood, romance and sexuality for example' (Brunsdon, 1981, p. 32).

This enables us to think of the subject in the social context occupying different positions in relation to different discourses which change across time. As particular discourses become central issues, they will affect the ways in which the social subject occupies, or resists, the subject position constructed by a text.

The viewing and reading of texts takes place, for the majority of people, within the domestic context. However, this is a context which is not singular and unchanging, but plural and open to different permutations, dependent upon the negotiations between members of the household and the particular texts involved. The VCR offers the potential for extended choice of viewing in terms of text and context. But in order to explore how this potential is being used the particular conditions of its consumption must be addressed. The viewing contexts and their associated texts which I have outlined here have emerged from my discussions with women who occupy different social positions and there are remarkable similarities in the ways in which all the women have spoken about their domestic viewing practices. However, it is simply not sufficient to have identified these similarities, and my analysis of the interview 'texts' continues in an attempt to make visible the important differences between the women's accounts of these practices. These differences must be seen in relation to their particular social positioning and the various specific discourses which they inhabit. The interview material I have gathered demands a framework of analysis which uses theories and concepts developed within different disciplines and will, I am sure, test their relative strengths and weaknesses in revealing the complexity of how women relate to television and video in their everyday lives.

NOTES

1. This research was initially funded by the Economic and Social Research Council and has taken the form of long, open-ended discussions with women whose age, social position, employment and family circumstances differ (race is a variable which has not been introduced). Part of my strategy has been to encourage open discussion and allow the women themselves to introduce topics which are of importance to them. By keeping the discussions open they can take pleasure in having the opportunity to explore and express their own ideas and feelings on these matters. For discussions on feminist research methods see Roberts (ed.), 1981; Stanley and Wise, 1983; Bell and Roberts, 1984.
2. There are notable exceptions (Hobson, 1981 and 1982; Morley, 1986; Collett, 1986).
3. I am grateful to Elizabeth Shove and Andrew Tudor for this working definition.
4. However, a recent publication by W. Faulkner and E. Arnold (eds), *Smothered by Invention Technology in Women's Lives*, Pluto Press, 1985, does address issues of domestic technology and gender.
5. These were ideas discussed at a seminar given by Cynthia Cockburn at York University, June 1985. See also Cockburn, 1985.
6. It is interesting to note that video tapes are now being distributed which are specifically aimed at a female audience; IPC and Videospace combined magazine and video to market their *Woman's Own Selection*, along with their more recent label *Image of Love*, while Polygram Video are offering a label, *Women's Choice*. However, in the North of England certainly, these have a very limited distribution.
7. These are the names which the women themselves gave to the different texts and genres.
8. Charlotte Brunsdon has made this point in relation to *Crossroads*, but we can see that it can apply to other 'women's genres' (Brunsdon, 1981).

REFERENCES

Barker, M. (ed.) (1984) *The Video Nasties*, London, Pluto Press.
Bell, C. and Roberts, H. (eds) (1984), *Social Researching*, London, Routledge & Kegan Paul.
Brunsdon, C. (1981), 'Crossroads: Notes on a soap opera', *Screen*, vol. 22, no. 4, pp. 32–7. [See Chapter 40 of this volume.]
Cockburn, C. (1983), *Brothers*, London, Pluto Press.
Cockburn, C. (1985), *Machinery of Dominance*, London, Pluto Press.
Collett, P. (1986), 'Watching the TV audience', paper presented to International Television Studies Conference 1986.
Deem, R. (1984), 'Paid work, leisure and non-employment: shifting boundaries and gender differences', paper presented to British Sociological Association Conference 1984.
Hobson, D. (1981), 'Housewives and the mass media', in Hall, S. *et al.* (eds), *Culture, Media, Language*, London, Hutchinson. [See Chapter 32 of this volume.]
Hobson, D. (1982), '*Crossroads': The Drama of a Soap Opera*, London, Methuen. [See Chapter 41 of this volume.]
Kuhn, A. (1984), 'Women's genres', *Screen*, vol. 25, no. 1, Jan/Feb, pp. 18–28.

Modleski, T. (1982), *Loving With a Vengeance*, Hamden, Connecticut, Shoe String Press. [See Chapter 38 of this volume.]
Morley, D. (1986), *Family Television: Cultural Power and Domestic Leisure*, London, Comedia.
Radway, J. A. (1984), *Reading the Romance*, Chapel Hill, University of North Carolina Press.
Roberts, H. (ed.) (1981), *Doing Feminist Research*, London, Routledge & Kegan Paul.
Rothschild, J. (1983), *Machina ex Dea*, New York, Pergamon Press.
Stanley L. and Wise, S. (1983), *Breaking Out*, London, Routledge & Kegan Paul.
Zimmerman, J. (1981), 'Technology and the future of women: haven't we met somewhere before?', *Women's Studies International Quarterly*, vol. 4, no. 3, p. 355.

35

MOMENTS OF TELEVISION: NEITHER THE TEXT NOR THE AUDIENCE

John Fiske

A group of people in front of the television set, spines curved weakly on the couch, drinks or snacks in hand, eyes glued to the screen is, I suppose, the commonsense model of television and its audience. What is on the screen is the text, the people watching, multiplied a millionfold, are the audience. In the not too distant past there have been theories of both the text and the audience that, unfortunately for them and us, have taken this model for the uninspected base of their assumptions, for the scene the model paints is both typical and realistic. Its problem lies in its easy categorization of the viewers into 'the audience' and the screen into 'the text'.

I wish to dissolve both categories. First, there is no such thing as 'the television audience,' defined as an empirically accessible object, for there can be no meaningful categories beyond its boundaries – what on earth is 'not the television audience'? The 'television audience' is not a social category like class, or race, or gender – everyone slips in or out of it in a way that makes nonsense of any categorical boundaries: similarly when in 'it' people constitute themselves quite differently as audience members at different times – I am a different television 'audience' when watching my football team from when watching *The A-Team* with my son or *Days of our Lives* with my wife. Categories focus our thinking on similarities: people watching television are best modeled according to a multitude of differences.

Similarly, the television text, or program, is no unified whole delivering the same message in the same way to all its 'audience.' The old literary idea of the organic, self-contained text has been exploded so comprehensively that there is no need for me here to contribute further to its demolition. But we still need the term, or something like it to refer to television's meaning-making potential, though we might do better to make it less concrete, less comfortable to handle, and to use the word 'textuality' whose abstraction signals its potentiality rather than its concrete existence. What the set in the living-room delivers is 'television,' visual and aural

From E. Seiter, H. Borchers, G. Kreutzner and E. M. Worth (eds), *Remote Control: Television, Audiences and Cultural Power* (London: Routledge, 1989) pp. 56–78.

signifiers that are potential provokers of meaning and pleasure. This potential is its textuality which is mobilized differently in the variety of its moments of viewing.

Textuality is realized in the making of sense and the production of pleasure, and central to this process is the inescapable intertextuality of our culture, a point I shall return to later. For the moment I wish only to point out that we have now collapsed the distinction between 'text' and 'audience.' The textuality of television, the intenextuality of the process of making sense and pleasure from it, can only occur when people bring their different histories and subjectivities to the viewing process. There is no text, there is no audience, there are only the processes of viewing, –that variety of cultural activities that take place in front of the screen which constitute the object of study that I am proposing.

THE VIEWER

[. . .]

Watching television is a process of making meanings and pleasures, and this process is determined by two parallel and interlocking sets of forces. I use the word 'determine' in its literal sense of setting the boundaries, not in its more common mis-sense of authoritarian social imperatives – thou shalt be, do, feel, react as society determines. Determination, then, refers to a bounded terrain within which people have the space to exercise some power over their meanings, pleasures, subjectivities. People can and do make their own culture, albeit within conditions that are not of their own choosing. How much power is available within this terrain, and how fixedly its boundaries are determined are matters of considerable debate, in which I align myself with those who propose that ideological and hegemonic theories of popular culture have overestimated the power of the determinations and underestimated that of the viewer.

The two intertwined sets of determination are the social and the textual, the one working upon the subjectivity of the viewer, the other upon the textuality of television, and I wish to argue that the correspondence between subjectivity and textuality is so close that the two leak into each other at every point of contact.

Viewers within this determined terrain are subjects constituted by late-capitalist societies. Such societies are characterized by heterogeneity – a vast shifting range of subcultures and groups which are finally structured by their relationship to the system by which power is unequally distributed in them. Any one person, or television viewer, forms a number of shifting alliances within this heterogeneity, she or he enters the social system via differently constituted and shifting social formations: the metaphor of a nomadic subjectivity is a productive one here.[1] Any one viewer, then, may at different times be a different viewing subject, as constituted by his or her social determinants, as different social alliances may be mobilized for different moments of viewing: to return to our spatial metaphor, the socially constituted viewing subject may occupy different spaces within the determined terrain according to the social alliances appropriate to this specific moment of making sense of and finding pleasure in the television experience. Hall refers to a similar process as 'articulation.'[2] Here he uses both senses of the word, first as speech, that is a symbolic system used to make sense of both self and experience, and second as flexible linkage. Hodge and Tripp's school students who made sense of *Prisoner* by aligning themselves with the prisoners, the wardens with school teachers, and the prison with the school were articulating, in both senses of the word.[3] They were using the television program to 'speak,' or make sense of their experience of institutionalized subordination and thus to make sense of themselves as subordinated subjects, and they did this by articulating (linking) their viewing of a soap opera set in a women's prison with their social experience of school.

But many of the same students also enjoyed *Sale of the Century* – *Prisoner* and *Sale of the Century* were the most popular programs amongst Australian junior high school students in 1983. Here, the program was articulated with school in a way that produced quite different meanings and pleasures.[4] Making sense of popular television, then, is the process of activating meanings from it, and this process is controlled within more or less determined boundaries by the socially situated viewer. The text will be a source of popular pleasure when these meanings become part of that larger cultural process by which the subject makes sense of his or her material existence. For social experience is like a text: it can only be made meaningful when a social subject brings his or her discursive competencies to bear upon it. The shifting alliance of formations that constitute social experience for the subject allows for a potentially unlimited range of social differences so that each person may be constituted differently, yet these differences are to be explained not by the individual differences of psychology but by the variety of intersections of social alliances and social relations.

Social experience is like intertextuality. It is a vast interlocking potential of elements that can be mobilized in an unpredictable number of ways. Any social system needs a system of meanings to underpin it, and the meanings that are made of it are determined only to an extent by the system itself. This determination allows adequate space for different people to make different meanings though they may use a shared discursive repertoire in the process. The subject is not fully subjected – the sense we make of our social relations is partly under our control – and making sense of social experience necessarily involves making sense of ourselves within that experience.

This potential of meanings that constitutes our social experience must not be seen as amoeba-like and structureless. Just as post-structuralism and discourse theory must not be allowed to evacuate a notion of material social relations, so too, my argument in favor of difference and a relatively empowered, relatively loosely subjected, subject must not blind us to the determining framework of power relations within which all of this takes place. In a similar vein, the emphasis on the power of the viewer to achieve certain meanings from the potential offered by the text can only be understood in terms of a textual power and a textual struggle that are remarkably similar to social power and social struggle. Making sense of social experience is an almost identical process to making sense of a text.

What television delivers is not programs but a semiotic experience. This experience is characterized by its openness and polysemy. Television is not quite a do-it-yourself meaning kit but neither is it a box of ready-made meanings for sale. Although it works within cultural determinations, it also offers freedoms and the power to evade, modify, or challenge these limitations and controls. All texts are polysemic, but polysemy is absolutely central to television's textuality.

TELEVISION AS CULTURAL COMMODITY

Television is a cultural commodity. It works within an economically determined capitalist economy, but when we have said that about it we have said both much and remarkably little. There is a financial economy within which wealth circulates, and a cultural economy within which meanings and pleasures circulate, and the relationship between them is not as deterministic as some theorists have proposed. In the financial economy television is programs and advertisements, not textuality. A program is a commodity produced and then sold to distributors. In distribution its role changes and it becomes not a commodity, but a producer, and what it produces is a new commodity, the audience which is then, in its turn, sold as a commodity to advertisers. The ramifications of this financial economy are fascinating, but they are not the topic of this paper. I wish to concentrate more on the cultural economy.

Here the role shift undergone by the program in the financial economy – that from commodity to producer – is now undergone by the audience, whom I left as a commodity sold to the advertiser. But in the cultural economy the audience rejects its role as commodity and becomes a producer, a producer of meanings and pleasures, and at this moment stops being 'an audience' and becomes different materializations of the process that we call 'viewing television.'

While the metaphor of a cultural economy is a productive one, we must not let it blind us to differences between it and the financial. Meanings and pleasures do not circulate in the cultural economy in the same way that wealth does in the financial. In the first place there is no exchange of money at the point of sale or consumption. Television *appears* to be free, however it may actually be paid for. Payment has no direct relationship to consumption – people can consume as much as they wish and what they wish with no thought of what they are able to afford. Watching an opera or a concert by Dire Straits costs no more than a quiz show or a rerun sitcom.

This liberation from economic constraints frees the viewer from the subordinate role in the market economy, that of 'consumer' who, by definition, gives more than he or she receives. This crucial difference between the television commodity and other more material goods in the market-place foregrounds the considerable freedom won by the viewer in the shift from consumer in the financial economy to producer in the cultural. Meanings and pleasures cannot be owned or bought and sold in a way that grants proprietorial rights over them to some but denies them to others. Bourdieu's theory of cultural capital needs re-examination: for him cultural capital works for one section of the bourgeoisie (the intelligentsia) similarly to the way that economic capital works for the business section.[5] It works to maintain power in the hands of the powerful, advantaged minority, whether that power be expressed in economic or cultural terms. We need to add to this notion that of a popular cultural capital that puts bourgeois culture under constant pressure. Hobson, for instance, has shown how the women viewers of *Crossroads* had made the program theirs, had constituted it as their cultural capital that they could draw upon to articulate their social relations and social identities – the meanings and pleasures of the program were theirs, not the male producers'.[6] Similarly, Hodge and Tripp have shown how Australian Aboriginal children have made American westerns into their cultural capital.[7] They constructed a cultural category, a tool to think with, that included them, American Indians, and American blacks in a way that enabled them to find in the western some articulation of their subordination to white imperialism and, presumably, to identify with instances of resistance to it. Such a reading position will, we may predict, affect the sense they make of the inevitability of the final narrative defeat of the Indians or non-whites. It was their ability to make a non-white sense from, and find non-white pleasures in, a genre of white imperialism and colonialism that made it popular with them. Without this ability to be the producers of their own culture, the makers of their own meanings and pleasures, it would be difficult to account for Aboriginals' choosing to watch westerns.

This freedom of the viewer to make socially pertinent meanings and pleasures out of television is considerable. Tulloch and Moran found that school students in working-class and middle-class areas made completely different sense out of an episode of the Australian soap *A Country Practice* which dealt with youth unemployment.[8] The working-class students articulated it with their social experience and found in it the sense that the economic system was at fault in not providing enough jobs for the people. The middle-class students, on the other hand, found meanings that supported the system and placed the blame upon the failures of the (working-class) individuals: for them the unemployed were the undereducated, and the episode's meanings for them were produced by the socially derived discourses of class, education, and economics that they brought to bear upon it. A group of Arab viewers in Katz and Liebes' study of different ethnic group readings of *Dallas* found it incompatible with their own culture that Sue Ellen, escaping with her baby from her husband, should return to her father; so they 'rewrote' it in their conversation about the program, making her return to her former lover, not to her father.[9] Of course, this freedom is inherent in all popular art, not just television: Michaels, for instance, has found that Aboriginal viewers of *Rambo*, who derived great pleasure from the movie, 'rewrote' considerable areas of it.[10] They found pleasure in Rambo's conflict with authority (presumably his Hispanic, non-white appearance, his verbal inarticulateness, and his opposition to the white officer class will have helped here), but could find neither sense nor pleasure in his 'patriotic' nationalistic motivation. Instead they constructed for him a tribal or family motivation by inserting him into an elaborate kinship network with those he was rescuing, which enabled them to make sense of the movie in a way that paralleled the way they made sense of their social relations both with each other and with white power. The fact that the film was a favorite with both Ronald Reagan and Australian Aboriginals must not lead us to assume any affinity between the two, nor between the meanings and pleasures that each produced from the same cultural commodity.

The (usually) scatological versions of television commercial jingles produced by school children provide an extreme example of this 'rewriting' process which is itself typical.[11] Most viewers of course do not need to rewrite television to this extent to find pleasurable meanings in it, but these examples demonstrate that the freedom is there; they are not a distinct form of perverse or aberrant viewing, but an exaggerated and therefore explicit example of the normal process of making meanings and pleasures from television.

This model differs essentially from that underlying political economy in stressing the relative autonomy of the cultural economy from the financial to which political economy traditionally grants considerable, if not total, determinate power. The political economy model is thus unable to progress beyond seeing the audience as a commodity, or in defining it other than in market terms, those of demographic headcounting. Equally it cannot conceive of the text except as the free lunch that catches the audience for the advertisers. Of course the audience is a commodity, of course the text is a free lunch: but neither definition comes within a mile of adequacy. Political economy cannot conceive of television audiences as being socially diverse and therefore capable of producing different socially pertinent meanings from the same commodity, nor of conceiving of this productive activity as pleasurable. It thus cannot conceive of the cultural commodity as a text that requires reading, and thus as capable of serving the contradictory interests of both the producers in the financial economy and of the viewers in the cultural: it cannot conceive of the text as a site of struggle for the power to make meanings; or of the notion that what finally determines the meanings and pleasures provoked by a text is the social situation of the viewer-reader, *not* the interests of the producers and their ideological investment in consumer capitalism. This leads to another crucial factor in the cultural economy which political economy is unable to take into account, and that is popular discrimination. The people choose to make some texts popular, and some not, and this process of choice is essentially a popular one: however hard the industry may try through market research, promotion, advertising, and scheduling to influence popular choice, its failure rate is enormous. It has thus been forced into producing what Garnham calls a 'repertoire' of products from which the public is invited to choose.[12] And it does not know which of its products will be chosen: if it did, it could concentrate on producing a narrower and thus more profitable repertoire. As it is, twelve out of thirteen records fail to make a profit, as do the vast majority of films on their cinema release. Television shows are regularly axed in mid-run. Political economy cannnot conceive of any audience activity that opposes the interests of the producers, whether this activity be one of semiosis or of discrimination.

My position differs from that of political economy in locating at least equal, if not greater, power in the cultural economy. The interests of the financial economy would be best served by producing and reproducing the smallest number of hit products: the cultural needs of the constantly shifting alliances of its audiences force the industry into its constant search for products that have enough originality to meet these shifts, but yet retain enough familiarily to meet both the audience expectations and developed competencies, and the routinized production practices of the producers. The major drive for innovation and change comes from the audience activity in the cultural economy, and from the relationship of this activity to larger movements in the political and social system. Television's rehabilitation of Vietnam in shows like *Magnum PI, Simon and Simon* or *The A-Team* has participated in the 1980s shift of American values to the Reaganite masculine right, but did not originate it. Similarly, shows like *Designing Women, Golden Girls*, and *Cagney and Lacey* are part of the redefinition of gender meanings, but the spur to redefine them came from the changing material conditions of women. In both cases, it was the cultural economy's dialectic relationship with the socio-political system at the level of the meanings of social experience that fed into the financial economy and caused the economic success and therefore the reproduction of these genres. Theorizing the audience as commodity blinds us to the subtleties and complexities of these social forces.

Of course the audiences' freedom and ability to make their socially pertinent meanings out of television's text, even though these meanings may be beyond both the prediction and the control of the producers, is, at one level, exactly what producers want: they neither know nor care what meanings and pleasures their audiences produce, their concern is solely with the headcount and the demographics. But only a tiny proportion of audience members are converted into purchasers or even potential purchasers. We must be chary of singular definitions of such multifarious (and ultimately untenable) categories as text and audience. Just as television's textuality can simultaneously serve the economic needs of its producers and the cultural pleasures of its audiences, however oppositional these functions may be to each other, so the audience can, at one and the same time, fill the contradictory roles of commodity and cultural producer. Russian Jews, newly arrived in Israel, read *Dallas* as capitalism criticizing itself: such a process can hardly be described as one of commodification.[13] Of course the industry will attempt, often successfully, to produce programs that invite and encourage the audiences' powers as meaning-producers, but their commercial intention can only describe a part and, I would argue, a small part, of the audiences' activities within the cultural economy.

[. . .]

CRITICAL INTERVENTION

Television's textuality is not bounded by the titles and credits of a program, subjectivity cannot be confined within the skin or history of an individual, and similarly viewing television cannot be confined to the periods when the set is switched on. Television is not only part of the process of viewing, or reading or talking about it, but it is also part of our cultural lives when its presence is less direct, less obvious. We need to investigate ways in which a television fan watches movies in a cinema or attends a live ballgame: we need to probe how a middle-aged fan of *Miami Vice* makes sense of his own shabby dress. Television is part of family relations and family politics, it is part of gender relations and politics, part of consumer relations and politics. Again, a comprehensive map of all the cultural processes, of which television viewing is only one, is both impossible and unnecessary. What is needed is the investigation of instances that are no more and no less typical than other instances. And the emphasis should be not on what people do, not on what their social experience is, but on how they make sense of it. Their recorded words and behaviors are not data giving us their reactions and meanings, but instances of the sense-making process that we call culture, clues of how this process works and can be actualized.

The ability of the critic to intervene in the politics of popular culture, to counter the forces of domination and support those of resistance or evasion, depends upon a far more sympathetic and detailed understanding of the cultural economy than we have so far achieved. The traditional critical emphasis from the left has focused upon the power of the industry and upon the power of ideology and hegemony. This has led us to locate the appropriate sites of intervention in the processes of production and representation. A more effective, if methodologically much more difficult, focus for intervention might be the diversity of sites of reception, but instrumental simplicity should not be the only factor in our choice of appropriate political action.

The main problem facing the critic today is to understand popular pleasures and popular discrimination, and on the basis of this understanding to decide how and if to intervene in both the production and reception of texts. It may be that open heteroglossic texts such as *Dallas* (which Altman characterises as a 'menu' from which viewers choose[14]) are actually socially and politically more progressive than more closed, monoglossic texts, even ones that prefer more apparently progressive meanings. The progressiveness of popular television may lie in heteroglossic programs that not only promote the dominant ideology but that also offer opportunities to resist, oppose, and evade it. As yet, we just do not know.

We can only find out by paying more attention to the moments of reception for only here can we determine which texts and which characteristics of those texts offer their polysemy for semiotic mobilization by the subordinate, and how these semiotic differences are produced and circulated subculturally. We also need to discover why some members of subordinated groups are more productive or more resistant viewers than others. The critic can only intervene effectively on the basis of adequate understanding, and on the basis of a deep respect for the pleasure that the subordinate make from their popular culture. It may seem unfortunate that it is commercially motivated mainstream television that is best able to offer these pleasures, but possibly the commercial imperative has brought its producers to a closer relationship with popular social experience than the more distantly theorized political-moral-aesthetic position of those with both a social conscience and a social power has been able to achieve.

The question facing progressive critics may now need reversing: rather than asking how it is that the culture industry makes people into commodities that serve its interests, we should now be asking how it is that the people can turn the products of the industry into *their* popular culture and can make them serve *their* interests.

Social differences are produced by the social system but the meanings of these differences are produced by culture: the sense of them has to be constantly produced and reproduced as part of the subject's experience of these differences. Viewer-driven meanings made from texts and subculturally driven meanings made of social experience involve the pleasures of producing meanings rather than the subjection of being produced by them, and make it possible to maintain a consciousness of those abrasive, uncomfortable social differences that hegemonic common sense works so hard to smooth over.

And television plays a crucial role in this; though it is produced by the culture industry and bears within it the lines of hegemonic force, it is met by the tactics of the everyday. De Certeau argues that social power and the power to make meanings that serve the interests of the dominant work strategically, that is, they work in the manner of an occupying army, in a massively organized structure of power.[15] But they are met by the tactics of guerrilla warfare, by tactical, fleeting raids upon their weak points which are not organized into any master plan, but which exploit the particularities and possibilities of each tactical moment. According to de Certeau, 'people make do with what they have,' and in the heavily bureaucratized and industrialized society of late capitalism, what people have is what is provided for them by the institutions and industries of capitalism. It is through these that the social strategy is put into practice, but its effectivity must not be read simply from its intent or from the strength of the forces at its disposal. It is not only the US army in Vietnam and the Soviet army in Afghanistan that have been unable to devise a strategy to beat guerrilla tactics. What we need to investigate, after de Certeau's provocative theorizing, is the everyday tactical, and therefore pleasurable, uses of these cultural resources (albeit industrially produced), the everyday deployment of the tactics of evasion, expropriation, and resistance.

The links between semiotic power/resistance/pleasure and the maintenance of resistive social differences, the role of television in this, and the part that all this can play in social change are theoretically arguable. What I would like to see is the methodologically daunting project of tracing actual instances of these links being made, of these processes being actualized, of the delineation of the multitude of cultural processes at work in the different moments of viewing television.

NOTES

1. Lawrence Grossberg, 'The In-Difference of Television,' *Screen* 28, no. 2 (spring 1987): 28–46.

2. Lawrence Grossberg (ed.) 'On Postmodernism and Articulation: An Interview with Stuart Hall,' *Journal of Communication Inquiry* 10, no. 2 (summer 1986): 45–60.

3. Robert Hodge and David Tripp, *Children and Television* (Cambridge: Polity Press, 1986). *Prisoner*, (screened in the US under the title *Prisoner – Cell Block H*) is an Australian soap opera set in a women's prison. Hodge and Tripp (p. 49) found that school students identified many similarities between school students and prisoners:
    1. pupils are shut in;
    2. pupils are separated from their friends;
    3. pupils would not be there if they were not made to be;
    4. pupils only work because they are punished if they do not and it is less boring than doing nothing at all;
    5. pupils have no rights; they can do nothing about an unfair teacher;
    6. some teachers victimize their pupils;
    7. there are gangs and leaders amongst the pupils;
    8. there are silly rules which everyone tries to break.
These similarities enable *Prisoner* to provide the students with an imaginative 'language' with which to think through their experience of powerlessness in the school. The meanings of subordination were those of the subordinate, not of the dominant, and there is evidence that students found these meanings both pleasurable and empowering.

4. *Sale of the Century* and *Prisoner* were both 'articulations' of school in that both could be linked with school and could be used differently to 'speak,' or make sense of, the school experience. See John Fiske, *Television Culture* (London and New York: Methuen, 1987).

5. Pierre Bourdieu, 'The Aristocracy of Culture,' *Media, Culture, and Society* 2, no. 3 (July 1980): 225–54.

6. Dorothy Hobson, *'Crossroads'*: The *Drama of a Soap Opera* (London: Methuen, 1982). [See Chapter 41 of this volume.]

7. Hodge and Tripp, *Children and Television*.

8. John Tulloch and Albert Moran, *'A Country Practice'*: *'Quality Soap'* (Sydney: Currency Press, 1986).

9. Elihu Katz and Tamar Liebes, 'Mutual Aid in the Decoding of *Dallas*: Preliminary Notes from a Cross-

Cultural Case Study,' in Phillip Drummond and Richard Paterson (eds) *Television in Transition*, (London: British Film Institute, 1985), pp. 187–98.

10. Eric Michaels, 'Aboriginal Content: Who's Got it – Who Needs it' (paper presented at the Australian Screen Studies Association Conference, Sydney, December 1986).

11. Fiske, *Television Culture*; e.g. Sydney children in 1982 and 1983 were singing their version of a Tooheys beer commercial: 'How do you feel when you're having a fuck, under a truck, and the truck rolls off? I feel like a Tooheys', I feel like a Tooheys', I feel like a Tooheys' or two' (Children's Folklore Archives, Australian Studies Centre, Curtin University).

12. Nicholas Garnham, 'Concepts of Culture: Public Policy and the Cultural Industries,' *Cultural Studies* 1, no. 1. (January 1987): 23–37.

13. See Tamar *Liebes and Elihu Katz*, in [Ellen Seiter et al. (eds), *Remote Control: Television, Audiences and Cultural Powers* (London: Routledge, 1989)].

14. Rick Altman, 'Television/Sound,' in Tania Modleski (ed.) *Studies in Entertainment: Critical Approaches to Mass Culture* (Bloomington: Indiana University Press, 1986), pp. 39–54.

15. Michel de Certeau, *The Practice of Everyday Life* (Berkeley, Calif.: University of California Press, 1984).

FURTHER READING

Ang, I., *Watching 'Dallas': Soap Opera and the Melodramatic Imagination* (London: Methuen, 1985).

Ang, I., 'The Battle between Television and its Audiences: The Politics of Watching Television', in P. Drummond and R. Paterson (eds), *Television in Transition* (London: BFI, 1985).

Ang, I., 'Culture and Communication: Towards an Ethnographic Critique of Media Consumption in the Transnational Media System', *European Journal of Communication* 5:2/3 (1990) pp. 239–60.

Ang, I., *Desperately Seeking the Audience* (London: Routledge, 1991).

Ang, I. and Hermes, J., 'Gender and/in Media Consumption', in J. Curran and M. Gurevitch (eds), *Mass Media and Society* (London: Edward Arnold, 1991).

Baehr, H. and Dyer, G. (eds), *Boxed In: Women and Television* (London: Pandora, 1987).

Brown, M. E. (ed.), *Television and Women's Culture* (London: Sage, 1990).

Collett, P. and Lamb, R., *Watching Families Watching Television*, Report to the Independent Broadcasting Authority (1986).

Curran, J., 'The New Revisionism in Mass Communication Research: A Reappraisal', *European Journal of Communication* 5:2/3 (1990) pp. 135–64.

Curran, J. and Gurevitch, M., *Mass Media and Society* (London: Edward Arnold, 1991).

Drummond, P. and Paterson, R. (eds), *Television in Transition* (London: BFI, 1985).

Drummond, P. and Paterson, R. (eds), *Television and its Audiences: International Research Perspectives* (London: BFI, 1988).

Feyes, F., 'Critical Communications Research and Media Effects: the Problem of the Disappearing Audience', *Media, Culture and Society* 6:3 (1984) pp. 219–32.

Fiske, J., *Television Culture* (London: Methuen, 1987).

Fiske, J., *Reading the Popular* (London: Unwin Hyman, 1989).

Fiske, J., *Understanding Popular Culture* (London: Unwin Hyman, 1989).

Frazer, E., 'Teenage Girls Reading *Jackie*', *Media, Culture and Society* 9 (1987) pp. 407–25.

Gray, A., 'Reading the Audience', *Screen* 28:3 (1987) pp. 24–35.

Gray, A., *Video Playtime; the Gendering of a Leisure Technology* (London: Comedia/Routledge, 1992).

Grossberg, L., 'Wandering Audiences, Nomadic Critics', *Cultural Studies* 2:3 (1988) pp. 377–91.

Hall, S., Hobson, D., Lowe, A. and Willis, P. (eds), *Culture, Media, Language* (London: Hutchinson, 1980).

Hartley, J., *Tele-Ology: Studies in Television* (London: Routledge, 1992).

Hodge, R. and Tripp, D., *Children and Television* (Cambridge: Polity, 1986).

Jenkins, H., *Textual Poachers: Television Fans and Participatory Culture* (London: Routledge, 1992).

Jensen, K. B., 'Qualitative Audience Research: Towards an Integrative Approach to Reception', *Critical Studies in Mass Communication* 4 (1987) pp. 21–36.

Lewis, J., 'The Encoding/Decoding Model: Criticisms and Redevelopments for Research on Decoding', *Media, Culture and Society* 5:2 (1983) pp. 179–97.

Lewis, J., 'Are You Receiving Me?', in A. Goodwin and G. Whannel (eds), *Understanding Television* (London: Routledge, 1990).

Lewis, J., *The Ideological Octopus: An Exploration of Television and its Audience* (London: Routledge, 1991).

Lewis, L. A., *The Adoring Audience: Fan Culture and Popular Media* (London: Routledge, 1992).

Livingstone, S. M., *Making Sense of Television: The Psychology of Audience Interpretation* (New York: Pergamon Press, 1990).

Lull, J. (ed.), *World Families Watch Television* (London: Sage, 1988).

Lull, J., *Inside Family Viewing: Ethnographic Research on Television's Audiences* (London: Routledge, 1990).

McGuigan, J., *Cultural Populism* (London: Routledge, 1992).

McRobbie, A., *Feminism and Youth Culture: From* Jackie *to* Just Seventeen (London: Macmillan, 1991).

McRobbie, A., *Postmodernism and Popular Culture* (London: Routledge, 1994).

Modleski, T., 'The Rhythms of Reception: Daytime Television and Women's Work', in E. A. Kaplan (ed.), *Regarding Television: Critical Approaches – An Anthology* (Frederick, Md.: University Publications of America, 1983).

Moores, S., 'Texts, Readers and Contexts of Reading: Developments in the Study of Media Audiences', *Media, Culture and Society* 12:1 (1990) pp. 9–30.

Moores, S., *Interpreting Audiences: The Ethnography of Media Consumption* (London: Sage, 1993).

Morley, D., 'Reconceptualizing the Media Audience', CCCS stencilled paper 9 (University of Birmigham, 1974).

Morley, D., *The 'Nationwide' Audience* (London: BFI, 1980).

Morley, D., 'Texts, Readers, Subjects', in S. Hall, D. Hobson, A. Lowe and P. Willis (eds), *Culture, Media, Language* (London: Hutchinson, 1980).

Morley, D., ' "The Nationwide Audience": A Critical Postscript', *Screen Education* 39 (1981) pp. 3–14.

Morley, D., *Family Television: Cultural Power and Domestic Leisure* (London: Comedia, 1986).

Morley, D., 'Where the Global meets the Local: Notes from the Sitting Room', *Screen* 32:1 (1991) pp. 1–15.

Morley, D., *Television, Audiences and Cultural Studies* (London: Routledge, 1992).

Morley, D. and Silverstone, R., 'Domestic Communication: Technologies and Meanings', *Media, Culture and Society* 12:1 (1990) pp. 31–55.

Nava, M., *Changing Cultures: Feminism, Youth and Consumerism* (London: Sage, 1992).

Nightingale, V., 'Women as Audiences', in M. E. Brown (ed.), *Television and Women's Culture* (London: Sage, 1990).

Oakley, A., 'Interviewing Women: A Contradiction in Terms', in H. Roberts (ed.), *Doing Feminist Research* (London: Routledge, 1981).

Press, A. L., *Women Watching Television: Gender, Class and Generation in the American Television Experience* (Philadelphia: University of Pennsylvania Press, 1991).

Radway, J., *Reading the Romance* (London: Verso, 1987).

Radway, J., 'Reception Study: Ethnography and the Problems of Dispersed Audiences and Nomadic Subjects', *Cultural Studies* 2:3 (1988) pp. 359–76.

Schlesinger, P., Dobash, R. E., Dobash, R. P. and Weaver, C. K., *Women Viewing Violence* (London: BFI, 1992).

Schroder, K. C., 'Convergence of Antagonistic Traditions? The Case of Audience Research', *European Journal of Communication* 2 (1987) pp. 7–31.

Seiter, E., Borchers, H., Kreutzner, G. and Warth, E.-M. (eds), *Remote Control: Television, Audiences and Cultural Power* (London: Routledge, 1989).

Seiter, E., 'Making Distinctions in TV Audience Research: Case Study of a Troubling Interview', *Cultural Studies* 4:1 (1990) pp. 61–84.

Shields, R., *Lifestyle Shopping: The Subject of Consumption* (London: Routledge, 1992).

Silverstone, R., 'Television and Everyday Life: Towards an Anthropology of the Television Audience', in M. Ferguson (ed.), *Public Communication: The New Imperatives* (London: Sage, 1990).

Silverstone, R., 'From Audiences to Consumers: The Household and the Consumption of Information and Communication Technologies', *European Journal of Communication* 6:2 (1991) pp. 135–54.

Silverstone, R. and Hirsch, E. (eds), *Consuming Technologies: Media and Information in Domestic Spaces* (London: Routledge, 1992).

Walkerdine, V., 'Video Replay: Families, Films and Fantasy', in V. Burgin, J. Donald and C. Kaplan (eds), *Formations of Fantasy* (London: Methuen, 1986).

Willis, P., *Common Culture* (Milton Keynes: Open University Press, 1990).

Part Two
Case Studies

Soap Opera

Soap Opera

Over the past fifteen years, soap opera has moved from being an object of academic and popular contempt to a major area of media study.[1] Much of the research which has contributed to this shift has been produced by feminist scholars, and can be seen as part of a wider commitment within feminist research to the re-evaluation of popular forms aimed at and enjoyed by women.[2] If this political commitment is one hallmark of feminist work on soap opera, a second is its focus upon the relationship of the popular text to its audience and the question of where, in this relationship, the power to determine meaning lies. This concern takes up many of the issues raised in Chapters 22–24 and 31–35 above, in particular that of the relationship between the 'ideal' spectator constructed, or positioned, by the text, and the socially situated 'real' spectator who reads, and enjoys, it. It is addressed, from a range of perspectives, in four of the six readings which follow.

The extract from David Buckingham's *Public Secrets:* EastEnders *and its Audience* (Chapter 36), which opens this section, however, focuses on the production determinants of the genre. In this chapter, which details the launch of the BBC's new soap opera in 1985, Buckingham describes the programme's promotion as a 'product', designed to fulfil a key role in the BBC's search for ratings and the reconstruction of its 'rather staid and middle-class "Auntie" image' – extremely important to the Corporation at a time in the mid- 1980s when it was under threat from government moves towards privatisation. The chapter also shows the *problems* which a popular soap like *EastEnders* can pose for a public service institution like the BBC, whose dominant discourse of 'quality' in television drama (see Chapter 20) adapts uneasily, and not without contradiction, to a popular success like *EastEnders*.

Christine Geraghty's analysis (Chapter 37) of the formal characteristics of the soap opera or 'continuous serial', which follows, first appeared in the 1981 collection of essays on *Coronation Street* published by the BFI. This collection signalled the resurgence of academic interest in soap opera, and Geraghty's structural analysis – of the soap opera's organisation of time, its narrative structure, its use of characters and its characteristic use of 'gossip', both within and beyond the text – forms the basis, in different ways, of all the remaining chapters in this section. Later chapters, however, focus much more explicitly on the *gendered* address of soap opera. Tania Modleski, then, analyses the structural features outlined by Geraghty in relation both to psychoanalytic theory and to the rhythms of women's work in the home (Chapter 38). Arguing that in their address to women's desires and 'collective fantasies', soap operas not only satisfy '*real* needs' but can also be said to make a contribution to the development of a feminist aesthetics, she nevertheless ends by framing her analysis within a 'mass culture' critique. Feminists, she insists, must find new and more empowering ways of meeting the utopian needs and desires which are at present expressed through the mass culture form of soap opera.

The extract from Ien Ang's *Watching Dallas* (Chapter 39), a study based upon a survey of Dutch viewers of the American prime-time soap opera – forty-two of whom responded by letter to an advertisement she placed in a women's magazine – also addresses the relationship between the pleasurable fantasies offered by soap opera and feminist politics. Ang rejects the 'moralism of the ideology of mass culture' which marks Modleski's conclusion, but her own conclusion can be seen as no less ambivalent. Despite its articulation of 'the contradictions which patriarchy generates', the 'fantasy positions and solutions' offered by soap opera are fundamentally conservative, she argues, and much of the pleasure which women viewers find in a soap opera like *Dallas* comes from their identification with its 'tragic structure of feeling'. Ang nevertheless argues for the *separation* of pleasurable fantasy and feminist politics, concluding that the space for fantasy offered by soap opera's 'tragic structure of feeling' enables women to experience *in fantasy* those feelings of resignation and despair which 'we can scarcely allow ourselves in the battlefield of actual social, political and personal struggles'. Although 'new fantasies' are needed, those offered by soap opera need not be at odds with a feminist politics.

Charlotte Brunsdon's 1981 article (Chapter 40) asks what it means to assume a gendered audience for soap opera. Her answer draws an important distinction between the subject positions proposed for their readers by texts and a 'social subject' who may or may not take up these positions. Brunsdon argues that in both their narrative structures and their 'moral and ideological frameworks', soap operas demand and set in play 'understandings and assumptions', discourses and cultural competencies, which in our society are traditionally gendered feminine and are therefore more likely to be possessed by female viewers. Thus, soap operas both appeal to and help to construct the 'culturally constructed skills of femininity' in their female viewers.

It is the 'social subject' of Brunsdon's model which is the object of investigation in the chapter by Dorothy Hobson (Chapter 41). This extract from Hobson's (1982) study of the producers and audience of ATV's soap opera *Crossroads* (1964–88) is taken from her ethnographic study of the viewers of the Midlands soap opera. Hobson went into the homes of viewers, watched the programme with these women and their families, and then discussed with them the meanings and pleasures which they found in it. Her conclusion, that 'there are as many different Crossroads as there are viewers', very much asserts the power of the *audience* in determining the meanings (and definition) of a text, and can be contrasted in this respect with Modleski's work. Indeed, her observation that 'the audience do not watch programmes as separate or individual items' can be seen as preparing the way for John Fiske's later (1989) celebration of 'semiotic democracy' – in which audiences are seen to be free to construct their own meanings, and the effectivity of the text (and its production context) disappears completely (see Chapter 35).

NOTES

1. This is not to deny that important research on soap opera was carried out before this period. See, in particular, Herta Herzog, 'On Borrowed Experience: An Analysis of Listening to Daytime Sketches' in *Studies in Philosophy and Social Science*, 9, 1. (1941), and 'What do we Really Know about Daytime Serial Listeners?' in P. F. Lazarsfeld & F. M. Stanton (eds.), *Radio Research: 1942–1943* (New York: Duell, Sloan & Pearce, 1944).
2. See, for example, the work by Janice Radway on romance (*Reading the Romance*. London: Verso, 1987), Janice Winship on women's magazines (*Inside Women's Magazines*. London: Pandora Press, 1987), and Tania Modleski on Harlequin romances and Gothic novels (*Loving with a Vengeance: Mass Produced Fantasies for Women*. London: Methuen, 1984). See also Chapters 22 and 23 in this volume.

36

EASTENDERS: CREATING THE AUDIENCE

David Buckingham

GRABBING THE RATINGS?

The BBC's decision to produce a new bi-weekly continuing serial dates back to 1981, well before the concern about declining viewing figures became a matter of urgency. The initial 'in principle' decision was made by Bill Cotton, then Controller of BBC1, and the early planning was commissioned by his successor, Alan Hart.

Michael Grade, who subsequently inherited *EastEnders*, certainly perceived its value in terms of the competition for ratings, and in particular as a means of increasing the BBC's early evening share, which had slumped to little more than half that of ITV:

> I think it was clear to the BBC that one of the reasons for the discrepancy in the share between ITV's audience and the BBC's audience was down to *Coronation Street, Emmerdale Farm* and *Crossroads*. The BBC did not have anything of that kind in its locker. ITV certainly didn't invent the soap opera. The BBC were doing *The Groves* and *Mrs Dale's Diary* and *The Archers* years before. So it was nothing new for the BBC to be in the soap business. But it had somehow gotten out of the soap business over the years, and it seemed the right time to get back into it, as a means also to boost the early evening schedule, which had been languishing for some time.[1]

The choice of a continuing serial as a means of building ratings would therefore appear at first sight to be an obvious one. Yet there were clearly significant risks. A new serial would involve a far greater financial outlay than any of the likely alternatives, such as game shows. While the running costs of a regular soap opera are comparatively small, it takes many years to recoup the substantial initial investment, and an early exit from the schedules would mean financial disaster as well as public embarrassment.

From D. Buckingham, *Public Secrets: Eastenders and its Audience* (London: BFI, 1987) pp. 7–33.

Furthermore, the number of soaps already being screened led many to doubt whether the public would be willing to accept yet another: indeed, the BBC's first audience research report on the subject in early 1984 concluded that enthusiasm for a new bi-weekly serial was 'at best moderate'.[2] The BBC's own past experience with continuing television serials could hardly be said to inspire confidence either: although 1970s serials like *The Brothers* and *Angels* had done fairly well in terms of ratings, and had lasted for several years, they had not been screened continuously for the full 52 weeks. The BBC's only experience in producing continuing serials on television was as long ago as the 1960s, with *Compact* (1962–65), *United* (1965–67) and *The Newcomers* (1965–69), of which only the first had achieved any substantial success in the ratings.

[. . .]

The decision to opt for a continuing serial was thus not merely informed by the desire to reach a large audience. Soap operas possess a symbolic importance for television institutions, above and beyond their function in terms of ratings. By building a loyal audience, often over decades, they can become a highly significant element in the way viewers perceive the institutions themselves. *Coronation Street*, for example, can be seen as providing a specific regional identity for Granada Television, despite the fact that the majority of its productions have no such regional flavour. If, as recent research has suggested, popular perceptions of the BBC remain to some extent tied to the rather staid and middle-class 'Auntie' image, a successful soap opera could clearly do much to alter these.[3]

Jonathan Powell, who became Head of Series & Serials in November 1983, and played a key role in the development of *EastEnders*, felt that a continuing serial could also serve as an important training ground for new talent, just as *Coronation Street* has done at Granada. Using new writers and directors alongside more experienced ones would provide his own department, and the industry in general, with 'a substantial injection of talent'.

While Powell acknowledged *EastEnders'* considerable strategic value in terms of ratings, he also saw it as filling a gap in the overall spread of drama programming:

> It was clearly an area of popular drama in which the BBC wasn't offering something to the public. . . . I think that the point of any department in the BBC as a matter of fact – although it's not my business to say so – is to offer the correct balance of material across the whole spectrum of taste. And I think that a drama department of this size without a bi-weekly is a drama department without a very important linchpin in the panoply of ground that it's covering.[4]

At the same time, Jonathan Powell and Michael Grade refuted the suggestion that *EastEnders* was merely a means of keeping the mass audience happy, and thereby enabling the BBC to get on with its real business of producing 'serious' television: both were keen to emphasise its dramatic 'quality' and the 'responsibility' with which it dealt with controversial issues. *EastEnders* was regarded as tangible proof that popularity did not necessarily mean 'catering to the lowest common denominator'.

If the drive for ratings was therefore not the only motivation behind the decision to produce *EastEnders*, it certainly assumed a central significance in the period immediately before and subsequent to its launch in February 1985. The Peacock Committee, the latest in a series of government enquiries into the running of the BBC, appeared set to recommend a degree of privatisation, which many advocates of public service broadcasting saw as the thin end of a very thick wedge which would eventually destroy the Corporation. More was clearly at stake in the 'Soap Wars' so enthusiastically reported by the tabloid press than the success or failure of individual programmes. If the supremacy of *Coronation Street* was in some sense symbolic of ITV's overall dominance of the ratings, the failure of *EastEnders* would doubtless have been seized upon with relish by the BBC's enemies.

[. . .]

LOCATING THE SERIAL

In re-entering the highly competitive 'soap business', the BBC inevitably had to exercise a considerable degree of caution. Key decisions in planning the serial had to be made with extreme care and forethought, as they would for the most part be impossible to reverse once the programme was on the air. The price of failure, in terms of both money and reputation, was very high indeed.

The choice of a location for the serial was clearly crucial, and required a number of considerations to be held in the balance.

[. . .]

As an area which has historically been populated by waves of different immigrant groups, and which has recently begun to be 'gentrified', the East End would provide a setting which could plausibly contain a broad mixture of characters. Furthermore, it would allow a greater potential for turnover of new characters, thus enabling the serial to remain contemporary – a distinct advantage over the relatively static community of *Coronation Street*, which they felt had become stuck in a 'timewarp' of the early 1960s, when it had been originated.

Like Julia Smith and Tony Holland*, Jonathan Powell felt that the East End location would provide 'roots' and 'identity', 'an attractive folklore and a sense of history', which was essential for the genre. He also argued that a 'flagship' programme like a continuing serial should provide a regional identity for the BBC, even though the Corporation as a whole has a national role. If the independent television companies had soap operas set in their own regions, then the BBC's should, he felt, be set in London.

Logistical factors were also significant here. In 1983 the BBC had purchased Elstree Studios, just outside London, from the independent company Central Television. Although the location of the new serial had not yet been decided at this stage, Elstree was clearly earmarked for it. While it would theoretically have been possible to make the programme at Elstree and set it in Manchester, Julia Smith was strongly opposed to the idea. In order to achieve the degree of authenticity she felt was essential, actors would have to be moved from Manchester down to London, and the cost of this operation would certainly have been prohibitive.

[. . .]

The balance of characters also had clear implications in terms of the kind of audience *EastEnders* was attempting to build. Prior to the launch of the BBC's new early evening package, its audience at this time of day tended to be predominantly middle-aged and middle-class. In order to broaden that audience, EastEnders would have to appeal both to younger and older viewers, and also to the working-class audience which traditionally watched ITV. The choice of a working-class setting, and the broad age range of the characters thus also made a good deal of sense in terms of ratings.

In addition, *EastEnders* sought to extend the traditional audience for British soaps, which is weighted towards women and towards the elderly. Having a number of strong younger characters, it was argued, meant that the programme would have a greater appeal for young viewers than other British soaps, as well as providing a means of regenerating the narrative in the longer term. Strong male characters would also serve to bring in male viewers who were traditionally suspicious of the genre. Julia Smith had a definite idea of her potential audience profile:

I'm not going for the stereotypical middle-class, BBC audience. The professional classes won't get home early enough to see the programme. I expect the audience to consist of working people who watch television around tea-time before going to bingo or the pub. Soap operas traditionally appeal to women, but we have to remember that men watch them too – even if they don't admit to it. And with at least five teenagers in the cast I expect to pick up a lot of young viewers.[5]

[. . .]

THE LAUNCH

After almost a year of frenetic activity, *EastEnders* was launched at 7 p.m. on 19 February 1985. Julia Smith's original target date of September 1984 had been postponed twice: firstly at the instigation of the new Controller of BBC1, Michael Grade, who had preferred a January start; and secondly when *EastEnders'* companion in the BBC's new early evening package, the chat show *Wogan*, had not been ready in time. Julia Smith was certainly uneasy about the late start: *EastEnders* no longer had the long winter months in which to build up a loyal following before the summer downturn in the ratings.

If the initial projections of *EastEnders'* audience size had been relatively modest, the publicity which surrounded its launch was rather less so. In an unprecedented move, the BBC had appointed a publicity officer specifically to promote the new serial. The programme had been trailed in *Radio Times* and on screen for many weeks beforehand, leading many newspaper critics to accuse the BBC of 'hype'. An ostentatious press launch, complete with lavish press pack and 'showbiz walkpast' of the cast, only fuelled their scepticism. The high profile certainly succeeded in giving the programme public visibility – and encouraged as many as 13 million viewers to tune in to the first episode – but it also increased the risks attached to failure. If *EastEnders* was going to make mistakes, it would do so in the public eye, without the opportunity to ease itself in gently.

[. . .]

One major reason for EastEnders' eventual success in the ratings was its careful scheduling. Michael Grade had arrived at the BBC with a reputation derived from his work at London Weekend Television of being a scheduling wizard. One of the problems he had identified very early on was the lack of fixed points in the BBC schedule – and in particular in the early evening. *EastEnders* and *Wogan*, in addition to pulling ratings, would also provide a much-needed stability at the start of the evening's viewing. The sheer longevity of a soap opera was also a significant point in its favour: as Grade observed, the BBC's past attempts to dent the ratings for *Coronation Street*, for example by scheduling a popular situation comedy against it, had only proved successful in the short term.

At the same time, Grade did not subscribe to the view that 'inheritance' was all-important – the idea that if you caught an audience at the start of the evening, it would stay with you until close down. Particularly in an era of remote control keypads, this approach was largely outdated. Nevertheless, if *EastEnders* were to be followed by a sequence of popular programmes, it would certainly go a long way to increase the BBC's overall audience share:

> If you've got good programmes that are following it, the audience look at it as a package. They say, 'Right, I'll watch BBC from 7.00 to 9.00 and then I'll switch to ITV because I want to watch their drama.' They'll watch a package of programmes, with a gem like that in the middle which attracts. So there is a package idea, but the pieces around it have to be the right pieces.

Nevertheless, the initial decision to schedule *EastEnders* at 7 p.m. represented something of a gamble since it meant competing with ITV's *Emmerdale Farm*, a rural soap opera with a steady and respectable share of the ratings. Michael Grade described this first phase of the 'Soap Wars' with considerable relish:

> I put *EastEnders* at 7.00 because *Emmerdale Farm* was not networked. As a response to it going at 7.00, ITV for once got its act together and networked *Emmerdale Farm*. That was a blow, but I knew – from my knowledge of ITV – that *Emmerdale Farm* went off the air in the summer for a number of weeks, and I only had to wait for that window, and then I would be away. What they did was that they somehow squeezed extra episodes and repeats, so there was no break in the clouds. So I thought, this is crazy, this is silly now, I'm going to have to move it. And because of the sort of press we have in this country, I didn't want them rubbishing the show – 'panic move' – they'd have written that as a failure story. I had to dress up the presentation of that move in such a way as to protect the show, so I gave all kinds of reasons for the move, trying to disguise the fact that I was having to move it because it had reached a plateau and wasn't moving off.

[. . .]

Following the shift to 7.30 in September 1985, *EastEnders'* ratings began a meteoric rise which eventually peaked at around 23 million in February and March of 1986. This rise co-incided with the regular seasonal upturn in the ratings, and also with the ending of the latest series of *Dallas*, but *EastEnders'* climb to the top of the ratings charts was both faster and earlier than even its most enthusiastic advocates could have expected. The appreciation indices also continued to rise, averaging a phenomenal 85 in the early months of the new year. Studies of the demographic profile of the audience showed that the programme was successfully reaching a genuine cross-section of the population in a way that no British soap opera had previously managed to do, and that it was particularly popular with teenagers, traditionally the least captive section of the television audience. Ironically, qualitative research suggested that it was precisely those features which had initially been found alienating – and in particular its abrasive treatment of 'social issues' – which viewers were now ready to praise.

[. . .]

SERVING THE PUBLIC

EastEnders' extraordinary popularity nevertheless means that it enjoys a rather ambiguous relationship with the 'official' Reithian definition of 'public service broadcasting'. The charge of 'catering to the lowest common denominator' could be made not only by the BBC's enemies, but also by those within the Corporation who believe in broadcasting as a means of uplifting public taste. While Tony Holland agreed that the BBC had allowed Julia Smith and himself a considerable degree of autonomy, he also acknowledged that their work was 'very commercial', and in some respects had more in common with the ethos of independent television than with that of the BBC. For example, part of the 'craft of script-making', as he defined it, lay in knowing the correct time of year to 'blow the big story': getting in a good story at Christmas meant that you might stand some chance of keeping your audience until Easter, despite the seasonal drop in the ratings.

> We are, in that sense, not typical of the BBC. It has been considered for some years, although I think it's changing, that to actually promote a product – and we're the only people in the BBC that I know of who call our show a product – a lot of people in

the corridors of power think it's terribly vulgar. But we like the packaging, we like the promotion, we like the hype.[6]

As Holland indicated, this Reithian view of public service broadcasting is gradually changing, although it remains influential. Michael Grade and Jonathan Powell both contested the view that popularity was incompatible with the principle of public service – a view which they described as both outdated and condescending:

> MICHAEL GRADE That's a patronising argument by people who believe that the BBC should be an elitist ghetto of cultural high ground, inaccessible to the working classes, or inaccessible to people who aren't highly educated, appreciative of the finer things of life.

At the same time, they refuted the suggestion that *EastEnders* was primarily about 'grabbing the ratings', or about popularity at any price. The idea that it was 'a lowest common denominator show' was incorrect, both on the basis of its broad demographic appeal, and on the grounds of its 'quality':

> JONATHAN POWELL If we really wanted to grab the ratings, we wouldn't make *EastEnders* like we make *EastEnders*. I think *EastEnders* has attracted a large audience because it's good, it's mature, it's grown up and it talks to people on their level. It talks to them on a mature level. It's an entertainment programme, fine: but entertainment is not a dirty word. It addresses, within a quite wide interpretation of an entertainment format, quite significant and human problems. There are good episodes and there are bad episodes, sure, but there are 104 a year, so there are bound to be. But there are episodes of *EastEnders* which I would frankly be very happy to put up as a one-off play.

Significantly, although popularity is clearly valued, 'quality' is still defined here by standards which derive from the 'cultural high ground' of the single play.

While Grade and Powell were therefore keen to argue the case for *EastEnders* as 'quality' television, they were also aware of its strategic role within the broader range of BBC programming, and within the context of public criticism of the Corporation. There was a sense in which the popularity of *EastEnders* enabled other, less popular, programmes to exist:

> JONATHAN POWELL I'm sure it helps our image to have programmes like this. I'm sure it helps to attract people to other programmes. And it creates space, too. . . . You have to create your space, allow yourself the space for specialised programming. It works when the balance is right. I don't think this department works with just *EastEnders* and *Bergerac*, but equally I don't think it just works with *Bleak House* and *Edge of Darkness*. They all complement each other.

Michael Grade argued that the BBC had always been in the business of producing popular programmes, although in the current context a major success like *EastEnders* could perform a particularly important function for the Corporation as a whole:

> It's a problem for our enemies, because they don't want us to be popular. If we weren't popular, then there is a case for breaking up the BBC and selling it off to private enterprise. We do stand in the way of a lot of people making a lot of money. My belief is that we need to be popular, but we don't need to be popular all the time, every day, every week of the year. We need to *prove* that we can be as popular as the other side with quality programmes when we want to be.

In many ways these comments reflect the broader dilemma which has faced public service broadcasting in this country since the introduction of commercial television, and which was brought to a head in the period immediately preceding the launch of *EastEnders*. On the one hand, the BBC is obliged to justify its monopoly over the licence fee by producing programmes of artistic 'quality' and 'responsibility'. Yet on the other hand, that monopoly can only be sustained if the BBC is seen to speak to the nation as a whole, rather than to a privileged minority, and it is therefore obliged to compete with ITV for a reasonable share of the mass audience. As Michael Grade argued, the BBC has always resisted the idea of catering merely to the educated middle class, yet in the context of a dwindling audience share, and a government committed to 'free market' economics, its delicate attempts to retain a balance between popular and minority tastes have inevitably been fraught with uncertainty.[7]

[. . .]

The very popularity of *EastEnders* thus highlights a number of tensions and contradictions in the relationships between the broadcasting institution, the programme-makers and the audience.

On the one hand, the programme has clearly served a very useful function for the BBC, in a period of increasing uncertainty. As a significant element within its early evening schedule, it has managed to maximise ratings, and to reverse the downturn in its audience share, thereby staving off a certain amount of public criticism. Yet, on the other hand, its success has also provoked further attacks on the Corporation from those on the political Right. *EastEnders* has been seen as a symptom of the BBC's abandonment of its 'public service' obligations, whereby 'quality' and 'responsibility' have simply been sacrificed in a cynical drive for ratings.

[. . .]

NOTES

1.   All quotations from Michael Grade are taken from an interview with the author.
2.   BBC Broadcasting Research Special Report, *Bi-Weekly Serial: The Appeal of Different Regional and Social Class Concepts*, February 1984.
3.   Laurie Taylor and Bob Mullan, *Uninvited Guests: the Intimate Secrets of Television and Radio* (London: Chatto & Windus, 1986).
4.   All quotations from Jonathan Powell are taken from an interview with the author.
5.   *Broadcast*, 26 October 1984.
6.   All quotations from Julia Smith and Tony Holland are taken from an interview with the author, unless otherwise indicated.
7.   For a useful account of contemporary developments, see Michael Leapman *The Last Days of the Beeb* (London: Allen & Unwin, 1986).

Editor's Note
* Julia Smith and Tony Holland, producer and script-editor, originators of the *EastEnders* proposal.

37

THE CONTINUOUS SERIAL: A DEFINITION

Christine Geraghty

[. . .]

THE CHARACTERISTICS OF THE CONTINUOUS SERIAL*

The Organisation Of Time

It can be argued that the most important influence on how the audience perceives the continuous serial is its regular appearance, in the same slot every week of the year. Twice a week, three times a week, five times a week, the familiar signature tune alerts us to the fact that the serial is about to begin. It does not disappear 'until the autumn' or 'until the next series'. It appears every week and the time which passes between each episode is always known to the audience. Because of this, the question of how time passes in a serial, of how time is constructed and perceived by the audience, is important in distinguishing the continuous serial from the series. The series, although it also uses the same characters across a number of episodes, normally deals with a particular story within a discrete episode. [. . .] Significantly, *The Archers*, on the other hand, is announced as 'the *everyday* story of country folk' even though it is only every week day. There is an appeal here to the audience's experience of time in the real world, as if we get through our own personal events during a day and then tune in to discover what has happened in Ambridge that day.

This feeling is usefully described, in terms of the novel, by Carl Grabo as being the

---

* This essay is concerned only with British television and radio serials and is not intended to cover American serials. Examples are mainly taken from four serials which were running at the time of writing – Granada's *Coronation Street*, ATV's *Crossroads* (then running four nights a week in the London area), *The Archers* and *Waggoner's Walk*, both on BBC Radio with a 15-minute episode every weekday.

From R. Dyer et al., *Coronation Street*, BFI TV Monograph no. 13 (London: BFI, 1981) pp. 9–26.

convention of 'unchronicled growth'. 'In the novel,' he argues, 'when the story shifts from one sub-plot to another, the characters abandoned pursue an unrecorded existence' (Grabo, 1978, p. 67). The characters in a serial, when abandoned at the end of an episode, pursue an 'unrecorded existence' until the next one begins. In other words, we are aware that day-to-day life has continued in our absence even though the problem we left at the end of the previous episode has still to be resolved.

[. . .]

In addition, the broadcast serial, whether it be daily or weekly, appears to have gone through a similar period of time as its audience, whereas in a series, narrative time within the episode is the only criterion for time passing.

[. . .]

The Sense of a Future

The second characteristic of the continuous serial is the sense of a future, the continual postponement of the final resolution. Unlike the series which is advertised as having a specific number of episodes, the serial is endless. The apparent multifariousness of the plots, their inextricability from each other, the everyday quality of narrative time and events, all encourage us to believe that this is a narrative whose future is not yet written. Even events which would offer a suitable ending in other narrative forms are never a final ending in the continuous serial: a wedding is not a happy ending but opens up the possibilities of stories about married life and divorce; a character's departure from a serial does not mean that s/he will not turn up again several years later. [. . .] It is perhaps this sense of a future which also explains the way in which deaths in serials [. . .] remain as high spots, remembered and indeed mysticised, not so much because of the characters involved, but because they are the only moments which are irreversible.

[. . .]

The Interweaving of Stories

The third characteristic of a continuous serial is the way in which two or three stories are woven together and presented to the audience over a number of episodes. It is interesting to compare this with how stories are handled in series. In series [. . .], the story, as I have pointed out, is usually resolved within a single episode. [. . .] It is characteristic of the continuous serial, however, that two or three stories dealt with are given approximately equal time in each episode and very often reflect on and play off each other. As one story finishes, another is begun so that at least two stories are always in progress. [. . .] It is possible for a serial to cover a wide range of stories and styles without disturbing the serial format by playing them against very familiar elements – the signature tune, the setting, long-standing characters. The audience is presented with a rich pattern of incident and characterisation – the dramatic is mixed in with the everyday, the tragic with the comic, the romantic with the mundane. The proportions will vary from serial to serial. [. . .] But because the unfamiliar is introduced within a context of the very familiar, the audience is able to cope with enormous shifts in style and material, even within one episode, which might otherwise be expected to occur across a whole evening's viewing.

These three characteristics, then, are the essential elements of the continuous serial and they distinguish it from other forms such as the series or the dramatisation of a novel. It is clear that all three – the organisation of time, the sense of an unwritten future, the interweaving of plots – are closely tied in with how narrative is handled in the serial. The next section therefore takes up the issue of narrative more directly.

NARRATIVE IN SERIALS

Much of the research done on narrative has concentrated on works which are read with the knowledge that they will come to an end. Narrative organisation is described as functioning through tension and the resolution of that tension by reaching a satisfactory ending (Scholes and Kellog. 1979, p.212). Todorov describes 'a minimum narrative … without which we cannot say that there is any narrative at all' as 'a movement between equilibriums which are similar but not identical' (Todorov, 1975, p. 163). The narrative ends, in other words, with the establishment of an equilibrium which balances that which was disturbed or disrupted at the beginning of the text. Barthes' work in *S/Z* has alerted us to the way in which narratives work by posing enigmas and questions which draw the reader through the text in search of an answer. The reader is kept involved through this pursuit which is in fact a pursuit of resolution. In the end, after delays, confusions and red herrings, comes the final resolution when 'all enigmas are disclosed' (Barthes, 1975, p. 209).

[. . .]

In the light of this emphasis on resolution and closure, work on serials and narrative offers a new perspective. As I have shown, serials are marked by their sense of the future, the promise which they hold out of being endless. While individual stories are resolved, the continuous serial must go on and the audience must be kept involved. In this section, therefore, I want to look at narrative in continuous serials in the light of their endlessness and, in particular, to concentrate on two devices of key importance – the use of the cliffhanger and of moments of temporary resolution. In addition, I will examine how the serial sets up different narrative conventions from those of the book and film and how this difference affects the audience's engagement with a continually unfinished text.

The Cliffhanger

The cliffhanger is often seen as the traditional hallmark of the serial. In this section, therefore, I want to look at how the use of the cliffhanger formally differentiates the serial from the complete novel or film and at how the serials I am discussing have adapted this device.

All fictional – and indeed non-fictional – forms attempt to engage the audience by the posing and working through of an enigma. [. . .] But the suspense in serials is forced on us, so that we are left waiting between one episode and the next, literally in suspense. The cliffhanger marks this enforced interruption.

The cliffhanger is normally thought of in terms of silent movie serials. The unfolding of the action is cut off at a crucial point so that the enigma is unresolved and the leading characters remain in danger. The audience is left with questions – how will the heroine escape, can the hero out-manœuvre the enemy? The tension which arises from the sudden break in the narrative is expressed by the cliffhanger so that the different directions which the story could take are frozen until the next episode. The serials I am writing about, however, only occasionally use the cliffhanger device with its original dramatic effect. It is important to note the narrative construction through which this shift has been achieved. Continuing problems run through every serial, which the audience can follow while missing specific episodes. [. . .] These overall stories contribute to the framework of the serial, within which each episode will have its own structure, working with two or more plots, of which one is often used as comic balance to a more serious drama. The weighting of this interweaving will vary from serial to serial. [. . .] In all serials, though, this episodic construction means that while major overall questions are left unanswered and unresolved, the cliffhanger can emanate from some minor matter, often comically presented and easily forgotten. It is, therefore, merely a formal device and is not necessarily related to the potential outcome of the story.

[. . .]

Moments of Temporary Resolution

[. . .]

[T]he cliffhanger is an important device in the narrative organisation of the continuous serial. Its use, however, is also balanced by the rarer moments of resolution in the serial, the points at which a new harmony is very temporarily reached. Serials vary in how much they use this strategy. *The Archers* quite often finishes, particularly at the end of the week, with the coming together of the family at a meal or a gathering. The other serials tend to save such moments for festivals such as Christmas or communal occasions like weddings or funerals. Such moments are marked by the suppression of other stories, even though they will be picked up in the next episode. For once, the harmony within the group of characters will be stressed so that quarrels and differences which would threaten the equilibrium are temporarily suspended. The final image of such an episode is not one which looks forward to the next instalment but one which rounds off this one – the bridal pair embracing, a toast at a family celebration, a group of characters at the end of a street party. Of course, there is never a final resolution since the audience is aware of stories which are to be continued, but such moments do provide a respite from the hermeneutic dramas of the cliffhanger. Indeed, the two alternatives, the temporary resolution and the cliffhanger, work together to provide variations within the established pattern of the serials' organisation.

The Use of the Past

So far, in this section on narrative, I have discussed how the serial form plays on the audience's desire to know what happens next. It is clear that the audience's engagement is also with what has happened in the past. The serial offers, as we have seen, an attenuated narrative which may in the case of successful serials go on for twenty or thirty years. In this situation, all viewers/listeners do not have the same knowledge of the serial's past and events remembered vividly by some are unknown to others. Episodes may have been missed; the viewers/listeners may be comparative newcomers to the programme; they may see/hear only a limited number of episodes, perhaps because of regular commitments elsewhere. Little attempt is made to bring the audience up-to-date with events it may have missed and the announcers who introduce the programmes obviously cannot offer a résumé of what has happened so far. There is therefore no guarantee that individual members of the audience will know very much about a particular serial's history.

It should be noted, however, that some viewers/listeners do remember a serial's past very clearly and expect any references to it to be accurate, down to the last detail. This accumulation of knowledge by the committed audience is recognised by those working on the programmes, who boast about the detailed attention to minutiae which their audience give the serial. The *Coronation Street* production team includes a programme historian who ensures that any references to the past are correct. Knowledge gained from watching or listening to the programme can be reinforced by reading the books based on the serials or magazines produced to mark special events. *Coronation Street*'s 2,000th episode, for instance, was celebrated with a 'souvenir album' which included the script of the first episode and a history of events in the Street over the last twenty years. The serial, therefore, operates in a situation in which it must be accessible to all viewers while, at the same time, be accurate about its own accumulated past.

[. . .]

Although the accumulated past is important to a serial, one could also say that the ability to 'forget' what has happened in the serial's past is equally crucial. If the serial had to carry the heavy weight of its own past it would not be able to carry on. The stories would grind to a halt while the implications of past events were explained to new viewers/listeners. Instead, the serials, while clearly accepting [. . .] that they have a past, cannot be bound by it. A rigid adherence to their own history is rejected in favour of a more flexible approach which allows serials to function in the present.

In this section, I have stressed the way in which the formal narrative strategies of the serial differ from those of the complete film or episode in a series and I have examined the use of the cliffhanger and the serial's past. These strategies are important because they allow the serial, while always operating within the familiar format, to provide sufficient variation to prevent a sense of complete repetition. Thus, the past can be actively used within a story, be fleetingly referred to, or remain a potential resource for the audience. The serial may break at a point of unfinished action or high tension, at moments of no particular dramatic importance or at moments of temporary resolution. These variations are limited but they are sufficient to give 'movement' and difference within the repetition described by Heath and Skirrow. [Heath and Skirrow, 1977, p. 15] The rest of this essay will show that this use of narrative strategies based on difference and repetition is backed up by similar variations at the level of characterisation and plot.

CHARACTERISATION AND PLOT

In this section, I want to study the way in which characterisation and plot in a serial interlock in a way which provides a familiar base for the viewer but which generates enough surprises to prevent tedium. Thus the same plots can be used again with different inflections, the same character can be used in various ways, new characters can be introduced and disappear without comment, the same situation can generate different expectations. We can see how this process works by looking first at how the characters in a serial are used and secondly at how they are placed within particular plots.

The Use of Characters

A serial always uses more characters than a play or even a series in order to give variety and so that characters do not get 'used up' too quickly. Although based on one community (the Street, Ambridge, Emmerdale), a serial will have a fairly wide variation among the characters in terms of age, relationships, and attitudes because, as we shall see, such variations permit a wider range of stories. A serial must have a core of characters who appear regularly over the years and who become familiar to the consistent viewer/listener. In addition, most serials introduce new characters for a small number of episodes featuring stories perhaps not applicable to the main characters.

[. . .]

I want to group the characters in serial in three ways which I will argue provide the base for their use within the narrative. One can see each character as an individuated character, as a serial type and as the holder of a position, distinctions which will become clear in the following comments.

The *individuated character* is the character marked by traits which are presented as uniquely his or her own. (It is this aspect which is emphasised by articles in the press.) Certain characters, very often but not always those used for comic effect, will be particularly marked by one such trait. [. . .] Others, especially the longstanding characters, will be constructed out of a number of such traits. Thus, Hilda Ogden is presented as a nag, a gossip and a woman who can occasionally take on a real dignity when confronted with her lot; David Hunter (*Crossroads*) is built up as a man with a smooth, suave exterior which conceals a capacity for feeling that real hurt. It is by emphasising the number of these individuated characters that the serial is able to reinforce the notion that it is giving us an endlessly rich pattern of life and people.

The second way of looking at these characters is by seeing them as *serial types*. I have mentioned before that our reference point for understanding a character is very often within the serial rather than outside it. It seems to me also that certain characters become types within whose range of traits other characters are also then shaped. Thus there is an 'Elsie Tanner type' – sexy, rather tartily dressed, hot-tempered, impulsive – who is also recognisable in other women in *Coronation Street* – Rita, Suzie, Bet (and I would also include Len Fairclough as a male equivalent). In addition, other women in the serial are defined by specifically *not* being an 'Elsie Tanner type' – Mavis, Emily and Gail, who has graduated from apprenticeship in this type to being its opposite.

[. . .]

The third way of grouping the same set of characters is as *holders of a status position*: by this, I am referring to the position they occupy in the serial in terms crucially of sex, age and marital position and sometimes in terms of class and work. Thus, in *Coronation Street*, Ken Barlow, Steve Fisher, Mike Baldwin, Eddie Yeats, Fred Gee and even Albert Tatlock, however different they may be as individuated characters and serial types, are all, at the time of writing, unmarried men and therefore available for stories centring on courtship and marriage.

[. . .]

Of course, characters may hold more than one position, depending on what is being emphasised. Thus Tony Archer is a husband, son and father as well as being a farmer, and the emphasis will clearly depend on the particular story he is involved in at a given moment.

It is important perhaps to stress that these three categories are not exclusive; all characters at all times can be seen as an individuated character, a serial type and the holder of a particular status position. It is the interaction of the three categories which allows the character to be used in different ways and which gives both stability and flexibility to the narrative.

Characters in the Narrative

This analysis of the serial characters makes it possible to see how they can be used within the narrative organisation of the serial. It is clear that while some plots are available to everyone, others will be limited to those of a particular type or status position. Big events – birth, marriage, death – are used sparingly to give them the feeling of a special occasion. (The complications of several characters dying and/or marrying at the same time could render *Coronation Street* something of a *Soap*-like farce.) Plots centring on marriage or birth are available to a limited, though still wide, range of characters; that of death is available to all, but different character traits will give the event its particular feeling of poignancy, grief, shock or even relief. When such events happen, they tend to take up a lot of time within an episode and, particularly in the case of television serials, are supported by off-screen coverage such as the production of special magazines.

General plots, on the other hand, are the staple of the serial, the basis of the output. They revolve – in the serials I am discussing – around problems of relationships such as arise within marriages, between generations, in friendships and through quarrels and difficulties at home. These general plots are available to all characters since everyone is involved, in one way or another, in this complex web of relationships. Variety is then available through the individuals involved, which makes for the difference between, for instance, the same story concerning Annie and Billy Walker, Ivy and Brian Tilsley or Gail and her mother.

[. . .]

It is important to note, though, that it is possible to add a further element of variety by surprising the audience with a change in position or a character acting against type. Thus, the revelation that Bet Lynch was a mother put her in a position unknown to and unexpected by the audience. The use of characters against type, rather than status position, is more common and very effective. Emily Bishop's anger, when expressed, is more surprising and moving than Elsie Tanner's simply because it comes from an unexpected source.

[. . .]

THE ROLE OF GOSSIP IN THE SERIAL

Gossip Within the Serial

In this final section, I want to try to analyse the role of gossip, which is frequently seen as being a characteristic of the serial and is quite often commented on within the serials themselves. On one level, gossip helps to create the feeling of day-to-dayness referred to at the beginning of this piece. [. . .] More importantly, gossip in the serial constitutes a commentary on the action.

Much of the gossip which takes place provides the audience with new information or gives more detail about what has been happening. It plays an important role formally in binding together the various plots and the different characters and making them coherent. Thus, a character involved in one story will, in apparently casual conversation, pass on information about that story and receive, in exchange, news about the other plots in which s/he is not involved. The locations in which gossip can easily take place are therefore among the most frequently used sets in the serial – the pubs and corner shops in *Coronation Street, The Archers, Waggoner's Walk* and *Emmerdale Farm*, Coronation Street itself, the village green or the church hall in *The Archers*. In these public locations, characters can appear and disappear, as required, in a way which seems quite natural. [. . .] A scene with two or three characters chatting about one story can wholly change direction with the arrival of another character with a different set of news. Such a setting means that the different plots can be brought together and commented on by characters who may not be directly involved in the action. This running commentary reveals the different moral positions which are taken up by the characters who comment on what is going on [. . .] and provide the audience with a range of perspectives from which to understand the action. In addition, such conversations nearly always move on to speculation about what will happen next and what the characters involved are likely to do. This kind of speculative gossip both encourages the audience to pursue the enigma dangled before it and provides us with an insight into the characters concerned.

Gossip very often has a part in the action itself. Stories very frequently revolve round questions of knowledge or ignorance on the part of different characters, and the decision to tell a character about a previously unknown event is often a major issue. Such questions occur continually in the serials.

[. . .]

Knowledge revealed through gossip becomes, in this situation, something almost tangible, to be given, withheld, revealed accidentally or hinted at. Gossip becomes then not just a running commentary but an important part of the action, and it is almost impossible to draw the line between action and comment on that action.

Gossip outside the Serial

We have seen how gossip operates within the serial, both playing an important part at the level of action and presenting the audience with information, ideas and speculation on what might happen next. I would also argue that, in terms of information and speculation, gossip operates in a similar way outside the programmes in the discussion which a serial generates among its regular followers. The attraction of a successful serial is that it offers us a place, a metaphoric elbow on the bar, as commentator on the events as they unfold and our years of watching/listening make us experts. Such conversations will involve being filled in on recent episodes ('What happened in *Coronation Street* last night?') or on events in the distant past. They then move on to speculation so that discussion [. . .] is carried on not only by the characters in the serial but by the audience as well. This is not to say that the audience in general has been conned into thinking that the world of the serial is the real world. Indeed, the pleasure of such discussions comes from performing the delicate balancing act of discussing the characters as if they were real people with histories, motivations and futures while at the same time recognising the formal conventions of the serial in which they appear. We are told in newspaper reports, for instance, that Suzie Birchall and Steve Fisher are to be written out of *Coronation Street*. We can use this knowledge to speculate on how this will be done; will Steve be sacked, will they go off together, will Suzie make a success, this time, of things in London? It is this kind of informed speculation among the audience which characterises the response to a serial and which differentiates it from any other television form.

CONCLUSION

In this essay, I have discussed the formal terms within which a continuous serial operates and have tried to assess some of the effects of this process. The continuous serial has to work with a punishing schedule, normally appearing on television more than once a week and sometimes, on radio, five times a week. In order to do this, it establishes a base which becomes increasingly familiar to its audience while maintaining sufficient flexibility to be able to present apparently different situations. It provides us with the feeling of an unwritten future while giving necessary access to the past. We are constantly left wondering what will happen next – occasionally with a real cliffhanger. It presents us with 'new' events which are endless variations on regular patterns and provides a range of characters which is both varied and limited. This balance of change and repetition is achieved through the organisation of narrative and character, and the succession of the narrative is cemented together by gossip, both inside and outside the text.

REFERENCES

Barthes, R., *S/Z* (trans. by R. Miller), Jonathan Cape, London 1975.
Chatman, S., *History and Discourse*, Cornell UP, Cornell 1978.
Grabo, C., *Technique of the Novel*, New York 1928 (quoted in Chatman).
Heath, S. and Skirrow, G., 'Television – a World in Action', *Screen*, vol. 18, no. 2, 1977.
Scholes, R. and Kellog, R., *The Nature of Narrative*, OUP, New York 1979.
Todorov, T., *The Fantastic*, Cornell UP, Cornell 1975.

38

THE SEARCH FOR TOMORROW IN TODAY'S SOAP OPERAS

Tania Modleski

[. . .]

Whereas the meaning of Harlequin Romances depends almost entirely on the sense of an ending, soap operas are important to their viewers in part because they never end. Whereas Harlequins encourage our identification with one character, soap operas invite identification with numerous personalities. And whereas Harlequins are structured around two basic enigmas, in soap operas, the enigmas proliferate: 'Will Bill find out that his wife's sister's baby is really his by artificial insemination? Will his wife submit to her sister's blackmail attempts, or will she finally let Bill know the truth? If he discovers the truth, will this lead to another nervous breakdown, causing him to go back to Springfield General where his ex-wife and his illegitimate daughter are both doctors and sworn enemies?' Tune in tomorrow, not in order to find out the answers, but to see what further complications will defer the resolutions and introduce new questions. Thus the narrative, by placing ever more complex obstacles between desire and fulfillment, makes anticipation of an end an end in itself. Soap operas invest exquisite pleasure in the central condition of a woman's life: waiting – whether for her phone to ring, for the baby to take its nap, or for the family to be reunited shortly after the day's final soap opera has left *its* family still struggling against dissolution.

According to Roland Barthes, the hermeneutic code, which propounds the enigmas, functions by making 'expectation . . . the basic condition for truth: truth, these narratives tell us, is what is *at the end* of expectation. This design implies a return to order, for expectation is a disorder.' [1] But, of course, soap operas do not end. Consequently, truth for women is seen to lie not 'at the end of expectation,' but *in* expectation, not in the 'return to order,' but in (familial) disorder.

[. . .]

The family is, for many women, their only support, and soap operas offer the assurance of its immortality.[2] They present the viewer with a picture of a family which, though it is always in

From T. Modleski, *Loving with a Vengeance: Mass-produced Fantasies for Women* (London:Methuen, 1984) pp. 85–109.

the process of breaking down, stays together no matter how intolerable its situation may get. Or, perhaps more accurately, the family remains close precisely because it is perpetually in a chaotic state. The unhappiness generated by the family can only be solved in the family. Misery becomes not, as in many nineteenth-century women's novels, the consequence and sign of the family's breakdown, but the very means of its functioning and perpetuation. As long as the children are unhappy, as long as things *don't* come to a satisfying conclusion, the mother will be needed as confidante and adviser, and her function will never end.

[. . .]

The subject/spectator of soap operas, it could be said, is constituted as a sort of ideal mother: a person who possesses greater wisdom than all her children, whose sympathy is large enough to encompass the conflicting claims of her family (she identifies with them all), and who has no demands or claims of her own (she identifies with no one character exclusively). The connection between melodrama and mothers is an old one. Harriet Beecher Stowe, of course, made it explicit in *Uncle Tom's Cabin*, believing that if her book could bring its female readers to see the world as one extended family, the world would be vastly improved. But in Stowe's novel, the frequent shifting of perspective identifies the reader with a variety of characters in order ultimately to ally her with the mother/author and with God who, in their higher wisdom and understanding, can make all the hurts of the world go away, thus insuring the 'essential "rightness" of the world order.' Soap opera, however, denies the 'mother' this extremely flattering illusion of her power. On the one hand, it plays upon the spectator's expectations of the melodramatic form, continually stimulating (by means of the hermeneutic code) the desire for a just conclusion to the story, and, on the other hand, it constantly presents the desire as unrealizable, by showing that conclusions only lead to further tension and suffering. Thus soap operas convince women that their highest goal is to see their families united and happy, while consoling them for their inability to realize this ideal and bring about familial harmony.

This is reinforced by the character of the good mother on soap operas. In contrast to the manipulating mother who tries to interfere with her children's lives, the good mother must sit helplessly by as her children's lives disintegrate; her advice, which she gives only when asked, is temporarily soothing, but usually ineffectual. Her primary function is to be sympathetic, to tolerate the foibles and errors of others.

[. . .]

It is important to recognize that soap operas serve to affirm the primacy of the family not by presenting an ideal family, but by portraying a family in constant turmoil and appealing to the spectator to be understanding and tolerant of the many evils which go on within that family. The spectator/mother, identifying with each character in turn, is made to see 'the larger picture' and extend her sympathy to both the sinner and the victim. She is thus in a position to forgive all. As a rule, only those issues which can be tolerated and ultimately pardoned are introduced on soap operas. The list includes careers for women, abortions, premarital and extramarital sex, alcoholism, divorce, mental and even physical cruelty. An issue like homosexuality, which could explode the family structure rather than temporarily disrupt it, is simply ignored. Soap operas, contrary to many people's conception of them, are not conservative but liberal, and the mother is the liberal par excellence. By constantly presenting her with the many-sidedness of any question, by never reaching a permanent conclusion, soap operas undermine her capacity to form unambiguous judgments.

[. . .]

These remarks must be qualified. If soap operas keep us caring about everyone; if they refuse to allow us to condemn most characters and actions until all the evidence is in (and, of course, it never is), there is one character whom we are allowed to hate unreservedly: the villainess, the negative image of the spectator's ideal self.[3] Although much of the suffering on soap opera is presented as unavoidable, the surplus suffering is often the fault of the villainess who tries to 'make things happen and control events better than the subject/spectator can.' The villainess might very possibly be a mother trying to manipulate her children's lives or ruin their marriages. Or perhaps she is a woman avenging herself on her husband's family because it has never fully accepted her.

This character cannot be dismissed as easily as many critics seem to think.[4] The extreme delight viewers apparently take in despising the villainess testifies to the enormous amount of energy involved in the spectator's repression and to her (albeit unconscious) resentment at being constituted as an egoless receptacle for the suffering of others.[5] The villainess embodies the 'split-off fury' which, in the words of Dorothy Dinnerstein, is 'the underside of the "truly feminine" woman's monstrously overdeveloped talent for unreciprocated empathy.'[6]

[. . .]

Soap operas, then, while constituting the spectator as a 'good mother,' provide in the person of the villainess an outlet for feminine anger: in particular, as we have seen, the spectator has the satisfaction of seeing men suffer the same anxieties and guilt that women usually experience and seeing them receive similar kinds of punishment for their transgressions. But that anger is neutralized at every moment in that it is the special object of the spectator's hatred. The spectator, encouraged to sympathize with almost everyone, can vent her frustration on the one character who refuses to accept her own powerlessness, who is unashamedly self-seeking. Woman's anger is directed at woman's anger, and an eternal cycle is created.

And yet, if the villainess never succeeds, if, in accordance with the spectator's conflicting desires, she is doomed to eternal repetition, then she obviously never permanently fails either. When, as occasionally happens, a villainess reforms, a new one immediately supplants her. Generally, however, a popular villainess will remain true to her character for most or all of the soap opera's duration. And if the villainess constantly suffers because she is always foiled, we should remember that she suffers no more than the good characters, who don't even try to interfere with their fates. Again, this may be contrasted to the usual imperatives of melodrama, which demand an ending to justify the suffering of the good and punish the wicked. While soap operas thrive they present a continual reminder that women's anger is alive, if not exactly well.

[. . .]

Another way in which soap opera stimulates women's desire for connectedness is through the constant, claustrophobic use of close-up shots. Often only the audience is privileged to witness the characters' expressions, which are complex and intricately coded, signifying triumph, bitterness, despair, confusion – the entire emotional register, in fact. Soap operas contrast sharply with other popular forms aimed at masculine visual pleasure, which is often centered on the fragmentation and fetishization of the female body. In the most popular feminine visual art, it is easy to forget that characters even have bodies, so insistently are close-ups of faces employed. One critic significantly remarks, 'A face in close-up is what before the age of film only a lover or a mother ever saw.'[7] Soap operas appear to be the one visual art which activates the gaze of the mother – but in order to provoke anxiety about the welfare of others. Close-ups provide the spectator with training in 'reading' other people, in being sensitive to their (unspoken) feelings at any given moment.

Chodorow* stresses the 'connectedness' of women's work in the home, but this is only half the picture. The wife's job is further complicated by the fact that she must often deal with several people with different, perhaps conflicting moods; and further she must be prepared to drop what she is doing in order to cope with various conflicts and problems the moment they arise. Unlike most workers in the labor force, the housewife must beware of concentrating her energies exclusively on any one task – otherwise, the dinner could burn or the baby could crack its skull (as happened once on 'Ryan's Hope' when the villainess became so absorbed in a love encounter that she forgot to keep an eye on her child). The housewife functions, as many creative women have sadly realized, by distraction. Tillie Olsen writes in *Silences*, 'More than in any other human relationship, overwhelmingly more, motherhood means being instantly interruptable, responsive, responsible. … It is distraction, not meditation, that becomes habitual: interruption, not continuity; spasmodic, not constant toil.'[8] Daytime television plays a part in habituating women to distraction, interruption, and spasmodic toil.

These observations have crucial implications for current television theory. In his book *Television: Technology and Cultural Form* Raymond Williams suggests that the shifts in television programming from one type of show to another and from part of a show to a commercial should not be seen as 'interruptions' – of a mood, of a story – but as parts of a whole. What at first appear to be discrete programming units in fact interrelate in profound and complex ways. Williams uses the term 'flow' to describe this interaction of various programs with each other and with commercials. 'The fact of flow,' he says, defines the 'central television experience.'[9] Against Williams I would argue that the flow within soap operas as well as between soap operas and other programming units reinforces the very principle of interruptability crucial to the proper functioning of women in the home. In other words, what Williams calls 'the central television experience' is a profoundly decentering experience.

'The art of being off center,' wrote Walter Benjamin in an essay on Baudelaire, 'in which the little man could acquire training in places like the Fun Fair, flourished concomitantly with unemployment.'[10] Soap operas also provide training in the 'art of being off center' (and we should note in passing that it is probably no accident that the nighttime 'soap opera' *Dallas* and its spinoffs and imitators are flourishing in a period of economic crisis and rising unemployment). The housewife, of course, is in one sense, like the little man at the Fun Fair, unemployed, but in another sense she is perpetually employed – her work, like a soap opera, is never done. Moreover, as I have said, her duties are split among a variety of domestic and familial tasks, and her television programs keep her from desiring a focused existence by involving her in the pleasures of a fragmented life.

Interruptions may be, as Benjamin thought, one of the fundamental devices of all art, but surely soap opera relies on them to a far greater extent than any other art.[11] Revelations, confrontations, and reunions are constantly being interrupted and postponed by telephone calls, unexpected visitors, counterrevelations, catastrophes, and switches from one plot to another. These interruptions are both annoying and pleasurable: if we are torn away from one exciting story, we at least have the relief of picking up the thread of an unfinished one. Like the (ideal) mother in the home, we are kept interested in a number of events at once and are denied the luxury of a total and prolonged absorption. Commercials constitute another kind of interruption, in this case from *outside* the diegesis. Commercials present the housewife with mini-problems and their resolutions, so after witnessing all the agonizingly hopeless dilemmas on soap operas, the spectator has the satisfaction of seeing something cleaned up, if only a stained shirt or a dirty floor.

Although daytime commercials and soap operas are both set overwhelmingly within the home, the two views of the home seem antithetical, for the chief concerns of commercials are precisely the ones soap operas censor out. The saggy diapers, yellow wax build-up and carpet smells making up the world of daytime television ads are rejected by soap operas in favor of 'Another World,' as the very title of one soap opera announces, a world in which characters deal only with the 'large' problems of human existence: crime, love, death and dying. But this antithesis embodies a deep truth about the way women function in (or, more accurately, around) culture: as both moral and spiritual guides and household drudges: now one, now the other, moving back and forth between the extremes, but obviously finding them difficult to reconcile.[12]

Similarly, the violent mood swings the spectator undergoes in switching from quiz shows, the other popular daytime television fare, to soap operas also constitute a kind of interruption, just as the housewife is required to endure monotonous, repetitive work but to be able to switch instantly and on demand from her role as a kind of bedmaking, dishwashing automaton to a large sympathizing consciousness. It must be stressed that while nighttime television certainly affords shifts in mood, notably from comedy to drama, these shifts are not nearly as extreme as in daytime programming. Quiz shows present the spectator with the same game, played and replayed frenetically day after day, with each game a self-contained unit, crowned by climactic success or failure. Soap operas, by contrast, endlessly defer resolutions and climaxes and undercut the very notion of success.

The formal properties of daytime television thus accord closely with the rhythms of women's work in the home. Individual soap operas as well as the flow of various programs and commercials tend to make repetition, interruption, and distraction pleasurable. But we can go even further and note that for women viewers reception itself often takes place in a state of distraction. According to Benjamin, 'reception in a state of distraction . . . finds in the film its true means of exercise'.[13] But now that we have television we can see that it goes beyond film in this respect, or at least the daytime programs do. For, the consumption of most films as well as of nighttime programs in some ways recapitulates the work situation in the factory or office: the viewer is physically passive, immobilized, and all his attention is focused on the object before him. Even the most allegedly 'mindless' program requires a fairly strong degree of concentration if its plot is to make sense. But since the housewife's 'leisure' time is not so strongly demarcated, her entertainment must often be consumed on the job. As the authors of *The Complete Soap Opera* Book tell us:

> The typical fan was assumed to be trotting about her daily chores with her mop in one hand, duster in the other, cooking, tending babies, answering telephones. Thus occupied, she might not be able to bring her full powers of concentration to bear on *Backstage Wife*.[14]

This accounts, in part, for the 'realistic' feel of soap operas. The script writers, anticipating the housewife's distracted state, are careful to repeat important elements of the story several times. Thus, if two characters are involved in a confrontation which is supposed to mark a final break in their relationship, that same confrontation must be repeated, with minor variations, a few times in order to make sure the viewer gets the point. 'Clean breaks' – surely a supreme fiction – are impossible on soap operas.

[. . .]

Ironically, critics of television untiringly accuse its viewers of indulging in escapism. In other words, both high art critics and politically oriented critics, though motivated by different concerns, unite in condemning daytime television for *distracting* the housewife from her real situation. My point has been that a distracted or distractable frame of mind is crucial to the housewife's efficient functioning *in* her real situation, and at this level television and its so-called distractions, along with the particular forms they take, are intimately bound up with women's work.

Given the differences in the ways men and women experience their lives, it is not surprising to find that 'narrative pleasure' can sometimes mean very different things to men and women. This is an important point. Too often feminist criticism implies that there is only one kind of pleasure to be derived from narrative and that it is an essentially masculine one. Hence, it is further implied, feminist artists must first of all challenge this pleasure and then out of nothing begin to construct a feminist aesthetics and feminist form. This is a mistaken position, in my view, for it keeps us constantly in an adversary role, always on the defensive, always, as it were, complaining about the family but never leaving home. Feminist artists don't have to start from nothing; rather, they can look for clues to women's pleasure which are already present in existing forms, even if this pleasure is currently placed at the service of patriarchy. Claire Johnston, a feminist film theorist, has argued for a strategy combining 'both the notion of film as a political tool and film as entertainment':

> For too long these have been regarded as two opposing poles with little common ground. In order to counter our objectification in the cinema, our collective fantasies must be released: women's cinema must embody the working through of desire: such an objective demands the use of the entertainment film. Ideas derived from the entertainment film, then, should inform the political film, and political ideas should inform the entertainment cinema: a two way process.[15]

Clearly, women find soap operas eminently entertaining, and an analysis of the pleasure these programs afford can provide feminists with ways not only to challenge this pleasure but to incorporate it into their own artistic practices.

The fact that soap operas never reach a full conclusion has usually been viewed in an entirely negative light. Here are the words of Dennis Porter, who, working from Roland Barthes' theories of narrative structures and ideology, completely condemns soap operas for their failure to resolve all problems:

> Unlike all traditionally end-oriented fiction and drama, soap opera offers process without progression, not a climax and a resolution, but mini-climaxes and provisional denouements that must never be presented in such a way as to eclipse the suspense experienced for associated plot lines. Thus soap opera is the drama of perepetia without anagnorisis. It deals forever in reversals but never portrays the irreversible change which traditionally marks the passage out of ignorance into true knowledge. For actors and audience alike, no action ever stands revealed in the terrible light of its consequences.[16]

These are strange words indeed, coming from one who purports to be analyzing the ideology of narrative form. They are a perfect illustration of how a high art bias, an eagerness to demonstrate the worthlessness of 'low' art, can lead us to make claims for high art which we would ordinarily be wary of professing. Terms like 'progression,' 'climax,' 'resolution,' 'irreversible change,' 'true knowledge,' and 'consequences' are certainly tied to an ideology; they are 'linked to classical metaphysics,' as Barthes observes. '[The] hermeneutic narrative in which truth predicates an incomplete subject, based on expectation and desire for its imminent closure, is . . . linked to the kerygmatic civilization of meaning and truth, appeal and fulfillment.'[17] To criticize classical narrative because, for example, it is based on a suspect notion of progress and then criticize soap opera because it *isn't* will never get us anywhere – certainly not 'out of ignorance into true knowledge.' A different approach is needed.

Luce Irigaray, describing woman's 'rediscovery' of herself, writes, 'It is a sort of universe in expansion for which no limits could be fixed and which, for all that, would not be incoherent.'[18] The similarities between this description and soap opera as a form are striking. They suggest the possibility that soap operas may not be an entirely negative influence on the viewer; they may also have the force of *a negation*, a negation of the typical (and masculine) modes of pleasure in our society. This challenge, is, moreover, very like the one being mounted in current literary and film theory. Theorists have recently been pointing out the pleasures of the kind of text which breaks the illusion of unity and totality provided the reader or spectator by the 'classic text.' Hence the emphasis since the structuralists has been on 'decentering the subject.' But, as we have seen, women are, in their lives, their work, and in certain forms of their pleasure, already decentered – 'off center.' As Mark Poster remarks in his *Critical Theory of the Family*, 'the feeling of being the center of creation is typical of the ego-structure of the bourgeois male.'[19] This fact seems to me to be of crucial importance to anyone interested in formulating a feminist aesthetic. Indeed, I would like to argue that soap operas are not altogether at odds with an already developing, though still embryonic, feminist aesthetics.

'Deep in the very nature of soaps is the implied promise that they will last forever.'[20] This being the case, a great deal of interest necessarily becomes focused upon those events which retard or impede the flow of the narrative. If, on the one hand, these constant interruptions provide consolation for the housewife's sense of missed opportunities, by illustrating for her the enormous difficulty of getting from desire to fulfillment, on the other hand, the notion of what Porter contemptuously calls 'process without progression' is one endorsed by many innovative women artists. In praising Nathalie Sarraute, for example, Mary Ellmann observes that she is not

> interested in the explicit speed of which the novel is capable, only in the nuances which must tend to delay it. In her own discussions of the novel, Nathalie Sarraute is entirely anti-progressive. In criticizing ordinary dialogue, she dislikes its haste: there not being 'time' for the person to consider a remark's ramifications, his having to speak and to listen frugally, his having to rush ahead toward his object – which is of course 'to order his own conduct.'[21]

Soap opera is similarly antiprogressive.[22] Just as Sarraute's work is opposed to the traditional novel form, soap opera is opposed to the classic (male) film narrative, which, with maximum action and minimum, always pertinent dialogue, speeds its way to the restoration of order.

In soap operas, the important thing is that there always be time for a person to consider a remark's ramifications, time for people to speak and to listen lavishly. Actions and climaxes are only of secondary importance. This may seem wilfully to misrepresent soap operas. Certainly they appear to contain a ludicrous number of climaxes and actions: people are always getting blackmailed, having major operations, dying, conducting extra-marital affairs which inevitably result in pregnancy, being kidnapped, going mad, and losing their memories. But just as in real life (one constantly hears it said) it takes a wedding or a funeral to reunite scattered families, so soap opera catastrophes provide convenient occasions for people to come together, confront one another, and explore intense emotions. One advantage of placing people in hospitals, for example, is that because they are immobilized they are forced to take the time to talk to others and listen to what others have to say to them. And friends and family members, imprisoned in waiting rooms (in some ways an apt metaphor for women's homes), can discuss their feelings about the latest tragedy, and, from there, since the waiting often seems interminable, go on to analyze the predicaments of their mutual friends, as well as the state of their own relationships. Thus, in direct contrast to the typical male narrative film, in which the climax functions to resolve difficulties, the 'mini-climaxes' of soap opera function to introduce difficulties and to complicate rather than simplify the characters' lives.

Furthermore, as with much women's narrative (such as the fiction of Ivy Compton–Burnett, who strongly influenced Sarraute), dialogue in soap operas is an enormously tricky business. Again, I must take issue with Porter, who says, 'Language here is of a kind that takes itself for granted and assumes it is always possible to mean no more and no less than what one intends.[23] More accurately, in soap operas the gap between what is intended and what is actually spoken is often very wide. Secrets better left buried may be blurted out in moments of intensity, or they are withheld just when a character most desires to tell all. This is very different from nighttime television programs and classic Hollywood films with their particularly naive belief in the beneficence of communication. The full revelation of a secret on these shows usually begins or proclaims the restoration of order. Marcus Welby can then get his patient to agree to treatment; Perry Mason can exonerate the innocent and punish the guilty. The necessity of confession, the means through which, according to Michel Foucault, we gladly submit to power, is wholeheartedly endorsed.[24] In soap operas, on the other hand, the effects of confession are often ambiguous, providing relief for some of the characters and dreadful complications for others. (Here too we can see how soap opera melodrama diverges from traditional melodrama, which Peter Brooks, following Eric Bentley, has defined by its impulse to excess, to the overcoming of inhibition and repression: 'The genre's very existence is bound to [the] possibility, and necessity, of saying everything.')[25] Moreover, it is remarkable how seldom in soap operas a character can talk another into changing his/her ways. Ordinarily, it takes a major disaster to bring about self-awareness – whereas all Marcus Welby has to do is give his stop-feeling-sorry-for-yourself speech and the character undergoes a drastic personality change. Perhaps more than men, women in our society are aware of the pleasures of language – though less sanguine about its potential use as an instrument of power.

Not only do soap operas suggest an alternate kind of narrative pleasure experienced by women, but they also tell us a great deal about what Johnston calls women's 'collective fantasies.' To the dismay of many feminist critics, the most powerful fantasy embodied in soap operas appears to be the fantasy of a fully self-sufficient family. Carol Lopate complains:

> Daytime television . . . promises that the family can be everything, if only one is willing to stay inside it. For the woman confined to her house, daytime television fills out the empty spaces of the long day when she is home alone, channels her fantasies toward love and family dramas, and promises her that the life she is in can fulfill her needs. But it does not call to her attention her aloneness and isolation, and it does not suggest to her that it is precisely in her solitude that she has a possibility for gaining a self.[26]

This statement merits close consideration. It implies that the family in soap operas is a mirror-image of the viewer's own family. But for most viewers, this is definitely not the case. What the spectator is looking at and perhaps longing for, is a kind of *extended* family, the direct opposite of her own isolated nuclear family. Most soap operas follow the lives of several generations of a large family, all living in the same town and all intimately involved in one another's lives. The fantasy here is truly a 'collective fantasy' – a fantasy of community, but put in terms with which the viewer can be comfortable. Lopate is wrong, I believe, to end her peroration with a call for feminine solitude. For too long women have had too much solitude and, quite rightly, they resent it. In her thought-provoking essay on the family, Barbara Easton points out that since the family is for many women their only support, those women who are abandoned to solitude by feminists eager to undermine this support are apt to turn to the right. People like Anita Bryant and Marabel Morgan, says Easton, 'feed on fears of social isolation that have a basis in reality.' [27] So do soap operas.

For it is important to recognize that soap opera allays *real* anxieties, satisfies *real* needs and desires, even while it may distort them. The fantasy of community is not only a real desire (as opposed to the 'false' ones mass culture is always accused of trumping up), it is a salutary one. As feminists, we have a responsibility to devise ways of meeting these needs that are more creative, honest, and interesting than the ones mass culture has supplied. Otherwise, the search for tomorrow threatens to go on, endlessly.

NOTES

1.   Barthes, *S/Z*, p. 76.

2.   Not only can women count on a never ending story line, they can also, to a great extent, rely upon the fact that their favorite characters will never desert them. To take a rather extreme example: when, on one soap opera, the writers killed off a popular female character and viewers were unhappy, the actress was brought back to portray the character's twin sister. See Madeleine Edmondson and David Rounds, *From Mary Noble to Mary Hartman: The Complete Soap Opera Book*, p. 208.

3.   There are still villains on soap operas, but their numbers have declined considerably since radio days – to the point where they are no longer indispensable to the formula. 'The Young and the Restless', for example, does without them.

4.   According to Kathryn Weibel (*Minor Mirror*), we quite simply 'deplore' the victimizers and totally identify with the victim (p. 62).

5.   'A soap opera without a bitch is a soap opera that doesn't get watched. The more hateful the bitch the better. Erica of "All My Children" is a classic. If you want to hear some hairy rap, just listen to a bunch of women discussing Erica.

"Girl, that Erica needs her tail whipped."

"I wish she'd try to steal my man and plant some marijuana in my purse. I'd be mopping up the street with her new hairdo." ' Bebe Moore Campbell, 'Hooked on Soaps,' p. 103.

6.   Dorothy Dinnerstein, *The Mermaid and The Minotaur*, p. 236.

7.   Dennis Porter, 'Soap Time: Thoughts on a Commodity Art Form,' p. 786.

8.   Tillie Olsen, *Silences*, pp. 18–19.

9.   Williams, p. 95.

10.   Benjamin, 'On Some Motifs in Baudelaire,' in *Illuminations*, p. 176.

11.   Benjamin, 'What is Epic Theater?' in *Illuminations*, p. 151.

12.   See Sherry B. Ortner's brilliant discussion of women's position in culture, 'Is Female to Male as Nature Is to Culture?'

13.   Benjamin, 'The Work of Art in the Age of Mechanical Reproduction,' in *Illuminations*, p. 240.

14.   Edmondson and Rounds, pp. 46–47.

15.   Claire Johnston, 'Women's Cinema as Counter-Cinema,' p. 217.

16.   Porter, pp. 783–84.

17.   Barthes, *S/Z*, p. 45.

18.   Luce Irigaray, 'Ce sexe qui n'en est pas un,' p. 104.

19.   Mark Poster, *Critical Theory of the Family*, p. 9.

20.   Edmondson and Rounds, p. 112.

21.   Ellmann, pp. 222–23.

22.   As David Grimsted points out, melodrama may always have been deeply antiprogressive, in spite of its apparent hopefulness and thrust toward a happy ending. First, the 'centrality of the villain in these plays, even though he was always eventually defeated, suggested a world where the evil and terror of which he was an incarnation were constant threats.' And second, in classic melodrama (as in soap operas), virtue is always allied with the past – with fathers, mothers, rural life styles, etc., while the present is conceived of as dangerous, confusing and perhaps even degenerate.' See *Melodrama Unveiled*, pp. 223–24.

23.   Porter, p. 788.

24.   Michel Foucault, *The History of Sexuality*, esp. pp. 57–73. In this connection, it is interesting to recall how in many detective stories, TV, shows, and films, the detective must overcome the reluctance of an *innocent*

party to yield some bit of information necessary to the solution of the crime. For an interesting discussion of Dragnet's Joe Friday as the Great Listener, see Reuel Denney, *The Astonished Muse*, pp. 82–92.

25.   Peter Brooks, *The Melodramatic Imagination*, p. 42. Or, as Eric Bentley puts it, 'melodrama is not so much the exaggerated as the uninhibited.' See *The Life of the Drama*, p. 206.

26.   Carol Lopate, 'Daytime Television: You'll Never Want to Leave Home,' p. 51.

27.   Easton, p. 34.

REFERENCES

Barthes, Roland. S/Z. Translated by Richard Miller. New York: Hill & Wang, 1974.

Benjamin, Walter. *Illuminations*. Translated by Harry Zohn. Edited by Hannah Arendt. New York: Schocken Books, 1969.

Bentley, Eric. *The Life of the Drama*. New York: Atheneum, 1974.

Brooks, Peter. *The Melodramatic Imagination: Balzac, Henry James, Melodrama, and the Mode of Excess*. New Haven: Yale University Press, 1976.

Campbell, Bebe Moore. 'Hooked on Soaps.' *Essence*, November 1978, pp. 100–103.

Denney, Reuel. *The Astonished Muse*. Chicago: University of Chicago Press, 1957.

Dinnerstein, Dorothy. *The Mermaid and the Minotaur: Sexual Arrangements and Human Malaise*. New York: Harper & Row, 1976.

Easton, Barbara. 'Feminism and the Contemporary Family.' *Socialist Review* 8, no. 3 (1978), pp. 11–36.

Edmondson, Madeleine and Rounds, David. *From Mary Noble to Mary Hartman: The Complete Soap Opera Book*. New York: Stein & Day, 1976.

Ellmann, Mary *Thinking about Women*. New York: Harvest Books, 1968.

Foucault, Michel *The History of Sexuality: Volume I: An Introduction*. Translated by Robert Hurley. New York: Vintage Books, 1980.

Grimsted, David. *Melodrama Unveiled: American Theater and Culture, 1800–1850*. Chicago: University of Chicago Press, 1968.

Irigaray, Luce. 'Ce sexe qui n'en est pas un.' In *New French Feminisms*. Edited by Elaine Marks and Isabelle Courtivron. Amherst: University of Massachusetts Press, 1980.

Johnston, Claire. 'Women's Cinema as Counter-Cinema.' In *Movies and Methods*. Edited by Bill Nichols. Berkeley: University of California Press, 1976.

Lopate, Carol. 'Daytime Television: You'll Never Want to Leave Home.' *Radical America* 2 (1977): 33–51.

Olsen, Tillie. *Silences*. New York: Dell Publishing Co., 1979.

Ortner, Sherry B. 'Is Female to Male as Nature Is to Culture?' In *Woman, Culture and Society*. Edited by Michelle Zimbalist Rosaldo and Louise Lamphere. Stanford, Ca.: Stanford University Press, 1974.

Porter, Dennis. 'Soap Time: Thoughts on a Commodity Art Form.' *College English* 38 (1977): 782–88.

Poster, Mark. *Critical Theory of the Family*. New York: Continuum Books, 1978.

Weibel, Kathryn. *Mirror Mirror: Images of Women Reflected in Popular Culture*. Garden City, N. Y.: Anchor Books, 1977.

Williams, Raymond *Television: Technology and Cultural Form*. New York: Schocken Books, 1975.

Editor's Note

*Chodorow, Nancy, *The Reproduction of Mothering: Psychoanalysis and the Sociology of Gender*. Berkeley: University of California Press, 1978.

39

DALLAS AND FEMINISM

Ien Ang

[. . .]

Feminism and the Tragic Structure of Feeling

As a political and cultural movement, feminism is sustained by collective fantasies of a social future in which the oppression of women will have ceased to exist. A future, in other words, in which women's lives will no longer be dominated and hindered by patriarchal structures and sexist practices. All feminist struggles into which women put so much energy in present-day societies are always related in some way or other to this (imaginary) Utopia. Feminist fighting spirit and solidarity today are always motivated by a desire to achieve that distant Utopia, however much that desire is repressed in concrete situations and in the thick of the fight in the deeper layers of day-to-day consciousness.

As a narrative, then, feminist discourse tends to move in the direction of an imagined happy ending. It is the belief in and the commitment to the necessity for this happy end that keeps feminists going. In this sense feminist discourse bears some similarity to the structure of popular romantic fiction, in which the search for a happy ending – for that orgastic moment of 'and they lived happily ever after' – also forms the motor of the narrative. However, the feminist notion of the happy ending has a totally different content from the happy ending of the popular romantic novel, in which the heterosexual, monogamous couple are eternally united in harmony. More strongly still, the way in which this romantic Utopia is achieved is generally deplored because it is seen to be in conflict with the feminist ideal: the heroine of the popular romantic novel wins happiness only after having given up her striving for independence and her resistance to the arrogance and violence of the male hero, and having subjected herself to his authority and paternalist protection.[1] In this sense the narrative of popular romantic fiction is one which asserts that the utopian situation can be realized within the framework of existing,

From I. Ang, *Watching* Dallas: *Soap Opera and the Melodramatic Imagination* (London: Methuen, 1985) pp. 121–36.

patriarchal power relations between men and women – an imaginary 'solution' totally at odds with the feminist scenario.

But what about soap operas, with their total lack of any sense of progress, a total absence of an outlook on any kind of happy ending? In soap operas it is by definition impossible for the characters to remain happy. A utopian moment is totally absent in soap opera narratives: circumstances and events continually throw up barriers to prevent the capture of that little scrap of happiness for which all the characters are none the less searching. Life is presented as inherently problematic. Unhappiness is the norm, the rule and not the exception. This is the core of the tragic structure of feeling.

As a consequence, women in soap opera can never be simply happy with the positions they occupy. On the contrary, it is often these positions themselves that give rise to many problems and conflicts. This holds pre-eminently for the traditional positions which are ascribed to women in contemporary society. So although motherhood is presented in soap opera as a feminine ideal, at the same time it is a source of constant care and worry. And marriage is not shown to be the blissful region of conjugal harmony but as subject to continual conflict. In a certain sense, then, a tense relationship is expressed in soap operas between the traditional destiny imposed on women by patriarchy and the non-viability of that destiny for women themselves. In other words, it would appear that some points made in feminist analysis of women's oppression are recognized in an intuitive way in soap operas: the contradictions which patriarchy generates are expressed time and again.

But it is precisely the lack of a prospect of a happy ending which makes any solution of these contradictions inconceivable. Women in soap opera never rise above their own problematic positions. On the contrary, they completely identify with them. In spite of all the miseries, they continue to believe in the ideals of patriarchal ideology: whatever the cost, the family must be held together (Miss Ellie); if your marriage breaks down you try again with another man or you become cynical (Sue Ellen); your happiness cannot be complete without children (Pamela). Hence the problems in *Dallas* can never be solved and are essentially cyclical: the patriarchal status quo is non-viable but remains intact.

Viewed in this way, the melodramatic sentimentality of *Dallas* is ideologically motivated by a sense of the essential impossibility of a fundamental alteration in the very structures which should be held responsible for all the trouble and unhappiness. This induces feelings of resignation and fatalism – sentiments which are not exactly conducive to resistance to those structures. From a feminist point of view the *Dallas* women therefore represent 'bad' positions: theirs are positions characterized by fatalism and passivity, while 'good' – feminist – positions should be accompanied by a fighting spirit and activity. It would seem, then, that the tragic structure of feeling is incompatible with a feminist sensibility.

[. . .]

PLEASURE, FANTASY AND CULTURAL POLITICS

What then about the 'feminist potential' of *Dallas*? What does it mean to get pleasure from *Dallas* by recognizing and identifying with its tragic structure of feeling, as so many female viewers seem to do?

Pleasure has so far not been discussed in this chapter. Yet pleasure is something that concerns many feminists and that is often seen as a problem for a feminist cultural politics. As part of a broader political issue, two questions can be asked concerning pleasure. First, what is the relevance of pleasure for a political project such as feminism? And secondly: what is the political and cultural meaning of the specific forms of pleasure which women find attractive?

There are no simple answers to these questions, but feminists certainly are convinced of the political importance of seeking satisfactory answers. Thus Michèle Barrett wonders: 'How can we widen the purchase of feminist ideas if we cannot understand why so many women read *Woman* and watch *Crossroads?*'[2] The relevance of pleasure is argued here by Barrett in a quite specific way. The understanding of women's existing pleasures, she appears to assert, can be useful for developing a more effective way of spreading feminist consciousness among the mass of women. Precisely how remains unclear for the present, but one positive point of Barrett's argument is that the enormous popularity among women of certain cultural forms is taken seriously. Thus she continues: 'We need to know why the "women's weepies" have an apparently enduring appeal . . . we need to examine much more open-mindedly and sympathetically their basis in our consciousness and subjectivity.'[3]

By presenting the problem in this way, Barrett avoids the moralism of the ideology of mass culture in which pleasure in 'mass culture' is regarded as illicit. Women's weepies and all other forms of popular culture for women (such as fashion, lyrical love songs and soap operas) must no longer be simply condemned: we must recognize that they have a positive value and meaning in women's lives. At the same time, however, Barrett does not attempt to fall into the opposite extreme; she does not endorse the populist position in which any pleasure is by definition justified and is above all discussion, because for her the understanding of these traditional pleasures of women is explicitly linked with a feminist aim. It is certainly not the aim to simply glorify those pleasures *because* they are popular among women – which would be a form of deceptive, populist solidarity – but to understand more thoroughly what concerns women today, so that feminists can connect up with it more efficiently. Women fortunately no longer need feel ashamed or guilty if they watch *Dallas*, but at the same time feminists must look for a way of making such pleasures politically productive by situating them in a feminist plan of action.

But it remains unclear what conclusion we must draw from Barrett's argument. How, for example, can the fact that so many women feel attracted to *Dallas* be made politically useful? Does it mean that feminists must make 'feminist soap operas' – whatever they might look like? Or is it a matter of creating contexts in which subversive readings of *Dallas* are promoted, so that the hope that Feuer and Seiter* nourish in the 'feminist potential' of soap operas is realized after all?

A serious theoretical problem arises here. This has to do with the danger of an overpoliticizing of pleasure. However much Barrett, for example, tries to approach women's weepies in an open-minded and sympathetic way, her basic premise nevertheless remains that its enjoyment is ultimately politically bad for women, because it does not lead to the adoption of feminist ideas. A new antagonism is constructed here: that between the fantasies of powerlessness inscribed in the tragic structure of feeling, and the fantasies of protest and liberation inscribed in the feminist imagination. But what does this antagonism imply? Does experiencing pleasure in fantasies of powerlessness necessarily lead to political passivity, as the antagonism suggests?

What is at stake here is the relationship between fantasy life, pleasure and socio-political practice and consciousness. In this context it is perhaps of less importance to wonder *why* women's weepies have such enduring appeal, as Barrett would have it, than to ask *what implications* the sentimental pleasure of identification with the tragic structure of feeling has for the way in which women make sense of and evaluate their position in society. And as the enduring popularity of women's weepies even among feminists would indicate, it is very doubtful whether the two are as intimately interrelated as is sometimes assumed. Must we see an imaginary identification with the tragic and masochistic positions of Sue Ellen or Pamela as a form of 'oppression in ourselves', a patriarchal 'remnant' that unfortunately women still have to hark back to because feminism has not yet developed any effective alternatives? Or can such fantasmatic scenarios have a meaning for women which is relatively independent of their political attitudes?

Although political activity certainly comprises a moment of pleasure because it provides one with a sense of positive identity, the project of feminism as a whole is not and never can be based on pleasure alone, because the project itself is impelled by an angry rejection of the existing social order as essentially unpleasurable, and by a projection of pleasure into a (mythical) ideal future. For that reason many feminist fantasies today are not pleasurable, but are linked with feelings of fury, frustration and pain. Political struggle is directed towards removing the distance between an ideal of the future and a given reality, but the harsh conditions in which this struggle must be waged inevitably create tensions in everyday life. Frustrations are always lurking but, from a political perspective, may not lead to giving up that ideal: the struggle must go on. A feeling of discomfort therefore always underlies, and is essential for, any political struggle for a better future, and for two reasons: because of the realization that that future does not yet exist, and because of the realization that a lot of energy has to be invested to bring that future closer.

But it is impossible to live solely with a feeling of discomfort. We cannot wait until the distant Utopia is finally achieved: here and now we must be able to enjoy life – if only to survive. In other words, any uneasiness with the present, with the social situation in which we now find ourselves, must be coupled with an (at least partial) positive acceptance and affirmation of the present. Life must be experienced as being worth the effort, not just because a prospect exists for a better future, but also because the present itself is a potential source of pleasure.

One dimension of life in which the distance between a (pleasurable) absent and an (unpleasurable) present can be eradicated is that of fantasy. Fantasies of the feminist Utopia, for example, can remove the feeling of unease by making the absent ideal present – in the imagination. Here it is not primarily a matter of the content of the fantasy, but mainly of the fact of fantasizing itself: producing and consuming fantasies allows for a play with reality, which can be felt as 'liberating' because it is fictional, not real. In the play of fantasy we can adopt positions and 'try out' those positions, without having to worry about their 'reality value'. In this sense then it is also little to the point to assume that imaginary identifications with the positions of 'cynical fatalism' (Sue Ellen) or 'false hope' (Pamela) would be politically bad because they would lead to pessimism and resignation in real social life. At the level of fantasy we can occupy these positions without having to experience their actual consequences. It may well be, then, that these identifications can be pleasurable, not because they imagine the Utopia to be present, but precisely because they create the possibility of being pessimistic, sentimental or despairing with impunity – feelings which we can scarcely allow ourselves in the battlefield of actual social, political and personal struggles, but which can offer a certain comfort if we are confronted by the contradictions we are living in. It is in this sense that we can interpret Terry Lovell's assertion that 'Soap opera may be [. . .] a context in which women can ambiguously express *both* goodhumoured acceptance of their oppression *and* recognition of that oppression, and some equally goodhumoured protest against it.'[4] But, we must add, this acceptance (just like protest) takes place within the world of fantasy, not outside it. It says nothing about the positions and standpoints that the same women occupy in 'real life'. After all, watching soap operas is never the only thing they do. In other activities, other positions will be (or have to be) assumed.

Fantasy is therefore a fictional area which is relatively cut off and independent. It does not function in place of, but beside, other dimensions of life (social practice, moral or political consciousness). It is a dimension of subjectivity which is a source of pleasure *because* it puts 'reality' in parentheses, because it constructs imaginary solutions for real contradictions which in their fictional simplicity and their simple fictionality step outside the tedious complexity of the existing social relations of dominance and subordination.

It seems therefore impossible to ascertain whether the pleasure of *Dallas* that is based on a recognition of and identification with the tragic structure of feeling is intrinsically progressive or conservative, and therefore politically good or bad – such a question would moreover contain an instrumentalist conception of pleasure, as though pleasure itself doesn't much matter – because that pleasure is first and foremost connected with the *fictional* nature of the positions and solutions which the tragic structure of feeling constructs, not with their ideological content. In terms of *content* the fantasy positions and solutions brought about by the tragic structure of feeling and the melodramatic imagination do seem indeed to incline to conservativism, and of course they can and must also be criticized for this – i.e. in so far as they are conservative representations. The politics of representation does matter. But the fact that we can identify with these positions and solutions when we watch *Dallas* or women's weepies and experience pleasure from them is a completely different issue: it need not imply that we are also bound to take up these positions and solutions in our relations to our loved ones and friends, our work, our political ideals, and so on.

Fiction and fantasy, then, function by making life in the present pleasurable, or at least livable, but this does not by any means exclude radical political activity or consciousness. It does not follow that feminists must not persevere in trying to produce new fantasies and fight for a place for them; at the level of cultural production the main issue of struggle is clear, as many feminist filmmakers, writers and artists have shown. It does, however, mean that, where cultural consumption is concerned, no fixed standard exists for gauging the 'progressiveness' of a fantasy. The personal may be political, but the personal and the political do not always go hand in hand.

NOTES

1. For an analysis of the narrative strategies of the popular romantic novel, see [T.] Modleski, *Loving with a Vengeance, Mass-Produced Fantasies for Women*, Shoe String Press, Hamden, 1982,/Methuen, London, 1984. [See Chapter 38 in this volume.]
2. M. Barrett, 'Feminism and the definition of cultural politics', in R. Brunt and C. Rowan (eds), *Feminism, Culture and Politics*, Lawrence and Wishart, London, 1982, p. 56.
3. Ibid., p. 57.
4. T. Lovell, 'Ideology and Coronation Street', in Dyer et al., *Coronation Street* [BFI, London, 1981,] p. 51.

Editor's Note

* Jane Feuer, 'Melodrama, Serial form and telivision today', *Screen*, vol. 25, no. 1, 1984, and Ellen Seiter, 'Eco's TV guide – the soaps', *Tabloid*, no. 5, winter 1982.

40

CROSSROADS: NOTES ON SOAP OPERA

Charlotte Brunsdon

Husband to wife weeping as she watches TV: 'For heaven's sake, Emily! It's only a commercial for acid indigestion.'

Joke on Bryant & May matchbox.

INTRODUCTION: A GENDERED AUDIENCE?

The audience for soap opera is usually assumed to be female.[1] In these notes I would like to examine this assumption, and the extent to which the notion of a gendered audience can be useful to us in the understanding of a British soap-opera, *Crossroads*.

Initially, I should like to make a distinction between the subject positions that a text constructs, and the social subject who may or may not take these positions up. We can usefully analyse the 'you' or 'yous' that the text as discourse constructs, but we cannot assume that any individual audience member will necessarily occupy these positions.[2] The relation of the audience to the text will not be determined solely by that text, but also by positionalities in relation to a whole range of other discourses – discourses of motherhood, romance and sexuality for example. Thus it may well be that visual pleasure in narrative cinema is dependent on identification with male characters in their gaze at female characters, but it does not necessarily follow that any individual audience member will unproblematically occupy this masculine position. Indeed, feminist film criticism usefully deconstructs the gendering of this 'you'. As J Winship has recently argued: 'A feminist politics of representation . . . has then to engage with the social reader, as well as the social text'.[3]

The interplay of social reader and social text can be considered by examining the extent to which a gendered audience is implied in programme publicity, scheduling and advertisements. The independent Broadcasting Authority, in its 1979 annual handbook, groups *Crossroads* with other Drama serials:

From Screen 22:4 (1981) pp. 32–7.

TV drama serials have for many years been an essential ingredient in the programme diet of a large and devoted audience. Established favourites such as *Coronation Street* and *Crossroads* continue to develop themes and situations which often deal with the everyday problems and difficulties to which many viewers can relate. Occasionally the more adventurous type of serial is produced.[4]

The feminity of the audience is specified, apart from the structuring dietary metaphor, in the opposition of 'devoted' and 'everyday' to 'adventurous'. There are a wide range of 'spin-off' materials associated with *Crossroads* – novels, special souvenir supplements, interview material, and a *Crossroads* Cookbook. I will take up the question of the incoherence of *Crossroads* narratives below.

In terms of scheduling, although *Crossroads* is broadcast at different times in different regions (stripped across four evenings a week),[5] it is always broadcast within the 5.15 pm – 7.30 pm slot. That is, with early evening, weekday transmission the programme is definitely not scheduled in the prime time in which it is expected to maximise on a male audience. If we accept Richard Paterson's argument that notions of the family and the domestic dominate the scheduling of British television programmes, then fathers are not expected to control television choice at this point. Paterson also suggests a relationship between scheduling and programme structure:

> Its narrative is constructed of multiple short segments, with continual repetition of narrative information, but no overall dramatic coherence in any episode. In part this structure reflects its place in the schedule: continual viewing has to be ensured even though meal times and other domestic interruptions might make it impossible to follow a coherent narrative.[6]

The broadcast slot of *Crossroads* is surrounded by magazine news programmes, panel games and other serials – all suitable for family, and interrupted, viewing. However, the advertising that frames, and erupts within, the programme is quite clearly addressed to a feminine consumer – beauty aids, breakfast cereals, instant 'man-appeal' meals and cleaning products: the viewer as sexual, as mother, as wife, as housewife, in contrast to the ads for lawn mowers, car gadgets, DIY equipment or large family purchases which dominate from 8.30 pm on. These 'extra textual' factors suggest that women are the target audience for *Crossroads*.

A DISCONTINUOUS TEXT

The ideological problematic of soap-opera – the frame or field in which meanings are made, in which significance is constructed narratively – is that of 'personal life'. More particularly, personal life in its everyday realisation through personal relationships. This can be understood to be constituted primarily through the representations of romances, families and attendant rituals – births, engagements, marriages, divorces and deaths. In marxist terms this is the sphere of the individual outside waged labour. In feminist terms, it is the sphere of women's 'intimate oppression'. Ideologically constructed as the feminine sphere, it is within this realm of the domestic, the personal, the private, that feminine competence is recognised. However, the action of soap-opera is not restricted to familial or quasi-familial institutions but, as it were, *colonises* the public masculine sphere, representing it from the point of view of the personal.

Thus in *Crossroads* we have a family run business, the Crossroads motel, with an attached garage. The motel is near a village, Kings Oak, which at various times has included a market-garden, a doctor's surgery, a post-office, an antique shop, and so on. Regular characters are members of one of three groups – the Crossroads family, the motel/garage workforce, or the village. The fictional community, clearly socially hierarchised through *mise-en-scène* and dialogue, is kept interacting through a series of interlocking economic relationships, but this business interaction is of diegetic importance only as the site of personal relationships. It is always emotionally significant personal interaction, often reported in dialogue, which is narratively foregrounded. This can be seen most clearly through the narrative construction of time and place.

There is no single linear time flow. The minimum three concurrent narratives proceed through a succession of short segments (rarely exceeding 2½ minutes). In contrast with classical narrative cinema,[7] the temporal relationship between segments is rarely encoded. Time in general moves forward, although there is repetition at the beginning of episodes. Relationships between segments can be read as in most cases sequential or simultaneous. One continuous scene can be broken into several segments – notoriously over commercial breaks and between episodes, but this is a standard intra-episodic suspense device. The lack of any overarching time scheme permits the rise and fall of different narrative threads. As each narrative has only its time of exposition, there is no loss of 'real' or referential time if a narrative lapses. Similarly, the very simplicity of the use of 'interruption' as the major form of narrative delay, extending dramatic action, also works against the construction of a coherent referential time. The different present tenses of the narrative co-exist, temporally unhierarchised.

Space in *Crossroads* is also organised in a way which is quite distinct from the conventions of classical narrative cinema, conventions which are carried over to some other forms of television drama. The shoestring budgets mean very restricted sets (all internal, usually no more than five in one episode) and few available camera positions.[8] Generally, sets have two distinct spaces arranged laterally to each other – that is, there are two distinct camera fields, and it is the articulation of these fields which constructs the space.[9] Some sets allow only one camera position. These camera set-ups are not variable, and camera movement is limited. Most scenes are shot in mid-shot or medium close up, opening with either a close-up or a longer shot. The narrative does not mobilise space within any particular set, not is there any attempt to make the different spaces of the different sets cohere. We are instead presented with a series of tableau-like views, more theatrical than cinematic. The sets thus function very literally as setting or background, seen always from the same points of view, as familiar as the room in which the viewer has the television.

I am thus arguing that the diegetic world of *Crossroads* is temporally and spatially fragmented, and that this fragmentation, accompanied by repetitious spatial orientation, foregrounds that dialogue of emotional and moral dilemma which makes up the action. The coherence of the serial does not come from the subordination of space and time to linear narrativity, as it does in classical narrative cinema, but from the continuities of moral and ideological frameworks which inform the dialogue. It is these frameworks which are explored, rehearsed and made explicit for the viewer in the repeated mulling over of actions and possibilities. *Crossroads* is in the business not of creating narrative excitement, suspense, delay and resolution, but of constructing moral consensus about the conduct of personal life. There is an endless unsettling, discussion and resettling of acceptable modes of behaviour within the sphere of personal relationships.

There are two key elements in this. Firstly, structurally, the plurality of story lines, which allows the use of the narrative strategy of interruption, and secondly, diegetically, the plot importance accorded to forms of lying and deceit. Structurally, although the different physical spaces of narratives do not cohere, except in the meeting place of the motel lobby, the same set of events, or the same dilemma, will be discussed, by different characters in 'their own' environments. A range of different opinions and understandings of any one situation will thus be voiced. At the same time, the use of interruption, the consistent holding off of *dénouement* and knowledge, invites the viewer to engage in exactly the same type of speculation and judgment. The viewer can, as it were, practise possible outcomes – join in the debate about how a particular event is to be understood.

The use of deceit in the narrative works slightly differently. By deceit, I mean the development of a narrative line which the audience knows that one character is consciously lying or misleading other characters. Here, the viewer is in a position of privileged knowledge in relation to the protagonists, and can see clearly what and who is 'right'. The drama of morality is here produced by the tension between the fact that 'good' characters must continue to be trusting, to remain 'good', but that they will suffer unless they 'find out' about the true nature of another character, x.

In both cases, what is being set in play, or exercised, are repertoires of understandings and assumptions about personal and familial relationships, in which the notion of individual character is central. Thus although soap-opera narrative may seem to ask 'What will happen next?' as its dominant question, the terrain on which this question is posed is determined by a prior question – 'What kind of a person is this?'. And in the ineluctable posing of this question, of all characters, whatever their social position, soap-opera poses a potential moral equality of all individuals.

A GENDERED AUDIENCE – 2

Recently, Tania Modleski has argued for the textual inscription of a female (maternal) subject in American soap-opera. She has suggested that the multiple narrative structure of soap-opera demands multiple identification on the part of the viewer, and thus constitutes the viewer as a type of ideal mother 'a person who possesses greater wisdom than all her children, whose sympathy is large enough to encompass the claims of all her family . . . and who has no demands of her own'.[10] I will consider the related question of the type of cultural competence that *Crossroads* as soap-opera narrative(s) demands of its social reader.

Just as a Godard film requires the possession of certain forms of cultural capital on the part of its audience to 'make sense' – an extra-textual familiarity with certain artistic, linguistic, political and cinematic discourses – so too does *Crossroads*/soap-opera. The particular competences demanded by soap opera fall into three categories:

1   Generic knowledge – familiarity with the conventions of soap opera as a genre. For example, expecting discontinuous and cliff-hanging narrative structures.
2   Serial-specific knowledge – knowledge of past narratives and of characters (in particular, who belongs to who).
3   Cultural knowledge of the socially acceptable codes and conventions for the conduct of personal life.

I will only comment on the third category here. The argument is that the narrative strategies and concerns of *Crossroads* call on the traditionally feminine competencies associated with the responsibility for 'managing' the sphere of personal life. It is the culturally constructed skills of femininity – sensitivity, perception, intuition and the necessary privileging of the concerns of personal life – which are both called on and practised in the genre. The fact that these skills and competencies, this type of cultural capital, is ideologically constructed as natural, does not mean, as many feminists have shown, that they are the *natural* attributes of femininity. However, under present cultural and political arrangements, it is more likely that female viewers will possess this repertoire of both sexual and maternal femininities which is called on to fill out the range of narrative possibilities when, for example, the phone rings. That is, when Jill is talking to her mother about her marriage (17 January 1979), and the phone rings, the viewer needs to know not only that it is likely to be Stan (her nearly ex-husband) calling about custody of their daughter Sarah-Jane (serial-specific knowledge) and that we're unlikely to hear the content of the phone-call in that segment (generic knowledge) but also that the mother's 'right' to her children is no longer automatically assumed. These knowledges only have narrative resonance in relation in discourses of maternal femininity which are elaborated elsewhere, already in circulation and brought to the programme by the viewer. In the enigma that is then posed – will Jill or Stan get Sarah-Jane? – questions are also raised about who, generally and particularly should get custody. The question of what should happen is rarely posed 'openly' – in this instance it was quite clear that 'right' lay with Jill. But it is precisely the terms of the question, the way in which it relates to other already circulating discourses, if you like, the degree of its closure, which form the site of the construction of moral consensus, a construction which 'demands', seeks to implicate, a skilled viewer.

I am thus arguing that *Crossroads* textually implies a feminine viewer to the extent that its textual discontinuities require a viewer competent within the ideological and moral frameworks, the rules, of romance, marriage and family life to make sense of it.

Against critics who complain of the redundancy of soap-opera, I would suggest that the radical discontinuities of the text require extensive, albeit interrupted, engagement on the part of the audience, before it becomes pleasurable. This is not to designate *Crossroads* 'progressive' but to suggest that the skills and discourses mobilised by its despised popularity have partly been overlooked because of their legitimation as natural (feminine).

NOTES

1. For example, early research on American radio soaps, either assumes a female audience, or only investigates one. (See H Herzog. 'On Borrowed Experience' in *Studies in the Philosophy of Social Science*, vol. 9 no. 65. 1941: Rudolph Arnheim. 'The world of the Daytime Serial' in *Radio Research* nos. 42–43. Lazarsfeld and Stanton (eds). New York 1944: H Kauffman, 'The Appeal of Specific Daytime Serials' *Radio Research*, op. cit.) It is of course precisely the perceived 'feminine' appeal of the genre which has fuelled recent feminist interest (see for instance, Richard Dyer et al. *Coronation Street*. BFI Television Monograph no. 13 London 1981, and Tania Modleski. 'The Search for Tomorrow in Today's Soap Operas', *Film Quarterly* vol. 33 no. 1, 1979).

2. See, for instance, Steve Neale. 'Propaganda', *Screen* vol. 18 no. 3 1977, Paul Willemen 'Notes on subjectivity', *Screen* vol. 19 no. 1 1978, and David Morley. The *'Nationwide'* Audience, BFI, London 1980.

3. J Winship. 'Handling Sex' *Media Culture and Society*, vol. 3 no. 1 1981.

4. *Television and Radio 1979*, Independent Broadcasting Authority, London 1979.

5. These notes are based on 1978 research when *Crossroads* was still four evenings per week, as opposed to the three at present.

6. Richard Paterson, 'Planning the Family: The Art of the Schedule', *Screen Education* no. 35. Summer 1980.

7. I recognise that 'classical narrative cinema' is not monolithic. David Bordwell and Kristin Thompson in *Film Art*, New York, 1979, give an account of the conventions of the narrative fiction film in the west.

8. Production constraints of *Crossroads* are discussed by Geoff Brown, 'I'm Worried about Chalet Nine', *Time Out* 24–30 November 1978, and R Miles 'Everyday Stories, Everyday Folk' MA Dissertation, University of Leicester, 1980.

9. I am indebted to Andy Lowe ('Narrative Spaces and Closure' Unpublished paper, Media Group, Centre for Contemporary Cultural Studies, Birmingham 1977) who originally discussed *Crossroads* in these terms.

10. Tania Modleski, op. cit. [See Chapter 38 of this volume.]

41

EVERYTHING STOPS FOR *CROSSROADS*: WATCHING WITH THE AUDIENCE

Dorothy Hobson

[...]

This chapter is about the viewers who watch Crossroads. It is written from different sources but it is all based on talking to people about the programme, and watching the programme with viewers. The data comes from interviews and observations which I made while watching episodes, and long unstructured conversations which we had after the programmes had finished. It is important to stress that the interviews were unstructured because I wanted the viewers to determine what was interesting or what they noticed, or liked, or disliked about the programme and specifically about the episodes which we had watched. I hoped that they would indicate the reasons for the popularity of the programme and also areas where they may have been critical. When a programme has fifteen million viewers it is, of course, not possible to speak to more than a minute percentage of those viewers. Different people watch television programmes for different reasons, and make different 'readings' of those programmes, and much of what they say is determined by preconceived ideas and opinions which they bring to a programme. The message is not solely in the 'text' but can be changed or 'worked on' by the audience as they make their own interpretation of a programme.

[...]

I began the project with the idea of linking the understanding of the production process of specific episodes or programmes with the audience reception and understanding of those same episodes or programmes. Although I have gone out to watch specific episodes and to talk about those episodes, the viewers have quickly moved the conversation to the programme in general and talked about other episodes through the medium of the storylines. This has not only been the case when I have watched Crossroads but also whenever I have watched other fictional programmes, whether they are drama series or situation comedies. I always began asking about the programme which we had just watched but quite quickly the women and their families

From D. Hobson, Crossroads: *The Drama of a Soap Opera* (London: Methuen, 1982) pp. 105–7 and 124–36.

began talking about the characters by name, and moved the conversations to the areas which most interested them.

The usual criticism which is made of any research which involves the intrusion into the privacy of a natural situation is that the presence of the researcher changes the situation. This is of course perfectly correct and the researcher, far from being neutral in the research situation, does affect that situation. In fact, the interaction between the interviewer and interviewee is an integral part of the research. However, since many of the viewers talked about programmes which they had seen when I was not there, nor did they know that months or years ahead they would be talking about them, it can be said that the effect which those programmes had had upon their audience had not been affected by my presence. In fact, it became clear through the process of the study that the audience do not watch programmes as separate or individual items, nor even as types of programmes, but rather that they build up an understanding of themes over a much wider range of programmes and length of time of viewing.

[. . .]

The basis of soap opera is its characters and their continuing stories. When the viewers say, 'I want to see what happens next,' it is what happens to the characters that interests them. What happens next? How will she get out of this problem? Will she meet someone rich, handsome, sexy? Will her children be all right? Storylines in soap opera are not arbitrary, they are stories which deal with everyday life and its 'ups and downs', problems and pleasures; the inclusion of personal, moral and emotional matters is an integral part of the genre.

'What happened in Crossroads last night?' or more familiarly, 'What happened to Jill last night?' No one has to explain which Jill is being talked about because the shared knowledge of the characters which is held by the viewers becomes part of the cultural capital which they exchange in normal conversation. In short digression, I once sat on a train returning from London to Birmingham when British Rail were running their £1.00 tickets during the winter of 1980. Four pensioners sat at a table next to me, complete with their sandwiches and flasks of coffee, and they talked together about many topics of mutual interest. The conversation moved to exchanges about their respective children and grandchildren and names were mentioned. Suddenly, without comment one of the women said, 'What about Emily's trouble with Arthur, what do you think about it all?' (This is not remembered verbatim.) The conversation continued about the mess that Emily was in now that it had been found that he was already married, and how it had seemed too good to be true for her to have found someone like him. How would she be, and how would it all end? As swiftly as the topic had arisen, it switched back to talking about other topics. The uninitiated or 'culturally deprived' would be forgiven for not realizing that the troubles of poor Emily and the misery which Arthur had brought to her were not the problems of the children or relatives of two of the speakers. However, anyone who was aware of the current storyline of the soap opera Coronation Street would have known instantly that it was the fate of the fictional characters which were being discussed. Yet from the conversation it was obvious that the speakers were playing a game with the serial. They did not actually believe that the characters existed; they were simply sharing a fantastic interest in the characters outside the serial. How many of us can honestly admit not to having done that ourselves? How many were not saddened at the fate of 'the beautiful young Sebastian' as he visibly declined before our eyes in Brideshead Revisited during this winter? It is a false critical elitism to allow the 'belief' and enjoyment in a fictional character in one programme and deny others the right to that belief or enjoyment in another.

Similarly, the knowledge which television viewers have about events within the programmes is a form of cultural capital which excludes those who do not watch the programmes. It is actually fun to talk about the characters in a soap opera, and yet the game that viewers play with one another is interpreted as some form of psychological disorder, when for the most part they are well aware that the game is going on.

It would be wrong, however, to create the idea that fans of Crossroads are uncritical of the programme. In fact, the contrary is true, and the viewers possess a level of knowledge about the storylines, the sets and the characters which few professional critics would be able to match. Their postive commitment to the programme does mean that when they make critical remarks their comments are more likely to be of a constructive nature rather than the blanket dismissive mode of some criticism. Their criticism is usually accompanied by a suggestion for improvement and they are unlikely to make comments which would be damaging to the programme as a whole.

Since the storylines are what holds the audience to Crossroads, it is not surprising that this is the area where they have most criticism to offer. However, they do not criticize the stories *per se*, but treat them rather benevolently, waiting to see how they will develop. Generally it is not the theme of any story which annoys them or fails to hold their interest; in fact their willingness to accept a wide variety of storylines would appear to be a *carte blanche* for producers. It is, however, in the length of time which a story runs which they sometimes find rather boring.

[. . .]

The viewers' criticism was often accompanied by suggestions for improvements. These were sometimes at the level of more interesting storylines which could develop the characters whom the viewers liked but thought could be more interesting. The character of Kath Brownlow was one who was particularly mentioned. Viewers liked the actress and the character and women were not impressed by the way that she was treated by her husband,

DH   Which characters do you particularly like or dislike?

L   Well, I dislike Arthur Brownlow, I can't stand him.

DH   And why don't you like him?

L   Because if he was my husband I would have kicked him out years ago – but that is obviously the character, not him. And his wife gets on your nerves, but then again they ought to be able to do something with her part, I think, because she's either laying the table or unlaying it or they are eating. Every time you see their living-room you know there is something on the table. That gets on your nerves.

When I pressed them about how the part could be improved the woman and her husband had different suggestions,

P   Put more meat into it.

L   Yes, she seems sort of downtrodden.

P   Take a lover!

L   Get her husband to lay the table for a change. It's just the character. She's probably doing a very good acting job.

The suggestion from the man is of a jokey nature, but the woman has identified one of the significant characteristics of Kath, who is written as an example of the ordinary, respectable working-class/lower-middle-class woman. She appears downtrodden and accepts Arthur's chauvinism, but not without a certain amount of eyebrow raising at his behaviour. The character as portrayed by the actress is seen as 'realistic', but what the viewers are asking for are stronger storylines so that the character can develop. Other women who talked about Kath have suggested that although the characterization might have been realistic when Kath was at home and without financial independence, now that she has returned to work, part-time in the motel kitchen, she would have gained more confidence and would not take Arthur's attitude and behaviour so readily. These women were often speaking from their own experiences of returning to work and they wished that Kath at least would be allowed to do something to establish her own independence.

The constant referencing of the events within the programme with ideas of what would be likely to happen in their own experience is the overriding way in which the viewers interact with the stories. They also have a remarkable amount of knowledge of what has happened in the serial and make judgements about it, always based in 'real life'. Sometimes these are at a small or trivial level, at others they are much more complex judgements. One woman commented that it was about time that Kath Brownlow had a new three-piece suite because the one which she had was getting to look old, and she added the comment, 'She will be able to when she's having the digs money off Kevin.' This comment was made at a lighthearted level but it did indicate that the viewer was questioning the realism of the serial. She knew that a woman of Kath's class would not be content with the old three-piece suite which the production tolerated. It was a nice example of the realism in the woman's experience being in conflict with the reality of the budget which constrained the production from buying Kath a new suite.

The knowledge of the way women react to stress in their own lives coloured the reactions that the viewers had to storylines within the serial. Stories about Jill's problems and her ways of coping with them were very interesting to the viewers. But they were not totally sympathetic to her reactions to her problems:

> I thought it was quite nitty gritty when – I'm going back a bit though – when Jill had that baby by Hugh Mortimer's son. I can't remember who he is now but I thought that was very good.

Another woman had no such problems with her memory, and told me stories from the serial in great detail, combined with a sharp critical assessment of the actions in the story, which were firmly rooted in her own assessments of everyday life:

> I thought when Jill was going through this drunken phase, you know, not so long ago, after this other fella ditched her, I thought was pathetic actually. Because she's been through it all before. It's about time she . . . you know. It is, it's part of life. We could all turn to the bottle but you just don't, do you, in real life like, you know. Some do. I agree some do, and I suppose that this is what they are trying to get over, that some do turn to the bottle. But there again, from the type of family that she's supposed to belong to, you wouldn't imagine that she would.

The woman was certainly not tolerant towards Jill. The fact that the character had been through many problems in her life meant in the eyes of this woman that she should have learned to cope with them better, and her class position should have stopped her from taking such a course. Even though there were areas of Jill's life of which the woman had no direct experience, there were assumptions about behaviour which were based on ideas which were common to all women of all classes. 'We could all turn to the bottle, but you just don't, do you, in real life,' but then again, 'some do,' so the authenticity of the serial is confirmed. Again, it shows that the actual stories are not criticized; it is the way that the characters react in the stories which determine whether the viewers will accept the 'true to life' aspects of the programme.

The idea that viewers 'escape' into a programme like Crossroads is clearly invalid, or at least it is not escapism in the conventional sense of the word. Escapism suggests that someone is running away from their problems and seeking diversions, even if momentarily. There are, of course, programmes which do provide escapism for the audience, but soap operas are definitely not in this category. They are precisely a way of understanding and coping with problems which are recognized as 'shared' by other women, both in the programme and in 'real life'. Differences in class or material possessions seem to be transcended in the realization that there are problems in everyday life which are common to all women and their families.

> It brings in every aspect of life, the poorer part and the rest, like Coronation Street as well. It does involve people getting drunk, having babies without being married and all this, that and the other. It is an everyday programme, you get involved in it. I mean, they have brought mugging into it now, haven't they. I think it's because they bring everything into it that it is so good.

One way to understand the appeal of Crossroads for its viewers is through the solutions to the problems or resolutions in fictional terms. In a series like Crossroads the solutions to problems are not obviously progressive and never revolutionary. The resolution to a difficult problem is sometimes achieved by some magical solution disguised as 'natural causes', sometimes helped along by other characters in the serial, and it is rare for resolutions to move outside the consensus. Indeed, Jack Barton* stated quite definitely that it was not his aim to move outside the consensus in the treatment of his storylines. However, although not revolutionary, sometimes the solutions can allow the status quo to be shaken up a little and maybe moved on a fraction. In fact, in soap opera much of the dramatic tension is achieved through the dynamics of the changing relationships and situations of the characters. Although the solutions to problems may not be seen as progressive, it is often in the raising of those problems in fictional forms that is important. The problems of facing an unwanted pregnancy and how to deal with it as explored in the storyline with Alison [. . .] provided a clue to why the ending was unimportant compared with the issues raised within the context of the story. From the perspective of a radical analysis the fortuitous miscarriage may be seen as a 'cop out', but in dramatic terms, the character, because of her sheltered life and intensively religious upbringing, would have been unlikely to have agreed to an abortion. However, the understanding of the situation and the responses which the raising of the problems elicit from the audience made the fictional resolutions almost irrelevant. For audiences recognize the restrictions imposed on the programme by its time schedule, but appreciate that it is portraying issues which they see as part of everyday life, therefore they can fill in their own understanding of the unseen events in the programme.

[. . .]

Sometimes storylines are touchstones for experiences which the viewers have and which they see reflected in the serial. One such incident brought home to me the futility of trying to estimate which stories would appeal to which sections of the audience. Marjory, an elderly widow with whom I watched the programme, continually surprised me throughout my time with her. The episode which we watched contained the storyline of Glenda's supposed frigidity and inability to have sexual intercourse with Kevin after they had returned from honeymoon. The sexual aspects of the story were not made explicit in any way and it was at one level a story where I felt one section of the audience might want the programme to go into more detail, yet I would have expected, from the image of older viewers which is prevalent, that someone like

Marjory may not have liked this particular storyline. I was proved to be completely mistaken in my speculation and again the incident revealed the intricate workings of the audience with the themes presented in the series.

> DH What do you think about the way the programme sometimes brings in subjects that are a bit difficult, like this story with Glenda at the moment? What do you think when it brings those kind of stories in?
>
> M Oh well, that kind of thing, her married life is not satisfactory, is it! That's the answer to that. Well, I'm going to say something to you. I never thought mine was when I was young. So I can understand how she felt, and it's rather a worry to you. In other words, well of course in my day they were terribly innocent, weren't they. We didn't really know what was what and what wasn't. And I think we were all a bit frightened. Well I said tonight, you never felt you could really let yourself go, you were frightened of having a kid, and all that kind of thing. Well I can understand that, you see. Now *that* is a thing, when I'm listening to that, I think, 'I can remember I used to be a bit like that.' So that is what I mean to say, whatever they put in Crossroads, it's appertaining to something what could happen in life. It doesn't seem fiction to me.
>
> DH No, no, that's interesting, because you think if any age group were going to think 'why have they bothered to have that story in,' it would be somebody older, and yet you understood it.
>
> M It comes to my age group. We used to say we were frightened of our husbands putting their trousers on the bedrail. You know, we had no pill, we had nothing. I mean, I'm speaking perfectly open to you, we were terrified really, if the man got anything out of it it's right, but you were too frightened to let yourself go, and that's just it.

Clearly, if a programme like Crossroads can transcend age to such an extent and evoke in one viewer the memories of her own early married life fifty years previously, it is making connections with its viewers which begin to indicate the importance of the genre. Crossroads viewers contribute to their own understanding of the programme and make their own readings of what the production sets out to communicate. They work with the text and add their own experiences and opinions to the stories in the programme.

It seems that the myth of the passive viewer is about to be shattered. They do not sit there watching and taking it all in without any mental activity or creativity. It seems that they expect to contribute to the production which they are watching and bring their own knowledge to augment the text. Stories which seem almost too fantastic for an everyday serial are transformed through a sympathetic audience reading whereby they strip the storyline to the idea behind it and construct an understanding on the skeleton that is left.

Popular fiction *should* connect with life and reality, indeed it is meaningless if it does not achieve this end, for fiction has always grown from experiences in life. Crossroads connects with its viewers. To look at a programme like Crossroads and criticize it on the basis of conventional literary/media analysis is obstinately to refuse to understand the relationship which it has with its audience. A television programme is a three part development – the production process, the programme, and the understanding of that programme by the audience or consumer – and it is false and elitist criticism to ignore what any member of the audience thinks or feels about a programme. Crossroads is a form of popular art and far from writing it off as rubbish we should be looking at what its popularity tells us about all programmes and indeed all forms of popular art. To try to say what Crossroads means to its audience is impossible for there is no single Crossroads, there are as many different Crossroads as there are viewers. Tonight twelve million, tomorrow thirteen million; with thirteen million possible understandings of the programme. Lew Grade is reported as saying, 'I don't make programmes for critics – I make programmes for the viewers.' His sentiments should be taken further, for in fact the viewers are the critics. Or at least, the only ones who should count.

Editors' Note
* Jack Burton, producer of *Crossroads* during the period of Dorothy Hobson's research.

FURTHER READING

Allen, R. C., *Speaking of Soap Operas* (Chapel Hill: University of North Carolina Press, 1985).

Ang, I., *Watching* Dallas: *Soap Opera and the Melodramatic Imagination* (London: Methuen, 1985).

Ang, I., 'Melodramatic Identifications: Television Fiction and Women's Fantasy', in Brown, M. E. (ed.), *Television and Women's Culture* (London: Sage, 1990).

Arnheim, R., 'The World of the Daytime Serial', in Lazarsfeld, F. and Stanton, F. (eds), *Radio Research 1942–3* (New York: Duell, Sloan & Pearce, 1944).

Brown, M. E., 'The Politics of Soaps: Pleasure and Feminine Empowerment', *The Australian Journal of Cultural Studies* 4:2 (1986) pp. 1–25.

Brown, M. E. (ed.), *Television and Women's Culture* (London: Sage, 1990).

Brown, M. E., 'Motley Moments: Soap Operas, Carnival, Gossip and the Power of Utterance', in Brown, M. E. (ed.), *Television and Women's Culture* (London: Sage, 1990).

Brunsdon, C., 'Writing about Soap Opera', in Masterman, L. (ed.), *Television Mythologies* (London: Comedia, 1984).

Brunsdon, C., 'Feminism and Soap Opera', in Davies, K., Dickey, J. and Stratford, T. (eds), *Out of Focus: Writings on Women and the Media* (London: Women's Press, 1987).

Brunsdon, C., 'Identity in Feminist Television Criticism', *Media, Culture and Society* 15:2 (1993) pp. 309–26.

Buckingham, D., *Public Secrets:* EastEnders *and its Audience* (London: BFI, 1987).

Buckman, P., *All for Love: A Study in Soap Opera* (London: Secker & Warburg, 1984).

Cantor, M. and Pingree, S., *The Soap Opera* (London: Sage, 1983).

Dyer, R., Geraghty, C., Jordan, M., Lovell, T., Paterson, R. and Stewart, J., *Coronation Street*, BFI TV Monograph, no. 13 (London: BFI, 1981).

Feuer, J., 'Melodrama, Serial Form and Television Today', *Screen* 25:1 (1984) pp. 4–16.

Feuer, J., 'Narrative Form in American Network Television', in MacCabe, C. (ed.), *High Theory: Low Culture* (Manchester: Manchester University Press, 1986).

Finch, M., 'Sex and Address in *Dynasty*', *Screen* 27:6 (1986) pp. 24–42.

Fiske, J., *Television Culture* (London: Methuen, 1987).

Geraghty, C., *Women and Soap Opera: A Study of Prime Time Soaps* (Cambridge: Polity, 1991).

Glaessner, V., 'Gendered Fictions', in Goodwin, A. and Whannel, G. (eds), *Understanding Television* (London: Routledge, 1990).

Herzog, H., 'On Borrowed Experience: An Analysis of Listening to Daytime Sketches', *Studies in Philosophy and Social Science* 9:1 (1941) pp. 65–95.

Herzog, H., 'What do we Really Know about Daytime Serial Listeners?', in Lazarsfeld, P. and Stanton, F. M. (eds), *Radio Research: 1942–1943* (New York: Duell, Sloan & Pearce, 1944). pp. 3–33.

Hobson, D., Crossroads: *The Drama of a Soap Opera* (London: Methuen, 1982).

Hobson, D., 'Soap Operas at Work', in Seiter, E., Borchers, H., Kreutzner, G. and Warth, E.-M. (eds), *Remote Control: Television Audiences and Cultural Power* (London: Routledge, 1989).

Katz, E. and Liebes, T., 'Mutual Aid in the Decoding of *Dallas*: Preliminary Notes from a Cross-Cultural Study', in Drummond, P. and Paterson, R. (eds), *Television in Transition* (London: BFI, 1986).

Kuhn, A., 'Women's Genres', *Screen* 25:1 (1984) pp. 18–28.

Press, A., 'Class, Gender and the Female Viewer: Women's Responses to *Dynasty*', in Brown, M. E. (ed.), *Television and Women's Culture* (London: Sage, 1990).

Seiter, E., Kreutzner, G., Warth, E.-M. and Borchers, H., ' "Don't Treat Us like We're so Stupid and Naive". Towards an Ethnography of Soap Opera Viewers', in Seiter, E., Borchers, H., Kreutzner, G. and Warth, E.-M. (eds), *Remote Control: Television Audiences and Cultural Power* (London: Routledge, 1989).

News

News

News, according to Denis McQuail, is 'the core activity according to which a large part of the journalistic (and thus media) profession defines itself'.[1] Its claims to objectivity, neutrality and balance, reinforced in Britain by the formal demands of a public service broadcasting structure, provide the basis of the media's claims to the status of a 'fourth estate' (see Chapter 10), independent of the workings of political or government agencies. As provider of independent information in and about the public sphere, its effective operation acts as guarantor both of the social responsibility of the mass media and of the healthy workings of a democratic society.

At the same time, however, news is also a media commodity. As a television genre, it exhibits all those features (segmentation, the open-ended series format, repetition, a sense of 'nowness') which John Ellis sees as characterising television as a medium (see Chapter 17), and in this respect can be seen to have more in common with soap opera than the account above might suggest. As Ellis concludes, 'After all, the first true use of the open-ended series format would seem to be the news bulletin, endlessly updating events and never synthesising them.'[2]

The news we get is inevitably, then, the product of institutional pressures and structures, of processes of both selection and construction. Its study focuses attention on issues of power, both in the relationship between media institutions and the state and in the internal workings of media institutions themselves, but it also raises issues about the gendered nature of definitions of the public sphere and about the range of audience readings generated by such an apparently neutral form. News is, in John Fiske's words, 'one of the most complex and widely studied' media forms.[3] It is also one of the most difficult to define. As discourse, its relation to the real is not as straightforward as claims to objectivity or neutrality might suggest, and the complex nature of its relationship to social and ideological power structures forms one of the major themes in the chapters which follow.

Chapter 42 comprises two extracts from Peter Golding and Philip Elliott's 1979 study (*Making the News*) of the operations of news organisations in three different countries. The first extract comes from their discussion of news values. Following Galtung and Ruge,[4] they define news values as 'qualities of events or of their journalistic construction, whose relative absence or presence recommends them for inclusion in the news product. The more of such qualities a story exhibits, the greater its chances of inclusion.' News values, however, do not act, as media institutions might claim, as prior guarantors of journalistic objectivity and impartiality. Rather, they are 'as much the resultant explanation or justification of necessary procedures as their source'. Working rules, they are organisational responses to 'the two immediate determinants of news making, perceptions of the audience and the availability of material'. The second extract discusses the consequences of these processes. News, argue Golding and Elliott, is ideology: the 'integrated picture of reality' which it provides is a picture which legitimates the interests of the powerful in society. It does this by omitting two key elements in the world it portrays. The first is social process: news renders invisible the processes of change, presenting the world as a succession of single events. The second 'absent dimension' is social power: news offers us politics in the form of the rituals of political office and omits consideration of economic power altogether. The result is a picture of a world which appears both unchanging and unchangeable.

Philip Schlesinger's study of the production processes of BBC television and radio news (Chapter 43) provides a more detailed picture of the routine practices referred to by Golding and Elliott. Arguing that the requirements of a daily news cycle mean that most news is prepared in advance, Schlesinger describes the 'newsday' structure and organisation. Far from being spontaneous or unanticipated, news is meticulously planned and structured. Inevitably, then, it is 'constructed within a framework of firm expectations' and guidelines which leave little scope for the operation of investigative journalism. The events which comprise news may be 'disorderly', but the picture of them which is produced fits a predetermined order.

Chapter 44, an extract from *Policing the crisis* (Hall et al. 1978), represents a powerful application of Gramsci's theory of hegemony to the processes of news production which have been outlined in the previous two chapters. This theorising of the '*ideological role*' of the news media argues, first, that the process of ordering 'disorderly' events – described by Schlesinger – is a process of assigning *meaning*, which operates by placing those events within 'maps of meaning' into which our social world is *already* organised and which it is assumed we all share. Thus news not only defines for us '*what* significant events are taking place' but also positions these events – events which by their definition as news are disruptive or problematic – within an interpretive framework which both '*assumes and helps to construct society as a consensus*'. Further, Hall et al. argue that the 'working rules' which ensure 'impartiality', 'balance' and 'objectivity' in news themselves operate in the interests of the powerful in society. The requirement to rely on 'accredited' sources for interpretations of events means a 'systematically structured *over-accessing* to the media' by the powerful, who then become the 'primary definers' of events. 'Oppositional' voices are usually confined to the accredited representatives of official opposition parties. The definitions of the powerful thus become the accepted definitions of social reality and consent to the existing social order is secured.

The work of the Glasgow University Media Group constitutes the most sustained analysis of television news content to have come out of British media studies. Chapter 45 is an extract from their fourth book, *War and Peace News* (1985), an analysis of television news coverage of the Falklands conflict and defence and disarmament issues. This study, like the group's other books, combines detailed quantitative analysis with an attempt to 'unpack' the cultural meaning of the news stories covered. Like their other books, too, it constitutes an attack on the claims of television news to present a balanced and impartial view of events. The book's Introduction outlines the group's method:

> Firstly, the identification of explanatory themes: these are the range of explanations which exist on a specific issue . . . The second dimension is a quantitative assessment of the appearance of each explanation. Finally we look at how each theme is developed in specific contexts such as in headlines or in news interviews.[5]

The extract included here analyses the construction of the image of 'the nation at war' during the Falklands conflict, through the coverage of 'Task Force families' at home. In contrast to the range of views found elsewhere, television news presented these families only as supporters of the campaign. As the war went on, interviews with the bereaved were banned entirely, effectively denying these relatives a voice. The second part of the extract examines the assumptions about 'a woman's role' revealed by the coverage. Women appear in the news as 'wives, mothers and fiancées', passive background figures, rarely speaking, who represent 'family life' or ' "sexual interest", marginal to the real business of the news'.

It is this last issue which is taken up in Patricia Holland's When a Woman Reads the News' (Chapter 46). Holland begins by noting women's marginality not only within the news itself but also within critical studies like some of those above. It is a marginalisation which would seem, however, to have been challenged in recent years. Today, nearly half of television's news readers are women; it is the meaning of this change which Holland's chapter addresses. Drawing on feminist film theory, she points to the quality of 'to-be-looked-at-ness' which has characterised women's screen images.[6] 'The authoritative address which issues from the head and shoulders image of the male newsreader, she argues, fits less easily with his female counterpart. It is women's *bodies* we are used to seeing; women's *speech* is usually 'downgraded as mere gossip or babble'. But the female newsreader in fact serves a number of quite specific purposes, none of which is to speak for women. Women are still excluded as actors from the content and reporting of news. Instead, they act as narrators, speaking a discourse which originates elsewhere, but acting as visible symbols of reassurance for their audience and a point of identification for the women in it, who would otherwise recognise their exclusion from this public discourse. Their presence is, then, a hegemonic device, a response to the challenge from groups who claimed that the news did not speak for them. In an application of Hall *et al.*'s model above – which reveals the gender blindness of the original – Holland concludes that the appearance of women newsreaders demonstrates 'the infinite flexibility of effortless power', which invites women to speak with the voice of an authority which simultaneously excludes them.

The final chapter in this section (Chapter 47) comes from one of the few qualitative empirical studies of audience responses to television news.[7] This study, by Greg Philo of the Glasgow University Media Group, reflects the recent move of the group into audience research, in order to 'examine how the structuring of news messages relate[s] to processes of understanding and belief within television audiences'.[8] In order to do this, the group devised a method which involved asking audience groups to write their own news programmes. Philo's research, published in *Seeing and Believing*, studied the responses of 169 people to the miners' strike of 1984–5. Groups of three to four people were given a set of photographs taken from television news programmes and asked to write their own 'news reports', which were then compared with actual news bulletins. Even one year after the strike had ended, which is when the exercise was carried out, there were 'extraordinary similarities'. Groups reproduced not only the general tone of bulletins but also actual phrases which had been used in the bulletins. Each group member was then asked a series of questions on issues such as picketing and violence in the strike. The extract included here discusses the sample groups' responses to these questions. Philo concludes that whether audiences accept television's account of events depends on 'what beliefs, experience, and information they bring to what they are shown'. Where people had personal experience of the events or access to other sources of information, they were able to negotiate or even reject television's account. However, even here 'the influence of media and especially television was central, since it established so firmly the issues which came to be associated with the strike'. The emphasis on picketing violence, for example, which was reproduced in both the constructed 'news reports' and people's memories of the strike, proved very damaging to the miners' cause. Even those whose direct experience of the strike contradicted television's account found it difficult to assert alternative meanings in the face of 'the dominant flow of images from the media'.

NOTES

1. D. McQuail, *Mass Communication Theory*, 2nd ed (London: Sage, 1987) p. 203.
2. See Chap. 17 of this volume.
3. Fiske, *Television Culture* (London: Methuen, 1987), p. 281.
4. See Johan Galtung and Mari Ruge, 'The Structure of Foreign News', *Journal of International Peace Research* I (1965) pp. 64–90, extract reprinted as 'Structuring and Selecting News', in S. Cohen and J. Young (eds), *The Manufacture of News* (London: Constable, 1973).
5. *War and Peace News* (Milton Keynes: Open University Press, 1985) pp. – x-xi.
6. See Laura Mulvey, 'Visual Pleasure and Narrative Cinema', *Screen* 16:3 (1975) pp. 6–18.
7. For another example, see Justin Lewis, *The Ideological Octopus* (London: Routledge, 1991).
8. G. Philo, 'Getting the Message: Audience Research in the Glasgow University Media Group', in J. Eldridge (ed.), *Getting the Message: News, Truth and Power* (London: Routledge, 1993) p. 254.

42

NEWS VALUES AND NEWS PRODUCTION

Peter Golding and Philip Elliott

Discussions of news values usually suggest they are surrounded by a mystique, an impenetrable cloud of verbal imprecision and conceptual obscurity. Many academic reports concentrate on this nebulous aspect of news values and imbue them with far greater importance and allure than they merit. We have stressed that news production is rarely the active application of decisions of rejection or promotion to highly varied and extensive material. On the contrary, it is for the most part the passive exercise of routine and highly regulated procedures in the task of selecting from already limited supplies of information. News values exist and are, of course, significant. But they are as much the resultant explanation or justification of necessary procedures as their source.

News values are used in two ways. They are criteria of selection from material available to the newsroom of those items worthy of inclusion in the final product. Second, they are guidelines for the presentation of items, suggesting what to emphasise, what to omit, and where to give priority in the preparation of the items for presentation to the audience. News values are thus working rules, comprising a corpus of occupational lore which implicitly and often expressly explains and guides newsroom practice. It is not as true as often suggested that they are beyond the ken of the newsman, himself unable and unwilling to articulate them. Indeed, they pepper the daily exchanges between journalists in collaborative production procedures. Far more they are terse shorthand references to shared understandings about the nature and purpose of news which can be used to ease the rapid and difficult manufacture of bulletins and news programmes. News values are qualities of events or of their journalistic construction, whose relative absence or presence recommends them for inclusion in the news product. The more of such qualities a story exhibits, the greater its chances of inclusion. Alternatively, the more different news values a story contains, the greater its chances of inclusion (see Galtung and Ruge, 1965). News values derive from unstated or implicit assumptions or judgements about three things:

From P. Golding and P. Elliott, *Making the News* (London: Longman, 1979) pp. 114–23.

1. The audience. Is this important to the audience or will it hold their attention? Is it of known interest, will it be understood, enjoyed, registered, perceived as relevant?
2. Accessibility – in two senses, prominence and ease of capture. Prominence: to what extent is the event known to the news organisation, how obvious is it, has it made itself apparent. Ease of capture: how available to journalists is the event, is it physically accessible, manageable technically, in a form amenable to journalism, is it ready-prepared for easy coverage, will it require great resources to obtain?
3. Fit. Is the item consonant with the pragmatics of production routines, is it commensurate with technical and organisational possibilities, is it homologous with the exigencies and constraints in programme making and the limitations of the medium? Does it make sense in terms of what is already known about the subject?

In other words, news values themselves derive from the two immediate determinants of news making, perceptions of the audience and the availability of material. Historically news values come to imbue the necessities of journalism with the lustre of good practice. They represent a classic case of making a virtue of necessity. This particularly applies to the broader values we have subsumed under the title of the occupational ideology – impartiality, objectivity, accuracy and so on. [. . .] News values are attached to the practice of the job, they are story values. Some of the more important are as follows. The first four derive from considerations of the audience, the remainder from a mixture of the three factors described above.

DRAMA

News stories are, as the term suggests, stories as well as news. Good ones exhibit a narrative structure akin to the root elements in human drama. To recall Reuven Frank, former President of NBC news in America, 'joy, sorrow, shock, fear, these are the stuff of news'. The good news story tells its tale with a beginning, a middle and an end, in that order.

[. . .]

Dramatic structure is often achieved by the presentation of conflict, most commonly by the matching of opposed viewpoints drawn from spokesmen of 'both sides of the question'. The audience is here felt to be served by being given the full picture as well as an interesting confrontation (cf. Epstein, 1973, pp. 168–9). [. . .]

VISUAL ATTRACTIVENESS

Television is a visual medium and the special power of television news is its ability to exploit this advantage. Television journalists are not obsessed by notions of 'good television' or 'good film'. They can't be, given the limited number of stories for which film is available. But the temptation to screen visually arresting material and to reject stories unadorned with good film is ever present and sometimes irresistible. In turn judgements about newsworthiness will be shaped by aesthetic judgements about film. A former editor-in-chief of the British Independent Television News has written that 'the key to putting more hard news on to the air effectively lies, I am sure, in putting more pictures and less talk into news programmes'. [. . .]

Just as audiences often justify their trust in the veracity of television news by reference to its use of film: 'you can actually see it happening', so newsmen refer to this quality in their favourite stories. 'Another good one was a building disaster. Three people died when it collapsed. We were the first station there and you could actually see people being rescued on camera.' (Head of News, WNBC)

A story may be included simply because film is available or because of the dramatic qualities of the film. A story narrated several days previously will be resurrected as film arrives simply to show the film. Film can also provide concrete evidence of the global surveillance of electronic journalism by demonstrating visually the journalist's presence at an event.

ENTERTAINMENT

News programmes seek, and usually find, large audiences. To do so they must take account of entertainment values in the literal sense of providing captivating, humorous, titillating, amusing or generally diverting material. The 'human interest' story was invented for just this purpose. Broadcast news is generally sober and serious, taking its social responsibility and constitutional position as demanding less frivolity than might be licensed in the popular press. Helen Hughes, who over 30 years ago wrote a book on the human interest story, considered that human interest was a dimension added to other types of story. ' . . . the news signalises [sic] a deviation from the expected, the normal and the traditional, which, when told with human interest is made human and comprehensible' (Hughes, 1942; see also Hughes, 1940). Although she was writing of the press this is especially true of broadcast news. The whimsical or bizarre events that are the currency of human interest stories, or the celebrities, children and animals that are their stars, are frequently too frivolous for broadcast news. But the human interest angle is an important way of making events palatable or comprehensible to audiences of broadcast news.

For some broadcast journalists there is a tension between the desire to ensure audience attentiveness and interest by following entertainment values, and a concern to maintain standards of seriousness and the plain honest narration of facts; between information and entertainment. This debate was alive in most newsrooms and linked back to arguments about how 'hard' or 'soft' news should be. It stems again from the dilemma of the journalist as producer of a marketable commodity, whose presentation and dressing up for the audience may cut across some of the professional ideals of the journalist *qua* journalist. The solution is normally the co-option of one ideal by the other, in the argument that to inform an audience you must first have its attention, and that there's no point preparing serious, well-intentioned, high-minded journalism if the audience registers its boredom by switching off. Thus entertainment is high on the list of news values both as an end in itself and as a means to other journalistic ideals.

IMPORTANCE

The most frequently cited reason for including a particular item in news bulletins is its importance. This is usually taken to mean that the reported event has considerable significance for large numbers of people in the audience. Most often importance is cited to explain the inclusion of items which might be omitted on the criteria of other audience-based news values. That is, items which may be boring, repetitive or non-visual must still be included despite audience disinterest. The item refers to something the audience needs to know. This news value is rooted in theories of the social role of journalism as tribune of the people. In broadcasting it has the further support that state-authorised corporations are expected to behave responsibly, informatively and educatively. Importance is often applied to political and foreign news. Both are assumed to be of greater interest to journalists than to their audience. Both are included however because of their unquestioned importance.

[. . .]

SIZE

The bigger the story the greater the likelihood of its inclusion, and the greater the prominence with which it will be presented. This simple rule of course begs the question of just how events are measured and which dimensions are relevant. The most common considerations are the numbers or type of people involved, or the scale of the event as an instance of a type. Thus the more people involved in a disaster or the presence of 'big names' at a formal occasion, enhance the initial visibility of such events and hence their consequent news value. Size as a news value normally qualifies other news values. That is, subsequent to the selection of events in the world as news, the criterion of size is applied to decide which are the most important news events. Less commonly events not normally registered as news become eligible by the sheer scale on which they occur.

PROXIMITY

Like size, the criterion of proximity derives partly from considerations of the audience, partly from problems of accessibility. Proximity has two senses, cultural and geographical. Stories are culturally proximate if they refer to events within the normal experience of journalists and their audience. They are the kinds of events which require a wide range of common language and shared cultural assumptions. For this reason they are normally, but not necessarily, domestic stories. Thus in Ireland the importance of the Church in secular life provides a background for stories on church or religion in other countries which might be ignored in more secularised nations. Cultural proximity can be applied to stories by, for example, putting foreign news into a domestic context to explain its importance or significance.

Geographical proximity refers to the simple rules of thumb that suggest the primacy of domestic news and the allocation of news from the rest of the world according to their nearness to the audience (see Schlesinger, 1978, p. 117). Here geography is distorted by the mechanics of news collection. As we have seen, the distribution of news gatherers is far from random, and in journalistic terms Lagos is far closer to London than to, say, Accra. Nonetheless the criterion is applied, and several Nigerian sub-editors adopted a three-tier news geography: Nigeria, Africa, the world. In the other countries, too, there was a sense of concentric spheres of influence. This design was of course totally disrupted by the availability of material. The geographical criterion thus moderates to two rules. Either, the further away an event the bigger it has to be, or, nearby events take precedence over similar events at a distance.

BREVITY

A story which is closely packed with facts and little padding is preferred to loose 'soft' news. Partly this relates to the journalistic role of informing rather than explaining, partly to concerns for what are seen as audience requirements and limitations. Audiences want just the facts and nothing but the facts. Since they also require comprehensiveness clearly no single item can be allowed to drag on too long. [. . .] News bulletins are normally between 15 and 30 minutes, and contain less than a couple of dozen items. Limiting news stories to their apparently more obvious elements is essential if there is to be room for even a minimal selection of the day's events. This limit seems to emphasise the necessary objectivity of broadcast news while in fact merely disguising the vast edifice of assumptions and cultural packaging which allow such brief items to make sense at all.

NEGATIVITY

Bad news is good news. As is often observed there is little mileage in reporting the safe arrival of aircraft, the continued health of a film star, or the smooth untroubled negotiations of a wage settlement. News is about disruptions in the normal current of events. In the literal sense it is not concerned with the uneventful. The concentration on negative events, that is events perceived or presented as damaging to social institutions, is not the result of a mischievous obsession with misery or discontent among journalists, but the outcome of the history of their occupation. News began as a service to groups directly concerned for the uninterrupted flow of commercial life. Interruptions included loss of merchandise at sea, financial upheavals in mercantile centres or, of course, war. These events remain paradigm instances of bad news, and as a result of news per se.

It is for this reason that news is described as a social surveillance, registering threats to the normal fabric of society and explaining their significance. The news value of negativity is therefore an important contributor to the social values in news, defining by default both the status quo and the sources and nature of threats to it. [. . .] It is worth noting that negativity is not a universal primary news value. What western journalists often see as the tediousness and irrelevance of broadcast news in eastern Europe has much to do with the conventions in many of these countries of presenting positive news (industrial production achievements, the award of honours, etc.) while excluding accidents, violence, crime and other negative categories prominent in news elsewhere (Varis, 1974; Lansipuro, 1975).

Some categories of negative news are disliked in broadcasting for their lack of other values. Crime was deliberately under-reported [. . .] in deference to the view that its presentation was pandering to the sensational news values more appropriate to the popular press. [. . .] Many broadcast journalists regretted this tendency to play down crime, and it was more often an executive than a 'shopfloor' view. Many journalists also subscribed to the view that showing too much violence was irresponsible. However, this view was frequently swamped by the power of news values such as drama and visual attractiveness. Again this is defined by reference to the audience. The point is made by Brucker (1973, p. 175):

> It is, of course, a basic principle of journalism that the bigger, the more off-beat, or the more bloody the spectacle, the greater the news value. This is not because newspapermen are more ghoulish or less sensitive to the finer things of life than their fellow men. It merely reflects the ineluctable fact that readers will flock to a story that has shock value but ignore one that is routine.

Or, as a journalist once pointed out, given a choice of two calamities news editors choose both, in the belief that the audience will be held by the dramatic power of tragic narrative.

RECENCY

The next three news values are derived more from production requirements than the perceived demands of the audience. Recency, the requirement that news be up to date and refer to events as close to transmission time as possible, derives from two factors. First, traditional journalistic competition puts a premium on the supply of 'earliest intelligencies' ahead of rivals. At its most successful this aim produces the 'scoop', an exclusive capture of a news event ahead of all competition. Second, the periodicity of news production itself sets the frame within which events in the world will be perceived. Thus daily production sets a daily frame, and news events must have occurred in the twenty-four hours between bulletins to merit inclusion. Although this is often impossible, especially for newsrooms dependent on air-freighted news film, the dictum that 'it's news when the audience first sees it' was only offered rather sheepishly, in the certain knowledge that it was an unhappy transgression of a root news value. The main point, however, is that processes which do not fit this daily cycle do not register as news by producing news events. Since daily reports are required the necessity of filling a daily quota becomes a laudable goal, and recency emerges as a journalistic virtue. Speed in collection and processing becomes paramount and is often cited as the particular merit of individual journalists or newsrooms. Conversely it is one of the main complaints against non-journalist broadcasters that they do not understand the need for speed and that technical and other facilities are inadequate for journalistic demands. The favourite accolade for Eurovision was that it permitted same-day film of European events. One of the most frequently cited problems was late arrival of unprocessed film and the inadequacy of film processing facilities.

The broadcasting equivalent of newspaper editions is the sequence of bulletins through the day, or evening on television. Journalists were acutely aware of the need to 'keep the picture changing'. [. . .] Journalists were fond of the fast-breaking story where the rapid movement of events pre-empted any need for the artificial injection of pace or change. Recency emphasises the task of news in topping up information on those events and institutions already defined as the substance of news.

ELITES

As a value within 'bigness' news values emphasise that big names are better news than nobodies, major personalities of more interest than ordinary folk. There is an obvious circularity in this in that well-known personalities become so by their exposure in news media. It is this that leads us to root this news value in production rather than in audience interests. Clearly audiences are interested in major rather than minor figures, people they all know about rather than the acquaintances of a few. But [. . .] elites are only partially exposed, and concentration on powerful or ruling groups is neither uniform nor comprehensive.

PERSONALITIES

News is about people, and mostly about individuals. This news value emphasises the need to make stories comprehensible by reducing complex processes and institutions to the actions of individuals. This aim is, like many news values, a virtue born of necessity. Brief, and especially visual, journalism cannot deal with abstractions and has to narrate in the concrete. Thus it becomes a news value to 'seek the personal angle' or to 'personalise' the news. The effect of this is to treat institutional and international relations either as the interaction of individuals, or as being analogous to inter-personal relations. For example, international political news deals almost entirely with the diplomatic globe-trotting of major politicians, and international relations are seen to depend on how well political leaders get on. The analogies appear in the terminology of the emotions which characterises institutional or national relations. Governments become 'angry', unions are 'hot-headed', nations are 'anxious' or 'eager'. This is most easily portrayed by personalising such acts in the presentation of individuals.

This list may not exhaust all news values but it includes the main ones. Their obviousness can be illustrated by compiling a list of antonyms. It is hard to imagine broadcast journalists anywhere seeking news which dealt with small events, the long term, dull, distant, visually boring, unimportant people, and so on. Yet many of these labels describe events and processes which may well have significance for news audiences, but which are not news. The application of news values is part of the process by which this labelling occurs.

BIAS, OBJECTIVITY AND IDEOLOGY

Peter Golding And Philip Elliott

[. . .]

It is possible to see broadcast news as simply the result of the bias of individual journalists, committed either to professional notions of how news should be structured, or to social views of the ideas it should convey. For David Brinkley, the authoritative American newscaster, 'News is what I say it is. It's something worth knowing by my standards' (Brinkley, 1964). Whether this is unguarded arrogance, or hyperbole to make a point about the essential indefinability of news, it represents to many people the most likely explanation of news output. The newscaster is the visible tip of the news production plant, a visual or aural reminder that it is a process handled by people; fallible, biased and opinionated, like the rest of us. The obvious weakness of this explanation is that the news changes very little when the individuals who produce it are changed. An occasional shift in partisanship may be detected in the reporting of particular issues, but the events covered, and the nature of their coverage, remain the same. [. . .] [E]ven in highly varied cultural and organisational settings broadcast news emerges with surprisingly similar forms and contents. In addition the division of labour required for production limits the impacts of individuals on news. [. . .] Epstein (1973, p. 28) describes how 'News executives decide on the development of correspondents and camera crews; assignment editors select what stories will be covered and by whom; field producers, in constant phone contact with the producers in New York, usually supervise the preparation of filming of stories . . . editors . . . reconstruct the story on film . . .' and so on.

From P. Golding and P. Elliott, *Making the News* (London: Longman, 1979) pp. 206–11.

Yet the notion of group, if not individual, bias persists. [. . .] The notion of bias is often contrasted with objectivity, and for clarity's sake two distinctions should be made. First impartiality and objectivity are distinct. Impartiality implies a disinterested approach to news, lacking in motivation to shape or select material according to a particular view or opinion. Objectivity, however defined, is clearly a broader demand than this. A journalist may well be impartial towards the material on which he works, yet fail to achieve objectivity – a complete and unrefracted capture of the world – due to the inherent limitations in news gathering and processing. Second, the bias of an individual reporter dealing with a single event may be reduced or even eliminated by, for example, the deliberate application of self-discipline and professional standards of process. In other words we should distinguish bias as the deliberate aim of journalism, which is rare, from bias as the inevitable but unintended consequence of organisation.

There are, then, three possible views of journalistic objectivity and impartiality. First, there is the professional view that it is possible to be both, based on the idea that objectivity and impartiality are attitudes of mind. Second is the view that objectivity may well be a nebulous and unattainable goal, but that impartiality is still desirable and possible.

[. . .]

The third view, that neither objectivity or impartiality are in any serious sense possible in journalism, comes from a change of analytical perspective, from the short-term and deliberate production of news stories to the long-term and routine, unreflective practices of journalism as we have analysed them in this study. Objectivity and impartiality remain the aims of most day-to-day journalism. But we should understand these terms as labels applied by journalists to the rules which govern their working routines. Objectivity is achieved by subscribing to and observing these sets of rules, which are themselves the object of our analysis. We have seen how these rules, both the explicit regulations of organisational charters and newsroom manuals, and the implicit understandings of news values, are derived from the currents of supply and demand which eddy round the newsroom.

The assumed needs and interests of audiences on the one hand, and the truncated supply of information into the newsroom on the other, both exert pressures to which the organisation of news production responds. What are the consequences of these pressures?

When we come to assess news as a coherent view of the world, that is to step up from news values to social values, we enter an altogether more complex and tangled argument. News is ideology to the extent that it provides an integrated picture of reality. But an ideology is more than this; it is also the world view of particular social groups, and especially of social classes. The claim that news is ideology implies that it provides a world view both consistent in itself, and supportive of the interests of powerful social groupings. This can come about in two ways.

First, news is structured by the exigencies of organised production which are the main concern of this study. These allow only a partial view of the reported world which may or may not coincide with a ruling ideology. The historical process by which this coincidence occurs is more than accidental, and is rooted in the development of news as a service to elite groups. [. . .] Thus most of the basic goals and values which surround journalism refer to the needs and interests of these groups. Second, in attempting to reach widespread, annonymous audiences news draws on the most broadly held common social values and assumptions, in other words the prevailing consensus, in establishing common ground for communication with its audiences. In the case of broadcast journalism the complex relationship with the state exaggerates this need to cling to the central and least challenged social values which provide implicit definitions of actions and events as acceptable or unacceptable, usual or unusual, legitimate or illegitimate.

[. . .]

There are two key elements to the world of broadcast news; the invisibility of social process, and the invisibility of power in society. We can discuss these two lacunae separately. First, the loss of a sense of social process. News is about the present, or the immediate past. It is an account of today's events. The world of broadcast news is a display of single events, making history indeed 'one damn thing after another'. Yet in this whirl of innumerable events the lingering impression is of stasis. Events are interchangeable, a succession rather than an unfolding. What is provided is a topping up of the limited range of regularly observed events in the world with more of the same. A reassuring sameness assimilates each succession of events to ready-made patterns in a timeless mosaic.

This fragmentation of social process, evacuating history, has been described as 'a kind of consecration to collective amnesia' (Glabel, 1967, p. 113). In a real sense reason disappears as actors flit across the journalistic stage, perform and hurriedly disappear. [. . .] Thus industrial relations appears not as an evolving conflict of interest but as a sporadic eruption of inexplicable anger and revolt (Hartmann, 1976; Glasgow University Media Group, 1976). Similarly the political affairs of foreign lands appear as spasmodic convulsions of a more or less violent turn, while international relations appear to result from the occasional urge for travel and conversation indulged in by the diplomatic jet-set.

The second absent dimension in broadcast news is that of power. News is about the actions of individuals, not corporate entities, thus individual authority rather than the exertion of entrenched power is seen to be the mover of events. News, and broadcast news in particular, is the last refuge of the great man theory of history. Yet faces change, power holders are replaced, and such changes take pride of place in the circumspection of the news. The continuing and consistent power of the position is masked by concentration on the recurrent changes of office-holder.

In domestic news the focus is on central political elites and their daily gamesmanship in the arenas of conflict resolution. Groups which may exert power but which do not make news disappear, by definition, from view, and with them the visibility of power itself. Prominent among the absentees are the owners of property and their corporate representatives. Of all the institutions which contribute to social process none is so invisible to broadcast news as the world of the company boardroom. In international news the world revolves round the news capitals in Europe and North America. For audiences in the Third World their fellows in three continents are invisible, a communality of interest cannot emerge and problems appear particular and separate to each watching nation. Thus it is not the *effect* of the rich and powerful nations on the Third World that is seen, but their attractiveness as models, benevolence as aid-givers and convenors of conferences, or wisdom as disinterested umpires in local disputes.

Power disappears in the institutional definitions the news provides, an agenda of issues and arenas to which attention is directed. In particular politics is separated from power. Power is seen only in the public display of formality, gesture and speech by major political actors. It is defined by reference to government and the central institutions of political negotiaion. Rositi has similarly drawn attention in his analysis of European television news to 'the primacy of formal politics' in the television news world (Rositi, 1975, pp.25–30), and remarks on the absence of financial and business elites. Thus power is reduced to areas of negotiation compromise, and politics to a recurrent series of decisions, debates and personalities. It is removed from the institutions of production. Thus news bears witness to the institutional separation of economics and politics, a precondition for the evacuation of power from its account of the world. Power is absent from news by virtue of this severance of politics from economics; power is located in authority not in control, in the office-holder not the property owner. News thus provides a particular and truncated view of power, and in this sense power is a dimension that is effectively missing from news.

With these two missing dimensions – social process or history, and power – news indeed provides a world view. The question remains to what extent this is a coherent ideology. Analyses which see news as necessarily a product of powerful groups, in society, designed to provide a view of the world consonant with the interests of those groups simplify the situation too far to be helpful. The occupational routines and beliefs of journalists do not allow a simple conduit between the ruling ideas of the powerful and their distribution via the airwaves. Yet the absence of power and process clearly precludes the development of views which might question the prevailing distribution of power, or its roots in the evolution of economic distribution and control. A world which appears fundamentally unchanging, subject to the genius or caprice of myriad powerful individuals, is not a world which appears susceptible to radical change or challenge.

There are three ways, then, in which broadcast news is ideological. First it focuses our attention on those institutions and events in which social conflict is managed and resolved. It is precisely the arenas of consensus formation which provide both access and appropriate material for making the news. Second, broadcast news, in studiously following statutory demands to eschew partiality or controversy, and professional demands for objectivity and neutrality, is left to draw on the values and beliefs of the broadest social consensus. It is this process which Stuart Hall (1970, p. 1056) describes as 'the steady and unexamined play of attitudes which, via the mediating structure of professionally defined news values, inclines all the media toward the status quo'. The prevailing beliefs in any society will rarely be those which question existing social organisation or values. News will itself merely reinforce scepticism about such divergent, dissident or deviant beliefs. Third, as we have seen, broadcast news is, for historical and organisational reasons, inherently incapable of providing a portrayal of social change or of displaying the operation of power in and between societies. It thus portrays a world which is unchanging and unchangeable.

The key elements of any ruling ideology are the undesirability of change, and its impossibility; all is for the best and change would do more harm than good, even if it were possible. Broadcast news substantiates this philosophy because of the interplay of the three processes we have just described.

REFERENCES

Brinkley, D. (1964) Interview, in *TI Guide*, 11 April.
Brucker, H. (1973) *Communication is Power: Unchanging Values in a Changing Journalism*, New York, Oxford University Press.
Epstein, E. J. (1973) *News from Nowhere – Television and the News*, New York, Random House.
Gabel, J. (1967) *La Falsa Conscienza*, Dedalo, Bari, quoted in Rositi (1975).
Galtung, J. and Ruge, M. (1965) The structure of foreign news, *Journal of Peace Research*, vol. 1, pp. 64–90.
Glasgow University Media Group (1976) *Bad News*, London, Routledge & Kegan Paul.
Hall, S. (1970) A world at one with itself, *New Society*, 18 June, pp. 1056–8.
Hartmann, P. (1976) *The Media and Industrial Relations*, unpublished, Leicester Centre for Mass Communication Research.

Hughes, H. M. (1940) *News and the Human Interest Story*, Chicago, University of Chicago Press.
Hughes, H. M. (1942) The social interpretation of news, *Annals of the American Academy of Political and Social Science*, vol. 219, pp. 11–17.
Lansipuro, Y. (1975) Joint Eurovision/Intervision news study, *EBU Review*, vol. XXVI, no. 3, May, pp. 37–40.
Rositi, F. (1975) The television news programme: fragmentation and recomposition of our image of society. Report presented to Prix Italia, Florence.
Schlesinger, P. (1978) *Putting 'Reality' Together: BBC News*, Constable, London. [See Chapter 43 in this volume.]
Varis, T. (1974) *Television News in Eurovision and Intervision*, Report to EBU Working Party on Television News, Lisbon.

43

THE PRODUCTION OF RADIO AND TELEVISION NEWS

Philip Schlesinger

Entrenched in newsmen's mythology about their work is the belief that news is somehow the product of a *lack* of organization. News, rather than being seen as the imposition of order upon the chaos of multifarious, often unrelated events and issues, is seen as a kind of recurring accident. [. . .] [However] the routines of production have definite consequences in structuring news. To delineate their main features goes some way towards providing a rational understanding of an important form of work. The news we receive on any given day is not as unpredictable as much journalistic mythology would have us believe. Rather, the doings of the world are tamed to meet the needs of a production system in many respects bureaucratically organized.

A related point is that the production of broadcast news, as presently constituted, is a *reactive* form of reportage. Broadly speaking, BBC newsmen wait for things to happen, and then register their occurrence. To some extent this results from the BBC doctrine that news refrains from investigation and elaborated interpretation. [. . .] Organization and ideology are in fact mutually reinforcing.

THE NEWSDAY CYCLE

News is produced in daily cycles known as 'newsdays'. Each newsday is divided by a number of transmission times for which bulletins and programmes have to be prepared. These transmission times constitute a series of deadlines towards which the entire production machine is oriented.

[. . .]

Production, therefore, is organized in relation to particular cycles, and is based on a division of labour within each newsroom.

From P. Schlesinger, *Putting 'Reality' Together: BBC News* (London: Methuen, 1987) pp. 47–80.

CONTROLLING PRODUCTION

A central theme of this study is how the production of news is controlled. There are two separate mechanisms through which day-to-day and minute-to-minute control production is exercised.

On a day-to-day basis, control is exercised through the daily editorial conferences which start each newsday in each of the News Departments. These are known as the 'morning meetings'. As the two News Departments* are organizationally separate, the meetings are also an important means of control at the Divisional level since they are linked each weekday by a radio circuit, over which discussion of mutual problems takes place and news judgements are exchanged.[1]

[. . .]

Certain features of the meetings can be distinguished. First, there is a retrospective discussion. At Radio News, where there has been overnight coverage, the chairman asks the night editor whether he has had problems, and often makes observations about the previous day's output.

[. . .]

Next, the morning meetings begin to address a definite agenda. This is the News Diary,[2] a document which lists home and foreign news stories which are thought to be newsworthy. Each service has its own diary. They are separately compiled overnight at Radio News, and in the late evening at Television News. The diary gives information on the availability of reporting staff at home and abroad; it lists the times at which circuits are available for feeding in reports from home and foreign correspondents, and reporters in various parts of the British Isles. The Television News diary contains a lot of detail about the arrival times of film from abroad, satellites and Eurovision link-ups.

[. . .]

Deployment and Logistics

At this early stage of the newsday there is much concern with the deployment of reporting resources. News organizations have limited manpower and can cover only those stories they think the most newsworthy. These arrangements are especially complex in television news, where there is a pre-eminent concern with 'logistics', with what is often described as 'the mechanics of the thing, getting the stuff in'. Because television has a more complex technology than radio, the morning meeting at Television Centre brings in people with technical expertise (such as film editors, graphics assistants and studio directors) as well as journalists. Discussion of 'satellite times' and 'picture lines' abounds, with talk of technique dominating far more than the substantive news judgements which actuate the quest for pictures. A senior news executive compared the problems of television coverage with those of radio:

> TV at its optimum working method uses much more complex equipment, it is also larger, more cumbersome and more obtrusive. The newspaper reporter is indistinguishable from the general public apart from his notebook and pencil. The radio reporter is also a single man with his own equipment. But the TV reporter will need a crew (cameraman, sound recordist, lighting man). To do the job effectively you need a certain amount of physical movement over varying distances in order to get the picture on the air. Compare this with radio: you can get a totally effective report through provided you can get to a phone anywhere in the world.

The news diaries contain detail of deployments which have already been made. The central problem is that of ensuring that reports are available to meet the transmission times.

[. . .]

The meetings last for about 20 minutes to half an hour. They provide a forum for the exercise of editorial control before the locus of decision-making shifts to the 'shopfloor' level of newsroom practice. Editorial attitudes emerge during the course of running through 'diary stories'; where they do not, it is because they are taken for granted.

[. . .]

There are two major mechanisms for controlling production at the newsroom level. The first is the morning meeting, which works out unwritten guidelines for treatment on a pragmatic day-to-day basis, and the second the editorial structure inside the newsroom.

[. . .]

Editorial autonomy is certainly stressed in the BBC's corporate ideology. But the scope of individual decision-making, although not subject to crude directives from above, *is* limited by the need to 'refer upwards' where doubts arise. Also, newsroom decisions are made within constraints set by the diaries which list the bulk of each day's likely output. The guiding principle behind the system is that, during each shift one (in Radio) or two (in Television) senior and trustworthy personnel are given as complete an overview of newsroom and news-gathering activities as possible, with the intention of securing an output which is 'reliable' in the BBC's terms. For reporters out in the field, and editorial staff inside the building, the editor of the day is a legitimate authority figure with a final say on the duration and content of reports. Within the News Department he is seen, as someone put it, as 'God for the Day'. The gods rotate according to the mundane dictates of the shift-system. But they are always represented.[3]

THE PRODUCTION OF BULLETINS AND PROGRAMMES

To understand the daily routines of news production the pre-eminence of deadlines needs to be recognized. The pattern of work falls into a series of phases, each of which is delimited by the period of time between transmission times. A radio news bulletin is composed of written copy read by the newsreader, 'voice' reports by correspondents and reporters, and 'actuality' (i.e., recorded sound of 'events' taking place – such as, shooting or rioting). Televised news is, as a product, a more complex combination of elements. It is composed of scripts spoken by the newsreader which are written to film, videotape, still photographs, maps, diagrams and other visual symbols; it contains 'on the spot' or studio reports from reporters and correspondents which may be edited film reports or 'live inserts'.

[. . .]

Planning the Bulletin
[. . .]

When the news diary has been discussed, the morning papers have been read, news agency copy sifted through and 'tip-offs' have been received from the BBC's correspondents, the two senior editors are able to draw up a 'provisional running order'. The running order is a list of news items which seems to the editors to make good sense in production terms. In general they broadly agree on their judgements, and where they do not, the editor of the day has the last word.

The day's production does not begin with a blank sheet. By that time of the morning, coverage of several stories, both home and foreign, is already in train. For example, 'Routine

Industrials', Northern Ireland Coverage, Ministerial Press Conferences, Court Coverage and the like are the kinds of diary story which would automatically be covered. Similarly, the arrival time of a film story from abroad is generally known a day in advance. The running order is expected to change as the morning wears on and new stories 'break'. The keystone of the bulletin is the 'lead', which is equivalent to the main front-page story in a newspaper. When the editors have found a story which they think is sufficiently newsworthy to head the bulletin, they have a yardstick against which to judge the newsworthiness of others.

[. . .]

A news bulletin is a collectively-assembled product, dependent upon the orchestration of a number of discrete skills. Once stories have been assigned, a series of parallel selection processes is set in train. These are woven together in the hour before the bulletin goes out over the air, and sometimes not finalized until transmission itself has begun.

[. . .]

The Updating Process

The concept of news presupposes a notion of change, and so 'updating' is integral to the entire production process. It involves accommodating 'new facts' in stories kept in the running order, and replacing entire stories by 'new' ones in line with the newsman's law of the survival of the newsworthiest.

While most news stories eventually broadcast can be predicted each morning, some cannot. The earlier they 'break' before the bulletin is due to go out over the air, the greater the chance for editors to arrange coverage.

[. . .]

Much of the selection of copy takes place within the framework of expectations about newsworthy stories which is embodied in the news prospects and the running order; in addition, the copy taster orients himself to the selection of news stories by having heard the most recent morning bulletins and having glanced through the most recent newspapers. Efficiency in selection is judged in terms of 'experience' – the development of a 'news sense' through time.

The updating process gives a dynamic structure to the production of bulletins. The editor of the day and the senior duty editor have to take account of a constant flow of information, and make changes in the sub-editing process which will accommodate it. Reporting is also affected as new requests may go out to reporters already working on stories. The role of the copy taster is particularly important when it comes to changes of fact in stories in the immediate period before the bulletin is transmitted. He knows which subs are working on particular stories and can directly inform them himself of changes, or pass messages through the senior duty editor. The updating process allows immediacy and accuracy to be maintained right up to transmission time.[4]

[. . .]

Transmission

A news bulletin, although a collective product, displays the characteristics of a unified one. The role of the newsreader as 'anchorman' in presenting the series of items which comprises a bulletin is a crucial one. He opens, intersperses, and concludes the sequence with his own voice, and, in television, his presence in vision.

[. . .]

Changes occur at this late stage, both in Radio and in Television News, because bulletins are routinely 'overset'; this occurs because editors like to leave their final selection to the last possible moment.

[. . .]

If an important 'newsbreak' occurs, and it is difficult to alter the running order, the story is accommodated by using phrases such as 'We've just heard that . . . ' or 'Some late news . . . ' at some convenient moment in the sequence.

[. . .]

News Intake: An Overview

The newsday begins with a structure of expectations about what is likely to make news. But the production process itself represents only one element of the behind-the-scenes activities of the News Department. Extensive logistical arrangements have to be made for news-gathering to meet the deadlines posed by the output times. 'News Intake' is the branch of the operation which makes these arrangements. It falls into two sections. One for 'Home News' which is under the supervision of the News Editor, and the other for 'Foreign News' which falls under the aegis of the Foreign News Editor. There is a further relevant division of labour. For both types of news there is both a daily function and also an advanced planning function.

Daily Intake

[. . .]

The intake desks produce the news diary [. . .], act as the logistical focus for incoming reports, and give briefings and updatings to the output desks.

Discussion at the morning meeting centres mainly on information contained in the news diary. In Radio News this document is compiled for distribution at 8.00 a.m. by the news organizer on the overnight shift on the basis of various sources: there are BBC advanced planning documents [. . .], from which stories relevant to the day are selected; the Press Association diary sent over the wires during the night; the various PR hand-outs from government departments and other institutions and groups; the morning papers which may provide a story which merits following up. At Television News, where the news operation ceases by midnight, the diary is prepared in the later hours of the evening, and additions made the following morning.

[. . .]

Future Planning

Home News

The day before the news diaries are drawn up in Radio and Television News, an earlier document called the advanced diary is compiled, by the Home News Editor (Planning) in Radio News, and by the News Organizer (Planning) in Television News. These intake editors arrange the deployment of reporters and the collection of recorded material one day ahead. It is estimated that 95 per cent of these advanced diary arrangements are embodied in the following day's diary, and that some 70 per cent on average are finally used, in some way or other, in the production of bulletins. Most news is not spontaneous, or unanticipated.

[. . .]

Every Thursday, at Television News, a Home News Futures meeting is held, which is attended by the Editor and Deputy Editor of Television News, the Home News Editor and his deputy, the five assistant editors who take it in turn to act as editor of the day, and the news organizer (planning). The agenda on this occasion is compiled by News Intake, and is called the Weekly Futures List. This list is divided into six distinct categories which indicate stable expectations of what is likely to make news: Ulster; Political; Industrial and Economic; General; Sport; Others.

[. . .]

Foreign News

There are similar foreign futures meetings held both at Radio News (on Tuesdays) and Television News (on Thursdays). Each is attended by the Editor and Deputy Editor of the Department, the Foreign News Editors from both radio and television services, the Diplomatic Correspondent, the foreign duty editors, the output editors, and a representative of the External Services News. The futures list is run through by the Foreign News Editor of the Department in question. It consists of a list of potential stories for transmission within the next month. The list is divided into continents and sub-continents, and within each of these sections are listed stories being pursued or as of likely interest. The Foreign News Editor (Television) described the meeting as a way 'for us to estimate the interest among the editors of the day – we wouldn't do anything without that'. Foreign news coverage – especially in television – is very expensive.

[. . .]

Foreign futures meetings combine, then, logistical and evaluative concerns. Much of the comment centres on the performance of given men in the field, and such reports as they likely to be filing. The meeting, like the others discussed in this chapter, acts as a forum for pooling intelligence. It provides a basis on which to plan coverage for the coming fortnight.

NEWS-GATHERING

News-gatherers consist of, on the one hand, specialist correspondents and, on the other, of general news reporters.

[. . .]

Home specialist correspondents cover defined areas of news interest. [. . .] The specialisms embody defined areas of news interest, and are expected routinely to generate stories. They all focus on major institutional spheres of British life, notably those of government and industry. One has simply to list the main areas to see what a staple diet they provide: Parliament and the major political parties; industry (the CBI and TUC), finance (the Stock Exchange and banks) and consumer affairs; Whitehall departments for education, labour, science and technology, home affairs, health, agriculture and fishing and local government; the Churches; the Monarchy. All are the stuff of the daily cycle of news.

News-gathering in this defined set of spheres contrasts with the generalist approach expected of reporters.

[. . .]

Like specialists in other news organizations, BBC correspondents have the status of an 'expert': they are internal pundits to be consulted by a non-specialists. The importance of this role is stressed in the BBC's *News Guide*, a codification of desired news practice:

> Any major story in an area covered by a specialist correspondent, e.g. education, should always be referred to that correspondent.[5]

The home correspondents are available for consultation in the London newsrooms. The foreign correspondents have routine discussions with London to assess longer-term trends and particular stories.

[. . .]

CONCLUSION

The production of broadcast news takes place in the context of a daily time-cycle. From the picture drawn in this chapter it is clear that there is a heavy reliance on a planning structure which creates a routine agenda of predictable stories which provide the backbone of each day's production requirement. There is nothing exceptional about the BBC's news operation in this respect. From such fragmentary indications as are available concerning its chief competitor in Britain, ITN, similar conclusions may be drawn.[6] Firm evidence is available about television news production practice in US networks in Epstein's account, and similarly detailed material on the major broadcast news operations of Ireland, Nigeria and Sweden is to be found in Golding and Elliott's work.[7] The analysis of routine practices given in these works shows the striking similarity of structure in different broadcast news organizations.

Most 'news' is constructed within a framework of firm expectations which are used to guide the deployment of available resources. For television in particular such planning is particularly important as there are technical requirements – such as having light to shoot film by, needing to wait for film to be processed – which make the time-factor particularly pressing. One might recall here Epstein's finding that despite the fact that news is defined by US television journalists in terms of immediacy, a high proportion of it is prepared in advance.[8] Most news is really 'olds', in the sense that it is largely predictable, but a powerful occupational mythology plays this fact down. [. . .]

A noteworthy feature of the planning structure outlined here is that it is not one which easily lends itself to what journalists call 'digging' or 'investigation'. Diaries are assembled from sources available to all the media in Britain. Given similar news judgements about the same stories there is a tendency to homogeneity. Rarely does broadcast news present stories which are the product of investigation. It is not 'set up' for the task. To do this one would need to set aside resources – reporters, film crews, production teams. Again, this is not a point to be made about British practice alone. Epstein notes how US television correspondents do little in the way of originating stories, and how the bulk of coverage is reactive, being based on agency and newspaper stories.[9] Golding and Elliott suggest that 'being a monopoly, broadcast journalism is less concerned with the "scoop", the triumphant capture of an exclusive story ahead of rivals'.[10] To talk of monopoly, or, in Britain, duopoly, forces us to focus on broadcasting's relationship to the state, and its inbuilt tendency to caution. There is an ideology at work here about what broadcast news ought – and ought not – to do as well as a production structure stressing routine and predictability, which is pre-eminently oriented to meeting that day's deadlines.

There is little in the belief that news production is chaotic. Certainly, to the complete outsider it might look so. And to the complete insider it might feel so. But neither of these positions takes us anywhere. Bulletin production itself works within a structure of expectations outlined each day at the morning meeting, which is subsequently embodied in the various planning documents, and which will, if 'spot news' comes along, be disturbed. The tendency of this system is to produce an orderly picture of events, which, being 'news', are often themselves disorderly.

NOTES

1. At weekends, when the outputs are more restricted, the editor of the day is generally in telephone contact with either the Editor or his deputy for routine consultations.

2. There are slight variations in name – News *Diary*, News *Prospects* – at Television Centre and Broadcasting House respectively. These don't indicate any distinction in purpose or content. At the BBC's External Services News, based in Bush House, London, the document in question is called the *Morning* Diary.

3. At Television Centre, there are five Assistant Editors who man the two desks, generally working a shift consisting of one planning day and two days on the desk. At Broadcasting House, there are two Assistant Editors acting as editor of the day, working three-day shifts.

4. This gives too neat a picture; there are, in fact, 'late' stories which have to be dealt with *after* this point in the production cycle.

5. *News Guide*, 1972: 61.

6. Glasgow Media group, 1976: Ch. 3; Day, 1961: Ch. 6; Tyrrell, 1972: Ch. 1; *Sunday Times Magazine*, 26.8.73: 29–33.

7. Golding and Elliott, 1976; Epstein, 1973.

8. Epstein, 1973: 133.

9. Ibid.: 141.

10. Golding and Elliott, 1976: 4/22.

REFERENCES

BBC Radio News, *News Guide*, revised edition, May 1972.

Robin Day, *Television: a personal report* (London: Hutchinson) 1961.

Edward Jay Epstein, *News from nowhere: television and the news* (New York: Random House) 1973.

Glasgow University Media Group, *Bad News* volume 1 (London: Routledge & Kegan Paul) 1976.

Peter Golding and Philip Elliott, *Making the News* (University of Leicester: Centre for Mass Communication Research) 1976. [See Chapter 42 in this volume.]

Robert Tyrrell, *The work of the television journalist* (London and New York: The Focal Press) 1972.

Editors' Note

* BBC Radio News and BBC Television News

44

THE SOCIAL PRODUCTION OF NEWS

Stuart Hall, Chas. Chritcher, Tony Jefferson, John Clarke and Brian Roberts

The media do not simply and transparently report events which are 'naturally' newsworthy *in themselves*. 'News' is the end-product of a complex process which begins with a systematic sorting and selecting of events and topics according to a socially constructed set of categories. As MacDougall puts it:

> At any given moment billions of simultaneous events occur throughout the world. . . . All of these occurences are potentially news. They do not become so until some purveyor of news gives an account of them. The news, in other words, is the account of the event, not something intrinsic in the event itself.[1]

One aspect of the structure of selection can be seen in the routine organisation of newspapers with respect to regular types or areas of news. Since newspapers are committed to the regular production of news, these organisational factors will, in turn, affect what is selected. For example, newspapers become predirected to certain types of event and topic in terms of the organisation of their own work-force (e.g. specialist correspondents and departments, the fostering of institutional contacts, etc.) and the structure of the papers themselves (e.g. home news, foreign, political, sport, etc.).[2]

Given that the organisation and staffing of a paper regularly direct it to certain categories of items, there is still the problem of selecting, from the many contending items within any one category, those that are felt will be of interest to the reader. This is where the *professional ideology* of what constitutes 'good news' – the newsman's sense of *news values* – begins to structure the process.

[. . .]

These two aspects of the social production of news – the bureaucratic organisation of the

From S. Hall et al., *Policing the Crisis: Mugging, the State, and Law and Order* (Basingstoke: Macmillan Education Ltd., 1978) pp. 53–60.

media which produces the news in specific types or categories and the structure of news values which orders the selection and ranking of particular stories within these categories – are only part of the process. The third aspect – the moment of the *construction* of the news story itself – is equally important, if less obvious. This involves the presentation of the item to its *assumed* audience, in terms which, as far as the presenters of the item can judge, will make it comprehensible to that audience. If the world is not to be represented as a jumble of random and chaotic events, then they must be identified (i.e. named, defined, related to other events known to the audience), and assigned to a social context (i.e. placed within a frame of meanings familiar to the audience). This process – identification and contextualisation – is one of the most important through which events are 'made to mean' by the media. An event only 'makes sense' if it can be located within a range of known social and cultural identifications. If newsmen did not have available – in however routine a way – such cultural 'maps' of the social world, they could not 'make sense' for their audiences of the unusual, unexpected and unpredicted events which form the basic content of what is 'newsworthy'. Things are newsworthy because they represent the changefulness, the unpredictability and the conflictful nature of the world. But such events cannot be allowed to remain in the limbo of the 'random' – they must be brought within the horizon of the 'meaningful'. This bringing of events within the realm of meanings means, in essence, referring unusual and unexpected events to the 'maps of meaning' which already form the basis of our cultural knowledge, into which the social world is *already* 'mapped'. The social identification, classification and contextualisation of news events in terms of these background frames of reference is the fundamental process by which the media make the world they report on intelligible to readers and viewers. This process of 'making an event intelligible' is a social process – constituted by a number of specific journalistic practices, which embody (often only implicitly) crucial assumptions about what society is and how it works.

One such background assumption is the *consensual* nature of society: the process of *signification* – giving social meanings to events – *both assumes and helps to construct society as a 'consensus'*. We exist as members of one society *because* – it is assumed – we share a common stock of cultural knowledge with our fellow men: we have access to the same 'maps of meanings'. Not only are we all able to manipulate these 'maps of meaning' to understand events, but we have fundamental interests, values and concerns in common, which these maps embody or reflect. We all want to, or do, maintain basically the same perspective *on* events. In this view, what unites us, as a society and a culture – its consensual side – far outweighs what divides and distinguishes us as groups or classes from other groups. Now, at one level, the existence of a cultural consensus is an obvious truth; it is the basis of all social communication.[3] If we were not members of the same language community we literally could not communicate with one another. On a broader level, if we did not inhabit, to some degree, the same classifications of social reality we could not 'make sense of the world together'. In recent years, however, this basic cultural fact about society has been raised to an extreme ideological level. Because we occupy the same society and belong to roughly the same 'culture', it is assumed that there is, basically, only *one* perspective on events: that provided by what is sometimes called *the* culture, or (by some social scientists) *the* 'central value system'. This view denies any major structural discrepancies between different groups, or between the very different maps of meaning in a society. This 'consensual' viewpoint has important political consequences, when used as the taken-for-granted basis of communication. It carries the assumption that we also all have roughly the same *interest* in the society, and that we all roughly have an equal share of power in the society. This is the essence of the idea of the political consensus. 'Consensual' views of society represent society as if there are no major cultural or economic breaks, no major conflicts of interests between classes and groups. Whatever disagreements exist, it is said, there are legitimate and institutionalised means for expressing and reconciling them. The 'free market' in opinions and in the media is supposed to guarantee the reconciliation of cultural discontinuities between one group and another. The political institutions – parliament, the two-party system, political representation, etc. – are supposed to guarantee equal access for all groups to the decision-making process. The growth of a 'consumer' economy is supposed to have created the economic conditions for everyone to have a stake in the making and distribution of wealth. The rule of law protects us all equally. This consensus view of society is particularly strong in modern, democratic, organised capitalist societies; and the media are among the institutions whose practices are most widely and consistently predicated upon the assumption of a 'national consensus'. So that, when events are 'mapped' by the media into frameworks of meaning and interpretation, it is assumed that we all equally possess and know how to use these frameworks, that they are drawn from fundamentally the same structures of understanding for all social groups and audiences. Of course, in the formation of opinion, as in politics and economic life, it is conceded that there will be differences of outlook, disagreement, argument and opposition; but these are understood as taking place within a broader basic framework of agreement – 'the consensus' – to which everyone subscribes, and within which every dispute, disagreement or conflict of interest can be reconciled by discussion, without recourse to confrontation or violence.

[. . .]

Events, as news, then, are regularly interpreted within frameworks which derive, in part, from this notion of *the consensus* as a basic feature of everyday life. They are elaborated through a variety of 'explanations', images and discourses which articulate what the audience is assumed to think and know about the society.

[. . .]

What, then, is the underlying significance of the framing and interpretive function of news presentation? We suggest that it lies in the fact that the media are often presenting information about events which occur outside the direct experience of the majority of the society. The media thus represent the primary, and often the only, source of information about many important events and topics. Further, because news is recurrently concerned with events which are 'new' or 'unexpected', the media are involved in the task of making comprehensible what we would term 'problematic reality'. Problematic events breach our commonly held expectations and are therefore threatening to a society based around the expectation of consensus, order and routine. Thus the media's mapping of problematic events within the conventional understandings of the society is crucial in two ways. The media define for the majority of the population *what* significant events are taking place, but, also, they offer powerful interpretations of *how* to understand these events. Implicit in those interpretations are orientations towards the events and the people or groups involved in them.

PRIMARY AND SECONDARY DEFINERS

In this section we want to begin to account for the 'fit' between dominant ideas and professional media ideologies and practices. This cannot be simply attributed – as it sometimes is in simple conspiracy theories – to the fact that the media are in large part capitalist-owned (though that structure of ownership is widespread), since this would be to ignore the day-to-day 'relative autonomy' of the journalist and news producers from direct economic control. Instead we want to draw attention to the more routine *structures* of news production to see how the media come in fact, in the 'last instance', to *reproduce the definitions of the powerful*, without being, in a simple sense, in their pay. Here we must insist on a crucial distinction between *primary* and *secondary definers* of social events.

The media do not themselves autonomously create news items; rather they are 'cued in' to specific new topics by regular and reliable institutional sources. As Paul Rock notes:

> In the main journalists position themselves so that they have access to institutions which generate a useful volume of reportable activity at regular intervals. Some of these institutions do, of course, make themselves visible by means of dramatization, or through press releases and press agents. Others are known to regularly produce consequential events. The courts, sports grounds and parliament mechanically manufacture news which is . . . assimilated by the press.[4]

One reason for this has to do with the internal pressures of news production – as Murdock notes:

> The incessant pressures of time and the consequent problems of resource allocation and work scheduling in news organisations can be reduced or alleviated by covering 'pre-scheduled events'; that is, events that have been announced in advance by their convenors. However, one of the consequences of adopting this solution to scheduling problems is to increase the newsmen's dependence on news sources willing and able to preschedule their activities.[5]

The second has to do with the fact that media reporting is underwritten by notions of 'impartiality', 'balance' and 'objectivity'. This is formally enforced in television (a near-monopoly situation, where the state is directly involved in a regulatory sense) but there are also similar professional ideological 'rules' in journalism.[6] One product of these rules is the carefully structured distinction between 'fact' and 'opinion'. [. . .] For our present purposes, the important point is that these professional rules give rise to the practice of ensuring that media statements are, wherever possible, grounded in 'objective' and 'authoritative' statements from 'accredited' sources. This means constantly turning to accredited representatives of major social institutions – MPs for political topics, employers and trade-union leaders for industrial matters, and so on. Such institutional representatives are 'accredited' because of their Institutional power and position, but also because of their 'representative' status: either they represent 'the people' (MPs, Ministers, etc.) or organised interest groups (which is how the TUC and the CBI are now regarded). One final 'accredited source' is 'the expert': his calling – the 'disinterested' pursuit of knowledge – not his position or his representativeness, confers on his statements 'objectivity' and 'authority'. Ironically, the very rules which aim to preserve the impartiality of the media, and which grew out of desires for greater professional neutrality, also serve powerfully to orientate the media in the 'definitions of social reality' which their 'accredited sources' – the institutional spokesmen – provide.

These two aspects of news production – the practical pressures of constantly working against the clock and the professional demands of impartiality and objectivity – combine to produce a systematically structured *over-accessing* to the media of those in powerful and privileged institutional positions. The media thus tend, faithfully and impartially, to reproduce symbolically the existing structure of power in society's institutional order. This is what Becker has called the 'hierarchy of credibility' – the likelihood that those in powerful or high-status positions in society who offer opinions about controversial topics will have their definitions accepted, because such spokesmen are understood to have access to more accurate or more specialised information on particular topics than the majority of the population.[7] The result of this structured preference given in the media to the opinions of the powerful is that these 'spokesmen' become what we call the *primary definers* of topics.

What is the significance of this? It could rightly be argued that through the requirement of 'balance' [. . .] alternative definitions do get a hearing: each 'side' *is* allowed to present its case. In point of fact [. . .] the setting up of a topic in terms of a debate within which there are oppositions and conflicts is also one way of *dramatising* an event so as to enhance its newsworthiness. The important point about the structured relationship between the media and the primary institutional definers is that it permits the institutional definers to establish the initial definition or *primary interpretation* of the topic in question. This interpretation then 'commands the field' in all subsequent treatment and sets the terms of reference within which all further coverage or debate takes place. Arguments *against* a primary interpretation are forced to insert themselves into *its* definition of 'what is at issue' – they must begin from this framework of interpretation as their starting-point. This initial interpretative framework – what Lang and Lang have called an 'inferential structure'[8] – is extremely difficult to alter fundamentally, once established. For example, once race relations in Britain have been defined as a 'problem of numbers' (i.e. how many blacks there are in the country), then even liberal spokesmen, in proving that the figures for black immigrants have been exaggerated, are nevertheless obliged to subscribe, implicitly, to the view that the debate is 'essentially' *about numbers.*

[. . .]

Effectively, then, the primary definition *sets the limit* for all subsequent discussion by *framing what the problem is*. This initial framework then provides the criteria by which all subsequent contributions are labelled as 'relevant' to the debate, or 'irrelevant' – beside the point. Contributions which stray from this framework are exposed to the charge that they are 'not addressing the problem'.[9]

The media, then, do not simply 'create' the news; nor do they simply transmit the ideology of the 'ruling class' in a conspiratorial fashion. Indeed, we have suggested that, in a critical sense, the media are frequently not the 'primary definers' of news events at all; but their structured relationship to power has the effect of making them play a crucial but secondary role in *reproducing* the definitions of those who have privileged access, as of right, to the media as 'accredited sources'. From this point of view, in the moment of news production, the media stand in a position of structured subordination to the primary definers.

It is this structured relationship – between the media and its 'powerful' sources – which begins to open up the neglected question of the *ideological role* of the media. It is this which begins to give substance and specificity to Marx's basic proposition that 'the ruling ideas of any age are the ideas of its ruling class'. Marx's contention is that this dominance of 'ruling ideas' operates primarily because, in addition to its ownership and control of the means of material production, this class also owns and controls the means of 'mental production'. In producing their definition of social reality, and the place of 'ordinary people' within it, they construct a particular image of society which represents particular class interests as the interests of all members of society. Because of their control over material and mental resources, and their domination of the major institutions of society, this class's definitions of the social world provide the basic rationale for those institutions which protect and reproduce their 'way of life'. This control of mental resources ensures that theirs are the most powerful and 'universal' of the available definitions of the social world. Their universality ensures that they are shared to some degree by the subordinate classes of the society. Those who govern, govern also through ideas; thus they govern with the consent of the subordinate classes, and not principally through their overt coercion. Parkin makes a similar point: 'the social and political definitions of those in dominant positions tend to become objectified in the major institutional orders, so providing the moral framework for the entire social system.'[10]

In the major social, political and legal institutions of society, coercion and constraint are never wholly absent. This is as true for the media as elsewhere. For example, reporters and reporting *are* subject to economic and legal constraints, as well as to more overt forms of censorship (e.g. over the coverage of events in Northern Ireland). But the transmission of 'dominant ideas' depends *more* on non-coercive mechanisms for their reproduction. Hierarchical structures of command and review, informal socialisation into institutional roles, the sedimenting of dominant ideas into the 'professional ideology' – all help to ensure, within the media, their continued reproduction in the dominant form. What we have been pointing to in this section is *precisely how one particular professional practice ensures that the media, effectively but 'objectively', play a key role in reproducing the dominant field of the ruling ideologies.*

[. . .]

NOTES

1. C. MacDougall, *Interpretative Reporting* (New York: Macmillan, 1968) p. 12.
2. For a fuller account of the impact of these 'bureaucratic' factors in news production, see P. Rock, 'News as Eternal Recurrence', in *The Manufacture of News: Social Problems, Deviance and the Mass Media*, ed. S. Cohen and J. Young (London: Constable, 1973).
3. L. Wirth, 'Consensus and Mass Communications', *American Sociological Review*, vol. 13, 1948.
4. Rock, 'News as Eternal Recurrence', p. 77.
5. G. Murdock, 'Mass Communication and the Construction of Meaning', in *Rethinking Social Psychology*, ed. N. Armistead (Harmondsworth: Penguin, 1974) p. 210.
6. For a historical account of the evolution of those rules, see J. W. Carey, 'The Communications Revolution and the Professional Communicator', *Sociological Review Monograph*, vol. 13, 1969.
7. H. Becker, 'Whose Side are We on?', in *The Relevance of Sociology*, ed. J. D. Douglas (New York: Appleton-Century-Crofts, 1972).
8. K. Lang and G. Lang, 'The Inferential Structure of Political Communications', *Public Opinion Quarterly*, vol. 19, Summer 1955.
9. See S. M. Hall, 'The "Structured Communication" of Events', paper for the Obstacles to Communication Symposium, UNESCO/Division of Philosophy (available from Centre for Contemporary Cultural Studies, University of Birmingham); Clarke et al., 'The Selection of Evidence and the Avoidance of Racialism: a Critique of the Parliamentary Select Committee on Race Relations and Immigration', *New Community*, vol III, no. 3, Summer 1974..
10. F. Parkin, *Class Inequality and Political Order* (London: MacGibbon & Kee, 1971) p. 83.

45

THE FALKLANDS CONFLICT:
THE HOME FRONT

Glasgow University Media Group

> Mrs Thatcher said it made us realise we are all really one family.
>
> BBC1, 21.00, 21.5.82

This chapter analyses the image TV news constructed of the nation at war. The bulk of TV news reports on the 'Home front' were about the relatives of the Task Force waiting at home. We look at this coverage in detail, finding that the Task Force families – the women in particular – were mainly presented as models of support for the war but were largely denied the possibility of expressing their own opinions and doubts.

TASK FORCE FAMILIES

The relatives and friends of those serving on the Task Force had a crucial part to play in reporting the home front. Although the viewing public was assumed to have an insatiable appetite for Falklands news, and the Prime Minister insisted that the Falklands 'were but a heartbeat away', most British people were not directly involved. Few had previously heard of the Falklands; the fighting was invisible, thousands of miles away, and (in the judgement of the *Financial Times* of 7 April, 1982) 'no vital national interest in any material or strategic sense' was at stake. But friends and families of men and women on the Task Force were 'deeply involved in the current events' (BBC2, 22.45, 5.5.82); reports on their plight became a familiar item on the news, appearing three or four times on each channel in the first week of the fighting. Their experiences were part of the national experience of the war; their human reactions and emotions were offered up to the rest of us via the TV, to provide the Falklands story with a 'human interest' angle, allowing us to share a surrogate personal involvement in the distant and confusing campaign. As one service man's wife put it: 'Ordinary people with no military involvement felt it was *their* lads out there, fighting for what they believed in' (Sara Jones, *Options* magazine, April 1983).

From Glasgow University Media Group, *War and Peace News* (Milton Keynes: Open University Press, 1985) pp. 93–104.

We analysed a total of 141 items relating to Task Force families from 390 bulletins recorded over the period 1 May to 14 June 1982. Seventy-one dealt with families waiting at home (twenty-three of these concerned the Royal Family), fifty-one with partings and reunions, and eighteen with memorial services. In some cases the views of relations were highlighted, as in these reports on the first deaths of British servicemen: 'The father of a Sea Harrier pilot who also died has said, "I'm proud to have a son who died for the country he loved"' (ITN, 13.00, 5.5.82).

When the *Sheffield* sank, one bereaved mother appeared, saying:

> I'm proud of him, I'm extremely proud of him, and if he's gone to war and fought for his country, and died for his country, I'd like everybody to feel that it's not in vain.
>
> BBC1, 21.00, 6.5.82

But during the whole period of the fighting we found only one case of a bereaved relative's doubts over the campaign being quoted – in this report on the casualties of HMS *Sheffield*:

> Twenty-year-old Neil Goodall had planned to get engaged at Easter. Instead he sailed with the Task Force . . . His mother who lived in Middlesex said, "My son never joined the Navy to die for something as wasteful as this."
>
> ITN, 22.00, 6.5.82

We found only two interviews with relatives suggesting that the loss of life might not be worth it: in one late-night bulletin on BBC2, a naval wife says:

> I didn't want them to go out there . . . I feel now I'd like to see it go to the United Nations . . . I feel there has been too much bloodshed already and I feel that if there is any more the nation is going to turn against the government.
>
> BBC, 22.45, 5.5.82

While in an interview on a lunchtime bulletin two naval wives give their opinion:

> I just think neither of them want to lose face, do they?

> Just give it back to them . . . I mean it's our men that's out there, if they can blow up one ship, how many more are going to go? It's ridiculous.
>
> BBC1, 12.30, 5.5.82

In the main bulletins on the same channel later in the same day, these less-than-supportive remarks are edited out and replaced with an interview with the wives of two survivors, in which the only question raised is: 'How did you pass the time?' (BBC1, 17.40, 5.5.82).

Apart from these exceptions in the first days of fighting, the Task Force families appeared only as supporters of the campaign; and as the losses mounted and their suffering increased, they disappeared from our screens, not to be readmitted until afterwards on the return of the survivors, to display what the TV journalists described as 'the indescribable joy of knowing that a loved one is safe' (ITN, 22.00, 11.6.82).

If this was the TV image, what was the true experience of those at home who were close to someone on the Task Force? Obviously it is not possible to measure or summarise all the varied attitudes and reactions of people who lived through the war knowing that someone close to them daily faced death or disablement. It is hard to imagine the full cost of war in human terms, the impact on people's lives when men were killed or injured. The Task Force friends and relatives, however, had no choice but to face up to and bear the human costs – this was precisely what made them such an important group for the TV coverage of the war at home. From this perspective, their views on the war understandably varied. Many remained loyal to the Task Force whatever happened. One bereaved mother said:

> I miss him terribly. Sometimes I would have felt better if I had gone to war. If I could have laid down my life for him I would. I loved him so much. But it was such a worthwhile thing. They went because they were needed. It wasn't a waste. I wouldn't ever accept that.
>
> Pamela Smith, mother of a corporal killed at Mount Harriet, *Sunday Times*, 3.5.82

Without denying the strength of such loyalty and pride, or the personal conviction that the British cause was just and 'it wasn't a waste', it is important to realise that not all relatives reacted in the same way. It would be facile to try to draw a line between 'supporters' and 'critics' of the campaign – relatives could feel both anger and loyalty:

> I'm bitter he went through Ireland and then got killed for an island nobody had ever heard of. They should have blown it out of the sea. But I knew he'd like it this way because he was so proud of his country.
>
> Jean Murdoch, mother of lance-corporal killed on the Falklands, *Glasgow Evening Times*, 8.7.82

However, many expressed definite opposition to the war in the light of their own experiences:

> We probably all thought it was worth it at the time . . . but when you finally do lose someone, it makes you wonder then whether it was worth it. I probably would've thought it was if my brother hadn't been lost in it, but it makes you look at it completely differently when you lose someone.
>
> Ben Bullers, brother of a sailor killed on *Sir Galahad*, *The Friday Alternative*, (Channel 4, 7.1.83)

> I think it should never have happened – this government virtually invited Argentina in . . . Throughout this whole crisis the only ones who really feel it are those who have actually lost someone or had someone injured. It just doesn't hit home with the rest of us, and that's the unpleasant reality – that's why they can yell and cheer on the quayside . . . There's no glory to war, and despite what's being said about patriotism really – what's there to be proud to be British about?
>
> Brenda Thomas, wife of a caterer on a Task Force aircraft carrier, *Spare Rib*, August 1982

> I am proud of my son, but not proud of the fact that he died for his country in a war which was not necessary. I accept that it's a serviceman's duty to fight, but in a futile situation like this, I think it's evil to put men's lives at risk when negotiations around a table can save so much heartbreak.
>
> Mrs Samble, mother of a sailor killed on HMS *Glamorgan*, *Bridport News*, 18.6.82

> David had to die because of crass error, and weakness disguised as boldness in high places.
>
> Hugh Tinker, father of lieutenant killed on HMS *Glamorgan*, *A Message from the Falklands*, Junction Books, 1982

He did not die for his country, he died because of his country. There were men in charge
of that strip who were paid to know better.

Mrs Gillian Parsons, mother of a Welsh Guard killed at Bluff Cove, *Week in Week Out*,
BBC Wales, 25.3.83

So there was a clear current of opinion among the Task Force relatives against the conduct
of the campaign. It could have been expressed, and might possibly have had some impact
on the views of the 'ordinary people with no military connection' who felt 'it was their lads
out there'. But the TV news representation of the Task Force relatives' emotions was carefully
controlled. The relatives' support for their loved ones was used to obscure their real thoughts
about whether they should have been sent to war at all.

Soon after the sinking of HMS *Sheffield* on 4 May 1982, the BBC Board of Governors issued a
firm ruling that the relatives of the dead would not be interviewed at all. The official grounds
were those of 'privacy' and 'taste', but the *effect* was to silence those who could have told us
most directly about the human costs of the fighting,[1] and to censor any doubts they may have
had about whether the fighting was worthwhile. The BBC did make certain special exceptions.
At an NCA meeting where fears of 'undermining the national will' were discussed, the chief of
current affairs programmes mentioned that:

> *Nationwide* had shown one [interview with a bereaved relative] which, was impeccable and
> had given him no concern on any score. He had referred to ADG [the Assistant Director
> General], had then discussed it with DG [the Director General], and had been given the
> go-ahead.

NCA minutes, 8.6.82

Nationwide's 'impeccable' interview featured a widow who worked for a naval wives' self-help
organisation, saying, 'I certainly don't feel bitter', and talking about another woman whose
husband was killed on the same ship – 'she's absolutely marvellous . . . coping fantastically'
(*Nationwide*, 4.6.82).

A number of assumptions were made by the TV reporters about the role that relatives were to
play on the screen. The BBC Assistant Director General's justification of the ban on interviews
with the bereaved is interesting here:

> Put brutally, interviewing a widow was an 'easy' story and he was strongly against an
> opening of the floodgates when restrictions were eased. The answers that the bereaved
> would give were, after all, largely predictable.

NCA, 8.6.82

The journalistic consideration (an 'easy' story) is put above the right of people directly affected
by the war to express their views. He dismisses as 'largely predictable' the whole variety of
reactions among people struggling to understand and judge a controversial war in which they
had to sacrifice a close relative. Most revealingly, reporting on the bereaved has to mean
'interviewing a widow'.

WIVES, MOTHERS AND SWEETHEARTS

This last assumption reveals one of the main preconceptions structuring the coverage of the
Task Force relatives: that those left behind are all women. Although those serving on the Task
Force had men and women close to them – fathers, brothers and lovers were left behind as well
as wives and mothers – the TV news framework evidently sees that it is *women* who wait while

the men go and fight; 'widows' who are left when they die. In a total of forty-eight interviews with relatives at home during the period of the fighting only four men appear: three 'proud' fathers, and Prince Charles who says that Prince Andrew is 'doing the most important job' (ITN, 21.15, 26.5.82).

All the remaining relatives are wives, mothers and fiancées. The conviction that waiting is the *women's* role is so total that 'wives' seems interchangeable with 'families' in the journalists' vocabulary:

> These remarks highlighted a particular problem for the *families* of servicemen, of which reports to believe and which to discount. [Our reporter] has been finding out how naval *wives* in Portsmouth have been coping.
>
> ITN, 17.45, 5.5.82

> The calls from distressed *families* for news about their men went on all night. But in the large naval estates around Portsmouth the grief is being shared by all the *wives*.
>
> ITN, 17.45, 5.5.82

> The company has invited *wives and families* of the crew of the QE2 to a meeting . . . The *wives and mothers* of merchant seaman have found the waiting war a lonely one.
>
> BBC1, 17.40, 3.5.82

A further indication of the way the news treated waiting at home as a 'women's affair' is that women reporters were more visible here than in any other area of the Falklands coverage. Over half the reports on families at home were done by women reporters, who covered only a small minority of the diplomatic, political news, and only one military story (on the Red Cross 'safe' zone in Port Stanley).

It is very unusual for married women in the home to appear on the news. An underlying assumption is that serious news stories should be about public events – government proposals, stock market movements, etc. The lives of women at home are taken as a sort of steady background, only 'newsworthy' in this case because the men are absent, and because the men are making news. Having selected 'ordinary' married women's thoughts and lives as an issue in these extraordinary circumstances, the TV journalists present them in a traditional women's role, which does not include expressing dissident views. Reports on the relatives are approached as 'human interest' items, 'soft' news stories where the issue at stake is how wives and mothers, sitting at home with emotions rather than political opinions, cope with the waiting. Given the rare chance of reports from naval housing estates to present an area of life that the news normally neglects, the TV journalists find themselves falling back on the old-fashioned stereotypes of women's role and family life.

According to the 1980 General Household Survey, conventional family units – couples living with children – make up only 31% of households.* Households where the woman is dependent on the man and stays at home to look after the children are only 13%. Altogether, two thirds of married women have paid jobs outside the home. This is not to cast doubt on the genuine warmth, security and family solidarity that the TV cameras captured, or the depth of joy and relief felt in reunions with survivors after the war. The point is that the TV news portrait of the

---

* This represents the percentage at a given moment in time but such family arrangements are a stage of life which many people pass through. Consequently at any given moment some people have just left such arrangements and others are about to enter into them.

nation at war was *selective*, and that it selected images of unity and families, concealing much of the real conflict and true attitudes within the country. This is as true of the image of family life as the image of broader public opinion.

The news reports present the conventional stereotypes. Women are shown in relation to men, and not at all as individuals in their own right. In the coverage of Task Force wives, mothers and fiancées, we do not hear any details of their jobs, for instance, or any activity at all apart from waiting for their men.[2] These are typical introductions to interviews with two women:

> Karen Murphin's only source of information was on news bulletins. She last saw her husband in November. Since then Kevin, who is a stoker, and his shipmates were in the Mediterranean before going to the Falklands.
>
> ITN, 22.05, 5.5.82

> He was the ship's NAAFI manager, although he had in fact served previously in the Army. His employers, the NAAFI, say they're proud of him; so are his family.
>
> BBC1, 21.00, 24.5.82

In one fairly long interview with a naval wife, the woman is not even named; instead the camera zooms in on her two-year-old son as she feeds him, and the reporter begins:

> Peter Goodfellow's father is a sailor too. He was the engineering officer aboard the frigate HMS *Antelope*. Commander Goodfellow was injured. When the news was first broken to his wife, the Navy still had no idea of the extent of his injuries. She had to wait.
>
> BBC1, 18.00, 4.6.82

He tells us about the man's job, and even the two-year-old boy's name is given, but we hear about the woman.

The women are most commonly interviewed with babies or young children on their knees. Every report from naval married quarters estates includes a shot of women with children, used as 'wallpaper footage', while the reporter's voice-over reminds us, 'But for the women and children life must go on' (ITN, 13.00, 5.5.82). We are shown close-ups of weeping widows at memorial services, but they only kneel and weep, they are given no chance to speak. When they are picked out of the congregation they are identified only in relation to their men:

> Wives of Acting Chef Michael Till and Petty Officer Anthony Norman. Both men died when an Exocet missile hit the *Sheffield*.
>
> ITN, 20.45, 9.5.82

> Early arrivals were the widows of two of the men who perished, Petty Officer Anthony Norman and Acting Chef Michael Till.
>
> BBC1, 21.30, 9.5.82

Since so few *male* relatives were featured, it is not possible to make a properly representative comparison with TV's presentation of men left at home in the same posiiton; but one was Prince Charles whose life is detailed elsewhere in the news; another is referred to by name and occupation:

> A second man that died as a result of the explosion that destroyed the frigate HMS *Antelope* on Sunday . . . Today his father Mr Stanley Stevens, who's a miner, said . . . Stevens had died for a good cause.

ITN, 17.45, 27.5.82

A third male relative appeared after his son was awarded a DSC. He is filmed at his radio as the reporter begins, 'At his home in Anglesey, Keith Mill's father Alan, who's a keen amateur radio enthusiast, has already passed the news to radio hams in Montevideo'; and is then interviewed declaring, 'I'm absolutely delighted . . . and obviously very very proud to be his father' (BBC1, 13.00, 4.6.82).

Female relatives, by contrast, are shown without occupations or interests outside the home, waiting anxiously for their men, listening to the news, looking after children and weeping for the dead. This is not confined to women in Britain: a report on a Falkland Islands woman who had escaped to Chile to have her child identifies her husband by his job and shows the woman, as usual, 'waiting':

> In spite of worries about the safety of her husband on the Falklands, the birth went beautifully, a fine 8 lb baby girl, Zoe Alexandra, born here in Chile, but nationality British Falkland Islander. And her lucky father is *Alex Betts, an accountant* in Port Stanley . . . In the next days Rosa will leave hospital to *wait* for her island home's liberation.
>
> BBC1, 17.05, 25.5.82

As well as being shown only within and in relation to their families, women are portrayed, not as active members of society, but more as vessels of emotion. TV reporters seem scarcely interested in what they think or what they do, but only in what they *feel*. There are only two cases in the period when any relatives are invited to speak for themselves about the political implications of the Falklands War:

> Now that Ian has been hurt, how do you feel about the Falklands crisis and Britain and Argentina? Do you still support Britain's stance?
>
> ITN, 20.45, 2.5.82

> What have been your thoughts since the Task Force left? Have you had any thoughts about what the government should be doing in all this?
>
> BBC2, 22.45, 5.5.82

On both occasions the women showed themselves perfectly able to give cogent answers. There were no intrinsic reasons to stop asking this sort of question, but none the less it is not raised again in the other forty-six interviews. Instead, we endlessly hear the question, 'How do/did you feel?'[3]

Whenever men are interviewed, there is a marked sex difference in the questioning, as if men are *not* expected to have feelings. For example, in a *vox pop.* on Londoners' reactions to the sinking of HMS *Sheffield* (ITN, 13.00, 5.5.82), the interviewer asks seven men in the street what they 'think' or 'believe' – the main question being, 'Do you *think* it was inevitable?' Only one woman appears, and for her the question is, 'Can we just ask you how you *felt* when you heard about HMS *Sheffield*?'

In a 'human interest' end-of-bulletin story about the wedding of a lieutenant commander who was about to leave for the Falklands ('Despite the crisis, wedding celebrations went ahead this afternoon at a country church . . . for all concerned the timing has proved exactly right' – BBC1, 22.10, 8.5.82), the bridegroom is asked whether his marriage is 'going to make things more difficult for you if it comes to action?', while the bride is asked how she *feels* about being separated so soon. Reporters sometimes see the answers as very 'predictable' in this sort of questioning:

Reporter. How were you feeling as the *QE2* came up? Did you glimpse him up on the deck? Did you see him?

Woman. No, I didn't have my glasses on.

Reporter. Through tears probably.

ITN, 22.00, 11.6.82

The reporter assumes, even before he asks, that the woman should feel like crying; although in the same report, an interview is broken off in embarrassment when a *man*, the captain of a sunken ship, understandably distressed, bursts into tears.

The same ideas of a woman's role are revealed elsewhere in the Falklands TV coverage, in casual remarks by journalists, treating women as 'sexual interest', marginal to the real business of the news. For instance, a woman at the dockside in black stockings delivering a singing telegram as the troops embark is picked out and described as 'some cheeky light relief' (BBC1, 21.00, 12.5.82); and over close-ups of women dancers a reporter comments: 'Hot Gossip gave the troops something of what they'll no doubt want to see' (ITN, 20.45, 30.5.82). Women actually involved in the campaign can receive the same sort of treatment: the caption given to the MoD photograph of soldiers talking to women in Port Stanley is '42 Commando met the more decorative of the Islanders'; while the commentary for film of nurses working in a military hospital is 'but now it's over and there's time to chat up a nurse' (both ITN, 22.15, 17.6.82).

An interview with the parents of a stewardess on the requisitioned *QE2* concentrates on her being surrounded by 3,500 men, and the journalists suggests that 'she might have got a taste for it by now . . . *(laughs)*' (BBC1, 11.40, 11.6.82). This sort of innuendo is mild and respectful compared to the coverage in the popular press at the same time. 'Sexy Capers on the Ocean Rave! Buxom blonde Jane Broomfield yesterday spilled the beans on saucy antics that turned the *QE2* into a floating love-nest,' began the *Sun*'s story on the *QE2* stewardess (12.6.82). But although the TV news is more dignified and restrained, it does share similar, very limited preconceptions about women's roles. When the first woman soldiers were sent out to the Falklands garrison after the British regained the islands, the news story (ITN, 22.00, 19.7.83) was about what *clothes* they would wear (evening dresses for off-duty and wellington boots for the mud).

NOTES

1. Servicemen too know the human costs of the fighting from direct experience; but the conditions of their service prevent them from expressing their views in public.

2. There are two possible exceptions: one woman is shown getting married (BBC1, 22.10, 8.5.82), but this is obviously before her husband leaves for the South Atlantic; and a group of women are shown talking to their MP (BBC1, 21.00, 26.5.82), but they are talking about waiting for information about their husbands.

3. The BBC's Assistant Director General notices this too. The NCA minutes of discussion about interviewing relatives record: 'Certainly, ADG said, he would seek the sacking of any reporter who asked "How did you feel?" ' (NCA, 8.5.82); 'The return of the *QE2* had been another example of superb coverage marred by constant repetition of "How did/do you feel?" ADG said enough was enough' (NCA, 15.6.82).

46

WHEN A WOMAN READS THE NEWS

Patricia Holland

ANGELA RIPPON'S LEGS

> The paradox is that the harder they strive being serious in the solemn business of inter-
> national news, the more delightfully coquettish and feminine they appear. By ignoring
> their femininity they heighten it. (*Evening Standard*, 6 June 1979, on what they describe as
> a 'newscasterette')

The *Evening Standard* is not alone in noting that the forms of femininity and sexuality required
of women are not readily compatible with the solemn business of the news. Philip Schlesinger's
study of news production in the BBC was written around the time of the introduction of
women as regular newsreaders, yet he describes his brief account of women in the newsrooms
as a 'digression' from his main discussion. He quotes the senior official who, according to
newsroom folklore, insisted that 'a good reporter needs a pair of balls.' Women reporters give
rise to 'tampax problems' and can't get the right sort of story, especially in situations like Belfast
'where you have to lean against the bar with army officers and swill down pints' (Schlesinger,
1978, p. 155). The imposed limits of femininity, it seems, cannot easily be cast off, especially
in the hard world of news reporting. Women remain a digression, confined to the incidental,
condemned never to break out of a circle in which they merely heighten their femininity if they
attempt to ignore or surpass it. This is despite the fact that from the beginning of broadcasting
in this country there have been examples of women at all levels, in front of and behind the
cameras.

[. . .]

Yet when women newsreaders began to appear regularly on British television in the mid
1970s – Angela Rippon from 1975 and Anna Ford from 1978 – they were greeted as a total
novelty by the press. They were seen as an opportunity for jokes, pictures and suggestive
comments. Every detail of their dress and appearance was commented on, their styles were
compared, their sexuality stressed:

From H. Baehr and G. Dyer (eds), *Boxed In: Women and Television* (London: Pandora Press, 1987) pp. 133–50.

> Could I suggest that Miss Ford cuts out the frosty lipstick and shiny blush-on which makes my screen look wet and slippery? (*Daily Express*, 5 July 1978)

> Angela, your lips are just smack on. (*Daily Mirror*, 29 December 1978)

> Angela is forceful, even dominant. In how many secret viewers' dreams does she deliver the *Nine O'clock News* in black leather. Anna has a twinkle in her eye, a tease in her manner. Together they achieve much for women's equality without loss of – indeed with enhancement of – femininity. (*Sunday Telegraph*, 30 April 1978)

They were described as deadly rivals, like Joan Collins and Linda Evans of *Dynasty*, unable to meet without exchanging a bitchy word. Most of all there was a call to see their legs. Resistance to this call itself became news:

> Forget about legs, storms Anna. Television news girl Anna Ford is fed up with people trying to compare her legs with Angela Rippon's. Anna is also unhappy with 'show us your legs' cat-calls wherever she goes. (*Sun*, 20 March 1979)

Angela Rippon decided to respond in the good-humoured way expected of women. She did a high kicking dance routine on the 1976 Morecombe and Wise Christmas show. The reaction to her performance included a worry that this sort of thing can trivialise the solemn business of public affairs (BBC TV *News: The First 30 Years*, Prod. Gordon Carr, TX 5 July 1984). Angela Rippon and Anna Ford were caught up in a familiar paradox. Women's very presence invites comment. They are associated with the trivial, forbidden the full seriousness of their job, but at the same time they must take the blame for reducing the seriousness of that job, for contaminating it with their own triviality. The public discourse which accompanied the introduction of women newsreaders in the 1970s – that chatter which circulated and continues to circulate as gossip in the newspapers and the club rooms and bars of the BBC and ITN – continually returned to a central problem. Women are about sexuality, the news is not.

Despite the work done by the newspapers at that time, and their efforts to discipline the women and remind them of their place, nearly half of today's television newsreaders are women.

[. . .]

These women face us with confidence. They appear on our screens, a calm, head and shoulders image, presented in the unemphatic way we have long taken for granted in the image of a man. I want to argue that this apparently unremarkable image is a deeply challenging one and that the efforts to limit and control women's appearance have not been overcome but continue, shifted from overt comment and ridicule to more subtle forms of redefinition. There is a continuing effort to remind women of their inescapable position as women, as 'not-men'. This is the repeated process of subordination. If that process is accepted as normal and is acquiesced in, the fact that it can never fully succeed is of little importance. The fact that a few women, or even many women, can escape from its enforced limitations makes little difference to the positioning of women as a group.

The newsreaders' confidence derives partly from the fact that the way they look is less important than what they have to say. The image is subordinate to the speech. For men this is something we take for granted – it is only to be expected – but for women it is an unfamiliar situation. As the newspaper reactions to Angela Rippon and Anna Ford demonstrated, women's right to speak in public may easily be subverted by drawing attention to their visual appearance. The authoritative male newsreader is a well established presence on the screen.

The image of a man, head and shoulders, in formal jacket and tie, is familiar across the media as a sign of assurance and power. It is used to introduce the company report, it appears on the business pages of the quality press, it presents politicians and statesmen. Characteristically it shows a middle-aged man of worldly experience and dignified presence, the lines on his face and his serious expression indicating the respect he commands. But it is an image which contains a problem. By refusing any hint of visual pleasure or sensuality, it attempts to deny its own image-presence. It suggests that this pictured man is not simply framed here to be looked at. His steady gaze, direct at the camera, appears to assert that he is the one doing the looking. He is the controller rather than the controlled, the active subject rather than the passive object. In its rigid formality his physical presence refuses to draw attention to itself, attempts to slide into invisibility. We take it for granted that, like the newsreader, what he has to say is more important than the way he looks. This paradoxical convention for men is in striking contrast to the familiar conventions for women, which contain a different set of problems and inconsistencies. We expect images of women to stress not head and shoulders, but faces and bodies. Women's faces, when they appear, are not normally poised for looking or for speech, but are painted, decorated, presented for beauty and the pleasure of the viewer (Berger, 1972).

[. . .]

On television the visual presentation of a head and shoulders image is always inadequate by itself. Something is missing; the image must be completed. In the case of a man it is unproblematically completed by what he has to say. In the case of a woman the commentators point to an absence of a different sort. For them what is missing is the woman's body. The *Sunday Telegraph* feels free to fantasise about Angela Rippon wearing the black leather of S/M, other newspapers discuss the absence metonymically as 'legs'. The head and shoulders of a man is completed by his speech, the head and shoulders of a woman only draws attention to the need to see her legs. As the *Evening Standard* said, 'By ignoring their femininity they heighten it'.

Women's speech, too, is beset by difficult problems, problems which, like those around the imagery of women, are linked to the very construction of femininity itself. Traditionally women's speech has been downgraded as mere gossip or babble (Spender, 1980). Some feminists want to reject this devaluation and lay claim to the 'neutral' language now appropriated by men. Others have embraced and celebrated a special 'women's language', a language that is more expressive and fluid, which is said to have sprung from a stage of development that was more creative, before the laying down of conventions and prohibitions (Daly, 1979). Yet the image of the woman newsreader has difficulty with both these options. Like the image of the man it claims to be completed not by 'legs' but by speech – a speech which is forbidden to be specifically feminine and must be taken seriously in the public world of the news. The tension between an image which may not forget its femininity and a speech which may not embrace the feminine is central to the challenge posed by women newsreaders.

THE NEWS AND ITS PLACE

The spaces on television that we describe as 'the news' must be understood both in continuity with and in opposition to the rest of the daily output. The audience is expected to understand and respond to 'news' in a way that is different from, say, sitcom, chat shows, or even its close relation 'current affairs' (Schlesinger, et al. 1983). One of the most striking characteristics of the news remains its dramatic under-representation of women.

[. . .]

In news bulletins women still appear on the screen in smaller numbers and more limited roles than men, while opportunities for them to speak are even more restricted. A glance at almost any randomly selected news programme will confirm that women tend to be seen in the background rather than as the main subjects of a news item. They are passing in the street, shopping, working in a canteen or hospital. Certain well-known women, like Princess Diana and other Royals, actresses and performers, make regular non-speaking appearances as part of the public spectacle, but women rarely appear in their own right as actors in those fields which are the central concern of the news and they are rarely selected as experts to comment on or interpret the news. When they are invited to speak it tends to be either as an anonymous example of uninformed public opinion, as housewife, consumer, neighbour, or as mother, sister, wife of the man in the news, or as victim – of crime, disaster, political policy. Thus not only do they speak less frequently, but they tend to speak as passive reactors and witnesses to public events rather than as participants in those events (compare Goulden et al., 1982, p. 81). The use of women as regular newsreaders and to a lesser extent as reporters, has made a dramatic difference to the gender balance of news programmes.

The expulsion of women from the news can only be fully understood when it is seen in the context of the whole of the television output. John Ellis has argued that the television flow is typically divided not into programmes, but into 'segments' of around two to five minutes in length – an advertisement, a news item, a single scene in a soap opera (Ellis, 1982). Faced with this irregular sequence, members of the audience do not turn on for discrete uninterrupted cultural events as in the cinema or theatre, but they compose their viewing from fragments, dropping in and out, catching the end of one programme or the opening titles of another, perhaps turning their backs or watching with only half their attention. Recent studies of the television audience have shown that it is actually made up of many audiences, each reacting differently to different parts of the programme output. Women and men, in particular, tend to have radically different tastes. Thus the experience of watching together becomes itself a re-enactment of the relations of power between them. The man of the house tends to be in charge of the programme selector. It is left to the woman to react to the imposition of programmes she dislikes by leaving the room, busying herself with other tasks or mentally switching off (see [Gray, 1987]; Collett, 1986; Morley, 1986). When we look at the way women are represented in the news it is not surprising that this is one area of television that women in the audience feel is not for them; they pay little attention to it even though it is frequently on in their presence.

However, the news is only part of a stream of material. It flows inexorably out of and in to the quiz shows, the sports reports, the American cops series that surround it and the advertisements which, on ITV, interrupt it. This is the mass of material from which the disparate audiences can select their imagery and construct their impressions. The reduced visibility of women in the news is more emphatic, carries more significance, precisely because of its routine juxtaposition with their heightened visibility in the rest of the output. Those qualities that are absent from the news are inescapably present elsewhere. When we watch the serious face of the newsreader we are reminded that women's faces on television normally display emotion (in soaps, feature films, dramas), that women's bodies are part of the spectacle of television (in the ads, in game shows, as entertainers), that women are characteristically placed in a domestic setting (in sitcoms, family dramas) and that their sexuality is never forgotten. Standing in sharp opposition to the rest of this output the news is presented as a space where emotion is inappropriate, where domestic issues are defined as private and as subordinate to public conflict and the world of hard politics, and where women's sexuality is trivialising and a distraction.

There are important distinctions of style and content to be made within news programmes themselves, the most significant being between two types of realism which operate simultaneously (Ellis, 1982, pp. 6–7). Each has a different implication for women. First there is the actuality of the filmed footage, the news items themselves. This is a realism of record. It seeks pictures from as close to an event as possible, transmitted to the audience as quickly as possible. Second there is a narrative realism provided by the studio and the presenters. A news programme takes place in the real time of the studio. Following the visual dazzle of the title sequence we are given a shot of the whole studio, an image of calm in its pale blues and greys, with the newsreaders relaxed yet prepared behind their sweeping desk. Firmly located in this secure and recognisible space, they greet us directly, then guide us through the programme. They act as narrators who can summon up other forms of input – stills, graphics, filmed reports – and weave them back into the overall shape of the programme. The actuality items are thus held together in a sequential narrative flow in which incoherences can be sorted out and contradictions contained.

[. . .]

Thus a double thread runs through the news and its imagery, a search for excitement and a concern with the seriousness of status and power. Both themes depend on values that are recognised as masculine and both deal with areas from which women are excluded. The actuality material is a collection of disparate and fragmented short items – characters and topics. Each item selects a high point from what could otherwise be seen as a complex of social and political relations. History is largely eradicated, depth of understanding sacrificed for the sense of immediacy, the effort to get as close as possible to the experience of an event.

[. . .]

The excitement of gathering this type of news calls for the competitive spirit of reporters who have 'balls' – 'The target is to be first and best. There are no second prizes,' declared the IBA's *Guide in Independent Broadcasting*, 1985.

We would expect such material to evoke a strong emotional response from the audience – a special sort of pleasure. We watch with fascinated horror the flames of the inner city riot, the suspense-filled moments of the hijacked aircraft waiting on the tarmac: events whose outcome is still unknown. But the pleasurable excitement to which these images give rise is rapidly transformed by their management and presentation as 'news'. We are allowed only a brief glimpse into the troubled and chaotic world before we are returned to the security of the studio and handed over to the reassuring presence of the newsreaders. The continuity they provide literally contains the unstable material of the actuality footage, dealing with it and making it manageable. It is their task to replace the moment of action with the serious face of the expert commentator, be it politician, academic or special correspondent, who can return that moment back to the responsible world of public affairs. The 'talking heads', public figures speaking responsibly on matters of import, form the main visual mode of the seriousness of the news. It is they who moderate the moments of excitement and it is they who deal with those other major topics of the news, what Chris Dunkley once described as the 'depressing agenda' of politics, industry, economics and defence (Dunkley, 1981). The high seriousness of these subjects and of those who are called on to present them temper and control the illicit pleasures of the actuality dramas with which they interleave.

This area of seriousness and responsibility excludes women in its own way. Women are vastly outnumbered by men in positions of social and political power, by those whose views are most likely to be reported on or whose opinions sought. They include prominent politicians, police chiefs, union leaders, judges and bishops. Stuart Hall and his colleagues describe them as 'primary definers' of the issues of the day (Hall et al., 1978). They are individuals who are likely to have built up relationships with those who make the news through both formal and informal channels. Women are not prominent among them. Women are expelled from the imagery of the news just as they are expelled from those areas of public life from which the news is derived.

Here I must add the reminder that I am discussing the main national news programmes and not the local and regional programmes. Local news deals in a completely different range of topics and imagery and includes many items on social problems and everyday life. Indeed, where the national news discusses policy and interviews policymakers, the local news of necessity looks at the effects of policies and speaks to those who must carry them out and those who suffer them, often predominantly women.

In the national news, the area where women now play an increasingly visible part is that of presentation – as reporters who speak over and appear in the actuality footage and as newsreaders in the studio. It is in the studio, where they have become part of the narrative continuity of the news, that their presence has made the most noticeable change. Is there some quality expected of newsreaders which, despite the apparent contradictions, is turning this into a suitable role for women to play? The readers sit between the audience and the news, not quite belonging to either, but offering themselves as a point of identification through which the news can be understood. They mediate between the audience and the rawness of the actuality items, distancing viewers from potential involvement, placing them as willing observers, as people who are eager to be informed but never to be involved, as witnesses rather than participants in the reported events. Is this role of mediation and management one that can be reconciled with the forms of femininity that have been constructed out of power relations between women and men? To understand what is happening when a woman reads the news we must look more closely at the ways in which newsreaders' speech has evolved.

THE VOICE OF AUTHORITY VERSUS SECTIONAL INTERESTS

Newsreaders belong to that group of performers on television who may look directly into the camera and hence directly at the viewer. This privilege is largely reserved for those whose presence and whose speech is sanctioned by the institution itself. By contrast, interviewees must direct their eyes slightly to one side of the camera where the interviewer sits and acts as mediator for their address. Yet for the newsreaders the intimacy of their direct gaze is in striking contrast to the formality of their speech. Apart from the relaxed moments at the beginning and end of each programme – 'That's all from us, we'll be back with you tomorrow' – they may not speak on their own behalf.

News is a form of knowledge. The newsreaders appear as those who know and whose job it is to pass their knowledge on. The professionals of the news are at pains to stress that this knowledge that constitutes news must not be partial. It cannot vary according to the knower and therein lies its jealously guarded objectivity. The newsreader, as the voice of that objectivity, may not present a point of view and may not speak from any recognised standpoint. To do so would be to admit to a 'sectional interest'. The newsreader must be the very voice of objective knowledge, must lay claim to a form of speech that can legitimately offer an account of the world and inhabit a position that will have universal validity. Yet the impartiality and objectivity of that voice is guaranteed from within the institution itself.

[. . .]

The voice of objective knowledge merges almost imperceptibly into the voice of authority, the claim to accuracy and truth of the one masking the power relations implied in the other.

Clearly these claims present a problem for women, who neither see themselves or their interests represented in the subject matter of the news, nor tend to be among those who can shape institutional authority. Yet this voice of objectivity also makes a claim to universality. The news institutions have appropriated the right to speak for all people, and the powerful institution feels it must defend itself against those who cry that it does not, in fact, speak for them.

[. . .]

Those outside this balance of power, women among them, must remain as a sectional interest. However, the claim of the BBC to speak with a single, authoritative voice is not natural or inevitable. It was fought for and achieved in the early days of sound broadcasting.

[. . .]

By the 1970s the confident assumptions of universality and neutrality shared by ITN and BBC news were challenged from many sides.

[. . .]

Many groups stood outside the recognised balance of power and were now demanding that their voices should be heard.

[. . .]

The notion that we now live in a complex and plural society has become part of the received wisdom of the programmers of the 1970s and 1980s and the news institutions have reacted defensively. The BBC *Year Book* for 1985 describes a 'polarised audience who sometimes find it difficult to accept the BBC's neutrality'. Krishan Kumar writing in 1977 saw the changing role of professional broadcasters – that is of the presenters, interviewers and newsreaders who speak on behalf of the organisation – as a kind of adaptive response to the fluctuating pressures on the BBC. The stress is now on professionalism and a certain kind of popular appeal rather than on the moral and cultural conviction of earlier days. It is in this context of a challenge to the claims to universality and an adaptable reassertion of those claims that women have become cautiously established as newsreaders.

WHEN A WOMAN READS THE NEWS

Women have become established as newsreaders, but they have not moved alongside men in the same way as those prestigious professional broadcasters, like Robin Day or David Dimbleby, whose popular presence is balanced by the political respect they command. Instead they are caught within the conflicting definitions of femininity and of 'the news' – themselves trivialised, they can be blamed for trivialising. Women represent the antithesis of news values. They are the very sign of dissent and disruption. Yet the job of the newsreader is to smooth over dissent, to provide the studio calm which receives and moderates the chaos from outside. Women newsreaders are called on to speak from a carefully constructed position, with the mythical neutrality of the universal voice, and yet, as women, they are defined as outside both the political consensus and the masculine structure of language. They cannot escape their femininity, yet the possibility of making a contribution that is specifically on behalf of women is ruled out. They may not speak as women or for women. Women newsreaders must search for a visual style that stresses their femininity yet defers to the seriousness of the news, that complements that of the man, yet takes care not to impinge on the male preserve. Hair that has not been 'done', lack of make-up, the less studied appearance associated with feminism, must be avoided. They must embrace the 'post-feminist' worked-on appearance of the young businesswoman of the 1980s, a style made current in advertisements and magazines directed at women executives. Their self-presentation must stress a rigid and unbridgeable *difference* between men and women, while distracting from the continuing process of *differentiation*.

However, it is not an eternal and unchangeable difference but the process of differentiation itself which works to secure and resecure the relations of domination and subordination between men and women. It is a process which is flexible, able to change its ground, to adapt to circumstances, to re-establish new forms of relations of power. The invitation to speak with the voice of authority may be nothing but an invitation, yet again, to be a decorative performer. Women have become accustomed to being asked to identify with men and to express themselves through men. Any attempt to speak with a universal voice within a system grounded in deep divisions of domination and subordination is doomed to failure. The question may not be, 'Can women speak from this position?' but 'Do they want to?' The feminine position in which we have been placed is surely one we would wish to recover and make use of rather than to deny. If the cost of being offered a public voice involves giving up the right to speak specifically as a woman, is it a price worth paying? Should we not argue that the voice of those who are subordinated can reach for an expression of truth to experience that is denied to an authority grounded in domination? Theirs is 'the sound mind whose soundness is what ails it' (Adorno, 1973).

The appearance of women newsreaders is not necessarily a step towards women's liberation. In the contemporary style of news presentation where the reader may be recognised as a front, a mask, a performer, a transmitter rather than an originator of news, it is not difficult to imagine news reading becoming a 'women's job'. After all women are easy on the eye, speak clearly and still add that element of spice that the press found so exciting in Anna, Angela and the rest. If we are not watchful we will find that once more, with the infinite flexibility of effortless power, women will have been put in their place yet again.

REFERENCES

Adorno, T. (1973), *Negative Dialectics*, trans. E. B. Ashton, London, Routledge & Kegan Paul.

Berger, J. (1972), *Ways of Seeing*, Harmondsworth, Penguin.

Collett, P. (1986), 'Watching the TV audience', paper presented to the International Television Studies Conference, London.

Daly, M. (1979), *Gyn-ecology*, Boston, Beacon Press.

Dunkley, C. (1981), 'The news that fits the view', in *Financial Times*, 4 February.

Ellis, J. (1982), *Visible Fictions*, London, Routledge & Kegan Paul. [See Chapter 17 in this volume.]

Goulden, H. et al. (1982), 'Consciousness razing', in S. Blanchard and D. Morley (eds), *What's this Channel Fo(u)r? An Alternative Report*, London, Comedia.

[Gray, A. (1987), 'Behind closed doors: video recorders in the home', in *Boxed In: Women and Television*, London, Pandara Press. [See also Chapter 34 in this volume.]

Hall, S. et al. (1978), *Policing the Crisis*, London, Macmillan [See also Chapter 44 in this volume.]

Kumar, K. (1977), 'Holding the middle ground', in J. Curran et al. (eds), *Mass Communication and Society*, London, Edward Arnold.

Morley, D. (1986), 'Family television: cultural power and domestic leisure', paper presented to International Television Studies Conference, London.

Schlesinger, P. (1978) *Putting 'Reality' Together*, London, Constable.

Schlesinger, P. et al. (1983), *Television Terrorism*, London, Comedia.

Spender, D. (1980), *Manmade language*, London, Routledge & Kegan Paul.

47

NEWS CONTENT AND AUDIENCE BELIEF

Greg Philo

[. . .]

The press and television are sometimes accused of selectivity in their reporting. The sheer scale of the events in the [Miners'] Strike [of 1984–5] meant that there were very many different stories and incidents which could potentially be highlighted. It is important to grasp the magnitude of the events in order to see how such a process of selection can work. At this time there were 190,000 mineworkers in total. There were also tens of thousands of police and workers from other unions and support groups who were involved in actions at different times in the strike. At Orgreave on 18 June 1984, there were 10,000 pickets present plus a very heavy police presence. Other picketing actions were much smaller, but spread over a very large number of locations. There were 174 pits, plus other sites such as power stations, ports, and steelworks. In such a huge sample of people over such a long period, we might expect to find many varieties of human behaviour. There would be miners trained in first aid, who would pause to help policemen who had fallen (which did happen), and we would find people who would throw bolts and bricks.

The political and economic events which surrounded the strike resulted in a conflict on a scale which had been unknown for many years. The police had a pivotal role in this and were seen as directly antagonistic to the strike by those who were pursuing it. When tens of thousands of police, miners, and their supporters confronted each other in such a stressed period, there was a very real possibility that there would be violent incidents. But it is the relentless focus on these by television and the press, accompanied by the comments on 'escalation' and 'new records', which establishes for many of the audience the belief that violence was a persistent feature of most picketing.

There was a remarkable unanimity of belief amongst the groups in this sample about what had actually been shown. In the general sample, 98 per cent believed that most picketing which they had seen on television news was violent. The remaining 2 per cent either were

From G. Philo, *Seeing and Believing: The Influence of Television* (London: Routledge, 1990) pp. 147–54.

unsure or believed the picketing shown was 'intimidatory' rather than physically violent. But perhaps what is most remarkable is the number of people who believed that these television images represented the everyday reality of picketing. There was occasionally a fear expressed of even going near a picket line, because of the high levels of physical fighting which were believed to be going on. In all, 54 per cent of the general sample believed that picketing was mostly violent.

The source for these beliefs was overwhelmingly given as television and the press, with the emphasis on TV, because of its immediate and more dramatic quality. Some people also indicated how their attitudes had altered as a result of what they had seen. For example, one of the secretaries in the solicitors' office in Croydon wrote that her opinion of the police had improved because 'you do not realise what they have to put up with'. It was clear that some key elements of belief were being provided by the media. But it would be wrong to see people as being totally dependent on such messages, as if they are simply empty vessels which are being filled up by News at Ten. To accept and believe what is seen on television is as much a cultural act as the rejection of it. Both acceptance and rejection are conditioned by our beliefs, history, and experience. A high degree of trust in the BBC, for example, might result from a knowledge of its history and its peculiar role in British society as an authoritative 'national' voice.

Television news itself works very hard at strategies to win our trust. It scorns the crude editorializing of newspapers and uses presentational techniques which suggest neutrality and balance. Whether the audience actually accepts television's presentation of itself depends very much on what beliefs, experience, and information they bring to what they are shown.

In this sample, some people clearly accepted the television account. But others adapted parts of the message and changed key elements of its meaning. For example, some believed that the strike was mostly violent because of what they had seen on television, but blamed the police for provoking the trouble. They could be quite aware that television news had not explained the origins of the violence in this way. The disjunction between what they had seen and what they believed was explained by saying that television 'only showed violence from miners, not police' (Glasgow woman). In such an example, what is finally believed results from news images being interpreted through beliefs about both the police and television.[1]

In the Glasgow retirement group, we encountered a different negotiation of the television message. In this group, there was a very high degree of trust in television news and most accepted its account of the violent nature of picketing. But there was also a high degree of sympathy with the miners and this contradiction was partly resolved by a focus on 'outsiders, infiltrators, and militants' as the cause of the trouble. This negotiation was not completely successful in rehabilitating the miners, as there was also deep unhappiness expressed about the violence and how it had reflected on the miners' cause.

The process by which people understand a television message depends in part on the beliefs which they bring to it and crucially on how these beliefs are utilized. There were cases amongst the group of electronics staff and the Bromley women where people had a critique of television latent in their beliefs. They stated at first that they thought picketing was mostly violent and then moved away from this position as they began to comment on the nature of television as a medium, with its tendency to select and to focus on the sensational. In these cases, the exercise itself seems to have provided the stimulus for the emergence of this view. But it is important that the belief about picketing had in a sense rested with them, until they were pressed to explain it. These again seem to be examples of the message being absorbed in spite of other beliefs which were held.

Where no critical view of television exists, the likelihood of accepting its account may be very great. One person in the Glasgow retirement group commented that television was the most important source of information and took her opinion of picketing from it because as she said:

Seeing is believing.

We also saw one case in this sample where the acceptance of the television message was underlined by indirect experience. One of the London Transport supervisors had stayed for a period in Yorkshire and had thought that the people there had a very 'them-and-us' attitude. This had led him to accept the television portrayal of picketing. But it was clear that in this study the overwhelming effect of indirect and direct experience was to produce a rejection of the television news account. This was most obvious in the case of people who had been at picket lines, whether police, pickets, or other observers. One interesting case was of the Scottish solicitor who had driven past a picket line during the strike and had compared what he had seen with television coverage of picketing. In the same office, a secretary commented that her experience of seeing how a dispute at Chrysler was treated in the news, had led her to question the coverage of the miners' strike.

In the general sample, 43 per cent believed that picketing was mostly peaceful. When giving reasons, about a third of these based their belief on the experience of knowing or having met policemen or miners. The effect of such experience could traverse class and political culture. We saw for example the two Bromley residents whose views were generally on the right and whose key memory of the strike was of 'Arthur Scargill talking rubbish/lies'. Yet they believed that picketing was mostly peaceful because of their contact with miners and their families whilst on holiday at Ollerton.

A second major reason for doubting television news was the comparison of it with other sources of information, such as the 'quality' and local press or 'alternative' current affairs programmes and radio. About 16 per cent of the general sample made such comparisons. These comments were sometimes linked to remarks on the tendency of television to exaggerate and focus on violence to the exclusion of other events. In the general sample, 14 per cent of the people made this criticism and gave it as a reason for rejecting the news presentation. This is a relatively low proportion given that it is sometimes thought that beliefs about the tendency of media to exaggerate are generally held in the population. It might in fact be that they are. But what is significant about this result is that even where such beliefs existed they were not always used to discount what was seen in the news. It was also noteworthy that where people relied only on this criticism to reject the news account, there was a tendency to estimate the level of violence as being very high. Some of the group in the Glasgow solicitors' office made such estimates, although their conclusion was that for a majority of the time picketing was probably peaceful.

These criticisms of television as a medium and the comparison of it with other accounts were made by people with varied political views. But there was another strand of criticism which saw the focus on violence as a conscious attempt to denigrate the miners' case.

This view was most prominent amongst the Scottish trade unionists. One of the London Transport supervisors had also commented that the media 'picked out the violence so as to get the majority of people against the miners'. The trade unionists had criticized several aspects of news presentation, such as the 'big thing' that was made of Ian MacGregor being knocked over and the focus on 'violence instead of support groups'. There was a strong belief amongst them that picketing was mostly peaceful. In arguing this, some also commented on the scale of the strike and the numbers involved, saying that people could not have been fighting most of the time. This deduction could apparently be made irrespective of sympathies with the strike. One woman in the Penge group said that she would have shot striking miners (has she been a working miner), but also argued that, 'because of the amount who were actually on strike . . . it can't all have been violent'. One of the print workers commented that 'if they had been really violent, the police couldn't have coped, it would have been the army' and a Bromley resident said that 'there would be a revolution'.

In the general sample, about 6 per cent of the people gave such deductions as an explanation for their beliefs on picketing, while 3 per cent gave their personal conviction that most people are not inclined to violence. These are relatively small proportions of the sample. We might remember that 54 per cent had believed that most picketing was violent. The source of this belief seems very clearly to have been the media. It is something of an indictment of news journalism that after coverage virtually every day for a year, such a large proportion of people had apparently no idea what a typical picket line was like. The eye-witness accounts which we have seen here were greeted with genuine surprise by many in the groups who had been convinced by what they had seen on the news.

MEMORY AND BELIEFS

The most frequently cited memories were of violence. Seventy-two per cent of the general sample thought that 'confrontation', 'clashes', 'picketing', and 'violence' were what was shown most on television news of the strike. [. . .] In the key memories, 'confrontation', 'violence', and 'picketing' were again cited more than any other issue. These were given by 27 per cent of the people in the general sample. There were other issues cited as key memories which had connotations of violence, such as the intimidation/treatment of non-strikers (6 per cent), police violence/causing trouble/charging miners on horseback (12 per cent), and the death of the Welsh taxi-driver (9 per cent). Arthur Scargill was named as being what was 'most shown' by 27 per cent of the general sample and was given as a key memory by 21 per cent, sometimes accompanied by pejorative comments. This was most noticeable in the south of the country. In the Shenfield group, for example, the miners' leader is named in eight out of the ten replies. For some respondents he was thought to be both what was shown most on television and also had the greatest impact upon them of anything in the strike. This suggests that judgements about the content of news were being affected by prior belief, in this case the intense antipathy which was felt for Scargill.

The assessment of what was on the news most could also be affected by direct involvement or close sympathy with the dispute. The Scottish trade unionists, the Yorkshire miners, and the printers in Fleet Street all included references to the return to work.

They had generally a very cynical view of the media and many saw the news emphasis on the breakdown of the strike as evidence of bias against the miners' cause. As one miner put it, television had shown 'returning miners, the more the better'. But the images were clearly also very significant in their own memories, because of what they represented in terms of the failure of union solidarity. This was very apparent in the case of the print workers who were involved in their own union dispute. For some in these groups, the return to work was given as the key memory of the strike and was also estimated to have been the issue most shown on the news. But there was not always such a clear correspondence between these two dimensions of memory. Some respondents made clear distinction between them. In the general sample, 9 per cent believed that negotiations, meetings, and arguments featured most in news coverage, but there were no references to these as key memories.

As we have seen, for most people the violent images were very salient and were thought to have predominated in the news. But many also made it clear that there were other memories which had an even more powerful impact upon them. For example the group of Scottish trade unionists had believed overwhelmingly that violence was the most shown issue on the news. But nearly half of the group did not include this in their key memories and instead spoke of the role of support groups and miners' wives and the attitude of the government and the Coal Board.

In the general sample, memories were clearly affected by political belief and class experience. The groups of women in Glasgow and Penge remembered people queueing for food and the loss of jobs in the dispute. But class experience was not synonymous with political belief. Some of the middle-class women in Bromley were very sympathetic to the miners' cause – yet none of these gave unemployment or hardship in the strike as a key memory.

The effect of experience on perception could apparently last for many years. One of the middle-class residents of Shenfield gave as her key memory of the strike the hopelessness of families and 'shortage of money'. She explained this by speaking of the harsh consequences of unemployment on her family when she was a small child.

Attitudes to police action in the strike could also be affected by past experience. One woman in the Glasgow retirement group commented on her belief that the police were 'causing the trouble' during the strike. She based this view on experiences when living in a large working-class housing estate, twenty years earlier. There were several examples of how direct contact with the police could have remarkable effects on memories of the dispute. Two people from the middle-class areas of Bromley and Beckenham gave 'police tactics' and 'use of police horsemen against miners and fear on people's faces', as their key memories of the strike. Both also gave accounts of how they had been stopped by the police – one of them for what was described as an 'April Fool's joke'.

In the general sample as a whole, there was apparently a growth in negative attitudes towards the police. Forty-three per cent of the people said that their attitude had changed for the worse in the period since the strike, while 11 per cent said that their attitude had improved (a further 12 per cent said that their attitude was already very good). Some of these changes in attitude related to media coverage of events which had nothing to do with the miners' dispute – such as the attack on the six youths in a police van in Islington in 1983 and the subsequent action against police officers.

Criticisms of the police which were featured in the media could sometimes be re-negotiated by people who were sympathetic with the force. They might say for example that the tougher stance of the police was being 'forced upon them', or the criticisms might simply be rejected. But negative contact with the police seemed to have a very powerful impact on the beliefs of people who might otherwise have been sympathetic.

This further underlines one of the key findings here, that direct experience can have a crucial influence on how new information from the media is understood. Such direct contacts, together with political culture, class experience, processes of logic, and comparisons made between accounts, were the most important factors in the relation between perception and belief.

These findings show that some of the media audience clearly negotiate the meaning of what they are told. However, the influence of media and especially television was central, since it established so firmly the issues which came to be associated with the strike. Some of these, such as the emphasis on violence and the return to work, were very damaging to the miners' cause. Those who sought to reject these accounts of the strike had in a sense to struggle against the dominant flow of images from the media. For those without access to direct experience, it was sometimes a losing battle.

[. . .]

NOTES

1.   None of these elements are static and they can all move in relation to each other. For example, several people said that their beliefs about television had been altered by what they had seen. They had believed it to be neutral until its presentation of the miners strike. This potential for change is important since there is a recent trend in media studies to present the interpretation of television messages as being subject to pre-existing cultural and political beliefs. Such beliefs are important dimensions to the reception of new information, but they cannot be treated as fixed entities. There is the constant possibility of their movement and renegotiation in relation to what we see and are told and as a result of new experience.

FURTHER READING

Boyce, G., Curran, J. and Wingate, P. (eds), *Newspaper History: From the Seventeenth Century to the Present Day*, (London: Constable, 1978).

Butcher, H. et al., 'Images of Women in the Media', in Cohen, S. and Young, J. (eds), *The Manufacture of News: Social Problems, Deviance and the Mass Media* (London: Constable, 1973).

Chibnall, S., *Law and Order News* (London: Tavistock, 1977).

Cohen, S., *Folk Devils and Moral Panics* (Oxford: Blackwell, 1987).

Cohen, S., and Young, J. (eds), *The Manufacture of News: Social Problems, Deviance and the Mass Media* (London: Constable, 1973).

Connell, I., 'Television, News and the Social Contract', in Hall, S., Hobson, D., Lowe, A. and Willis, P. (eds), *Culture, Media, Language* (London: Hutchinson, 1980).

Cumberbatch, G., McGregor, R., Brown, J. and Morrison, D., *Television and the Miners' Strike* (London: Broadcasting Research Unit, 1986).

Curran, J. and Gurevitch, M. (eds), *Mass Media and Society* (London: Edward Arnold, 1991).

Curran, J., Gurevitch, M. and Woollacott, J. (eds), *Mass Communication and Society* (London: Edward Arnold, 1977).

Curran, J. and Seaton, J., *Power without Responsibility: The Press and Broadcasting in Britain*, 4th edn (London: Routledge, 1991).

Dahlgren, P., 'The Modes of Reception: For a Hermeneutics of TV News', in Drummond, P. and Paterson, R. (eds), *Television in Transition* (London: BFI, 1985).

Dahlgren, P., 'What's the Meaning of This?: Viewers' Plural Sense-Making of TV News', *Media Culture and Society* 10:3 (1988) pp. 285–301.

Dahlgren, P. and Sparks, C. (eds), *Communication and Citizenship: Journalism and the Public Sphere* (London: Routledge, 1991).

Davis, H. and Walton, P., *Language, Image, Media* (Oxford: Blackwell, 1983).

Ericson, R., Baranek, P. and Chan, J., *Visualizing Deviance: A Study of News Organization* (Milton Keynes: Open University Press, 1987).

Ericson, R., Baranek, P. and Chan, J., *Negotiating Control: A Study of News Sources* (Milton Keynes: Open University Press, 1989).

Fiske, J., *Television Culture* (London: Methuen, 1987).

Fiske, J., *Reading the Popular* (London: Unwin Hyman, 1989).

Fiske, J. and Hartley, J., *Reading Television* (London: Methuen, 1978).

Galtung, J. and Ruge, M., 'Structuring and Selecting News', in Cohen, S. and Young, J. (eds), *The Manufacture of News: Social Problems, Deviance and the Mass Media* (London: Constable, 1973).

Gans, H., *Deciding What's News* (London: Constable, 1979).

Glasgow University Media Group, *Bad News* (London: Routledge, 1976).

Glasgow University Media Group, *More Bad News* (London: Routledge, 1980).

Glasgow University Media Group, *Really Bad News* (London: Writers and Readers Co-operative, 1982).

Glasgow University Media Group, *War and Peace News* (Milton Keynes: Open University Press, 1985).

Glasgow University Media Group, *Getting the Message: News, Truth and Power*, ed. J. Eldridge (London: Routledge, 1993).

Golding, P. and Elliott, P., *Making the News* (London: Longman, 1979).

Golding, P. and Middleton, S., *Images of Welfare* (Oxford: Blackwell and Martin Robertson, 1982).

Goodwin, A., 'TV News: Striking the Right Balance', in Goodwin, A. and Whannel, G. (eds), *Understanding Television* (London: Routledge, 1990).

Hall, S., 'The Determinations of News Photographs', in Cohen, S. and Young, J. (eds), *The Manufacture of News: Social Problems, Deviance and the Mass Media* (London: Constable, 1973).

Hall, S., 'Introduction' to A. C. H. Smith (with E. Immirzi and T. Blackwell), *Paper Voices: The Popular Press and Social Change 1935–1965* (London: Chatto & Windus, 1975).

Hall, S., Connell, I. and Curti, L., 'The Unity of Current Affairs Television', in Bennett, T., Boyd-Bowman, S., Mercer, C. and Woollacott, J. (eds), *Popular Television and Film* (London: BFI, 1981).

Hall, S., Critcher, C., Jefferson, T., Clarke, J. and Roberts, B., *Policing the Crisis: Mugging, the State, and Law and Order* (London: Macmillan, 1978).

Hartley, J., *Understanding News* (London: Methuen, 1982).

Jensen, K. B., *Making Sense of the News* (Aarhus: University of Aarhus Press, 1986).

Jensen, K. B., 'The Politics of Polysemy: Television News, Everday Consciousness and Political Action', *Media, Culture and Society* 12:1 (1990) pp. 57–77.

Lewis, J., 'Decoding Television News', in Drummond, P. and Paterson, R., (eds), *Television in Transition* (London: BFI, 1985).

Lewis, J., 'Behind the News', in Lewis, J. *The Ideological Octopus: An Exploration of Television and its Audience* (London: Routledge, 1991).

Negrine, R., *Politics and the Mass Media in Britain* (London: Routledge, 1989).

Philo, G., *Seeing and Believing* (London: Routledge, 1990).

Schlesinger, P., *Putting 'Reality' Together: BBC News* (London: Methuen, 1978).

Schlesinger, P., 'From Production to Propaganda', *Media, Culture and Society* vol. 2 (1989) pp. 283–306.

Schlesinger, P., 'Rethinking the Sociology of Journalism: Source Strategies and the Limits of Media Centrism', in Ferguson, M. (ed.), *Public Communication: The New Imperatives* (London: Sage, 1990).

Schlesinger, P., Murdock, G. and Elliott, P., *Televising 'Terrorism': Political Violence in Popular Culture* (London: Comedia, 1983).

Schudson, M., *Discovering the News* (New York: Basic Books, 1987).

Schudson, M., 'The Sociology of News Production', *Media, Culture and Society* 11: (1989) pp. 263–82.

Schudson, M., 'The Sociology of News Production Revisited', in Curran, J. and Gurevitch, M. (eds), *Mass Media and Society* (London: Edward Arnold, 1991).

Tuchman, G., *Making News* (New York: Free Press, 1978).

Wallis, R. and Baran, S., *The Known World of Broadcast News* (London: Routledge, 1990).

White, D. M., 'The Gatekeeper: A Case Study in the Selection of News', *Journalism Quarterly* 27:4 (1950) pp. 383–90.

Advertising

Advertising

The study of advertising takes us into wider and more contested areas of study than do the other two case studies in this book. In the first place, advertising is an *industry* which wields considerable power within Western capitalist society. It is tied in more directly to economic structures than other media forms, being linked into a chain of marketing practices which function to sustain the flow of goods on which the economic system depends. It also exerts economic force upon mass media structures themselves, since it acts, as James Curran argues (Chapter 49), as a 'concealed subsidy system' to whose demands the mass media must be responsive. A consideration of its relations of production, therefore, must deal not only with its internal processes but with the influence it exerts at this level upon the media system as a whole.

Secondly, advertising has often been seen within cultural theory as emblematic of the culture in which it has become so all-pervasive. For F. R. Leavis, writing in 1930 in defence of what he termed 'minority culture', advertising epitomised the 'exploitation of the cheap response' which characterises contemporary 'mass civilisation'[1] In 1947, Theodor Adorno and Max Horkheimer – though writing from the very different, Marxist perspective of the Frankfurt School (see Chapter 2) – argued similarly that advertising pervades what has now become the 'culture industry', subsidising the 'ideological media' and turning culture into an 'assembly-line' whose standardised products it furhishes with artificial differences.[2] For contemporary theorists, too, advertising functions in this emblematic way. Jean Baudrillard, for example, argues that it 'invades everything': both 'public space' and 'private space', and the separation between them, disappear, to be replaced by 'great screens on which are reflected atoms, particles, molecules in motion', in the 'era of hyperreality'.[3] For these theorists, advertising functions as a key reference point rather than an object of sustained study.

Thirdly, as part of a marketing industry, advertising has conducted its own audience research. This *marketing* research has at times been closely identified with the audience research produced within the American 'mass communication' tradition. Todd Gitlin, for example, in a 1978 critique of what he termed the 'dominant paradigm' of American media sociology, makes this attack on the American tradition:

> It is no secret that mass communications research descends directly from the development of sophisticated marketing techniques. The theory of 'effects' was first developed for the direct, explicit use of broadcasters and advertisers, and continues to be used mostly in those circles, to grow more sophisticated there.[4]

His conclusion, that, by its complicity with the advertising industry, American media sociology has functioned to 'legitimize . . . mid-century capitalism',[5] is one echoed from elsewhere within the 'critical' tradition of media research. Stuart Hall, for example, writes in 1982 that this approach, 'though advanced as empirically-grounded and scientific, was predicated on a very specific set of political and ideological presuppositions. These presuppositions, however, were not put to the test, within the theory, but framed and underpinned it as a set of unexamined postulates'.[6] Thus advertising becomes a ground on which opposing traditions of audience research may be fought out.[7]

Finally, its links with the processes of consumption mean that advertising is caught up in wider arguments about the power of audiences/consumers to resist the meanings and pleasures produced by the powerful. For example, John Fiske's assertion of a semiautonomous 'cultural economy' which operates in parallel to the 'political economy', and in which consumers rather than producers are empowered, involves a view of shopping as 'an oppositional . . . act' whose 'guerrillas' – particularly women – always cause advertising to fail: 'There is so much advertising only because it can never finally succeed in its tasks – those of containing social diversity within the needs of capitalism and of reducing the relative autonomy of the cultural economy from the financial . . . '[8]

The chapter by Raymond Williams (written in 1960), which opens this section, takes up several of the issues outlined above. Advertising, he argues (Chapter 48), is both crucial to the economic functioning of capitalism and a form of 'social communication', offering us new ways of understanding ourselves. Advertising, then, categorises us as 'consumers' rather than 'users', offering in response to real human needs – the 'problems of death, loneliness, frustration, the need for identity and respect' – the illusory satisfaction provided by the consumption of material goods. In advertising's 'magic system' these goods are identified with human values and desires, in order to obscure the 'real sources' of satisfaction whose discovery would involve radical change in our way of life. Williams, however, is far less pessimistic than, for example, Adorno and Horkheimer; advertisers, he writes, are as confused as their consumers and the confused society for which they speak still has a choice: between 'capitalism and socialism . . . man as consumer and man as user.'

James Curran (in Chapter 49) offers an overview of the impact of advertising on the range and nature of Britain's mass media. Advertisers, he argues, have played a central role in shaping Britain's media system in three ways. First, the allocation of advertising finance *between* media influences the overall shape of Britain's media industries. Changing trends in advertising allocation cause the expansion or contraction of specific media sectors. Secondly, advertising allocation *within* media sectors influences the character of each medium, causing, for example, the political imbalance of the press and the overwhelming orientation of women's magazines towards the young middle-class reader. Finally, the need to respond to advertising pressures produces highly conservative television and commercial radio schedules and a popular press which is largely depoliticised.

The chapter by Kathy Myers (Chapter 50) takes a closer look at one area included in Curran's analysis: that of women's magazines. Like Curran, Myers argues that the financial dependency of these magazines on advertising revenue crucially determines magazine content, so that advertisements and journalism alike (the two often being indistinguishable) are geared to the process of consumption. Myers also argues, however, that the determinations exerted by the advertising industry are less coherent and more contradictory, and the advertisements themselves more polysemic, than is often supposed. Finally, she argues that readers' responses to advertisements can be read off neither from the economic interests of the advertisers nor from the advertising text itself: meanings 'may be radically altered and realigned in accord with usage'. What is needed is an analysis which recognises 'the spectrum of alternative audience readings' as well as the complex forces of production and the varieties of advertisement form which they produce.

Judith Williamson's (1978) *Decoding Advertisements* is the most sustained application of structuralist methods to advertising texts to have appeared. Like Williams, she argues that the 'need for relationship and human meaning appropriated by advertising is one that, if only it was not diverted, could radically change the society in which we live'[9] Her analysis of 'how ads work', which draws on semiotics, Lacanian psychoanalysis and Althusserian Marxism, constitutes an engagement 'in a sort of running battle' with advertising, a battle waged in order to make that change possible.[10] The extract reproduced here (Chapter 51) outlines her argument that, as sign systems, advertisements are parasitic, appropriating existing symbolic systems and their associated cultural values as their '*referent systems*'. Thus, ads 'use distinctions existing in social mythologies to create distinctions between products'.

Janice Winship's analysis of the use of hands in advertisements (Chapter 52) continues Williamson's argument that ads not only reflect but also help to construct the ideological structures and frameworks in our society. Hands, she argues, are always gendered in advertisements, and through her analysis of specific examples she explores the meanings of 'masculinity' and 'femininity' constructed through these representations.

Although Winship argues that a 'feminist politics of representation . . . has to engage with the social reader, as well as the social text', she, like Judith Williamson, concentrates wholly on the advertising *text*. In contrast, the chapter by Mica Nava and Orson Nava (Chapter 53) is unusual within work on advertising in being based upon an ethnographic study: of young people's readings of advertisements. Nava's and Nava's work offers a challenge to the emphasis on the power of advertisers in determining meaning, which can be found in different ways in the work of both Curran and Williamson. Like John Fiske and Angela McRobbie, Nava and Nava emphasise the creative play of advertising's users, arguing that both the 'critical tools' evidenced by young people's decodings, and the pleasures generated by the 'increasingly . . . sophisticated cultural form' of advertising, may be used to 'subvert and fragment existing networks of power-knowledge'.

The final chapter in this section, which is taken from a more general discussion of consumer culture, takes issue with Nava's conclusion. There is a double danger, argues Alan Tomlinson (Chapter 54), in this 'illusion of freedom'. Firstly, while the sphere of consumption is indeed that in which 'many will seek to express their sense of freedom, their personal power', it remains the case that this sense of personal identity 'is created by others and marketed aggressively and seductively'. Secondly, the emphasis on consumption as the sphere of individual empowerment ignores the material realities of a society whose unequal distribution of wealth disenfranchises millions from this 'sphere of freedom'.

NOTES

1.   See F. R. Leavis, *Mass Civilisation and Minority culture* (Cambridge: Minority Press, 1930). This quotation is taken from J. Storey (ed.) *Cultural Theory and Popular Culture: A Reader* (Hemel Hempstead: Harvester Wheatsheaf, 1994) p. 12.

2.   See 'The Culture Industry: Enlightenment as Mass Deception', in J. Curran, M. Gurevitch and J. Woollacott (eds), *Mass Communication and Society* (London: Edward Arnold, 1977) pp. 380, 381.

3.   See 'The Ecstasy of Communication', in H. Foster (ed.), *Postmodern Culture* (London: Pluto Press, 1985) pp. 129, 130. See also Chapter 8 in this book.

4.   Todd Gitlin, 'Media Sociology: The Dominant Paradigm', *Theory and Society* 6 (1978) p. 232.

5.   Ibid. p. 245.

6.   Stuart Hall, 'The Rediscovery of "Ideology": Return of the Repressed in Media Studies', in M. Gurevitch, T. Bennett, J. Curran and J. Woollacott (ed.), *Culture, Society and the Media* (London: Methuen, 1982) p. 59.

7.   See also len Ang's examination of advertising audience research in *Desperately seeking the Audience* (London: Routledge, 1991) which, as its title suggests, concludes that this research is doomed to failure, since the practices and experiences of actual audiences always remain beyond the reach of its quantitative research methods.

8.   See 'Shopping for Pleasure' in J. Fiske, *Reading the Popular* (London: Unwin Hyman, 1989) pp. 13–42 and 'Commodities and Culture', in J. Fiske, *Understanding Popular Culture* (London: Unwin Hyman, 1989), p. 30. [See also Chapter 35 in this volume.]

9.   *Decoding Advertisements* (London: Marion Boyars, 1978) p. 14.

10.   Ibid pp. 167, 178

48

ADVERTISING: THE MAGIC SYSTEM

Raymond Williams

[. . .]

In the last hundred years, [. . .] advertising has developed from the simple announcements of shopkeepers and the persuasive arts of a few marginal dealers into a major part of capitalist business organization. This is important enough, but the place of advertising in society goes far beyond this commercial context. It is increasingly the source of finance for a whole range of general communication, to the extent that in 1960 our majority television service and almost all our newspapers and periodicals could not exist without it. Further, in the last forty years and now at an increasing rate, it has passed the frontier of the selling of goods and services and has become involved with the teaching of social and personal values; it is also rapidly entering the world of politics. Advertising is also, in a sense, the official art of modern capitalist society: it is what 'we' put up in 'our' streets and use to fill up to half of 'our' newspapers and magazines: and it commands the services of perhaps the largest organized body of writers and artists, with their attendant managers and advisers, in the whole society. Since this is the actual social status of advertising, we shall only understand it with any adequacy if we can develop a kind of total analysis in which the economic, social and cultural facts are visibly related. We may then also find, taking advertising as a major form of modern social communication, that we can understand our society itself in new ways.

It is often said that our society is too materialist, and that advertising reflects this. We are in the phase of a relatively rapid distribution of what are called 'consumer goods', and advertising, with its emphasis on 'bringing the good things of life', is taken as central for this reason. But it seems to me that in this respect our society is quite evidently not materialist enough, and that this, paradoxically, is the result of a failure in social meanings, values and ideals.

It is impossible to look at modern advertising without realising that the material object being sold is never enough: this indeed is the crucial cultural quality of its modern forms. If we were sensibly materialist, in that part of our living in which we use things, we should find most advertising to be of an insane irrelevance. Beer would be enough for us, without the additional

From R. Williams, *Problems in Materialism and Culture* (London: Verso, 1980) pp. 184–91.

promise that in drinking it we show ourselves to be manly, young in heart, or neighbourly. A washing-machine would be a useful machine to wash clothes, rather than an indication that we are forward-looking or an object of envy to our neighbours. But if these associations sell beer and washing-machines, as some of the evidence suggests, it is clear that we have a cultural pattern in which the objects are not enough but must be validated, if only in fantasy, by association with social and personal meanings which in a different cultural pattern might be more directly available. The short description of the pattern we have is *magic*: a highly organized and professional system of magical inducements and satisfactions, functionally very similar to magical systems in simpler societies, but rather strangely coexistent with a highly developed scientific technology.

This contradiction is of the greatest importance in any analysis of modern capitalist society. The coming of large-scale industrial production necessarily raised critical problems of social organization, which in many fields we are still only struggling to solve. In the production of goods for personal use, the critical problem posed by the factory of advanced machines was that of the organization of the market. The modern factory requires not only smooth and steady distributive channels (without which it would suffocate under its own product) but also definite indications of demand without which the expensive processes of capitalization and equipment would be too great a risk. The historical choice posed by the development of industrial production is between different forms of organization and planning in the society to which it is central. In our own century, the choice has been and remains between some form of socialism and a new form of capitalism. In Britain, since the 1890s and with rapidly continuing emphasis, we have had the new capitalism, based on a series of devices for organizing and ensuring the market. Modern advertising, taking on its distinctive features in just this economic phase, is one of the most important of these devices, and it is perfectly true to say that modern capitalism could not function without it.

Yet the essence of capitalism is that the basic means of production are not socially but privately owned, and that decisions about production are therefore in the hands of a group occupying a minority position in the society and in no direct way responsible to it. Obviously, since the capitalist wishes to be successful, he is influenced in his decisions about production by what other members of the society need. But he is influenced also by considerations of industrial convenience and likely profit, and his decisions tend to be a balance of these varying factors. The challenge of socialism, still very powerful elsewhere but in Britain deeply confused by political immaturities and errors, is essentially that decisions about production should be in the hands of the society as a whole, in the sense that control of the means of production is made part of the general system of decision which the society as a whole creates. The conflict between capitalism and socialism is now commonly seen in terms of a competition in productive efficiency, and we need not doubt that much of our future history, on a world scale, will be determined by the results of our competition. Yet the conflict is really much deeper than this, and is also a conflict between different approaches to and forms of socialism. The fundamental choice that emerges, in the problems set to us by modern industrial production, is between man as consumer and man as user. The system of organized magic which is modern advertising is primarily important as a functional obscuring of this choice.

'CONSUMERS'

The popularity of 'consumer', as a way of describing the ordinary member of modern capitalist society in a main part of his economic capacity, is very significant. The description is spreading very rapidly, and is now habitually used by people to whom it ought, logically, to be repugnant. It is not only that, at a simple level, 'consumption' is a very strange description of our ordinary use of goods and services. This metaphor drawn from the stomach or the furnace is only partially relevant even to our use of things. Yet we say 'consumer', rather than 'user', because in the form of society we now have, and in the forms of thinking which it almost imperceptibly fosters, it is as consumers that the majority of people are seen. We are the market, which the system of industrial production has organized. We are the channels along which the product flows and disappears. In every aspect of social communication, and in every version of what we are as a community, the pressure of a system of industrial production is towards these impersonal forms.

Yet it is by no means necessary that these versions should prevail, just because we use advanced productive techniques. It is simply that once these have entered a society, new questions of structure and purpose in social organization are inevitably posed. One set of answers is the development of genuine democracy, in which the human needs of all the people in the society are taken as the central purpose of all social activity, so that politics is not a system of government but of self-government, and the systems of production and communication are rooted in the satisfaction of human needs and the development of human capacities. Another set of answers, of which we have had more experience, retains, often in very subtle forms, a more limited social purpose. In the first phase, loyal subjects, as they were previously seen, became the labour market of industrial 'hands'. Later, as the 'hands' reject this version of themselves, and claim a higher human status, the emphasis is changed. Any real concession of higher status would mean the end of class-society and the coming of socialist democracy. But intermediate concessions are possible, including material concessions. The 'subjects' become the 'electorate', and 'the mob' becomes 'public opinion'.

Decision is still a function of the minority, but a new system of decision, in which the majority can be organized to this end, has to be devised. The majority are seen as 'the masses', whose opinion, *as masses* but not as real individuals or groups, is a factor in the business of governing. In practical terms, this version can succeed for a long time, but it then becomes increasingly difficult to state the nature of the society, since there is a real gap between profession and fact. Moreover, as the governing minority changes in character, and increasingly rests for real power on a modern economic system, older social purposes become vestigial, and whether expressed or implied, the maintenance of the economic system becomes the main factual purpose of all social activity. Politics and culture become deeply affected by this dominant pattern, and ways of thinking derived from the economic market – political parties considering how to sell themselves to the electorate, to create a favourable brand image; education being primarily organized in terms of a graded supply of labour; culture being organized and even evaluated in terms of commercial profit – become increasingly evident.

Still, however, the purposes of the society have to be declared in terms that will command the effort of a majority of its people. It is here that the idea of the 'consumer' has proved so useful. Since consumption is within its limits a satisfactory activity, it can be plausibly offered as a commanding social purpose. At the same time, its ambiguity is such that it ratifies the subjection of society to the operations of the existing economic system. An irresponsible economic system can supply the 'consumption' market, whereas it could only meet the criterion of human use by becoming genuinely responsible: that is to say, shaped in its use of human labour and resources by general social decisions. The consumer asks for an adequate supply of personal 'consumer goods' at a tolerable price: over the last ten years, this has been the primary aim of British government. But users ask for more than this, necessarily. They ask for the satisfaction of human needs which consumption, as such can never really supply. Since many of these needs are social – roads, hospitals, schools, quiet – they are not only not covered by the consumer ideal: they are even denied by it, because consumption tends always to materialize as an individual activity. And to satisfy this range of needs would involve questioning the autonomy of the economic system, in its actual setting of priorities. This is where the consumption ideal is not only misleading, as a form of defence of the system, but ultimately destructive to the broad general purposes of the society.

Advertising, in its modern forms, then operates to preserve the consumption ideal from the criticism inexorably made of it by experience. If the consumption of individual goods leaves that whole area of human need unsatisfied, the attempt is made, by magic, to associate this consumption with human desires to which it has no real reference. You do not only buy an object: you buy social respect, discrimination, health, beauty, success, power to control your environment. The magic obscures the real sources of general satisfaction because their discovery would involve radical change in the whole common way of life.

Of course, when a magical pattern has become established in a society, it is capable of some real if limited success. Many people will indeed look twice at you, upgrade you, upmarket you, respond to your displayed signals, if you have made the right purchases within a system of meanings to which you are all trained. Thus the fantasy seems to be validated, at a personal level, but only at the cost of preserving the general unreality which it obscures: the real failures of the society which however are not easily traced to this pattern.

It must not be assumed that magicians – in this case, advertising agents – disbelieve their own magic. They may have a limited professional cynicism about it, from knowing how some of the tricks are done. But fundamentally they are involved, with the rest of the society, in the confusion to which the magical gestures are a response. Magic is always an unsuccessful attempt to provide meanings and values, but it is often very difficult to distinguish magic from genuine knowledge and from art. The belief that high consumption is a high standard of living is a general belief of the society. The conversion of numerous objects into sources of sexual or pre-sexual satisfaction is evidently not only a process in the minds of advertisers, but also a deep and general confusion in which much energy is locked.

At one level, the advertisers are people using certain skills and knowledge, created by real art and science, against the public for commercial advantage. This hostile stance is rarely confessed in general propaganda for advertising, where the normal emphasis is the blind consumption ethic ('Advertising brings you the good things of life'), but it is common in advertisers' propaganda to their clients. 'Hunt with the mind of the hunter', one recent announcement begins, and another, under the heading 'Getting any honey from the hive industry?', is rich in the language of attack:

> One of the most important weapons used in successful marketing is advertising. Commando Sales Limited, steeped to the nerve ends in the skills of unarmed combat, are ready to move into battle on any sales front at the crack of an accepted estimate. These are the front line troops to call in when your own sales force is hopelessly outnumbered by the forces of sales resistance . . .

This is the structure of feeling in which 'impact' has become the normal description of the effect of successful communication, and 'impact' like 'consumer' is now habitually used by people to whom it ought to be repugnant. What sort of person really wants to 'make an impact' or create a 'smash hit', and what state is a society in when this can be its normal cultural language?

It is indeed monstrous that human advances in psychology, sociology and communication should be used or thought of as powerful techniques *against* people, just as it is rotten to try to reduce the faculty of human choice to 'sales resistance'. In these respects, the claim of advertising to be a service is not particularly plausible. But equally, much of this talk of weapons and impact is the jejune bravado of deeply confused men. It is in the end the language of frustration rather than of power. Most advertising is not the cool creation of skilled professionals, but the confused creation of bad thinkers and artists. If we look at the petrol with the huge clenched fist, the cigarette against loneliness in the deserted street, the puppet facing death with a life-insurance policy (the modern protection, unlike the magical symbols painstakingly listed from earlier societies), or the man in the cradle which is an aeroplane, we are looking at attempts to express and resolve real human tensions which may be crude but which also involve deep feelings of a personal and social kind.

The structural similarity between much advertising and much modern art is not simply copying by the advertisers. It is the result of comparable responses to the contemporary human condition, and the only distinction that matters is between the clarification achieved by some art and the displacement normal in bad art and most advertising. The skilled magicians, the masters of the masses, must be seen as ultimately involved in the general weakness which they not only exploit but are exploited by. If the meanings and values generally operative in the society give no answers to, no means of negotiating, problems of death, loneliness, frustration, the need for identity and respect, then the magical system must come, mixing its charms and expedients with reality in easily available forms, and binding the weakness to the condition which has created it. Advertising is then no longer merely a way of selling goods, it is a true part of the culture of a confused society.

49

THE IMPACT OF ADVERTISING ON THE BRITISH MASS MEDIA

James Curran[1]

INTRODUCTION

Senior officials at the Independent Broadcasting Authority are adamant that advertising has no effect on commercial television. 'If the suggestion is' writes Ian Haldane, the head of the IBA research department, 'that advertising has some "impact" or influence on ITV programmes, this is not so: the two are absolutely separate as laid down in the IBA Act under which we broadcast, and neither has any influence on the other.'[2] Even the suggestion that the policy of commercial broadcasting companies is influenced, in some way, by advertisers' requirements, provokes sharp denials. 'The programme controllers (of the ITV companies) are more Reithian than the BBC,' declares Stephen Murphy, a TV officer at the IBA with a distinguished record as a BBC producer, ' . . . Advertising pressure is simply not transferred through.'[3]

Royal Commissions on the Press are almost equally dismissive about the effect of advertising on the Press. The first Commission concluded that attempts by advertisers to influence editorial policy 'appear to be infrequent and unsuccessful' (RCP, 1949: 143). Similar conclusions were reached by its two successors, neither of which found substantiated evidence that advertisers had ever significantly influenced editorial policy (RCP, 1962: 86–87; 1977: 104–105).

Indeed, the whole question of advertising influence on the media is authoritatively judged to be closed since such marginal influence, as may exist, cannot be adequately measured. 'No Royal Commission can expect to learn,' argued the last Commission, 'what happens from those directly concerned, for it would not be in their interest to speak about the success of advertisers in exerting pressures . . . ' (RCP, 1977: 105). 'In its nature', opined its predecessor, 'the subject is one in which one has to rely largely on impression' (RCP, 1962: 86). The head of the IBA research department was even more forthright: this research study, he warned, was likely to be 'sadly lacking in substantial material, even were such material available'.[4]

From *Media, Culture and Society* 3:1 (1981) pp. 43–69.

Such intimidating scepticism, combined with consistent denials of significant advertising influence, would seem to suggest that further enquiry is pointless. Nevertheless, there are grounds for wondering whether the verdict of successive Royal Commissions on the Press and of experienced officials at the IBA is correct.[5] Their conclusions are largely based on a rather narrow definition of advertising influence in terms of overt attempts by advertisers to influence media content to their advantage by withholding or giving advertising favours.[6] This reflects the way in which the influence of advertising is often presented by critics from the Left. Thus, Sheridan and Gardiner (1979: 121–122) have recently argued, for instance, that the editorial policy of the press is shaped and moulded by a combination of 'subtle and crude financial pressure' from advertisers, exemplified by some advertisers' boycott of *The Guardian* during the Suez Crisis. In a similar vein, the Glasgow University Media Group (1976: 71) alleged, to the fury and outrage of many in the IBA and elsewhere, that Independent Television News not infrequently suppresses news stories in response to, or in anticipation of, pressure from advertisers.[7]

It is worth investigating, however, alternative ways in which advertisers may influence the mass media other than by overt attempts to influence its content. In particular, attention needs to be given to ways in which advertising as a concealed subsidy system has shaped the mass media; and to ways in which the media have adapted to the marketing needs of advertisers in order to compete for these subsidies.

The nature of these influences has been obscured by the conventional representation of advertisers as having interests identical with those of audiences (e.g. Advertising Association, 1975). Since advertisers want to reach the public in order to sell their products, it is argued, they naturally support the media which are popular with the public. Advertisers are thus portrayed as neutral and passive intermediaries who allocate their media budgets according to the likes and dislikes of media consumers and who consequently *exercise no independent influence of their own*. As John Whale puts it, 'advertising doubles the price on each reader's head . . . but there is not much a newspaperman can do to differentiate a double from a single dose of zeal to attract new readers' (Whale, 1979: 93).

This portrayal of advertisers is based on a misleading representation of media planning and marketing practice. Advertisers rarely think of the media exclusively as a distribution system for advertisements: they also generally make judgements about the effectiveness of different media as agencies of persuasion. They are not 'neutral' in their desire to reach all members of the public: they usually wish to reach – and will pay more to reach – particular segments of the market rather than others. They are not 'passive' and unchanging in the criteria they adopt for media buying: on the contrary, changes in marketing perspectives, research procedures and data inputs have produced changes in how advertisers have spent this money with important long-term consequences for the development of the media. Finally advertisers are not a uniform group with a common approach and shared objectives: indeed, changes within the economy have resulted in a significant shift in the pattern of advertising expenditure, reflecting the emergence of new advertisers and the decline of others, which have had major repercussions on the media system as a whole.

What this exploratory study will seek to do, therefore, is to examine ways in which the allocation of advertising, and media competition for this allocation, has influenced the character of the British mass media, and consider how this allocation has been influenced, in turn, by economic and social structures external to the media. To see the impact of advertising only in terms of overt attempts by individual advertisers to influence media content is, it will be argued, to misconceive both the true nature and the significance of advertising influence: advertising

Table [49.]1. *Proportion of press revenue derived from advertising in 1979**

National dailies	National Sundays	Regional daily and Sunday papers	Local weeklies	Total newspapers	Trade, technical and professional journals	Other periodicals	Total periodicals
44%	44%	66%	85%	59%	64%	47%	54%

* Derived from Department of Industry (1979).

patronage is essentially an impersonal means by which Britain's mass media are fashioned according to the marketing needs of the economic system and the class inequalities of power, influence and consumption within British society.

ADVERTISING ALLOCATION BETWEEN MEDIA

Advertisers make a larger contribution to the finances of the British mass media than audiences. Commercial broadcasting derives nearly all of its revenue from advertising while newspapers and magazines both derive over half their revenue from advertisements (see Table [49.]1).

Advertising does not constitute a straight media subsidy. Receipts from advertisers must be set against the costs involved in securing and producing advertisements, and these sometimes represent, as we shall see, a very large proportion of advertising revenue. Generally speaking, though, advertising generates a surplus after relevant costs have been deducted, so that advertising allocations crucially affect the financial resources available to competing media sectors as well as to competing companies within each media sector.

Advertising allocations between media are not closely tied to the pattern of media consumption. Newspapers and magazines absorb much less time, on average, than commercial TV and radio. Yet the press obtains almost three times as much advertising as commercial broadcasting (see Table [49.]2). The continuing ascendancy of the press as an advertising medium (largely due to government restrictions on the development of commercial broadcasting) has helped it to fend off the challenge of TV. During the period of rapid growth of TV ownership during the 50s and early 60s, the press was able to charge very low cover prices and spend very much more heavily on editorial outlay as a result of the rising advertising income it obtained. This contributed, in turn, to its remarkable resilience. The proportion of the adult population reading newspapers and magazines remained stable during the period of TV's rise, while newspaper consumption (when measured adequately) actually increased (Curran, 1970).[8] There is also no close correspondence between the pattern of demand and the amount of advertising expenditure on different sectors of the press. Although the circulation of the regional press was only about two-thirds that of the national press,[9] the regional papers still obtained £246 million more advertising than national papers in 1979. The success of the regional press in attracting advertising has helped to make it more profitable than Fleet Street.

The trade, technical and professional press also has a very much smaller circulation than that of the rest of the magazine press,[10] but nonetheless still attracts more advertising (see Table [49.2]). This high level of support has helped to sustain a large number of specialist titles many of which have only small sales.

Table [49.2]. *Media advertising expenditure (£m) in 1979**

National newspapers	Regional newspapers	Magazines and periodicals	Trade and technical	Total press	TV	Cinema	Radio
347	593	180	203	1496	471	17	52

* Source: Advertising Association (1980: 45).

CHANGES IN ADVERTISING ALLOCATIONS

Important shifts in the pattern of media advertising expenditure have taken place during the last 40 years, which have altered the character of the media. Before considering these, it is necessary to refer, however, to government economic controls which temporarily distorted advertising trends. Newsprint rationing was maintained on a statutory basis between 1940 and 1956, and on a voluntary basis until 1959. During the height of its severity, newsprint rationing caused national newspapers to shrink to less than a quarter of their pre-war size, and severely curtailed advertising in national newspapers, (Gerald, 1956). Imposed with less severity on the regional press, rationing caused advertising to be redistributed to the provinces (Henry, 1979). And because magazines were exempted from economic controls before newspapers, there was a temporary boom in magazine advertising in the early 1950s (Silverman, 1954). These distortions need to be distinguished from long-term changes.

The most important of these long-term changes have been the decline of traditional mass market advertising media and the linked rise of television; the shift of advertising to the provinces; and the redistribution of advertising within the magazine sector in favour of specialist magazines (see Table [49.3]).

[. . .]

ADVERTISING ALLOCATION WITHIN MEDIA SECTORS: SOME CONSEQUENCES

The last Royal Commission on the Press recoiled from the thought of redistributing advertising according to public service criteria partly on the grounds that it would introduce political judgements in the free processes of the market (RCP, 1977: 117). It did not pause to consider whether free market processes also have political and cultural consequences. It merely assumed that free market allocation of advertising was neutral and consequently that it did not warrant careful investigation.[11] Whether the Commission's assumption is justified remains to be seen.

THE CONSERVATIVE BIAS OF ADVERTISING: A REAPPRAISAL

The national newspaper press is predominantly conservative – very much more so than its readers, to judge from a comparison of newspapers' and readers' political affiliations (Seymour-Ure, 1977).[12] It also derives a substantial proportion of its revenue from advertisers. This has prompted some commentators to assume that the two things are connected: advertisers, it is reasoned, use their financial power to fashion the press according to their political prejudices (Steed, 1938; Labour Research Department, 1946; Orwell, 1970; Hoch, 1974).

It is undoubtedly the case that political bias on the part of advertisers helped to stifle the development of the radical press during the late nineteenth and early twentieth century

Table [49.3]. *Distribution of advertising expenditure between media**

	1938 %	1948 %	1954 %	1960 %	1965 %	1970 %	1975 %	1979 %
National newspapers	25	14	17	20	20	20	17	16
Regional newspapers†	27	31	31	21	24	26	29	28
Magazines and periodicals	15	13	19	12	11	9	8	9
Trade and technical journals	12	16	13	10	9	10	9	10
Other publications‡	2	1	1	1	1	2	2	3
Press production costs§	5	8	6	5	4	6	5	6
Total press	85	83	88	71	70	72	70	70
Television	–	–	–	22	24	23	24	22
Poster and transport	8	14	9	5	4	4	4	4
Cinema	3	4	3	2	1	1	1	1
Radio	3	–	1	–	1	–	1	2

* Sources: Kaldor and Silverman (1948), Silverman (1951), Advertising Association (1951, 1962, 1972, 1980), Critchley (n.d.). All forms of non-media promotional expenditure are excluded. All percentage figures have been rounded off to the nearest whole number.
† Including London evening newspapers.
‡ Directories, guide books, yellow pages, etc.
§ According to the Advertising Association's definition which does not include all relevant costs.

when the national press evolved in its modern form (Curran, 1977). The subsequent growth of advertising also helped to perpetuate this historical legacy by forcing up press costs and making the launch and establishment of new papers more costly and difficult[13] (Curran and Seaton, 1981).

Nevertheless, the political bias of advertisers was only one factor contributing to the conservative domination of the press in the early twentieth century. In any case, important changes have taken place in the procedures adopted by advertisers in selecting advertising media, which has significantly reduced the influence of political bias on media appropriations (Curran, 1980).

Disparities still persist however in the advertising revenue per copy obtained by Conservative and Labour papers. For example, the net advertisement revenue of the generally Conservative *Sunday Times* was almost four times that of the Labour *Sunday Mirror* in 1975, despite the fact that it had less than half the *Sunday Mirror*'s circulation (Curran, 1978: T7). These disparities do not arise from political prejudice but from the fact that, generally speaking, Conservative papers reach readers who have more money to spend, more influence over corporate spending, and watch less ITV than readers of Labour papers.[14]

The pattern of advertising expenditure has consequently enabled some Conservative papers to be economically viable with audiences much smaller than those of Labour papers.[15] The four quality dailies constitute half the national daily titles in Britain, yet they accounted for only 15% of national daily circulation in 1980.[16] Although they charged high cover prices, they still derived over half their revenue from advertising. Mostly Conservative in their politics, they have continued in publication largely because of the high advertising receipts they have obtained as a result of being read by a socially select readership. A similar pattern has developed in the national Sunday press, where three out of seven papers, heavily endowed with advertising, accounted for only 18% of national Sunday circulation in 1980. They have survived and grown only with the aid of advertising bounty.[17] The obverse to this is that Labour papers have died with circulations far larger than those of some Conservative papers. In 1964, for instance, the Labour *Daily Herald* was forced to close with a readership well over that of *The Times and The Financial Times* combined (National Readership Survey, 1964: T1A).

The political imbalance of the press thus partly reflects class inequalities within society which have generated unequal advertising subsidies between Labour and Conservative papers. This has helped to reinforce Conservative domination of the national press by making it easier for Conservative papers to survive and flourish.

INEQUALITIES OF CULTURAL PROVISION

Women's magazines tend to be oriented towards the middle class. This is a consequence of the much higher advertising subsidies that middle-class women readers generate by comparison with working-class readers. Bird (1978) found, for instance, that the correlation between the advertisement revenue of the five big women's weeklies and the size of their ABC1 (i.e. upper middle, middle and lower middle class) readerships was 0.997, very much higher than that between circulation and advertising revenue which was only 0.782.

[. . .]

This pattern of advertising expenditure has profoundly affected the development of the women's magazine press. The majority of women's magazines sell at prices (after discounts to distributors) that do not cover costs (Coopers and Lybrand, 1975). Whether they make a profit depends upon whether they attract adequate advertising. Only in the children's and young teenage market are magazines largely dependent on sales. In other sectors of the women's magazine market, the average magazine has relied upon advertising for the majority of its revenue.[18]

Consequently, the majority of adult women's magazine titles are oriented towards the middle class, even though it constitutes little more than one-third of the population.[19] Even some mass market publications pay disproportionate attention to the middle class because of its importance to advertisers. As Michael Bird (then marketing director of the National Magazine Company) stressed in an influential paper, magazines are forced to seek not the largest but the 'optimum circulation' defined in relation to advertisers' priorities. 'Pushing circulations to ruinous heights' can be counterproductive if 'the audience profile is diluted' (Bird, 1978: 150; cf. Bird, 1979).

Publications that have not conformed to advertisers' requirements have simply disappeared. For example, *Everywoman* folded in 1967 with the fourth highest sale out of 21 women's magazines sold through newsagents, but with a majority of its readers being drawn from the working class (National Readership Survey, 1966: T19A). This gravitational pull towards the middle class, exerted by advertising, has contributed to the remarkable conservatism of much women's journalism. It has also resulted in a broad range of cultural provision being geared disproportionately to one section of the community.

The class bias of much magazine publishing is matched by an age bias. As early as the 1950s, market researchers were stressing the importance of the age cycle and family structure on the demand pattern for products (e.g. Wheeler, 1954). The relative affluence of the 15–24 age group, at a time of sharply rising consumption, encouraged advertisers to pay increasing attention to youth markets. This orientation was further reinforced by the 'accessibility' of youth markets due to the greater willingness of young people to try out new consumer products. This encouraged publishers to cater for this much-prized advertising market by launching a succession of publications aimed at young people.[20] In marked contrast, few publications have been directed towards elderly people because their disposable income – and consequently advertising utility – is much less than that of young people. Inequalities between age groups are thus reproduced in the market structure of the magazine press through the mediational rôle of advertisers.

Inequalities of age and class have coalesced to produce a further distortion in the women's magazine press. Many of the new women's magazines aimed at the late teen and twenties market have been oriented towards the middle class. Consequently many more magazines now cater primarily for the young (under 35) middle class than for the older (over 35) working class, although the former number about five and a half million and the latter 16 million (Bird, 1979).

THE BIAS OF ADVERTISERS' PRIORITIES

Which sections of the public are serviced with a multiplicity of publications depends, in part, upon their importance to advertisers. Two groups – distribution agents and those influencing corporate spending decisions – are so important that they have over a thousand publications catering for their needs. For example, there were 161 medical publications in 1974, many of which were heavily subsidized by advertising designed to influence spending within the National Health Service.[21]

Another distorting effect of advertising has been to encourage the growth of what may be broadly defined as 'consumer' magazines, but not a whole range of publications that fail to conform to the marketing requirements of advertisers. A good example of this latter group are political periodicals that, generally speaking, are found wanting on three counts. They do not provide an editorial environment conducive to buying particular products or services; they do not 'cover' a consumer market; and they do not reach specialized groups of corporate spenders or distribution agents. Consequently whereas advertising subsidies have assisted the growth of consumer and specialist publications by lowering their cover prices and funding their editorial costs, the lack of large-scale advertising has retarded a comparable development of the political periodical press in Britain.

[. . .]

DICTATES OF THE MASS MARKET

TV companies make their money from selling audiences rather than programmes. TV companies therefore seek to make and transmit programmes that *produce* the audiences advertisers want to reach. As Simon Broadbent, the vice-chairman of a leading agency, put it, 'the spot therefore is the packaging, the product inside the package is an audience'.

Contrary to popular belief, advertisers generally do not want to reach a mass audience in an indiscriminate way. As the standard advertising textbook puts it, 'It is wasteful and often futile to aim advertising at everybody' (Broadbent, 1979: 149). Many advertisers would like ideally commercial TV to produce large but variegated and selected audiences.

[. . .]

A small number of programmes do 'select' particular groups and, no less important for the media planner, also deter particular groups of consumer.[22] But generally speaking, the pattern of commercial TV programme viewing is very unselective and would seem to be influenced more by the availability of the viewer to watch TV than by what is being shown. As Goodhardt et al. (1975) have shown, specialized programmes do not tend to generate specialized audiences; light viewers do not tend to be especially discriminating but tend to watch the most popular programmes; even many regular series have a minority of viewers who saw the previous episode.

The desire of most advertisers to use TV as a medium for reaching selected groups is thus partly frustrated by the relative lack of selectivity of TV viewing. Thus would-be selective, targeting pressure has been converted into a powerful impetus for TV companies to deliver the largest possible audience since this produces the largest possible number of people within the prospect groups that advertisers want to reach. This, in turn, enables TV companies to charge high rates.

Advertisers also exert a strong pressure for commercial TV companies to produce stable, reliable and predictable audiences. Advertisers pay money for spots in anticipation that these will deliver certain quantities of viewers. Most sophisticated agencies also run retrospective checks to see what value for money they obtained from their schedules. If the TV companies do not deliver what is expected of them, there is generally a loud chorus of complaint from their clients.

Advertisers also seek quantity rather than quality.

[. . .]

The effect of this pressure for large audiences is for priority to be given to programmes that are of universal appeal – notably soap operas, situation comedies, the main news bulletin and variety programmes. In 1978–79, for instance, what may be broadly defined as drama, light entertainment, news and news magazine programmes, accounted for 61% of ITV's total output, and the overwhelming proportion of its peak time transmission (IBA, 1979). Programmes that are not of universal appeal such as documentary and current affairs programmes tend to be transmitted outside peak time hours.

Commercial TV companies have also developed scheduling strategies designed to maintain a stable and predictable audience. This generally involves transmitting light entertainment programmes early in the evening, followed by a sequence of programmes that expand and consolidate the mass audience throughout the evening. If ITV contractors are forced as a consequence of IBA pressure, direct or indirect, to transmit a programme of low audience appeal during peak viewing hours, they often take steps to minimize audience fall-out either by matching it with an equally unpopular programme on BBC1 or by 'hammocking' the programme between two 'bankers' (i.e. programmes with proven audience appeal). The scheduling philosophy of the ITV system is thus essentially cautious and conservative: it is wary of programme innovation during peak time viewing of a sort that might lose viewers to another channel for the rest of the evening.

The pursuit of viewers in crude terms of quantity rather than in terms of their quality of appreciation also provides a built-in bias within the ITV system against current affairs programmes. As Barwise, Ehrenburg and Goodhardt (1979) have shown, 'information' programmes generally gain higher appreciation scores than 'entertainment' programmes, even though they generally attract smaller audiences. Whether reliance on ratings results in advertisers undervaluing the 'pull' of minority programmes is less than clear. Barwise, Ehrenburg and Goodhardt (1979) found that, within the two broad categories of information and entertainment programmes, there was a positive correlation between size of audience and appreciation.[23]

The development of mass audience programming and scheduling strategies within the private sector of broadcasting has compelled a fundamental change of policy within the BBC. When in 1958 its audience share slipped to below 30%, senior BBC executives became convinced that the BBC had to imitate, to some extent, the programme and scheduling policy of ITV. Increasingly, the output and schedules of BBC1 have come to resemble those of its principal rival. The change has produced an increasing uniformity in the content of broadcasting and an increasing reluctance to experiment. As Weldon, then managing director of the BBC, euphemistically put it, 'once you are locked in competition, you cannot afford losers' (Weldon, 1971: 9).

Commercial radio has also responded to mass marketing pressures. Between 6 am and 6 pm, commercial local radio stations are largely geared to satisfying the largest possible audience. This has given rise to styles of radio production very different from those pioneered by the BBC: to programming as distinct from separate programmes, that is to say a miscellany of short items that will include something of interest for almost everyone in the local community, organized in a flexible way and set on 'a music bed'. Within this format, priority is given to those sections of the audience available to listen. It is only in the evening that more conventional programmes are transmitted, including some aimed at minority audiences. These include programmes directed at specialist markets that will attract specialized advertising such as 'Race Track' (Radio Victory) which generates car accessory advertising, and 'Hullaballoo' (Capital Radio) which generated advertisements aimed at teenagers. The shift reflects an attempt to deliver a differentiated audience (which, again, is partly frustrated by unselective radio listening behaviour) of value to advertisers, at a time when the mass audience has been surrendered to TV.

The fluid, fast-moving programming formula of local commercial radio has been highly successful in attracting substantial local audiences to local commercial radio during peak listening times. Its overall share of radio listening in ILR areas in 1980 was 34%, significantly higher than that of any national or local BBC radio channel (JICRAR, 1980). This share is still substantially lower, however, than the BBC service as a whole, and has not compelled an adjustment on the part of the BBC comparable to the radio reorganization and change in broadcasting philosophy that followed the incursion of illegal commercial radio stations into the mass audience during the 1960s.

A striking feature of local commercial radio output is its inclusion of a substantial local news content. This is a reflection of the pattern of consumer demand. IBA surveys reveal, for example, that 'local news coverage' was rated more favourably than any other aspect of commercial local radio output.[24] The provision of local news is thus consistent with maintaining large audiences in order to maximize advertising, just as the provision of news bulletins is consistent with maximizing TV audiences.

The same is not true of national newspapers. Research undertaken by publishers over a 40-year period shows that most categories of news about public affairs have obtained below-average attention in national papers both before and after the arrival of TV. In particular, public affairs items have generally appealed less to women and to the young than to men and the older age-groups. In contrast, human interest stories and certain entertainment features have been found to have a universal appeal, transcending differences of sex, age and class. As economic pressures have built up for popular newspapers to maximize their sales and advertising revenue by winning bigger audiences, so the proportion of space devoted to public affairs has declined, while common-denominator material has steadily increased. The only departure from this trend over a 50-year period has been the period of strict economic controls when popular newspapers were temporarily insulated from the economic pressures for audience maximization (Curran, Douglas and Whannel, 1980).

There has not been a comparable trend towards depoliticization of the quality press. This is not because there is a wide chasm between reading preferences of mass and elite audiences: the pattern of quality and popular reader interest is in fact rather similar, with certain categories of human interest story being the most read items in both quality and popular papers (Curran, Douglas and Whannel, 1980: 304 *et passim*). Publishers of quality newspapers have merely been restrained from providing more common-denominator material for fear of diluting the social quality of their audiences, and consequently undermining their utility to advertisers as selective media reaching small elite groups.

[. . .]

CREATING THE RIGHT ENVIRONMENT

Subjective judgements about whether a medium provides a favourable environment for advertisements has always played a part in some advertisers' choice of media. This has generated pressure on media to create a suitable environment for advertising in order to maximize revenue.

Subjective judgements of media 'communication value' have been based on a number of considerations: whether specific editorial or programme content will attract the attention of particular groups of consumers to adjacent advertising; whether such advertising will gain their attention when they are in the right mood to respond; whether media content will induce a frame of mind that will be responsive to the advertised message; whether the authority or prestige of the medium or particular programme/column will rub off on the client's product; whether the style and tone of the media content harmonizes with the advertisement in a way that reinforces its effectiveness; and whether, in crude terms, the editorial content supports the product that is being advertised.

Such subjective considerations have become much less important in media selection than they were 50 years ago. They are now generally outweighed by calculations of cost of exposure to the target audience and 'experience' based on previous advertising campaigns. There has been, however, a significant shift towards a more intuitive approach to media selection during the last 12 years and this has increased pressures on the media to provide an environment conducive to advertising.

Commercial television is the mass medium least affected by pressure of this kind. The prohibition of advertising sponsorship within commercial TV has insulated programme controllers from direct influence on programme content. Advertisers do have foreknowledge of programme schedules and consequently are able to select space beside specific programmes. Programmes are sometimes selected because their content is thought to complement a particular advertising campaign. In theory, at least, this could give rise to pressure for more programmes complementing advertising commercials. But in practice, the selection of spots in terms of programmes is unusual.[25] Advertisers generally buy viewers rather than programme environments. The fact that the connection between programmes and audience types or profiles is so elusive, as mentioned earlier, further reduces pressure on TV companies to deliver a suitable programme ambience. Moreover, a belief has developed within agencies that commercials create 'their own environment' unaided by programme content.

When there is a conflict between a commercial and a programme – such as the announcement of an airline crash with an airline advertisement scheduled to follow – the conflict is sometimes eliminated by the withdrawal of the advertisement. But programmes or programme items are not suppressed to protect the commercial interests of advertisers. Commercial TV companies have a monopoly as the sellers of TV airtime and are in a powerful position to resist illicit advertising pressure. Indeed, it is very much in their economic interests not to submit to advertisers' censorship since this would put their franchises at risk.

Commercial radio stations are also insulated, to some extent, from overt advertising pressures. Subject to surveillance by the IBA, local radio companies have a vested interest in maintaining their autonomy from advertisers. The fact that the majority of local radio advertising is bought in packages rather than in spots, with the times of transmission being rotated by radio contractors, further contributes to radio's independence from crude advertising influence.

Newspapers have been more influenced by advertisers, and in some ways less resistant to advertising pressure. Service features on investment, travel, property, motoring and fashion have grown as a proportion of editorial space in national newspapers during the postwar period (Curran, Douglas and Whannel, 1980). Their expansion has been geared, to a large extent, to the advertising they have generated. They represent an efficient means of selling selected subgroups within a mass audience, packaged in a suitable editorial environment. Yet their narrow orientation to readers as consumers has distorted their content (Curran, 1978). Their advertising orientation has encouraged the specialist journalists working on these pages to develop a dependent and generally uncritical relationship with advertisers (Tunstall, 1971). The result has been the development of a subservient genre of journalism in which, as Ian Breach, the former motoring correspondent of *The Guardian*, puts it, 'there is a pervading fear that valuable advertising will drain away in the face of persistent criticism that names names and condemns specific products' (Breach, 1978).

This crude form of influence is largely restricted to the advertising-oriented sections of national papers. It is extremely rare for news items to be suppressed or rewritten in order to placate potential advertisers. Attempts by advertisers to influence general news reporting and comment by withholding advertising is also much less frequent than is generally supposed. The *Sunday Times* continued to receive advertising from Distillers, for example, even when it was campaigning against the company for its 'heartless treatment' of Thalidomide drug victims Advertisers are a much more pervasive influence on women's magazines than they are on national newspapers. There is generally less commitment to non-revenue goals within consumer magazine organizations than there is within national news organizations, and consequently less suspicion of advertisers. Consumer magazines are also subject to more advertising pressure because advertisers attach more weight to the editorial environment of magazines than to the content of any other medium.[26]

Pressure from advertisers has crucially influenced the balance of contents of the magazine press. A growing proportion of women's magazines during the 50s and 60s, for instance, were devoted to material consumption partly in order to provide a conducive environment for advertisements. This expansion tended to squeeze out more general articles on social and even political issues (White, 1970).

[...]

CONCLUSION

Advertisers have thus played a central rôle in shaping Britain's media system. Firstly, recent changes in advertising allocation *between* media sectors have tended to undermine traditional mass media, promote the growth of specialized media and favour the development of the regional press.

Second, advertising appropriations *within* each media sector have profoundly influenced the character and development of each medium. In particular, they have reinforced the conservative domination of the national press, caused the women's magazine press to be heavily oriented towards the young middle class, and contributed to a growing financial imbalance between the public and private sectors of broadcasting.

Third, the media have adapted to the requirements of advertisers in the ways they have sought to maximize revenue. This has resulted in a growing polarization between popular and quality newspaper journalism, the adoption of limiting programme strategies for producing large and predictable audiences on television, and the increasing subordination of the consumer magazine press to creating a conducive editorial environment for advertisements.

NOTES

1.   School of Communication, Polytechnic of Central London.
2.   Letter to the author, 30 August 1980.
3.   Interview with Stephen Murphy, 22 September 1980.
4.   Letter to the author, 30 August 1980.
5.   Not least because not all IBA officials I spoke to were of the same mind: some of the younger executives, in particular, were more inclined to perceive advertising as an influence on broadcasting output.
6.   This was not true of the considered comments of S. Murphy of the IBA nor of the last Royal Commission on the Press, although the Commission only seriously addressed itself in its report to a conspiracy model of advertising influence.
7.   The page numbering in the reference refers to the proof copy of *Bad News*. Allegations of direct advertising influence (which were almost certainly untrue) were withdrawn following the threat of a libel action.
8.   Adjusting to declining advertising profits during the 70s, national newspapers sharply increased retail prices appreciably more than the rate of inflation, thereby losing the large price differential they had compared with papers in many Western countries (documented, for instance, by the Royal Commission on the Press (1962 Appendix 9). It is perhaps no coincidence that the audience for newspapers began to decline as a proportion of the adult population during the 1970s.
9.   In 1976, its aggregate circulation was 65% of that of the national press (calculated from RCP, 1977, Annex 3, T1).
10.   The aggregate circulation of the trade, technical and professional press is unknown, but for an indication of its smallness by comparison with the rest of the periodical press, see Coopers and Lybrand (1975: T1. 7).
11.   In so far as the Commission was interested in the advertising process, it was largely in order to forecast future trends (see RCP, 1977: Appendix E).
12.   Seymour-Ure's valuable analysis is confined to the national daily press. The political imbalance is less marked in the case of national Sunday papers.
13.   Since 1918, only three new national papers have been successfully established and only one of these (currently accounting for at most 0.2% of national daily circulation) is on the left. Such adaptation as there has been to the increased strength of the left in the country, has been through changes of ownership and editorial staffing rather than through the launch of new papers.
14.   There are, of course, exceptions such as the Conservative *Sun* which has a below-average (among national dailies) advertising revenue per copy. But it is not a typical Conservative paper since more of its readers voted Labour than Conservative in the last three General Elections.
15.   This remains true despite the erosion of advertising profit margins because Conservative papers generally have suffered less from this erosion than Labour papers.
16.   The *Morning Star* has been excluded since it does not have an audited circulation.
17.   The papers concerned are the *Times, Financial Times, Guardian, Sunday Times, Sunday Telegraph* and *Observer*. Four of these six papers are generally aligned with the Conservative Party. In addition to a high level of advertising support, some of them have also obtained large subsidies from multinational conglomerates.
18.   Advertising accounted for, on average, 60% of young women's magazines and of women's monthlies, and 55% of women's weekly revenue in 1973–74 (RCP Secretariat, 1977: T24).
19.   Significantly, this targeting towards the middle class is much less marked in the case of juvenile and young teen publications. Children's periodicals derived, on average, 90% of their revenue from sales, while teenage magazines obtained, on average, 70% of their revenue from sales, in 1973–74.
20.   Social changes, inducing a change in the pattern of reader demand, also encouraged this shift. See White (1970, 1977).
21.   For an interesting examination of the wider implications of having a medical press heavily subsidized by drug companies in an American context, see Gandy (1980).
22.   For example, Sunday afternoon football on TV has a particular appeal among lager drinkers.
23.   Whether this would have remained true if very heavy viewers – 'lumpers' who will watch most programmes that are being screened – had been eliminated, remains to be investigated. For rather different findings from those of Barwise, Ehrenburg and Goodhardt (1979), see Prue (1979).

24. 'Local news coverage' scored + 86%, the highest score out of 19 aspects of commercial local radio output based on subtracting 'likes' and 'dislikes' from the question 'which of these aspects do you like, which do you dislike, and which makes no difference to you?' asked in each one of 19 local surveys in the various ILR areas over a period of five years (IBA, unpublished material).

25. Instances of commercials skilfully harmonizing with programmes, that were mentioned to me, included an advertisement for 'Black Magic' with a romantic drama, a James Bond commercial alongside 'The Professionals' (a security police drama), a Kattomeat commercial alongside a programme about the conservation of tigers, and so on. They were remarked upon *because* they were unusual.

26. This is partly because agencies are encouraged to evaluate the editorial content of magazines in terms of advertising effectiveness by the way in which many magazines sell advertising space. This is very much less true of other media.

REFERENCES

Advertising association (1962). *Advertising Expenditure 1960*, Advertising Association, London
Advertising association (1972). Advertising expenditure 1960–71, *Advertising Quarterly*, vol. 32 and 33
Advertising association (1975). *Evidence to Royal Commission on the Press* 1974–77, HMSO
Advertising association (1980). Advertising expenditure tables, 1960–1979, *Advertising Magazine*. vol 64
Barwise, T. P., Ehrenburg, A. S. C. and Goodhardt, G. J. (1979). Audience appreciation and audience size, *Journal of the Market Research Society* vol. 21, 4
Bird, M. (1978). Magazines, markets and money, in Henry, H. (ed.) *Behind the Headlines – the Business of the British Press*, Associated Business Press, London
Bird, M. (1979). Women's magazines – survey of the 70s, *Options*, Spring
Breach, I. (1978). The gentlemen of the road, *Sunday Times Colour Magazine*
Broadbent, S. (1979). *Spending Advertising Money* (3rd edition), Business Books, London
Coopers and Lybrand (1975). The periodical publishing industry, unpub., Royal Commission on the Press 1974–77
Critchley, R. A. (n.d.) *U.K. Advertising Statistics*, Advertising Association, London
Curran, J. (1970). The impact of TV on the audience for national newspapers 1945–68, in Tunstall, J. (ed.), *Media Sociology*, Constable, London
Curran, J. (1977). Capitalism and control of the press, 1800–1975, in Curran, J., Gurevitch, M. and Woollacott, J. (eds) *Mass Communication and Society*, Arnold, London
Curran, J. (1978). Advertising and the press, in Curran, J. (ed.) *The British Press: A Manifesto*, Macmillan, London
Curran, J. (1980). Advertising as a patronage system, *Sociological Review Monograph*, 29
Curran J., Douglas, A. and Whannel, G. (1980). The political economy of the human-interest story, in Smith, A. (ed.) *Newspapers and Democracy*, Massachusetts Institute of Technology Press, Cambridge, Mass.
Curran, J. and Seaton, J. (1981). *Power Without Responsibility: Press and Broadcasting in Britain*, Fontana, London
Department of Industry (1979). Newspapers and periodicals, *Business Monitor* (PQ485), Fourth Quarter, HMSO, London
Gandy, O., Jr. (1980). Information in health: subsidised news, *Media, Culture and Society*, vol. 2
Gerald, J. E. (1956). *The British Press under Government Economic Controls*, University of Minnesota Press, Minneapolis
Glasgow University Media Group (1976). *Bad News*, Routledge, Kegan & Paul, London
Goodhardt, G. J., Ehrenburg, A. S. C. and Collins, M. A. (1975). *The Television Audience: Patterns of Viewing*, Saxon House, Westmead
Henry, H. (1977). Some observations on the effects of newsprint rationing (1939–1959) on the advertising media, *Journal of Advertising History*, vol. 1
Hoch, P. (1974). *The Newspaper Game*, Calder & Boyars, London
Independent Broadcasting Authority (1979). *Annual Report 1978–9*, IBA, London
Jicrar (1980). Independent local radio network surveys, Spring/Autumn
Kaldor, N. and Silverman, R. (1948). *A Statistical Analysis of Advertising Expenditure and of the Press*, Cambridge University Press, Cambridge
Labour Research Department (1946). *The Millionaire Press*, L.R.D., London
National Readership Surveys (1956–67). Institute of the Practitioners in Advertising, London
Orwell, G. (1970). London letter to partisan review, in Orwell, S. and Angus, I. (eds), *The Collected Essays, Journalism and Letters of George Orwell*, vol. 2, Penguin, Harmondsworth
Prue, T. (1979). The rate for the job, *Options*, vol. 3
Royal Commission on the Press 1947–1949 (1949). HMSO, London
Royal Commission on the Press 1961–1962 (1962). HMSO, London
Royal Commission on the Press 1974–1977 Final Report (1977). HMSO, London
Royal Commission on the Press Secretariat (1977). Periodicals and the alternative press, *Royal Commission on the Press Research Series 6*, HMSO, London

Seymour-ure, C. (1977). National daily newspapers and the party system, in *Studies on the Press*, Royal Commission on the Press Working Paper No. 3, HMSO, London
Silverman, R. (1951). *Advertising Expenditure in 1948*, Advertising Association, London
Silverman, R. (1954). *Advertising Expenditure 1952*, Advertising Association, London
Steed, H. Wickham (1938). The Press, Penguin, Harmondsworth
Tunstall, J. (1971). *Journalists at Work*, Constable, London
Weldon, H. (1971). *Competition in Television*, BBC, London
Whale, J. (1979). *The Politics of the Media* (rev. edition), Fontana, London
Wheeler, D. (1955). *A New Classification of Households*, British Market Research Bureau, June
White, C. (1970). *Women's Magazines 1963–1968*, Michael Joseph, London
White, C. (1977). *The Women's Periodical Press in Britain 1946–1976*, Royal Commission on the Press Working Paper No. 4, HMSO, London

50

UNDERSTANDING ADVERTISERS[1]

Kathy Myers

One of the problems with cultural analysis of advertising is the tendency to isolate a single preferred reading or decoding of a text or image[2]. There has been a marked reluctance to consider either the production practices and deliberate persuasive strategies which affect the design of an advert or the variety of possible interpretations which audiences may make. In particular, readings of advertisements have failed to take into account the fact that advertisements are selectively targeted, that they are encoded in such a way as to maximize their appeal for a preselected social group or target audience.

Selective targeting is a strategy for selective selling, designed to secure a predictable level of demand for an advertised product. In marketing terminology, the ability to predict the level of demand represents the difference between 'trial selling' and 'branding'. For a product to become a brand it needs to establish and maintain a position in the market over a defined period of time. Market stability ultimately depends upon repeat purchases.

Ralph Horowitz put the case for manufacturers' investment in advertising as follows: 'The role of advertising is to diminish uncertainty. Advertising sets out to secure a predetermined level of demand for a given future and to diminish fluctuations around that predetermined level.'[3] The ability to predict total revenue from advertised products is crucial if manufacturers are to accurately plan future output, product development and capital investment.

It is therefore the need to take the trial and error out of selling that motivates advertisers to create a clear picture of the audience they are selling to, and what role or function the product could play in people's lives. An agency report on consumer research emphasized the importance of 'consumer orientation' in campaign planning:

> Consumer orientation is the difference between looking through the eyes of the manu-
> facturer and looking through the eyes of the consumer . . . consumer orientation means
> thinking of advertising strategies in terms of what it will do to them. Understanding the

From H. Davis and P. Walton (eds), *Language, Image, Media* (Oxford: Blackwell, 1983) pp. 205–23.

target audience, how they will use the advertising and respond to it, are the subjects of advertising planning. (Ogilvy, Benson & Mather 1978)

It is important to make the distinction between the ability of an audience to comprehend or decode an advertisement in terms of its product message, and the possibility that the audience will react or respond to it by buying the product. Agency consumer research is geared to understanding the relationship between advertisement comprehension and purchase. The report quoted above went on to say:

> [Advertisers] need understanding of the consumer's relationships with the product – how the target consumer thinks and feels about the product and how it is used and the way it fits in with their lives. It is wrong to begin thinking about the brand and its attributes and how to compete with rivals without first thinking of basic consumer requirements and habits and basic thoughts and beliefs.

Attention to the 'needs' and 'desires' of the consumer informs every level of marketing strategy: the design of the campaign, the kind of media exposure given, the amount of exposure, the choice of packaging, distribution, etc. The advert which we see is only one part of this highly coordinated marketing offensive.

The rest of this paper is divided into two sections. The first section considers the problem of identifying advertisements in women's magazines. The second section looks at advertisers' intentions: the concepts of branding and selling in relation to the advertisers' image of the consumer. Both issues have been neglected in the cultural analysis of advertising to the detriment of theory and interpretation.

IDENTIFYING ADVERTISEMENTS IN WOMEN'S MAGAZINES

Pateman [. . .] suggests that recognizing an advertisement is an easy business; something which audiences 'routinely accomplish'. For Pateman it appears to be the implicit 'intention to sell' which differentiates advertisements from other kinds of messages conveyed by the media. In fact, advertisements differ from each other in significant ways which lead to three distinct kinds of advertising: Direct Advertising, Shared Advertising and Indirect Advertising. It would seem that in women's magazines, the intention to sell is what unites the commercial content of these publications rather than the basis for distinguishing between advertisements and other kinds of journalistic copy.

Direct advertising.   This refers to advertisements commissioned by manufacturing companies and produced by agencies. It is what most commentators [. . .] appear to mean by 'advertisements'.

Shared advertisements.   The expense of an advertisement may be shared by two or more interested companies, or, in the case of 'advertorials', by the magazine and manufacturer. Because of expense and problems of organization, this kind of advertising tends to be limited.

[. . .]

Indirect advertising.   All forms of advertising depend on the support which successful promotion or marketing can provide. Manufacturing companies or hired agencies and public relation services work to provide magazines with up-to-date product information. This kind of promotion aims to encourage journalistic attention in the hope that it will reap favourable 'free' advertising benefits. The scale and significance of indirect advertising is hard to detect, as it may be incorporated into a magazine article or consumer advice page at the discretion of journalists and editors.

[. . .]

The benefits of information accrue to both advertisers and publishers. Advertisers need to expose their products or services but magazines also need up-to-date product information if they are to keep their publication topical and competitive.

[. . .]

It is surprising that Raymond Williams's early observations on the close relationship between advertising and editorial within the context of women's magazines have been overlooked by other writers. He said: 'It is often not easy to separate advertising from editorial material. It is not only that the styles of presentation are remarkably similar. It is also that a good deal of more or less direct advertising is normally included in certain editorial features.' (1962, pp. 55–6) This overlap is neither a coincidence nor is it just a matter of stylistic convention. Both advertiser and publisher may benefit from the development of all overall 'house' style which gives predictability, consistency and coherence to the entire range of content.

To understand advertisements it is also important to know that without exception all women's magazines are financially dependent upon advertising revenue. Paid advertisements account for up to a third of total page space. That publicity and product promotions are partly a consumer and partly an advertiser service is illustrated by the convention of giving front cover make-up or fashion credits to lucrative advertisers. Magazine styles have also been influenced by presentation and design innovations made within commercial advertising.

From the advertiser's point of view, women's magazines are a highly reliable way of reaching the female consumer. Readership profiles are available for each magazine on the market. The Target Group Index and National Readership Survey suggest that women make 80 per cent of domestic consumer decisions, and that one of the most cost-efficient ways of reaching this market is through the medium of women's magazines. The readership profiles also provide a detailed analysis of the female market by social group which is broken down by age, class, occupation and other variables. Magazines may sell advertising space on the strength of their ability to reach a precise social group or target audience. For example, the copy for a National Magazines advert which appeared in *Campaign* read:

> ABC 1 × 3 million. Spend a month in colour with National Magazines and Cosmospolitan, Harper and Queens, Good Housekeeping, She and Company will put you in touch with 33% of all ABC 1 women. Independent, discriminating, intelligent and above all affluent. Britain's most desirable women. Spend six months with National Magazines, and the figures are even more glamorous: 51% of all ABC 1 women; 65% of all ABC 1 women under 35. No other publishing company reaches so many desirable ABC 1 women at so little cost. Be they fashion-conscious younger women, discerning housewives, or decision-making business women. Taken all in all, National Magazines are the best-written, most beautifully designed magazines now available for Britain's ABC 1 women and ABC 1 Advertisers, too.[4]

One unquantifiable benefit to advertisers is that magazines provide a 'hospitable environment' for the digestion and assimilation of advertised information. Glossy, colourful and eye-catching, women's magazines are reputed to have a 'keep' value. They may be read at leisure, used for reference, shown to friends or left about the house. Publishers and advertisers believe that these magazines provide a source of information, advice, solidarity and companionship, and that women have grown to trust the opinions voiced. It is a credibility jealously guarded by editors and highly valued by advertisers, for both groups feel that some of the journalistic credibility is carried over into the advertisements. The magazine environment as an essential ingredient of advertising success was the message of an IPC advert for their Women's Group of magazines. The copy quoted a Saatchi and Saatchi spokesman on the subject of Anchor Butter:

> While our TV advertising is promoting the use of Anchor Butter in the family, we are looking to posters and women's magazines to reinforce our branding for us. We want the housewife to be absolutely certain that Anchor is the name she can rely on for real butter goodness, and we are confident that in the relaxed, intimate environment of women's magazines our message carries complete conviction.[5]

The two-way relationship between advertisers and the medium is not always untroubled. Magazine editors feel some responsibility towards readers as well as advertisers and are concerned for the integrity of their product. This may produce a conflict of loyalties between publisher, editor and advertiser. In 1980, this tension precipitated the sacking of the editor of one women's magazine. She had exercised her editorial rights and refused to carry cigarette advertising which she felt compromised the health and beauty ethos of the magazine.

Some advertisers may seek to stretch the credibility of their advertisement by plagiarizing the 'house style' of the magazine. Agency personnel I interviewed believed that this approach could make advertisements immediately accessible and appealing, especially to the younger audience. It is one way of seducing readers into paying attention to advertisements which they might otherwise selectively avoid. However, some agencies despised this approach, not because they considered it underhand, but because they felt it lacked distinction and impact, advertisements tending to 'blur' into the overall background provided by the magazine. There seemed to be a consensus of opinion among the agencies that this method could provide a useful way of 'educating' a young audience into 'product benefit'; especially when, for certain products, there are severe constraints on advertising in other media (for example, adverts for sanitary protection, vaginal deodorants). Under these circumstances teenage magazines may provide advertisers with the sole means of access to their target audience.

[. . .]

The publisher's planning department has to be aware of the implications of stylistic overlap between advertisement and journalism. If advertisements are not signalled clearly, and look too much like editorial copy, readers may lose faith in the journalistic values of the magazine. Hence magazines often cover themselves by placing the word 'Advertisement' over some ads. However, the actual course of action taken will depend on the importance of the advertiser for the revenue of the magazine. Over-stringent policies which prevent advertisers from producing advertisements in the style of the magazine may result in the buyer moving elsewhere, in what is a highly competitive market.

Advertisers need to strike a delicate perceptual balance between making an advertisement appear 'at home' in the environment of the magazine, and designing it to stand out – maximizing 'brand impact'. The tension between environment and brand impact particularly affects the design of advertisements for products in close competition, like Martini and Cinzano aperitifs.[6] The problem may be less acute in press advertising than in television commercials because the audience can dwell on a printed image for longer, but room for confusion still exists. Because brand impact is felt to be essential for successful advertising, those advertisements which directly trade off other advertisements or editorial style tend to be in the minority. The fact that magazines also engage in this borrowing of style means that advertisers have to constantly find new ways of expressing the product message whilst keeping within the parameters of the overall stylistic conventions laid down by the magazine.

In the context of women's magazines the ability to recognize an advertisement will therefore depend on how it is signalled to the audience. Accurate recognition cannot be taken for granted, for the difference between advertisement and the varieties of journalism is often hard to define either linguistically or visually. The form which an advertisement ultimately takes will depend on a combination of advertisers' intentions, economic criteria, editorial policy and legal and voluntary restraints on practice, as well as technical developments within the medium.

ADVERTISERS' INTENTIONS: BRANDING, SELLING AND THE IMAGE OF THE CONSUMER

Advertisers' intentions could be described loosely as consisting of the overall marketing strategy for a specific campaign. However, within any agency there is unlikely to be a consensus of opinion on exactly how a campaign should be executed. For example, the creative team responsible for the production of artwork and copy may feel that the aesthetic form of the advertisement has been prostituted in the interests of economic or diplomatic considerations. The account director – an agency middle man – has the job of harmonizing the ideas of the creative team with the demands of the client. The relationship between client and agency is essentially that of employer and employee, and is not necessarily a smooth one. Agencies are very dependent on the diplomatic skills and organizational ability of the accounts department to ensure the smooth running of the campaign. The advertisement which emerges from these processes of imagination, financial control and human management must be a product of compromise, argument, bargaining and tight deadlines.

Attitudes expressed by agency staff on the role of advertising are often contradictory and eclectic. There is a danger in the analysis of advertising of assuming that it is in the interests of advertisers to create one 'preferred' reading of the advertisement's message. Intentionality suggests conscious manipulation and organization of texts and images, and implies that the visual, technical and linguistic strategies work together to secure one preferred reading of an advertisement to the exclusion of others.

If we take as an example the Benson and Hedges campaign [. . .], the advertisement can be said to work on three levels.

From the advertiser's point of view it has two related functions at the level of denotation: to attract the attention of the target audience for the product and to maximize brand impact. The connotative associations work in two different ways. One is to connect the product with a visual system familiar in abstract art, so that we may read off connotations of advertising as an art form, a 'commercial' artifact which transcends its origins and acquires the prestige of art. In the other, the connotations are left open. The reader is required to do the work of making associations within and between the images present within the advertisement. Advertisers may deliberately trade on the polysemic nature of these images to hold interest and entertain the viewer. The ambiguity and complexity of the image adds richness and texture to the advertisement itself, and, in a highly competitive product field, may provide a way of securing audience attention. It may not be in the advertiser's interests to foreclose the entire range of alternative readings. It is interesting to note that a number of abstract advertisements in the same genre (e.g. Guinness, White Horse, Number 6) were pioneered by the drink and tobacco companies whose advertising is heavily constrained by voluntary agreements with the Department of Health and Social Security, the Independent Broadcasting Authority and the Advertising Standards Authority which proscribe many associations or comments which advertisers might make for their product. As a consequence of these restrictions, advertisers have had to find an alternative way of branding which does not rely on 'country scenes', 'virility', 'social success' and similar associations.

The openness of the connotative codes may mean that we have to replace the notion of 'preferred reading' with another which admits a range of possible alternatives open to the audience. In certain cases it may also be that 'brand impact' is achieved more by single features (e.g. colour) than by the deeper and more complex levels of coding and signification within the image or text. With Benson and Hedges the intention is clearly to brand a product in a particular way. But preferential reading of the image operates only in so far as the advertisement secures the attention of a specific target audience. In other words, the determinants of the 'readings' are not present *within* the advertisement and cannot be read out of it without reference to the implicit marketing strategy of the agency concerned. It can be misleading to search for the determinations of a preferred reading solely within the form and structure of an advertisement.

Conflicts within agency strategy are reflected in the system of beliefs which validate the industry as a whole. On the one hand members of the advertising profession see advertising mythically as consistent with the needs of a democratic egalitarian society: it helps to make the consumer aware of available market choices', it 'educates' the consumer into 'product benefit' and so on. But the vision of advertising as a democratic information service is distorted by the fact that it is the job of each individual agency to promote one product at the expense of competing products and, implicitly, to systematically foreclose the appeal of alternatives in the eye of the consumer. The apparent contradiction between these two aspects of commercial philosophy is rationalized in terms of the 'Darwinian' survival of the fittest product. In the Western economy, where 95 per cent of the new products introduced onto the market each year fail to maintain a market position, successful marketing and advertising is felt to be essential to give products a competitive chance.

Agencies are commissioned to promote specific products for their clients, but the cumulative effect of advertising is to promote product fields or categories. From the advertisers' point of view this effect is double-edged. On the one hand, their specific brand may benefit from the increase in public awareness of, and interest in, the product field. On the other hand, consumers may start to favour less expensive alternatives. Advertisers are aware that brand loyalty is at best idealistic, and that in terms of consumer behaviour, its probability is low. Successful marketing and promotion of a product therefore cannot depend on advertising alone. Advertising has to be seen as an integral part of a much wider marketing offensive which extends from product development through to retail distribution. It is this spectrum of product promotion which gives a commodity its total image and style. Advertisers, if not their critics, realize that they cannot rely on the linguistic or visual significations internal to the advertisement to do the selling. As one account executive put it: 'You can't sell a product if it's naff – if a need for it doesn't exist. You need the right product, the right distribution and the right sales staff. Advertising can't go it alone, it's all got to work together.' 'Good' advertising is therefore a combination of market research, intuition and so-called 'creative talent'.

One requirement of successful branding is to recognize or create the 'right' consumer for the product. As a consequence, advertisements are constructed so as to be highly selective in their form of address and appeal. Account executives tend to talk about their products fulfilling 'social needs', although they seem unclear about the aetiology of these 'needs' or the role which advertising plays in structuring them. They typically describe advertising as both 'reflecting' social needs, and as 'creating a market'. As an account executive for a men's aftershave advertisement put it, the product 'created the market, or rather, satisfied a need that was already there'.

Whatever inconsistency there may be in notions of demand, the consumer is never absent from agency strategy. The consumer profile which they build informs all levels of agency discourse. The agency concept of 'consumer experience' is supported by a complex social map which details how a product will be used, how it will fit into, shape and alter the lifestyle of the prospective consumer. An illustration of this is the concept of the female consumer.

Since most domestic purchasing decisions are made by women, agencies tend to refer to the consumer as 'she', or as the 'housewife'. Women are recognized as a social group by virtue of gender, but certain 'lifestyle' differences within this 'all housewives' group are recognized. In fact the need for a refined view of 'lifestyle' is stressed:

> Beware the 'all housewives' target audience – select your prime prospect. The more accurately you pinpoint your prime prospect, the higher your conversion rate [to the product] . . . and when your prime prospect is defined, paint a picture of him/her using all the attitudinal data you can find. Do not settle for media jargon categories. Persil Automatic was not launched merely at 'front loading washing machine users'; its success has demonstrated a precise and continuing understanding of the attitudes and lifestyle of the women who own such a machine.[7]

However, the nebulous concept of 'lifestyle' used by agencies is not guaranteed to provide a precise understanding of consumer practice. Imported from the USA marketing industry it provided an alternative description of social difference from that of 'class'. 'Lifestyle' was felt to provide a more accurate estimation of purchasing power and actual market choices made by consumers. Advertisers' resistance to the concept of class as a structuring principle is due partly to the consensual view of society which they appear to favour, and partly to the inadequacies of the class model employed. Agencies do use the Registrar General's scale which categorizes people on the basis of occupation of head of household, but they feel that this gives a misleading picture of consumers' disposable income because women are subsumed in the general socioeconomic categories.

Lifestyle categories are said to cut across the hierarchies of occupation and status, so that social stratification is contradictory and complex. Women are stereotyped in similar ways and unified by their common interests in beauty, youth, the family, home and relationships. At the same time, however, they are segmented according to lifestyle variables: the kind of beauty look, the size of the family, the location of the house, or the woman's marital status. Typical constellations of social experience may be described euphemistically as 'sophisticated' or 'accessible' lifestyles. The effect of using 'lifestyle' categories and of separating social experiences from structured inequalities of occupation, income and ideology is to perpetuate the myth of classlessness and to promote the idea of embourgeoisement in agency thinking.

The ostensible purpose of these categories is to tailor 'aspirations' to the material circumstances of the potential consumer. Agencies are concerned that messages should be 'accessible' and not 'too farfetched' so as to encourage audience identification with the lifestyle portrayed in the advertisement.

[. . .]

How people actually respond to campaigns is hard to determine except in hard sales terms. Most agencies receive little feedback about who buys the advertised product, or why they chose it. This is due partly to the expense of post-campaign research and partly to the problems of conducting it. Successful branding is supposed to mean the securing of the 'right' consumer for the product. In practice, however, advertising success is usually measured in terms of the quantity of sales rather than the quality or characteristics of the consumer. Eventually, as products become established, incorporated into the pattern of everyday life, their significance changes. Hence, the relationship between advertising strategy and actual consumer response is rarely stable. Advertising is what René König has termed a 'restless image'. Meanings which are injected into products through advertising may be radically altered and realigned in accord with usage.

CONCLUSION

> Consumer orientation means thinking of advertising strategies in terms of what people do with advertising, not what it will do to them; understanding the target audience, how they will use the advertising and respond to it, are the subjects of advertising planning. (Ogilvy, Benson & Mather 1978)

Like the advertisers, cultural analysis has as yet no coherent theory of audience response to advertisements, or of how and why people consume. Existing definitions of consumption, or what is meant by relations to consumption, tend to be eclectic, ambiguous and confused. Especially within contemporary Marxist thought and cultural analysis, theories of consumption have been subordinated to theories of production. As Simon Frith has commented:

> The concept [of cultural consumption] means different things according to the analytic framework involved: in the marxist economic theory it refers to a moment in the circulation of value, in recent literary and film theory it refers to a kind of pleasure, in historical sociology it refers to an institutional process. Cultural theories of consumption are left in a muddle – 'passive consumption' for example is a term used by theorists of all persuasions but as a rhetorical rather than a theoretical device. (Frith 1980)

A prerequisite for any theoretical progress is that, like consumer market research, we have to reject the notion that people consume in a passive way. And since most advertising is aimed at women, and women make the majority of domestic consumer decisions, we need a theory of consumption which will explain not only how people in general relate to advertisements, but subsequently, how this affects women's purchasing decisions. Such a theory must be concerned to reassess the significance of women's place in the home. There has been a tendency to assess women's position in the home solely as an unpaid contribution to production: for example, in housework, child care and nurturing the workforce. But the home is also the focal point for consumption. This is where most advertised goods are consumed. It is also where most advertising is directed: on television, on the radio, in magazines, by mailing, etc. Women play a crucial role within this important sphere.

The general poverty of consumption theory has not only affected our analysis of marketing but has also allowed advertising to be conceptually isolated as a social form. A theory of consumption would be enriched by incorporation into a broader theory of social communications. This would mean getting out of the ghetto of 'cultural' as opposed to 'economic' analysis and the polarities of production/consumption or encoding/decoding. The role of advertising cannot be inferred simply from a knowledge of economic interests nor deduced from structuralist or language-based theories. In future, the analysis of marketing, publicity and advertising must pay closer attention to the diversity of advertisement form and the variety of advertising strategies employed. It must also recognize the spectrum of alternative audience readings which invariably exist. Perhaps where these features are acknowledged in empirical investigation, codes and conventions of advertising practice and consumer response will emerge which can be shown to be sensitive to the whole social structure.

NOTES

1.   The empirical evidence used in this paper was gathered during the period January–August 1980. Interviews were conducted in ten leading advertising agencies which have cosmetic accounts. I would like to thank Don Slater for his assistance.
2.   See Williamson 1978, and Pateman 1983 [. . .] for examples of this tendency.
3.   R. Horowitz, 'The case for advertising', *Campaign*, 24 Aug. 1979.
4.   National Women's Magazine Group advertisement *Campaign*, 18 Apr. 1980.
5.   IPC Women's Magazine Group advertisement *Campaign*, 26 Oct. 1979.
6.   T. Fawley of (TABS) has voiced the anxiety of the advertisers: 'In general product fields there is a multiplicity of brands competing for attention . . . unless a commercial is very well branded, how many of the target audience will be unable to differentiate between competing brands?' 'Analysis of the ITV strike', *Campaign*, 18 Jan. 1980.
7.   A. Gibson, managing director of Benton and Bowles, '5 vital steps to prevent a launch disaster', *Campaign*, 18 Apr. 1980.

REFERENCES

Davis, H. and Walton, P. 1983: *Language Image, Media*. Oxford: Blackwell.
Frith, S. 1980: Music for pleasure. *Screen Education* 34, Spring.
Horowitz, M. J. 1970: *Image formation and cognition*. New York: Meredith.
König, R. 1973: *The restless image. A sociology of fashion*. London: George Allen & Unwin.
Ogilvy, Benson & Mather 1978: *A consumer's view of how advertising works*. London: Ogilvy, Benson & Mather Planning and Research Unit.
[Pateman, T. 1983: How is understanding an advertisement possible? In Davis and Walton 1983.]
Williams, R. 1962: *Communications*. Harmondsworth: Penguin.
Williamson, J. 1978: *Decoding Advertisements*. London: Marian Boyars.

51

DECODING ADVERTISEMENTS

Judith Williamson

[. . .]

There is very little real difference between brands of product within any category, such as detergents, margarine, paper towels and so on. Therefore it is the first function of an advertisement to *create* a differentiation between one particular product and others in the same category. It does this by providing the product with an 'image'; this image only succeeds in differentiating between products in so far as *it* is part of a system of differences. The identity of anything depends more on what it is *not* than what it is, since boundaries are primarily distinctions: and there are no 'natural' distinctions between most products. This can be seen by the fact that a *group* of products will sometimes be marketed with the same 'image', in a set or 'range' [. . .] – these usually have names, like 'Maybelline' or 'Spring Bouquet' etc.: the limits of identity are chosen arbitrarily, it is clear, because in other cases two identical products from the very same manufacturer will be given different names and different images. If two different bottles of cleansing milk can have the same name – 'Outdoor girl' or suchlike, but a third, apparently similar, can appear with a different name and therefore with supposedly different properties, it immediately becomes apparent that there are no logical boundaries between most products. Surf and Daz essentially contain the same chemicals. Obviously there *are* products with special qualities or particular uses, but these do not usually need extensive advertising campaigns: the bulk of advertising covers exactly the areas where goods are the same: cigarettes, cornflakes, beer, soap.

I am taking a group of perfume advertisements – two of which come from the same manufacturer: these provide a good example of the creation of 'images' since perfumes *can* have no particular significance. This is a type of ad which can give no real information about the product (what information can be given about a smell?) so that the function of differentiation rests totally on making a connection with an image drawn from outside the ad world.

From J. Williamson, *Decoding Advertisements* (London: Marion Boyars, 1978) pp. 24–7.

CHANEL NO. 5

Catherine Deneuve's face and the Chanel bottle are not linked [in the ad] by any narrative, simply by juxtaposition: but there is not supposed to be any *need* to link them directly. They are as it were in apposition in the grammar of the ad, placed together in terms of an assumption that they have the same meaning, although the connection is really a random one. For the face and the bottle are not inherently connected: there is no link between Catherine Deneuve *in herself* and Chanel No. 5: but the link is in terms of what Catherine Deneuve's face *means to us,* for this is what Chanel No. 5 is trying to mean to us, too. The advertisement presents this transference of meaning to us as a *fait accompli,* as though it were simply presenting two objects with the same meaning but, in fact, it is only *in* the advertisement that this transference takes place. Chanel No. 5 only has the 'meaning' or image that it shares with Catherine Deneuve by having become associated with Catherine Deneuve through this very advertisement. So what Catherine Deneuve's face means to us in the world of magazines and films. Chanel No. 5 seeks to mean and comes to mean in the world of consumer goods. The ad is using another already existing mythological language or sign system, and appropriating a relationship that exists in that system between signifier (Catherine Deneuve) and signified (glamour, beauty) to speak of its product in terms of the same relationship; sothat the perfume can be substituted for Catherine Deneuve's face and can also be made to signify glamour and beauty.

Using the structure of one system in order to give a structure to another, or to translate the structure of another, is a process which must involve an intermediate structure, a system of systems or 'meta-system' at the point where the translation takes place: this is the advertisement. Advertisements are constantly translating between systems of meaning, and therefore constitute a vast meta-system where values from different areas of our lives are made interchangeable.

Thus, the work of the advertisement is not to invent a meaning for No. 5, but to translate meaning for it by means of a sign system we already know. It is only because Catherine Deneuve has an 'image', a significance in one sign system, that she can be used to create a new system of significance relating to perfumes. If she were not a film star and famous for her chic type of French beauty, if she did not *mean* something to us, the link made between her face and the perfume would be meaningless. So it is not her face as such, but its position in a system of signs where it signifies flawless French beauty, which makes it useful as a piece of linguistic currency to sell Chanel.

The system of signs from which the product draws its image is a *referent system* in that the sign lifted out of it and placed in the ad (in this case, Catherine Deneuve's face) *refers back to it*. It is not enough simply to know who Catherine Deneuve is: this will not help you to understand the ad. Someone from another culture who knew that Catherine Deneuve was a model and film star would still not understand the significance of her image here, because they would not have access to the referent system as a whole. And it is only by referring back to this system as a system of *differences* that the sign can function: it is hollow of meaning in itself, its signified is only a distinction rather than a 'content'. Only the form and structure of the referent system are appropriated by the advertisement system; it is the relationship and distinction between parts, rather than the parts themselves, that make an already-structured external system so valuable to advertising. The links made between elements from a referent system and products arise from the *place* these elements have in the whole system rather than from their inherent qualities. Thus Catherine Deneuve has significance only in that she is not, for example, Margaux Hemingway.

'BABE'

The 'image' of this ad derives its impact from the existence of precisely such ads as [that for Chanel No. 5], as it is able to 'kick off' against the more sedate Catherine Deneuve image and others like it. This new perfume, 'Babe', has been launched in a campaign using the new 'discovery' Margaux Hemingway. The significance of her novelty, youth and 'Tomboy' style, which has value only *in relation* to the more typically 'feminine' style usually connected with modelling, is carried over to the perfume: which is thus signified as new and 'fresh', in relation to other established perfumes. There would be no significance at all in the fact that Margaux Hemingway is wearing a karate outfit and has her hair tied back to look like a man's, were it not for the fact that *other* perfume ads show women wearing pretty dresses and with elaborately styled hair. The meaning is not, however, generated *inside* the advertisement system; there is a meaning in terms of 'women's liberation' and 'breaking conventions' in a model's having a tough 'liberated' image (in one TV ad for 'Babe', Margaux Hemingway mends the car while her boyfriend watches) rather than a passive, 'feminine' one. In the widest sphere of meaning which the ad draws on, even outside modelling and images, the meaning still depends on a contrast, since the very idea of women doing karate is only significant because most women do *not* and have not done anything of the sort. [. . .]

So this advertisement uses the 'Margaux Hemingway' image, *which itself depends for its significance on not being Catherine Deneuve's image* to give 'Babe' a distinct place in the inventory of perfumes, emphasising its novelty (It's *not being like* what has gone before) and its difference from all the others. It uses a contrast made in social terms, 'feminine' vs. 'liberated', as signified by two models, to make a contrast between products.

In the mythological system of fashion and publicity Catherine Deneuve and Margaux Hemingway are mutually differentiated and can only have value as signs in relation to each other: as Saussure says: 'in all cases, then, we discover not *ideas* given in advance but *values* emanating from the system. When we say that these values correspond to concepts, it is understood that these concepts are purely differential, not positively defined by their content but negatively defined by their relation with other terms of the system. Their most precise characteristic is that they are what the others are not.'[1] Thus with Catherine Deneuve and Margaux Hemingway it is the *difference* between their significances (taking them not as women but as signs, for this is what they are in this context) that makes them valuable in advertising. Advertisements appropriate the formal relations of pre-existing systems of differences. They use distinctions existing in social mythologies to create distinctions between products.

[. . .]

NOTES

1.   Saussure, *Course in General Linguistics*, quoted in *Saussure* by Jonathan Culler, Fontana, 1976, p. 26.

52

HANDLING SEX

Janice Winship

Attention to women's and men's hands in ads may not seem *the* most burning issue to be tackled on the question of representations of femininity and masculinity in ads. Yet it is not just feminist nit-picking. As Erving Goffman has commented in his glossy book, *Gender Advertisements*, gender is 'something that can be conveyed *fleetingly* in any social situation' (Goffman, 1979: 7, my emphasis). If only a brief *time* suffices to communicate gender to us, similarly only a small part of our anatomy need be represented in that communication. A representation of a hand, or even only a part of one, will then do quite as well to signify cultural aspects of gender, as a full length portrayal. That this is so, is sure evidence of the pervasiveness and depth to which gender construction penetrates.

However, there are other reasons why I have chosen the representation of hands to focus this discussion of gender difference and its construction in forms which, I argue, are oppressive to women. Firstly, there is a partly empirical consideration. In ads women are frequently represented in a 'fragmented' way, or as Trevor Millum describes, photographically 'cropped' (Millum, 1975: 83–84). Women are signified by their lips, legs, hair, eyes or hands, which stand, metonymically – the bit for the whole – for, in this case, the 'sexual woman' (Winship, 1980). Men, on the other hand are less often 'dismembered' and the only bit of them which is represented with any frequency seems to be the hand. Since women's hands also appear in ads this allows us to make a limited but fine analysis which begins to compare the representations of femininity with those of masculinity by beginning from a similar point. The *difference* of the meanings conveyed by a gendered hand, which the analysis then goes on to demonstrate, is only highlighted by this formally equivalent beginning. In the ad context we find that a woman's hand can never be substitute for a man's, nor a man's for a woman's: the gender difference the hand stands for is always crucial to the meaning of the ad.

This singular focus on hands also has a further pedagogic benefit in so far as it allows us to argue a particular theoretical position more clearly. Briefly, that position holds that ads as a

From *Media, Culture and Society* 3:1 (1981) pp. 25–41.

discourse do have their own 'specificity' but that the order of that specificity must be pinned down. Simultaneously we must also conceptualize them in their 'external' relations, especially in their relation to the social reader and to other discourses. Behind this formulation is the political concern posed by the title, 'Handling sex'. *Who* is handling? The ad makers certainly, but we as readers of the ad also 'handle' what we understand there. A feminist politics of representation with respect to ads has then, to engage with the social reader, as well as the social text.

[. . .]

To return now to the choice of hands, this focus allows us to illustrate that, clearly, one of the ideological fields these ads are working within, is that of feminity and masculinity; that feminity and masculinity can be constructed by means quite specific to ads – the hand – but also alongside other means; that femininity and masculinity are constructed with particular ideological inflections, and nearly always have a class specificity; that the hand can be used as a visual mode of address which is also verbally repeated. In what follows it is these aspects which I examine in a selection of ads, paying particular attention to how ads mean differently for women and men reading them.

1. NATURALLY: 'MEN OF THE WORLD' AND 'WOMEN AT HOME'

In most ads where we see a hand there is no doubt about it: it just *has* to be a woman's or a man's hand which we see there: the other sex would not do. It is not, however, the intrinsic qualities of each hand which makes that so. Rather it is the tightly organized production of the *whole* representation in the ad – of which the hand is only a part – which constructs a gender difference from which the hand accrues, as well as contributes meaning. If we were merely to change the hands in the next two ads so that a woman's hand (signified by, say, painted nails and a gold bracelet) was offering that packet of cigarettes, and a man's hand (signified by, say, shirt cuff and jacket) was pouring that custard there would be a disruption of the meanings. 'Hand' and text would rudely jar, signifying contradictorily: a woman's hand does not signify 'world leader'; a man's hand does not signify 'home-made'. But as it is, the appropriately gendered hand allows us to key into familiar ideologies of masculinity and femininity. Those ideologies seem 'naturally' masculine or feminine, and the represented hand is 'naturally' a man's *or* a woman's.

Rothman's cigarettes (*Observer*, 28 September 1980)

At one level the background of deep blue, *royal* blue (royal confirmed by the royal insignia and 'By special appointment') only repeats the blue band across the packet. Yet at another it signifies, as we know from other texts outside the ad, the universe, the span of the sky, or the world's seas. That meaning is corroborated by the globe represented by (some of) the constituent flags (what imperialism is perpetrated here with Britain's union jack at the centre of the world, which the packet too occupies?); and by the assignation: 'world leader'. This label is linked to 'Filter tipped' on the packet: both are against a red background, both cut diagonally across the page. The cigarette is visually confirmed by this exchange of meaning, which we make, as the 'world leader', as 'King Size' in status as well as size. At the same time the male hand, marked as male by what seems the customary middle class code in ads – the white shirt cuff, and accompanying jacket sleeve (here dark blue, with conveniently superimposed insignia), the well manicured and unblemished hand – partakes of that leadership. These are all

the signs that *he* is a leader, the 'officered (naval?) gentleman'. Cigarette and man add stature to each other.

But to whom is this packet of gourmet or snobbish fare proffered? The 'world', which includes 'you': 'the best tobacco money can buy'; the best tobacco *your* money can buy. But who is 'you'? Men. For the claims of a *masculine* leadership, over which hand and packet egg each other on in complicit and seemingly natural agreement, allows men a point of participation in the signification of the ad – via hand or packet. If that 'you' is a woman we can only submit to this dominating hand offering us a cigarette, and capitulate to the meaning of the *ad from which we are excluded*, even if we buy the cigarettes. How can we enter 'world leadership'?

Bird's custard (*Woman's Weekly*, 24 March 1979)

If we were to replace the woman's hand here by a man's we would no longer have 'Home-made goodness' as an appropriate caption. It might as a chef's hand signify a 'culinary delight', but then jam sponge would have been transformed from its 'homely' associations. This woman's hand (as woman herself) is synonymous with home; the meaning emerges 'naturally', something we recognize from what we know outside ads. But how do we know that *inside* the ad? Note what the hand looks like: *un*varnished nails, no indication of elegant long fingers which are the usual signs for that other non-homely femininity, the signification for 'beauty' or 'sex', and which definitively mark the hand as different from a man's. Here that difference is less visually established by the hand than by other visual and verbal cues in the ad. 'Home-made goodness' is conjured up not only by the 'plain' hand but by the unadorned plate, the old-fashioned, English pudding and custard itself. There is an implicit appeal to tradition, to the idealized value of femininity as 'home-making' which cuts across any class specificity: the absence of any background detail which would place this hand in class terms aids this signification. But see not only how easily and effortlessly that tradition is kept alive, but the *narrowness* of what it includes: *just* pour a jug of Bird's custard (as world leadership in the Rothman's ad *just* needed a packet of cigarettes). Modes of femininity and masculinity are achievable, then, through consumption.

If we delve a little deeper into the ad's rhetoric, as Alvarado puts it, to make an analysis which 'releases that frozen moment' (Alvarado, 1979: 8) of the representation, we might want to ask: who made the jam sponge and custard? And who is going to eat this homely fare? Who is she serving? There are three sorts of answer here. One concerns who produced the *commodity*, Bird's custard. The second is concerned with who made the pudding, or the mock-up, for the purposes of the photograph. The third is the narrative the ad fictionally traps into this moment of representation, as if it were the 'natural' narrative, so 'natural' that we don't even have to think about it. The answers are sewn up. Obviously, she who owns the hand, a 'mum', a 'wife' has made the pudding and custard; Obviously 'he' or 'they' – children and/or husband are going to eat it. Home-making is, unremittingly, for others. There she is preparing something which she is unlikely to eat herself: jam sponge at 250 calories a portion, uncompromisingly on all those diet lists of taboo foods. What woman dare eat that without feelings of self-damnation? This is truly men's and children's fare.

Reading this ad we are not verbally addressed as 'you'. Yet visually we are placed so that the hand which pours this custard could be ours: it is *our* body, if we are women, which completes the person off page. This is a frequent and useful artifice for ads, a means of visually addressing us as powerful as the verbal exhortations to 'you'. We are inevitably caught up in this 'natural' association of the feminine hand and homemade goodness – for the family. To reject that on any grounds other than feminism, that is, to wrench apart some of this 'natural meaning', we are thrown into '*not*' goodness.' What guilt to bear! Meanwhile, men enjoy the pudding, their masculinity unthreatened. Representationally their dominance is signified in their absence: they are being served.

2. BEAUTY AND THE BOSS

We have seen then, that these two hands, a man's and a woman's, signify seemingly naturally and unquestionably the 'worldly' and the 'homely', masculinity and femininity.

However, there are other gendered qualities called into play by ads. John Berger's pithy statement on the subject of gender representations that 'Men act and women appear' (Berger, 1972: 47), has awesome applicability.

(a) *Men at work* . . .

Scotcade shirts (*Observer*, 21 September 1980)

On the question of how masculinity is represented differently from femininity there is one simple point to be made here. 'Man the (middle class) worker' is signified both by what his hand is doing *and* by his appearance – the creaseless shirt and business tie. We can just about imagine that women's blouses might be advertised with this same caption which, by emptying our usual understanding of 'white, blue collar workers' to which the ad refers, and refilling with a 'commodity' meaning, trivializes that original understanding while *appearing* to extend it – 'cream collar workers' too. Workers are now differentiated by what they consume rather than by their place in any social division of labour, Judith Williamson considers this aspect of ads in some detail (Williamson, 1980). We can even imagine that a woman could

be shown doing the same activities; they are not particularly masculine tasks. But what is extremely unlikely is this mutual support between 'doing' and 'appearance'. Either the whole stress would be on the women's *looks* in the blouse (and the ad might show her face, or emphasize her sexuality by her bosom or even her hand) and/or there would be some dis-juncture between what she was doing and how, and for whom, she was looking. Men's sexuality is not in play in this ad; if the 'worker' were a woman it undoubtedly would be.

[. . .]

(b) . . . *and men at play*

JVC **video (***Observer*, **4 November 1979)**

As readers of the ad we are clearly put in the position of the viewer of the TV screen; moreover that position is occupied by a man whose hand we see controlling the screen. *If* we are men that could be our hand. The hand is marked as masculine both by its *lack* of feminine marks – no varnished nails – the caption – 'Who, said slow motion replays were just for "Match of the Day"?' – and the TV image – the fanciful strip 'girls'. As if an appeal to the most popular TV programme for men were not enough, adding insult to injury, the ad relies on that other 'spectator sport', peculiarly masculine in style, that of 'bird' watching. I use this sexist term only because the 'Simulated picture' indicates only too well the calculating construction of the ad: not just any old picture from the telly, but one showing women who are decoratively attired *like* extravagant birds. They are caught at some moment in a striptease act posing with what Goffman has neatly described as 'the bashful knee bend' (Goffman, 1979: 45). However his interpretation of this as representing 'a foregoing of full effort . . . the position adds a moment to any effort', and his assertion that because women are seen supporting each other in this pose the question of gender relations does not arise, seems not to be quite the point. The gesture is surely one of submission in which the

Who said slow motion replays were just for 'Match of the Day'?

JVC 3660 – the first colour home video recorder with slow motion and freeze frame.

woman is pausing to gaze or to be gazed at – by men. And it is this representation of women which the male hand is seen to control; at the press of a button 'you' (he) can stop and start, obliterate or bring into gaze the strip act, like the director of a film. As the ad says, 'All you need now is a canvas chair with "Director" on it.' What is being advertised is the video and the control of the image which it provides, but what seems to be at stake is a control of women's sexuality: women as fare for men's play. Further in a reversal which gives them no power or status at all, *women work* on the screen, while men play – with them.

Sony stereo cassette player (*Observer*, 22 June 1980)

When a woman's hand appears in what is formally a similar mode – at the controls of a cassette player – its place and meaning bear no comparison with the controlling hand of masculinity. The limp-wristed way she holds her hand, finger delicately resting on a switch hardly suggests she is actively working the equipment. [. . .] This elegantly attired, black gloved hand, with ring and silver bracelets, complements and repeats the metallic tones of the cassette player. The hand and the hi-fi are interchangeable; not only through their colours, but also their size and, importantly, what they are meant to stand for. The cassette player is called 'Stowaway': it is tiny; so are women's hands (well, so the stereotypes say). But this gloved hand is also classy, daring, demonstrating style; so is the cassette player. If the hand signifies the ultimate in the 'lady of leisure', a female dilettante who has money and more to spend (or be spent on her), so too the cassette player is in a class of its own: 'Sony's little masterpiece.' Even Sony think they've done quite well.

The ad primarily addresses men – hi-fi freaks – who may 'want to know about its performance in Hz, SPL, and watts per channel . . . ' They are urged, 'To see how small it is put your hand over the picture.' 'Your' (his) hand is then caught up in that of the dazzling

The way Sony have drawn hi-fi stereo sound from their new pocket sized Stowaway is a brilliant technical achievement.

Even Sony think they've done quite well.

This is Sony's new Stowaway, actual size. To see how small it is put your hand over the picture. Tiny, isn't it? Yet it plays standard music cassettes and rates as a serious piece of hi-fi equipment.

If you really want to know about its performance in Hz, SPL and watts per channel ask your Sony dealer or any of the staff at Sony's showrooms, 134 Regent Street, London.

In layman's terms, though, Stowaway's sound is its true colour stereo to dazzle your ears.

Since it is the world's smallest cassette player it comes as no surprise to learn it is equipped with a set of the world's smallest, lightest hi-fi headphones. They can pick up the tiniest tinkle of a triangle, or rasp the inside of your brain with the deepest bass of a synthesiser. You can plug in a second set of 'phones should you ever want to share your favourite music with a favourite friend.

Sony's little masterpiece runs off batteries, so you can tuck it in a pocket to play your own choice of music on the train, the plane or in a hotel room far from home. Or you can buy an adaptor to run it off the mains.

Listen to Stowaway for yourself. You won't believe it till you hear it, and even then you may find it difficult. **SONY.**

The world's smallest stereo cassette player.

lady; the electric touch only affirms the effect of Sony's technical achievement: 'to dazzle your ears.' Obviously it would not have been appropriate to encourage two male hands to touch: how could that signify 'dazzlement'?

Finally note the differences between Sony and their 'brilliant technical achievement' (*Who* are Sony? *Whose* achievement is it?), and the woman's hand; production and consumption; masculinity and femininity.

Elbeo tights (*Honey*, August/September, 1980)

Here gender difference is organized explicitly around sexuality: blatantly a man's hand 'touches her up', but in a class mode which would refuse that idiom. Visually all is there for us to guess; verbally like middle class manners, double-talk is the key note. If a hand can be used in representation so that we are placed as the owner of it, off the page, it can also pose the riddle of what exactly is happening to the owner of the hand off the page. And when it is a man's hand resting on a woman's leg the answer is clear: sex, however harmless. Yet the caption belies such a sexual appeal: 'Your appreciation of the finer things in life has always impressed me, Sir Giles.' With what are fast becoming tedious middle class significations for masculinity – white shirt cuff etc. – *plus* large dress ring, which definitely ups the class position, this 'gentleman', Sir Giles, could not be concerned with anything so brash as sex, but rather with 'the finer things in life'. What are they? Outside the context of the ad we might guess: good wine, antiques, tailor made suits, caviar and truffles, those accoutrements of a certain class position which his hand, the finely upholstered sofa, are signs for in the ad. (Note how the background here is important whereas it was purposely obliterated in the Bird's ad. The scene conforms to what Goffman refers to as 'commercial realism' in relation to which 'the viewer is to engage knowingly in a kind of make-believe, treating the depicted world as if it were real-life but of course not actually real' (Goffman, 1979: 6). But for the ad the apotheosis of 'fineness' is, of

"Your appreciation of the finer things in life has always impressed me, Sir Giles"

Supersheer 15 Denier 'Nymphe' by Elbeo, fashion tights that are more than a shade superior

ELBEO

course, Elbeo tights which drain 'fineness' from the classy environment – ' . . . are more than a shade superior'.

If the man's hand signifies class, the bit of woman which is represented primarily signifies sexuality, and would do so, *even* if the man's hand were not there. A focus on legs, like a focus on the lips, bottom, or breasts of a woman, always signifies sexuality. Yet the gold chain round her ankle and mini (*c.* 1980), black, broderie anglaise dress, support a sexual signification. There is also something classy about her representation too: the stylishness of black patent court shoes, gold chain and black dress. Indeed, a 'fine' sexuality which carries over to the 'Supersheer 15 Denier "Nymphe" ' tights, which in turn, themselves deliver that fineness to whoever wears them. The sexual loading behind the term 'fine' is not only carried in the name of the tights – Nymphe – what kind of femininity does that suggest – but also in the placing of his hand: literally it is his appreciation of the tights which is being referred to. But really?

Since it is in a woman's magazine, and since it is an ad for tights, it is women who read this ad. A woman appears to have the speaking voice. But what she speaks of is only to be impressed that *he* appreciates, what *she* appreciates; and the latter is only what he has set up in the first place. She speaks to accept a male possession – the hand on her knee: the 'man's eye view' of her legs.

3. GENDER (DIS)PLACEMENT

The next two ads are similar in so far as they show a woman and a man, respectively, in the 'wrong place'. In the Veuve du Vernay ad a woman has invaded what is visually purported to be the male terrain of a commuter train. In the Carling ad a man has been and gone from what is verbally assumed to be a woman's place – around the kitchen sink. These displacements serve, however, not to be innovative, only to reinforce particular ideologies of masculinity and

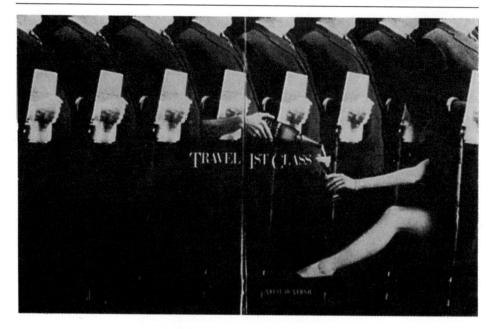

femininity. Moreover the *form* of each ad – different in each case – heightens the separation between femininity and masculinity which is being constructed.

Veuve du Vernay (*Observer*, 13 July 1980)

While the Elbeo ad corresponds to what Goffman describes as 'commercial realism', this ad uses a kind of montage technique: the incongruous chain of colour composed of the curiously emerging man's hand pouring the drink, and the woman's ridiculously placed arm and leg, seem to be superimposed against the background of drab grey and white businessmen. This achieves two effects: one of playing up a 'naughty' fantasy element, and perhaps of generating humour (funny for whom though?); the other of differentiating that brazen couple from the boring and repeated motif of the city gents.

Clearly the 'chain of colour' signifies excitement and sex. In the Elbeo ad a man's hand corroborated the sexual meaning of the woman's legs. Here the sexually explosive mixture constituted from the man's hand, the woman's hand and leg, still has the woman's leg as the core of the sexual signification. Imagine the ad *without* that leg: neither so ridiculous nor so sexually 'ripe'. Yet the man's hand does have some sexual meaning – in its difference from the suited arm of the city gent clutching his *Times* and umbrella. The latter is middle aged, portly and formal; the former is probably young and certainly 'naked' – or shirtless – with bronzed arm, full of sexual potency. The potency is symbolized by her position, not quite supine, but certainly awkwardly below him who could be standing; she sexually submits as the drink is poured (coincidentally at crotch level?) into her glass: a metaphor for a 'sexual filling'.

'Travel 1st Class' exhorts the ad, and we can add, 'you will find sex and excitement'. But to whom is this addressed? Perhaps 'you' are a woman and the drink a woman's drink, for where is *his* glass? 'You' (she) reels with the effect, of him, or the drink, and see the same businessman many times over: woman out of control. She drinks it but *he* has bought it and offers it to her, a sign not of his service to her, but of her *dependence* on him. But we can also read the ad as perhaps the fantasy of that city gent. He imagines himself in the place of the one who pours the drink: their arms are almost in the same place. What he gets travelling first class is not the drink, but *her*. But then contrarily, we are put into the position of looking *up* to the line of men; as the crouching woman who extends her vulnerable limbs? If we are women what other position is offered us? While men revel in sweet fantasy.

Carling (*Cosmopolitan*, June 1980)

A difference is marked here not by the contrast between colour and black and white, but between the background of the kitchen and the focal inset of the woman's hand pouring a can of lager. What the difference is about is not sexuality/asexuality or excitement/mundanity, contrasts which the woman primarily introduces into the Veuve du Vernay ad, but femininity and masculinity of another order: femininity as domestic and masculinity as definitely not.

The 'commercial realism' of the kitchen scene has all the signs of construction. Who can spot the visual clues which indicate, what we are told in text and caption, that a man (her husband – note the wedding ring we can usefully just see on her finger) has not only done the washing up, but that it is not taken for granted that he will do it: it is not his natural rôle? He needs reminding – 'Your turn xx'. Does she when it's her turn? The crockery needs putting away, the cloth hasn't been hung to dry; the bin hasn't been emptied, i.e. she still has work to do. Would *men* looking at this ad recognize those signs of masculine domesticity which are only *too* familiar to women? Yet here she is so thankful for this small lightening of her load, that she is rewarding him. What reward does she get each day? It is *such* an (extra)ordinary task for him to do that both a 'little feminine charm' is required to encourage its execution, and because the task is such a strain, so mammoth a chore – 'The things men do for . . . ' – only Carling with its 'thirst shattering flavour' will suffice to quench this man-size thirst this task has generated. And there we see her pouring it for him; the inset of femininity restoring what is absent from

that kitchen. Despite her absence from the kitchen then, she is confirmed in her domestic rôle; despite his presence he is affirmed as 'a man' – and non-domestic, naturally.

What we have seen in these ads are the ways in which the hand becomes a central mark of femininity or masculinity. If we were to look just at our friends' *hands* we might well *not* be able to tell whether the hand was a woman's or a man's. But of course, then, as in the ads, we *do* always know whose hand it is primarily from what the person as a whole looks like, if not from the hand itself. Usually, however, the hand is not the chief means by which we recognize femininity or masculinity, though this has not always been the case. Leonora Davidoff explains how the appearance of hands was a preoccupation of the middle classes in the nineteenth century; it was as much a concern about establishing class differentials as it was to separate women and men (Davidoff, 1976: 127). Even today the difference between rough and calloused hands, and smooth white ones has both a class and gender reference, which we all recognize ideologically, but do not entirely rely on in our judgement of people as working class or middle class, women or men. What is specific to representation and ads is how they are able to 'elevate' this, in many cases, 'unmarked' part of our bodies and embue it with gender, even when it is detached from any body: it becomes the focal sign of femininity or masculinity. Yet though as we look at the ads it appears that it does this *by itself*, that the gendered meaning is there 'naturally', in the hand, this is by no means so. The biological hand is parasitic on *cultural* markers for this 'natural meaning'. Thus either the hand itself is marked – the bracelet, or shirt cuff – or the text and visuals apart from the hand are marked – 'Home-made goodness' and sponge pudding in the Bird's Custard ad, caption and the TV image in the JVC video ad – and these fill the hand with gendered and therefore cultural meaning. This process of representation occurs equally for masculinity and femininity. Inequality lies in the cultural meanings themselves to which representation only gives a heightened and particular expression.

REFERENCES

Alvarado, M. (1980). Photographs and narrativity, *Screen Education*, no. 32/33, Autumn/Winter 1979/80
Berger, J. (1972). *Ways of Seeing*, London, Penguin
Davidoff, L. (1976). The rationalisation of housework, in Barker, D. and Allen, S. (eds) *Dependence and Exploitation in Work and Marriage*, London, Longman
Goffman, E. (1979). *Gender Advertisements*, London, Macmillan
Millum, T. (1975). *Images of Woman*, London, Chatto & Windus
Williamson, J. (1978). *Decoding Advertisements*, London, Marion Boyars
Williamson, J. (1979). The history that photographs mislaid, *Photography/Politics: One*
Winship, J. (1980). Sexuality for sale, in Hall, S., Hobson, D., Lowe, A. and Willis, P. (eds) *Culture, Media, Language*, London, CCCS/Hutchinson

53

DISCRIMINATING OR DUPED? YOUNG PEOPLE AS CONSUMERS OF ADVERTISING/ART

Mica Nava and Orson Nava

This chapter is based on research commissioned by Paul Willis in his capacity as director of the Gulbenkian Enquiry into Arts and Cultural Provision for Young People. It is drawn on, as are similarly commissioned investigations by other authors, in Willis' final report *Common Culture* (1990). The Enquiry was prompted in the first instance by the recognition 'that most young people see the arts as remote and institutional, not part of everyday life. Art is what they are forced to do at school . . . the preserve of art galleries, theatres and concert halls' which they do not attend. The project of the Enquiry was therefore to explore the wide range of cultural forms and symbolic expressions through which young people establish their identities, the ways in which they consume and invest with meaning the practices and spaces that surround them. 'The Enquiry sets out to investigate creativity wherever it is and whatever its forms' (Willis, 1988: 1).

It is in the context of these terms of reference that the following arguments about young people, advertising and art must be understood.

An interesting TV commercial made by the agency Ogilvy and Mather was shown on Channel 4 each Sunday during the spring of 1988. Entitled *Chair*, its object was to promote the agency's own advertising services to potential 'marketing decision makers'. The advert opens with a shot of a modern young man in a stylish flat watching television. At the commercial break he gets up and goes to make a cup of tea. For a moment the camera focuses on the empty chair and the abandoned TV set. Then it cuts to the kitchen but we can still hear the noise of the ads coming from the unwatched television. The young man returns to his chair with his cup of tea just as the commercial break ends. Over the final frame a voiceover informs us that there are 600 commercials on TV every day; 'what's so special about yours?' it enquires of the potential advertisers among us.

From M. Nava, *Changing Cultures: Feminism, Youth and Consumerism* (London: Sage, 1992) pp. 171–82.

As the press release for Ogilvy and Mather states, 'The film confronts the viewer with the question of whether or not people pay attention to commercial breaks.' At the same time it conveys another message. It represents young people as discriminating and hard to reach and suggests that they are likely to ignore all but the most challenging and entertaining commercials. This view of young people is one which is increasingly prevalent among advertisers and their clients and was frequently expressed to us in interview. Articles in trade magazines like *Campaign*, research conducted by advertising agencies like the *McCann-Erickson Youth Study*, advertisements themselves, and a spate of recent conferences organized for marketeers about the difficulties of targeting and persuading contemporary youth are further evidence of this growing preoccupation (Nava, 1988). Within the world of advertising today, concern is regularly expressed about how to reach young people (since they watch less TV than any other age group, even the under-fours) and how to persuade and gratify them, given what is referred to in the trade (and is illustrated in the Ogilvy and Mather ad) as their high level of 'televisual literacy'. Bartle Bogle Hegarty, the agency responsible for the Levi ads, have put it thus: 'Young consumers are sophisticated, video literate and acutely sensitive to being patronised. They pick up clues and covert messages quicker than you would believe.'

This image of young people and advertising is not, however, the one that circulates most frequently. The way in which advertising and consumerism are generally viewed today (although challenged by, for example, Myers, 1986; Nava, 1987) remains deeply influenced by the work of cultural theorists of the 1950s and 1960s such as Vance Packard, who argues in his seminal book *The Hidden Persuaders* (1981, first published in 1957) that people are 'influenced and manipulated [by advertisers] far more than we realize. . . . Large scale efforts are being made, often with impressive success, to channel our . . . habits, our purchasing decisions and our thought processes' (1981: 11). For Herbert Marcuse (1964) one of the most influential thinkers of the Left in this sphere, advertising – as an inherent aspect of consumer capitalism and its pursuit of profit – is capable not only of convincing us to buy, but of creating false needs, of indoctrinating us into social conformity and thus ultimately of suppressing political opposition. More recently, commentators of both the Left and Right who have been preoccupied by what they consider to be a decline in moral standards (see for example the work of Jeremy Seabrook on the one hand and statements issued by Mary Whitehouse on the other) as well as more academic analysts of advertising (Dyer, 1982) have been concerned to establish the effects of a constant diet of television programmes and commercials, particularly on young viewers who are considered to be those most at risk of being corrupted and duped by entreaties to buy.

Given the pervasiveness of these debates, it is not surprising that certain ideas have now become part of received wisdom, a commonsense way of viewing the world. Thus we have a context in which the question of television advertising and youth is likely to conjure up images of undereducated undiscriminating and undisciplined young people who are addicted to TV and who mindlessly imbibe the advertisers' messages along with the materialist values of the consumer society. Characteristic of this view is the notion that there exists a simple cause and effect relationship between advertising and the purchasing of commodities. It is not only assumed that advertisements work but that the young are more likely than any other sector of the population to be taken in by the psychologically informed scheming of the marketeers. Youth are considered to be more vulnerable, more gullible and more inclined to be persuaded to buy totally useless things.

Significantly and interestingly, this is a far more demeaning view of youth than that held by the advertisers themselves. As has already been indicated, the British advertising industry is highly respectful of the critical skills and visual literacy of young people. Indeed, as emerges clearly from our research, no other age group is considered as discriminating, cynical and resistant to the 'hard sell'. Furthermore, no other group is as astute at decoding the complex messages, cross-references and visual jokes of current advertising (except perhaps the industry itself). These critical skills are untutored and seem to arise out of an unprecedented intimacy with the cultural form of the television commercial. No other generation has been so imbued with the meanings produced by quick edits, long shots, zooms, by particular lighting codes and combinations of sound. The young have a unique mastery of the grammar of the commercial; one might say that they have an intuitive grasp of the visual equivalent of the semicolon. This is the case even where, as one bemused advertiser put it, 'they are not very intellectually clever'.

Advertisers work hard to capture this discerning audience and to win its esteem. Indeed many ads appear to utilize the codes that are most likely to appeal to that sector of the population with the most developed analytical skills – that is, the young – regardless of the suitability of the product for this kind of treatment. The British Telecom commercial about the unfortunate Jewish grandson who managed to pass only his pottery and sociology exams, which emerged as the preferred ad in a small-scale survey of young people, is an example of this. In return, young people will watch and rewatch the commercials they consider successful. The tea will wait (or will be made by someone else) while judgement is exercised. Favourite ads will be recorded and viewed again with friends. Phrases will be selected and replayed. Comparisons and connections will be made, messages identified and effectivity assessed. Repetition and familiarity might enhance the rating of some commercials (for example the celebrated Levi Strauss Launderette ad) but others will not survive such close scrutiny. They will be taped over and forgotten.

It is not only 'youth' (fourteen to twenty-four-year-olds) who watch and enjoy TV ads in this way. Research carried out by the Association of Market Survey Organizations indicates that commercials also come high on the list of younger children's preferred television viewing. Favourite ads among those in the six to fourteen-year-old category include Carling's Black Label, Anchor Butter's dancing cows and Mates condoms. They too like advertisements promoting items which they are unlikely to buy.

What emerges quite clearly from this picture is that young people consume commercials independently of the product that is being marketed. Commercials are cultural products in themselves and are consumed for themselves. The success of any particular commercial is, in this respect, completely divorced from its effectivity in promoting sales. Evaluations are made on the basis of criteria which are indistinguishable from those employed in the appreciation of other cultural forms. Our argument therefore is twofold: an analysis of the mode in which the commercial is consumed not only gives us insight into the cultural skills of young people, it also radically interrogates conventional divisions between art and advertising.

[. . .]

Among the technologies and forms which have been requisitioned by the makers of advertisements since the turn of the century are painting, photography, cinema, graphics, animation, pop music, video promos and video scratch. Examples are numerous: Dada and surrealism have been used in cigarette advertising; Michelangelo's drawings have been used by Parker pens. As John Berger pointed out in *Ways of Seeing* (1972), publicity regularly quotes from works of art. Of the popular cultural forms, hip hop and rapping have most recently been in vogue. More critical avant-garde forms like video scratch are also increasingly drawn on, though not always with much understanding. On the whole, however, what is interesting is that these techniques are not only appropriated and 'quoted', they are also developed (this is particularly so for photography, graphics and animation) in the innovative and generously funded climate of advertising today.

At the level of ideas we see that advertisements not only draw specific narratives and images from the other forms, and parody them, they increasingly cross-reference each other. In this sense they constitute the classic postmodernist form (if such a thing exists) wherein boundaries between forms and between their high and popular versions are effaced (Jameson, 1985). Works of art, despite ideologies to the contrary, have always been derivative; in so far as they make use of existing technologies, artistic conventions and archetypal themes, they are collaborative projects. In advertising, however, this process of the appropriation and reworking of ideas and motifs already in the public domain is not only not concealed, it is celebrated. Pastiche is increasingly becoming an integral part of the form.

References are made to different genres of cinema. The Pirelli Tyre ad is a miniature *film noir*, complete with murder plot, *femme fatale* and moody lighting. Carling Black Label has made an ad for its lager which references the cinematic preoccupation with Vietnam yet also appears to be a critique of war films and traditional masculinity: the hero is an intellectual and a refusenik – an inversion of the archetypal Rambo figure. Barclays Bank has made use of the style and images of *Blade Runner* as well as its director, Ridley Scott. The Holsten Pils advertisements are famous for taking quotations from old movies and incorporating them into their own narratives; thus we witness an unlikely encounter in the ladies washroom between Griff Rhys Jones and Marilyn Monroe.

Cross-referencing between ads occurs frequently, particularly where an ad has been success-ful. In its recent campaign Carling Black Label has made parodic references of this kind its trademark, hence its detailed and witty re-enactment – even the same extras are used – of the famous Levi's Launderette ad, which itself draws on images from 1950s youth movies. In the same vein Carling Black Label references an Old Spice commercial in its ad about a surfer riding a wave into a pub. Another example of an obscure and in this case more laboured reference occurs in a Wrangler ad where the hero puts on a pair of jeans and drives a double-decker bus across a row of parked motorbikes. This is a very coded allusion to Eddie Kidd, star of a 1987 ad for Black Levi 501s, who as a real-life stunt man in the 1970s held the world record for jumping his motorbike across parked double-decker buses.

The fusion of the commercial with other cultural forms is exemplified in an interesting way by a 1988 Independent Broadcasting Authority ruling on an ad for Pepe jeans. This was banned from appearing either immediately before or immediately after a normal programme because stylistically it looked more like a TV drama than a commercial and might delude people about its status. Influences operate in both directions. *Network 7*, for example, a now defunct Channel 4 programme for young people, developed a style of editing and presentation which owed a great deal to television advertising. The employment of cinema and TV actors in commercials also contributes to this merger of forms; not only do such actors draw on theatrical skills and conventions which are then subsumed into the commercial form, they also carry with them their theatrical identities which then work to enhance selected meanings.

[. . .]

At the level of behind-the-camera personnel there has in recent years been an escalating rate of crossover between commercials and cinema and TV. For some time now directors have been cutting their teeth on ads and progressing thereafter – where possible – to bigger things, even to Hollywood. Alan Parker, Ridley Scott and Tony Scott are examples of these. More recently, however, the movement has been in the other direction and already established cinema and television directors from a range of political and stylistic backgrounds have been recruited to direct commercials. Thus Ken Russell, director of *Crimes of Passion*, made an ad for Shredded Wheat; Peter Greenaway (*Draughtman's Contract*) and Stephen Frears (*My Beautiful Launderette*) have both directed commercials in the last few years. Ken Loach (*Kes*) made the award-winning ad for *The Guardian* in which the skinhead saves a passer-by from falling scaffolding, and John Amiel (*The Singing Detective*) and Nic Roeg (*Bad Timing*) made two of the government AIDS warnings. Amiel has described the condensed quintessential dramas currently being made for British advertisers by himself and other established directors as 'little haikus' (Rusbridger, 1988). They exist and are recognized as autonomous creations.

[. . .]

Here we must return to young people. How do youth fit into this analysis of the commercial as (at its best) an increasingly innovative and sophisticated cultural form – as 'art'? What has the relationship of young people been to this redefinition? Is it possible to argue that, as audience, they have contributed to the complexity, elegance and wit of some contemporary television commercials?

In order to unravel and respond to these questions it is necessary to investigate in a little more detail the current state of advertising and marketing theory and practice. What has emerged quite clearly in recent years, concurrently with the refinements in form, is that advertisers no longer have confidence in the old theories about how ads promote sales. This view was frequently confirmed in the interviews we conducted with members of the industry and was reiterated in papers delivered by advertisers at a number of conferences we attended.[1] Beliefs in the power of subliminal messages to penetrate and manipulate the mass psyche no longer have currency. Advertisers are now as aware as other cultural producers that there is no formula or scientific method which can guarantee success. Market research has not come up with the answers. Marketing managers cannot precisely identify the components of a successful campaign; they are unable to anticipate what will spark the public imagination; they do not know exactly who their target audience is, nor how to reach it; and, at a more pedestrian level, they do not even know whether an ad is more effective if placed before or after a particular programme. Some go so far as to insist that advertising is hardly effective at all, that what is required is consistent media coverage in order to shift a product. So what we see is that marketing is a far more haphazard process than the intellectual orthodoxies would have us believe. There are no rules. There is no consensus.

These uncertainties do not mean though that the classic objectives of the industry have been abandoned. Advertisers still aim to increase sales for their clients, and to do so they need to take into account the culture and preferences of young people who constitute a significant proportion of the market both in terms of their own disposable income and their influence on friends and family. They must be recruited, their cynicism must be overcome. Yet in the absence of the confident and clear guidelines of earlier times, how is this to be achieved?

Although the industry continues to be enormously productive, the undermining of old convictions and the growing anxiety about public (youth) cynicism combine to reveal a picture of the advertising process itself in a state of crisis. Indeed the paradox is that the industry's productivity appears to be both a symptom and a cause of its malaise. More numerous and more subtle and sophisticated advertisements have generated more discriminating audiences. As we have already argued, at the forefront of these are the young themselves, whose scepticism and powers of analysis are, in this respect, a great deal more developed than those of older generations. It is through the exercise of these refined critical skills and through the consumption of the ad rather than the product that the young have contributed to the spiralling crisis.

Given the current climate of uncertainty and the lack of clarity about what might be an appropriate response to the crisis, the solution of the marketeers has been to turn to the creative departments within their agencies, to hand over responsibility to individuals largely trained in art schools, who rely not on research and surveys, for which they have little respect, but on imagination, inventiveness and intuition.[2]

Alternatively they have hired film-makers from outside the industry with already established 'artistic' credibility. There is no doubt that the experimental forms produced in this way have had unprecedented success in recruiting and retaining viewers. Above all they have been able to satisfy the gourmet appetites of the discerning young. What emerges quite clearly from this account is that young people, in their capacity as active consumers, have, as Willis (1988) suggests, 'shaped the contours of the commercial culture' which they inhabit. Unlike the young man in the Ogilvy and Mather commercial described at the beginning of this chapter, they do watch the ads. But they do not necessarily buy.

In this chapter we have developed an argument about young people and their relation to contemporary advertising. In order to do this we have used a very undifferentiated model of youth, we have not investigated – or even postulated – distinctions based on class, race or gender because our argument does not require these refinements. Not all youth – and certainly not only youth – read advertisements in the ways in which we (and the advertisers themselves) have argued, though sufficient numbers do to justify our thesis. Our central preoccupation here has been with the consumption of advertising and the skills brought to bear in this process. This has included examining not only transformations in the production of advertisements but also the ways in which historically advertising has been defined. Our argument has been that although ads have in the past been primarily concerned to promote sales, they increasingly offer moments of intellectual stimulation, entertainment and pleasure – of 'art'. To focus on this phenomenon is not to exonerate advertisers and their clients from responsibility in the formation and perpetuation of consumer capitalism. Nor is it to deny totally the influence of advertising in purchasing decisions. Our intention has been to bypass these debates. Instead we recognize the relative autonomy of the ad as product and view it as no more or less inherently implicated in the economic organization of life than any other cultural form. (Advertisements can after all also promote progressive products and causes, like Nicaraguan coffee and the Greater London Council: Myers, 1986.) More importantly, [. . .] we have emphasized in this chapter the very considerable though untutored skills that young people bring to bear in their appreciation of advertisements and that they exercise individually and collectively, not in museums and public galleries, but in millions of front rooms throughout the country – and indeed the world.

The critical question arising from this is whether or not the possession of such decoding skills by young people, and the revolution in the advertising process itself, can be interpreted as progressive. Debates of this kind have always surrounded new stages in the dissemination of knowledge. Reading the written word was considered a contentious activity in the nineteenth century: some people thought it would serve to discipline and pacify the population while others feared (or hoped) it would prove subversive. Earlier in this century Walter Benjamin (1973, originally published in 1936) claimed that the new technology of film would help to develop in spectators a more acute and critical perception. Film as cultural form was not only more popular and democratic, it was potentially revolutionary. Arguing against this position, Adorno and Horkheimer (1973), condemned the culture industry for what they alleged was its taming both of critical art and the minds of the people. More recently Fredric Jameson

(1985) has asked similar questions about the advent of 'postmodernism'. To what extent can postmodern forms be considered oppositional or progressive? Is there a way in which they can resist and contest the logic of consumer capitalism? Our answer must be that the forms alone cannot be subversive, but that the critical tools as well as the pleasures they have generated, and from which they are in any case inseparable, may indeed subvert and fragment existing networks of power-knowledge.

NOTES

1.   See for example papers given by Neil Fazakerly, Creative Director at Davidson Pearce, at the Institute of Contemporary Arts 'Talking Ideas' event, July 1988; Winston Fletcher, Chairman of Delaney Fletcher Delaney, at the *Marxism Today* 'New Times' conference, October 1989; and Richard Phillips, Creative Director at J. Walter Thompson at the Forum Communications 'New Wave Young: Targeting the Youth Market' conference, March 1988.
2.   See note 1.

REFERENCES

Adorno, Theodor and Horkheimer, Max (1973) *Dialectics of Enlightenment*. London: Allen
Benjamin, Walter (1973) 'The work of art in the age of mechanical reproduction', in *Illuminations*. London: Fontana. (Originally published in 1936.)
Berger, John (1972) *Ways of Seeing*. Harmondsworth: Penguin.
Dyer, Gillian (1982) *Advertising as Communication*. London: Methuen.
Foster, Hal (1985) *Postmodern Culture*. London: Pluto Press.
Jameson, Fredric (1985) 'Postmodernism and consumer society', in Foster (1985).
Marcuse, H. (1964) *One-Dimensional Man*. Boston: Beacon Press.
Myers, Kathy (1986) *Understains: The Sense and Seduction of Advertising*. London: Comedia.
Nava, Mica (1987) 'Consumerism and its contradictions', *Cultural Studies*, 1/2.
Nava, Mica (1988) 'Targeting the young: what do the marketeers think?' unpublished paper for the Gulbenkian Enquiry into Young People and the Arts.
Packard, Vance (1981) *The Hidden Persuaders*. Harmondsworth: Penguin. (Originally published in 1957.)
Rusbridger, Alan (1988) 'Ad men discover a fatal attraction', *The Guardian*, 3 March.
Willis, Paul (1988) Unpublished 'Position paper' for the Gulbenkian Enquiry into Arts and Cultural Provision for Young People.
Willis, Paul (1990) *Common Culture*. Milton Keynes: Open University Press.

54

CONSUMER CULTURE AND THE AURA OF THE COMMODITY

Alan Tomlinson

[. . .]

As we near the end of the second millennium, we will no doubt see '2000' used as a dramatic landmark in the development of human civilization. But if '1984' symbolized debates about political freedom and citizenship, '2000' will come to symbolize issues concerning economic freedoms and consumerism. In Britain media institutions already offer an example of how things might move. Rupert Murdoch's takeover of *The Times*, for instance, led to the appointment of an editor whose editorial direction was, in Hugo Young's words, a drift from the notion of citizen as victim to a notion of citizen as consumer (*New Statesman*, 2 November 1984). We may have survived in 2000. Many of us may be free. But free for what? By then, worldwide, the sign of satisfactory survival might well be the colour television set and video, the personal transport system, the personal organizer, the personalized deodorant.

It is in the sphere of consumption – conspicuous leisure on the basis of adequate disposable income – that many will seek to express their sense of freedom, their personal power, their status aspirations. The effect of such a trend upon collective consciousness and cultural relations in particular societies cannot be understated. Popular culture and everyday life have always been of great concern to our political and economic masters. If popular culture can be reduced to a set of apparent choices based upon personal taste then we will see the triumph of the fragmented self, a constant lust for the new and the authentic among a population of consumer clones. That is why the issue of leisure, lifestyle, and consumption is a political one. If religion was, in Tawney's celebrated phrase, vital to the rise of capitalism, it is consumption which has become vital to its continuation and expansion.[1]

Markets have developed, throughout this century, which have radically altered the act of consumption. Take, for instance, mail order. Montgomery Ward and Co. began the mail order business in the United States in 1872, an opportunistic business initiative intended to constitute

From A. Tomlinson (ed.), *Consumption, Identity and Style: Marketing, Meanings, and the Packaging of Pleasure* (London: Routledge, (1990) pp 5–13.

frontier pioneers as a consumer market. The more famous Sears, Roebuck and Co. issued its first catalogue in 1893, diversifying beyond Sears's and Roebuck's initial interest in jewellery and watches. From 200 pages of listings in 1893, it had expanded to over 1100 pages by 1900. The emphasis was very much on the honest sale, the good deal, the reliable source. The inside back cover [. . .] of the 1900 catalogue simply depicts the size and scale of the buildings from which the stock was dispatched. The front and back cover pictures were both the same [. . .], placing strong emphasis on value for money in the sticks as well as the city.[2]

Consumer goods were mimetically represented in the catalogue. Illustrations were simply faithful reproductions of what you would get for your money. If you wanted some gentlemen's suspenders, Sears Roebuck showed you what you'd get and also threw in a bit of advice: 'While we quote cheap suspenders, we do not warrant or recommend them. The better qualities are the cheapest in the end.'[3] From suspenders to leggings, rubber boots to toys, open lavatories to corsets, the emphasis was upon the integrity of the product, rather than its aura or its effect upon the consumer. Contemporary mail order catalogues might still stress value for money and consumer choice, but there is a fundamental difference in emphasis: the commodity has acquired, in late consumer capitalism, an aura beyond just its function. The commodity now acts *on* the consumer, endows him/her with perceived qualities which can be displayed in widening public contexts; consumption becomes a riskier business. It is the difference between buying an object mainly for its function, and acquiring an item for its style. Motor cars or jeans, for instance, are produced and consumed as more than functional means of mobility or clothing.

The role of the car in contemporary culture has altered in precisely this way. As early as 1949 Ford advertised its new model as 'a living room on wheels', with soft seats, modern fabrics and 'picture-window' visibility.[4] For the super rich and uninhibitedly status conscious, the car is only the raw material for the 'King of the Kustomisers', George Barris, to display his talents on. Barris painted Elvis Presley's Cadillac limousine with a gold murano pearl. Hub-caps and grille were gold plated. Even the telephone in the centre seat's pull-down section was gold. The interior of Liberace's Cadillac Eldorado included a piano keyboard motif on the seats and a musical score of his themesong 'I'll be seeing you', with a miniature candelabra on its hood. Poor chicanos restyle second-hand models with brightly coloured carpets and chandeliers. The commodity itself is altered into an object of individual fantasy for the purpose of display.[5]

Shifts in production principles and advances in industrial technology brought the car into the mass market. Stephen Bayley points to three key structural shifts: Henry Ford's application of Frederick Taylor's principles of scientific management; breakthroughs in design after the Second World War, which produced a technically sophisticated small car; and recent development in process efficiency in Japan which makes the perfect product an everyday reality.[6] Important changes in the production process might involve new techniques in selling, 'but the taste for symbolism, as ineradicable in human beings as the parallel appetites for love and sustenance, is going to stick around'.[7] It is this taste to which contemporary Japanese designers are seeking to appeal, with designers styling previously invisible parts such as suspension frames and engine bays. Buying a car has become, increasingly, a declaration of consumer choice on the level of symbols as well as cash. The amazing success of the Ford Cortina, launched in 1962 at a cost of £13 million, was certainly helped by its contemporary styling and continental naming:

> This new Ford was named after Cortina d'Amppezzo, the North Italian hill town that hosted the 1960 Winter Olympics. This gave the first generation of British tourists to benefit from cheap jet travel a symbol of European awareness to park in their drives.[8]

Twenty years on, the Ford Sierra was launched with a new preoccupation with interior design, on the basis that the driver must be made to feel important. More recently, the city whizzkid drives a Porsche. Production constantly seeks to respond to an identifiable consumer mentality, but also to redirect it and sometimes shape it anew. The marketing of the product has come increasingly to flatter the individual consumer, to fuel his or her aspirations, dreams, and fantasies; consumption resolves insecurity, offering status to the nouveau riche. The commodity becomes an object of passion, a source of potential distinctiveness, of constant renewal. Judith Williamson generalizes on this, equating consumer need with thrill and excitement:

> The power of the purchase – taking home a new thing, the anticipation of unwrapping
> – seems to drink up the desire for something new, the restlessness and unease that must
> be engendered in a society where so many have so little active power, other than to
> withdraw the labour which produces its prizes.[9]

However much genuinely subjective passion for the commodity motivates the individual consumer, such subjectivity and consciousness is not unrelated to the process of packaging. Legends have been forged, fortunes made by producer-designers who have their fingers on the pulse (or throat) of the consuming public. And packaging, in the era of market segmentation, has become more and more sophisticated in its targeting, in its modes of address to selected markets. Benson and Hedges and Guinness perhaps, are the best British examples of 'understated' ways of really boasting about the elite status of the product.[10] But whether the commodity is targeted at a large mass market, or at the more lucrative high-earning and high-spending end of the market in a time when production structures are chasing a differentiated niche-market, it is still the aura of the commodity which the consumer is offered and attracted to or seduced by. It is, to paraphrase Roland Barthes, not what the object is or does, in any concrete sense, which gives it its attractiveness: rather, it is what it signifies.[11] In the middle of the 1980s there was perhaps no better example of this phenomenon than the advertising war over jeans.

In the late 1970s and early 1980s, after an all-time low in non-American sales of 501 jeans, Levi's began to tackle the image of the blue jeans. The 501s, baggier jeans with fly buttons, were earmarked for United Kingdom and European marketing. Tim Lindsay, of the British agency Bartle, Bogle, and Hegarty, identified three reasons why such a 're-launch' could work. First, 501s had a practicality about them which was in vogue. Second, the cut of the 501s offered a different style (familiar but different). And third, 501s 1950s image linked with a new generation of youth's view of that period as cool, mythical, stylish. Levi's put £10 million by to draw in new youthful buyers, whilst retaining fashion-conscious established buyers. Lindsay's agency created two television/cinema commercials: Nick Kamen undressing down to his boxer shorts in a fifties launderette, and washing his 501s; and James Mardle wearing his pair in the bath, to shrink them to the ideal fit. This was enough to catapult the unknown model Kamen to high-profile superstardom as beautiful young man, actor, pop star or whatever. It was also enough to increase 501 sales from 80,000 in 1985 to 650,000 in 1986. For the follow-up campaign two story lines were chosen. 'Parting' had a young girl remembering her lost 'drafted' boyfriend by slipping on the 501s – symbol of civilian freedom and style – which he presents to her on parting. 'Entrance' featured Eddie Kidd, former motor-bike stuntman, as a hunky male wearing black 501s as he passes a 'No blue jeans' sign and enters a 1950s nightclub. The budget for these two productions was £500,000.[12]

In America, four expatriates from Marseilles run the Guess company, aiming for a more discriminating exclusive consumer. Guess jeans have aimed for the Calvin Klein designer jeans market, and now sell $250 million worth of merchandise annually, 95 per cent in the United States. The sales really boomed when a moody, provocative black and white approach was introduced in the advertising. In the words of one of the brothers: 'We wanted a difference, some drama, an emotional intense movement. We wanted Italian movie, Fellini atmosphere, *Dolce Vita*, 1950s St Tropez, Brigitte Bardot.[13] These moments included ripped clothes, exposed bras, and cleavages. In Paul Marciano's words 'it is about sensuality and relationships between girls and guys'. Marciano's annual budget for Guess advertising is $20 million.

Guess's first two commercials, made by English director Roger Lunn, were inspired by a classic fifties film (Monroe, Montgomery Clift and Clark Gable in *The Misfits*) and a clever 1970s film depicting the fifties (Bogdanovich's *The Last Picture Show*, shot in black and white). In the third commercial Lunn spent £350,000 on a ninety-second film featuring Rolling Stone Bill Wyman's then little-girl friend, now wife, Mandy Smith, and a dissipated looking older male actor. Smith had already had an earlier modelling deal with Brutus jeans. Marciano took little persuading: 'She goes directly on Guess image. Meaning – sensual, attractive, provocative and youth.' In the commercial this couple arrive in late 1960s London to be hounded by press photographers. At no time in 'Paparazzi' do either of these lead players ever wear a pair of Guess jeans. The star endorses not the product, but the image around the product. 'Branding' is actually forsaken for the cultivation of desirable images. With a hounded sugar-daddy, you too could afford guess what.

With jeans as well as cars, we are now buying so much more than the object or artefact. We are buying into the imagery that surrounds the object. Cars, Peter York has commented in his review of the Marsh/Collett and Bayley books, must:

> Share the stage with a lot of other choices now – so many other things to buy. The notion of 'lifestyle' supposes a fine-stitch tapestry of many small choices with brands attached – a Filofax here, a Tizio lamp there. In these terms, a car's just another *accessory* – though a hugely important one – and it has to fit in.[14]

Our personal identity is created out of elements created by others and marketed aggressively and seductively.

This is the key to what have emerged as the dominant modes of consumption, based upon an individualized sense of selfhood and well-being and the notion of free choice. But if we think we are free when our choices have in fact been consciously constructed for us, then this is a dangerous illusion of freedom. And if in paid work with money to spend we define ourselves as free human actors in a drama in which we can all have the choice of a part, we by inference define all of those without parts too as free. Those who are not able to consume are simply the weak-willed, unable to exploit their freedom!

There is a double danger in this illusion of freedom. First, consumer choice is highly constructed. Second, millions unemployed by anyone and uninvited by Visa are, simply and brutally, excluded from the sphere of freedom. Freedom of goods for some goes hand-in-hand with subordination for others. Critics of consumerism must always remember this. It is a privilege to critique women's romantic novels in the pages of the increasingly glossy 'left' periodicals; it is an exclusion and a deprivation not to be able to afford a second-hand Mills and Boon because that is the price of a loaf.

[. . .]

NOTES

1. R. H. Tawney, *Religion and the Rise of Capitalism: A Historical Study* (1926), Harmondsworth: Penguin, 1938.
2. Sears, Roebuck, and Co., Inc., *Consumers' Guide* (Fall 1900), Northfield, Illinois: DBI Books, 1970.
3. Ibid., p. 541.
4. Peter Marsh and Peter Collett, *Driving Passion – The Psychology of the Car*, London: Jonathan Cape, 1986, p. 11.
5. Ibid., pp. 132–3. See also Martin Pawley, *The Private Future – Causes and Consequences of Community Collapse in the West*, London: Pan, 1974, pp. 50–6, where the car is discussed as an example of the 'pathology of privacy'.
6. Stephen Bayley, *Sex, Drink and Fast Cars: The Creation and Consumption of Images*, London: Faber & Faber, 1986, p. 101.
7. Ibid., p. 103.
8. Ibid., p. 88.
9. Judith Williamson, *Consuming Passions: The Dynamics of Popular Culture*, London: Marion Boyars, 1986, p. 13.
10. See Deyan Sudjie, in *Cult Objects*, London: Paladin Granada, 1985, ch. 6, 'Putting pack art onto the shelves' for some interesting examples of the art of successful packaging.
11. I offer no excursions into semiotic discourse here, just a key reference. See Roland Barthes, 'Myth Today', in *Mythologies* (1957), London: Paladin, 1973, pp. 109–59.
12. The details of the Levi's 501 advertisements are from Hugh Sebag-Montefiore, 'The bottom line', *Sunday Times Magazine*, 1 February 1987, pp. 60–5.
13. Matthew Gwyther, 'Mandy keeps us guessing', *Observer Magazine*, 26 July 1987, pp. 26–9. The following quotes from Marciano are from this piece.
14. Peter York, 'Crash of a sex symbol', *The Observer*, 23 November 1986, p. 57.

FURTHER READING

Adorno, T. and Horkheimer, M., 'The Culture Industry: Enlightenment as Mass Deception', in Curran, J., Gurevitch, M. and Woollacott J. (eds), *Mass Communication and Society* (London: Edward Arnold, 1977).

Ang, I., *Desperately Seeking the Audience* (London: Routledge, 1991).

Baehr, H., *Women and Media* (Oxford: Pergamon Press, 1980).

Barthes, R., *Mythologies* (London: Paladin, 1973).

Berger, J., *Ways of Seeing* (Harmondsworth: Penguin, 1972).

Bonney, B. and Wilson, H., *Australia's Commercial Media* (Melbourne: Macmillan, 1983).

Bonney, B. and Wilson, H., 'Advertising and the Manufacture of Difference', in Alvarado M. and Thompson J. O. (eds), *The Media Reader* (London: BFI, 1990).

Chapman, S. and Egger, G., 'Myth in Cigarette Advertising and Health Promotion', in Davis H. and Walton P. (eds), *Language, Image, Media* (Oxford: Blackwell, 1983).

Cook, G., *The Discourse of Advertising* (London: Routledge, 1992).

Coward, R., *Female Desire* (London: Paladin, 1984).

Curran, J., 'Capitalism and Control of the Press, 1800–1975', in Curran, J., Gurevitch, M. and Woollacott, J. (eds), *Mass Communication and Society* (London: Edward Arnold, 1977).

Curran, J., 'Advertising and the Press', in Curran J. (ed.), *The British Press . . . A Manifesto* (London: Macmillan, 1978).

Curran, J., 'Advertising as a Patronage System', *Sociological Review Monograph* 29 (1980).

Curran, J. and Seaton, J., *Power without Responsibility: The Press and Broadcasting in Britain*, 4th edn (London: Routledge, 1991).

Davis, H. and Walton, P. (eds), *Language, Image, Media* (Oxford: Blackwell, 1983).

Dyer, G., *Advertising as Communication* (London: Methuen, 1982).

Earnshaw, S., 'Advertising and the Media: The Case of Women's Magazines', *Media, Culture and Society* 6:4 (1984) pp. 44–21.

Ewen, S., *Captains of Consciousness* (New York: McGraw Hill, 1976).

Ewen, S. and Ewen, E., *Channels of Desire* (New York: McGraw Hill, 1982).

Fiske, J., *Television Culture* (London: Methuen, 1987).

Fiske, J., *Reading the Popular* (London: Unwin Hyman, 1989).

Fiske, J., *Understanding Popular Culture* (London: Unwin Hyman, 1989).

Goddard, J., 'Editorial', in Alvarado, M. and Thompson, J. O. *The Media Reader* (London: BFI, 1990).

Goffman, E., *Gender Advertisements* (London: Macmillan, 1978).

Goldman, R., *Reading Ads Socially* (London: Routledge, 1992).

Goldman, R. and Papson, S., 'Advertising in the Age of Hypersignification', *Theory, Culture and Society* 11:3 (1994) pp. 23–53.

Hebdige, D., *Subculture: The Meaning of Style* (London: Methuen, 1979).

Hebdige, D., *Hiding in the Light: On Images and Things* (London: Routledge, 1988).

Inglis, F., *The Imagery of Power* (London: Heinemann, 1972).

Janus, N., 'Advertising and the Mass Media: Transnational Link between Production and Consumption', *Media, Culture and Society* 3:1 (1981) pp. 13–23.

Jhally, S., *The Codes of Advertising: Fetishism and the Political Economy. Of Meaning in the Consumer Society* (London: Routledge, 1990).

Leiss, W., *The Limits to Satisfaction* (London: Marion Boyars, 1978).

Leiss, W., Kline, S. and Jhally, S., *Social Communication in Advertising*, 2nd edn (London: Routledge, 1990).

Myers, K., *Understains: The Sense and Seduction of Advertising* (London: Comedia, 1986).

Nava, M., *Changing Cultures: Feminism, Youth and Consumerism* (London: Sage, 1992).

Packard, V., *The Hidden Persuaders* (Harmondsworth: Penguin, 1979).

Pateman, T., 'How is Understanding an Advertisement Possible?', in Davis, H. and Walton, P. (eds), *Language, Image, Media* (Oxford: Blackwell, 1983).

Schudson, M., 'Criticizing the Critics of Advertising: Towards a Sociological View of Marketing', *Media, Culture and Society* 3:1 (1981) pp. 3–12.

Schudson, M., *Advertising: The Uneasy Persuasion* (London: Routledge, 1993).

Sinclair, J., *Images Incorporated: Advertising as Industry and Ideology* (London: Routledge, 1989).

Tomlinson, A., (ed.), *Consumption, Identity and Style: Marketing, Meanings, and the Packaging of Pleasure* (London: Routledge, 1990).

Tuchman, G., Kaplan Daniels, A. and Benet, J. (eds), *Hearth and Home: Images of Women in the Media* (New York: Oxford University Press, 1978).

Wernick, A., *Promotional Culture: Advertising, Ideology and Symbolic Expression* (London: Sage, 1991).

Williams, R., *Problems in Materialism and Culture* (London: Verso, 1980).

Williamson, J., *Decoding Advertisements* (London: Marion Boyars, 1978).

Williamson, J., 'Woman is an Island: Femininity and Colonization', in Modleski, T. (ed.), *Studies in Entertainment: Critical Approaches to Mass Culture* (Bloomington: Indiana University Press, 1986).

Willis, P., *Common Culture* (Milton Keynes: Open University Press, 1990).

Willis, S., *A Primer for Daily Life* (London: Routledge, 1991).

Winship, J., 'Sexuality for Sale', in Hall, S., Hobson, D., Lowe, A. and Willis, P. (eds), *Culture, Media, Language* (London: Hutchinson, 1980).

ACKNOWLEDGEMENTS

Grateful acknowledgement is made to the following sources for permission to reproduce material previously published elsewhere. Every effort has been made to trace copyright holders, but if any have been inadvertently overlooked, the publisher will be pleased to make the necessary arrangement at the first opportunity.

Paul F. Lazarsfeld and Robert K. Merton, 'Mass Communication, Popular Taste and Organized Social Action', from *The Communication of Ideas*, ed. Lyman Bryson, Harper & Bros., 1948.

Theodor Adorno, 'Culture Industry Reconsidered', trans. Anson G. Rabinbach, from *The Culture Industry: Selected Essays on Mass Culture*, ed. J. M. Bernstein, Routledge, 1991.

Marshall McLuhan, 'The Medium is the Message', from *Understanding Media*, by Marshall McLuhan, Routledge, 1964.

Raymond Williams, ' "Mass Communication" and "Minority Culture" ', from *Communications*, by Raymond Williams, Penguin Books, 1962, copyright © Raymond Williams, 1962, 1966, 1976.

Stuart Hall, 'Encoding/Decoding', from *Culture, Media, Language*, eds Stuart Hall, Dorothy Hobson, A. Lowe and P. Willis, Hutchinson, 1980. Reproduced by permission of Routledge and Stuart Hall.

Annette Kuhn, 'The Power of the Image', from *The Power of the Image*, by Annette Kuhn, Routledge, 1985.

Jürgen Habermas, 'The Public Sphere', trans. Shierry Weber Nicholson, from *Jürgen Habermas on Society and Politics: a Reader*, ed. Steven Seidman, Beacon Press, 1989, copyright © Beacon Press, 1989. Reprinted by permission of Beacon Press.

Jean Baudrillard, 'The Masses: The Implosion of the Social in the Media', trans. Marie MacLean, from *Jean Baudrillard: Selected Writings*, ed. Mark Poster, Polity Press, 1988. Reproduced by permission of the John Hopkins University Press.

Nicholas Garnham, 'On the Cultural Industries', from *Capitalism and Communication*, by Nicholas Garnham, Sage, 1990, copyright © Nicholas Garnham, 1990. Reprinted by permission of Sage Publications Ltd.

Colin Sparks, 'The Media and the State', from *Bending Reality*, eds James Curran et al., Pluto Press, 1986.

Graham Murdock, 'Redrawing the Map of the Communication Industries: Concentration and Ownership in the Era of Privatization', from *Public Communication: the New Imperatives*, ed. Marjorie Ferguson, Sage, 1990, copyright © Sage Publications Ltd 1990. Reproduced by permission of Sage Publications Ltd.

Jeremy Tunstall, 'Producers in British Television', from *Television Producers*, by Jeremy Tunstall, Routledge, 1993.

Asa Briggs, 'Suez 1956', from *Governing the BBC*, by Asa Briggs, BBC Publications, 1979. Reproduced by permission of BBC Worldwide Ltd.

Andrew Crisell, 'Radio Signs', from *Understanding Radio*, by Andrew Crisell, Methuen & Co., 1986.

John Fiske, 'The Codes of Television', from *Television Culture*, by John Fiske, Methuen & Co., 1987. Reproduced by permission of Methuen and John Fiske.

Raymond Williams, 'Programming as Sequence or Flow', from *Television, Technology and Cultural Form*, by Raymond Williams, Fontana, 1974. Reproduced by permission of Routledge.

John Ellis, 'Broadcast TV Narration', from *Visible Fictions: Cinema, Television, Video*, by John Ellis, Routledge, 1982.

Stuart Hall, 'The Whites of their Eyes: Racist Ideologies and the Media', from *Silver Linings*, eds George Bridges and Rosalind Brunt, Lawrence & Wishart, 1981.

Janet Woollacott, 'Fictions and Ideologies: The Case of Situation Comedy', from *Popular Culture and Social Relations*, eds T. Bennett, C. Mercer and J. Woollacott, Open University Press, 1986.

John Caughie, 'Progressive Television and Documentary Drama', from *Screen*, vol. 21, no. 3, 1980. Reproduced by permission of John Caughie.

Andrew Tolson, 'Televised Chat and the Synthetic Personality', from *Broadcast Talk*, ed. Paddy Scannell, Sage, 1991, copyright © Sage Publications Ltd, 1991. Reproduced by permission of Sage Publications Ltd.

Janice Winship, 'Survival Skills and Daydreams', from *Inside Women's Magazines*, by Janice Winship, Pandora Press, an imprint of HarperCollins Publishers Ltd, 1987.

Danae Clark, 'Cagney & Lacey: Feminist Strategies of Detection', from *Television and Women's Culture: The Politics of the Popular*, by M. E. Brown, Sage, 1990, copyright © Sage Publications Ltd. Reproduced by permission of Sage Publications Ltd.

Patricia Holland, 'The Page Three Girl Speaks to Women, Too', from *Screen*, vol. 24, no. 3, 1983. Reproduced by permission of Patricia Holland.

E. Ann Kaplan, 'Whose Imaginary? The Televisual Apparatus, the Female Body and Textual Strategies in Select Rock Videos on MTV', from *Female Spectators: Looking at Film and Television*, ed. E. Deidre Pribram, Verso, 1988.

Angela McRobbie, 'Postmodernism and Popular Culture', from *ICA Documents 4: Postmodernism*, 1986. Reproduced by permission of Free Association Books Ltd and Angela McRobbie.

Hans Eysenck and D. K. B. Nias, 'Desensitization, Violence and the Media', from *Sex, Violence and the Media*, by Hans Eysenck and D. K. B. Nias, Maurice Temple Smith, 1978.

James D. Halloran, 'On the Social Effects of Television', from *The Effects of Television*, ed. James Halloran, Panther Books, 1970.

Denis McQuail, Jay G. Blumler and J. R. Brown, 'The Television Audience: a Revised Perspective', from *Sociology of Mass Communications*, ed. Denis McQuail, Penguin Books, 1972, copyright © Denis McQuail, Jay G. Blumler and J. R. Brown, 1972.

Philip Elliott, 'Uses and Gratifications Research: A Critique and Sociological Alternative', from *The Uses of Mass Communications: Current Perspectives on Gratifications Research*, eds Jay Blumler and Elihu Katz, Sage (US), 1974, copyright © Sage Publications, Inc., 1974. Reprinted by permission of Sage Publications, Inc.

David Morley, 'Cultural Transformations: The Politics of Resistance', from *Language, Image, Media*, eds H. Davis and P. Walton, Blackwell, 1983.

Dorothy Hobson, 'Housewives and the Mass Media', from *Culture, Media, Language*, eds Stuart Hall et al., Hutchinson, 1980. Reproduced by permission of Routledge.

Ien Ang, 'Wanted: Audiences. On the Politics of Empirical Audience Studies', from *Remote Control: Television, Audiences and Cultural Power*, eds E. Seiter, H. Borchers, G. Kreutzner and E. M. Warth, Routledge, 1989.

Ann Gray, 'Behind Closed Doors: Video Recorders in the Home', from *Boxed In: Women and Television*, eds H. Baehr and G. Dyer, HarperCollins Publishers Ltd, 1987.

John Fiske, 'Moments of Television: Neither the Text nor the Audience', from *Remote Control: Television, Audiences and Cultural Power*, eds E. Seiter et al., Routledge, 1989.

David Buckingham, '*EastEnders*: Creating the Audience', from *Public Secrets: EastEnders and its Audience*, by David Buckingham, BFI, 1987. Reprinted by permission of the British Film Institute.

Christine Geraghty, 'The Continuous Serial: A Definition', from *Coronation Street* (BFI TV Monograph No. 13), by R. Dyer, C. Geraghty, M. Jordan, T. Lovell, R. Paterson and J. Stewart, BFI, 1981. Reprinted by permission of the British Film Institute.

Tania Modleski, 'The Search for Tomorrow in Today's Soap Operas', from *Loving with a Vengeance: Mass-Produced Fantasies for Women*, by Tania Modleski, Methuen, 1984.

Ien Ang, '*Dallas* and Feminism', from *Watching Dallas: Soap Opera and the Melodramatic Imagination*, by Ien Ang, Methuen & Co., 1985.

Charlotte Brunsdon, '*Crossroads*: Notes on a Soap Opera', from *Screen*, vol. 22, no. 4, 1981. Reproduced by permission of Charlotte Brunsdon.

Dorothy Hobson, 'Everything Stops for *Crossroads*: Watching with the Audience', from *Crossroads: The Drama of a Soap Opera*, by Dorothy Hobson, Methuen, London, 1982.

Philip Schlesinger, 'The Production of Radio and Television News', from *Putting 'Reality' Together: BBC News*, by Philip Schlesinger, Methuen & Co., 1987.

Peter Golding and Philip Elliott, 'News Values and News Production' and 'Bias, Objectivity and Ideology', from *Making the News*, by Peter Golding and Philip Elliott, Longman, 1979.

Stuart Hall, Chas. Critcher, Tony Jefferson, John Clarke and Brian Roberts, 'The Social Production of News', from *Policing the Crisis: Mugging, the State, Law and Order*, by Stuart Hall et al., Macmillan Education, 1978.

'[The Falklands Conflict:] The Home Front', from *War and Peace News*, by Glasgow University Media Group, Open University Press, 1985, copyright © Lucinda Broadbent, 1985.

Patricia Holland, 'When a Woman Reads the News', from *Boxed in: Women and Television*, eds H. Baehr and G. Dyer, HarperCollins Publishers Ltd, 1987. Reproduced by permission of HarperCollins and Patricia Holland.

Greg Philo, 'News Content and Audience Belief', from *Seeing and Believing: The Influence of Television*, by Greg Philo, Routledge, 1990.

Raymond Williams, 'Advertising: The Magic System', from *Problems in Materialism and Culture*, by Raymond Williams, Verso/New Left Books, 1980.

James Curran, 'The Impact of Advertising on the British Mass Media', from *Media, Culture and Society*, vol. 3, no. 1, 1981. Reprinted by permission of Sage Publications Ltd.

Kathy Myers, 'Understanding Advertisers', from *Language, Image, Media*, eds H. Davis and P. Walton, Blackwell, 1983.

Judith Williamson, 'Decoding Advertisements', from *Decoding Advertisements*, by Judith Williamson, Marion Boyars, 1978.

Janice Winship, 'Handling Sex', from *Media, Culture and Society*, vol. 3, no. 1, 1981. Reprinted by permission of Sage Publications Ltd.

Mica Nava and Orson Nava, 'Discriminating or Duped? Young People as Consumers of Advertising/Art', from *Changing Cultures: Feminism, Youth and Consumerism*, by Mica Nava, Sage, 1992, copyright © Mica Nava and Orson Nava. Reproduced by permission of Sage Publications Ltd.

Alan Tomlinson, 'Consumer Culture and the Aura of the Commodity', from *Consumption, Identity and Style: Marketing, Meanings and the Packaging of Pleasure,* ed. Alan Tomlinson, Routledge, 1990.

INDEX OF NAMES

SUBJECT INDEX